Organization and Administration of Physical Education

THEORY AND PRACTICE

Second Edition

Organization and Administration of Physical Education

THEORY AND PRACTICE

Second Edition

Jayne D. Greenberg

Judy L. LoBianco

Library of Congress Cataloging-in-Publication Data

Names: Greenberg, Jayne Debra, author. | LoBianco, Judy L., 1969- author.
Title: Organization and administration of physical education : theory and practice / Jayne D. Greenberg, Judy L. LoBianco.
Description: Second edition. | Champaign, IL : Human Kinetics, [2026] | Includes bibliographical references and index.
Identifiers: LCCN 2024044015 (print) | LCCN 2024044016 (ebook) | ISBN 9781718217652 (paperback) | ISBN 9781718217669 (epub) | ISBN 9781718217676 (pdf)
Subjects: LCSH: Physical education and training–United States–Management. | School sports–United States–Management.
Classification: LCC GV343.5 .O74 2026 (print) | LCC GV343.5 (ebook) | DDC 796.06/9–dc23/eng/20240923
LC record available at https://lccn.loc.gov/2024044015
LC ebook record available at https://lccn.loc.gov/2024044016

ISBN: 978-1-7182-1765-2 (print)

The online learning content that accompanies this product is delivered on HK*Propel*, **HKPropel.HumanKinetics.com**. You agree that you will not use HK*Propel* if you do not accept the site's Privacy Policy and Terms and Conditions, which detail approved uses of the online content.

The web addresses cited in this text were current as of October 2024, unless otherwise noted.

Acquisitions Editor: Mark Manross; **Senior Developmental Editor:** Melissa Feld; **Senior Managing Editor:** Anne E. Mrozek; **Copyeditor:** Joanna Hatzopoulos Portman; **Proofreader:** Leigh Keylock; **Indexer:** Ferreira Indexing; **Permissions Manager:** Laurel Mitchell; **Senior Graphic Designer:** Nancy Rasmus; **Layout:** MPS Limited; **Cover Designer:** Keri Evans; **Cover Design Specialist:** Susan Rothermel Allen; **Photograph (cover):** © Jayne Greenberg; **Photographs (interior):** © Human Kinetics, unless otherwise noted; **Photo Asset Manager:** Laura Fitch; **Photo Production Manager:** Jason Allen; **Senior Art Manager:** Kelly Hendren; **Illustrations:** © Human Kinetics, unless otherwise noted; **Printer:** Premier Print Group

Printed in the United States of America 10 9 8 7 6 5 4 3 2 1

Human Kinetics
1607 N. Market Street
Champaign, IL 61820
USA

United States and International
Website: **US.HumanKinetics.com**
Email: info@hkusa.com
Phone: 1-800-747-4457

Canada
Website: **Canada.HumanKinetics.com**
Email: info@hkcanada.com

E8920

This book is dedicated to the many transformational leaders in my life and throughout my career who—through their vision, inspiration, and motivation—have enabled me to be more than I could have ever imagined. The true meaning of leadership, which I hope emerges from the work in this book and the pages that follow, is exemplified in those who unselfishly give of themselves to their profession, their organization, and especially to those whom they lead and mentor. To that end, I would like to extend my deepest feelings of gratitude to Drs. Michael and Dorothy Marge, Dr. Laurie Whitsel, Dr. Gillian Hotz, Mogens Kirkeby, Jacob Schouenborg, Saska Benedicic Tomat, and especially Dr. Bill Kohl, who once told me that he saw more potential in me than I knew I had in myself. Those were the powerful words of a true leader that opened up so many doors and opportunities for me.

To my immediate and extended family, friends, colleagues, and the plethora of teachers whom I have worked with throughout my career, I give my heartfelt thanks for always supporting me through your love, understanding, and patience as I navigated my path in living my passion to serve ALL children and youth. My journey continues.

—Dr. Jayne D. Greenberg

I dedicate this book to my parents, Michael and Ethel, who encouraged me throughout my life to be of service to others, and to my wife, Alison, for pushing me to be my very best. I also dedicate this book to the South Orange-Maplewood Schools for giving me opportunities to lead.

I would like to personally thank SHAPE America for helping me become a lifelong student of my profession, providing opportunities for me to serve in leadership, and offering me countless moments of connection and community. Thank you for serving the profession with unwavering support for all health and physical educators.

Finally, to all of my former students and every teacher I have had the pleasure of working with: When it comes time to pass the torch to a new generation of administrative leaders, it is my hope that I have contributed in a positive way to our vital work.

—Judy L. LoBianco

Contents

PART IV Communication, Legal Issues, and Human Resources

PART V Financial Management

PART VI Meeting Social Issues and Challenges

Preface

As a current or future physical education administrator and leader, you have or will have the unique opportunity to ensure that all students benefit from participating in quality physical education programs. As a result, you will make a positive difference in the current and future lives of your students.

According to the U.S. Department of Education Every Student Succeeds Act (ESSA) of 2015, physical education is part of a well-rounded education. Therefore, it is essential that schools be staffed with trained physical education administrators who are prepared to enter into a leadership role. The main purpose of this book is to assist the undergraduate and graduate student in understanding the roles and responsibilities of a physical education administrator through theoretical and practical perspectives as well as to assist the physical education teacher or department chairperson in entering the role of a physical education administrator. In this book, the term *physical education administrator* refers to the physical education administrator, the department chairperson, or any physical education teacher who is assigned administrative duties.

Another purpose of this book is to assist the current physical education administrator in securing new skills and innovative ideas in order to expand present efforts and skills. The most significant change to this second edition of *Organization and Administration of Physical Education: Theory and Practice* is the transition from using the 2014 National Standards for Physical Education & Grade-Level Learning Outcomes to the 2024 National Physical Education Standards and Grade-Span Learning Indicators. SHAPE America developed and published the 2024 version to address student learning across the psychomotor, cognitive, affective, and social learning domains, which is an essential approach in supporting PreK-12 learners as they progress along their own meaningful physical literacy journey.

This book's authors, editors, and contributors have a vast array of combined experiences, including teaching at the elementary school, middle school, high school, and college levels in urban, suburban, and rural settings; serving as a school site administrator; and holding physical education administrative positions at the regional and district levels. Drawing on our experience as teachers at all levels and our administrative experience in a large urban school district and a small suburban environment, we are excited to present innovative ideas and practical scenarios that work in diverse settings. In addition, many chapter contributors lend their expertise both from higher education and from the field. Thus, reader, whether you are a student or a professional educator, we are hopeful that this text will help you gain both the theory and application necessary to prepare for becoming an effective administrator. Further, contributors include a mix of veterans and young up-and-comers, so they bring both lived experience and new ideas that align with today's students. Finally, successful physical education administrators and leaders from district, state, and professional organizations across the United States have provided tips from their successful programmatic implementations. Each chapter includes at least one Leadership in Action sidebar to provide advice from the field.

This book is divided into six major sections, each representing a major job responsibility that is inherent in most physical education administrative positions. Many physical education administrators at the district level oversee more than one subject area. Although the focus of this book is on physical education, most of these skills can be applied easily to other subjects, including health education, driver education, and athletics.

Part I (Leadership, Management, Organization, and Planning) includes three chapters that take a theoretical look at leadership and management styles while presenting practical theories of motivation, development, and planning. We believe that all future administrators should have a thorough understanding of leadership theory and management qualities that would enable them to lead others to meet the goals and objectives of their organizations and school districts. Chapter 3 in particular takes an in-depth look at the benefits of a quality physical education program, the role of the National Standards for PreK-12 Physical Education in program development, how to plan for the essential components of a quality physical education program, how to align the physical education program with the overall strategic initiatives of your school or district, and how the school or district environment can serve as the hub of a comprehensive school physical activity program.

Part II (Curriculum, Instruction, Assessment, and Special Events) takes a deep dive into the role that curriculum and instruction play in developing a high-quality, effective physical education program to support student learning outcomes. Curriculum and instructional models, curriculum theory and mapping, and teacher and program evaluation round out the concepts required in the systematic process of planning, designing, and implementing a high-quality standards-based instructional physical education program. This section concludes with a chapter on event planning, special programs, and field trips, which are major components of a district administrator's responsibilities for internal and external advocacy as well as fundraising, team building, and securing community connections.

Part III (Facilities, Equipment, and Technology) assists the physical education administrator in planning and designing new or existing school sites, presents new concepts in universal design and sustainable and environmental design, and facilitates understanding of state-specific educational specifications for construction projects. It familiarizes you with how Title IX and accessibility standards play a role in planning and constructing facilities to meet legal requirements. Chapter 9 focuses on technology in physical education, a topic that ever evolves as new technologies constantly emerge. The chapter offers ideas on how a school's infrastructure should be planned to enable the use of technology in the district or school site environment. It explores ideas on how to incorporate technology to meet the needs of 21st-century learners. In addition, it covers how technology is used to enhance learning and engagement in physical education, what infrastructure is needed to integrate new technologies into the classroom, and how artificial intelligence (AI), virtual reality (VR), augmented reality (AR), and robotics can be used in delivering instruction and communication.

Part IV (Communication, Legal Issues, and Human Resources) explores many of the critical elements involved in administrative duties, such as written, verbal, and electronic communication as well as lobbying and advocating for physical education. Legal issues, laws, policies, and administrative directives are presented in a stand-alone chapter, chapter 11. All administrators need to be aware of these matters in relation to how the legal system affects what can be done in a school setting, the rights and responsibilities of teachers and students, and what teachers and administrators need to know to prevent entanglement with the law. The chapter includes topics regarding legal personnel issues as well as bullying and harassment. Next, chapter 12 presents human resources and human capital management issues. It addresses recruiting, selection, and hiring of quality physical education teachers, interview techniques, professional development for both professional growth and teacher support, and labor relations and collective bargaining.

Part V (Financial Management) provides a thorough explanation of the fiscal responsibilities inherent in every administrative position. The chapter on budgets, bids, and purchasing provides sample budgets with detailed examples of object codes and functions as well as the policies and procedures set by district-specific office of procurement management rules and regulations. You will become familiar with the various types of budgets, how to place a purchase order, and what to expect in an audit situation. This section concludes with a chapter on how you can secure funding for your programs independent of any district or local funding. Several examples of grants and fundraising opportunities are presented, including sample letters and grant applications.

Part VI (Meeting Social Issues and Challenges), which is new to this book, provides a thorough understanding of issues related to all administrative positions. Chapter 15 focuses on the connection between physical education content, pedagogy, and practices and social and emotional learning (SEL). Chapter 16 provides legal and practical approaches that administrators can implement to elevate the participation of underrepresented students in physical education.

In addition to the content just outlined, we have included several resources through URLs in the chapters as well as an online resource in HK*Propel* that offers supportive material and documents. See the Accessing the HK*Propel* Online Content page at the front of this text for instructions on how to access the HK*Propel* materials for book purchasers. Many figures in the book are available for download via HK*Propel*; they are marked with a WWW icon.

For instructors who adopt this text, we provide an instructor guide, PowerPoint presentation, and test package to assist with the course delivery, all available at HK*Propel*.

We are hopeful that this book serves as a perpetual resource to provide you with both present and future theoretical knowledge and practical support.

Accessing the HK*Propel* Online Content

Instructors

If you received this book or ebook as a desk copy, you should use the access instructions provided by your sales representative instead of the access code printed on this page.

All Other Users

Throughout *Organization and Administration of Physical Education, Second Edition* you will notice references to HK*Propel* online content. This online content is available to you for free upon purchase of a new print book or an ebook.

HK*Propel* offers access to sample resources from the book in PDF format.

Follow these steps to access the HK*Propel* online content. If you need help at any point in the process, you can contact us via email at HKPropelCustSer@hkusa.com.

If it's your first time using HK*Propel*:

1. Visit HKPropel.HumanKinetics.com.
2. Click the "New user? Register here" link on the opening screen.
3. Follow the onscreen prompts to create your HK*Propel* account.
4. Enter the access code exactly as shown below, including hyphens. You will not need to re-enter this access code on subsequent visits.
5. After your first visit, simply log in to HKPropel.HumanKinetics.com to access your digital product.

If you already have an HK*Propel* account:

1. Visit HKPropel.HumanKinetics.com and log in with your username (email address) and password.
2. Once you are logged in, navigate to Account in the top right corner.
3. Under "Add Access Code" enter the access code exactly as shown below, including hyphens.
4. Once your code is redeemed, navigate to your Library on the Dashboard to access your digital content.

Access code: GREENBERG2E-774T-CD3M-DYSK

Once you have signed in to HK*Propel* and redeemed the access code, navigate to your Library to access your digital content. Your license to this digital product will expire two years after the date you redeem the access code. You can check the expiration dates of all your HK*Propel* products at any time in My Account.

For technical support, contact us via email at HKPropelCustSer@hkusa.com. **Helpful tip:** You may reset your password from the log in screen at any time if you forget it.

Acknowledgments

In the preparation of this manuscript, the authors would like to thank all of the exemplary and ethical leaders and educators who contributed to the chapters in the first edition of this textbook providing a sound foundation to build upon. A special thank you goes out to Lori S. Dunn, Sheri J. Brock, Leah H. Robinson, Kara K. Palmer, Miriam Kenyon, Christopher Hersl, Collin Brooks, Richard Benvenuti, Jessica de Koninck, Shawn Ladda, and Alexandra Reyes. Your contributions will have an everlasting impact on this important work in organizing and administering quality physical education programs.

We would further like to extend a heartfelt thanks to Ray Vallese, VP and Director, Academic Division, and the staff at Human Kinetics for their expertise and attention to detail during the writing, editing, and revision process and for their patience and guidance in making this book possible. In particular, a special thanks is extended to acquisitions editors Scott Wikgren (retired) and Mark Manross (former); senior developmental editor Melissa Feld; senior managing editor Anne E. Mrozek; editorial services manager Karla Walsh; copyeditor Joanna Hatzopoulos Portman; proofreader Leigh Keylock; indexer Ferreira Indexing; permissions manager Laurel Mitchell; senior graphic designer Nancy Rasmus; marketing and implementation manager Lynn Kincaid; layout professionals MPS Limited; cover designer Keri Evans; cover design specialist Susan Rothermel Allen; photo asset manager Laura Fitch; photo production manager Jason Allen; senior art manager Kelly Hendren; illustrator Matt Harshbarger; and printer Premier Print Group.

PART I

Leadership, Management, Organization, and Planning

CHAPTER 1

The Role of a Physical Education Administrator as a Leader

Jayne D. Greenberg

LEARNING OBJECTIVES

After reading this chapter, you will be able to do the following:

- Describe the role of the physical education administrator.
- Differentiate between the styles and philosophies of leadership.
- Differentiate between theories of leadership.
- Identify the roles and responsibilities of the physical education administrator.
- Explain the value of ethics in leadership.
- Discuss the role that strategic planning plays in meeting programmatic goals and objectives.
- Identify strategies to develop and expand a culture of diversity in leadership positions.

KEY CONCEPTS

conflict resolution
diversity in leadership and management
dualism
eclecticism
ethical leadership and management
existentialism
idealism
leadership development
leadership styles
leadership theories
motivation theories of leadership
philosophy of leadership
pragmatism
realism
strategic planning
visionary leadership

The decision to become an administrator comes with a deep desire to effect change and affect school culture at a higher level. Improving the curriculum, teacher practices, delivery of instruction, and educational experiences for students is a task for those who have both the ability to lead and the drive to improve what is happening in the classroom. The reward for this work is that physical education administrators, who assume a leadership role, can truly make a difference in the instructional outcomes in their school districts. Just as teachers in the classroom affect the lives of their students, administrators have a profound effect on staff. True leaders inspire, promote self-reflection, and advocate for programs and children. Administrators have the whole picture in sight, and they act mindfully and deliberately to make the mission and vision for their programs a reality.

The landscape of education changes rapidly. In the United States, there is more emphasis than ever before on teacher and program accountability in the nation's schools. It is through effective leadership that instructional improvements can be realized in order for U.S. educational systems to prepare all students for life in the 21st century as well as prepare teachers to provide instruction in the 21st century. Many of the jobs that current students may compete for do not even exist yet. With that reality in mind, a true administrative leader can advocate, teach, and effect positive changes in schools.

One of the most important roles of a physical education administrator is to constantly advocate for and about the profession. Many decades ago, physical education was characterized as a nonessential subject area with very little to offer the academic world besides giving students a so-called break from their classes. The field of physical education has evolved considerably since that time. One can use the known research to catapult physical education to the forefront of the learning process, linking physical activity and physical education to academic performance outcomes. It is the responsibility of all leaders in physical education to promulgate these facts in order to connect students with physical activity for a lifetime. It is essential that the professional leader be a visionary—constantly on the cutting edge of best practices—and have the skill set to be able to communicate those practices to a variety of stakeholders both inside and outside the profession.

As you begin to explore administration and organization in physical education, it is important to understand what inherent qualities are necessary for both leadership and management positions. Throughout this chapter, you will learn about the philosophies, styles, and theories inherent in leadership as well as the evolving role of the physical education administrator as a leader.

Roles and Responsibilities of the Physical Education Administrator

As you take the next career step and transition from physical education teacher to district-level physical education administrator, your roles and responsibilities, subject area focus, and technical expertise will broaden. The focus shifts from a daily classroom schedule providing instruction to students assigned to your classes to the day-to-day responsibilities of providing district-wide leadership with an increased workload. The key to successful school district administration is embedded in preparation, time management, communication skills, and becoming a lifelong learner whose passion for teaching and making a difference remains the cornerstone. As the physical education teacher, your day was consumed with providing high-quality instruction, ensuring student safety, attending to discipline issues, and carrying out other responsibilities such as bus duty, cafeteria duty, parent meetings, and after-school activities. What seemed manageable during your school day will now test your leadership and management skills while learning the "art of street level bureaucracy" (Marshall, 1985, p. 39) (see figure 1.1).

Once you assume your new position as the district-level administrator, your responsibilities shift from student-centered duties to supervising and facilitating the development of leadership and technical skills of all certified staff. Major responsibilities include supervising the development, implementation, and evaluation of all physical education and health

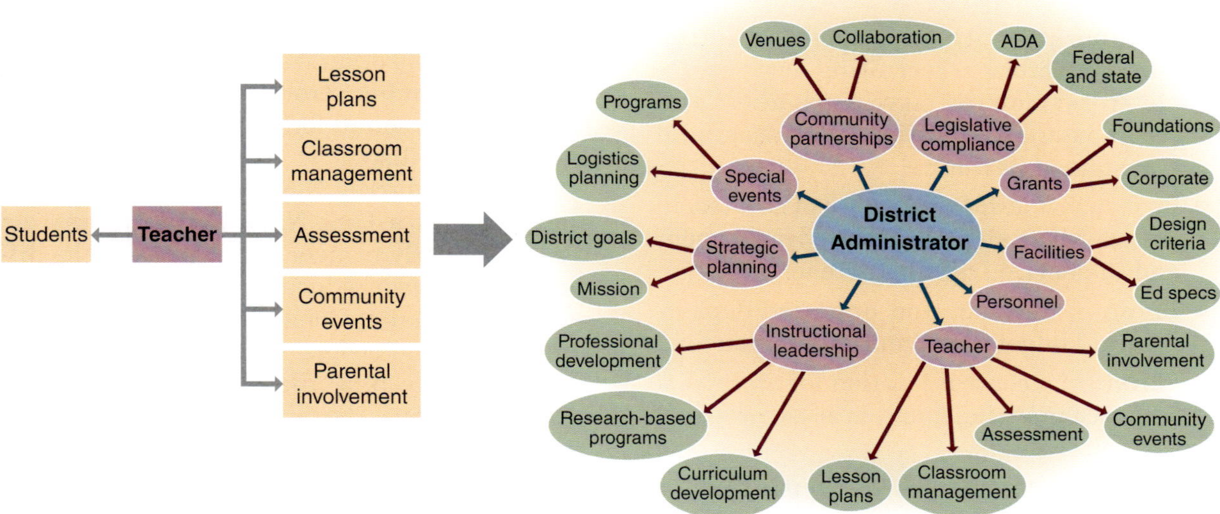

FIGURE 1.1 Shifting your role from teacher to administrator greatly expands your responsibilities.

delivery programs to ensure congruency with the written, taught, and tested curriculum; supervising the work of staff to ensure that the quality of the work is congruent with district needs and expectations and to evaluate according to the district's strategic plan and adopted evaluation system; supervising staff to ensure that the district's fiscal resources are managed efficiently and appropriately; becoming active in the community to develop a close working relationship between the schools and community at large; assisting in the planning and implementation of the district's professional development program; and modeling the personal and professional expectations for district physical education personnel by demonstrating a commitment to growth and ethical leadership. You must be able to lead by example and guide teachers—and, ultimately, students—in the right direction to ensure programmatic excellence.

Specific duties may include the following:

- Work collaboratively with school site administration to develop and improve physical education and wellness programs in grades K through 12.
- Be responsible for all aspects of curriculum and program planning for grades K through 12 in physical education and other related subject areas, as assigned, to ensure compliance and alignment with state and national standards including curriculum writing or special projects.
- Plan, organize, and administer the programs and activities in the department.
- Assist principals and teachers in implementing programs for students with disabilities and in compliance with the Individuals with Disabilities Education Act (IDEA) and 504 requirements.
- Inform administrative superiors of all pertinent concerns related to the department.
- Assist principals in the supervision of teachers and with observations and evaluations.
- Represent the department at administrative–supervisory meetings, as required, for both the school and the district.
- Arrange or assist in arranging teaching schedules of staff according to school or district needs.
- Establish and maintain an office climate that encourages innovation, productivity, and a high level of morale among staff.
- Conduct staff meetings while providing leadership, instruction, and motivation for transparency, efficiency, and professional growth of staff.
- Provide the necessary organization, supervision, guidance, and direction for

all special programs or events related to the department.

- Collaborate with and assist building administrators in recruiting new personnel, interviewing new personnel, and recommending additions, releases, and transfers of personnel.
- Be responsible for orientation of new teachers as well as all professional development and in-service training of teachers.
- Prepare, develop, and organize departmental budget, bids, and requisitions.
- Maintain a central location for storage of resource materials, and oversee property control.
- Serve on committees as consultant or coordinator of special programs, and represent the school system as directed or self-initiated.
- Model exemplary ethical practices at all times.
- Perform other duties as assigned by supervisors or under the authority of the school board.

Daily, administrators in leadership positions face mounting and constant demands on their time. Communication with subordinates, peers, superiors, parents, and community members must be constant. The district-level physical education administrator must also learn to work within, and adapt to, the school district's climate and how to navigate policies, school board rules, budgetary requirements, and union issues and labor laws while always remembering that the ultimate goal is student achievement.

Leadership Versus Management

In an educational setting, whether in a school site or a district-level position, the terms *leadership* and *management* are often used interchangeably with reference to the administrator. However, although there are distinct differences between the roles and responsibilities of a leader and a manager, there is often a crossover effect. The true leader is often the *visionary*, who sets the goals and direction for the organization in addition to having the capacity to inspire and motivate people toward achieving those goals. The manager, on the other hand, focuses on the actual work and organizational tasks to achieve the goals. Having strong management skills can provide a sound foundation for productive leadership skills.

As Grace Murray Hopper, who was both an educator and a U.S. Navy Rear Admiral as well as an early pioneer in delineating the differences between educational leadership and educational management, stated, "You manage things; you lead people" (Educational Business Articles, 2015, p. 3). Based on that thought, table 1.1 depicts the differences between the two.

Kotter (1990) further explained that the functions of management and leadership are distinctly dissimilar; while leadership produces a change and movement within an organization, management seeks order and stability (table 1.2). Distinct differences are further discussed by Bennis and colleagues (1985) and Bennis and Nanus (2003), who assert that leaders and managers have fundamentally different values and approaches.

Conversely, it should be noted that scholars such as Yukl and Gardner (2020) and Nickles and colleagues (2010) view leadership as a function of good management such that they are not mutually exclusive notions. Although several thoughts have emerged on the difference between leadership and management, throughout this chapter the emphasis is on the physical education administrator as a leader, whereas in chapter 2 the emphasis is on management.

Leadership Defined

To begin to fully understand leadership, one needs to acknowledge that varying definitions of leadership have evolved, since leadership is a difficult construct to define in universally accepted terms. However, there seems to be consensus that strong leadership is often the most critical element in determining the success of any organization. In early research literature, Koontz and O'Donnell (1955) define leadership in terms of persuasion, as "the activity of persuading people to cooperate in the achievement

TABLE 1.1 Educational Management Versus Educational Leadership

Subject	Manager	Leader
Makeup of role	Stability	Change
Decision making	Makes	Facilitates
Approach	Plans detail around constraints	Sets and leads direction
Vision	Short-term today	Long-term horizon
Control	Formal influence	Personal charm
Appeals to	The head	The heart
Culture	Endorses	Shapes
Action	Reactive	Proactive
Risk	Minimizes	Takes
Rules	Makes	Breaks
Direction	Existing direction; keeps status quo	New direction; challenges norms
Values	Results	Achievement
Concern	Doing the thing right	Doing the right thing
Focus	Managing work	Leading people
Human resources	Subordinates	Followers

Based on "Leadership Versus Management Debate: What's the Difference?" Educational-Business-Articles.com.

of a common objective" (cited in Bass & Stogdill, 1990, p. 15).

From the perspective of goal attainment, Davis (1942), Urwick (1953), and Davis (1963) all looked at the role of the human factor that brings a group together to work toward common goals. W.G. Bennis, a true pioneer and scholar in leadership studies as seen in his book, *On Becoming a Leader* (2009), defines leadership as "the capacity to create a compelling vision, translate it into action and sustain it" (p. 46). Burns (1978) and Bass (1985) further define leadership in transformational terms: The leader transforms followers, sets the vision, and defines a path for the followers to attain a goal.

TABLE 1.2 Functions of Management and Leadership

Management Produces Order and Consistency	Leadership Produces Change and Movement
Planning and budgeting • Establish agendas. • Set timetables. • Allocate resources.	Establishing direction • Create a vision. • Clarify the big picture. • Set strategies.
Organizing and staffing • Provide structure. • Make job placements. • Establish rules and procedures.	Aligning people • Communicate goals. • Seek commitment. • Build teams and coalitions.
Controlling and problem solving • Develop incentives. • Generate creative solutions. • Take corrective action.	Motivating and inspiring • Inspire and energize. • Empower subordinates. • Satisfy unmet needs.

Adapted from Kotter (1990).

Social theorists, such as Bogardus (1929) and Pigors (1935), view leadership through a social process in which it is the interaction of people that leads them to pursue a common cause. In contrast, Stogdill (1948), a trait theorist, asserts that through this social interaction, a person who holds a leadership position in one situation may not necessarily be the leader in a different situation. Other early trait theorists such as Cowley (1932) and Yukl asserted that "Leadership is the process of influencing others to understand and agree about what needs to be done and how to do it, and the process of facilitating individual and collective efforts to accomplish shared objectives" (Yukl & Gardner, 2020, p. 6). Additionally, according to Yukl (Yukl & Gardner, 2020), most definitions of leadership involve a process whereby intentional influence is exerted over other people to guide, structure, and facilitate activities and relationships in a group or organization.

There is no right or wrong definition of leadership; rather, it is characterized by individual differences, behaviors, and the situations in which they occur. Leadership philosophies and styles also play a vital role in the development of leadership behaviors.

Characteristics of Effective Leaders

Now that you have a sense of the various definitions of leadership, note that although there is no consensus on the characteristics of effective leaders, inherent characteristics are present in all leaders. To begin with, it should be noted that an effective leader is a visionary who has the tenacity to make things happen; builds trust, confidence, and motivation in constituents; and works toward achieving a goal. An effective leader must also be an effective communicator and possess the ability to inspire others.

Kouzes and Posner (2007) maintain that five practices of exemplary leaders foster collaboration by promoting mutual goals, building trust, and strengthening others. These principles are as follows:

1. *Model the way.* Leaders establish principles on how people should be treated and how goals should be pursued, and they set the example for others to follow.
2. *Inspire a shared vision.* Leaders believe they can make a difference and create a vision of what the organization can become.
3. *Challenge the process.* Leaders search for opportunities to change the status quo.
4. *Enable others to act.* Leaders foster collaboration, embrace mutual respect, and empower others.
5. *Encourage the heart.* Leaders recognize the contributions of others and reward their efforts.

Bennis (2009) asserts that leadership involves six personal qualities:

1. *Integrity*: Aligning words and actions with inner values; a leader with integrity can be trusted and admired for sticking to strong values.
2. *Dedication*: Exerting time and energy on a task to get the job done.
3. *Magnanimity*: Crediting people with success and accepting personal responsibility for failures.
4. *Humility*: Recognizing that you are not inherently superior to others and consequently that they are not inferior to you.
5. *Openness:* Being able to listen to ideas that are outside your current mental models, being able to suspend judgment until after you have heard someone else's ideas.
6. *Creativity:* Thinking differently, being able to get outside the box and take a new and different viewpoint on things.

A meta-analysis of literature indicates that other qualities of effective leadership are communication skills, consistency, cooperation, direction, drive, decisiveness, dependability, energy, emotional stability, foresight, fairness, honesty, human relations skill, initiative, judgment, objectivity, reliability, and technical skills.

Developing Leaders

As discussed throughout this chapter, leadership is a component that is critical to the success of any organization in reaching its goals and objectives. Today's leaders take on a more dynamic role than in the past, and they have to develop a skill set ready to meet the demands of 21st-century organizations. They are required to have a vision and to motivate and inspire followers, as well as to initiate change and develop a positive culture where subordinates feel that they are each an important and contributing member of the organization. Therefore, in the complex role of **leadership development**, organizations in every facet of society are continuously seeking the best way to both identify people with leadership abilities and develop leaders through a variety of methods. We will explore how an organization develops leaders, as well as how leaders develop subordinates into leaders, from a historical perspective.

Throughout history, there has been much discussion of whether leaders are born or made. The great man theory, a 19th-century idea supported by Thomas Carlyle, asserts that great leaders are born with all the required internal features such as intelligence, confidence, social skills, and charisma and that these features make them leaders who are naturally born. In contrast, Warren Bennis asserts that leadership is not a set of genetic characteristics but rather the result of the lifelong process of self-discovery. Jay Conger, a leading authority on leadership development, states that "leaders are both born and made and that on-the-job experience, work on special projects, and participation in assignments assist people in learning about building and leading teams" (2004, p. 137, cited in Scott, 2014, p. 190). For the purpose of this chapter, we look at leadership development as a learning process in the belief that given select qualities, anyone is capable of taking on a leadership role in some capacity and that leadership development is formed through a process of experiences and learning opportunities.

The following practices, as identified by Scott (2014), involve areas of leadership development embedded in empirical studies as well as practical implications.

- *Self-development* is an approach in which individuals learn about themselves in a variety of leadership areas, usually through the use of self-rating instruments, experiences, and interaction with leaders.
- *360-degree feedback* is an approach in which important information is anonymously solicited from an employee's subordinates, direct reports, colleagues, and supervisors, as well as self-evaluation by the employees themselves. Although the information received is helpful in identifying strengths and weaknesses, the feedback can be harmful if poorly administered.
- *Mentoring* is a common approach used by many organizations to develop personnel with leadership interests and abilities. Mentoring can have a positive impact on an organization by improving employee retention and engagement and by shaping culture. Mentoring also serves a strategic purpose when linked to talent strategy, leadership development, workforce planning, and organizational goals. The key to a successful mentoring program lies in the match between the mentor and mentee and in the forged relationship with regard to knowledge sharing, leadership growth, and succession planning.
- *Experiential learning*, more commonly known as on-the-job training, or learning by doing, has been used by organizations in the development of leadership competencies; this is in contrast to traditional leadership training programs. Experiential learning involves discovery and exploration with a focus on learning through experience (Warnick & Schmidt, 2014).
- *Employer-based action learning*, originated by Reginald Revans, is an organizational approach to solving real problems that involves taking action and reflecting on the results. When this approach is used for leadership development, it can assist in improving individual and team problem-solving processes.
- *Succession planning* is a systemic process for identifying, assessing, and developing staff. Through this process, organizations can plan for sustainability since they are investing in their employees to be future leaders. The key elements inherent in succession planning lie in the identification of key talent, developing that talent so people are ready for the next level, then

> providing opportunity and monitoring progress. Kouzes and Posner (2007) further assert that "The domain of leaders is the future. The leader's unique legacy is the creation of valued institutions that survive over time. The most significant contribution leaders make is not simply to today's bottom line; it is to the long-term development of people and institutions so they can adapt, change, prosper, and grow" (p. xiv).

The importance of high-quality leadership development is articulated throughout this section of the chapter. Although there are different approaches and beliefs regarding leadership development, the underlying premises are that for productive sustainability, every organization needs to identify qualified personnel to fill future leadership roles and responsibilities, attract talent, retain employees, and implement leadership development programs.

Understanding Your Philosophy of Leadership

The term *philosophy* comes from Greek words meaning "love of wisdom." Philosophy uses the tools of logic and reason to analyze the ways in which humans experience the world. It enables educators to use critical thinking and logical analysis in decision-making processes. The study of philosophy gives you the ability to question why things are and how you can change them. It also enables you to comprehend how your belief system helps shape your system of values. These are all critical elements in understanding what drives leaders and how individual decisions are made.

As a physical education administrator, you have adhered to the relationship between mind and body in the overall attainment of educational goals. Understanding **dualism** and the early works of Socrates, Plato, Aristotle, and Descartes further helps you to embrace the relationship between mind and body in the field of physical education and how that drives your educational decisions. Your foundations in the **philosophy of leadership** can be based on your understanding of the schools of philosophy as explained next.

Idealism

Idealism asserts that reality is fundamentally mental and that the only concern is with the mind or spirit and the self. It asserts that experience through the senses is not the real world; rather, the real world is the world of ideas. Idealism emphasizes a person's rationality and the cultivation of reason.

Thus, idealism applied to physical education contends that a healthy and fit body is a requisite to reaching full potential. Idealists believe that physical, intellectual, spiritual, and moral growth are desirable constructs. Physical education not only looks after the physical factor but also consists of those experiences that fulfill the needs of the individual and bring the individual a sense of satisfaction or well-being. It provides for physical education teachers to be role models for students while developing a sense of character and sporting behavior, and it guides the physical education administrator in meeting SHAPE America's National Physical Education Standards 3 and 4 through programmatic development. Plato, well known as a true idealist, described a utopian society in which "education to body and soul all the beauty and perfection of which they are capable" as an ideal (Parkinson, 1897, p. 8).

Realism

Realism is the philosophy that the world exists in terms of matter, separate from the world of ideas and independent of it. Aristotle, the father of realism and a student of Plato, held that the existence of objects is what is real, separate from the human mind. This philosophy is based on the assumption of a scientific approach to the development of knowledge. Because of its foundation in scientific reasoning, realism has had a great impact on educational philosophy.

A curriculum based on realism emphasizes a subject matter in which the teacher organizes and presents content systematically within a discipline, demonstrating use of criteria in making decisions. Teaching methods focus on mastery of facts and basic skills through demonstration and recitation. For the physical education administrator, curriculum should be scientifically approached, standardized, and based on a distinct discipline. Realists also see the role of physical fitness as omnipotent,

LEADERSHIP IN ACTION

Organizing for Success as a District Leader in Health and Physical Education

Kymm Ballard, EdD

Health and Physical Education Teacher Education Coordinator, Campbell University

The only certainty in this job is change. Our schools and students have changed tenfold in the last five years. Between an increase in school shootings and the impact of COVID-19 alone, our school culture has forever changed how we teach and learn. There has never been a time when our teachers needed us more. There is no book for what we have faced; there was no warning or perception that these things could happen. All we can do is ask ourselves what did we learn, and can we prepare for the unknown?

I will not pretend to have any answers. We cannot prepare for the unknown other than by continuing to cultivate a Whole School, Whole Community, Whole Child (WSCC) approach. However, with this CDC model in place, it is the closest thing we have to protecting our children and being prepared for any foreseeable thing with the contacts to come together quickly for a plan.

Luckily, we are not faced with high-level chaos every day. My version of chaos is more like too many people calling on me at once, upset people, nagging people, and turning in late documents in addition to keeping track of what is going on with my own children at home. However, this level of stress can be dangerous to our health; I know from experience. How can I be an administrator who cultivates a supportive environment so that teachers can reach their potential and deal with everything else?

Effective leaders do not try to do it all. If you follow that approach, then when chaos hits, your brain is fresher to think and plan than the brain that always goes 100 miles per hour. The following tips are helpful for new administrators and also serve as a good refresher for seasoned ones:

1. *Know the expectations*. Understand your bosses' expectations of you, your expectations of your administrator (if you are lucky enough to have one), your expectations of your key personnel, and your expectations of your teachers.

2. *Empower your teachers*. Help them take some ownership in their professional growth. Have some grade-level leaders or teams to assist in the issues that should go to you and what they can discuss together. I call this my 911 (emergency) level. Have them ask themselves if it is a 911 or if they can solve it together. The leaders take notes to share with you and meet only if necessary.

3. *Communicate*. Establish a line of communication between the department chairs in your district. Establish guidelines for which that chain is used so it is not abused. You should be included on that chain so that you can stay informed.

    - Show up to professional development sessions. First, discuss the chain of command and why it exists, then give them a side of you they can relate to. This approach is an excellent way to communicate to them that you care and are working hard through the systems you create to make things happen.
    - While open-door policies are friendly, sometimes they create more problems. An open door sometimes encourages a break of a chain of command and demolishes any chain link present, and you are right back handling little things. However, of course, I am not talking about something serious for which they cannot go to anyone else. In this case, they should come to you; it is a 911.
    - Keeping your superiors informed is the same. They most likely only want to know something if it can help them in a situation. I call this approach *Make them smart before you make them mad*. In such a case, prepare superintendents with every scenario possible that may come back to them so that they are ready to respond. Never let them get caught without information. Again, these cases may occur mostly during policy development or involve hot topics such as comprehensive sex education.

4. *Show respect*. Showing respect is essential in a leadership position. However, it is always important to remember for everyone—not just the decision makers. I call this approach *make friends before you need them*. No one likes someone coming to you only when they want something and never giving you any courtesy any other time. Everyone will need everyone else at some time.

(continued)

Organizing for Success as a District Leader in Health and Physical Education *(continued)*

- Acknowledge the custodians, the mail person, the cafeteria workers, and the administrative assistants (not only yours but those of others also). Just say hello when you walk by, offer a smile, or drop off a cookie from where you went to lunch that day once in a while. It truly means the world. Everyone deserves respect.

5. *Keep your word.* Do not overpromise. If you can do it, then do it—and keep your word. If you need more time, then say so—and give it your best. If you cannot do it, then find someone who can, or say no—even when it hurts. Be reliable and dependable.

6. *Be a team player.* You do not always have to agree. Even after disagreeing, standing your ground, and clearly making your point does not get the votes, you are still all united.

7. *Listen.* Listen to the words people say. Try to hear and learn what they are saying from their perspective and why they need, want, or feel what they do. Then, if you understand, ask questions for clarity. Do not make assumptions from your point of view.

    - Listen and think about constructive feedback rather than get offended by it. You may disagree with others, but ask yourself what they see from their view. The way you provide and receive constructive criticism should be thought out carefully. Maybe you are sending the wrong message to another culture without knowing it.

8. *Have a vision and strategy.* Always have a plan. Where do you want to be in the next 3, 5, and 10 years? Create a strategic plan, and check it yearly to see if you are progressing. Set a positive environment for the energy to create. The following is a sample (not inclusive of all) of the people who may help you with your goals and strategic planning. Of course, depending on your school size, you want a manageable number; it gets messy.

    - Grade-level health and physical education teachers (Try not to only get your doers but also one or two naysayers if possible; let them help create the path forward.)
    - Juniors and seniors
    - Principals
    - Parent–teacher association (PTA) (if possible, so they understand your fundraising efforts)
    - Funding director, or representative if you have one (They may not need to come until the end, when you look at the strategic plan draft for realistic funding or finding grants, which they can help with.)
    - Your boss (invited at strategic times)
    - Anyone who will be involved, such as community partners

9. *Practice sound time management and organization.* This will help you manage chaos more than anything.

    - Set a to-do list, and mark things off. Warning: Do not list everything under the sun. If you have too long a list to remember, pick the most important things for the day and save the other tasks for a later time.

10. *Take time for yourself.* You must take time for yourself. It is extremely hard for me to do this. My family needs just as much attention as my work does, but I cannot give them my excess energy when I don't take time for myself as well. Give your work what you can, leave it there, and devote the rest to yourself and your loved ones.

    - Try to find time to reflect at night before going to bed. Be careful; if you think about what you have to do tomorrow, you may wake up in the middle of the night! Reflect on *you*. Did you do all the things on this list of tips? Could you do better? Do you need to reach out to someone to amend something? Did you eat well today? Set your personal goals for tomorrow, then get some rest.
    - Do not think about the tasks you must do tomorrow. That list is at work, and you need a good night's sleep.

We all want to be the best versions of ourselves. Many people have a mindset that they must keep going at full speed all day, but no one can do that. Something will give out, whether it is patience, anger, stress, diet, energy, sleep, or a combination such as your health. Too much of one thing is a trade-off from the other; there is no way around it.

Effective leaders can model both work and well-being. With this balanced approach, you will ultimately create a more positive and thriving educational environment and foster successful relationships.

believing that a healthy and fit body enables a person to act more efficiently and be more productive. SHAPE America's National Physical Education Standards 1 and 2 can be met through a realist approach to curriculum development and instructional planning.

Pragmatism

Pragmatism, founded in the United States by Charles Sanders Pierce, is a philosophy rooted in the belief that the truth or meaning of an idea lies in its observable practical results. For pragmatists, only those things that are experienced or observed are real. Pragmatists believe that reality is constantly changing and that people learn best through applying their experiences and thoughts to problems as they arise. There is no absolute and unchanging truth; rather, truth is what works.

John Dewey, an American philosopher, applied pragmatist philosophy in his progressive approaches to education. He believed that learners must adapt to each other and to their environment. Therefore, schools should emphasize the subject matter of social experience. All learning is dependent on the context of place, time, and circumstance. Different cultural and ethnic groups learn to work cooperatively and contribute to a democratic society. The ultimate purpose of education and democratic politics is the creation of a new social order. Character development is based on making group decisions in light of consequences.

For pragmatists, teaching methods focus on hands-on problem solving, experimenting, and projects, often having students work in groups. Curriculum should bring the fields of study together to focus on solving problems in an interdisciplinary way. Pragmatists believe that learners should apply their knowledge to real situations through experimental inquiry. This approach prepares students for citizenship, daily living, and future careers. Physical education administrators incorporating programs such as Project Adventure and other outdoor education programs will embrace the pragmatism philosophy. Bringing recess to schools and emphasizing the importance of play will further support the socializing effects and experiences that influence students' lives, as will field trips to enhance individual experiences. For the purpose of socialization and experiential learning, team sports would be the preferred type of activities over dual and individual sports.

Existentialism

Existentialism is a philosophy that is more subjective, lies within the individual, and emphasizes that the physical world has no inherent meaning outside of human existence. Individual choice and individual standards (rather than external standards) are central. Existentialists define themselves in relationship to that existence by the choices they make, acknowledging that one must take personal responsibility for the rational decisions one makes. The focus is on personal freedom and choice. Søren Kierkegaard and Friedrich Nietzsche, 19th-century philosophers, are credited with the origin of existentialism.

As related to education, existentialists believe that there is a common core of knowledge that needs to be transmitted to students in a systematic, disciplined way and that the curriculum should have academic rigor. The subject matter of existentialist classrooms should be a personal choice. Character development emphasizes individual responsibility for decisions. Real answers come from within the individual, not from outside authority. Existentialists are opposed to thinking about students as objects to be measured, tracked, or standardized. Such educators want the educational experience to focus on creating opportunities for self-direction and self-actualization. They start with the student rather than with curriculum content. For the physical education administrator and teacher using this approach, activities should be varied, allowing students to choose an activity of their interest with the understanding that play will lead to creativity. As a 20th-century leading educational visionary and founder of the Coalition of Essential Schools, Theodore Sizer was a proponent of existentialism in education.

Eclecticism

Eclecticism is a blend of diverse philosophies that draws upon multiple theories rather than adhering to the tenets of any particular one. Eclecticism was first recorded to have been practiced by a group of ancient Greek and

Roman philosophers who attached themselves to no real system; instead, they selected from the existing philosophical beliefs those doctrines that seemed most reasonable to them. In the education setting, this allows the teacher to select among a variety of approaches, methods, and techniques that can be adjusted to different educational settings and different groups of students. Different approaches are used for the teaching of different skills. Johann Heinrich Pestalozzi, a Swiss social reformer and educator, believed that education is the development of the inherent capacities of a child and that as such, education should develop to the fullest extent the physical, mental, and moral capacities of a child. He believed that children learn through three elements—hands, heart, and head. He further stressed that children should learn through their own interests and activities and that teaching should be child centered rather than teacher centered.

This section briefly introduced and defined the various philosophical schools of thought, and it discussed how they affect physical education and the role of the physical education administrator. Based on your individual values and beliefs, you cannot separate your individual philosophical beliefs in your approach to the development of physical education curriculum and programs as an administrator, or the implementation of physical education curriculum and instruction, methodology, and teaching styles. However, as you continue to see how philosophy guided the development of physical education throughout the years, you will begin to gain a greater understanding of the evolution of physical education programs. To date, these varying philosophies still account for programmatic differences in delivery, goals, and objectives.

Determining Your Leadership Style

In addition to philosophies of education, **leadership theories** and **leadership styles** are often studied with respect to goal attainment of an organization. A person's leadership style is affected by many factors, including their philosophy of education, their beliefs, their values, and their personalities, as well as the situations and the types of followers they deal with. Despite the many diverse styles of leadership, a good or effective leader inspires, motivates, and directs activities to help achieve group or organizational goals and objectives. This section describes the five most commonly recognized styles: authoritarian, democratic, laissez-faire, servant, and eclectic.

Authoritarian leaders, also known as *autocratic* leaders, exhibit a leadership style characterized by individual control in which strategic decisions are made without input from their subordinates or group members. These leaders are highly disciplined, and they have a clear view of where they are and in what direction they want to lead their subordinates. This style of leadership is best used when control of a situation is necessary and there is little room for error; it works best when an immediate decision needs to be made. Since it is often a more rigid style of leadership that could affect the motivation of others, the leader should make a concerted effort to be respectful of others, communicate frequently, ensure that everyone is aware of and understands the expectations, and listen to all opinions.

Democratic leaders, also known as *participative* leaders, make the final decisions but seek out input from their subordinates. Participative leaders emphasize the concept of planning *with* people, not *for* them. They consider meeting the goals of the organization to be a collaborative effort on the part of all participants through building trust and commitment and encouraging creativity. They have a clear vision of where everyone should be, and they incorporate the ideas of their subordinates to make that vision happen. Team members have a higher level of satisfaction than they might otherwise since they take a more participative role in the decision-making process. Through this leadership style, group members are encouraged to share ideas and opinions, and they can freely exchange ideas.

Laissez-faire leaders, also known as *delegative* leaders, consider their subordinates fully capable of doing their jobs without direction and allow a high degree of autonomy on the part of their subordinates. Laissez-faire leaders work to build a strong team and give people the power to make decisions about their own work. They provide teams with resources and advice (if needed), but otherwise, they do not get involved. This leadership style can be effective if the leader monitors performance and gives feedback to team members regularly. The laissez-faire style of leadership is most often found where a high degree of creativity is needed.

Servant leaders move the focus from the needs of the organization to the people who are being led. There is no sense of self-interest on the part of the leader, who steps back and supports only the interests of the followers before considering her own interests in order to be effective. The leader exists to serve the people. These leaders enhance the growth of the organization through factors such as teamwork and shared decision making. Guidance, empowerment, and a culture of trust are inherent in this style of leadership. A servant leader puts complete trust in the process and in his followers, assuming that individuals within the organization will align with its goals. Servant leaders develop people through modeling behavior and listening more than speaking.

Eclectic leaders do not subscribe to any one style of leadership but rather borrow from many as the situation arises. Eclectic leaders are flexible in their styles and can incorporate aspects of various leadership styles based on the situation and their constituents. Using the eclectic approach enables leaders to shape their environment and take action either through their own decision-making powers or through collaborative efforts with input from subordinates.

Regardless of the leadership style implemented, the end result will always have a focus on moving the organization forward toward achieving goals, providing direction for staff, and motivating people to succeed and feel as though they are a valuable part of the organization.

Theoretical Approaches to Leadership

Leadership as a complex, multidimensional concept has been studied for decades in order to define what makes a great leader. There are as many different theories of leadership as there are philosophies and styles. Throughout the years, the study of leadership has shifted focus from traditional trait (personality-based) theories to situation theory. However, it has become apparent throughout time that leadership theories comprise three main categories: (1) as dependent on a set of traits or characteristics that an individual possesses, (2) as a set of behaviors or actions that an individual performs, and (3) as an interactive process that depends on a particular situation (Jenson & Overman, 2003).

Trait Theory

The concept underlying trait theory is that leaders inherently possess certain physical, intellectual, and personality qualities (traits) that make them more suited to be leaders. Early trait theorists asserted that leadership qualities are innate and that these traits are consistent across a variety of situations and remain stable over time. The trait theory approach focuses on the leader rather than the follower; it holds that leaders are born, not made. Early researchers believed that if these traits could be identified in people, then they could become great leaders. These traits were identified as (1) intelligence, (2) self-confidence, (3) determination, (4) integrity, and (5) sociability (Northouse, 2013). Stogdill (1974) identified certain traits and skills as critical to leaders (table 1.3).

Behavioral Theory

Unlike trait theorists, behavioral theorists emphasize the style and behaviors of the leader. They believe that leaders can be made rather than born. Successful leadership is based on the actions of the leader, not innate qualities. The belief is that leaders can be developed through training and observation. Two types of behaviors were found to have greater importance: task behaviors and relationship behaviors. *Task behaviors* are concerned with goal accomplishment and emphasize organizational structure and operating procedures, whereas *relationship behaviors* focus on the needs of people and assist employees in feeling comfortable with themselves and with others in the organization. The root of this theory can be found in the Leader Behavior Description Questionnaire (LBDQ) conducted by Ohio State University (in 1945) and by the University of Michigan (in the 1950s).

TABLE 1.3 Traits and Skills Critical to Leaders

Traits	Skills
• Adaptable to situations	• Clever (intelligent)
• Alert to social environment	• Conceptually skilled
• Ambitious and achievement-oriented	• Creative
• Assertive	• Diplomatic and tactful
• Cooperative	• Fluent in speaking
• Decisive	• Knowledgeable about group task
• Dependable	• Organized (administrative ability)
• Dominant (desire to influence others)	• Persuasive
• Energetic (high activity level)	• Socially skilled
• Persistent	
• Self-confident	
• Tolerant of stress	
• Willing to assume responsibility	

From Stogdill (1974).

Contingency or Situational Theory

The contingency or situational theory of leadership is based on the premise that the success of leadership lies in the specific situation and circumstances in which it occurs. Different styles of leadership may be more appropriate for different types of decision making. According to this theory, no single style of leadership is appropriate in all situations, and successful leaders possess the ability to align their behaviors and actions in accordance with the situation. Gill (2011) explains, "Contingency theories suggest that there is no one best style of leadership. Successful and enduring leaders will use various styles according to the nature of the situation and the followers" (p. 79).

A number of different approaches to contingency theory have emerged over the years. The following are the ones most frequently referenced.

Fiedler's Contingency Theory

One of the first contingency theories was proposed by Fiedler in the 1960s. Fiedler's theory (Fiedler & Chemers, 1974) proposes that a leader's effectiveness hinges on how well her leadership style matches the current context and task (figure 1.2).

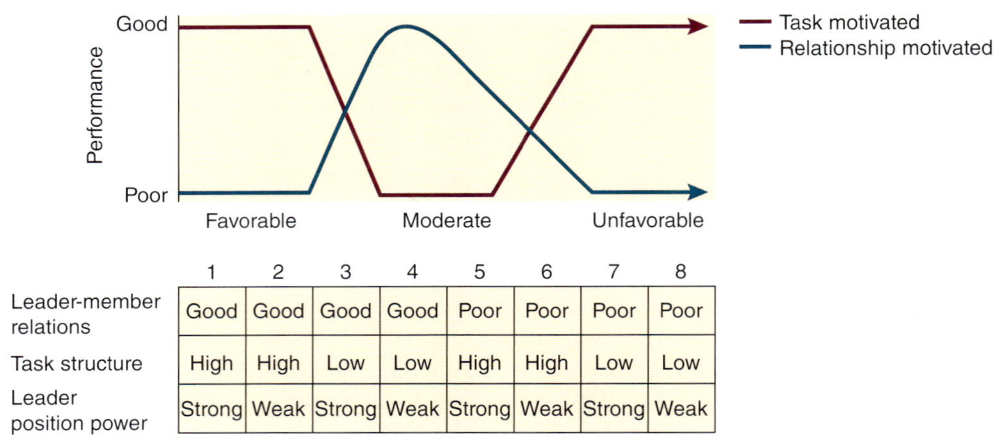

	1	2	3	4	5	6	7	8
Leader-member relations	Good	Good	Good	Good	Poor	Poor	Poor	Poor
Task structure	High	High	Low	Low	High	High	Low	Low
Leader position power	Strong	Weak	Strong	Weak	Strong	Weak	Strong	Weak

FIGURE 1.2 Fiedler's contingency model of leader–situation matches.

Reprinted from F.E. Fiedler and M.M. Chemers, *Leadership and Effective Management* (Scott Foresman, 1974).

Fiedler's theory asserts that leaders fall into one of two different leadership styles: task oriented or relationship oriented. The effectiveness of a person's style in a particular situation depends on how well defined the job is; how much authority, or power, the leader has; and the relationship between the followers and the leader.

The Evans and House Path–Goal Theory

The path–goal contingency theory of leadership, first proposed by Evans (1970) and expanded by House (1971), focuses on how leadership behavior and style can help followers achieve the group's goals. Four key types of leader behavior are identified as directive, supportive, achievement oriented, and participative, and the type of behavior applied should depend upon the nature of the task and the characteristics of the followers (figure 1.3).

Hersey and Blanchard's Situational Theory

Hersey and Blanchard (1988) proposed a situational theory of leadership in which the leadership depends on the individual situation and no single leadership style is considered best. The style that should be used in a particular situation depends on the maturity level of the subordinates. For example, if followers lack both knowledge and responsibility, the leader should adopt a directive leadership style in that situation. This leadership theory has two pillars, leadership style and the maturity level of the followers. The four basic leadership styles are S1, telling; S2, selling; S3, participating; and S4, delegating. These styles correspond to four maturity levels: M1, basic incompetence or unwillingness to do the task; M2, inability to do the task but willingness to do it; M3, competence to do the task but lack of belief in the ability to do it; and M4, readiness, willingness, and ability to do the task on the part of the group. Hersey later added four levels of commitment: D1, low competence and low commitment; D2, low competence and high commitment; D3, high competence and low or variable commitment; and D4, high competence and high commitment.

Vroom-Yetton Contingency Model

The Vroom-Yetton contingency model (developed in 1973 and later with Jago in 1988) further contends that the best style of leadership is contingent on the situation and takes into account varying styles of leadership: autocratic, consultative, and group based. Vroom defined motivation as "a process governing choice made by persons . . . among alternative forms of voluntary activity" (cited in Moniz, 2010, p. 53). This model takes into account how to involve followers in making group decisions.

Transactional Theory

Transactional theory, also known as *management theory*, was first developed by Weber in 1947. It focuses on the role of supervision, organization, and group performance and the exchanges that take place between leaders and followers. Transactional leadership focuses on results, conforms to the existing structure of

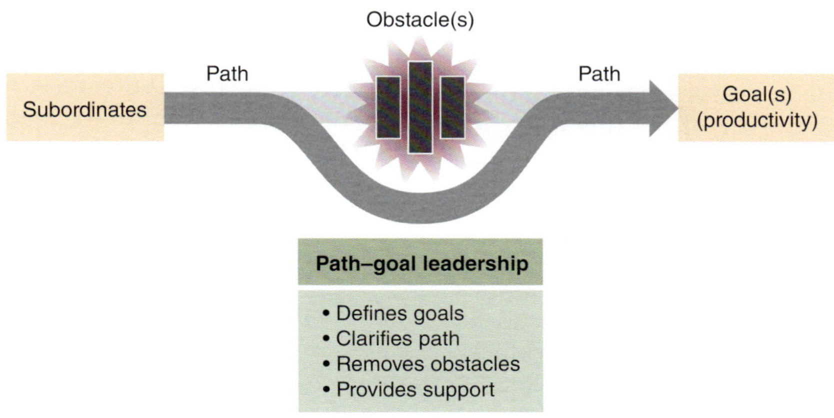

FIGURE 1.3 The Evans and House path–goal theory.

an organization, and measures success according to that organization's system of rewards and penalties (Charry, 2012). Transactional leaders have formal authority and positions of responsibility in an organization. The objective of the transactional leader is to ensure that barriers to goal attainment are removed in order to achieve stated goals. This type of leader is responsible for maintaining routine by managing individual performance and facilitating group performance (Spahr, 2014).

Transformational Theory

Transformational leadership, introduced by Burns (1978), asserts that leaders are people who transform their followers into becoming leaders themselves by creating a vision to guide the change through inspiration and motivation. A transformational leader has a vision and a passion to achieve great things. Followers and leaders must realize that their goals are mutually held, and both leaders and followers benefit from their interdependent relationship. Transformational leaders motivate and inspire people by helping group members see the importance and higher purpose of the task. These leaders are focused on the performance of group members, but also on each person with respect to fulfilling his potential. Leaders with this style often exhibit a high degree of ethical and moral standards (Charry, 2012).

Charismatic Leadership Theory

Charismatic leadership theory, introduced by Weber (1968), was based on the theory that leaders inspire eagerness in their followers and are energetic in moving people forward. It is rooted in the personal and behavioral characteristics of the leader. Charismatic leaders share many common traits such as dynamic personalities and an air of confidence; they are great communicators and have the ability to connect with their audience on an emotional level. They share an intangible quality that attracts and inspires loyal followers and motivates them to action. Under the guidance of a charismatic leader, organizations can be energized and transformed as the workforce supports the leader's vision and goals. Charismatic leadership resembles transformational leadership in that both types of leaders inspire and motivate their team members to execute at higher levels and be fully committed to the cause or organization.

Visionary Leadership

Visionary leadership theory seeks to identify what makes a great leader by studying leaders who inspire high levels of achievement in their followers through an inspiring vision and through other behaviors. A visionary leader is a leader who articulates a vision to followers, has the ability to create and sustain a vision for the organization, motivates individuals to share and commit to this vision, can align human and fiscal resources to accomplish the vision, and has the passion and necessary knowledge to achieve long-term goals and objectives.

Although several definitions of visionary leadership have been documented, the works of Burt Nanus (1992) emerge with regard to understanding the role of visionary leadership in organizational productivity and success. Nanus, in his book *Visionary Leadership: Creating a Compelling Sense of Direction for Your Organization*, states,

> *There is no more powerful engine driving an organization toward excellence and long-range success than an attractive, worthwhile, and achievable vision of the future, widely shared . . . there is no mystery about this. Effective leaders have agendas; they are totally result oriented. They adopt challenging new visions of what is both possible and desirable, communicate their visions, and persuade others to become so committed to these new directions that they are eager to lend their resources and energies to make it happen. (1992, pp. 3-4)*

Visionary leadership has further positive effects on follower outcomes, resulting in trust in and commitment to the leader, high levels of performance among followers, and high overall organizational performance.

Power, Authority, and Influence

Physical educators in administrative leadership positions are provided with the unique opportunity and responsibility to make organizational changes in a positive direction. How you exert your power, influence, and authority over people to achieve your desired results will determine how your followers perceive your leadership ability to effect change and gain support.

The general notion of *power*, according to Yukl and Gardner (2020), is helpful in understanding how some people are able to exert *influence* over others in an organization. Leaders need to exert some source of power to influence others in achieving organizational goals and objectives. One of the most influential theories of power is attributed to the work of French and Raven (1959), who developed a taxonomy to determine the sources of power leaders use to influence others. Through their work, five bases of power emerged:

1. *Legitimate:* This base comes from the belief that a person has a formal right to make demands, and to expect others to be compliant and obedient. Legitimate power is based on the position a person holds, not on the person.
2. *Reward:* This base results from one person's ability to compensate another for compliance. Reward power enables a leader to give out raises, promotions, and favorable assignments while knowing that if people receive an award, they will more likely do what the leader wants them to do.
3. *Expert:* This base refers to a person's high levels of skill and knowledge. Followers will listen to leaders who use solid judgment and leaders they can trust.
4. *Referent:* This base results from a person's attractiveness, worthiness, and right to others' respect. Leaders with referent power make people feel good, so they tend to exert influence.
5. *Coercive:* This base comes from the belief that a person can punish others for noncompliance. This type of power is least desirable as it has a tendency to cause negative effects and resentment.

Six years after the original bases of power were identified, Raven added another power base:

6. *Informational:* This base results from a person's ability to control the information that others need to accomplish something. This type of power is often data driven when decisions are made.

By understanding these different forms or bases of power, an effective leader can learn to use the positive ones to full effect. It should also be noted that power is dynamic and that it changes as the situations and conditions change.

Authority is the power that is formally given to an individual or group because of the position the person or group holds in an organization. Leaders' authority provides them with the right to make certain decisions for the organization and to ensure that subordinates follow those decisions. Such decisions might include work rules for the organization or the distribution of work assignments. How authority is exerted will be contingent on the culture of the organization, the amount of authority given to the leader, and the preferred management style of the leader.

Motivation Theories of Leadership

Understanding what inspires and motivates people toward goal attainment is a critical component of effective leadership. Gaining insight into the various needs and motives of your peers, subordinates, and supervisors will have a positive impact on the organization as a whole. In an attempt to answer the complex question of what motivates individuals to reach their fullest potential in the pursuit of individual excellence and organizational success, this section explores several **motivation theories of leadership**.

Maslow's Hierarchy of Needs

Maslow's hierarchy of needs is a theory proposed by American psychologist Abraham Maslow in his 1943 paper "A Theory of Human Motivation" (see figure 1.4). Maslow's theoretical framework was based on understanding motivation that arises from the needs and wants of an individual. These needs further drive people through action and work, and they are based on the theory that people have a distinct set of needs: physiological needs, safety needs, love and belonging needs, esteem needs, and needs for self-actualization. Maslow proposed that

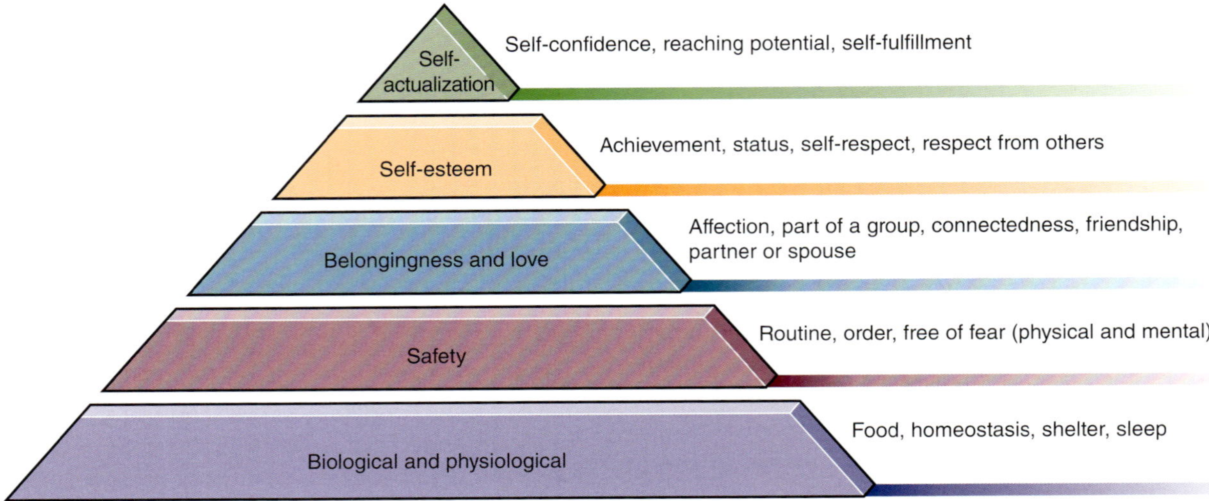

FIGURE 1.4 Maslow's hierarchy of needs.

people focus on meeting their basic needs and then move up the hierarchy until they reach the need for self-actualization. This level of need refers to what a person's full potential is and the realization of that potential. As Maslow put it, "What a man can be, he must be" forms the basis of the perceived need for self-actualization (p 370-396).

Herzberg's Motivation–Hygiene Theory

Frederick Herzberg constructed a two-dimensional paradigm of factors, also known as the *two-factor theory* or *dual-factor theory* (figure 1.5), through which he sought to understand how work activities and the nature of an employee's job influence motivation and performance. Herzberg's 1959 theory involved what he termed *motivators* and *hygiene factors*.

Motivators are intrinsic factors that give positive satisfaction and arise from intrinsic conditions of the job itself, such as recognition, achievement, or personal growth. According to Herzberg, motivators are the conditions that encourage individuals to work harder. In contrast, hygiene factors are external factors, such as company policies, supervision, working conditions, salary, and job security. These factors are part of the context in which the job is performed, as opposed to the job itself. Herzberg noted that good hygiene could prevent dissatisfaction, but it could not necessarily create a positive attitude or motivation to work. Herzberg (1959) further argued that work motivation is influenced to a large extent by the degree to which a job is intrinsically challenging and provides opportunities for recognition and reinforcement.

Motivators	**Hygiene factors**
Leading to satisfaction	Leading to dissatisfaction
• Achievement • Recognition • Work itself • Responsibility • Advancement • Personal growth	• Company policy • Supervision • Work conditions • Status • Job security • Salary • Relationship with peers and boss

FIGURE 1.5 Herzberg motivation–hygiene theory.

Alderfer's ERG Theory

The ERG theory, developed by Clayton Alderfer in 1969, holds that the main motivational factors are *existence*, *relatedness*, and *growth* (figure 1.6). In relation to Maslow's work, Alderfer distinguishes three categories of human needs that influence a person's behavior in the workplace: Existence needs are the physiological and safety needs; relatedness needs are the social and esteem needs; and growth needs

LEADERSHIP IN ACTION

Leading the Nation's Largest Urban School District: Building a Model Program

Lindsey Harr

Executive director, (2011-2021), Hip Hop Public Health

Establishing rigorous PE for all students—especially in urban school districts—requires us to reach beyond pedagogical knowledge and fluency with research that eloquently makes the case for PE as an essential part of every child's education. Education leaders need a nuanced understanding of the political realities that surround education locally and nationally so they can be nimble in positioning PE as a central part of the conversation. They must also seek partners in a variety of sectors to create diverse networks of stakeholders who can help to move the PE agenda forward. In New York City, this two-pronged approach, coupled with an uncompromising commitment to prioritize physical education instruction, enabled us to embark on an unprecedented initiative to revitalize PE in all of our 1,600 schools for each one of our 1.1 million students.

Central support for PE at the New York City Department of Education (DOE) largely disappeared following the city's brush with bankruptcy in 1970s. When a small central team was reestablished in 2003, PE as a core instructional area was still far from being an educational or political priority. Too many students had inadequate physical education, if they had it at all. In the DOE's Office of School Wellness Programs, which is partially funded through the city's health department, our vision and mission was to establish PE as an essential element of the K-12 academic program, which is a given rather than an afterthought.

Our approach was to proactively align ourselves not only with the educational priorities of our agency in any given year but also with the city's public health agenda, where growing concerns about childhood obesity led to expanded opportunities for collaboration, resource development, and messaging. In this endeavor, our success required that we stay well-informed and well-connected. We built relationships with a range of partners, from community-based organizations to national groups. We engaged those inside and outside of the DOE with whom we had complementary priorities, and we educated stakeholders who could amplify our message about systematically addressing barriers to PE and who could advocate in settings where we did not have access. Over time, growing and informed awareness about the importance of PE and the challenges to providing it for every student moved physical education into the political conversation; ultimately, it resulted in Mayor Bill de Blasio making an investment of $100 million in 2016 to bring New York City schools into compliance with state PE requirements over four years.

When the mayor asked us to "fix PE," we knew what the main barriers were; so did our partners. We were able to quickly design a plan to establish PE as a core academic area due in part to the groundwork we laid helping our constituents understand the reality-based barriers to PE and due to our smaller-scale efforts to test effective solutions for those barriers.

PE Works combined a rigorous pedagogical approach with a strong customer service model that tackled very real and practical challenges that our schools face, including generations of educators who had never experienced the full potential of physical education. We partnered with DOE Human Resources and local colleges to build a pipeline for the 400+ new certified PE teachers being hired under PE Works. We expanded and reorganized our team to be responsive to the varying needs of teachers, principals, and district leaders, with Central Office staff who had a diverse mix of expertise.

For our PE teachers, we focused on improving instructional quality and developing them as teacher-leaders, with dedicated instructional coaches assigned to each school, new professional development, one-on-one coaching cycles, professional learning communities, and more. For our principals, we used on-site needs assessments to collaboratively create individualized, multi-year action plans, providing them with specific, customized assistance and resources to create the conditions for PE to thrive in their school. At the district level, we partnered with other divisions to make policy changes, solve problems, and build buy-in for the school-level transformations required. At all levels, this work benefited from an extensive network of partnerships with community-based and advocate organizations as well as our education and public health colleagues.

The PE Works initiative will be judged not by its success after 4 years, but by the state of PE in New York City 10 and 20 years from now. Did we shift the culture in schools and in the district so that PE is not an afterthought, but an essential component of every child's education? Is there a thriving group of physical

(continued)

Leading the Nation's Largest Urban School District: Building a Model Program *(continued)*

education leaders with a central role in their educational community as they help develop the next generation of leaders? Is every child in New York City receiving rigorous, high-quality physical education that enables them to live a healthy life? Sustaining the investment we have made in New York City will rely on the same strategies that have brought us to this point: keeping PE relevant and central to the conversation throughout whatever education, public health, and political shifts lie ahead and continuing to expand our network of partners and advocates in every sector who understand the value of PE and will never stop demanding it for our students.

Reprinted by permission from Lindsey Harr

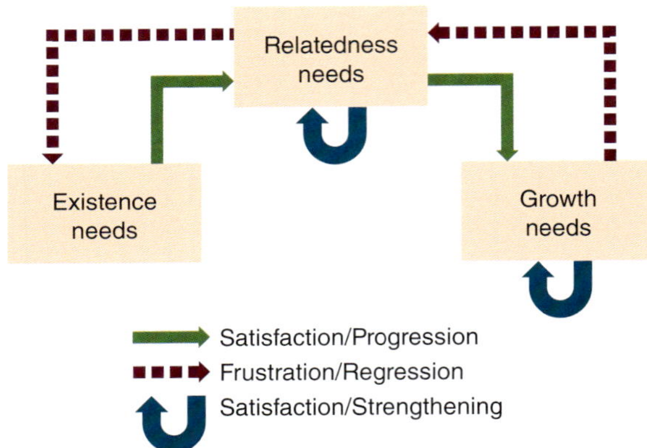

FIGURE 1.6 Alderfer's ERG theory.
Based on Wikipedia, https://en.wikipedia.org/wiki/ERG_theory.

are the self-actualization needs. Although these categories are not hierarchical in any way, all three categories of needs must be met to enable the subordinate to pursue personal achievement.

McGregor's Theory X and Theory Y

In 1960, Douglas McGregor developed a leadership premise based on two opposing presumptions about people and work. McGregor postulated that there are two types of assumptions regarding employees: theory X and theory Y. Theory X assumes that employees are naturally lazy, avoid work as much as possible, do not like to take responsibility, and have no ambition. Therefore, theory X suggests that in order to motivate employees, a relatively autocratic style of management is required. Conversely, theory Y assumes that workers enjoy work, are motivated and committed to the objectives of the organization, and are self-directed in the attainment of organizational goals and objectives. Therefore, subordinates according to this assumption do not require external control. There is some balance to be achieved between these two perspectives; however, theory Y motivators tend to have the preferable approach to building strong collaborative cultures.

Hawthorne Effect

Although not a theory, the Hawthorne effect is noteworthy since as an administrator you are always looking for ways to increase performance and productivity, whether in an organization, a school district, or a classroom. The Hawthorne effect, as described by Henry A. Landsberger in 1958, reflected a tendency for people to work harder and perform better when they were being observed. Originating out of an experiment with lighting conducted in 1924 through 1932 at Hawthorne Works in the Chicago area, it was noted that worker productivity increased when changes were made to the lighting at both higher and lower levels. The conclusion was that lighting had nothing to do with productivity; what resulted in a greater motivational effect on the workers was the attention being paid to them. This is a valuable lesson to leadership at all levels.

This section explored many theories of motivation that have an impact on group and individual motivation toward goal attainment. Although the list is far from exhaustive, the theories of Maslow, Herzberg, Alderfer, and McGregor should provide insight as to the importance of motivation in the workplace, which is a critical component of individual and group performance in working toward a common goal. As an effective leader, having a thorough knowledge of motivational factors will assist you in understanding the basic needs of your employees and staff and how to get the most out of productivity, performance, and job satisfaction.

Strategic Planning

Regardless of whether you hold a leadership position within a corporation or an educational setting, **strategic planning** is a crucial element necessary to obtain the goals, objectives, and mission of the organization. A school district's strategic plan further serves as a means of focusing on specific goals and objectives, developing strategies for attaining those goals and objectives, then selecting measures to ensure attainment through a systematic process. The overall plan should focus on providing broad guidance so that all aspects of the school district can work toward the common goal of attaining specific identified goals to meet both student and management needs. The goals and objectives are usually determined based on the results of a needs assessment. District-level funding will also follow the goals identified in the strategic plan to ensure that both human and fiscal resources are allocated where the greatest needs are. To ensure departmental involvement, the physical education administrator would then review the district's strategic plan; it would use that review as a launching point for developing the department's annual plan as well as developing the physical education strategic plan. In many cases, administrative staff at all levels would be evaluated based on how they met their key performance indicators aligned with the strategic plan. See chapter 2 for examples.

In most districts, to ensure transparency and accountability, the planning, or steering, committee is usually composed of the superintendent, senior-level district administrators, community and business members, parents, and a student representative. In larger school districts, a chief strategy officer would be hired by the school district with the sole responsibility of leading the development team, communicating the strategic plan with all employees and community members, executing and monitoring implementation of the plan, and reviewing and revising the plan on an annual basis. The process of developing a district-wide strategic plan is complex, especially since it involves consensus among all committee members on focused goals and strategy decisions.

Strategic Planning Process

Once the planning committee is determined, the next phase is to determine what should be included in the strategic plan. Several articles have been published on the strategic planning process; for the most part, there is agreement that the strategic planning process should follow a sequence for development, including the following steps:

- *Identify* the goals, objectives, and mission of your school district, then *prioritize* which goals and objectives to focus on. These priorities would usually be determined by a specific needs assessment such as looking at student achievement scores, district fiscal management, community engagement, student health and social needs, and any category based on local needs.
- *Develop* strategies to achieve the selected objectives under each priority area. They could be district-wide or department-level strategies to ensure that they are specific to either the subject area or the office with oversight responsibilities.
- *Assess and evaluate* attainment of goals and objectives through continuous data points. This process could guide both mid-year and end-of-year department and personnel evaluations.
- *Revise* strategies if key performance indicators are not met.

Since strategic plans usually follow a three- to five-year planning cycle, through continuous evaluations the school district could monitor progress in meeting the goals and objectives. Convening the planning committee on an annual basis to review the data collection points ensures that transparency and communication among all stakeholders are occurring and that there is a sense of trust between the community and district leadership.

The leader plays several roles in the development of strategic plans (Bryson & Crosby, 1995, pp. 357-381; cited in Scott, 2014). Table 1.4 provides an illustration of these processes.

TABLE 1.4 Leader's Role in Making Strategic Planning Work

Understand the Context	1. Leaders should help constituents view their organization and organizational change in the context of relevant social, political, economic, technological, and ecological systems and trends.
Understand the People Involved, Including Oneself	1. Understanding oneself and others is particularly important for developing the strength of character and insight that invigorate leadership and increase the chances that strategic planning and implementation will help the organization. 2. Leaders should seek to understand the strengths and weaknesses of the people who are or should be involved in strategic planning and implementation, including themselves. 3. Perhaps the most important strength is a passion for fulfilling the organization's mission and contributing to the well-being of multiple stakeholders.
Sponsor the Process	1. Articulate the purpose and importance of strategic planning effort. 2. Commit necessary resources—time, money, energy, and legitimacy. 3. Emphasize at the beginning and at critical points that action and change will result. 4. Encourage and reward creative thinking, constructive debate, and multiple sources of input and insight. 5. Be aware of the possible need for outside consultants. 6. Be willing to exercise power and authority to keep the process on track.
Champion the Process	1. Keep strategic planning high on people's agendas. 2. Attend to the process without promoting specific solutions. 3. Think about what has to come together at or before key decision points. 4. Organize time, space, materials, and participation needed for the process to succeed. 5. Pay attention to the language used to describe strategic planning and implementation. 6. Keep rallying participants and pushing the process along. 7. Develop champions throughout the organization. 8. Be sensitive to power differences.
Facilitate the Process	1. Know the strategic planning process, and explain how it works at the beginning and at many points along the way. 2. Tailor the process to the organization and the groups involved. 3. Convey a sense of humor and enthusiasm for the process, and help groups get unstuck. 4. Ensure that participants (rather than the facilitators) are doing the work. 5. Press groups toward action and the assignment of responsibility for specific action. 6. Congratulate people whenever possible.
Foster Collective Leadership	1. Rely on teams. 2. Focus on network and coalition development. 3. Make leadership and followership development an explicit strategy. 4. Establish specific mechanisms for sharing power, responsibility, and accountability.
Create a Meaningful Process	1. Understand the design and use of forums. 2. Seize opportunities to be interpreters and direction givers in areas of uncertainty and difficulty. 3. Reveal and name real needs and real conditions. 4. Help coleaders and followers frame and reframe issues and strategies. 5. Offer compelling visions of the future. 6. Champion new and improved ideas for dealing with strategic issues. 7. Articulate desired actions and expected consequences.
Implement Decisions in Arenas	1. Understand the design and use of arenas. 2. Mediate and shape conflict within and among stakeholders. 3. Understand the dynamics of political influence and how to target resources appropriately. 4. Build winning, sustainable coalitions. 5. Avoid bureaucratic imprisonment.
Enforce Norms, Settle Disputes, and Manage Conflicts	1. Understand the design and use of formal and informal courts. 2. Foster organizational (collaboration, community) integrity, and educate others about ethics, constitutions, laws, and norms. 3. Apply constitutions, laws, and norms to specific cases. 4. Adapt constitutions, laws, and norms to changing times. 5. Resolve conflicts among constitutions, laws, and norms.

From J. Greenberg and J. LoBianco, *Organization and Administration of Physical Education,* 2nd ed. (Human Kinetics, 2026). Based on Bryson and Crosby (1995, p. 357-381).

Strategic Management

Strategic management, according to Rollinson, "is the comprehensive collection of ongoing activities and processes that organizations use to systematically coordinate and align resources and actions with mission, vision and strategy throughout an organization" (n.d.). Strategic management further involves examining data points against a set of performance measures to make future decisions about the direction of the organization. Once the strengths and weaknesses are determined, decisions can be made as to where to best allocate the organization's resources, both fiscal and human. Strategic planning is a future-oriented activity, whereas strategic management is the execution of the strategies to achieve the goals and objectives. Through sound strategic management practices, strategies can be more readily revised if the data show that target points are not being met. This carefully monitored process could lead to a higher probability of meeting your goals and objectives.

Ethical Leadership

The ability to develop a culture of ethics within an organization begins with the ethical and moral character of the leader. Leaders develop the climate and create the culture where values, trust, and respect are woven into every level of the organization. Ethical leaders place the interests of their followers and the organization ahead of their own interests, and they show overt respect for others' feelings, decisions, values, and beliefs.

Ethical leadership should also be understood through the lens of its influence over other leadership theories. Being ethical is a core part of other leadership styles, and a strong ethical foundation is required for styles such as transformational and charismatic leadership. While a strong ethical outlook is required for these leadership theories, ethical leadership places the greatest emphasis on implementing ethical values within every aspect of leadership.

Ethical leadership and management should be omnipresent in every organization; this precept is no different in school districts, where the ethical conduct of the superintendent sets the tone for the district office, schools, and all employees at every level. Most school districts develop their own code of ethics through school board rules; as an example, figure 1.7 provides sections I through III of the Code of Ethics for Miami-Dade County Public Schools. School board rules further include individual state statutes for the code of ethics for the education profession.

Developing ethics in leadership is a multidimensional, complex practice; leaders have to juggle many different competing situations while working with different personalities and needs. This task requires leaders to be introspective about how decisions are made beyond their own special interests and how they have to hold themselves accountable for those decisions. Through this process of ethical leadership, the culture transforms itself to one of trust and credibility where all employees feel respected, engaged, and part of the organization.

To create this ethics-focused organizational culture and climate, according to Linda Fisher Thornton (2013), "Effective leaders focus on what's right and exemplify to their people that they are there to help, and not to exploit the vulnerability of others." Thornton further outlines several steps to ethical leadership:

1. *Model ethical behavior.* Be a leader who adheres to high ethical standards in your own professional life, consistently treating others with respect and authenticity.
2. *Adopt transparency in decision making and communications.* Have an open-door policy and regular one-on-one meetings so employees know their suggestions and insights are welcome and valued.
3. *Establish a formal ethics or values statement.* This statement should be a living, breathing, foundational document that helps center your staff and guide them as they navigate ethical gray areas. The values communicated in this document must be modeled.
4. *Insist that everyone meet ethical expectations.* Allow no excuses. Make sure that no one is exempt from meeting the adopted ethical standards. Maintain the status of ethics as a total, absolute must in the organization.

FIGURE 1.7 Sections I, II, and III of the Code of Ethics for Miami-Dade County Public Schools

I. INTRODUCTION

All members of The School Board of Miami-Dade County, Florida, administrators, teachers and all other employees of Miami-Dade County Public Schools, regardless of their position, because of their dual roles as public servants and educators are to be bound by the following Code of Ethics. Adherence to the Code of Ethics will create an environment of honesty and integrity and will aid in achieving the common mission of providing a safe and high quality education to all Miami-Dade County Public Schools students.

As stated in the Code of Ethics of the Education Profession in Florida (State Board of Education Rule 6B-1.001):

1. The educator values the worth and dignity of every person, the pursuit of truth, devotion to excellence, acquisition of knowledge, and the nurture of democratic citizenship. Essential to the achievement of these standards are the freedom to learn and to teach and the guarantee of equal opportunity for all.
2. The educator's primary professional concern will always be for the student and for the development of the student's potential. The educator will therefore strive for professional growth and will seek to exercise the best professional judgment and integrity.
3. Aware of the importance of maintaining the respect and confidence of one's colleagues, students, parents, and other members of the community, the educator strives to achieve and sustain the highest degree of ethical conduct. Further, non-academic and elected officials are bound to accept these principles since these groups reflect critical policy direction and support services for the essential academic purpose.

II. APPLICATION

This Code of Ethics applies to all members of The School Board of Miami-Dade County, Florida, administrators, teachers, and all other employees. The term "employee," as used herein, applies to all these groups regardless of full or part time status. It further applies to all persons who receive any direct economic benefit such as membership in School Board funded insurance programs.

Employees are subject to various other laws, rules, and regulations including but not limited to "The Code of Ethics for the Education Profession in Florida and the Principles of Professional Conduct of the Education Profession in Florida," Chapter 6B-1.001 and -1.006, F.A.C., the "Code of Ethics for Public Officers and Employees," found in Chapter 112, Part III of the Florida Statutes, and School Board Rule 6Gx13- 4A-1.212, Conflict of Interest, which are incorporated herein by reference and this Code of Ethics should be viewed as additive to these laws, rules and regulations. To the extent not in conflict with any laws, School Board rules or governmental regulations, this Code of Ethics shall control with regard to conduct. In the event of any conflict, the law, regulation or School Board Rule shall control.

III. FUNDAMENTAL PRINCIPLES

The fundamental principles upon which this Code of Ethics is predicated are as follows:

- Citizenship—Helping to create a society based upon democratic values; e.g., rule of law, equality of opportunity, due process, reasoned argument, representative government, checks and balances, rights and responsibilities, and democratic decision-making.

- Cooperation—Working together toward goals as basic as human survival in an increasingly interdependent world.
- Fairness—Treating people impartially, not playing favorites, being open minded, and maintaining an objective attitude toward those whose actions and ideas are different from our own.
- Honesty—Dealing truthfully with people, being sincere, not deceiving them nor stealing from them, not cheating nor lying.
- Integrity—Standing up for your beliefs about what is right and what is wrong and resisting social pressure to do wrong.
- Kindness—Being sympathetic, helpful, compassionate, benevolent, agreeable, and gentle toward people and other living things.
- Pursuit of Excellence—Doing your best with the talents you have, striving toward a goal, and not giving up.
- Respect—Showing regard for the worth and dignity of someone or something, being courteous and polite, and judging all people on their merits. It takes three major forms: respect for oneself, respect for other people, and respect for all forms of life and the environment.
- Responsibility—Thinking before you act and being accountable for your actions, paying attention to others and responding to their needs. Responsibility emphasizes our positive obligations to care for each other.

Each employee agrees and pledges:

1. To abide by this Code of Ethics, making the well-being of the students and the honest performance of professional duties core guiding principles.
2. To obey local, state and national laws, codes and regulations.
3. To support the principles of due process to protect the civil and human rights of all individuals.
4. To treat all persons with respect and to strive to be fair in all matters.
5. To take responsibility and be accountable for his or her actions.
6. To avoid conflicts of interest or any appearance of impropriety.
7. To cooperate with others to protect and advance the District and its students.
8. To be efficient and effective in the delivery of job duties.

5. *Recognize and reward examples of ethical behavior.* Be a proactive ethical leader, championing high ethical conduct and emphasizing prevention.
6. *Talk about ethics as an ongoing learning journey, not a once-a-year training program.* Integrate ethics into every action of the organization—everything people do, touch, or influence.

Ethical leaders work under the principle that everyone is valued and an important part of the organization. As a physical education administrator, maintaining a high level of professionalism and ethical leadership will further assist your efforts in working with teachers, especially when it comes time to advocate for your programs or make programmatic changes in the adoption of new curriculum or district-level mandates. Exhibiting traits such as respect, honesty, integrity, and moral character at department chair meetings or in staff professional development will enable you to focus more on team building and implementation of innovative concepts while earning the trust and support of your colleagues and teachers. In other words: *lead by example.*

Conflict Resolution

Conflict resolution is another relatively common issue that leaders confront on a regular basis in all organizations. The key for effective leaders is to learn to manage the conflict so that it does not disrupt or interfere with the work of the team, whole department, or organization. Astute leaders must be able to recognize when conflict is occurring and be prepared to handle it. Avoiding conflict could lead to an unhealthy work environment.

Conflicts arise from differences among people when they disagree over values, motivations, perceptions, or ideas. To the leader, they may seem of lesser importance within the scope of the daily responsibilities; to those involved, however, conflicts often trigger strong feelings. To gain an understanding of conflict resolution theory and models, this section explores the work of Thomas and Kilmann (1974) and Fisher and Ury (1981).

Thomas and Kilmann (1974) identified five main styles of dealing with conflict that vary in their degrees of cooperativeness and assertiveness. They discovered that people have a preferred conflict resolution style, and to identify that style they developed the Thomas-Kilmann conflict mode instrument (TKI) (figure 1.8). Here are the styles identified:

- *Competitive*: People who gravitate toward a competitive style take a firm stand and know what they want. They usually draw from a position of power, rank, and expertise.
- *Collaborative*: People who gravitate toward a collaborative style try to meet the needs of all people involved. They can be highly assertive, but unlike those who adopt the competitive style, they cooperate effectively and acknowledge that everyone is important.
- *Compromising*: People who gravitate toward a compromising style try to find a solution that will at least partially satisfy everyone. Everyone is expected to give up something on both sides of the conflict.
- *Accommodating:* People who gravitate toward an accommodating style display a willingness to meet the needs of others at the expense of their own needs. This person is not assertive, but highly cooperative.

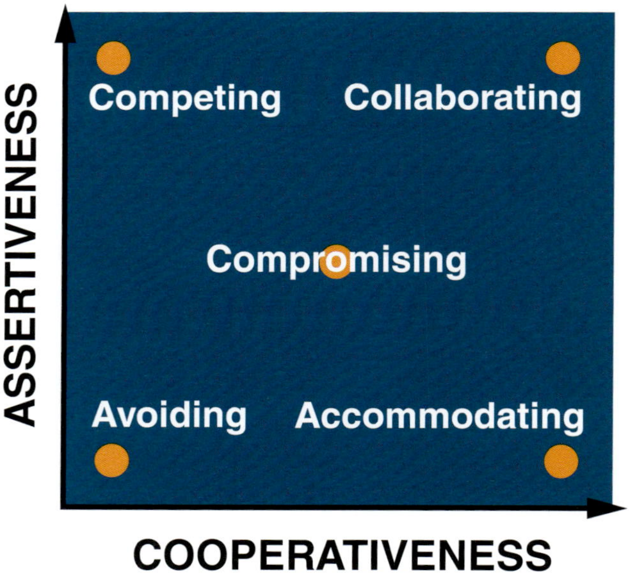

FIGURE 1.8 Thomas-Kilmann Conflict Mode Instrument.

- *Avoiding*: People who gravitate toward this style seek to evade conflict entirely. This style is exemplified by delegating controversial decisions and not wanting to hurt anyone's feelings.

As a leader using the TKI, a thorough understanding of the different styles will assist you in deciding on the most appropriate approach to use for the present situation. Various situations will require various approaches.

Fisher and Ury (1981) developed the interest-based relational (IBR) approach to conflict resolution. This approach asserts that you resolve conflicts by separating people and their emotions from the problem. It is built on establishing mutual respect and understanding, which enables the leader to resolve conflicts in a cooperative manner. To be effective, the parties in conflict need to follow these six steps:

1. *Make sure that good relationships are the first priority.* As far as possible, make sure that you treat the other calmly and that you try to build mutual respect. Do your best to be courteous to one another and remain constructive under pressure.
2. *Keep people and problems separate.* Recognize that in many cases, the other person is not just being difficult; real and valid differences can lie behind conflictive positions. Through separating the problem from the person, real issues can be debated without damaging working relationships.
3. *Pay attention to the interests that are being presented.* By listening carefully you'll most likely understand why the person is adopting her position.
4. *Listen first; talk second.* To solve a problem effectively, you have to understand where the other person is coming from before defending your own position.
5. *Set out the facts.* Agree on and establish the objective, observable elements that will have an impact on the decision.
6. *Explore options together.* Be open to the idea that a third position may exist and that you can get to this idea jointly.

Although conflicts arise in every organization due to the ongoing dynamics and interactions of the people that make up the organization, it behooves leaders at every level to learn the skills inherent in conflict resolution. The TKI and IBR approaches to conflict resolution should assist the leader in identifying which approaches would be most beneficial in situation-specific disputes. Conflicts should be addressed as soon as they arise, and a quick solution that all parties can agree on will keep the organization moving forward toward the common mission, goals, and objectives.

Diversity in Leadership

Since the mid-1970s, major organizations as well as educational institutions have acknowledged the need to address **diversity in leadership and management** positions. In more recent times as the population of the United States has become more diverse, so have the number of students of color, ethnicities, and number of students with culturally and linguistically diverse backgrounds in U.S. schools. Understanding cultures different from your own is also becoming increasingly important due to the globalization of business and education. As a result, there has been a deliberate focus in school districts and corporations on hiring diverse leaders as well as incorporating programs to develop a pool of diverse personnel to assume leadership roles as they become available. This focus has become especially important since a diverse workforce could prevent a school district from becoming too insulated and removed from its increasingly changing student base.

Although there have been many U.S. federal laws throughout the years to address equality and equity in education, for both students and personnel (such as Title 6 of the Civil Rights Act of 1964, Title 7 of the Civil Rights Act of 1964, Executive Order 11246 as amended by Executive Order 11375, Equal Pay Act of 1963, Title IX of the Education Amendments Act of 1972, and the Lilly Ledbetter Fair Pay Act of 2009) as well as state administrative laws that affect school districts, in many cases, the practices of adhering to these laws have not kept up with the intent of the law. However, although the lack of diversity in leadership positions may be based on unintentional past practices, deliberate actions can be implemented to change course.

Developing and expanding a culture of diversity and inclusion means developing respect for and appreciation of differences in ethnicity, gender, age, national origin, disability, sexual orientation, education, and religion. It means creating and maintaining an environment—which starts at the top—in which all employees feel that they are valued, empowered, and respected and that they have the same opportunities as everyone else. This goal can be accomplished through the recruitment and selection process regarding qualified personnel, identification and development of diverse talent, providing opportunities for training and personal growth while eliminating preconceptions of roles and abilities, pairing of mentors and mentees, and developing a synergy among team members across all departments.

Women in Leadership: Breaking the Glass Ceiling

Prior to the adoption of Title IX in 1972, women faced barriers in advancement to upper-level leadership and management positions, in part because of sex-based biases and beliefs, stereotypes, and role expectations (Stogdill, 1974). There is no shortage of qualified women. However, regardless of the increasing amount of research on barriers to the advancement of women (Bell & Nkomo, 2001) and the advancement of civil rights and education reform movements, men still outnumber women when it comes to holding CEO positions and top educational leadership roles.

The United States Federal Glass Ceiling Commission (U.S. Department of Labor, 1995, p. iii) defined the *glass ceiling* as "the unseen yet impenetrable barrier that keeps minorities and women from rising to the upper rungs of the corporate ladder, regardless of their qualifications or achievements." Accordingly, 6 percent of the companies in the Standard and Poor's 500 index had female chief executive officers; 10 percent of the Fortune 500 companies had female CEOs (Hinchliffe, 2023); in education, 26 percent of superintendent positions were held by females (AASA, 2021) although 77 percent of public school teachers were women (NCES, 2023), and 27 percent of posts in Congress were held by females (CAWP, 2022). For women of color (Asian, Black, and Hispanic), the percentages were even lower. Although there is limited research on the role of women in physical education leadership, research supports that male athletic directors continue to outnumber the women in the field of sport.

Through these disparities in equity access, women are denied opportunities for status, monetary compensation, and the ability to make a difference in the workforce. Another pronounced barrier that prevents women from advancing to upper levels of leadership is their "exclusion from networks and conversations that open doors to further development and promotion" (Groysberg & Connolly, 2013, p. 70). Women need to assertively prepare for the opportunity to climb the corporate ladder by taking advantage of training and development opportunities as well as networking among peers, mentors, and leaders within various organizations. Organizations and school districts need to develop a human resource plan to identify, nurture, and actively recruit qualified women for positions. However, only through proactive measures and overcoming stereotypes and biases can change occur.

Managing Diversity

Managing diversity in the workforce is a major responsibility of leaders in the 21st century, and leaders can do many things to foster an appreciation of and tolerance for people of diverse backgrounds (Yukl & Gardner, 2020, p. 369). Figure 1.9 offers guidelines for leaders to follow as a means of managing diversity.

Today's leaders in organizational and educational settings have an essential role in the management of diversity in developing a new workforce to meet the growing needs for the next generation of leaders. It is the responsibility of leaders to ensure that organizations encourage tolerance and appreciation of diversity within their settings and that equal opportunity as well as the elimination of discrimination are exercised in selection and promotion decisions.

Conclusion

This chapter examined the formal role of leadership inherent in organizations and educational settings. Within the physical education environment, whether you are a district-level

FIGURE 1.9 Guidelines for Managing Diversity

- Set an example in your own behavior of appreciation for diversity.
- Encourage respect for individual differences.
- Promote understanding of different values, beliefs, and traditions.
- Explain the benefits of diversity for the team or organization.
- Encourage and support others who promote diversity.
- Discourage use of stereotypes to describe people.
- Identify biased beliefs and role expectations for women or underrepresented ethnic groups.
- Challenge people who make prejudiced comments.
- Speak out to protest against unfair treatment based on prejudice.
- Take disciplinary action to stop harassment of women or underrepresented ethnic groups.

administrator or a physical education department chairperson, the role of the leader is complex; it will vary depending on the situation, the culture of the organization, and the people involved. There are as many definitions of leadership as there are characteristics that make up an effective leader. Empirical studies on the theories of leadership, philosophies of leadership, and motivational theories of leadership all influence people's personal styles of leadership along with their various personalities, values, and beliefs.

However, regardless of the leadership style, the true leader is often the *visionary*, who sets the goals and direction for the organization as well as has the capacity to inspire and motivate people toward achieving those goals. Leaders build direction to bring about change while connecting their vision with the needs, goals, and aspirations of their followers. Leadership is also about setting a positive example for staff to follow and exhibiting honesty, integrity, trustworthiness, and high ethical standards. When leaders can motivate and influence people in accepting that vision, the organization can move forward toward the successful attainment of goals and objectives.

Review Questions

1. Describe the various roles and responsibilities of the physical education administrator, and explain the impact they have on leadership in an educational setting.
2. Identify the various philosophies of leadership, and describe their impact on physical education.
3. Differentiate between the various theories of leadership and how each one plays a part in the educational process.
4. Identify the various motivational theories, and describe how they would be used to inspire staff.
5. Describe the importance of strategic leadership and planning to meet goals and objectives.
6. As an educational leader, describe how diversity management would have an impact on providing opportunities and future leaders.
7. Describe why ethics in leadership is a critical component in an educational setting.

» Visit HK*Propel* for reproducible forms.

CHAPTER 2

Management and Operations

Jayne D. Greenberg

© Courtesy of Crittenden LLC

LEARNING OBJECTIVES

After reading this chapter, you will be able to do the following:

- Identify the theories of management.
- Identify motivation theories of management.
- Discuss change theory.
- Describe how to supervise employees.
- Summarize the roles and responsibilities of the physical education administrator as a manager.
- Identify day-to-day operations.

KEY CONCEPTS

change theory
department chairperson
effective communication
emotional intelligence (EI)
management function
management theory
motivation theory
social intelligence (SI)
systems thinking
teachers as leaders
time management

As discussed in chapter 1, although differences exist between the definitions and roles described in leadership and management as delineated by function, they are not mutually exclusive. The success of any organization's ability to attain its goals and objectives is contingent on the complementary and collaborative efforts of both the leader and the manager. However, although theoretical differences exist in defining leadership versus management, most researchers agree that in order to be a successful manager or administrator one must have an inherent degree of leadership.

The role of the leader is often seen as that of a visionary who sets the mission of the organization as well as inspires and motivates people to believe in that vision. Managers focus on the systems and structure of the organization in working with people to maintain the day-to-day operations and logistics, workflow, and achievement of tasks to reach the desired goals and objectives; nevertheless, they can also serve in the capacity of a leader.

This chapter focuses on understanding management theories; motivation theories; skills, competencies, and functions of effective managers; managers as change agents; and the day-to-day operations of the physical education administrator as both a leader and a manager.

Management Theories

Through the years, researchers have proffered a variety of **management theories** and **motivation theories** in order to better understand how organizations work as well as how people behave within organizations. Gaining a theoretical understanding of managerial effectiveness is key to developing an effective workforce that can attain organizational goals and objectives in an environment that is conducive to greater productivity.

Peter Drucker, who introduced the theory of management by objectives (MBO), has been described as the founder of modern management. Under the MBO theory, Drucker states that objectives must be realistic, achievable, measurable, and motivating or else they are useless. Drucker's reputation as a leader in management was established with *The Practice of Management* (1954), a work still highly regarded by theorists. His five basic principles of management focus on

1. setting objectives,
2. organizing,
3. motivating and communicating,
4. establishing measurements of performance, and
5. developing people.

Drucker asserts that these objectives are more likely to be achieved when developed cooperatively between management and employees in open discussions.

The earliest research in the study of managerial effectiveness, conducted during the 1930s and 1940s, attempted to look at an individual's traits, such as personality, temperament, needs, motives, and values (Yukl & Gardner, 2020). Linking individual traits to successful leadership was originally suggested by Carlyle (1837) and then supported by Galton (1869), Cowley (1931), Allport (1937), Guilford (1959), Cattell (1965), and Eysenck (1967, 1970). In a meta-analysis of early leadership research, Stogdill (in 1948 and again in 1974) found that although some traits were important, many skills were also necessary to be an effective leader. Stogdill (1974) suggested that there were no consistent traits that differentiated leaders from nonleaders across situations, and he further asserted that a leader with certain traits and skills can be effective in one situation but ineffective in another situation. Stogdill's combination of traits and skills can be seen in table 1.3.

Need Achievement Theory

Need achievement theory (Atkinson, 1974; McClelland, 1961) asserts that personal and situational factors are equally important as predictors of behavior toward the attainment of success, or excellence. According to this theory, five major components contribute to achievement behavior: personality factors, situational factors, resultant tendencies, emotional reactions, and achievement-related behaviors (figure 2.1). This theory was built on the previous work of McClelland's human motivation theory (discussed next).

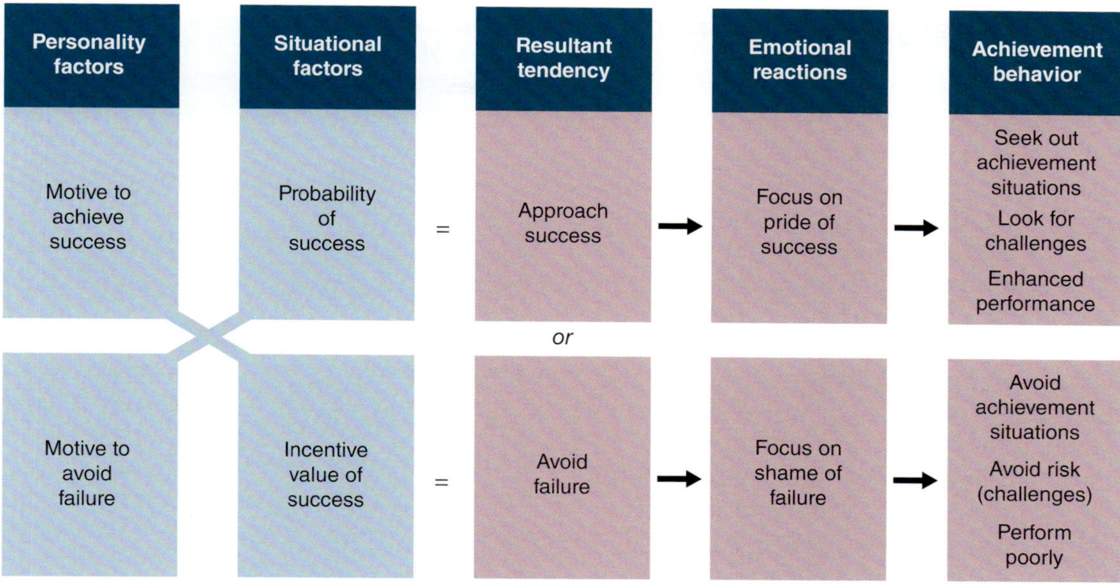

FIGURE 2.1 McClelland's need achievement theory.

Reprinted by permission from R.S. Weinberg and D. Gould, *Foundations of Sport and Exercise Psychology,* 8th ed. (Human Kinetics, 2024), 70.

David McClelland, most noted for his work on motivation need theory during the 1950s, conducted some of the fundamental research on managerial motivation. McClelland's human motivation theory (1961), or theory of needs, is based on an individual's desire for accomplishment; it supports the premise that every person possesses one of three main driving motivators: the need for achievement, the need for affiliation, and the need for power. It is asserted that these motivators are learned and further developed through cultural and life experiences as opposed to inherent qualities. People motivated by achievement have a desire to excel, have a drive to succeed, need challenging tasks, like to solve problems, and like to achieve goals. Those with a strong need for affiliation work best in a group environment, they do not like to stand out or take risk, and they value relationships above anything else. Those with a strong power motivator have a desire to be influential and have impact on an organization, they work best when they are in charge, and they perform best with goal-oriented projects. Those with a strong power motivator are often divided into two groups: personal and institutional. People with a personal power drive want to control others, while people with an institutional power drive like to organize the efforts of a team to further the company's or organization's goals.

Through an understanding of McClelland's theory, physical education administrators can identify the dominant motivators of staff; using this information enables them to set appropriate goals, provide feedback, and motivate and reward team members.

Miner's Managerial Role Motivation Theory

Miner (1965), through the study of relationships between managerial motivation and advancement, formulated a theory of managerial role motivation to describe the traits required for management positions in large organizations. Through the use of the Miner Sentence Completion Scale, Miner discovered a significant correlation between a manager's overall score on motivation and advancement to higher levels of management, particularly on the need to exercise power, compete with peers, and possess a positive attitude toward figures of authority. However, it should be noted that through Miner's research, managerial motivation for advancement was more predictable in large, bureaucratic organizations than in small organizations (Yukl, 2010).

Henry Mintzberg's Management Theory

Henry Mintzberg (1973), a management theorist, described leadership as one of 10 managerial roles (summarized in table 2.1). Leadership includes motivating subordinates and creating favorable conditions for doing the work. The other roles, such as resource allocator and negotiator, involve distinct managerial responsibilities; however, leadership is viewed as an essential managerial role that pervades the other roles (Yukl, 2010, p. 29). According to Mintzberg, an organization's structure affects the relationships between the organization's strategy, external forces, and the organization itself. Mintzberg suggests that organizations can be configured into five types of structures: The *entrepreneurial*, or *simple structure*, uses direct supervision in which the organization consists of a top manager and a few workers; the *machine*, or *bureaucracy*, uses standardization of work processes with a high degree of formalization and work specialization. There are many levels in the chain of command from top management to the lower levels of the organization. The *professional* structure is relatively formalized but decentralized to provide autonomy to professionals. The top management is small, which allows for more middle managers. The *divisional*, or *diversified structure*, is decentralized with little coordination among the separate divisions. The corporate headquarters provide services to all divisions, with support staff located in each division. And lastly, the *innovative*, or *adhocracy structure* uses the support staff as its key part and maintains a sense of decentralization. Adhocracies engage in nonroutine tasks and use sophisticated technology. The primary goal is innovation and rapid adaptation to changing environments.

When organizations are structured in such a way that these relationships are optimal, the organization itself operates smoothly and performs well. Advocating a less traditional process of training, Mintzberg believes that management skills cannot be taught through formal classroom lessons but rather can be acquired and enhanced through authentic experiences. The management theory of Mintzberg divides the manager's tasks into three areas: interpersonal, information processing, and decision making; these areas are based on the Katz (1974) theory of managerial skills. Mintzberg further believes that when managers or leaders understand the tasks they perform and where they fit in the organization, it can help them in effectively fulfilling all of the various roles of a leader (see table 2.1).

TABLE 2.1 Mintzberg's Categories and Roles of a Leader

Categories	Roles
Interpersonal	Figurehead Leader Liaison
Informational	Monitor Disseminator Spokesperson
Decisional	Entrepreneur Disturbance handler Resource allocator Negotiator

Tannenbaum and Schmidt Theory

Tannenbaum and Schmidt (1958, 1973) developed a continuum model, consisting of seven defined levels of delegated freedom, to express the range involved in leader behavior that moves from the manager-centered, autocratic style to the subordinate-centered, democratic style (figure 2.2). The major component of this model shows the relationship between the levels of freedom that a manager chooses to give to a team and the level of authority exerted by the manager. This approach is team centered with the development of the team, but it is also a reminder that regardless of the amount of freedom provided to subordinates, the manager is ultimately responsible and accountable for all outcomes. The seven levels of delegated freedom are as follows:

1. The manager decides and announces the decision.
2. The manager decides and then "sells" the decision to the group.
3. The manager presents the decision with the background ideas and invites questions.
4. The manager suggests a provisional decision and invites discussion about it.

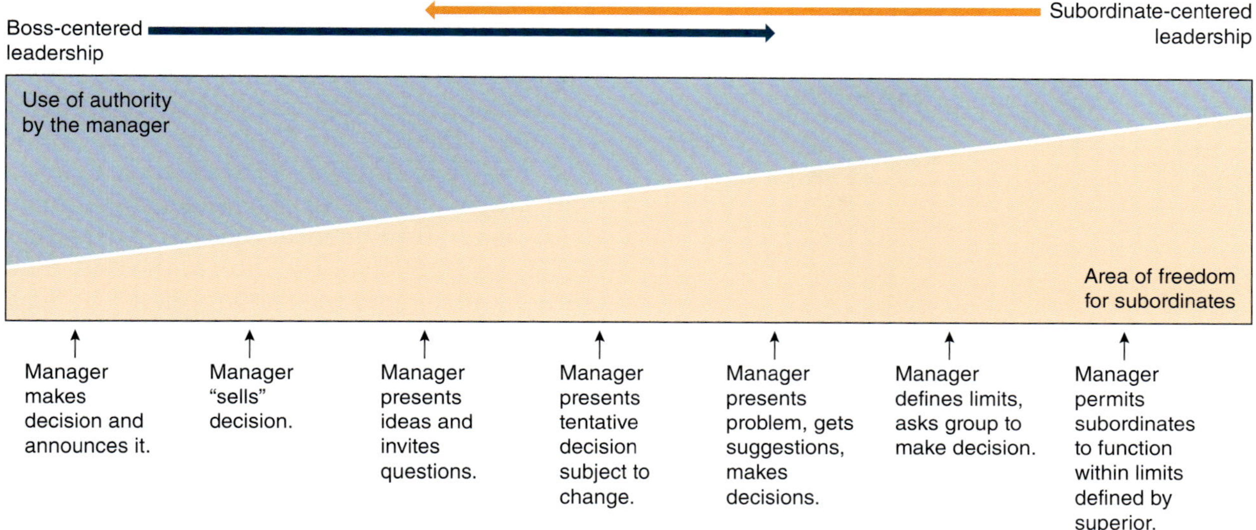

FIGURE 2.2 Continuum of leadership.

Based on R. Tannenbaum and W. Schmidt, "How to Choose a Leadership Pattern," *Harvard Business Review* 51, no. 3 (1973): 162-180.

5. The manager presents the situation or problem, gets suggestions, then decides.
6. The manager explains the situation, defines the parameters, and asks the team to decide.
7. The manager allows the team to identify the problem, develop the options, and decide on the action, within the manager's received limits.

Management Skills and Competencies

The traits and skills necessary to be an effective manager are universal regardless of the type of organization. Management skills, as developed by Robert L. Katz (1974) and as expressed by Yukl (2010, pp. 48, 62-64), are divided into three categories related to managerial effectiveness (see figure 2.3):

1. *Technical skills* represent the knowledge that managers must have with respect to methods, procedures, and processes within the organization. This type of knowledge is usually secured through formal training and on-the-job experiences. Technical skills and a strong knowledge base are required of managers who supervise personnel, so they have the ability to lead based on organizational and program knowledge.

2. *Conceptual skills* are the analytic ability of managers, which includes logical thinking, proficiency in concept formation, and conceptualization of complex and ambiguous relationships. These skills also include problem-solving ability, ability to analyze events and perceive trends, ability to anticipate changes, and ability to recognize opportunities and potential problems. Managers must also be able to exert good judgment when decisions need to be made and be able to coordinate activities through planning, organizing, and problem solving.

3. *Interpersonal skills*, also known as social skills, relate to knowledge about human behavior and interpersonal processes and the ability to understand feelings, attitudes, and motives of others. These skills are also required for effective communication, the ability to establish effective and cooperative relationships, and the ability to influence people. Specific interpersonal skills include empathy, charm, tact and diplomacy, persuasiveness, and oral communication.

Katz viewed managerial skills as a hierarchy. Technical skills are particularly important for lower-level management; interpersonal skills (human) are needed for all levels of management; and conceptual skills are significantly important for top-level management. Other relevant competencies necessary for managerial effectiveness, according to

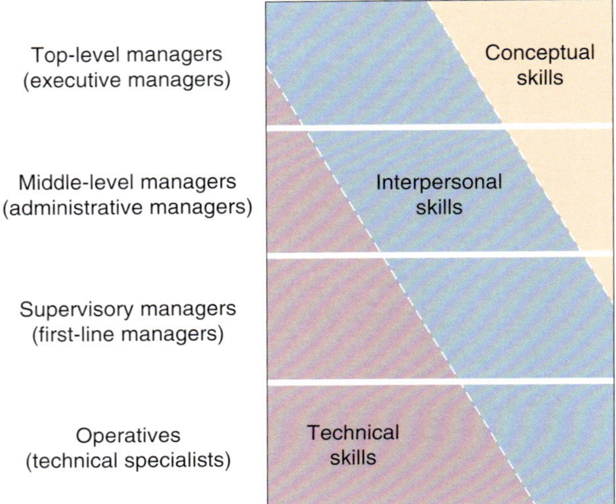

FIGURE 2.3 Katz's hierarchy of managerial skills.

Reprinted by permission from J. Quarterman, M. Li, and J.B. Parks, "Managerial Leadership in Sport Organizations," in *Contemporary Sport Management,* 3rd ed., edited by J.B. Parks, J. Quarterman, and L. Thibault (Human Kinetics, 2007), 348.

Yukl (2010, pp. 65-68), are emotional intelligence, social intelligence, systems thinking, and ability to learn.

Emotional Intelligence

Since organizations and educational institutions are made up of people, it is expected that at times, emotions become a factor when decisions are made. **Emotional intelligence (EI)** is therefore viewed as the ability to recognize and understand one's own feelings and emotions as well as those of others and to use that information to manage emotions and relationships. Following the early work of Gardner (1983) in his book *Frames of Mind: The Theory of Multiple Intelligences*, Salovey and Mayer (1990), in their seminal article "Emotional Intelligence," asserted that cognition and emotion are interconnected. The authors introduced the framework for EI "as a set of skills hypothesized to contribute to the accurate appraisal and expression of emotion in oneself and in others, the effective regulation of emotion in self and others, and the use of feelings to motivate, plan, and achieve in one's life" (p. 189). The growth of this work in EI can further be attributed to Daniel Goleman (1995) in his book *Emotional Intelligence*. Goleman noted that people's ability to lead goes beyond their IQ, and that people must understand and recognize how their emotions drive their own behavior as well as how they affect other people in a positive way. Four important aspects of EI as proposed by Daniel Goleman are shown in figure 2.4 and described as follows:

1. *Self-awareness:* People with high EI understand their feelings. Because of this awareness, they do not let their emotions rule them or get out of control.
2. *Self-management:* People with high EI are able to control their emotions. The key

FIGURE 2.4 Daniel Goleman's emotional intelligence.

Goleman/Boyatzis Emotional Intelligence Leadership Competency Model. Reprinted by permission from Daniel Goleman.

components are transparency, adaptability, and optimism as well as whether they respond or react to situations. They think before they act, and they engage the rational part of their brain.

3. *Social awareness–empathy:* People with high EI are empathetic. They are able to understand the needs, feelings, and wants of others around them; in doing so, they excel in managing relationships.
4. *Relationship management or social skills:* People with high EI are typically team players, thrive on developing others, have high communication skills, are masters at building relationships, and serve as inspiring catalysts for change.

   In 2021, Goleman introduced a fifth component:

5. *Self-regulation:* People with high EI can master the skill of self-regulation, and they are able to deal with conflict and create a nurturing environment by leading by example.

As a physical education administrator, understanding the concept behind EI is important in understanding how you interact with teachers and how you manage your own departments within the overall organization. The importance is further seen when one attempts to implement new programs or change those that exist in cases in which emotional attachments are evident. For physical education teachers, this is an important concept to teach children with respect to how to handle and react to their emotions, especially in a game situation.

Social Intelligence

Social intelligence (SI), originally proposed by Thorndike (1920, p. 228), divided intelligence into three broad classes pertaining to the ability to understand and manage ideas (abstract intelligence), concrete objects (mechanical intelligence), and people (social intelligence). Thorndike's classic formulation was as follows: "By social intelligence is meant the ability to understand and manage men and women, boys and girls – to act wisely in human relations" (cited in Cantor & Kihlstrom, 1987, p. 564). Unlike genetic levels of intelligence, or IQ, social intelligence is mostly learned behavior. It develops from experiences with personal interactions in social settings, as well as ways in which people react to those situations. Social intelligence includes an awareness of situations and the social dynamics that govern them. Through understanding these dynamics, leaders can achieve their goals in working with others. Success depends on how each leader secures an understanding of people and then how that leader interacts with them.

After proposing his theory of emotional intelligence, which at the time was based on the newly emerged field called affective neuroscience, Daniel Goleman looked at the study of brains and emotions. In his book *Social Intelligence: The New Science of Human Relationships*, Goleman (2006) asserted that through exploring the newly emerging field known as social neuroscience, people gain a better understanding of what is going on in their brains when they interact. Therefore, social intelligence is the interpersonal part of emotional intelligence; it's the new science of human relationships. Goleman further indicates that the human brain is mainly designed to connect to the brains of other humans; moreover, people's interactions work both ways when making these connections in developing emotional states. Connection is what keeps people's interactions in synchrony, which has vast implications for daily interactions. In other words, people are *wired* to connect.

Although differences exist, it should be noted that emotional intelligence and social intelligence share many similarities. In addition, they are linked in that they both include cognitive and behavioral components and they respond to social and emotional cues.

Systems Thinking

Systems thinking involves understanding a system by examining the linkages and interactions between the components that compose the entire organization, or system. In order to be successful, managers must be able to collaborate across a number of functional systems. The success of the whole system requires collaborative efforts, which include understanding policies, group- or team-level goal setting, communication, a rewards system, and accountability. The aim is to focus on what binds individuals together and what binds systems together rather than working in so-called silos (Tate, 2009). Tate (2009) further asserts that a systems approach is defined as "Improving the way an organization is led, based on an understanding of the organization as a system, focused on the interdependency between leadership and the organization, concerning how leadership is applied, managed, and developed" (p. 275).

In applying the systems approach to physical inactivity, Kohl and colleagues (2012) asserted that changing behavior requires systems thinking through a public health approach. A systems approach identifies schools as the focal point, but schools cannot be solely tasked with increasing physical activity due to the multiple systems and sectors that influence the adoption of a healthy lifestyle (Institute of Medicine, 2013, p. 23). The systems approach further recognizes that the ability to get youth physically active goes beyond what happens only during physical education; it extends throughout the school environment as well as before, during, and after school (figure 2.5; Institute of Medicine, 2013, p. 24).

Ability to Learn

Since organizations are dynamic, one of the most important competencies of effective managers is the ability to learn from past experiences and adapt to change. This competency involves "learning how to learn," which is the ability to introspectively analyze one's own cognitive processes and find ways to improve them (Yukl, 2010, p. 68). According to Spreitzer and colleagues (1997), these traits are somewhat related to emotional and social intelligence, in which achievement motivation, emotional stability, intelligence, self-monitoring, and internal locus of control are all relevant for learning from experience.

Yukl (2010, pp. 52-60), through a meta-analysis of research, further asserts that these eight managerial traits are inherent in effective managers: (1) high energy level and stress management, (2) self-confidence, (3) internal locus-of-control orientation, (4) emotional maturity, (5) personal integrity, (6) socialized power motivation, (7) moderately high achievement orientation, and (8) low need for affiliation.

Roles and Responsibilities and Administrative Functions

Irrespective of the type of organization, an administrator must perform certain functions in order to successfully attain the goals and objectives of the organization, school district, department, or school. Throughout the years, scholars and researchers have identified the interactive processes of managers as

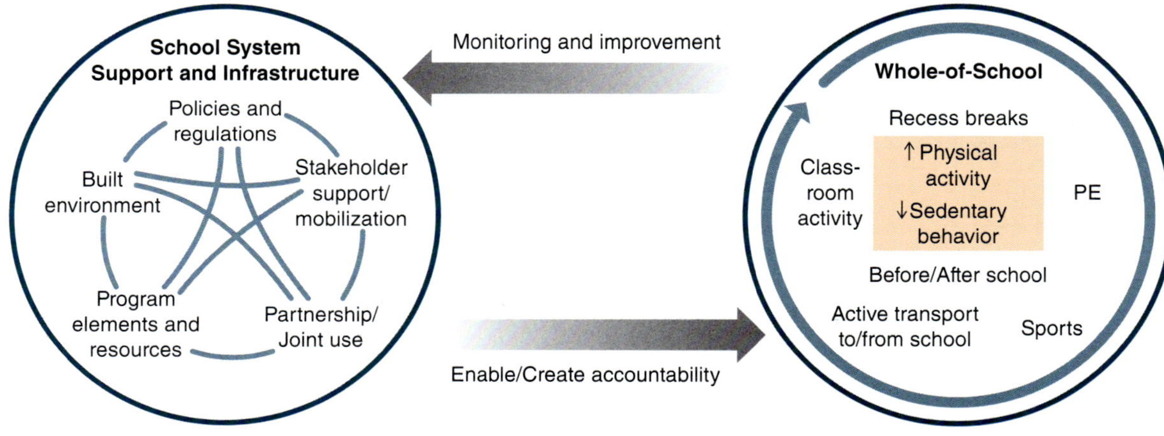

FIGURE 2.5 Systems approach to student physical activity.

Reprinted by permission from Institute of Medicine, *Educating the Student Body: Taking Physical Activity and Physical Education to School* (National Academies Press, 2013), 24.

administrative functions. The five elements of administration—planning, organizing, staffing, directing, and controlling—were originally identified in the works of Henri Fayol (1916), followed by those of Gulick and Urwick (1937), Drucker (1967), Hersey and Blanchard (1988), and Chelladurai (2001). These **management functions** provide a structured overview of the tasks that are performed by managers, but they do not necessarily address the informal relationships between managers and subordinates within the complexities of organizations. In more recent times, management leaders such as Chelladurai (2005) have condensed them into four: planning, organizing, leading, and controlling. Staffing as a fifth function was added to the roles of management.

Planning

Successful advance planning assists the administrative leader and manager in meeting the goals and objectives of an organization regardless of its size or structure. According to Jensen and Overman (2003), "Planning should accomplish two broad objectives: it should enable the administrator to foresee and control situations more effectively, and it should help an administrator shape the future of the organization" (p. 55). Whether with respect to developing the organization's or department's strategic plan (as discussed in chapter 1) or event planning (as discussed in chapter 7), the concerted and deliberate effort put into planning plays a critical role in the effective implementation of curriculum, programs, or projects. This effort further allows you to formulate and convene a planning committee and develop timetables for implementation and interim assessment to evaluate progress.

Given the ever-changing dynamics of education, it would benefit the physical education administrator to review the strategic plan of the school district, evaluate the previous school year's programmatic implementation, and set the course for the upcoming school year. It will assist in ensuring that all staff and teachers understand the direction and priorities the district physical education office is undertaking. These plans, goals, and objectives should also be communicated to the district's physical education teachers as early as the opening of schools meeting. For example, if the school district is looking to mandate fitness assessment as part of its fitness education curriculum, decisions will need to made about which fitness assessment to use, how the teachers will be trained to administer the assessment, how data will be input to the district's server, and what will be appropriate use of the fitness assessment scores. It will take a fair amount of preplanning before the start of the school year. For physical education administrators, planning for the upcoming school year usually begins in the spring before the close of schools, with the majority of the plans finalized during the summer months when school is out of session.

Organizing

A second administrative function following the planning phase is the organizing phase. This function requires the manager to organize the workforce efficiently and align the activities with the goals and structure of the organization. Organizing further involves identifying the individual and group responsibilities that are assigned to various departments or divisions, breaking down the job functions and defining the relationships between people and the jobs, and providing resources (Chelladurai, 2001). Within the department of physical education, the administrator would apply this function through organizing staff to work on different projects by providing purpose and direction (either collaboratively or independently, depending on their skills) to meet the goals and objectives of the department.

Leading

As another important management function, leading involves influencing and motivating employees to implement the activities developed in the organizing step during the planning process. The manager takes an active role in directing the activities of the staff in achieving the organizational goals. The ability to lead staff also requires effective communication skills as well as those skills identified in chapter 1. In addition, leading involves supervising employees and their work productivity, managing change, and delegating responsibilities to employees.

Controlling or Evaluating

Controlling or evaluating is used to determine whether the activities chosen to reach the goal are progressing satisfactorily or are deviating from the desired plans, policies, instructions, and outcomes. Controls are used to set performance standards while monitoring progress, which allows the manager to take appropriate action to prevent problems and address weaknesses. The major objective of controlling is to get people to work more effectively toward goal attainment while collecting data and analyzing information on how the job is being performed. Evaluating would further entail conducting a final analysis of the outcome of the process as well as the outcome of the intended objectives. This objective would be evident in the implementation of a new physical education program such as fitness assessment, where the physical education administrator would be responsible for monitoring the activities of staff assigned to conduct professional development, implementing the fitness education curriculum and assessment program, and monitoring the teachers inputting fitness scores to generate a district profile report. If problems occur during the process, the administrator can step in and take appropriate action to correct the problem area and keep the program and activities aligned with the plans and final outcome.

Delegation

Delegation is defined as assigning duties, tasks, and responsibilities to others and granting them authority to make decisions. According to Jensen and Overman (2003), "Delegation is distinct from simply assigning work to someone else . . . it means that you pass on to a subordinate a portion of your *responsibilities*, along with the *authority* to carry them out, and the *accountability* for how well they are carried out" (p. 57). It is a way to complete more tasks in a shorter time while building team capacity, increasing motivation, and nurturing professional growth among subordinates or staff. It is one of the most important skills of any administrator, but it is often the most difficult one to practice. The initial response of any new administrator is often "Since I am granted the responsibility to make the decisions, I'll do the task myself, because I can do it better." Additionally, as accountability and responsibilities increase, many managers are reluctant to relinquish any authority for fear that the work will not be completed successfully or on time. As a result, the manager's workload keeps piling up until the manager feels completely overwhelmed.

To feel comfortable successfully delegating responsibilities, first you must decide which tasks to delegate. You should prioritize, in order of complexity and importance, which ones you will accomplish and which ones you are ready to relinquish.

The second step is selecting the right person to delegate the task and authority to. As the administrator, you must be comfortable with the skill set of the staff member you are delegating to, and you must be cognizant that the staff member is ready to accept the responsibility and to be committed to the task at hand. At that point, you need to be clear and concise in communicating what the task is, what resources are available, what the expectations are, and what the time frame is for completing the assignment. If the staff member is accepting of the authority but not committed to completing the task in the given period, it will end up back on your desk.

The third step is deciding how you will monitor progress, and how often and in what way the completed project will be evaluated. Two-way communication and accountability are critical components of delegation. Without the follow-up, you run the risk that the task may not be completed in a timely manner.

An example of delegating authority might be assigning a staff member to oversee the ordering of bus transportation for the Special Olympics track and field competition. In preparing for the task, the staff member needs to know which schools are registered; what the pickup and drop-off times for each school are; how many students are participating, which will determine how many buses to order for each school; whether schools can be paired for bus transportation if participation at some schools is low; who the coordinator at the bus depot will be; who the contact person at each school is if any issues arise; and whether all field trip forms for student participation have been completed. An evaluation of the process would be completed if there were no issues regarding transportation and if all students were able to participate in the event after arriving on time. Data can be secured from the school site administrator, the person in charge of the program at each school, the bus depot contact person, and the Special Olympics staff coordinator. If the task was successfully implemented, the staff member should be recognized and congratulated for a job well done.

Once you begin to get comfortable with delegating assignments, the process will become easier for you to implement. However, you should always remember that even though specific assignments or tasks may be delegated, the physical education administrator always retains the ultimate responsibility for all programs and assignments within the department.

Effective Communication

Chapter 1 and this chapter both emphasize that **effective communication** is an essential leadership and management skill for motivating staff. Without the manager's having strong communication skills, subordinates or staff will not understand what they are supposed to accomplish. The lines of communication must be established so that the information being shared is understood by all. Communication must be clear, concise, and frequent in order to be effective; it can take many forms, including in-person meetings, either one-on-one or in group or team settings; electronic communication such as email; and written communication, which can be in the form of memoranda, policy manuals, and other hard copy formats. Another form is social media, which can include social networks, text messaging, videos, and discussion boards.

To be an effective communicator, you need the following skills:

- Using active and engaged listening
- Using nonverbal communication and appropriate body language
- Asking questions
- Being clear, concise, and succinct
- Clarifying and summarizing
- Showing empathy
- Asking for and providing feedback
- Acknowledging barriers
- Establishing trust and rapport
- Identifying the desired outcome

Effective communication is a skill necessary for every leader and manager to be successful in meeting the goals and objectives of any organization or department. Excelling in written and verbal communication will enable you to increase your ability to motivate and inspire staff in their work, build and maintain relationships, facilitate innovation, and develop an environment built on trust and transparency.

Time Management

As a district-level administrator, managing your workload and juggling several programs, projects, meetings, and deadlines becomes a way of life. Learning how to manage your time is one of the most critical elements leading to your success. Since many administrators function on a high energy level, they also put in more hours in a day than many others until they feel satisfied that they are at a place where they can stop working and leave for the day. Managing your time is really about how you manage yourself. **Time management** also allows you to maintain a balance between work and personal time.

As already stated, becoming comfortable with delegating tasks will assist you in managing your time and in prioritizing your assignments and job responsibilities. As a new physical education administrator, developing a time management system that works for you, as well as learning to set priorities, is the first step in alleviating some of the work-related (and at times stressful) decisions.

Aside from prioritizing your tasks, setting and controlling your schedule is a helpful strategy. Once your mandatory meetings are in place and on your calendar, you can look at the rest of your day and determine what can reasonably fit in. Advance planning as a function of time management is as critical as the actual time you are trying to manage. People often spend a lot of their time doing, but they don't spend as much time on advance planning. The key is to work smarter, not harder. Keep in mind that if you work in a large urban community and will be attending an off-site meeting, there may be unforeseen circumstances such as heavy traffic flow; therefore, it will be advantageous for you to allocate plenty of time on your calendar to get to the meeting on time as well as return to your office. This way, you will not be overbooking your time. By placing tasks and meetings on your calendar, you will be able to determine how effectively you are spending your time.

On days when you are in the office all day, determine how much time you will spend on conference calls and written assignments, and how much time you will spend on formal and informal communication with colleagues, community members, staff, teachers, and parents. Organizing your time and files will also help you complete tasks more quickly as the information needed will be readily available. Managing your paperwork effectively and using office and secretarial staff to assist will help you discriminate between what is important now and what can be stored for a later date. In-person office meetings should have a start and end time set in advance so that you can stay on schedule and move on to the next task or meeting. This careful planning will also show sensitivity regarding your time as well as that of others.

Another tool for managing your time is to maintain a to-do list. Your to-do list will work in conjunction with your calendar and keep you on task for the work that needs to be done immediately versus what can be delayed for a later time. Along with your to-do list, maintaining an activity log will further assist you in addressing the tasks that need immediate attention as well as tracking the time you are allocating to each activity. Monitoring the amount of time you spend on prioritized tasks will also keep you from procrastinating on starting tasks that are necessary but not as urgent. On days when you are under a very tight deadline for an assignment requested by senior-level management and need to focus, remember that it is perfectly OK to reduce the number of interruptions and distractions and actually close your door!

Last but not least, something that is extremely difficult for leaders and managers alike is learning how to say no. While you should develop and work in a collaborative environment that stresses the importance of teamwork and support for colleagues, you have to be realistic and know when your plate is too full to take on another assignment at a particular time. If it is something you could do in the near future, propose a later time for completion when other projects are finalized.

Learning and practicing the skills involved in time management will not only enable you to become more effective and efficient in your use of time, it will reduce or eliminate the stress and subsequent burnout often associated with administrative positions. Being prepared and organized will help you understand what needs to be done and how to accomplish tasks while effectively managing your time.

Change Theory

So far, this chapter has discussed several theories on management effectiveness, roles, and responsibilities. Now, the discussion turns to one of the most challenging tasks seen in every dynamic organizational setting: bringing about change. Organizational change is a complex process, but it is a necessary one. The most efficient way to effect planned change is to ensure that it is purposeful, is calculated, and occurs within a collaborative environment.

As you explore models for organizational change, you must first understand why there is resistance to change. Lewin's model of organizational change will serve as the theoretical framework for understanding the basis of managerial change, and the discussion begins with Kotter's eight-step process for creating major change.

Resistance to Change

Resistance to change is not an uncommon behavior across organizational structures; nevertheless, change is inevitable as people learn more and seek to increase productivity in the workplace or improve outcomes such as student academic scores or fitness scores. The adoption of new ideas, new technologies, and new innovations makes change inevitable in organizations and education. How managers implement change is the deciding factor as to whether the change process will be successful. Resistance to the change initiative cannot be ignored, and managing the resistance is a critical skill for an effective manager.

According to Connor (1995), people resist change for a number of reasons, including lack of trust, belief that change is not necessary, belief that change is not feasible, economic threats, relative high cost, fear of personal failure, loss of status and power, threats to values and ideals, and resentment of interference. Kotter (1995) adds that many employees resist change because they become suspicious of the motives, fear that management is incompetent, fear the unknown, or fear that change will bring about extreme conflict. In other cases, there is a lack of communication about the need for change, people have low trust in management, or people are not part of the change process.

Kurt Lewin: Change Theory

As a new physical education administrator or as one who has attempted to change a program, curriculum, or type of assessment, you have probably heard the outcry from a select group of teachers who utter the common saying "because that's the way we have always done it." As true as this statement may be, it is no excuse for accepting the status quo. As a change agent, you need to understand why people are resistant to change and then determine the most effective way to positively accomplish change.

One of the early pioneers in addressing how and why change occurs in organizations was Kurt Lewin (1951), who focused on individual behavior that must be addressed to bring about organizational change. Having developed a framework called force field analysis, Lewin asserted that in any organization attempting to effect change, two forces are operating within the change effort: driving forces and restraining forces (see figure 2.6). Driving forces are the factors that initiate, assist, and support the change, whereas restraining forces are those factors that resist change and work against the change. Lewin further recognized that if equilibrium exists, then no change will occur between the driving and restraining forces; however, he noted that equilibrium can be changed when changes occur between the driving and restraining forces.

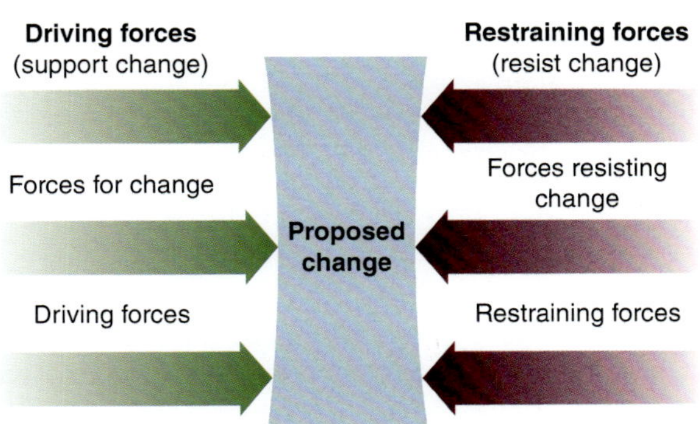

FIGURE 2.6 Kurt Lewin's driving and restraining forces.

Following identification of the forces that affect change through the force field analysis, Lewin proposed a theory of how to implement successful change through this three-stage process:

1. The *unfreezing stage* works on reducing the forces that are attempting to maintain the status quo and works toward getting people to recognize the need for change.
2. The *change or moving stage* works on developing new behaviors, values, and attitudes whereby people begin to embrace the change.
3. The *refreezing stage* is when the desired change becomes the new norm. Reinforcement and support are provided for the refreezing to occur.

To influence effective change, the manager must carefully work through the three-step process of implementing change. Lewin further asserts that successful change rests in *unfreezing* the equilibrium by enhancing the driving forces, or by removing the resisting forces, and then *refreezing* in a new equilibrium state. When the desired outcomes become the new norm, then change has effectively occurred.

John Kotter: Implementing Change

John Kotter, a foremost authority on the topics of leadership and change, is best known for his work on how organizations achieve successful transformation. His 1995 article in the *Harvard Business Review* identified eight errors managers make when attempting to implement change. After identifying the errors, Kotter developed an eight-step process for implementing positive change (figure 2.7). In order to secure the desired results, it is important to include people in the change process.

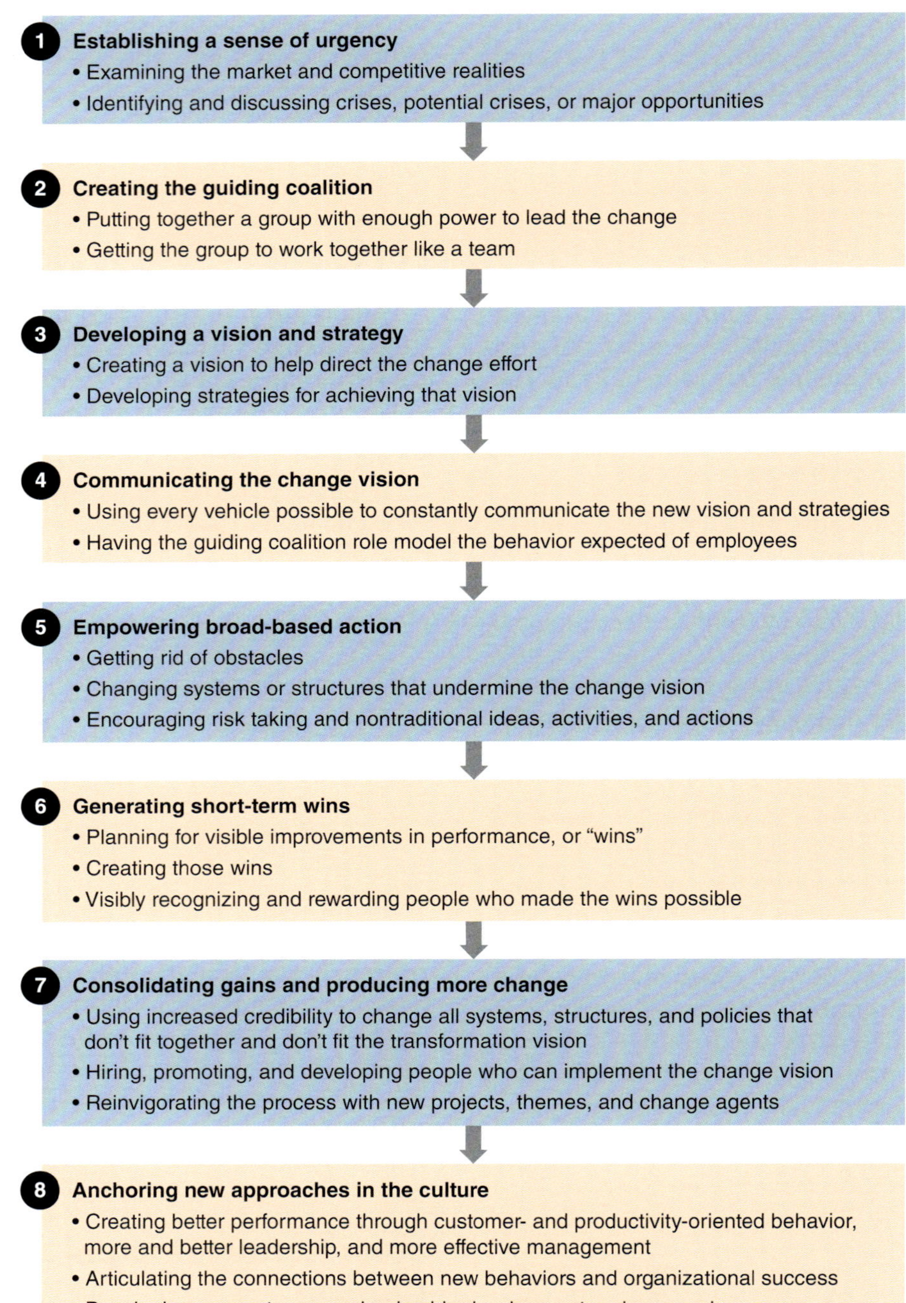

FIGURE 2.7 John Kotter: The eight-step process for creating major change.
Adapted from Kotter (1995).

Although the focus for this chapter is on the models developed by Lewin and Kotter, they are in no way inclusive of all **change theory** models. For a greater understanding of how change takes place in organizations, you are encouraged to explore Lippitt's phases of change theory, Prochaska and DiClemente's stages of change theory, and social cognitive theory. Developing an understanding of various change models and theories will help you develop your own management style in achieving organizational goals and objectives.

Plan Do Study Act (PDSA) Model: Continuous Change

Once change is implemented in an organization, it must be monitored and studied in order to determine its effectiveness and whether change actually occurred. A continuous improvement model is based on best practices; the four components of the Plan Do Study Act (PDSA) model provide for continuous monitoring of performance. This type of model can be used for any subject area; one way you can use it in physical education is to assess the effects of a new curriculum on cognitive knowledge, professional development, parent participation logs, and student attendance. The greatest benefit of the PDSA is that it both supports data-driven decision making and provides a structure for improvement efforts. Of special note is that the process does not start or stop; rather, it is a continuous process involving learning, reflecting, monitoring, and evaluating successes. The PDSA model provides checks and balances for determining what you are trying to accomplish, whether the change is actually an improvement, and what alterations can be made to ensure improvement (figure 2.8).

Continuous improvement models can be used at the state level, school district level, or school site level to determine the effectiveness of the change. In a similar fashion, collective impact can also be reviewed as part of the change process.

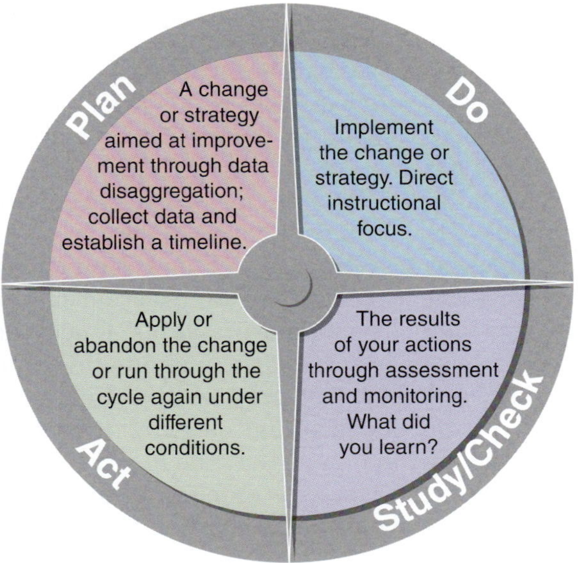

FIGURE 2.8 Plan Do Study Act (PDSA) model.

Day-to-Day Operations

The role of the physical education administrator not only involves managing programs and staff; it also involves managing the day-to-day operations of the office. How you implement your managerial skills will have a direct impact on the efficiency and effectiveness of your department, which will eventually filter down to support and program delivery at the school site level. These responsibilities include supervision of staff; conducting meetings; managing projects, contracts, and budgets; and approving payroll. Fiscal management is extensively discussed in chapter 13. The responsibilities discussed next represent just a portion of what an administrator can expect on a daily basis.

Supervising Office Employees and Support Staff

Supervising office staff is another daily function of the physical education administrator. One of the most important assets of an effective leader and manager is having a supportive office staff and a senior secretary who can do more than the required clerical duties such as typing, filing, and photocopying. In most district-level offices, the first line of communication for incoming calls is the secretary, who can respond to questions by providing information, forwarding the calls, or taking messages. As an administrator, you are also responsible for ensuring that your staff is prepared to respond to questions and carry out assignments based on the programs and projects you are implementing. For example, if your office is collecting information from schools on the School Health Index, the secretary can provide information as to which (if not all) modules must be submitted, what must be included in the responses and action plans, and what the deadline for submitting the information is. With a secretary who is knowledgeable about your present projects and programs, teachers and school site administrators can get an immediate response so the given task can be completed in a timely manner. Therefore, preparing your staff saves you time in terms of returning phone calls or responding to a plethora of emails. In addition, your secretary can maintain your calendar to ensure no overlaps occur in scheduling meetings or calls and can reschedule appointments if a more pressing or unforeseen issue emerges.

Strong administrative support and office staff can further assist in processing purchase orders and communicating with vendors; can take minutes at your staff meetings; can maintain grant records and data collected for audit purposes; and can keep you informed on fiscal spending and budgets, in particular, when funds need to be transferred from one program object or function to another based on need. These personnel may also have great technology skills and can process professional travel requests, monitor and restock office supplies, monitor service needs for office machines, and monitor annual department events and send out notifications. Most importantly, they can be your confidants in ensuring the integrity of your office.

Planning for Effective Meetings

Scheduling meetings, developing agendas, and providing follow-up meeting minutes constitute another important role of the physical education administrator. The size of your district staff, the number of committees you oversee, and the types of projects you are planning on implementing during the school year will determine the number and types of meetings you will need to schedule. Keep in mind that since several of your meetings will involve administrators from other departments, teachers, community and business partners, and parents, you will need to be sensitive to their time commitments and level of responsibilities when assigning tasks. In a more formal context, for standing committees, such as the district wellness committee, it is highly recommended that you develop an annual schedule of monthly meetings at the beginning of the school year, and that you conduct the meeting on the same day and at the same time each month. For example, holding meetings on the third Thursday of every month at 9:00 a.m. will allow committee members to adjust their calendars so that attendance is high and you have a voting quorum at each meeting. These district meetings operate in the sunshine (they are open to the public). Therefore, scheduling in this way will also allow you to place the meeting notices on the district's community calendar so that public notices are in place well in advance of each meeting. Sending out correspondence to committee members as meeting reminders could also be a function of your office support staff. Less formal meetings, such as those with your department staff, could be scheduled on a weekly, monthly, or as-needed basis. From experience, I have found that conducting meetings with staff on Monday mornings allows the team to discuss the activities for the week, plan trainings, or support one another if a member has an event that week. The involvement of all staff provides for a more collaborative and supportive work environment.

Developing an agenda is one of the most important elements of planning and conducting a meeting. Having a written agenda in advance of the meeting allows you to organize your thoughts, identify the important topics and items for discussion, assign speakers and presenters for those items, set a time limit for discussion for each item, and keep the meeting focused and on time so that you can cover all items within the designated time limits of the meeting. Soliciting agenda items from the committee members and allowing time at the end of the meeting for open discussion provide an opportunity for full engagement of the members.

Once the agenda is fully set, it should be sent electronically to all members a couple of days before the meeting such that they receive a reminder about the meeting, the location, and the times. It would also be advantageous to attach any additional information to the meeting agenda so that the committee members can review the documents in advance and be prepared to engage in discussion or vote on actionable items. It is of utmost importance to follow the agenda during the meeting to ensure that all of the items are covered.

Learning how to organize and conduct an effective meeting is another function of the physical education administrator. Once the agenda has been set and the meeting information forwarded to all committee and staff members, the day of the actual meeting arrives. It is extremely important that the meeting start on time so that you can complete your agenda items within the designated period. The same holds true whether it is an in-person or virtual meeting. Since most committee members will come from off site for an in-person meeting, having refreshments and beverages set up in advance of the meeting start time will encourage attendees to arrive early. Sign-in sheets should also be displayed at the entrance so committee members can sign in as they arrive. As the meeting organizer, you also have a responsibility to ensure that everyone understands the meeting ground rules, which can be set during the initial meeting at the beginning of the school year; that you stay on topic according to the agenda and keep the discussion on target and moving; and that you make sure all attendees have an opportunity to be heard and voice their opinion. For more formal meetings, Robert's Rules of Order, a means for facilitating discussions and group decision-making, can be used as the standard. At the conclusion of the meeting, take time to summarize the discussion and decisions made so everyone is knowledgeable about the meeting outcome. As you bring closure to the meeting, remind attendees of the date and time of the next meeting, then thank them for their input and for attending.

Providing meeting minutes is an essential follow-up to the meeting itself. First and foremost, minutes should be taken by designated support staff to allow you, the organizer, to pay careful attention to the discussion taking place and to manage the meeting. From a logistics standpoint, minutes should always include the day and date of the meeting, the actual start time, and the names of committee members and guests in attendance. The minutes should follow the agenda items and state any decisions made, motions or actions taken, tasks assigned, next steps, new business, and items to be held over if time runs out or if further discussion is warranted. Once you review and approve the minutes, they should be sent out to all committee members in advance of the next meeting. This step will give the members a chance to review them so the opening agenda item can be a quick review and revision or approval of the minutes.

Managing Paperwork and Records

The amount of correspondence an administrator receives on a daily basis can be overwhelming when one considers the number of required forms, phone messages, electronic communications, and paper communications (yes, hard copy memoranda do still exist in this technological age) involved.

For efficiency and effectiveness in managing communication, an administrator must address all forms of communication on a regular basis. With reference to phone messages, as stated previously, an effective secretary or administrative assistant can respond to most phone inquiries. However, maintaining a phone log will allow you to review your messages, keep notes on when phone calls are returned, and make notations as to the content of the call. As a rule of thumb, calls should be returned within a 24-hour period but no later than 48 hours. Prioritize your calls based on level of importance and who the call came from. Senior staff can reach you on your cell phone when they need immediate information, but calls from parents should be returned as soon as possible. By the time parents have called the district office, they have usually been through the channels and have reached a point of needing higher-level assistance.

Electronic communication in the form of emails should also be returned as soon as possible and based on priority. Unfortunately, immediate access to cell phones and personal mobile devices means that you can potentially be available through email all the time. However, as an administrator, you will need to set time constraints regarding the number of hours spent responding to work-related emails after the close of your regular workday; otherwise, it will consume your personal and family time.

The correspondence you receive through hard copy communication, such as interoffice memoranda, U.S. mail, or commercial delivery systems, is usually informative in nature or contains vendor invoices that need to be processed and paid. In many cases, electronic notifications of the content will be sent to you in advance of receipt of the hard copy.

Managing records also involves managing paperwork and data collection forms for grants and for other resources such as fitness assessment records and School Health Index self-assessments. In situations involving federal, state, or foundation grants, all records must be kept (including student data for three to five years), depending on the grant requirements for record retention policies. Additional information can be found in chapter 14.

Record-Keeping and Filing Systems

Maintaining records of hard copy paperwork and electronic communication will require you to develop your own filing system as well as assign some of the filing responsibilities to your secretary. Electronic communication can be kept in labeled computer files for easy retrieval, but important electronic files should be backed up on a separate device in case of unexpected computer issues. For very important electronic files, it is highly recommended that hard copies also be kept and filed for future use.

Records such as grant paperwork, invoices, and purchase orders can be assigned to your secretary for filing; staff should have immediate access if you need to follow up, if your grants are being audited, or if vendors are inquiring about a payment schedule. Internal communication as well as travel records can also be filed or kept in binders according to subject, type, and date of correspondence.

Anything that requires immediate attention should be in folders and readily available on your desk so that it stays on your radar for completion. Communication that is marked "confidential" should be kept in a secure file cabinet or desk drawer so that it is out of sight lines for anyone entering your office. Personnel records, including annual evaluations or any paperwork that involves administrative disciplinary action on employees, should be kept in locked file cabinets or drawers.

Other paperwork such as payroll sign-in sheets, payroll approvals, budget transfers, equipment checkout forms, equipment transfer or disposal forms, forms for acceptance of distribution of keys, and other important documents should also be filed in a safe and secure place but be readily available in case any follow-up attention is needed.

Teachers as Leaders

One of the greatest attributes of a successful and confident leader and manager is the ability to identify talent, mentor that talent, and nurture individuals through support and experiential opportunities. As the district-level physical education administrator, through professional development trainings, committee work, and official communication, you will eventually see which physical education teachers and department chairpersons either have exhibited the potential for professional growth or have an expressed desire to be included in professional growth opportunities. As a leader and manager, these interactions can give you the opportunity to expand your staff, without hiring additional administrators, by empowering teachers to take the lead on programs and projects, either at the district level or at the school site level, while lending support and guidance throughout their growth.

In addition to leadership training, the physical education administrator can serve as a mentor to a new physical education **department chairperson** at the school site with respect to day-to-day operations and responsibilities. Responsibilities worth mentioning include how to

- plan for physical education instruction as well as the organization of instruction, including team teaching;
- develop teachers' schedules and assign instructional space;
- work with counselors in assigning and monitoring appropriate class sizes;
- order and monitor equipment and supplies inventory;
- develop student grading policies;
- ensure student safety;
- develop policies for the management of locker rooms;
- handle locker and lock distributions as well as student physical education uniform sales and distribution;
- develop and manage annual budgets; and
- work with the community in developing partnerships for before- and after-school programming.

Additionally, the physical education department chairperson should work collaboratively with the special education department in implementing the individual education plan (IEP) for students in either adapted physical education classes or in inclusion settings.

LEADERSHIP IN ACTION

Importance of Training Teachers as Leaders

Rachel Winsten, MS

Health and physical educator, Viera High School; former district resource teacher for health and physical education for 10 years, Brevard Public Schools, Florida

Health and physical education teachers have a significant role as leaders within the educational system. While we may not hold formal leadership positions like principals or administrators, teachers have a major influence on students, colleagues, and the overall educational environment. Teachers play a crucial role in curriculum development and execution. We are unpacking standards, designing learning goals, developing assessments, and implementing effective teaching strategies. We make decisions about adapting to meet the diverse needs of all students. Through our instructional leadership, we impact student learning and performance outcomes as well as foster a lifelong love of physical activity.

As health and physical educators, we have a unique perspective on the needs and challenges of students, and we should advocate for their rights and well-being. We should use our voice and expertise to advocate for policies and reforms that benefit students and the profession as a whole. Teachers as leaders can be powerful advocates. We are well positioned to speak out on important issues from the classroom level to entire educational systems. Effective teacher leaders continuously engage in their own professional growth by pursuing professional development opportunities, staying abreast of the latest research, technologies, pedagogical best practices, and seeking continuous improvement of their teaching skills.

Teacher leaders often serve as mentors, providing guidance and support to both developing and experienced colleagues. They share their knowledge and experiences, helping others improve their instructional practices and navigate the unique challenges of teaching health and physical education. Effective teachers as leaders invest in the professional growth and development of themselves and their peers through professional association membership. Professional association membership and involvement is vital because it provides opportunities for leadership, such as serving on a committee, being part of the governing board, or just presenting at conferences or conventions. Local, state, and national professional organizations support teachers as leaders as they provide opportunity and expertise within our specific content areas.

Developing relationships with colleagues from within your district, county, state, region, nation, and the world will further provide an invaluable network of support as you navigate your career in education. Effective teachers and leaders build strong relationships not only with a network of colleagues but also with their students, parents, and local community. These relationships foster trust and create a supportive network for continuous growth. Collegial relationships are the cornerstone of a successful school environment for teachers. Student–teacher relationships are the cornerstone of a successful classroom environment. Teachers who are willing to ask for help, learn from one another, and support one another are not only going to have greater job satisfaction but also model those positive behaviors for their students, thereby creating an overall supportive school environment. Health and physical education teacher leaders have a significant impact on student achievement, school culture, and the overall quality of education. Their leadership extends beyond the walls of their gymnasiums, pavilions, courts, classrooms, pools, and other activity spaces, influencing the educational community and society as a whole.

Enabling physical education teachers to develop as physical activity leaders in the school setting is supported by Castelli and Beighle (2007), Beighle and colleagues (2009), Carson (2012), and Kim (2021). Physical education **teachers as leaders** can play a key role in providing instructional leadership at the school, ensuring that the curriculum being delivered aligns with the state and national standards, and coordinating the activities and efforts of schools in implementing the Comprehensive School Physical Activity Program (CSPAP) (Carson, 2012). Rink and colleagues (2010) assert that to address the physical activity needs at the local level, the physical education teacher must be the go-to person to promote

Keeping Physical Education Students Safe in an Active Shooter Situation

Jayne D. Greenberg

The K-12 school environment has long been viewed as a safe haven for developing healthy and active students. Today, however, physical education administrators and teachers must be prepared to face the harsh reality of dealing with an active shooter situation. Our students must be kept safe from any potential emergency situation. This task is especially challenging during physical education, recess, before- and after-school activities, or athletics, when students and teachers are most vulnerable in an open space such as the physical education field.

On a personal note, I live 20 minutes south of Parkland, Florida. I have always been upset by school shootings and often wondered what would make a person deliberately take away such innocent lives full of promise. On February 14, 2018, the issue hit home. It made me take a deep dive and look for some type of guidance for physical education teachers. After reviewing many documents and having conversations with personnel from several national organizations, school districts, and experts in the school security field, it was determined that although there are procedures in place for the classroom teacher and school personnel inside the building, there is nothing written explicitly for the physical education teacher. Given this void, and with the support of personnel from those highly respected organizations, following are some guidance points for consideration, taking into account that every school and every school district is unique.

First and foremost are two extremely important recommendations that every school should embrace: (1) Every physical education teacher (or at least the physical education department chairperson) should be a part of the school safety plan committee and should be in attendance at all planning and implementation meetings to ensure that a plan is in place that is disseminated and practiced like every other evacuation and lockdown drill; and (2) all physical education teachers should be provided with a communication device so that they can immediately receive important information from the front office if there is an active incident inside the school as well as immediately send information to the front office if they observe an active incident or a potential incident outside of the school walls. Following are two scenarios inherent in every physical education setting: inside the gymnasium, weight room, wellness center, or classroom; and outside on the physical education field, intramural field, athletic field, and recess or play area.

Inside the School

Chances are that if you are conducting physical education classes inside the school building and you hear the all call for "Code Red" or any other adopted signaling call, you will take immediate action as to whether to lock down in the classroom or evacuate the building in a predetermined orderly fashion until you are far away and in a safe location. Most U.S. schools practice fire or evacuation drills as well as lockdown drills, so there is a sense of familiarity when the alarm is sounded. Therefore, if you hear the call for lockdown while in physical education class, you should follow the procedures set and practiced within your school, which most commonly involve these steps:

- Direct all students, staff, and approved visitors to enter classrooms or secure rooms.
- Lock the door, turn off the lights, close the blinds (if possible), and (where and when possible) cover internal windows to prevent a visual line.
- Direct students to sit or lie on the floor out of the sight line from the doors or windows or to enter an interior closet, locker room, or other internal space.
- Direct students to be quiet, with no talking, and to turn off or silence cell phones.
- Remain calm, and try to keep students calm at all times.

- Do not open the doors for anyone under any circumstance until an all-clear announcement is sent from the designated person in charge (usually the principal or second in command).
- Communicate with other teachers and administrators through email if important information needs to be shared.

Outside the School

When you are conducting physical education outside the school on the playing field or on a hard court and you receive emergency communication from inside the school that there is an active incident in the building, your plan of action would be to evacuate rather than to seek shelter inside the building. If you see an active or potential situation outside of the building, your plan for action would be to go inside the building and follow the plans as stated for lockdowns.

If the critical incident is occurring inside the school and the plan of action is to evacuate, these are some procedures for consideration:

- Activate the evacuation plan for physical education as developed and practiced in the school safety plan.
- After surveying the situation, direct and guide the students to a predetermined off-site unification location, where they stay together until an all-clear is sent to your communication device. Designated well in advance by the school safety plan committee, the unification site can be a department store, restaurant, or any other safe space where the students and staff can be led to safety.
- Direct students to leave all of their belongings on the court or field and move as quickly as possible, either in a line or in a zigzag formation, while leaving the school grounds. They must all stay together with you.
- Do not release any students to parents until directed to do so by the person in charge (usually the principal or second in command).
- Have your communication device and keys with you at all times in case you need to unlock a gate to evacuate in emergency situations. (However, external gates should be locked at all times when school is in session to prevent unauthorized outsiders from entering the school grounds.)

As stated previously, every scenario is different and each situation must be assessed individually to make the correct decision, but it cannot be stressed enough how important it is for physical education teachers to be a part of the school safety plan committee and to practice these drills specific to physical education (possibly at the beginning of each semester) to ensure that students are prepared in case action needs to be taken. Since school safety plans are dynamic documents with information evolving continuously, it is recommended that you evaluate your physical education plan annually so that you can be an active contributor at the next planning committee meeting. The best scenario is that you will never need to be engaged in such a horrific incident, but planning ahead greatly reduces the sense of confusion in a panic situation or when a critical incident occurs.

Many thanks are extended to the following organizations for spending as much time on the phone with me as they did to provide guidance and recommendations:

The National Association of School Resource Officers (NASRO): https://nasro.org

The National Center for Spectator Sports, Safety, and Security (NCS4): www.ncs4.com/home

The National Federation of State High School Associations (NFHS): www.nfhs.org

Printable resources are available here:

Guide for Developing High-Quality School Emergency Operations Plans: U.S. Department of Education, U.S. Department of Health and Human Services, U.S. Department of Homeland Security, U.S. Department of Justice, Federal Bureau of Investigation, and Federal Emergency Management Agency: https://rems.ed.gov/docs/rems_k-12_guide_508.pdf

(continued)

Keeping Physical Education Students Safe in an Active Shooter Situation *(continued)*

Department of Homeland Security:

Active Shooter Preparedness: www.dhs.gov/publication/active-shooter-how-to-respond

Active Shooter: How to Respond: www.dhs.gov/xlibrary/assets/active_shooter_booklet.pdf

FEMA:

www.fit.edu/media/site-specific/wwwfitedu/security/documents/FEMA_ActiveShooter_OnePagerv1d15_508_FINAL_2.pdf

www.ready.gov/sites/default/files/2024-03/ready.gov_active-shooter_hazard-info-sheet.pdf

ALICE Training: www.alicetraining.com/alice-training-for-schools

Sandy Hook Promise: www.sandyhookpromise.org

change in the schools. The physical education teacher is the physical activity expert in the building and therefore should take on the role of physical activity leader for the school. The focal point of the program is the understanding, promotion, and implementation of the Comprehensive School Physical Activity Program (CSPAP), a multicomponent approach for school districts and schools to develop strategies enabling all students to participate in 60 minutes of physical activity daily, which will be discussed in-depth in chapter 3. Note that physical education as an academic subject serves as the foundation of this comprehensive model.

The responsibilities should include the following:

- Being an active member of the school wellness committee
  - Helping in the evaluation and planning process for the school
  - Actively learning about and promoting opportunities for physical activity in the community
- Serving as a resource person for classroom teachers
  - Informing classroom teachers about the need for and benefits of adding small bouts of physical activity to the school day
  - Providing resources and training to the classroom teachers
  - Aiding teachers in understanding and implementing appropriate practices for physical activity
  - Providing opportunities for the teachers to engage in physical activity before or after school
- Organizing school-wide physical activity experiences
  - Planning school-wide activities such as field day, fun runs, a walking program, and morning exercise breaks
  - Encouraging fundraisers that promote physical activity

The physical education teacher can also take the lead in planning or assisting others in planning before- and after-school clubs and intramural programs.

Conclusion

The major goal of this chapter is to identify the concept of management with respect to organizational effectiveness and the impact that managers have on the people they work with in attaining the goals and objectives of the organization. Although there is some overlap between leadership and management, distinct theories, roles and responsibilities, and administrative functions differentiate the two. It is important to note that skills and competencies such as technical skills, human skills, and conceptual skills are critical elements involved in managing dynamic systems. It is equally important to appreciate that for managers who work with people, an understanding of emotional and social intelligence is a necessary competency in relation to the decision-making process.

As a physical education administrator, whether new to the administrative team or a veteran, you hold the key to developing teachers as leaders and providing a space for growth opportunities for those professionals who aspire to be future leaders and managers.

Review Questions

1. Differentiate among the various theories of management, and explain how each one plays a part in the educational process.
2. Identify and differentiate between McClelland's and Miner's motivation theories.
3. Emotional intelligence and social intelligence are relevant competencies of a manager. Explain the difference between the two and how they can be applied in a physical education setting.
4. Describe the four functions of management and how you would apply them to physical education administration.
5. What are the managerial roles and responsibilities of a physical education administrator?
6. Given that school districts are dynamic educational organizations, describe change theory and how you would implement change using Kotter's eight-step process.
7. Explain why it is important to develop teachers as physical activity leaders and what plan you would put in place to provide professional growth opportunities.

CHAPTER 3

Organizing and Planning a Quality Physical Education Program

Jayne D. Greenberg

Photo courtesy of Victor Spadaro at Abingdon Elementary of Arlington Public Schools.

LEARNING OBJECTIVES

After reading this chapter, you will be able to do the following:

- Identify the benefits of a quality physical education program.
- Create mission statements and policies and procedures.
- Establish goals and objectives.
- Identify the essential components of a quality physical education program.
- Develop a comprehensive school physical activity program.
- Align physical education programs with the school's or district's strategic initiatives.
- Develop program scheduling.

KEY CONCEPTS

community engagement
Comprehensive School Physical Activity Program (CSPAP)
curriculum development
essential components
grade-span learning indicators
instructional strategies
mission statement
national standards
program planning
student assessment

One of the cornerstones of effective physical education administration is planning for and executing a quality physical education program. Without this foundational principle, appropriate practices around teaching and learning simply cannot occur. The role of the administrator is multifaceted, ensuring that programs are standards based; incorporate grade-span learning indicators; are age and developmentally appropriate; are committed to inclusion and equality; and address the cognitive, affective, social and emotional, and psychomotor domains of all students.

Developing curriculum aligned to state and national standards, implementing instructional strategies, and providing evidence of growth through meaningful assessments are all among the necessary steps to ensuring a quality program. Understanding the components of an effective program at the district and school site levels, and expanding the physical education teacher's reach beyond the gymnasium and playing field through a comprehensive school approach, are part of a comprehensive physical education program.

The research supporting the need for daily, quality physical education programs is compelling. Several research studies and national and international reports provide supportive evidence of the benefits of engaging in physical education and physical activity through the lens of a public health agenda, academic support, and the need to address all learning domains. This chapter explores several of the components that encompass a quality physical education program, and it provides available resources to assist in the development and planning of the program. Many of these components are explored in greater depth and breadth in subsequent chapters.

Definition of Physical Education

The definitions of physical education have changed throughout the years based on philosophical ideals, medical concerns, curricular issues and needs, and political climate. If you were to browse the Internet for definitions of physical education, you would encounter a series of key phrases that relate to a theme, from the teaching of sport to the development of physical fitness. From the time of ancient Greece and the birth of the Olympic Games all the way through the modern day, people have recognized that movement of the body is a critical part of the human condition.

Early physical education began with global influences in the area of gymnastics and programs that began to emerge in the United States in the 1800s. With a dramatic expansion of content beyond the original Swedish and German gymnastics programs of the 19th century, physical education evolved into a content area with diverse learning goals that facilitate the holistic development of children. By the turn of the 20th century, personal hygiene and exercise for bodily health were incorporated in the physical education curriculum as the major learning outcomes for students (Institute of Medicine [IOM], 2013).

It was well documented after World War I, which the United States entered in 1917, that one in three of the men in the military had not been physically fit enough to do battle. The Korean War proved once again that Americans were not as fit as they should be, and the nation began to focus on the importance of physical fitness. This focus led to the development of physical education programming in schools and a requirement for physical fitness prior to military service. As World War II approached, the United States again saw a shift, from physical education involving games and sport to physical conditioning. This new focus led to the Kraus-Weber study (which determined that school-aged children failed to meet minimum standards of muscular strength), which led to the development of the Kraus-Weber Test and ultimately the formation of the President's Council on Physical Fitness. In the 21st century, history is repeating itself; according to a 2020 Pentagon study, 77 percent of the young men and women wishing to enlist in the military were not accepted due to their low levels of fitness (Novelly, 2022).

The focus on physical education during the last decades of the 19th century and early 20th century was attributed to John Dewey's progressive ideas, which focused on the role that activity plays in learning. Child's play became recognized as an important aspect of child development. It was during this time that physical education was accepted as contributing to the physical well-being of children as well as to their social, emotional, and intellectual development—a concept adhered to in today's educational environment. Moving into the 21st century, today's physical education programs focus on increasing the amount of time students are physically active during physical education and improving the fitness of students engaged in physical education. This improvement can be accomplished by implementing a variety of curriculum models such as the Sport Education Model, Tactical Games Model, Skill Theme Approach model, and fitness education model, to name a few. These models are discussed more comprehensively in chapter 4.

Although it is not the main focus of this chapter, the history of physical education is rich in theory and practice. Credit should be given to those leaders whose work brought the field to where it is today: Thomas D. Wood, Rosalind Cassidy, Catharine Beecher, Charles H. McCloy, Clark W. Hetherington, Luther H. Gulick, Jay B. Nash, Jesse Feiring Williams, Charles Bucher, Edward L. Thorndike, Dudley A. Sargent, Dio Lewis, John Dewey, Edward Hitchcock, Delphine Hanna, and many others.

According to an Association for Physical Education (afPE) health position paper (2008, cited in United Nations Educational, Scientific and Cultural Organization [UNESCO], 2015a), quality physical education (QPE)

> *is the planned, progressive, inclusive learning experience that forms part of the curriculum in early years, primary and secondary education. In this respect, QPE acts as the foundation for a lifelong engagement in physical activity and sport. The learning experience offered to children and young people through physical education lessons should be developmentally appropriate to help them acquire the psychomotor skills, cognitive understanding, and social and emotional skills they need to lead a physically active life. (p. 9)*

Ennis (2011), with a direct focus on student learning, states,

> *Educational physical education focuses first and foremost on student learning. The content and scope of the curriculum emphasizes in-depth instruction in a range of physical activities that students need to learn to be physically active; want to learn because the activities lead to opportunities in competitive sport and recreation; and enjoy learning because the activities are meaningful and relevant in their lives today. (p. 6)*

Understanding what physical education is helps you to appreciate what goes into the development of state and **national standards**. As the *National Standards & Grade-Level Outcomes for K-12 Physical Education* (2014) redefined physical education in terms of pursuit of the physically literate individual, the 2024 *National Physical Education Standards* replaced the term *physical literacy* with the term *physical literacy journey*. These standards "consider the psychomotor, cognitive, social, and affective learning domains essential to facilitating the physical literacy journey of preK-12 learners" (SHAPE America, 2025, p. 3).

The Centers for Disease Control and Prevention (CDC) (2013a, p. 12) recommends that a well-designed physical education program

- meet the needs of all students,
- keep students active for most of physical education class time,
- teach self-management,
- emphasize knowledge and skills for a lifetime of physical activity, and
- be an enjoyable experience for all students.

Through these definitions, SHAPE America (2015b) developed a position statement, "Physical Education Is an Academic Subject," which affirmed its position as a fundamental part of the American public school curriculum. Physical education is designated in this way because it

1. is required by schools,
2. has national and state standards,
3. has a course of study via curriculum,
4. has textbooks and resources available,
5. requires student assessments,
6. requires grading,
7. requires teacher preparation program accreditation, and
8. requires teacher certification.

It is important to differentiate the definition of physical education from the activities that are designed for the classroom. Having children play games and learn about sport is not the sole purpose or intent of this subject area. Defining physical education helps you better understand its significance in the educational landscape and its contribution to a lifetime of health and wellness for school-aged children.

Benefits of a Quality Physical Education Program

The benefits of a quality physical education program have long been established in relation to the health and academic outcomes for students. Compelling research-based evidence from national and global organizations and agencies supports both the need for daily, quality physical education and the benefits of engaging in a quality physical education program. Research literature (provided by CDC; IOM; U.S. Department of Health and Human Services [HHS]; President's Council on Sports, Fitness and Nutrition; UNESCO; Physical Activity Alliance [PAA]; National Association of State Boards of Education; World Health Organization [WHO]) and organizations (such as SHAPE America, Alliance for a Healthier Generation, GENYOUth, Personal Health Investment Today [PHIT] America, Active Schools, Voices for Healthy Kids, National Fitness Foundation, Robert Wood Johnson Foundation, American Heart Association, American Cancer Society, American Lung Association, American Academy of Pediatrics, Action for Healthy Kids, Active Schools, Mission Readiness, American College of Sports Medicine's [ACSM] Exercise is Medicine initiative [ACSM, 2011], and the Aspen Institute's Project Play) have provided guidance, research, advocacy, and programming to ensure and assist with the implementation of quality physical education and physical activity opportunities. The benefits of 60 minutes or more of daily physical activity for youth, predominantly through physical education and within the school environment, include the following:

1. Improving cardiorespiratory fitness
2. Strengthening bones and muscles
3. Controlling weight
4. Reducing risk of obesity
5. Reducing symptoms of anxiety and depression
6. Reducing risk of type 2 diabetes and metabolic syndrome
7. Reducing risk of some cancers
8. Reducing risk of high blood pressure
9. Reducing risk of osteoporosis
10. Improving classroom behavior
11. Reducing absenteeism

According to the *Physical Activity Guidelines for Americans, Second Edition,* by the U.S. Department of Health and Human Services (HHS),

> *Since more than 95% of youth are enrolled in schools, they provide an ideal setting to provide physical activity to schools . . . which includes enhanced physical education with increased lesson time, a well-designed physical education curriculum, delivery by well-trained specialists, and instructional practices that provide substantial moderate to vigorous physical activity. (HHS, 2018, p. vii)*

According to the HHS (2018, p. 48), it is recommended that school-aged children and adolescents ages 6 through 17 should do 60 minutes or more of moderate-to-vigorous physical activity daily. Most of this activity can be accumulated in the school environment through before-school programming, recess, physical education, after-school programming, intramurals, clubs, and interscholastic sports. In particular, children and adolescents should participate in these activities:

- *Aerobic*: Most of the 60 minutes or more per day should be moderate- to vigorous-intensity aerobic physical activity at least three days per week.
- *Muscle strengthening*: As part of the 60 minutes or more of daily physical activity, children and adolescents should include muscle-strengthening activity at least three days per week.
- *Bone strengthening*: As part of the 60 minutes or more of daily physical activity, children and adolescents should include bone-strengthening physical activity at least three days per week.

Move Your Way, the physical activity campaign from the U.S. Department of Health and Human Services (HHS) Office of Disease Prevention and Health Promotion, provides recommendations and activities to get Americans physically active. Resources can be found at www.health.gov/moveyourway.

HHS is also responsible for setting data-driven national health objectives in its 10-year plan, the Healthy People initiative. Through an independent panel, the Community Preventive Services Task Force (CPSTF), HHS released Healthy People 2030. The CPSTF

> *recommends enhanced school-based physical education (PE) to increase physical activity based on strong evidence of effectiveness in increasing the amount of time students spend in moderate- or vigorous-intensity physical activity. Enhanced school-based PE involves curricular and practice-based changes that increase the amount of time that PreK-12 students engage in moderate- or vigorous-intensity physical activity, including aerobic and muscle-strengthening activities during PE classes and activity time (The Community Guide, 2018, para 3).*

The objectives for physical activity are shown in figure 3.1.

The National Physical Activity Plan (NPAP) (Physical Activity Alliance, 2022b) is a comprehensive set of recommended policies, programs, and initiatives designed to increase physical activity in all segments of the population. Acknowledging the role that schools play in affecting the development of physical education and physical activity programs for youth who attend PreK-12 programs, the plan offers a number of strategy recommendations, along with tactics and objectives, for the education sector (see figure 3.2).

Linking the research to practical applications is a major role of the physical education administrator; it is essential in developing the program at the district level as well as in assisting physical education department chairpersons and teachers to design their programs at the school site level. It is important to encourage young people to participate in physical activities that are appropriate for their age, are enjoyable, and offer variety.

The benefits of daily physical education and physical activity on the academic performance of youth have been well documented in evidence-based studies. Much of the research that focused on the relationship between physical activity and brain activity was disseminated to the general public and to senior-level district administrators with the release of *Spark: The Revolutionary New Science of Exercise and the Brain* by John Ratey (2008). According to research cited in the IOM (2013) report,

> *physically active and aerobically fit children consistently outperform their inactive*

FIGURE 3.1 Healthy People 2030 Physical Education and Physical Activity Objectives

ECBP-01 Increase the proportion of adolescents who participate in daily school physical education.

PA-R01 Increase the proportion of children aged 3 to 5 years who do at least 60 minutes of physical activity a day.

PA-06 Increase the proportion of adolescents who do enough aerobic physical activity.

PA-07 Increase the proportion of adolescents who do enough muscle-strengthening activity.

PA-08 Increase the proportion of adolescents who do enough aerobic and muscle-strengthening activity.

PA-09 Increase the proportion of children who do enough aerobic physical activity.

PA-11 Increase the proportion of adolescents who walk or bike to get places.

PA-12 Increase the proportion of children and adolescents who play sports.

Data from U.S. Department of Health and Human Services, https://health.gov/healthypeople/objectives-and-data/browse-objectives/physical-activity.

FIGURE 3.2 National Physical Activity Plan: Education Sector Strategies

Strategy 1
States and school districts should adopt strong policies that support implementation of the Comprehensive School Physical Activity Program (CSPAP) model.

Strategy 2
Schools should provide high-quality physical education programs.

Strategy 3
Providers of after-school, holiday, and vacation programs for children and youth should adopt policies and practices that ensure participants are appropriately physically active throughout the program.

Strategy 4
States should adopt evidence-based standards for childcare and early childhood education programs to ensure children aged zero to five years are appropriately physically active throughout their time in such programs.

Strategy 5
Colleges and universities should provide students and employees with opportunities and incentives to adopt and maintain physically active lifestyles.

Strategy 6
Educational institutions should provide pre-service professional training and in-service continuous professional development programs that prepare educators to deliver effective physical education and activity programs for students of all types.

Strategy 7
Professional and scientific organizations should develop and advocate for strong policies that promote physical activity among all students.

The complete list of tactics that accompany the seven education sector strategies, along with the entire National Physical Activity Plan, can be found at https://paamovewithus.org/national-physical-activity-plan.

From J. Greenberg and J. LoBianco, *Organization and Administration of Physical Education,* 2nd ed. (Human Kinetics, 2026). Reprinted by permission from "Physical Activity Plan," Physical Activity Alliance, accessed September 26, 2024, https://paamovewithus.org/for-transfer/education/

and unfit peers academically on both a short-term and long-term basis. Time spent engaged in physical activity is related not only to a healthier body but also to enriched cognitive development and lifelong brain health. (p. 186)

According to research by the CDC (2010, p. 6) and Michael and colleagues (2015), the relationship is further supported by the following:

- There is substantial evidence that physical activity can help improve academic achievement, including grades and standardized test scores.
- The articles in this review suggest that physical activity can have an impact on cognitive skills and attitudes and on academic behavior, all of which are important components of improved academic performance. They include enhanced concentration and attention as well as improved classroom behavior.
- Increasing or maintaining time dedicated to physical education may help, and does not appear to adversely affect, academic performance.

In support of including fitness assessment, the Presidential Youth Fitness Program (PYFP) as part of the physical education curriculum (Grissom, 2005) found a consistent positive relationship between overall fitness and academic achievement on the California Standardized Assessment. Similar findings were reported in Delaware (Gao & Kaplan, 2012), New York (Bezold et al., 2014), and Texas (Janak et al., 2014). The relationship between fitness and academic performance has been further supported by Dwyer and colleagues

(2001); Hillman and colleagues (2005); Castelli and colleagues (2007); Martin and Chalmers (2007); Hillman and colleagues (2008); and Van Dusen and colleagues (2011). It is important to note that although fitness assessment should be used as part of the educational program to assist students in improving their fitness levels, it should not be used in any way to grade students or as part of the teacher evaluation. The district physical education administrator could also use the school's overall fitness scores to determine whether the physical education teachers are including enough fitness education opportunities in their curriculum, which would enable students to improve their fitness levels and overall scores.

The CDC's publication *The Association Between School-Based Physical Activity, Including Physical Education, and Academic Performance* (2010) provides a comprehensive meta-analysis on the research linking school-based physical activity to academic performance and cognitive processes. The recommended 60 minutes or more of physical activity in the school environment can be achieved through physical activity, classroom physical activity breaks, recess, and before- and after-school programs (IOM, 2013). A growing body of evidence supports a relationship between physical activity and brain structure and function. Research by Trost (2007) and Rosenbaum and colleagues (2001), and cited by the CDC (2010, p. 9) and Dai and Xu (2022), further identified the interaction that occurs between cognitive skills and motor skills to support the link to increased academic performance. Behringer and colleagues (2022), the Youth Sport Trust (2022), and Donnelly (2017) further found a positive relationship between physical fitness and academic achievement. Physical movement affects the physiology of the brain by increasing the following:

- Cerebral capillary growth
- Blood flow
- Oxygenation
- Production of neurotrophins
- Growth of nerve cells in the hippocampus (center of learning and memory)
- Neurotransmitter levels
- Development of nerve connections
- Density of neural network
- Brain tissue volume

As a result of these physiological changes in the brain, increases in academic performance may be associated with the following effects:

- Improved attention
- Improved information processing, storage, and retrieval
- Enhanced coping
- Enhanced positive affect
- Reduced sensations of cravings and pain

The research supporting the relationship between physical education and physical activity and better grades, improved academic performance, higher academic achievement test scores, and better classroom behavior is compelling. An understanding of how physical activity positively influences overall cognitive, behavioral, and physical skills will lend further support for the need to develop and implement a standards-based, quality physical education program in schools across the United States and globally. How these benefits affect the development of physical education policy and environment is explored later in this chapter.

Program Planning

As previously stated, the cornerstone of effective physical education administration includes planning for and executing a quality physical education program. Foundational to the job requirements is ensuring that your physical education instructional program is embedded in a standards-based curriculum encompassing **grade-span learning indicators** and intended outcomes as well as incorporating age- and developmentally appropriate instructional practices. **Program planning** should also take into account the needs of all students, ensuring that your program addresses the cultural needs of an ever-changing diverse population; is committed to equity and inclusion; and addresses the cognitive, affective, social and emotional, and psychomotor domains of all students.

Other **essential components** for consideration that will impact your program planning responsibilities include the certification of teachers delivering the curriculum, the district's policies and procedures (especially relating to class size and scheduling patterns), and available facilities. With deliberate time and effort dedicated to program planning, your end result will be physically literate students; they will successfully achieve the intended learning indicators and outcomes throughout their educational experiences, with the skills, knowledge, competence, and confidence to be physically active throughout their life span.

Role of the National PE Standards in Program Planning

The most significant change reflected in the current edition of this book is the transition from the 2014 *National Standards & Grade-Level Outcomes for K-12 Physical Education* (SHAPE America, 2014) to the 2024 *National Physical Education Standards*. Developed by SHAPE America (2025), the National Physical Education Standards, Grade-Span Learning Indicators, and Learning Progressions address learning across the psychomotor, cognitive, affective, and social learning domains, which is essential to supporting PreK-12 learners as they progress along their own meaningful physical literacy journey. While the National PE Standards, Grade-Span Learning Indicators, and Learning Progressions articulate the knowledge and skills students are expected to learn across grades PreK-12 and a general trajectory for that learning, physical literacy is not about mastery; rather, it is an ongoing process (Castelli et al., 2015). "These National PE Standards, along with their corresponding Grade-Span Learning Indicators and Learning Progressions, can be used to create relevant and developmentally appropriate learning experiences that engage all PreK-12 learners on a physical literacy journey of holistic competence, to include opportunities to develop the skills, knowledge, confidence, appreciation, and motivation to live an active life—across and beyond their PreK-12 years" (chapter 2, p. 1). It should also be noted that where there were previously five national standards, the updated 2024 version includes four national standards for PreK-12 physical education (figure 3.3). Many states and local school districts use these documents to develop curriculum, ensure alignment, and provide guidance to establish the intended outcomes of their physical education programs.

The Grade-Span Learning Indicators, intended to support the National PE Standards, provide a framework for what students should be able to do at each grade span. The measurable learning indicators and intended outcomes provide the bridge between the national standards and the physical education curriculum. The grade-span learning indicators and the intended outcomes are grounded in scholarly literature in motor development, skill competency, motor learning, physical activity, and student engagement and motivation. Taken together, the intention of the physical literacy journey, the four national standards (previously five), and the grade-span learning indicators is to operationalize the concept of the physical literacy journey and to provide a framework for teachers to use in developing curricula and lesson plans. What follows is an overall view of what students should know by the end of each grade span (SHAPE America, 2025).

Tables 3.1 through 3.4 provide examples of how each of the four National PE Standards & Grade-Span Learning Indicators can be applied for each grade span: PreK through 2

FIGURE 3.3 SHAPE America 2024 National Physical Education Standards

Standard 1: Develops a variety of motor skills.

Standard 2: Applies knowledge related to movement and fitness concepts.

Standard 3: Develops social skills through movement.

Standard 4: Develops personal skills, identifies personal benefits of movement, and chooses to engage in physical activity.

Reprinted by permission from SHAPE America, *National Physical Education Standards* (Champaign, IL: Human Kinetics, 2025).

TABLE 3.1 Sample PreK-2 National PE Standards and Grade-Span Learning Indicators

Standard 1: Develops a Variety of Motor Skills	
Locomotor skills	1.2.1 Demonstrates a variety of locomotor skills with the concepts of space, effort, and relationship awareness. 1.2.2 Demonstrates jumping and landing in a nondynamic environment. 1.2.3 Demonstrates transferring weight on multiple body parts.
Dance and rhythms	1.2.4 Demonstrates locomotor, nonlocomotor, and manipulative movements based on a variety of dance forms. 1.2.5 Demonstrates jumping rope in a nondynamic environment.
Nonlocomotor skills	1.2.6 Demonstrates nonlocomotor skills with the concepts of space, effort, and relationship awareness. 1.2.7 Demonstrates balancing on different body parts in a nondynamic environment.
Manipulative skills	1.2.8 Demonstrates the ability to manipulate small implements.
Bouncing	1.2.9 Demonstrates bouncing a ball in a variety of practice tasks.
Rolling	1.2.10 Demonstrates rolling a ball in a variety of practice tasks.
Catching/throwing	1.2.11 Demonstrates catching in a variety of practice tasks. 1.2.12 Demonstrates throwing in a nondynamic environment.
Kicking	1.2.13 Demonstrates kicking a ball in a nondynamic environment.
Striking with hands	1.2.14 Demonstrates striking with hands in a variety of practice tasks.
Striking with implements	1.2.15 Demonstrates striking with short-handled implement in a non-dynamic environment. 1.2.16 Demonstrates striking with a long-handled implement in a variety of practice tasks.
Aquatics	1.2.17 Demonstrates water safety skills. If a pool facility is available demonstrates water safety and basic swimming skills. Please reference the American Red Cross Learn to Swim program.

From J. Greenberg and J. LoBianco, *Organization and Administration of Physical Education,* 2nd ed. (Human Kinetics, 2026). Reprinted by permission from SHAPE America, *National Physical Education Standards.* (Human Kinetics, 2025).

(table 3.1); 3 through 5 (table 3.2); 6 through 8 (table 3.3); and 9 through 12 (table 3.4). Keep in mind that all four standards are applied to each grade span; they can be found at www.shapeamerica.org.

Sample PreK-2 National PE Standards and Grade-Span Learning Indicators

The preschool and early elementary years have been recognized as critical in the development of fundamental movement skills. The grade-span learning indicators inform teachers about what children in grades PreK through 2 (PreK-2) should know and be able to do, and they guide teachers in designing meaningful learning experiences. Children in PreK-2 are in the fundamental movement phase of motor development. PreK (ages 4-5) students are progressing through the emerging elementary stage of fundamental motor skill development (SHAPE America, 2025, chapter 3, p. 1). See table 3.1.

Sample Grade 3-5 National PE Standards and Grade-Span Learning Indicators

Children's physical literacy journey in grades 3 through 5 is developing as they combine fundamental movement skills (manipulative, locomotor, nonlocomotor) with movement concepts (space, effort, relationships) to acquire specialized movement skills. These specialized movement skills are applied with varied movement forms (e.g., games, dance, gymnastics). The three stages of the specialized movement phase are transition, application, and lifelong utilization (SHAPE America, 2025, chapter 4, p. 1). See table 3.2.

TABLE 3.2 Sample Grade 3-5 National PE Standards and Grade-Span Learning Indicators

Standard 2: Applies Knowledge Related to Movement and Fitness Concepts	
Tactics and strategies	2.5.1 Applies movement concepts and strategies for safe movement within dynamic environments. 2.5.2 Demonstrates knowledge of offensive strategies in small-sided invasion practice tasks. 2.5.3 Demonstrates knowledge of defensive strategies in small-sided invasion practice tasks. 2.5.4 Demonstrates knowledge of appropriate movement concepts for efficient performance of manipulative skills. 2.5.5 Demonstrates problem-solving strategies in a variety of games and activities.
Dance, gymnastics, and individual activities	2.5.6 Applies movement concepts to different types of dances, gymnastics, rhythms, and individual performance activities.
Fitness concepts	2.5.7 Defines and provides examples of movement activities for developing the health-related fitness components. 2.5.8 Establishes goals related to enhancing fitness development. 2.5.9 Defines and explains how to implement the FITT Principle for fitness development. 2.5.10 Defines and provides examples of movement activities for developing the skill-related fitness components. 2.5.11 Identifies the need for warm-up and cool-down relative to various physical activities. 2.5.12 Identifies location of pulse and provides examples of activities that increase heart rate.
Physical activity knowledge	2.5.13 Explains the benefits of physical activity. 2.5.14 Recognizes and explains how physical activity influences physiological changes in their body. 2.5.15 Recognizes the critical elements that contribute to proper execution of a skill. 2.5.16 Identifies technology tools that support physical activity goals. 2.5.17 Describes the impact of food and hydration choices on physical activity.
Aquatics	2.5.18 Demonstrates knowledge of water safety skills. Demonstrates knowledge of basic swimming skills.

From J. Greenberg and J. LoBianco, *Organization and Administration of Physical Education*, 2nd ed. (Human Kinetics, 2026). Reprinted by permission from SHAPE America, *National Physical Education Standards*. (Human Kinetics, 2025).

Sample Grade 6-8 National PE Standards and Grade-Span Learning Indicators

The physical literacy journey for students in grades 6 through 8 reflects the influence of early and emerging adolescence on their psychomotor, cognitive, social, and affective learning. Transitions prompted by changes (e.g., biological, social, emotional, cognitive) during early and emerging adolescence directly impact learning in physical education. During the middle school years, individual differences in growth and maturation rates will require differentiated instruction and developmentally appropriate accommodations. Through learning experiences in physical education, the students use their knowledge of movement concepts, tactics, and strategies across a variety of environments. This knowledge helps students become more versatile and efficient movers (SHAPE America, 2025, chapter 5, p. 1). See table 3.3.

Sample Grade 9-12 National PE Standards and Grade-Span Learning Indicators

The development of an adolescent's physical literacy journey in grades 9 through 12 is

TABLE 3.3 Sample Grade 6-8 National PE Standards and Grade-Span Learning Indicators

Standard 3: Develops Social Skills Through Movement	
Social awareness	3.8.1 Understands and accepts others' differences during a variety of physical activities. 3.8.2 Demonstrates consideration for others and contributes positively to the group or team. 3.8.5 Explains the value of a specific physical activity in culture.
Communication	3.8.3 Uses communication skills to negotiate strategies and tactics in a physical activity setting. 3.8.4 Implements and provides constructive feedback to and from others when prompted and supported by the teacher.
Working with others	3.8.8 Solves problems amongst teammates and opponents. 3.8.9 Applies and respects the importance of etiquette in a physical activity setting.
Safety	3.8.6 Demonstrates the ability to follow game rules in a variety of physical activity situations. 3.8.7 Recognizes and implements safe and appropriate behaviors during physical activity and with exercise equipment.

From J. Greenberg and J. LoBianco, *Organization and Administration of Physical Education*, 2nd ed. (Human Kinetics, 2026). Reprinted by permission from SHAPE America, *National Physical Education Standards*. (Human Kinetics, 2025).

significant; during this time, the student exists in a transitional stage between childhood and early adulthood. As students enter high school, they receive their (often final) structured pedagogical exposure to instruction related to physical activity before entering early adulthood. According to SHAPE America (2025, chapter 6, p. 1), the knowledge, skills, and dispositions acquired by students prior to and during this pivotal time frame will shape their ability and likeliness to maintain a health-enhancing and physically active lifestyle through adulthood. In addition,

> *Through learning experiences in physical education, the student develops an understanding of how movement is personally beneficial and subsequently chooses to participate in physical activities that are personally meaningful (e.g., activities that offer social interaction, cultural connection, exploration, choice, self-expression, appropriate levels of challenge, and added health benefits). The student develops personal skills including goal setting, identifying strengths, and reflection to enhance their physical literacy journey. (p. 11).*

See table 3.4.

These documents should serve as the basis for developing or revising a district's curriculum, developing a scope and sequence by grade-span, and determining what should be assessed to ensure that the learning indicators and intended outcomes have been achieved. States and local school districts could use a crosswalk to ensure alignment with the national standards. The 2024 National Physical Education Standards & Grade-Span Learning Indicators can be accessed at www.shapeamerica.org.

Developing a Mission Statement

Since many definitions of physical education have evolved throughout the years, as a physical education administrator, before you begin to plan your program you first must decide what your definition of physical education is and then work collaboratively to develop a **mission statement** (see figure 3.4). Through careful consideration and planning, the mission statement should reflect the philosophy and core purpose of your department or office. It can be written as a short sentence; however, it is usually written in paragraph form, in simple and concise terms. Development of the mission statement assists all physical education teachers and stakeholders in understanding the direction the physical education program is moving in as well as in defining your overall long-term focus. When developing your mission statement, you should vet it with teachers and other staff members to ensure that there is buy-in and consensus on the purpose of, and vision for, physical education in the school district. Once the mission statement

TABLE 3.4 Sample Grade 9-12 National PE Standards and Grade-Span Learning Indicators

Standard 4: Develops Personal Skills, Identifies Personal Benefits of Movement, and Chooses to Engage in Physical Activity	
Self-expression and social interaction	4.12.1 Selects and participates in physical activities (e.g., dance, yoga, aerobics) that meet the need for self-expression. 4.12.2 Selects and participates in physical activities that meet the need for social interaction.
Self-management and personal health	4.12.3 Identifies and participates in physical activity that positively affects health. 4.12.8 Analyzes and applies self-selected techniques to manage one's emotions in a physical activity setting.
Choice	4.12.4 Chooses and participates in physical activity based on personal interests. 4.12.5 Chooses and successfully participates in self-selected physical activity at a level that is appropriately challenging.
Goal setting	4.12.6 Sets and develops movement goals related to personal interests.
Reflection	4.12.9 Reflects on movement experiences during physical education to develop understanding of how movement is personally meaningful.
Participation in PE	4.12.7 Analyzes factors on regular participation in physical activity after high school (e.g., life choices, economics, motivation, accessibility).

From J. Greenberg and J. LoBianco, *Organization and Administration of Physical Education,* 2nd ed. (Human Kinetics, 2026). Reprinted by permission from SHAPE America, *National Physical Education Standards*. (Human Kinetics, 2025).

has been developed and accepted, you can proceed with determining the goals and objectives of the program. The goals and objectives provide a guide on how to operationalize your mission.

Developing Goals and Objectives

According to SHAPE America (2025), the National Physical Education Standards, Grade-Span Learning Indicators, and Learning Progressions were developed with the understanding that the goal of high-quality physical education is to support PreK-12 students in their physical literacy journey (the ongoing acquisition and application of knowledge, skills, and dispositions necessary for engagement in a lifetime of healthful and meaningful physical activity) so they have the "ability, confidence, and desire to be physically active for life" (Farrey & Isard, 2015; SHAPE America, 2025, p. 9). Program goals are broad statements with intended outcomes that

FIGURE 3.4 Sample School District Mission Statement

Physical education provides students the opportunity to attain their optimal level of fitness, motor, and sports skills while participating in a continuous, carefully planned program of physical activities, essential for developing physical, mental, emotional, and social skills. To that end, the division provides direction and assistance to enable schools to nurture high student achievement and foster academic excellence through quality curriculum development, enriched learning opportunities through outdoor education and environmental pursuits, research-based instructional strategies leading to evidence-based results, technology-infused instruction, career path exploration through the implementation of school-based academies, real-world learning, enhanced parental involvement, and programs that include partnerships and collaborations in a multiculturally rich and diverse community. All programs use full inclusion models, allowing for participation of ALL students.

express what you are striving to achieve and that are linked with the mission statement. A clearly stated goal should be focused and concrete, and it should have definitive objectives regarding what you want to accomplish throughout the program. The CDC asserts that program goals and objectives are used to establish criterion standards to determine whether your program is effective. Through the identification of goals and objectives, the program content can be evaluated to determine if the intended outcome has been achieved. Through this assessment and feedback, modifications can be implemented to ensure future success.

One common denominator in all quality physical education programs is that they have written goals and objectives aligned with the state and national standards. Goals and objectives should be developed for the overall physical education program as well as for **instructional strategies** and student achievement. As an academic class, physical education is essential to student achievement and learning outcomes; therefore, it should have established goals and objectives.

When you are developing goals and objectives for your program, the recommended format to ensure that they are well thought out and aligned to the expected outcomes involves the SMART principle (discussed in chapter 14). When following the SMART principle, goals and objectives should be developed as follows:

***S**pecific*: Goals and objectives should clearly define what you are going to do and achieve.

***M**easurable*: The focus should be on how to assess and how much change can be expected.

***A**chievable*: The goals and objectives should be realistic yet challenging.

***R**elevant*: Sufficient resources must be available to ensure achievement of the goals and objectives.

***T**ime-bound*: The start and end dates should ensure that the goals and objectives can be met within the designated time frame.

See figure 3.5 for sample SMART goals for both middle school and high school physical education classes.

The objectives developed for your program can be based on both process and outcome. Process-based objectives describe the curriculum and instructional strategies that will be delivered during the program implementation process. Outcome-based objectives specify what is to be achieved as a result of the program's implementation; they can be identified as short-term, intermediate, or long-term objectives. Both process- and outcome-based objectives should be measurable to enable determination of program effectiveness in achieving the intended outcomes. The activities selected to implement your program should support its goals and objectives. Physical education teachers have the opportunity to develop their own goals and objectives aligned with those developed by the district once they establish their instructional units and lesson plans. These goals and objectives will vary from school to school, and they are often based on the scheduling configurations and local decisions. Therefore, the physical education teacher (whether a veteran or a beginning teacher) should seek the assistance of the physical education administrator in the development process.

FIGURE 3.5 Sample SMART Goals for Physical Education Classes

Middle School Class Goal

By the fourth week of the first semester, through the use of a pedometer, students will exhibit measurable progress by increasing the number of steps they take during a 30-minute time period by 3 percent from individual baseline measures.

High School Class Goal

During the 2025-2026 school year, 80 percent of the students will improve their scores on the Personal Fitness End of Course exam by 5 percent as established by the pretest assessment.

Essential Components of Physical Education

In December of 2015, the U.S. Congress passed the Every Student Succeeds Act (ESSA), which reauthorized the Elementary and Secondary Education Act. The ESSA provides great opportunities for physical education. Designation as a part of a well-rounded education elevates physical education and health education to the same level of importance as other academic subjects; moreover, it provides physical educators with the opportunity to develop more rigorous curriculum and seek U.S. federal funding through their state departments of education from Title I, Title II, and Title IV. In an effort to transform physical education with respect to rigor and focus, SHAPE America has identified four essential elements, termed the *essential components of physical education*, to guide the structuring of physical education to meet the needs of districts, schools, and students. As identified in figure 3.6, these elements are (1) policy and environment, (2) curriculum, (3) appropriate instruction, and (4) student assessment.

Policy and Environment

Well-defined and well-implemented physical education policies serve to ensure that students engage in physical education programs that

Policy and environment	Curriculum	Appropriate instruction	Student assessment
• Every student is required to take daily physical education in grades K–12, with instruction periods totaling 150 minutes/week in elementary and 225 minutes/week in middle and high school. • School districts and schools require full inclusion of all students in physical education. • School districts and schools do not allow waivers from physical education class time or credit requirements. • School districts and schools do not allow student exemptions from physical education class time or credit requirements. • School districts and schools prohibit students from substituting other activities (e.g., JROTC, interscholastic sports) for physical education class time or credit requirements. • Physical education class size is consistent with that of other subject areas and aligns with school district and school teacher/student ratio policy. • Physical activity is not assigned or withheld as punishment. • Physical education is taught by a state-licensed or state-certified teacher who is endorsed to teach physical education.	• School districts and schools should have a written physical education curriculum for grades K–12 that is sequential and comprehensive. • The physical education curriculum is based on national and/or state standards and grade-level outcomes for physical education. • The physical education curriculum mirrors other school district and school curricula in its design and schedule for periodic review/update.	• The physical education teacher uses instructional practices and deliberate-practice tasks that support the goals and objectives defined in the school district's/school's physical education curriculum (e.g., differentiated instruction, active engagement, modified activities, self-assessment, self-monitoring). • The physical education teacher evaluates student learning continually to document teacher effectiveness. • The physical education teacher employs instructional practices that engage students in moderate to vigorous physical activity for at least 50 percent of class time. • The physical education teacher ensures the inclusion of all students and makes the necessary adaptations for students with special needs or disabilities.	• Student assessment is aligned with national and/or state physical education standards and established grade-level outcomes, and is included in the written physical education curriculum along with administration protocols. • Student assessment includes evidence-based practices that measure student achievement in all areas of instruction, including physical fitness. • Grading is related directly to the student learning objectives identified in the written physical education curriculum. • The physical education teacher follows school and school district protocols for reporting and communicating student progress to students and parents.

FIGURE 3.6 SHAPE America's essential components of physical education.

Reprinted by permission from SHAPE America, *The Essential Components of Physical Education* (Reston VA; SHAPE America), 9, www.shapeamerica.org/upload/TheEssentialComponentsOfPhysicalEducation.pdf

are standards based with intended learning outcomes to ensure the delivery of a quality educational program. It is well documented in the literature that active kids do better and that quality physical education programs contribute to the physical, cognitive, mental, and emotional health of children. As administrators look toward increasing the amount of time designated to physical education in schools, increasing the physical education graduation requirements, addressing teacher certification issues, and addressing the quality of physical education being offered, they need to look at the factors that affect policy decisions.

Dyson (2014) asserts that several powerful forces are coming together to affect the policy environment; these forces include the public health agenda, which is based on childhood obesity and other medical concerns due to physical inactivity and increases in sedentary behavior; educational issues, including standards, accountability, assessment, and other measures affecting teachers and students; and finally, a recognition that schools alone cannot solve all of the problems of student inactivity. However, achieving enhanced physical education policies has not been an easy process, and much more work needs to be done. This need is clearly evident in the Physical Activity Alliance's (PAA's) (2022a) *The 2022 United States Report Card on Physical Activity for Children and Youth*; it assigned a letter grade of D− to schools. The primary indicator was the proportion of high school students attending at least one physical education class in an average week. Results from the 2019 Youth Risk Behavior Surveillance System (YRBSS; CDC, 2019) indicate that only 52 percent of high school students attended at least one physical education class in the previous week versus 29.9 percent of students attending physical education on all five days. The 2018 School Health Profiles further reported that the percentage of schools requiring a PE course be taught in each grade decreases from 97 percent in grade 6 to 43 percent in grade 12. The 2021 YRBSS (CDC, 2021) continues to show a downward trend; only 46.8 percent of high school students attended physical education on one or more days, and only 19 percent of high school students attended physical education on all five days (see figure 3.7). This trend has a great impact on meeting the recommendations in the *Physical Activity Guidelines for Americans, Second Edition* (HHS, 2018) as well as meeting the Healthy People 2030 objectives.

Ward (2011, pp. 3-4), as well as Cooper and colleagues (2016), through a synthesis of research about school policies on physical education and physical activity, obtained the following findings:

- *Children who attend regularly scheduled physical education classes get significantly more physical activity than those who attend them less often.*
- *Physical education programs that include the use of standardized curricula, goals for active classes, and staff development result in children who are more physically active.*
- *Quality in-service training for teachers, either for PE specialists or for classroom teachers, increases students' levels of physical activity at school.*

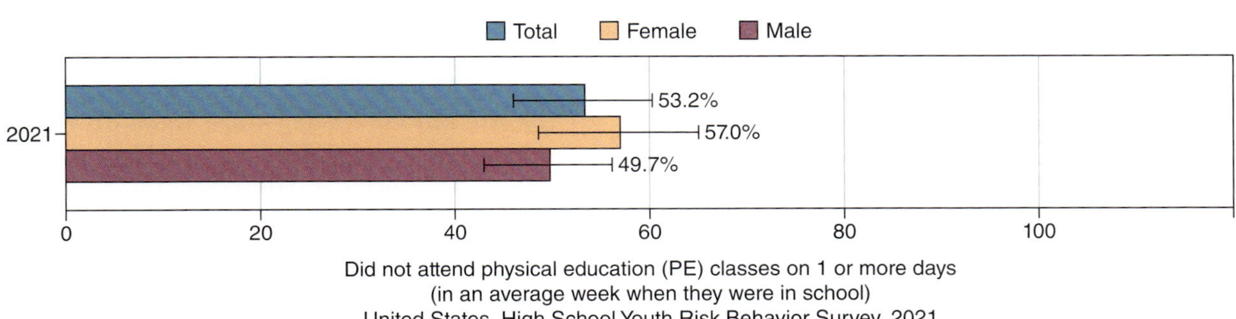

FIGURE 3.7 Percentage of high school students who did not attend physical education classes on all five days.

Data from CDC (2021).

- *Whole school programs that provide additional opportunities for physical activity across the school day—through recess, in-class breaks, and after-school events—increase children's physical activity levels.*
- *Schools that provide ample time for supervised recess and access to equipment, as well as those that make low-cost modifications to improve play spaces, have more physically active students.*
- *Additional activity breaks during classes not only increase physical activity, they also help children focus better on academic tasks and enhance academic achievement.*
- *School environments with well-designed playgrounds; open spaces; and facilities and equipment that are available, accessible, and inviting to children encourage more physical activity, both during and after school.*
- *After-school programs may contribute additional physical activity beyond that which children obtain during school hours, but more research is needed.*
- *Joint-use agreements between schools and communities encourage physical activity after school and on weekends by opening school grounds so children have places to play.*
- *State policies requiring that children engage in a specific amount of physical activity at school each day have the potential to affect large numbers of children and are an effective strategy for promoting regular activity.*

These findings have global implications for future policy decisions, with consideration for state and federal policies as well as local school district and local school wellness policies.

Since well-defined policies can create an environment that ensures that students receive quality physical education with standards-based outcomes, SHAPE America (2015a) asserts that the following policies should be included in the local school wellness policy:

- Every student is required to take daily physical education in grades K through 12, with instruction periods totaling 150 minutes per week in elementary and 225 minutes per week in middle and high school.
- School districts and schools require full inclusion of all students in physical education.
- School districts and schools do not allow waivers from physical education class time or credit requirements.
- School districts and schools do not allow student exemptions from physical education class time or credit requirements.
- School districts and schools prohibit students from substituting other activities (e.g., Junior Reserve Officer Training Corps [JROTC], interscholastic sports) for physical education class time or credit requirements.
- Physical education class size is consistent with that of other subject areas and aligns with school district and school teacher-to-student ratio policy.
- Physical activity is neither assigned nor withheld as punishment.
- Physical education is taught by a state-licensed or state-certified teacher who is endorsed to teach physical education.

Additional attention should be paid to the equipment and facilities provided for the instructional program. Equipment should be age and size appropriate to ensure student safety, in full operational order, and aligned with the instructional program needs. Facilities—whether the gymnasium, classroom, or outdoor playing fields—should represent a safe environment that is free from hazards.

Data from the 2016 School Health Policies and Practices Study (SHPPS) (CDC, 2016) reflected some promising progress, showing that

> *for all school levels, more than 89% of districts require schools to teach physical education, and this requirement increased significantly for elementary schools since 2000. In addition, for all school levels, the majority of districts follow national standards for physical education; have time requirements for physical education; and*

> *have staffing policies that require staff who teach physical education to be certified, licensed, or endorsed by the state to teach physical education. (p. 81)*

However, additional progress needs to be made as to the percentage of schools that have a written scope and sequence and assess students on fitness and other learning outcomes.

The 2016 Shape of the Nation report was developed in collaboration between SHAPE America and Voices for Healthy Kids as a joint initiative of the American Heart Association and the Robert Wood Johnson Foundation. It was conducted to gather information and identify state statutes and regulations in support of physical education and physical activity in schools and to advocate at the federal and state levels. As schools strive to implement 60 minutes of daily physical activity with physical education as the cornerstone of a comprehensive physical activity program,

> *[A]n ongoing challenge is the diversity of state education legislative and regulatory activity and the resulting variety in policies and implementation approaches. Standards differ widely from state to state and many state policies are broad, leaving implementation details open to interpretation at the local level. (SHAPE America, 2016, p. 4)*

The data secured from the report's executive summary (SHAPE America, 2016) demonstrate the following:

- *Only Oregon and District of Columbia meet the national recommendations for weekly time in physical education at both the elementary and middle school levels.*
- *Few states set any minimum amount of time that elementary (19), middle/junior high (15), and high school (6) students must participate in physical education.*
- *Just 15 states have additional funding available for physical education programs.*
- *Nearly all states (50) have set standards for physical education programs.*
- *Many states require physical education teachers to meet state professional requirements as well, but it varies by school level: elementary (35), middle school/junior high (43) and high school (48).*
- *Most states require students to participate in physical education during elementary school (39), middle school/junior high (37) and high school (44).*
- *More than half of state policies (28) require a type of assessment.*
- *Many states (31) allow other activities as substitutions for physical education credit and more than half of state policies (30) allow student exemptions from physical education class time or credit.*
- *A few states (15) allow school districts to apply for a waiver from the state physical education requirements.*
- *Only a handful of states (10) prohibit withholding physical activity as punishment.*
- *Just a few states (13) prohibit using physical activity as a form of punishment. (p. 3)*

Although the Shape of the Nation Report shows that the majority of youth are still not participating in adequate physical education programs, it does provide information for policymakers to use as a launching point to increase physical education programs and get more students active and healthy in the school environment. From a policy perspective, the report lends to the promotion of more frequent and effective physical education in schools as the cornerstone of comprehensive physical activity before, during, and after the school day. It further acknowledges the need to address standards-based curriculum, appropriate professional development for teachers, teacher certification, student assessment, and accountability.

From a global perspective, the World Health Organization (WHO) called for increased physical activity and physical education in its 2017 publication, the *WHO Global Action Plan on Physical Activity 2018-2030*. Finalized and adopted on June 4, 2018, the plan highlights the WHO's Sustainable Development Goals

(SDGs). Although the plan identifies several opportunities for physical activity through four strategic objectives and 20 policy actions, physical education is referenced under sustainable goal 4 (SDG 4): Ensure inclusive and equitable quality education and promote lifelong learning for all (WHO, 2017).

The policy implication from the WHO (2017) recommended the proposed action:

> *Action 3.1: Strengthen the provision of positive experiences in physical education and physical activity for girls and boys, applying the whole-of-school approach in all pre-primary, primary, secondary and tertiary educational institutions to establish and reinforce life-long health, physical literacy, and promote the enjoyment of, and participation in physical activity according to capacity and ability. (p. 36)*

The full Global Action Plan can be found at www.who.int/initiatives/gappa and www.who.int/publications/i/item/9789241514187.

The data in these reports and studies clearly show support for strengthening physical education policies at the federal, state, local, and individual school levels. The passing of the ESSA (2015) opens up new opportunities to advance the role of physical education in the school environment, especially at the state and school levels, for enhanced physical education curriculum, program expansion, and funding opportunities. Policy language including waivers, exemptions, and substitutions should be used with caution or eliminated where possible so that all students can be provided with a quality physical education experience. Physical education administrators, teachers, parents, and other stakeholders play a critical role in supporting positive policies for enabling all students to engage in quality and equitable physical education programs. Strong policy is important for ensuring that state requirements are implemented throughout school districts and schools at all grade levels and for all students. Determining the appropriate practices and procedures for advocating for physical education is discussed in chapter 10.

Curriculum Development

A well-designed physical education curriculum provides students with the knowledge, skills, and confidence to be physically active for a lifetime. Developing or implementing a curriculum that meets the goals and objectives of your program is key to determining the overall academic content that teachers are expected to deliver; the scope and sequence of the content that should be taught; the lessons, resources, and materials to deliver that content; and the strategies for student assessment. The physical education curriculum provides a framework for what is to be taught and the diverse learning experiences that all students should have access to in all grade levels from PreK through grade 12. The overarching goals and objectives in any physical education program should be the attainment of state and national standards to ensure that students are achieving the educational objectives identified in each course and at each grade level. Tables 3.1 through 3.4 present a clearly articulated plan for how students will meet the physical education standards and outcomes resulting in physical literacy.

Developing a curriculum—a collaborative process that engages a variety of stakeholders (including physical education teachers) in the planning process—should have standards-based outcomes aligned with the PreK-12 program. Consideration should be given to which curriculum models will best meet your district's philosophy and needs. The process should ensure that instructional strategies are culturally and linguistically appropriate and that assessment is directly tied to the achievement of the standards and grade-level outcomes. Since a standards-based outcome is the desired result, most educational curriculum developers use a backward design approach; they start with the standards in mind and work toward the instructional strategies.

Furthermore, the curriculum should be developmentally based with progressively sequenced and well-defined goals, objectives, and intended learning outcomes balanced between knowledge and motor skill development. Once you have developed your curriculum and aligned the specific learning standards for grades PreK-12 both vertically and horizontally to ensure that the skills and knowledge are attained across grade levels, the next step is to prioritize the standards, especially in scheduling configurations in which the students are enrolled in physical education for a semester as opposed to a full academic school year. This step will further assist teachers in their planning to ensure that the instructional processes and content are delivered in depth, enabling mastery of the standards. Development of a curriculum map gives the development team the ability to visually determine that the standards have been aligned and implemented within a course or grade level. This overview gives teachers the opportunity to plan accordingly to ensure that the content and skills necessary to attain the standards are delivered and that there is scope and sequence across the curriculum.

As district physical education administrative personnel provide the guidance for delivery of the physical education curriculum in terms of the program mission statement, goals, instructional models to address all learning domains, and grade-level outcomes and assessments, it is usually up to the physical education teacher to determine which curriculum models will be used to develop unit and lesson plans. As also discussed in chapter 4, the most common physical education curriculum models (Metzler, 2017; Mitchell & Walton-Fisette, 2016) are the following:

- Teaching Personal and Social Responsibility (TPSR) model
- Tactical Games model
- Sport Education model
- The Conceptual Physical Education or Fitness Education model
- Skill Theme Approach model
- Adventure Education model
- Outdoor Education model

In developing the district or individual school physical education program, you should consider several other factors that may be unique to a geographical location. For example, physical education teachers in Vermont might teach skiing and snowboarding as part of their curriculum, whereas those in Florida would consider kayaking and sailing. The same could hold true with regard to linking the school physical education program to community-based events and partnerships that would enable lifelong physical activity participation. The high school and middle school curriculum, in particular, could match up with opportunities your students will have as adults in your community. In Vermont, fishing, hunting, skiing, mountain biking, and hiking are readily available in the local environment, whereas sailing, kayaking, canoeing, cycling, and swimming are readily available in South Florida. The types of facilities and equipment are also factors for consideration in developing your physical education program; for example, you need to consider whether you have the equipment to teach archery as a target sport or the appropriate space for field hockey in a team sports unit.

As a physical education administrator, aside from distributing your curriculum or curriculum guide to your physical education teachers or posting your district's curriculum on your website, providing professional development to your teachers will assist them in making the most appropriate decisions for their school and program. Through district-wide meetings, it will also give senior staff the opportunity to be educated about the district's curriculum, ensuring equitable access and the standardization of curriculum across all schools. **Curriculum development**, evaluation, and revisions are covered in depth in chapter 4.

Appropriate Instruction and Instructional Strategies

It is a foundational role for the physical education administrator to ensure that appropriate instructional practices are taking place in all instructional spaces including gymnasiums, playing fields, weight rooms, and fitness centers under their supervision. Delivering appropriate instruction in physical education that is aligned with the district's goals and objectives involves a variety of factors, such as the needs and developmental stages of the students as well as the content and pedagogical knowledge of the teachers and the instructional environment (e.g., class size, allocated time, and availability of facilities and equipment). Many instructional models, aligned with curriculum models, incorporate research-based practices designed to maximize learning opportunities for all students to ensure success in attaining expected learning outcomes. An instructional model as defined by Metzler (2017), based on theoretical frameworks, is

> *a comprehensive and coherent plan for teaching that includes descriptions of*

> *students' needs and abilities, statements of learning outcomes, teacher's content knowledge, developmentally appropriate and sequenced learning activities, expectations for teacher and student behaviors, unique task structures, measures of learning outcomes.* (p. 8)

Appropriate instruction involves using a variety of teaching strategies to ensure that students are engaged in physical activity for at least 50 percent of the class time, and that students are provided with enough activity time to enable mastery of content knowledge and skill attainment.

The physical education administrator plays a critical role in providing leadership and guidance to teachers to assist them in delivering appropriate instruction to a diverse student population. Through professional development opportunities, on-site school visits, and individual interactions, teachers can strengthen their instructional offerings and delivery systems.

From the national perspective, in working toward quality instruction, SHAPE America (2015a, p. 6) advises using these four key practices:

1. The physical education teacher uses instructional practices and deliberate-practice tasks that support the goals and objectives defined in the school district's or school's physical education curriculum (e.g., differentiated instruction, active engagement, modified activities, self-assessment, self-monitoring).
2. The physical education teacher evaluates student learning continually to document teacher effectiveness.
3. The physical education teacher employs instructional practices that engage students in moderate-to-vigorous physical activity for at least 50 percent of class time.
4. The physical education teacher ensures the inclusion of all students and makes the necessary adaptations for students with special needs or disabilities.

At the school level, physical education teachers should hold high expectations for student learning, provide well-designed lessons that are age and developmentally appropriate, vary the teaching styles to meet the individual student learning styles, provide constructive feedback, incorporate the use of technology where appropriate, and maximize participation time. Lessons should be culturally and linguistically sensitive and meet the needs of all students. For the learning environment to be effective, students should be motivated, engaged, and interested in the activities being presented. Opportunities to provide authentic learning experiences outside of the school environment should be part of the instructional program. The time spent on managerial tasks, such as attendance, locker room time, and other issues, should be kept to a minimum.

Students With Disabilities

Because students with disabilities are less physically active than their peers, they are more prone to chronic health conditions along with secondary conditions related to their disability. Providing educational opportunities for inclusion of students with disabilities should be a priority for all instructional programs; it is mandated under federal law. These laws include Public Law 93-112, which is known as the Rehabilitation Act of 1973; Rehabilitation Act Section 504, which stipulates that no person with a disability shall be discriminated against or denied opportunity equal to that afforded to nondisabled individuals in any programs or activities that receive federal funding; Public Law 94-142, which is known as the Education for All Handicapped Children Act; and Public Law 108-446, which is known as the Individuals with Disabilities Education Improvement Act (IDEIA) of 2004. IDEIA states that instruction must meet the needs of the student at no cost to the parents, services must be provided by qualified personnel, and students with disabilities must have individualized education plans (IEPs). It is highly recommended that the physical education teacher attend the IEP meetings so that they can have a better understanding of the individual and unique needs of all students with disabilities who receive services.

This area may be one where physical education teachers could use physical education administrative support. According to the

National Consortium for Physical Education for Individuals with Disabilities (NCPEID) and the Adapted Physical Education National Standards (APENS) (NCPEID & Kelly, 2020), "Adapted Physical Education is physical education which has been adapted or modified, so that it is as appropriate for the person with a disability as it is for a person without a disability" (p. 1). Programs such as I Can Do It! (managed by the administration for Community Living, HHS), or resources from the NCPEID, BlazeSports, Inclusive Fitness Coalition, Special Olympics, and Paralympics, to name a few, provide opportunities for physical activity participation and inclusion for students with disabilities. Students with disabilities should be provided with appropriate instruction and assessed using a variety of methods including authentic assessment, portfolios, and rubrics (Lieberman et al., 2025). Because regular physical activity contributes significantly to quality of life, people of all ages and abilities can benefit from regular activity (Kasser & Lytle, 2005). Students with disabilities should also be assessed on fitness measures using the FitnessGram, where appropriate, along with the Brockport Fitness Test for modified test components. A combination of FitnessGram and Brockport assessment measures is appropriate as well.

As an additional resource, *Appropriate Instructional Practice Guidelines, K-12: A Side-by-Side Comparison* (SHAPE America, 2009) can be accessed at www.shapeamerica.org/Common/Uploaded%20files/uploads/pdfs/Appropriate-Instructional-Practices-Grid.pdf. Appropriate instruction and instructional strategies will be covered more comprehensively in chapter 5.

Student Assessment

Student assessment, the final component of the delivered curriculum, involves collecting data about student progress and achievement of the desired and intended learning outcomes. A wide variety of assessments are used in physical education; they range from traditional summative assessments to other forms such as checklists, rating scales, and rubrics that link directly to the intended student outcomes. Assessment can occur both through formative measures to determine student progress in skills and knowledge, and through summative assessment to determine achievement of standards at the conclusion of the course or unit. According to SHAPE America (2025), student assessment provides accountability for standards-based learning, and it should include the following:

- Student assessment is aligned with national and state physical education standards and established grade-span learning indicators and intended outcomes, and it is included in the written physical education curriculum along with administration protocols.
- Student assessment includes evidence-based practices that measure student achievement in all areas of instruction, including physical fitness.
- Grading is related directly to the student learning objectives identified in the written physical education curriculum.
- The physical education teacher follows school district and school protocols for reporting and communicating student progress to students and parents.

Instruction in physical education should include content through the learning domains—cognitive, affective, social and emotional, and psychomotor. Appropriate assessment tools should be selected to properly assess content through those domains. Assessing students during physical education provides an opportunity for teachers to determine student progress in achieving the learning outcomes as well as providing feedback to teachers on instructional effectiveness and student grading (Lund & Veal, 2013). Student assessment could also be addressed using the third edition of *PE Metrics* (SHAPE America, 2019) through a broad range of performance indicators to perform cognitive and motor skill assessment using a standards-based assessment tool. Although not fully comprehensive in terms of what is taught in every physical education class *PE Metrics* provides valid and reliable assessments of student performance for the most critical skills and knowledge inherent in the National Standards & Grade-Level Outcomes for K-12 Physical Education (SHAPE America, 2019).

LEADERSHIP IN ACTION

Importance of Standards-Based Physical Education Programs

Keri Schoeff, BS

Title IV—A Safe, Healthy & Active Students Specialist, Arizona Department of Education.

Standards are the foundation of any quality educational program, and physical education is no exception. As a state director, ensuring that teachers create lesson plans that are aligned to state and national standards is vital to the success and sustainability of our physical education programs across Arizona. Physical education teachers should provide sequential, structured, organized lessons to maximize learning and increase physical literacy for their students. We often can't change the amount of time we have with our students, or the curriculum that we are given to teach, but the one thing that we can change is the quality of lessons that we deliver and how we assess them. This fact is the greatest reason why implementing a standards-based physical education program, including effective lesson planning and assessment, has the biggest impact on students' achievement of physical literacy.

Administrators must monitor the frequency and type of assessments that are occurring in the classroom and ensure their rigor. Assessments should be based on lesson objectives and standards. Different teachers teaching the same courses should be using similar assessments to make sure that students are participating in equally rigorous experiences regardless of the teacher. Common assessments should be reviewed by the administrators and the teachers who are delivering the content.

Being dressed appropriately and being on time or present for class are expectations, not assessments. A strong instructional leader will offer resources to develop teachers in the area of grading and ensure that students' grades are based on the integrity of their actual work in physical education.

Part of maintaining a quality program is to monitor grading in physical education and be prepared to hold teachers accountable for grading practices that are realistic and promote the individual success of each child. Administrators are often on the phone with parents who want to know how the teacher can substantiate and explain a poor grade in physical education. At the other extreme, teachers need to substantiate and explain circumstances when most or all of their students are achieving an A.

As with student assessment, the *curriculum* should be evaluated at least every five years. The Physical Education Curriculum Analysis Tool (PECAT) (CDC, 2019), developed by the CDC, is a self-assessment tool that can be used at the district or individual level to determine whether the content described in the curriculum and assessments aligns with the national standards. The major components are the philosophy and goals, standards, content, vertical alignment, instructional materials, format, and assessment. If any of these components are not present, then the curriculum should be revised or modified to include the missing elements. The School Health Index (SHI), another self-assessment tool developed by the CDC, is further recommended to secure school-level data to identify strengths and weaknesses in school health and safety policies as well as to develop an individualized action plan that can be incorporated into school improvement plans.

Defining the essential components of physical education facilitates the ability to raise awareness about the critical policies and practices that guide school districts and schools in addressing students' education needs, identifying program accountability, and delivering a quality physical education program embedded in evidence-based research and driven by state and national standards. District-level physical education administrators, school site administrators, and physical education teachers should incorporate the Physical Education Program Checklist (SHAPE America, 2015a) to determine if their physical education program is meeting the essential components of physical education (policy and environment, curriculum, appropriate instruction, and student assessment), along with the national and state standards for physical education. The program checklist can be accessed at www.shapeamerica.org/Common/Uploadedfiles/document_manager/standards/guidelines/Physical-Education-Program-Checklist.pdf.

Program Planning Considerations

As discussed earlier, you must consider many factors when organizing a quality physical education program. Physical education programs should be based on the district's goals and objectives, and the curriculum should be aligned with the state and national standards to ensure that students have the opportunity to achieve the intended educational outcomes. Aside from the focus on the essential components such as policy and environment, curriculum, appropriate instruction, and assessment, factors such as teacher certification, developing and implementing policies and procedures, developing lesson plans, class scheduling and size, and legal issues should also be addressed and reviewed.

Certified Physical Education Teachers

Certified and licensed physical education teachers play a critical role in the design and implementation of a quality physical education program; create learning environments that motivate students; support the physical, cognitive, social, and emotional development of children; foster positive social interactions; and provide opportunities for *all* students to engage in age- and developmentally appropriate standards-based education. Certified physical education teachers also serve as facilitators to provide opportunities for students to engage in physical activity before, during, or after school in a variety of settings within and outside of the school environment. In many states, physical education teacher certification and adapted physical education teacher certification are separated into two different areas, whereas in other states, physical education certification includes adapted physical education. For physical education administrators who are not very familiar with appropriate curriculum and instructional strategies for working with students with disabilities, a plethora of references, resources, and textbooks can provide guidance.

In addition to the essential components inherent in a quality physical education program, the importance of having certified and licensed physical education teachers provide instruction is well documented in the research and organizational reports cited previously. Overall, teachers who are certified or licensed possess skills and knowledge, and they adhere to professional standards required for effective classroom instruction and student achievement. Mandigo (2003) determined that physical education specialists during critical developmental years at the elementary level are vital for developing the skills, knowledge, attitude, and health benefits related to an active, healthy lifestyle and that principals may be more inclined to devote more time to physical education if taught by a specialist. Faulkner and colleagues (2008) and Schempp and colleagues (1998) asserted that given the importance of subject- and pedagogically specific knowledge, physical education specialists who have received more intensive and subject-specific training than generalist teachers are more likely to teach all areas of a physical education curriculum. Physical education teachers can also have a direct impact by developing more opportunities for physical activity throughout the school day (McKenzie et al., 2000), whereas classroom teachers do not have the pedagogical content knowledge and experiences to match those that physical education specialists receive during four years of training (McKenzie et al., 1995). Lounsbery and colleagues (2014) found that physical education specialists were more likely to track student learning through formal assessment than teachers who were not. Further findings discovered that certified physical education teachers have an impact on student academic achievement, participation in physical activity, and moderate-to-vigorous physical activity (MVPA) (Kern et al., 2018; Mears, 2010; Weaver et al., 2018; Lounsbery et al., 2014). Using a district physical education coordinator and teachers with appropriate qualifications, in addition to offering staff development opportunities on physical education, may enhance school physical education programs (Davis et al., 2005).

The UNESCO revised International Charter of Physical Education, Physical Activity and Sport (2015a) asserts the following in Article 4, 4.3:

> *As the only area of school curricula concerned with developing students' competence and confidence in sport and physical activity, physical education provides a learning gateway for the skills, attitudes and knowledge necessary for lifelong physical activity and sport; quality and inclusive physical education classes, taught by qualified physical education teachers, should be mandatory in all grades and levels of education. (p. 4)*

The ability to deliver a quality physical education program is contingent not only on the available curriculum but also on the effectiveness of certified and well-trained physical education teachers. High-quality pre-service training and certification undergraduate programs are an essential component in producing a skilled physical education teacher workforce with the capacity to deliver a quality physical education program. There is no substitute for teacher effectiveness in the achievement of student learning outcomes. Ongoing professional development throughout a teacher's tenure and annual systematic teacher evaluations should contribute to the continuity of quality programs. Chapter 12 explores the importance of professional development on teacher effectiveness in greater detail.

Policies and Procedures

As a physical education administrator, it is important to instill in your physical education teachers that as they plan their programs at the beginning of the school year, they have an established set of policies and procedures for their students. Your leadership is critical so that there is consistency and compliance with district policies across all school sites. At your first back-to-school meeting with the district physical education teachers, you may begin the conversation by asking them to think back to their first day of physical education, whether in elementary, middle, or high school. For example, you might say the following:

> *You probably were asked to enter the class and sit on either the hard court, gymnasium court or bleachers, or the benches in the locker room—or in the auditorium or at tables in the media center. In any case, you all had one thing in common: Your physical education teacher introduced herself, welcomed you to class, and then proceeded to explain the physical education policies and procedures. This is the one component that has remained constant and occurs on an annual basis. To avoid any circumstances that might lead to problems or possible litigation, it is crucial that you review the established program policies and procedures with your students and that they are familiar with class management expectations.*

It is at this time that you also discuss policies involving attendance: arriving to class on time and not leaving before the bell sounds; dressing out and other hygiene expectations; grading policies (including medical excuses and making up assignments); behavioral expectations; locker room regulations; gymnasium regulations; and safety and discipline policies. For record-keeping purposes, it would be beneficial to have students sign a copy of the policy as well as having a parent or guardian sign a second copy to ensure that everyone has had an opportunity to review the expectations as well as to request clarification if needed. It is also common practice to assign your first letter grade for the student based on having the form signed and returned; the signed form is the first page of their portfolio. From an administrative standpoint, this signature provides evidence that all students have read and understood the policies and procedures and could avoid future parental complaints to the district office.

The physical education administrator can assist a new teacher, a teacher new to the school, or the physical education department chair in developing the policies and procedures to ensure that they are aligned with the school district's grading policies and district's code of conduct policies. Having clear expectations in writing at the beginning of the school year or semester will greatly assist in class and program management.

Class Scheduling and Class Size

Depending on your school district or individual school, class scheduling can involve many configurations. At the elementary school level, hopefully your school district follows the recommended 150 minutes per week of physical education, taught daily for 30 minutes by a certified physical education teacher. This recommendation is a doable practice, and sample schedules are available for preview (IOM, 2013). One of the best ways to schedule the 30 minutes of daily physical education is to have it take place during the classroom teacher's planning time. Other creative ways can be incorporated following a thorough examination of how the minutes of the school day are being divided. When the students may have daily physical education, it is not always delivered by the physical education teacher. In many school districts, the physical education teacher may see the students once a week or once every 10 days, and the classroom generalist teacher delivers physical education the rest of the days. Although students would achieve some level of physical activity, this option would not guarantee that they receive a standards-based education and that they are properly assessed on learning outcomes.

At the middle or high school level, the preferred practice is to have daily physical education, with the class period commensurate with that of other academic subjects. Other forms of scheduling at the secondary level include various forms of block scheduling. There are pros and cons to block scheduling, and it takes more planning time on the part of the teacher to ensure that the selected standards are met. It also challenges the physical education teacher to incorporate other methods of teaching, including blended classrooms and more use of class time, as well as to plan for out-of-class experiences and resources. Some of the most common types of block scheduling are the 4 × 4 schedule, the A/B alternate day schedule, the four-day block schedule (the fifth day is a traditional period school day), the 4 × 8 model, hybrid models, the tri-semester block schedule, the reconfigured school year, and the extended year schedule. Each model can be modified from its original form as the school district sees fit.

Class size and teaching loads have been an ongoing concern for physical education teachers. Although it has been recommended that the size of the physical education class be consistent with that of other classes, various policies regarding class size reduction for math, science, language arts, and social studies have pushed all electives to class sizes larger than preferred. With instructional spaces such as gymnasiums and playing fields larger than the educational specifications for a standard-size classroom, the argument should not center on the assumption that you can handle it because you have more student teaching stations. Instead, the conversation should focus on student safety, supervision issues, and (most importantly) the ability to effectively deliver a standards-based instructional program. The inability to properly assess students if they have not had enough opportunity to achieve the intended outcomes would put the students at a gross disadvantage, and it would put physical education teachers in a position to consistently defend their program and teaching strategies. In situations in which double classes are evident in the elementary school and extremely large classes are evident in the secondary schools, the physical education administrator would appropriately intervene with a conversation with the school's administration. Additional professional development workshops would also be warranted to provide assistance on innovative ways to deliver instruction in large-group settings.

Unit and Lesson Planning

Developing unit and lesson plans is a way for you to organize your instructional program to ensure that you have properly planned and delivered a standards-based program with grade-level outcomes. The unit plan is the broad picture of what you want to achieve across the school year, taking into account whether the school has four nine-week grading periods, as an example, or across semesters at the secondary level. The lesson plan builds out the unit plan in determining what instructional opportunities you plan to deliver on a selected day. All lesson plans should be tied to the physical education standards and have grade-level outcomes (Holt/Hale & Hall, 2016). According to Mitchell and Walton-Fisette (2016), lesson plan formats should include the following:

1. Lesson focus
2. Learning objectives and standards
3. Teacher goals
4. Management plan
5. Equipment needs

6. Resources
7. Instructional and activity tasks
8. Modifications
9. Teaching cues and questioning
10. Organization of tasks
11. Closure
12. Assessment

Advance lesson planning should also contain contingency plans for unexpected situations that may cause an interruption in the delivery of instruction for a particular day. Examples include inclement weather (which would move your outdoor activity indoors) and use of the gymnasium by the school administration for testing or other school-wide events. Another situation involves the need for an emergency plan if a physical education teacher is out and the substitute teacher is not comfortable teaching physical education or comes to school without appropriate attire for teaching physical education.

A well-developed lesson should meet the needs and interests of all students and incorporate the best practices in physical education. Appropriate instructional strategies have been discussed earlier in this chapter, and they are covered more extensively in chapter 5.

Legal Issues

Legal issues are often the most difficult to deal with in an educational setting, so careful advance program planning can help prevent future negative issues. Many of the legal issues that teachers and administrators face involve lack of supervision, access and equity, facilities and equipment, student safety, and disciplinary concerns. It would be an understatement to say that common sense could eliminate some of these issues.

For example, students should be supervised at all times—in the locker room, gymnasium, playing field, and line-up and dismissal area. If you are the only physical education teacher at the school, you need to prepare accordingly or ask for an assistant or paraprofessional to assist at times when the students are in multiple locations, such as when some are still in the locker room changing while others are outside. If there are multiple teachers, the physical education department chairperson should develop a schedule for supervision. Locker room doors should always be locked once they are cleared of all students. Teachers should avoid giving students their keys, which would give them unsupervised access.

Appropriate instruction that is age and developmentally appropriate should be provided at all times. Through a scope and sequence, there should not be any issues in determining whether a student has received sequenced instruction to ensure learning progressions. Proper warm-up and cool-down for activity-specific movements should be included every class period to avoid injuries. Developing a curriculum map would further ensure that appropriate instruction is being delivered through both vertical and horizontal alignment. Facilities and equipment should be checked in advance of each lesson to ensure that the facilities are clear of any debris or obstacles, especially in outdoor facilities after the weekend, when the fields are open for community use. Excessive cracks on the hard court that could cause a tripping incident should be brought to the attention of the school administrator immediately so a request for repair can be issued. Sometimes declaring the request as a safety to life issue gets the maintenance staff out more quickly; it can be catastrophic if a student falls on his head and incurs a serious injury.

Checking equipment in advance of any lesson to determine working order and ensuring that there are no cracks or chips that would cause a danger should be part of everyday planning. Appropriate size of striking objects such as tennis rackets, softball bats, and field hockey sticks should also be used based on size and age of the students. If a sport or activity requires the use of safety equipment, such as a mask for the catcher in a class softball unit, it is up to the teacher to ensure that the equipment is readily available and that the catcher wears the mask. Modified equipment must also be used for students with disabilities to ensure inclusion in all lessons. A physical education teacher should be careful when assigning students to set up and take down equipment, especially if they have difficulty lifting or easily moving the equipment.

Access and equity for programming, instruction, facilities, and equipment refer to programs for students with disabilities as well as issues relating to Title IX. In these instances, federal laws require access and opportunity, and the physical education teacher needs to be familiar with them. These issues are discussed more fully throughout the book, with emphasis in chapter 8.

With respect to student behavior and legal issues that could affect the physical education teacher, there are many times in physical education classes when student behavior causes a disruption in the teaching process. A physical education teacher needs to be prudent to ensure that no impulsive actions occur that would have negative consequences and are deemed unnecessary and inappropriate. For example, having students run excessive laps because of behavioral concerns, using exercise for punishment, or withholding hydration from students on exceptionally hot days as punishment should be avoided by any professional teacher. Parental contact should be made and documented for students who excessively disrupt the learning environment. Telephone and email contact logs should be readily available in case further disciplinary action at a higher level becomes necessary. Keeping all students safe in class—even from other students' actions—should be one of the highest priorities.

Physical education teachers should have some basic first aid emergency training, be certified in cardiopulmonary resuscitation (CPR), and be aware of any medical issues that particular students have. Always have an emergency plan in place and a way to immediately contact the front office. Chapter 11 presents a more comprehensive review of legal issues and policies.

The School and Community Connections National Framework: Comprehensive School Physical Activity Plan

As stated throughout this chapter and based on the recommendations in several national and international reports, it is highly recommended that all children participate in 60 minutes or more of physical activity daily. Since over 95 percent of children spend between seven and nine hours a day in school, the school environment is uniquely positioned as a place for students to reach those activity minutes. However, although this chapter focuses on organizing and planning a quality physical education program, it has become evident through the *Physical Activity Guidelines for Americans, Second Edition* (HHS, 2018), Healthy People 2030, YRBSS (CDC, 2021), the 2022 United States Report Card on Physical Activity for Children and Youth (PAA, 2022), the Shape of the Nation report (SHAPE America, 2016), and SHPPS (CDC, 2016) reports that physical education programs around the country alone cannot provide the critical 60 minutes a day of physical activity. Building **community engagement** and school capacity becomes a necessary component for expanding student physical activity to achieve the recommended goal. The **Comprehensive School Physical Activity Program (CSPAP)** (figure 3.8) has been recognized as the national framework for physical education and physical activity for young people since 2014 (CDC, 2014a, p. 2).

The CDC (2019) states,

> *A Comprehensive School Physical Activity Program (CSPAP) is a framework for planning and organizing activities for school physical education and physical activity. It can help schools be strategic in addressing*

FIGURE 3.8 Comprehensive School Physical Activity Program (CSPAP).

Reprinted from CDC (2018).

Teaching CSPAP in Physical Education Teacher Education Programs

Brian Dauenhauer, PhD, Professor, Kinesiology, Nutrition and Dietetics and Director, University of Northern Colorado Active Schools Institute
Charlene Burgeson, Former Chief Program Officer and Active Schools Executive Director, Action for Healthy Kids

Having a trained Active School Champion or Physical Activity Leader (PAL) on school campuses is considered best practice for implementing comprehensive school physical activity programs (CSPAPs) (Beighle et al., 2009; Carson, 2012; Castelli & Beighle, 2007). According to Stoepker and colleagues (2021), there are four main characteristics of a successful Champion or PAL: (a) advocating for physical education and physical activity, (b) training school staff on the importance of health and physical activity, (c) being one of the primary organizers of school-wide physical activity and health events, and (d) understanding each component of CSPAP (p. 24). Carson and colleagues (2020) further emphasize knowledge of organizational structures and leadership skills such as planning, communication, collaboration, and delegation. According to SHAPE America (2017), the National Standards for Initial Physical Education Teacher Education states in Standard 1 that physical education teacher candidates should learn to "demonstrate knowledge of promotion/advocacy strategies for physical education and expanded physical activity opportunities that support the development of physically literate individuals" as part of their professional responsibilities.

Some PETE programs in the United States have been integrating elements of CSPAP into their undergraduate and graduate programs. A special issue of the *Journal of Physical Education, Recreation & Dance* (*JOPERD*) (Carson et al., 2017; Castelli et al., 2017) overviewed 12 pioneering PETE programs that include CSPAP-related learning experiences. For example, the Physical Education and Physical Activity Leadership program at the University of Northern Colorado teaches undergraduate students the foundations of CSPAP in a course called Physical Activity and Fitness in Schools, encourages students to engage in service-learning experiences outside of physical education, and has students present to a panel of school professionals from the local community on their ideas for CSPAP. At the master's level, in-service teachers learn to plan, implement, and evaluate a new physical activity initiative in their school and report on outcomes as part of graduation requirements (Dauenhauer et al., 2017). PreK-12 schools should seek to hire teachers with strong CSPAP knowledge and skills and encourage their teachers to pursue ongoing professional development to maximize the number of educators on school campuses that are trained and committed to promoting an active school culture (Active Schools, 2022).

this aspect of the WSCC model. The goal of a CSPAP is to increase physical activity opportunities before, during, and after school and to increase students' overall physical activity and health. Healthy and physically active students tend to have better grades, school attendance, cognitive performance (e.g., memory), and classroom behaviors (e.g., on-task behavior). (p. 2)

The main goal of the CSPAP is to increase physical activity opportunities before, during, and after school and increase students' overall physical activity and health. More specifically, these are the CSPAP goals (CDC, 2014a, p. 12):

- To provide a variety of school-based physical activities to enable all students to participate in 60 minutes of moderate-to-vigorous physical activity each day.
- To provide coordination among the CSPAP components to maximize understanding, application, and practice of the knowledge and skills learned in physical education so that all students will be fully physically educated and well equipped for a lifetime of physical activity.

The CSPAP is a multicomponent approach by which school districts and schools use all opportunities for students to be physically active throughout the school day in order to meet the national physical activity recommendation (CDC, 2013a, p. 12). Through this model, there is coordination and synergy across all of its five components: physical education as the foundation of the program, physical activity during school, physical activity before and after school, staff involvement, and family and community engagement (CDC, 2013a, p. 12, SHAPE America, 2023). At the heart of the framework, physical education is the academic subject that serves as the foundation of a CSPAP (2023, p. 4), which provides youth with the fundamental education and skills needed to make decisions regarding physical activity. Physical activity during the school day includes active recess and physical activity integrated into classroom lessons. Physical activity before and after school includes opportunities through active transport, activity clubs, intramurals, interscholastic sports, and during, before, or after school in extended day school programs. Staff involvement allows for staff members to become engaged as positive role models and support programs for school-based physical activity. Family and community engagement enables parents, staff, and community members to work together to increase physical activity opportunities before, during, and after the school day. Community organizations can establish shared-use agreements with schools that allow them to use school facilities for physical activity opportunities or events (CDC, 2013b, p. 14; 2017, p. 3). The physical education administrator has a unique role in guiding those discussions, seeking out resources and funding and monitoring action plans in order to support schools, teachers, staff, parents, and students (SHAPE America, 2015a, 2023). Additional community programs and events to support the CSPAP can be found in chapter 7.

The Whole School, Whole Community, Whole Child Model

The Whole School, Whole Community, Whole Child (WSCC) model (figure 3.9), in collaboration with key leaders from the fields of health, public health, education, and school health, expanded on the eight elements of the CDC's coordinated school health (CSH) approach and combined with the Whole Child framework of the Association for Supervision and Curriculum Development (ASCD) (2014) to strengthen a unified and collaborative approach designed to improve learning and health in our nation's schools and create a greater alignment between health and educational outcomes (Lewallen et al., 2015). The model was designed to put the students at the center, making them the focal point, followed by the five tenets of the Whole Child: Healthy, Safe, Engaged, Supported, and Challenged. The ring surrounding the child or student stresses the need for coordination among policy, process, and practice. The outer ring of the WSCC model reflects greater integration and alignment between health and education by incorporating the components of the CSH approach and emphasizing the school as an integral part of the community. The importance of sectors and individuals working together, with emphasis on the community, to implement policies, practice, and process is now prominent in this integrated approach that addresses health and learning. These are the 10 components of the outer ring:

1. Health Education
2. Nutrition Environment and Services
3. Employee Wellness
4. Social and Emotional School Climate
5. Physical Environment
6. Health Services
7. Counseling, Psychological, and Social Services
8. Community Involvement
9. Family Engagement
10. Physical Education and Physical Activity

This model further provides greater alignment, integration, and collaboration between health and education across the school setting to improve each child's cognitive, physical, social, and emotional development. The CSPAP provides a framework to implement the physical education and physical activity sector of the WSCC model to increase physical activity opportunities before, during, and after school to increase both physical activity and student health.

FIGURE 3.9 The Whole School, Whole Community, Whole Child (WSCC) model.
Reprinted from ASCD, *Whole School, Whole Community, Whole Child: A Collaborative Approach to Learning and Health* (CDC, 2014).

Conclusion

Throughout this chapter it became evident that organizing and planning a quality physical education program is no easy task. As you explore the components integral to a quality program—policy and environment, curriculum, appropriate instruction, and student assessment—you begin to see how dependent you become on the National Physical Education Standards and Grade-Span Learning Indicators for both intended outcomes and guidance for student achievement. The physical education administrator not only takes on the multifaceted role of ensuring age- and developmentally appropriate instruction but also operates in an environment committed to inclusion and equality to provide opportunities for learning for *all* students. The chapter has also addressed the roles and responsibilities of the physical education teacher in delivering quality physical education.

This chapter considered several national and international reports that specify the need for quality physical education and the need for youth to engage in 60 minutes or more of daily physical activity, using the school environment as the main vehicle. The need for daily physical activity is further supported by the evidence-based relationship between physical activity and academic performance. The continued emphasis of the CSPAP and the WSCC models used to provide increased physical activity opportunities for youth serves as an ongoing framework for future programmatic considerations.

Review Questions

1. Identify and explain the benefits of a quality physical education program.
2. The National Physical Education Standards and Grade-Span Learning Indicators are critical to the development of a quality physical education program. Discuss the role that they play in the development process.
3. Identify and describe the essential elements of physical education.
4. Explain how the information in the YRBSS and SHPPS reports assists in the development of quality programs.
5. Describe how the CSPAP and the WSCC models provide a framework for increasing physical activity and improving health of students.
6. Identify how planning for units of instruction and daily lessons assists the physical educator in developing a quality program.

» Visit HK*Propel* for reproducible forms.

PART II

Curriculum, Instruction, Assessment, and Special Events

CHAPTER 4

Curriculum Development and Evaluation

Nichole D. Barta and Jayne D. Greenberg

Photo courtesy of Elizabeth Cabrera

LEARNING OBJECTIVES

After reading this chapter, you will be able to do the following:

- Describe how state and national standards affect curriculum development.
- Apply the steps of the curriculum development process.
- Discuss how to design a standards-based curriculum.
- Describe how curriculum models can be used to select, structure, and sequence instruction.
- Explain the purpose of curriculum maps.

KEY CONCEPTS

backward design
curriculum models
grade-span learning indicators
horizontal alignment
standards-based curriculum
vertical alignment

The quality of a physical education program relies heavily on the quality of the curriculum. A well-designed physical education curriculum provides a clearly articulated plan for how students will gain the knowledge, skills, and confidence to be physically active for life. The curriculum shapes instruction by articulating how developmentally appropriate learning will occur and be assessed. Curriculum that is aligned with standards, assessments, and policies can increase student achievement by enhancing a teacher's instructional capacity. The lack of a coherent curriculum can negatively impact student learning as teachers have no direction on what and when to teach and to assess.

While there are U.S. national standards for physical education, there is not a national physical education curriculum or policy that guides the development of the curriculum in schools. Different states have different legislation requirements for the number of minutes that students must take physical education each week, how many credits of physical education are required for graduation, and how curriculum is adopted. The compliance of those requirements and how they are implemented within the school day are planned at the local level. Legislation in most states requires districts to use a curriculum that is aligned with national standards, state standards, or both, and that meets the minimum requirements for allotted time or credits. Therefore, district physical education administrators must engage in the curriculum development process to select or design curriculum resources for their physical education programs. Engaging physical education teachers in the development process is highly recommended so that there is buy-in from the instructors who will be implementing the curriculum.

Curriculum development is a planned and purposeful process of designing, organizing, selecting, and evaluating learning experiences for a defined population for all subject areas. Curriculum development occurs at multiple levels and creates different products for select grade levels. For example, a district curriculum committee can create a curriculum guide that describes the philosophy, goals, grade-span learning indicators and intended outcomes, assessments, and instructional procedures of the K-12 educational program. A school-level curriculum committee may develop (or implement) curriculum maps for the physical education courses or grade levels in their building. Curriculum development at the teacher level results in unit plans and daily lesson plans.

Whether you are on a district-level curriculum committee or writing unit plans, it is important to understand the curriculum development process so that you can create positive learning experiences for students. Successful curriculum development requires collaboration among many individuals. Contemplating answers to the following questions may help you understand why you cannot effectively develop curriculum in isolation:

- What knowledge and skills are students learning before entering this class?
- What knowledge and skills are students expected to have upon leaving this class?
- Is this class setting students up to be successful in subsequent courses and experiences?
- What activities are students interested and engaged in?

If teachers are not seeking the answers to these questions before developing units, then they risk consequences such as reduced student engagement, lower levels of achievement, and possibly a negative view of physical activity resulting in a sedentary lifestyle (Cothran & Ennis, 1998).

In the past, physical education curriculum involved very little development; it was simply a list of activities that would be taught over the course of an academic year (Mitchell & Walton-Fisette, 2016). However, physical education, which was once viewed as a recreation or activity class, has changed with a renewed emphasis on student learning that centers on the students developing skills through their physical literacy journey (SHAPE America, 2025). The purpose of this chapter is to discuss curriculum development as a strategic process for designing high-quality physical education learning experiences.

What is taught (curriculum) and how it is taught (instruction) will directly affect students' experience in physical education and possibly their long-term participation in physical activity (Phillips & Silverman, 2015). Students who have positive experiences in physical education are more likely to develop positive attitudes toward physical activity, engage in it more frequently, and remain physically active as adults (Graham et al., 2011; Ladwig et al., 2018). Many studies reveal that students' physical education experiences affect their attitude toward physical activity and their adoption of a physically active lifestyle. Therefore, helping students to have a positive experience in physical education is crucial to accomplishing the goal of lifetime physical activity (Castillo et al., 2020; Ladwig et al., 2018; Trudeau & Shephard, 2008).

Motivation is another critical determinant of student learning and engagement in physical education (Chen & Ennis, 2009). A quality physical education program will increase students' motivation to engage in physical activity, both within the school environment and in the community. Many factors that influence students' motivation to engage in physical education include perceived competence, student autonomy, varied activities, differentiated practice opportunities, and cooperative learning (Cairney et al., 2012; Leyton-Román et al., 2020; Manninen & Yli-Piipari, 2021; Silverman, 2011). Table 4.1 outlines several curricular aspects that can reduce students' motivation to engage in physical education and potential solutions that the curriculum development process can address to improve the physical education experience. Curriculum development involves identifying solutions to common problems such as a lack of motivation to engage.

The Curriculum Development Process

There is not a single agreed-upon approach to curriculum development. Most school districts have published procedures for curriculum design and implementation because they are required to deliver educational programs in accordance with state standards. Those procedures guide curriculum developers in creating curricula that adhere to board policy, district administration procedures, legislative requirements, and the district's vision for teaching and learning. The common goals of a curriculum development process are shown in figure 4.1.

WWW **TABLE 4.1** Increasing Motivation Through Curriculum Development

Curricular Aspect	Description	Curriculum Development Solutions
Repetitive content	The same sports and activities are taught each year.	• Creating a K-12 vertical alignment • Curriculum mapping to vary the activities
De-emphasis on learning: physical activity, not physical education	Participation in class is primarily focused on activity and playing games rather than on learning developmentally appropriate knowledge or skills. Perceived competence increases motivation to engage in physical activity.	• Creating standards-based outcomes and grade-span learning indicators • Using assessments for and of learning • Using appropriate curriculum models • Differentiation in lesson plans
Lack of autonomy	Students have no or limited voice in selecting what they learn and how they learn it.	• Following a program philosophy • Using appropriate curriculum models • Surveying students
Lack of relevance	There is no connection to life outside of physical education class or to student interest.	• Culturally responsive content and strategies • Following a program philosophy • Selecting an appropriate curriculum model
Competitive environment: social comparisons	Winning and losing are highly emphasized; competition is against others instead of within oneself. There is a lack of cooperation and collaboration in activities.	• Using appropriate curriculum models • Following a program philosophy

FIGURE 4.1 Goals of the K-12 Curriculum Development Process

- Align curriculum and instruction with national or state standards, or both.
- Structure the learning experience for quality, consistency, and equity.
- Provide a basis for resource management and decision making.
- Establish common goals and expectations for schools in the district.
- Establish a context for program evaluation.
- Provide guidance for teachers in delivering instruction.
- Make learning meaningful and relevant.

Since instructional standards are the driving force of education programs, this chapter presents a **standards-based curriculum** development process. The term *standards-based* indicates that the desired results of the curriculum are achieving district, state, or national standards, and that curriculum is developed by identifying the skills, knowledge, and behaviors that students need to demonstrate in order to meet those standards (Lund & Tannehill, 2015). A standards-based curriculum development process uses the backward design approach to curriculum planning. **Backward design** is a curriculum planning process that starts with identifying the desired results of the curriculum before designing the assessments, selecting the appropriate content or activities, and planning the learning experiences (Wiggins & McTighe, 2005). The term *backward* implies that the developer starts with the end in mind and then creates a plan to reach that goal (see figure 4.2).

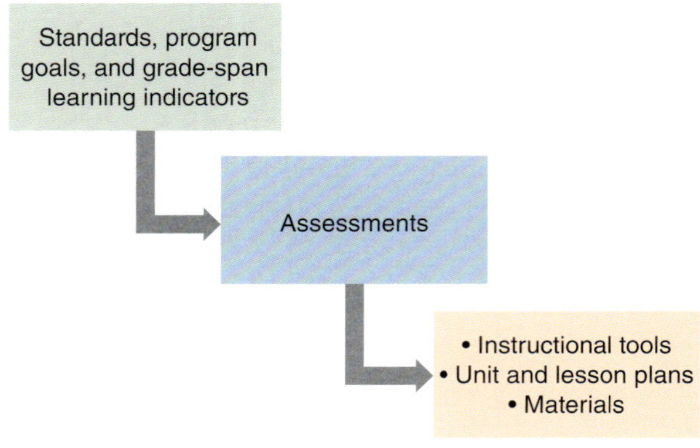

WWW **FIGURE 4.2** Backward design approach.

Understanding Standards-Based Curriculum Development

A common misconception in standards-based curriculum development is that teachers are designing a scripted, cookie-cutter program that centers on assessment results (Lambert, 1996). Standards-based curriculum development is not about a prescription for learning; rather, it is about providing a comprehensive, student-centered learning experience. A standards-based curriculum framework is a safeguard to ensure that all students have the opportunity to learn the knowledge and skills necessary for a lifetime of physical activity. Adherence to a standards-based curriculum means that teachers are not picking and choosing what they want to teach based on preference. Without such a framework, some knowledge and skills may be overlooked or disregarded, which can limit students' enjoyment of and competence in a variety of physical activities.

The process presented in this chapter is about creating a curriculum framework that guides student-centered instruction aligned to standards with the intent of developing physically literate students. Table 4.2 outlines various action steps for developing a standards-based curriculum within each of the curriculum development phases from a district-level perspective as well as an individual-level perspective.

TABLE 4.2 A Standards-Based Curriculum Development Process

Development Phase	District-Level Steps	Teacher-Level Steps
Analysis	• Analyze district and community characteristics. • Conduct a needs assessment. • Evaluate required resources (e.g., budget, equipment, technology, instructional materials, facilities).	• Analyze learner characteristics (e.g., culture, interests, abilities). • Evaluate available resources (e.g., equipment, space, time).
Planning	• Identify a curriculum leader and assemble a curriculum development committee. • Develop a program philosophy, mission, and vision, and create program goals.	• Review district grade-level outcomes and curriculum maps • Develop course, unit, and lesson outcomes. • Review national grade-span learning indicators.
Design	• Determine common assessments. • Develop a K-12 scope and sequence of grade-level outcomes and national grade-span learning indicators. • Create a curriculum delivery system. • Select instructional materials.	• Design formative and summative assessments. • Select appropriate curriculum model. • Create unit and lesson plans.
Implementation	• Provide ongoing professional development and support in putting program into practice. • Educate stakeholders (e.g., parents, administrators). • Work with community partners.	• Deliver curriculum. • Use formative feedback to guide future instruction. • Reflect on and record what is working and not working.
Evaluation	• Analyze assessment data. • Collect data (e.g., teacher surveys, input). • Make recommendations for revisions.	• Analyze student achievement and assessment data. • Collect student input. • Make revisions based on data and input.

The Analysis Phase

The analysis phase is the first step in the curriculum development process. The main objective of this phase is to ascertain the current state of the program. During this phase, the administrator should gather as much data and information as possible to form a realistic picture of the program and identify context-specific needs of the target audience.

Designing curriculum is similar to architecture in that it is a process of planning, designing, and building. Before construction begins, an architect first gathers information by conducting preliminary research, surveying the scene, and taking measurements. It would be foolish to start building without using data about the building site to create a blueprint. In the same way, the first step in the curriculum development process must be to research information relevant to the planning process such as that listed in figure 4.3. A curriculum leader needs to gather and analyze information that will guide the direction of the curriculum development process.

Decisions in education are often governed by federal mandates, state legislation, and district policies as accountability procedures and funding are linked to them. States have different legislation requirements for the number of minutes that students must attend physical education each week and how many credits of physical education are required at the high school level. While curriculum is a local decision, districts are held accountable for providing an educational program that meets state

LEADERSHIP IN ACTION

What Is Adapted Physical Education, and What Do Adapted Physical Educators Really Do?

Jennifer Houston, PhD

Arizona State University (Mesa, AZ); Mesa Public Schools (Mesa, AZ)

What is adapted physical education? When students with disabilities need extra support to benefit from general physical education, or when these students need a special physical education program, they qualify for specially designed physical education, or adapted physical education. Adapted physical education is a sub-discipline of physical education with an emphasis on physical education for students with disabilities. The term *adapted physical education* generally refers to school-based programs for students aged 3 to 21; the more global term *adapted physical activity* refers to programs across the life span, including post-school programs. Determining who is qualified to provide services to students with disabilities (including physical education services) is left up to each state.

Qualified means that a person has met state educational agency approved or recognized certification, licensing, registration, or other comparable requirements, which apply to the area in which the person is providing special education or related services.

Services provided can be either direct (not related service providers) or on a consult basis. *Consultation services* means the adapted physical education teacher does not necessarily provide direct service to students with disabilities. Instead, the physical education teacher consults with the general education teachers who have students with disabilities in their classrooms, providing possible modifications or accommodations for the various activities. For districts who are lucky enough to have adapted physical educators that provide

FIGURE 4.3 Researching Relevant Information

- District policies and procedures related to physical education
- State legislation related to physical education (e.g., graduation requirements, required days per week, and required minutes per day)
- National and state standards
- Current district curriculum documents (e.g., curriculum maps, guides)
- Current offerings and time allotted to physical education
- Community culture and characteristics (e.g., values, language, socioeconomic status, traditions)
- Resources (e.g., equipment, money, materials, access to technology, facilities)
- Personnel (e.g., number of teachers, paraprofessionals, instructional specialists)

requirements. Therefore, curriculum leaders must first know the legislative requirements for their state as well as their state standards for physical education so that they create a curriculum that complies with those expectations. For state-specific resources, go to www.shapeamerica.org/advocacy/advocacyresources_state.aspx.

A crucial step in the analysis process is gathering data on the community and students. Cultural and ethnic norms can influence students' physical activity preferences; therefore, an effective curriculum needs to be culturally relevant to motivate students to succeed and participate in physical activity (Hill & Cleven, 2006). Cultural relevance can be established by direct services, they typically each have a caseload of students they work with at several different schools. Some districts divide their caseloads by grade level, some by regions, and some by student disabilities.

Services can be provided in various settings depending on the student's least restrictive environment (LRE). LRE, under Individuals with Disabilities Education Act (IDEA), states that to the maximum extent appropriate, children with disabilities are educated with children who are nondisabled (U.S. Department of Education, n.d.). It could include the general physical education class, where teachers may work with several students with disabilities from a self-contained classroom in an adapted physical education class (small group); alternatively, teachers may see an entire class of students in a modified or unified physical education class, some with nondisabled peer buddies and some without.

There are so many different settings where we service our students. Therefore, the process of creating a schedule that aligns with the general physical education classes, with the days and times the classroom teachers will allow us to work with their students, and with available space to work with students, can be a bit of a puzzle. Moreover, this puzzle is constantly changing throughout the school year as new students are enrolling in and others are leaving the district. Sometimes, a certain class time just doesn't work with the classroom teacher.

Along with teaching classes and working with students—which is the fun part—adapted physical educators are also required to attend IEP meetings for every student on their caseload, writing goals and objectives for those IEPs, determining appropriate placements according to the student's LRE, conducting ongoing assessments to document progress, planning the lessons and carting equipment in and out of their cars, calling parents, collaborating with other specialists such as physical and occupational therapists as well as the classroom teacher, and working with and training the paraprofessionals who work with the student when we are not there.

From my perspective, it's the best and most rewarding job in education!

---

using knowledge of how community dynamics influence the educational process in designing and selecting learning experiences (Flory & McCaughtry, 2011). Community dynamics may include the level of parental support students receive, languages spoken, religious observances, socioeconomic status, crime rates, and ethnicity (Flory & McCaughtry, 2011). Curriculum leaders and teachers can collect demographic data from a variety of sources to inform decisions as well as survey students on their physical activity preferences to reduce marginalization based on cultural norms.

The Planning Phase

The planning phase is the second step in the process. The main objective of this phase is to establish the goals and structure for managing the curriculum work. Planning phase strategies include the following:

- Recruiting committee members
- Defining program purpose
- Developing action plans

Recruiting Committee Members

Curriculum leaders may choose to ask for volunteers, send out applications, or appoint teachers to the committee. It is important that the committee represent the district demographics. In order to balance the need for representation with getting the job done, it is recommended that a reasonable size for a committee be 7 to 10 members (Carr & Harris, 2009). Figure 4.4 identifies some considerations for assembling a committee that will best represent varied viewpoints and experience from within the district.

Defining the Program Purpose

Education is a collaborative effort. The proverb *It takes a village to raise a child* adequately reflects the approach that curriculum leaders must take in developing a program; the educational system relies on parents, teachers, administrators, and community members working together to help students reach educational goals. Since there are so many stakeholders in a student's learning experience, it is important

FIGURE 4.4 Considerations for Committee Representation

- Experienced and beginning teachers
- Teachers from different grade levels and different schools in the district
- Students (high school level)
- Gender and ethnic diversity
- Parents and community members
- Administrators (e.g., athletic directors, principals, instructional specialists)
- Representatives from different departments (e.g., athletics, special education, and English language learning [ELL])
- People with experience on curriculum committees and no experience on curriculum committees

to have a program philosophy that provides a unifying framework for decision making. For various people to work together, there must be agreement about how and what students will learn in the program and the level of commitment and support required. A program philosophy creates that agreement by stating the common belief system that guides policy and practice in assisting students to reach identified goals. If an education program does not have a philosophy, developing one should be the first task to accomplish after researching and analyzing the community needs. Figure 4.5 lists several questions that can be used in developing or revising a program philosophy. These same questions can also be used to develop a teaching philosophy for a particular course or grade level; simply replace "program" with "course" or "experience." Figure 4.6 shows a sample philosophy statement.

Once a program philosophy has been established, the curriculum committee can work on creating program goals. Program goals are a written description of what students should be able to do when they graduate. These goals establish the criteria for how program performance can be measured, and they provide guidance for developing all of the objectives and resources that will be used in the program (Centers for Disease Control and Prevention [CDC], 2017a). Many programs choose to adopt the SHAPE America National Physical Education Standards as their program goals since they are written as grade-span learning indicators for a PreK-12 program.

Developing an Action Plan

After the direction of the program has been clearly articulated with a philosophy and program goals, the curriculum leader or committee can plan the work by developing an action plan. The action plan needs to identify the objectives of the curriculum development process, the tasks, and a time line to accomplish the objectives. See figure 4.7 for an action plan template.

FIGURE 4.5 Developing a Philosophy Statement

- Why do students need this program?
- How does the district's mission inform the program?
- What are the goals of the program?
- What are the beliefs about learners' capabilities and motivations?
- How will program success be measured?
- What support is necessary for student success?
- How is the program linked to community interests and values?

FIGURE 4.6 Sample Philosophy Statement

Highline School District's Physical Education Program Philosophy Statement

The goal of physical education is to develop physically literate individuals who have the knowledge, skills, and confidence to enjoy a lifetime of healthful physical activity. It is our goal that our students will know the benefits of being physically active and consistently choose to be active in order to sustain a healthy lifestyle. Movement is critical to the development and maintenance of good health for both the body and the mind. Studies have shown a correlation between physical activity, physical fitness, and academic performance. Overall, our students will experience a greater quality of life through consistently participating in physical activity and obtaining a high level of physical fitness.

To ensure that our students are receiving high-quality physical education that will lead to lifelong health and fitness, the physical education department is implementing a standards-based curriculum and assessment system. This system has been developed through looking at the national and state standards; identifying the skills, knowledge, and dispositions that students should demonstrate to meet these standards; and identifying activities that will allow students to reach the goals stated in the standards. A standards-based framework provides teachers, parents, and students with specific information about the knowledge and skills students should be developing as they progress through their physical education programs. With the standards serving as clearly defined targets, parents, teachers, and community members will be able to become partners in helping children achieve physical literacy and educational success.

FIGURE 4.7 Action Plan Template

GOAL:

ACTION STEPS *What will be done?*	**RESPONSIBILITIES** *Who will do it?*	**TIME LINE** *By when (day, month)?*	**RESOURCES** *A. Resources available* *B. Resources needed*	**POTENTIAL BARRIERS AND SOLUTIONS** *A. Potential barriers for completing the task* *B. Potential solutions*	**COMMUNICATIONS PLAN** *Who is involved?* *What methods?* *How often?*
Step 1:			A. B.	A. B.	
Step 2:			A. B.	A. B.	
Evaluation process *(How will you determine that your goal has been reached? What are your measures?)*					

The Design Phase

The main objective of the design phase is to develop and select resources to support student learning. What students will learn is determined in the planning phase with the program goals, so the design phase seeks to answer the question *How and when are students going to learn it?* As with all subjects, there is much to learn in little time. Teachers may feel overwhelmed when reading through the National Physical Education Standards, state standards, and grade-span learning indicators; they may wonder, "How will I be able to teach all of this?" The design phase is about creating a curriculum that uses the standards, grade-span learning indicators, and intended outcomes in a manageable and coherent way, through the support and guidance of the physical education administrator, so that both teachers and students can succeed. This section focuses on the following design phase strategies:

- Establish K-12 alignment.
- Prioritize the standards.
- Determine grade-span learning indicators.
- Unpack the standards and grade-span learning indicators.
- Decide how and when student learning will be assessed.
- Create curriculum maps.
- Select instructional materials.
- Determine appropriate curriculum models.

Establish K-12 Alignment

In a standards-based curriculum, alignment exists when (1) all of the knowledge, skills, topics, and concepts that are taught to students—and the lessons, assignments, materials, and assessments used in the teaching process—are aligned with specific learning standards; and (2) all of the learning experiences at each grade level are sequenced so that new concepts build on previously taught concepts, preventing gaps and avoiding instructional overlaps (Great Schools Partnership, 2015b). Establishing both vertical and horizontal alignment works to ensure progressive skill development through continuity of instruction based on standards, and it helps to maximize instructional time by identifying what should be taught and when.

Vertical alignment refers to the progression of skills, knowledge, rigor, and content across grade levels (Blackburn, 2017). A vertically aligned curriculum provides teachers with an understanding of what students should have already learned, what the teachers currently have to teach, and what students will learn in future courses or years (Connecticut State Department of Education, 2006). **Horizontal alignment** refers to aligning learning activities within a grade level or course so that students in the same course or grade level are receiving similar learning experiences despite having a different teacher. In grade levels in which textbooks are used, it is extremely helpful to develop pacing guides so that regardless of what teacher the student has within the same school, or what school a student in a given district attends, all students will be receiving the curricular continuity across the district. Creating a curriculum that is aligned K-12 is a complex process because it is difficult to plan 13 years of learning experiences that result in students accomplishing defined goals. All of the strategies listed in this section can help curriculum leaders and teachers in aligning a curriculum K-12.

Prioritize the Standards

The adage "Less is more" refers to the importance of prioritizing our work so that we direct our effort and energy toward what is essential. When educators provide in-depth instruction on fewer concepts rather than superficially covering multiple concepts, students are more likely to remain engaged, retain information, and develop the confidence to use what they have learned (Ainsworth, 2003). The standards describe what students should know and be able to do as a result of participating in a physical education program. However, the standards may contain more concepts and skills than students can realistically master in a school year or semester due to lack of time. A district committee may rank standards in terms of their importance at different grade levels to help teachers provide more in-depth instruction on those standards as shown in table 4.3. Prioritized standards are those that have been

TABLE 4.3 Example of Prioritizing the Standards

Grade Span	Priority Standards	Supporting Standards
K-2	1, 2	3, 4
3-5	2, 1	3, 2
6-8	2, 3	4, 1
9-12	3, 4	3, 1

identified as most essential to a particular grade level, content area, or course. Teachers devote more time and resources to ensure that students demonstrate proficiency on the priority standards. Supporting standards act as instructional scaffolds to help students master the priority standards (Ainsworth, 2013). To select priority standards, the committee can consider the following criteria:

- *Readiness:* What prerequisite knowledge and skills are important to subsequent courses or grade levels?
- *Endurance:* What knowledge and skills will be of value beyond the classroom?
- *Leverage:* What knowledge and skills will help students in any academic discipline?
- *Assessment:* What knowledge and skills will be evaluated on state/district assessments? (Ainsworth, 2013).

Determine Grade-Span Learning Indicators

After the standards have been prioritized, the next step is to determine the accompanying grade-span learning indicators. **Grade-span learning indicators** describe age and developmentally appropriate outcomes for students to demonstrate meeting the standards. They articulate the progression of skill development and content knowledge across the grade levels (SHAPE America, 2025). As an example, in the PreK-5 grade-span for National Standard 1, there are 53 different motor skills and movement patterns with multiple indicators for each of those sub-categories. How will districts align each of those categories in a scope and sequence? When determining grade-span learning indicators, districts may choose to (1) select either the national grade-span learning indicator or state grade-level outcomes and use one or the other exclusively, (2) pick and choose grade-span learning indicators or outcomes that meet their needs from both state and national outcomes, or (3) create their own grade-span learning indicators or grade-level outcomes. Several factors will influence how a district selects its grade-level outcomes:

- *Time:* The number of days per week and the number of minutes per class period that students have physical education
- *Resources:* The space, equipment, and materials available to provide instruction
- *Community and culture:* What is appropriate for the student population
- *District policies and mission:* What the district priorities and learning goals are

Unpack the Standards and Grade-Span Learning Indicators

Standards and grade-span learning indicators provide a framework that defines what students should know and be able to do as a result of the physical education program, but they are not a "how-to" manual. You must be able to take an indicator or outcome and design activities and assessments that allow students to show you they know it and can do it. A process for identifying what you want students to achieve from the selected outcomes and how to measure their success is *unpacking the standards* (Lund & Tannehill, 2015). When teachers unpack the standards, they clarify the knowledge and skills students will need to master the outcome and can develop assessments and lesson plans matched to that knowledge and those skills. At the district level, this process can help the curriculum committee decide on common grade-level assessments and may help to select instructional materials for teaching outcomes. At the individual level, this process can help teachers design standards-based units and lessons. Figure 4.8 shows an example of unpacking a grade-span learning indicator for Standard 2.

Decide How and When Student Learning Will Be Assessed

Assessment is an essential component of the curriculum development process as it shows a student's progress in achieving the grade-span learning indicators and meeting standards. It is the "proof" of progress and achievement. Assessment is the process of gathering data. It is the *way* teachers and districts gather data about students' learning progress, academic readiness, skill acquisition, and the effectiveness of instruction. There are four types of assessment used in curriculum development: diagnostic, formative, summative, and common.

FIGURE 4.8 Sample Unpacking of a Grade-Span Learning Indicator (Standard 2)

What is the standard/grade-span learning indicator? Defines and provides examples of movement activities for developing the health-related fitness components (2.5.6)

Targeted grade-span? Grade 3-5

Identify the purpose of teaching this standard and grade-span learning indicator:

- Students will provide examples of what kinds of physical activities they can do independently or with others, to develop health-related fitness so they can remain active for life.

Knowledge or concepts needed to master the standard and grade-span learning indicator (what students need to *know*). Knowledge—Awareness of something; the state of being aware of something.	*Skills* needed to master the standard and grade-span learning indicator (what students need to be able to *do*). Skill—The ability to do something that comes from training, experience, or practice.
• *Motivation to participate:* What activities do I enjoy doing the most, and where can I do them? • *Availability of physical activity opportunities:* What do you know about opportunities to be active (at recess, during physical education, in after-school programs, in the community, and so on)? • *Various types of physical activities:* Identify a physical activity that you can do by yourself, or with friends, to develop increased levels of health-related fitness.	• *Accessing information:* How can you find out what physical activity opportunities are available to you to increase your health-related fitness levels? • *Communication skills:* How would you ask someone to join you in participating in activities that will lead to increased levels of health-related fitness? • *Various motor skills:* How can I use _____ (list skills learned in PE) in being physically active? • *Analytical skills:* How can I change select activities so that they provide opportunities to enhance my personal level of health-related fitness?

Learning objectives: What daily learning objectives will lead to students being able to master this standard and grade-span learning indicators?

- I can list at least three physical activities that I can do to increase my level of health-related fitness.
- I can explain what I can do during the school day to be physically active.
- I can demonstrate how to organize _________ activities at recess.

Assessment: Physical activity in the after-school program. Students will identify three different physical activities (what, where, and with whom) that they can do after school.

Each type of assessment has a different purpose in the teaching and learning process.

- *Diagnostic assessment* can be used to identify students' current knowledge of a subject, their current skill capabilities, and potential misconceptions before teaching takes place. Knowing students' strengths, weaknesses, and interests can help instructors better plan what to teach and how to teach it.
- *Formative assessment* is an assessment of learning that allows students to receive immediate, corrective feedback and provides teachers with information to guide future instruction. Using formative assessments helps students remain focused on the process of learning and the purpose of activities within the classroom. This type of assessment is informal (not attached to a student's grade) and can use peer-, self-, or teacher-led tools to determine progress.
- *Summative assessment* is an assessment of learning given at the end of an instructional unit or at the end of the semester to evaluate what has been learned and how well it was learned. Grades are typically an outcome of summative assessment, and they indicate whether the student has an acceptable level of proficiency for the identified learning indicators and intended outcomes.
- *Common assessments* are assessments that districts may require at specified times during a curriculum sequence to evaluate students' knowledge and skills of identified standards. Such assessments have the same format, are administered in consistent ways, align to specific standards or curricular goals, and use the

same scoring guides so that the results from multiple classrooms and schools can be compared (Great Schools Partnership, 2015a). The data from common assessments can be used to monitor and evaluate program effectiveness and to inform decision making related to recommending resources, curriculum, and instructional strategies. Table 4.4 shows an example of how a common assessment plan guides instructional decisions.

Create Curriculum Maps

One of the most powerful tools for aligning and implementing **standards-based curriculum** is a curriculum map. A curriculum map shows where student learning indicators and intended outcomes are taught and assessed for a program, course, or grade level. In the curriculum development process, it maps out a student's learning experience across a specified time. When created at a program level, a curriculum map shows where the prioritized standards or program content, skills, instruction, and grade-span learning indicators and intended outcomes are taught and assessed. Teachers will create unit plans and daily lessons according to the scope and sequence outlined in each curriculum map.

Table 4.5 provides an overview of when the required content, fitness, and skills are to be taught and the required assessments. This template shows an example of what could be used in the initial stages of curriculum mapping to outline the essential content and required assessments. Then, the grade-level curriculum map (table 4.6) gives a very detailed description of all of the activities, content, and standards that are expected to be taught during the school year. As you can see by the design and content of each map, student learning would be greatly enhanced if all teachers in the district followed the curriculum maps for their grade levels. Using the maps avoids repetitious or unnecessary content and activities and progressively prepares students for more challenging work. The maps also help teachers in providing a well-rounded physical education experience by including the cognitive, affective, and psychomotor domains.

www **TABLE 4.4** Sample Common Assessment Template

Type	Elementary School	Middle School	High School
Cognitive assessment	Concepts of health and fitness assessment	FITT principle assessment	Personal fitness planning assessment
Fitness assessment	FitnessGram pre and post • PACER • Push-ups • Curl-ups • Sit and reach Grades 3-5	FitnessGram pre and post • PACER • Push-ups • Curl-ups • Sit and reach Grades 6-8	FitnessGram pre and post • Mile • PACER • Push-ups • Curl-ups • Sit and reach Grades 9-12
Motor skills assessment	Locomotor skills • Hopping • Grades PreK-2 and 3-5	Locomotor skills • Running Grades 6-8	Locomotor skills • Walking lunge Grades 9-12
	Nonlocomotor skills • Ready position Grades PreK-2 and 3-5	Nonlocomotor skills • Pivot Grades 6-8	Nonlocomotor skills • Body-weight squat Grades 9-12
	Manipulative skills • Jumping rope (two-foot basic jump) Grades 3-5	Manipulative skills • Throwing (overhand) • Catching Grades 6-8	Manipulative skills • Striking with a racket • Forehand • Underhand Grades 9-12

TABLE 4.5 Sample Year-at-a-Glance Curriculum Map for Grades K-5

	Sep-Oct	Nov-Dec	Jan	Feb-March	April	May-June
Required Health and Fitness Academic Content	Five components of fitness	Nutrition	Goal setting	Bone health Muscle motion	Heart health Physical activity promotion	Review health and fitness content and goals First aid, injury prevention
Required Fitness-Related Activities	Prefitness assessments Fitness circuits	Nutrition-related games	Pedometers	Fitness activities Fitness circuits	Postfitness assessments	Postfitness assessments, continued Circuit training
Required Motor Skills	Locomotor skills Nonlocomotor skills Low-organized games Soccer skills	Basketball skills	Throwing and catching Rhythmic movement	Developmental gymnastics skills	Volleyball Jump rope Bike safety	Racket and paddle skills
Required Social and Emotional and Safety Content	Rules, behavior, safety, and fair play	Media awareness Celebration of differences	Perseverance	Self-esteem	Stress reduction	Integrity
Required Assessments	[See required district prefitness assessments.] Summative Motor Skill Mastery Point (5th grade): Uses various speeds, levels, directions, and decision-making skills in a game situation	Summative Motor Skill Mastery Point (5th grade): Dribbles with hand while moving in any direction	No required assessments this month	No required assessments this month	Summative Motor Skill Mastery Point (4th grade): Two-foot basic rope jump Let's go, bike and ped safety: pre- and postassessment	OSPI developed assessment 3rd-5th postfitness assessments Summative Motor Skill Mastery Point (2nd grade: Jumping and hopping) (3rd grade: Galloping, skipping, and ready position) Summative 3rd grade assessment: Correctly identifies 5 components of fitness Summative 4th grade assessment: Classifies fitness assessment to fitness components Summative 5th grade assessment: Classifies various fitness activities to fitness components

From J. Greenberg and J. LoBianco, *Organization and Administration of Physical Education,* 2nd ed. (Human Kinetics, 2026). Reprinted by permission from Seattle Public Schools.

TABLE 4.6 Sample Yearlong Curriculum Map for Grades 1-3

Time Frame: Sep-Oct	Health and Fitness Academic Content	Fitness-Related Activities	Motor Skills	Social and Emotional Safety
Essential questions	What is fitness?	What is my individual fitness level? How do I improve my fitness?	Which motor skills are necessary to improve my fitness level?	What makes a safe learning environment during PE class?
Content	Section 1: Five components for fitness Unit: Five for Life	Section 4: Fitness-related activities Unit: Fitness Measurements K-5 Unit: Circuit Training	Locomotor/ nonlocomotor skills Recess activities Manipulative skills	Rules Behavior Safety Fair play
Skills and activities	Unit: Five for Life • Student introduction • Cardiorespiratory activity • Muscular strength and endurance activity • Flexibility activity • Body composition explanation	Fitness testing protocol preparation • Introduction of protocols but no measurements taken until 3rd grade Unit: Fitness Measurements (required starting in 3rd grade) • Introduction • Push-ups • Curl-ups • Sit and reach • PACER • Heath and weight (opt-in required for BMI) Unit: Circuit training introduction	Locomotor/ nonlocomotor skills • Locomotor skills (run, gallop, hop, jump, walk, chase, flee, skip) • Nonlocomotor skills (twist, turn, curl, ready position) Low-organized activities Suggested recess activities • Four square • Kickball Suggested manipulative skills: ball skills • Trap the ball • Kick with inside of dominant foot • Kick to a partner	Rules • Team-building activities • Responsibility • Care of equipment Behavior • Cooperation • Self-control • Anti-bullying Safety • Emergency procedures • Play structure: safe use and rules • PE equipment: protocols for safe use Fair play • Conflict resolution

Selection of Instructional Materials

Once the state and local intended outcomes, or national grade-span learning indicators, and assessments have been developed, the curriculum team can select instructional resources that will support students in reaching those outcomes. Districts have policies and procedures that guide the selection and adoption of instructional materials. They typically require that the curriculum team review, possibly pilot, and evaluate materials such as texts, videos, and software to determine whether they will be effective resources in meeting the program's goals. Figure 4.9 shows examples of various physical education curriculum resources. Although they are sometimes affected by budgetary constraints, districts may use a combination of various curriculum resources and materials that can be identified in the curriculum map, determining which instructional materials are aligned to specific grade-span learning indicators and intended outcomes.

Identify Appropriate Curriculum Models and Determine the Delivery System

After establishing the outcomes, assessments, and instructional materials, the next step is to determine how to organize those components to

FIGURE 4.9 Physical Education Curriculum Resources

- *Coordinated Approach to Child Health (CATCH) PE Journeys (https://catch.org/program/physical-education)*: CATCH PE Journeys is an evidence-based, developmentally appropriate physical education program that teaches physical literacy, movement skills, physical fitness, social-emotional learning, skill competency, and cognitive understanding about the importance of lifelong physical activity. It is standards-aligned and designed to promote motivation and participation in moderate-to-vigorous physical activity while emphasizing non-elimination games for K-8 children of all skill levels and physical abilities.
- *Five for Life Curriculum (www.schoolhealth.com/5forlife-k-5):* The Five for Life program is an evidence-based, K-12 fitness and health curriculum that aligns with SHAPE America National Physical Education Standards. Using age-appropriate academic instructional units in an activity-based setting, the Five for Life basic, intermediate, and advanced programs move students through a continuum of learning without compromising activity time for students.
- *SPARK PE K-12 program (www.sparkpe.org):* The focus of SPARK is the development of healthy lifestyles, motor skills, movement knowledge, and social and personal skills. Each SPARK program is a coordinated package of research and standards-based teacher resources, interactive teacher training, content-matched equipment sets, and extensive follow-up support/consultation.
- *Online Physical Education Network (OPEN) (http://openphysed.org):* OPEN is a backward-designed curriculum project that targets SHAPE America's National Physical Education Standards. It is a free online resource that provides rigorous, outcomes-based curriculum tools.
- *Presidential Youth Fitness Program (PYFP) (www.pyfp.org):* The PYFP promotes health-related fitness and provides physical education programs with quality resources and tools to empower youth to be fit for life. The program provides schools with access to best practices, including training for physical educators, fitness assessment standards, and grants for equipment and professional development.

deliver instruction. **Curriculum models** are theme-based frameworks with distinct characteristics that help educators organize content into meaningful patterns to deliver coherent instruction (Mitchell & Walton-Fisette, 2022). Models have defined pedagogical approaches that intentionally impact a student's learning experience around a central theme and that have a stronger emphasis on different standards and outcomes (e.g., affective, psychomotor, cognitive) (Gurvitch & Metzler, 2013).

The predominant model used in physical education programs in the United States has been the multi-activity, sport-based approach, which is characterized by short units (5-10 lessons) of skills, drills, and game play (Ennis, 2014). Also termed *exposure curriculum*, this model favors breadth over depth so that students develop a basic understanding of the different skills and rules associated with multiple sports. Unfortunately, in some instances, this teaching approach appears to contribute to negative attitudes toward physical education and physical activity, specifically for less-skilled students who are embarrassed by their lack of competence (Bernstein et al., 2011; Capel & Blair, 2007). It is recommended that educators avoid using a multi-activity approach and instead use a multimodel approach to physical education (Quay & Peters, 2008). *Multimodel* means that teachers use more than one curriculum model to deliver a physical education program. It is critically important for the district physical education administrator to provide professional development so that physical education teachers are properly versed on the various curriculum models and feel comfortable when implementing a comprehensive program.

PHYSICAL EDUCATION CURRICULUM MODELS

Teaching Personal and Social Responsibility (TPSR) Model

Grade Levels: PreK-12

Standard Emphasis:

- **Standard 3:** Develops social skills through movement.
- **Standard 4:** Develops personal skills, identifies personal benefits of movement, and chooses to engage in physical activity.

Curricular Focus: To teach personal and social responsibility through physical activity

Description: The Teaching Personal and Social Responsibility (TPSR) model emphasizes development of character through physical activity. Students are deliberately taught how to cooperate and act respectfully as opposed to assuming they will instinctively learn or use those skills when interacting with others. The model suggests using levels of responsibility, or a hierarchy of values, to design learning experiences in which students can practice and apply the various attributes of social and personal responsibility. Table 4.7 shows an example of how the levels could be structured so that teachers and students know the expectations pertaining to personally and socially responsible behavior.

Curricular Design Considerations: The suggested curricular structure for ensuring that personal and social responsibility is the driving theme of the class is to use a daily format that includes the following five components:

- **Relational or counseling time:** A check-in with individual students on how they are doing (can be done at any point in the class).
- **Awareness talk:** The class opener; the teacher describes the purpose of TPSR in relation to the objectives for the class period.
- **Physical activity content:** The physical activity in which students apply the levels of responsibility.
- **Group meeting:** Class discussion near the end of the period that allows students to provide feedback on the lesson and the importance of using the TPSR levels.
- **Reflection time:** The lesson closure; students conduct a self-evaluation related to their level of personal and social responsibility.

Model Resource: Hellison, D. (2011). *Teaching personal and social responsibility through physical activity* (3rd ed.). Human Kinetics.

TABLE 4.7 Example of the TPSR Levels of Responsibility

Level	Teaching Components	Student Expectations
I: Respect	• Self-control • Conflict resolution • Understanding the rights of self and peers • Consideration of others' feelings	I can take turns and share the equipment.
II: Effort	• Self-motivation • Cooperating with others • Participating in new tasks	I can try new things without complaining.
III: Self-direction	• Personal goal setting • Self-starting • Accountability • Resilience and resourcefulness	I can participate fully without the teacher always watching me.
IV: Helping	• Leadership roles • Responding to others' needs • Encouraging and supporting others	I can make sure no one feels left out when playing the game.
V: Transfer	• Being a positive role model • Using values and skills learned in all aspects of life	I can be respectful and play well with others on the playground.

Adapted from Hellison (2011, p. 21).

PHYSICAL EDUCATION CURRICULUM MODELS

Tactical Games Model

Grade Levels: PreK-12

Standard Emphasis:

- **Standard 1:** Develops a variety of motor skills.
- **Standard 2:** Applies knowledge related to movement and fitness concepts.
- **Standard 4:** Develops personal skills, identifies personal benefits of movement, and chooses to engage in physical activity.

Curricular Focus: To increase students' interest in games by developing and improving their tactical awareness, skill performance, and overall game performance

Description: The Tactical Games Model (TGM) uses games to teach decision making, problem solving, communication, skills, and teamwork. All games are designed so that students can solve a tactical problem. Students participate in practice tasks that allow them to develop the skills needed to appropriately respond to game situations. A major focus is the transfer of tactical approaches so that students can use the decision-making skills in similar games.

Curricular Design Considerations: A planning framework for lesson design using the TGM includes first identifying the tactical problem to be addressed, then creating a lesson focus on how the tactical problem can be solved and writing a lesson objective for how students will demonstrate their tactical knowledge and skills. Once those criteria have been established, the TGM suggests designing and implementing lessons following a specific sequence of steps as outlined in table 4.8.

Model Resource: Mitchell, S., Oslin, J.L., & Griffin, L.L. (2021). *Teaching sport concepts and skills: A tactical games approach for ages 7 to 18* (4th ed.). Human Kinetics.

TABLE 4.8 Tactical Games Lesson Format

Lesson Component	Description
Game 1	Students play a game that exposes them to a tactical problem and allows them to try to solve the problem. The teacher creates specific conditions that promote tactical problem solving in the game.
Questioning	After the game, the teacher gathers students together and asks questions related to the tactical problem and solution. Question stems for this critical thinking regarding tactical problems: "How do you . . . ?" (Skill and movement execution) "When is the best time to . . . ?" (Time) "What do you . . . ?" (Tactical awareness) "Where is/can . . . ?" (Space) "Which choice . . . ?" (Risk)
Practice tasks	Teacher assigns practice tasks that involve improving a skill specific to the tactical problem.
Game 2	Students play another game, which may be the same as game 1 or with a different condition designed to reinforce the use of the skill that was just practiced.
Closure	It comprises questions and discussion about being able to accomplish the objective.

Based on Mitchell, Oslin, and Griffin (2021).

PHYSICAL EDUCATION CURRICULUM MODELS

Sport Education Model

Grade Levels: 3-12

Standard Emphasis:

- **Standard 1:** Develops a variety of motor skills.
- **Standard 2:** Applies knowledge related to movement and fitness concepts.
- **Standard 3:** Develops social skills through movement.
- **Standard 4:** Develops personal skills, identifies personal benefits of movement, and chooses to engage in physical activity.

Curricular Focus: For students to become competent, literate, and enthusiastic sportspersons so that they are motivated to continue to learn and improve in the sport and engage in lifelong participation by engaging in authentic sport experiences

Description: In the Sport Education Model (SEM), the curriculum and instruction are delivered in a way that simulates an athletic team in season. The teacher selects a sport, dance, or exercise activity and designs all lessons around aspects associated with participating and competing in that activity. SEM promotes an in-depth learning experience so that students become competent and confident in performing the activity. Students learn teamwork, fair play, skills, rules, and career-related responsibilities all through participation in authentic sport experiences.

Curricular Design Considerations: Key features of the model that influence lesson planning and curriculum organization include the following:

- **Sport seasons:** Instead of units are sport seasons with formal practice schedules and a longer duration devoted to the sport. Seasons typically last a minimum of 12 lessons so that students can experience all the various aspects of a sport season and have a more in-depth learning experience. (It means that fewer sports or activities will be taught during a school year due to the duration of the seasons.)
- **Diverse roles and responsibilities:** Students aren't just players; they take on roles such as coach, referee, or scorekeeper that are a necessary part of the sport. Students are actively engaged in an assigned role at all times.
- **Affiliation:** Students work with the same mixed-ability team throughout the season to build team spirit and camaraderie by creating team names, mottos, and cheers as well as fulfilling specific roles.
- **Formal competition:** There can be a series of mini competitions throughout the season, such as 1v1, 2v2, or 4v4, and then a culminating competitive event, or championship, which highlights the season and provides a goal for teams and players to work toward.
- **Record keeping:** Records of performance are tracked and displayed to show team standings, individual improvement, and various statistics. Students are assigned the role of statistician during the season. This information can be used to ensure fair teams, to develop practice plans, and to assign awards.
- **Authenticity and festivity:** The season is intended to be an authentic sport or dance experience that focuses on the social element of bonding with teammates. It includes a final event that celebrates the season with a recognition of accomplishments and awards.

Model Resource: Siedentop, D., Hastie, P.A., & van der Mars, H. (2020). *Complete guide to sport education* (3rd ed.). Human Kinetics.

PHYSICAL EDUCATION CURRICULUM MODELS

Conceptual Physical Education or Fitness Education Model

Grade Levels: PreK-12

Standard Emphasis:

- **Standard 1:** Develops a variety of motor skills.
- **Standard 2:** Applies knowledge related to movement and fitness concepts.

Curricular Focus: To prepare and motivate students to engage in health-enhancing physical activity by providing them with the knowledge and skills they will need to be physically active for life

Description: In the Conceptual Physical Education (CPE) model, which is also known as the fitness education model, curriculum and instruction are delivered in a lecture–laboratory approach so that students are taught the conceptual fitness content and then apply it in a physical activity lab session (Houston & Kulinna, 2014). This model emphasizes both the how and why of physical activity and fitness by incorporating exercise science and physiology concepts. Students engage in health-enhancing physical activity while learning both the purpose and importance of physical fitness. Students are taught the benefits of physical activity and the fitness requirements of specific activities, and they learn to develop a plan to achieve and maintain a health-enhancing level of fitness (Ayers & Sariscsany, 2011).

Curricular Design Considerations: In developing a lesson framework for the CPE model, teachers will have to plan for how to deliver the cognitive concepts and then design physical activity experiences that allow students to apply those concepts. Table 4.9 shows an example of structuring the content so that students are learning the material in the classroom and then applying it in the physical activity setting. Teachers may not have the ability to use a classroom; in this case, they could instead deliver short 5- to 10-minute content lectures in the gym before the students participate in the activity.

The Stairway to Lifetime Fitness (see figure 4.10) presents a means for teachers to organize content and guide students toward lifelong physical activity. They must learn foundational information and skills such as how to manage time, self-assess, set goals, and train for the health-related components of fitness to achieve lifelong fitness. Teachers can design lessons using these skills so that students can become physically literate and achieve lifelong health and wellness.

Model Resource: Corbin, C.B., Castelli, D.M., Sibley, B.A., & Le Masurier, G.C. (2022). *Fitness for Life* (7th ed.). Champaign, IL: Human Kinetics.

TABLE 4.9 Sample CPE Curriculum Delivery

Monday	Tuesday	Wednesday	Thursday	Friday
Location: Gym	Location: Classroom	Location: Gym	Location: Classroom	Location: Track
Activity: Circuit training	Topic: Benefits of cardiorespiratory fitness	Activity: Circuit training	Topic: Calculating target heart rate zone	Activity: Interval training

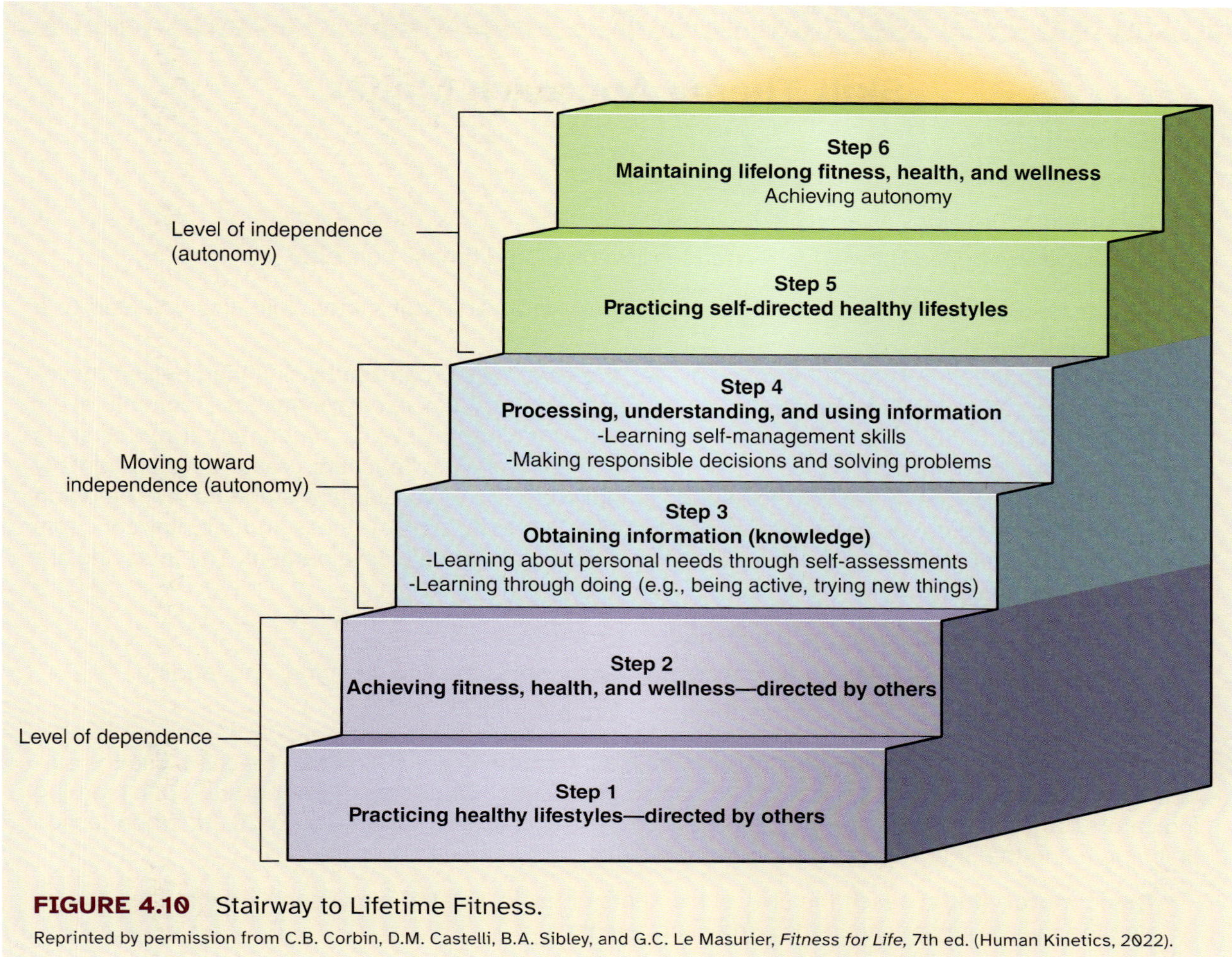

FIGURE 4.10 Stairway to Lifetime Fitness.

Reprinted by permission from C.B. Corbin, D.M. Castelli, B.A. Sibley, and G.C. Le Masurier, *Fitness for Life,* 7th ed. (Human Kinetics, 2022).

The physical education administrator should provide teachers with a curriculum guide, including the program philosophy, program goals, and curriculum maps with all of the grade-span learning indicators, required assessments, and recommended resources without any guidance on how to deliver the curriculum. This approach will ensure that all teachers receive training on how to deliver the curriculum and can ask questions if any clarification is needed. This section summarizes five of the most commonly used and researched physical education models to provide a basic understanding of how curriculum models will contribute to the curriculum development process and student learning. Other models not addressed in this chapter include the outdoor education, adventure education, and the cultural studies models.

Curriculum models offer a framework for organizing and delivering the curriculum, and they can be adapted to fit a particular school setting, course, or grade level. For example, at the high school level, a weight training class may use the Fitness Education model while a racquet sports class at the same school employs a combination of the Sport Education Model (SEM) and the fitness education model. Selecting appropriate curriculum models helps instructors design units and lessons to effectively teach the prioritized standards.

PHYSICAL EDUCATION CURRICULUM MODELS

Skill Theme Approach Model

Grade Levels: PreK-5

Standard Emphasis:

- **Standard 1:** Develops a variety of motor skills.
- **Standard 2:** Applies knowledge related to movement and fitness concepts.

Curricular Focus: For students to develop proficiency in a variety of motor skills that will lead to a physically active lifestyle

Description: In the Skill Theme Approach model, the content is organized by skill themes and movement concepts rather than by activities such as sports, games, dance, or gymnastics (Tannehill et al., 2015). The initial focus of this approach is on helping children develop fundamental motor skills and then applying them within different physical activity contexts. Teachers create developmentally appropriate experiences that reflect the needs of individual students, so many students may be doing different tasks based on their skill proficiency (Lund & Tannehill, 2015). Fitness and fair play concepts are interwoven throughout the lessons, and they are secondary to skill development. The following are skill theme examples:

- **Locomotor skills:** Walking, skipping, hopping, running, galloping.
- **Non-manipulative skills:** Turning, twisting, balancing, stretching, jumping, and landing.
- **Manipulative skills:** Throwing, catching, kicking, punting.

Curricular Design Considerations: This model is truly student centered in that teachers use the students' current motor development abilities to plan instruction rather than age- or grade-span learning indicators, so that students are taught based on their skill level (Graham et al., 2013). When lesson planning using the Skill Theme Approach model, teachers address the following:

- **Basic motor skills:** Teach the critical elements of basic isolated movements so that they can be applied in a variety of situations and environments.
- **Developmental levels:** Use individual students' developmental levels to match the task difficulty to the ability of the child. Differentiate the activities based upon an appropriate challenge level for the students.
- **Scope and sequence:** Spiral the skills so that they are visited and revisited across the school year such that practice sessions are distributed across a longer period of time rather than as extensive short units (Tannehill et al., 2015).
- **Instructional alignment:** Use a backward design approach to determine what is to be learned, design the practice sessions, and then assess what students have been practicing.

Model Resource: Graham, G., Holt/Hale, S., & Parker, M. (2013). *Children moving: A reflective approach to teaching physical education* (9th ed.). McGraw-Hill.

The Implementation Phase

The main objective of the implementation phase is to deliver the curriculum to meet the stated grade-span learning indicators and intended outcomes. Teachers should implement the following strategies to meet this objective:

- Reflect on and record what is working and not working.
- Participate in professional development opportunities.

One of the most challenging parts of the curriculum development process is to align the written, delivered, and experienced curricula. The written curriculum is what the district intends for the students to learn; the delivered curriculum is what is taught by the teachers; and the experienced curriculum is what is learned by the students. Sometimes the written curriculum may only slightly influence the delivered curriculum, and often there is a significant gap between the delivered curriculum and the experienced curriculum

(Glatthorn et al., 2001). In the case of physical education, the experienced curriculum should be one in which students are learning concepts and skills that support lifelong physical activity.

An essential part of curriculum implementation is establishing time for teachers to meet in grade-level teams to discuss how they are delivering the content, identify what is working, design lesson plans for the grade-span learning indicators, and ask for necessary support. Based on teacher need, the district physical education administrator can connect teachers to community partners, peer mentors, or other resources that can help them deliver effective standards-based instruction. Without ongoing professional development opportunities and established professional learning time, the written curriculum may be left on the shelf.

The Evaluation Phase

The main objectives of the evaluation phase are to determine whether goals were achieved and to improve program effectiveness. The following are evaluation phase strategies:

- Follow an evaluation framework.
- Collect data from different sources for decision making.
- Identify strengths, weaknesses, and potential gaps.
- Make revisions as necessary.

Curriculum development is a continuous process; it never ends. After the curriculum is designed and implemented, curriculum leaders and teachers reflect on and evaluate its effectiveness. Then the cycle starts over again as the evaluation phase informs the planning phase to revise the curriculum, implement the changes, and then evaluate those changes.

The evaluation phase is critical to the success of the program as it seeks to discover how to improve the program to better meet the needs of students. For this reason, most school districts require that programs conduct and submit a formal evaluation on a specified schedule, such as every five years. An evaluation can identify curricular strengths and weaknesses so that necessary revisions can be made to ensure that the program is successful in accomplishing its goals. Similar to classroom assessments, curriculum evaluation can be formative or summative. Formative evaluation typically occurs during the implementation phase, and it allows teachers to make modifications and adjustments as necessary. Formative evaluation can also be used on a yearly basis to make revisions before a formal or summative evaluation is conducted. Summative evaluation occurs at the conclusion of a program or at a designated time to measure the success in meeting the identified goals. Summative evaluations tend to produce formal reports that show the progress and accomplishments of the learners within the program using specific sources of data.

The evaluation phase is a process in itself in that curriculum leaders must follow several steps in order to obtain and analyze information that will guide decision making for changes in the curriculum. Table 4.10 shows an example of a curriculum evaluation framework modeled after the CDC framework for program evaluation (CDC, 2017b).

As a curriculum leader, it is important for you to understand that an effective evaluation will provide information on the written, delivered, and experienced curricula. The written curriculum can be quickly assessed through a simple evaluation checklist (as shown in table 4.11) or by an in-depth analysis using, for example, the Physical Education Curriculum Analysis Tool (PECAT). The PECAT is a self-assessment tool that can be used at a district or individual level and that determines whether the contents described in the curriculum and assessments align with the national standards. The PECAT is available in print and as an interactive online version at www.cdc.gov/healthyschools/pecat/index.htm.

The written curriculum can also be evaluated by analyzing the level of student achievement on the grade-span learning indicators and intended outcomes, such as motor skill proficiency scores, fitness assessment data, and cognitive assessment scores. Tools for evaluating the delivered and experienced curricula include administrator, teacher, parent, and student surveys. Tables 4.12 and 4.13 provide examples of survey questions that can be used to gather information on the delivered curriculum and the experienced curriculum, respectively.

TABLE 4.10 Curriculum Evaluation Framework

Focus the Evaluation	• Determine the purpose of the evaluation. • Select key questions to be answered and indicators of progress and success. • Determine the data collection process (focus groups, surveys, test scores, observations, etc.).
Engage Stakeholders	• Communicate the importance and purpose of the process. • Indicate how stakeholders can provide feedback.
Collect Data	• Establish clear procedures for collecting credible information (quality control, sources, reliability of measurements, etc.). • Determine the amount of information necessary to make informed decisions before stopping data collection.
Analyze and Interpret	• Use appropriate methods of analysis and synthesis to summarize findings. • Use the evidence to make claims regarding the curriculum.
Use and Share	• Determine the most effective way to inform stakeholders of the findings and how the data will affect decisions in changing the curriculum. • Share the conclusions and potential revisions.

Adapted from CDC (1999), www.cdc.gov/mmwr/PDF/rr/rr4811.pdf.

TABLE 4.11 The Written Curriculum: Evaluation Checklist

		Yes	No
Philosophy and goals	Do the grade-span learning indicators and common assessments align with the district philosophy and program goals?		
Standards	Does the curriculum thoroughly cover foundational concepts that help students achieve the state standards?		
Content	Is the content the most updated, rigorous, and culturally relevant to meet the stated objectives?		
Vertical alignment	Are the grade-span learning indicators and intended outcomes appropriately sequenced to allow students to complete progressively more complex work?		
Instructional materials	Are the instructional materials the best available for meeting the program goals and grade-span learning indicators and intended outcomes?		
Format	Do the format and design facilitate easy navigation and understanding of the curriculum expectations?		
Assessments	Are the assessments feasible and developmentally appropriate for the grade level assigned?		

Evaluations have the potential to shape the curriculum into an effective and relevant working document that helps all students succeed. They can support teachers in revising instructional strategies, lesson plans, and curriculum models. They can support districts in choosing instructional materials, offering professional development, revising grade-span learning indicators and intended outcomes, and revising content. Remember that the major objective of the evaluation phase is to improve the program, which means that you must make revisions using the analyzed data. Recognize that every evaluation should result in revisions because no curriculum is perfect, especially since education itself is dynamic and ever-changing.

TABLE 4.12 The Delivered Curriculum: Teacher Curriculum Survey

	1 Strongly Disagree	2 Disagree	3 Neutral	4 Agree	5 Strongly Agree
1. My instruction is guided by the grade-span learning indicators and intended outcomes. Comments:					
2. I follow the sequence of content and learning activities outlined in the curriculum map. Comments:					
3. I assessed (either formative or summative) all the grade-span learning indicators and intended outcomes for my grade level. Comments:					
4. I used formative assessment data to guide my instruction toward students meeting the standards. Comments:					
5. My students were well prepared for the common assessment(s) for my grade level. Comments:					

TABLE 4.13 The Experienced Curriculum: Student Curriculum Survey

	1 Strongly Disagree	2 Disagree	3 Neutral	4 Agree	5 Strongly Agree
1. I have learned new information and skills this year in my PE class. Comments:					
2. I learned enough about a new sport or activity to participate in it outside of school. Comments:					
3. Participating in PE class motivates me to be physically active. Comments:					

(continued)

TABLE 4.13 *(continued)*

	1	2	3	4	5
4. The content and activities in the class were enjoyable and relevant to me.	Strongly Disagree	Disagree	Neutral	Agree	Strongly Agree
Comments:					
5. I am physically active more than 50% of the time in PE class.	Strongly Disagree	Disagree	Neutral	Agree	Strongly Agree
Comments:					

Conclusion

Curriculum development is a collaborative and cyclical process. Creating a well-designed curriculum that supports student learning and positive attitudes toward physical education and physical activity requires research, planning, communication, constant monitoring, evaluating, and revising. Curriculum must consistently change to meet the diverse needs of your students, and you must be willing and able to provide input to make those changes. Quality curriculum can be developed by following a systematic process of planning, designing, implementing, and evaluating what students are learning and how they are learning it.

As you implement different assessments, you may find that they are too rigorous or not rigorous enough or that students aren't adequately prepared for some assessments based on different grade-span learning indicators and intended outcomes. You may find that certain curriculum models are not as effective in certain settings. Each of these discoveries can help to modify the curriculum so that future students will benefit from the lessons you have learned. Use the curriculum development process to ensure that students are receiving the highest-quality physical education you can provide.

Review Questions

1. What are four curricular aspects that can negatively affect students' motivation to participate in physical education? Identify a potential solution for each aspect.
2. What factors may influence how districts determine grade-span learning indicators?
3. Identify two different curriculum models, describe their key characteristics, and explain why they may be used in the curriculum development process.
4. What strategies can be used to align the written, delivered, and experienced curriculum?
5. Why is it important to develop a curriculum map?

» Visit HK*Propel* for reproducible forms.

CHAPTER 5

Quality Instruction

Nichole D. Barta and Jayne D. Greenberg

Photo courtesy of Miriam Kenyon, DC Public Schools

LEARNING OBJECTIVES

After reading this chapter, you will be able to do the following:

- Define the physical literacy journey.
- Describe common physical education instructional models and their purposes.
- Describe key practices in delivering appropriate instruction in physical education.
- Explain the legal responsibility of physical educators to provide instruction to students with disabilities.
- Explain strategies for developing an inclusive environment.
- Summarize various factors that affect the quality of instruction in physical education.

KEY CONCEPTS

appropriate instruction	inclusion	physically literate
fitness education	instructional models	waivers

After reading chapter 4, as a physical education administrator, you can see that the field of physical education has evolved from a sports-focused activity time or supervised play into a standards-based, learning-oriented class with clear objectives. What was once considered a marginalized profession due to its lack of valuable content and meaningful application has become a key element in a well-rounded education for all students. This shift is due primarily to the work of the Society for Health and Physical Educators (SHAPE America), who published the *National Physical Education Standards* (2025), the revised national standards among many other online documents that guide quality physical education (see References), as well as the passage of the Every Student Succeeds Act (ESSA). The ESSA lists physical education as one of the subjects that all students need as part of a well-rounded education (ESSA, 2015, p. 298). A well-rounded education provides students with the opportunity to develop a broad set of skills and interests that will help them to be successful in college, career, and life. Looking at the national standards, as shown in chapter 3, you can see that physical education contributes to a well-rounded individual by teaching the knowledge, skills, and confidence to enjoy a lifetime of healthful physical activity.

No other content area teaches students how to develop motor skills and health-enhancing fitness and how to use social skills in a range of physical activity contexts primarily through movement. Movement skills do not automatically develop in children; they must be taught, practiced, and reinforced (Robinson et al., 2012). Physical education may provide the only opportunity for many children to develop proficient motor skills; therefore, effective instructional strategies for motor skill acquisition are essential to enhance physically active lifestyles (Calkins, 2017). Studies have shown that physical education does in fact develop skills (how to be physically active), knowledge (ways to be physically active and why), positive attitudes (the valuing of physical activity), and physical fitness in students (Bernstein et al., 2011; Sallis et al., 2012; Zeng et al., 2011; Greenberg et al., 2022). In other words, physical education promotes physical literacy, which is a necessary component in increasing an individual's functional capacity and quality of life. It is foundational to a well-rounded individual.

Physical education is a comprehensive, progressive, and articulated program that aims to provide learners with quality PreK-12 instruction. In 2014, the goal of physical education was to develop **physically literate** learners who possess the knowledge, skills, and confidence to enjoy a lifetime of healthful physical activity as in the 21st century. Professional organizations, school districts, and teachers nationwide were promoting, creating, and implementing physical education programs designed to meet the overall goal of physical education: to develop physically literate individuals. According to the Aspen Institute (2015), "physical literacy is the ability, confidence, and desire to be physically active for life" (p. 9). Whitehead (2019) further asserts that "as appropriate to each individual, physical literacy can be described as the motivation, confidence, physical competence, knowledge and understanding to value and take responsibility for engaging in physical activities for life" (p.8). However, with the development of the 2024 National Physical Education Standards & Grade-Span Learning Indicators (SHAPE America, 2025), physical literacy has been replaced with the concept of a physical literacy journey, which aims to

> *create relevant and developmentally appropriate learning experiences that engage all PreK-12 learners on a physical literacy journey of holistic competence, to include opportunities to develop the skills, knowledge, confidence, appreciation, and motivation to live an active life—across and beyond their PreK-12 years. (p.1)*

As delineated in chapter 3, SHAPE America has outlined four essential components for structuring programs to support the development of physically literate individuals. Those components essential to achieving physical literacy as a program outcome include curriculum, appropriate instruction, student assessment, and policy and environment (SHAPE America, 2015a). The previous chapter focused on how to develop what to teach (the curriculum), and this chapter focuses on how to teach (instruction and assessment) and how to create an environment (policy and environment) that promotes learning for lifelong health and fitness.

Appropriate Instruction

Appropriate instruction in physical education involves using instructional approaches that allow teachers to organize and deliver the content in the most effective manner possible. Instruction is a complex process because students have a variety of unique physical, social, and emotional needs, and there may be limited resources to meet those needs. In working toward quality instruction, SHAPE America (2015a) advises utilizing these four key practices:

1. *The physical education teacher uses instructional practices and deliberate-practice tasks that support the goals and objectives defined in the school district's / school's physical education curriculum (e.g., differentiated instruction, active engagement, modified activities, self-assessment, self-monitoring).*
2. *The physical education teacher evaluates student learning continually to document teacher effectiveness.*
3. *The physical education teacher employs instructional practices that engage students in moderate to vigorous physical activity for at least 50 percent of class time.*
4. *The physical education teacher ensures the inclusion of all students and makes the necessary adaptations for students with special needs or disabilities. (p. 6)*

In short, appropriate instruction meets the needs of all students, promotes maximum physical activity during class, and emphasizes learning the necessary knowledge and skills for a lifetime of physical activity. As mentioned in the previous chapter, what you teach and how you teach it will affect your students' experience in physical education and possibly their long-term participation in physical activity. Therefore, implementing appropriate instruction is vital to your students' ability and desire to become more physically literate. Evidence-based curriculum programs such as SPARK, CATCH, and Five for Life, aligned with the national and state physical education standards, serve as examples for increasing physical activity levels and cognitive knowledge during physical education. These programs can easily be implemented by both novice and veteran teachers. The Online Physical Education Network (OPEN) further provides standards-based lesson plans for teacher use.

Factors That Influence Quality Instruction and Environment

Several factors influence the quality of instruction and the environment in a physical education setting. These factors can generally be classified into two categories: teacher related (factors that the teacher has control over and can change) and institutional (factors that teachers typically do not have direct control over and may have difficulty changing) (Morgan & Hansen, 2008). Table 5.1 lists several examples of the factors that can affect instruction and the environment. Understanding these factors and their influences can help prevent them from becoming barriers to quality physical education. This chapter addresses a number of these factors so that you understand how you

TABLE 5.1 Factors That Influence Instruction and Environment

Teacher-Related Factors	Institutional Factors
• Pedagogical and content knowledge	• Attitudes and beliefs about purpose of physical education
• Management skills	• Class size and class scheduling
• Beliefs and knowledge about learners	• Time allotted to physical education
• Ability to create an inclusive environment	• Quality of facilities and equipment availability
• Confidence	• Professional development provided
• Assessment and instruction	• Certified versus noncertified PE teachers
• Content knowledge	• Exemptions and waivers
	• Online physical education

can improve the quality of instruction in your program. The teacher-related factors that are discussed more extensively are pedagogical and content knowledge and the ability to create an inclusive environment. The institutional factors addressed are time allotment to physical education, class size and scheduling, and attitudes and beliefs about the purpose of physical education.

Teacher-Related Factors

Physical education is different from other content areas in that it is "education through the physical" (Kirk, 2014, pp. 77-91). It is a curriculum that emphasizes learning in the cognitive, affective, and psychomotor domains in a physically active setting. Teaching these three learning domains effectively in a diverse classroom demands that teachers have advanced content and pedagogical knowledge (see table 5.2).

Pedagogical Knowledge

Pedagogical knowledge is the knowledge needed to create and optimize teaching–learning situations (Voss et al., 2011). It includes knowledge of classroom management, effective teaching methods, classroom assessment, feedback mechanisms, and knowledge about how students learn. Teachers with expert pedagogical knowledge can maximize student learning and physical activity through established routines, effective management procedures, differentiated instruction, and feedback matched to student need. They can set up a learning experience in which all students will be successful while not sacrificing physical activity time.

In physical education, understanding how to use curriculum and instructional models is paramount to optimizing teaching–learning situations. As you recall from chapter 4, curriculum models are structured theme-based frameworks for deciding how to select, organize, sequence, and deliver the content. **Instructional models**, like curriculum models, are frameworks or specific approaches that can be used to shape the curriculum, guide instruction, and establish a management system (Metzler, 2011). Instructional models provide a plan for how theory, planning, classroom management, learning activities, and assessment tie together (Metzler & Colquitt, 2021). You may have access to the best curriculum, world-class facilities, and all the equipment that you need; however, if you are unable to deliver appropriate instruction and manage your class, those resources are powerless.

Table 5.3 shows the eight instructional models that Metzler (2011) has identified as those most commonly used in physical education. The first five models listed are instructional models from other content areas that can be adapted for the physical education setting and content. Notice that the remaining three are also curriculum models that were introduced in chapter 4. These three models were developed exclusively for physical education, so their curricular goals align directly with physical education objectives and their instructional strategies support reaching those curricular goals. As mentioned in chapter 4, each model (whether curriculum or instructional) is designed to promote specific intended learning outcomes and grade-span learning indicators, and each model addresses different combinations of the national standards. Some have a greater emphasis on Standards 1 and 2, while others may have a greater emphasis on

TABLE 5.2 Learning Domains in Physical Education

Learning Domain	Sample Learning Objectives	Alignment With 2024 Standards
Psychomotor domain—Includes physical movement, coordination, and use of motor skills.	Demonstrate Perform Throw	1 and 2
Affective domain—Includes motivation, attitudes, behaviors, and feelings.	Accept responsibility for Express Respond appropriately	3 and 4
Cognitive domain—Includes understanding concepts, principles, and strategies.	Identify Discuss Describe	1 and 2

TABLE 5.3 Physical Education Instructional Models

Instructional Models	Themes	Common Learning Activities	Sample Assessment Tools
Direct instruction	Teacher is the leader and director of the feedback.	• Skill drill • Full-version games	Teacher observation with defined checklist or rubric
Personalized system for instruction	Students make progress at a personalized pace. Students are largely independent of the teacher.	• Self-analysis of skill and tactics • Situated learning tasks	Student workbook or journal
Cooperative learning	Students learn with each other and are dependent on one another. Teacher facilitates students providing each other with feedback.	• Jigsaw • Discussion strategies	Member contributions evaluation
Peer teaching	*I teach you; you teach me*: Teachers instruct tutors who then teach other students.	• Partner teaching • Skill drill	Peer skill checklists
Inquiry teaching	Learner is a problem solver. Teacher stimulates student thinking.	• Inquiry task and problem solving • Critical thinking and decision-making tasks	Student journal inquiry with answer
Sport Education Model (SEM)	Model involves learning to be a competent, literate, and enthusiastic sportsperson, working as a team to learn knowledge and skills.	• Modified games • Cooperative tasks	Fair play behavior rubrics
Tactical Games Model (TGM)	Model involves teaching games for understanding. Teacher facilitates problem-solving activities.	• Modified games • Situated learning tasks	Game performance assessments
Teaching Personal and Social Responsibility (TPSR) model	Model entails teacher–student relationships, empowering students to make decisions.	• Partner teaching • Cooperative task and problem solving	Self-assessment of personal responsibility

Adapted from R. Gurvitch and M. Metzler, “Aligning Learning Activities with Instructional Models,” *Journal of Physical Education, Recreation, and Dance* 84, no. 3 (2013): 30-37.

Standards 3 and 4. These differences will affect the choice of learning activities, instructional strategies, lesson plan design, and classroom routines.

For example, the Tactical Games Model (TGM) primarily focuses on Standard 2, so the content of the units centers on understanding tactics and strategies related to games. To learn tactics and strategies, the model recommends an instructional delivery system for how to accomplish that curricular focus based on assumptions about how students learn to use skills and strategies in a game. This system includes a lesson plan format that emphasizes cognitive learning before psychomotor learning, specific questioning techniques to assess cognitive learning, and physical activities centered on strategies and tactics in the form of modified games and situated learning experiences. Every decision about how to teach and what to teach can be guided by the TGM framework.

Using curriculum and instructional models is equivalent to following a teaching blueprint designed to enhance a student’s physical education experience and opportunity to learn meaningful knowledge and skills. To select an appropriate instructional model, teachers should answer the following questions:

- What are the main ideas that I want students to learn from the curriculum?
- Which models support learning those main ideas?

- What key strategies or concepts do these models use to teach the main ideas? How do these strategies or concepts align with my district's or my personal philosophy (or both) about student learning?
- Of those models, how well does my context (equipment, time, space, students' abilities, students' interests) meet the requirements for implementation?

Even though some models emphasize certain learning outcomes over others, there are foundational outcomes (e.g., how to lead a healthy lifestyle) that should not be neglected in a quality physical education program. As stated earlier in this chapter, physical educators can affect students' health-related fitness, and this objective is supported by several public health organizations (e.g., World Health Organization [WHO], Centers for Disease Control and Prevention [CDC], American Alliance for Health) as a strategy to combat rising obesity rates and promote physically active lifestyles (Houston & Kulinna, 2014). Physical education can make such an impact by utilizing an approach in which teachers embed fitness education into all instructional units (Institute of Medicine [IOM], 2013). **Fitness education** is considered a subcomponent of the total physical education program; it is more than conducting fitness testing or making sure that students sweat and get their heart rates up in class. It is an instructional approach and a learning process "of acquiring knowledge, skills and values; experiencing regular participation in physical activity; and promoting healthy nutrition choices to attain life-enhancing health-related fitness" (SHAPE America, 2012, p. 1). Implementing programs such as the Presidential Youth Fitness Program (PYFP) will assist in the delivery of fitness education as well as assessing students on fitness gains. To support physical educators in delivering fitness education, SHAPE America created a guidance document, *Instructional Framework for Fitness Education in Physical Education*, which suggests grade-level applications for helping students to adopt a healthy lifestyle. This framework, along with the *Appropriate and Inappropriate Practices Related to* Fitness *Testing* position statement (which can be found at www.shapeamerica.org/Common/Uploaded%20files/uploads/pdfs/2018/advocacy/position-statements/Appropriate-and-Inappropriate-Uses-of-Fitness-Testing-FINAL-3-6-17.pdf) can and should be used with any curriculum or instructional model to ensure that students are obtaining the knowledge and skills necessary to obtain and maintain a health-enhancing level of fitness.

The instructional model that you choose to implement can greatly affect your students' motivation to participate in physical education. As shown in table 5.3, the model will influence decisions about activities, assessment tools, feedback mechanisms, and how you will interact with students during the lesson. By linking curriculum, instruction, and assessment, you will greatly improve students' ability to succeed. For more detailed information on instructional models and using them to link curriculum, instruction, and assessment, look at Metzler's 2011 book, *Instructional Models for Physical Education.*

Assessment in Instruction

Chapter 4 discusses how formative and summative assessments can be used to document students' progress in meeting grade-span learning indicators and intended outcomes. Districts may require that teachers utilize common grade-level assessments, but outside of those obligations, teachers have to select appropriate assessment tools to monitor student learning. Remember that continuously evaluating student learning to determine your effectiveness is a key element in delivering appropriate instruction. Embedding assessment into the curriculum and instruction will greatly benefit students in that it allows you to adapt instruction to what your students need in order to progress. Assessment data may show that you need to reteach a concept or that you can provide more challenging tasks for students.

Curriculum and instructional models can help you decide what to assess and how to assess it. They recommend specific ways to deliver feedback so that students can meet the stated grade-span learning indicators and intended outcomes. Since each model has a primary learning domain, some assessment tools will be more useful than others in reaching the identified objectives. Rubrics, checklists, portfolios, written exams, and skills tests are all tools that you can use to assess learning. Choosing how to assess student learning can be difficult. Figure 5.1 lists several questions that can guide you in choosing an effective assessment tool. Keep in mind that you don't want to create or select assessments independent of your curriculum and instruction. If you are creating your own assessments, the References and Resources list for this chapter (located at the back of this book) provides numerous sources with information on developing formative and summative assessments.

Content Knowledge

Content knowledge is knowledge of the subject matter students will learn and use in physical activities. In physical education, it includes knowledge of fundamental movements, motor learning, motor development, exercise physiology, sport-specific technical and tactical strategies, and motivational theories. Content knowledge enables teachers to identify what their students are to learn and why they need to learn it. There is no end to the depth of content knowledge that you can use to enhance your teaching. Ongoing professional development in areas related to your position can help you better implement a high-quality physical education program. You must expect to never stop learning. Increasing your content knowledge is foundational to instruction; you can't confidently teach what you don't know.

Physical educators are in a unique position in the education of a child in that they can potentially affect health-related fitness and motor skill acquisition, which are extremely influential in the path to lifelong health and fitness. Understanding the physiological principles of training for the health-related components of fitness and the critical elements of various motor skills will enhance your instructional strategies. Since physical education is largely learning through moving, lessons are often training sessions in which students are working to develop the five components of physical fitness (cardiorespiratory fitness, muscular strength, muscular endurance, flexibility, and body composition) as well as improve motor skills. For example, you can use training methods such as circuit training or interval training (moderate or high intensity) to help students improve their cardiorespiratory endurance; for flexibility, you can design lessons using dynamic, static passive, or static active stretches. Students will learn the fundamental motor skills necessary to achieve health-enhancing levels of fitness by participating in developmentally appropriate activities that are improving their fitness. Your ability to deliver instruction that allows students to learn while doing primarily comes from understanding motor development, exercise physiology, and motor learning concepts.

A recommended strategy for increasing your content knowledge is to thoroughly study your curriculum and develop a study plan for learning the content. If your school or district does not have an established curriculum, then

FIGURE 5.1 Questions for Choosing and Designing Effective Assessments

- Does the assessment match the specific instructional objectives and targeted learning domains?
- Does the assessment enable students to demonstrate their progress and proficiency level?
- Does the assessment use authentic, relevant tasks?
- Can the assessment be structured to measure several objectives?
- Does the assessment provide students with feedback they can use to improve future performance?
- Is the assessment time-efficient and realistic for my context?
- Does the assessment meet student-intended learning outcomes?
- Is the chosen assessment free of bias?

Adapted from J. Herman, P. Aschbacher, and L. Winters, *A Practical Guide to Alternative Assessment* (ASCD, 1992)

LEADERSHIP IN ACTION

Quality of Instruction

Don Cain, PhD

Physical education and health coordinator, Columbus City Schools, Ohio

Quality instruction starts with the end goal in mind. We ask our health and physical educators, *What do you want the students to demonstrate as a result of your student learning objectives, lessons, and units? Are the objectives, lessons, and units aligned to the district's standards and benchmarks?* The final question is *How will you know that your students have reached your stated learning objectives?*

To answer all of these questions, school districts must provide an appropriate curriculum. Here at Columbus City Schools in Ohio, we provide a comprehensive and appropriate health and physical education curriculum. To ensure that we have a comprehensive and appropriate curriculum, our district elicits assistance from practicing teachers to help with the development of the curriculum. The district provides a balanced approach in which the state of Ohio has identified required state evaluations and the district develops (with considerable teacher input) the outcomes. Our teachers enrich and adapt the curriculum and determine the appropriate instructional strategies through these evaluations and outcomes.

The next area in quality instruction is having access to all the curriculum materials and resources that were developed. Gone are the days when teachers pulled from a shelf of curriculum materials in a binder. In the 21st century, teachers need to have access to resources 24 hours a day, seven days a week—in an environment that is easily accessible. Our district is able to post all curriculum resources so that teachers can place these materials on their mobile devices and view them when needed while in the gym, at home, or in the office.

The last area within quality instruction is addressed at the beginning of each year, through three full days of professional development activities. During these three days, teachers are instructed through lecture and hands-on demonstrations on how best to implement the posted curriculum. During this time, updates and best practices are shared throughout the day to ensure that teachers have the ability to implement all newly acquired instructional strategies that were delivered. At this point, it's up to the individual teacher to place all of these strategies in action by delivering the best-quality lesson for all students.

---

use the national standards or your state standards and grade-span learning indicators and intended outcomes as your curriculum. In your study plan, identify strengths and weaknesses related to your understanding of the content and then identify resources that you can use to improve on your weaknesses. Throughout the school year, commit to increasing your knowledge in at least one content area. Additional resources for improving your content knowledge and instructional strategies that can help students learn through movement are listed in the References and Resources.

Creating an Inclusive Environment

Classrooms are composed of diverse learners who are of different ethnicities, races, cultures, abilities, and genders. Being able to deliver quality instruction requires that you learn who your students are. As mentioned in the previous chapter, physical activity preferences can be influenced by cultural and ethnic norms. In addition, students' cognitive, physical, and communicative abilities will guide how you deliver the curriculum and choose instructional strategies. Possibly one of the most challenging aspects of instruction is to develop a positive and inclusive environment in which all students feel safe, supported, and challenged to achieve.

Not only is it considered appropriate instruction to develop an inclusive environment, but it is also a legal responsibility for physical educators. The Individuals with Disabilities Education Act (IDEA) is a federal law mandating that all children with disabilities receive physical education and that they be educated in the least restrictive environment (LRE) to meet their unique needs. The LRE is one that allows children with disabilities to interact and participate with their peers to the maximum extent possible while affording them the most success. For some students with disabilities, the LRE may involve inclusion, which means integrating them into the general physical education setting. **Inclusion** requires providing adapted physical education since the student with a disability is learning alongside peers without disabilities and will need modifications or accommodations (or both) to fully participate. Adapted physical education is a service, not a placement, that is provided to students with disabilities in the most appropriate environment (Lieberman et al., 2025). For some, the LRE may be a segregated class; however, removal from the general classroom setting is to be used only when the nature or severity of the disability will not allow for inclusion with the use of supplementary aids or services. The following are reasons that students with disabilities may require an alternative environment:

- There is a probability of harm to the student with a disability or probability of harm to other participants inside the general education classroom (based on reasonable medical judgments).
- The student with a disability is a disruptive force; the student detracts from other students' ability to learn.
- The student with a disability will not derive educational benefits in the general classroom, and the benefit of having a separate instructional setting significantly outweighs the benefits of inclusion (French et al., 1998; Yelm, 1998).

It is possible that in a classroom of 30 students you may have 3 students with Individualized Education Programs (IEPs), because roughly 15 percent of the public school population, or 7.5 million students, receive special education services (National Center for Education Statistics, 2024). What does this statistic mean for you in delivering appropriate instruction to all students in that class? It means that you will want to understand the students' disabilities and instructional strategies that you can use to meet their unique needs. Table 5.4 presents the 13 categories of disabilities as defined by IDEA, listed in order according to the greatest number of students receiving services for that disability. Students diagnosed with any of these disabilities may require an IEP, which outlines a plan to ensure the student receives specialized instruction and services to reach personalized goals. An IEP team will examine a variety of factors and determine the appropriate placement for the student. Typical components of a physical education IEP include present level of performance, short-term goals, annual goals, evaluation procedures, assessment modifications, support services, and supplementary aids (Lieberman & Houston-Wilson, 2025). Successful inclusion occurs when a physical education teacher can use the information in the IEP and adapt or adjust the regular curriculum setting to meet the needs of the student. There are several strategies that physical educators can use for improving the learning outcomes of students with disabilities in an inclusive environment. Using these strategies can help students become fully included in the class as opposed to being mere spectators. The strategies include the following (Lieberman et al., 2021; Grenier et al., 2017; Qi & Ha, 2012):

- Implementing peer tutoring and cooperative learning strategies
- Enlisting the help of paraprofessionals and adapted physical education specialists or occupational therapists
- Collaborating with all members of the IEP team
- Utilizing a Universal Design for Learning framework to plan for and structure learning experiences

Additionally, some students in your classroom may have 504 plans as governed by another federal law known as Section 504 of the Rehabilitation Act of 1973. This law prohibits discrimination based on disability. It applies to students who have a disabling condition that is not specifically listed under IDEA but who need accommodations or services (French et al., 1998). According to Section 504, "An individual with a disability means any person who: (i) has a mental or physical impairment that substantially limits one or more major life activity; (ii) has a record of such an impairment; or (iii) is regarded as having such an impairment" (U.S. Congress, 1973). For example, in physical education, many students with asthma or diabetes may have a 504 plan that requires the teacher to modify exercise intensities to meet their needs but does not require a specialized program.

Students without diagnosed disabilities may also bring a unique set of individual constraints (e.g., fitness level, motor skill competency,

TABLE 5.4 IDEA Disability Categories

Federal Disability Term	Alternative Terms, Descriptions	Percentage of Students Receiving Special Education Services (12.9%)*
Autism	Autism spectrum disorder	11.5
Deaf-blindness	Significant hearing and vision loss	>0.1
Developmental delay	Nonspecific disability category for students aged 3-9 who may need special education services due to delays in physical, cognitive, communicative, social-emotional, or adaptive development, or more than one of these	6.8
Emotional disturbance	Behavior disorder, emotional disability	4.9
Hearing impairment	Deafness or hard of hearing	1.0
Intellectual disability	Neurodevelopmental disorders	6.0
Multiple disabilities	Presence of two or more disabilities so that one cannot be identified as the primary disability	1.8
Orthopedic impairment	Physical disability; impaired ability to move or perform motor activities	0.5
Other health impairment	Disease, disorder, or condition that limits a child's strength, energy, or alertness, such as cancer, diabetes, or heart disease	15.3
Specific learning disability	Disorders related to difficulty in processing information (reading, writing, and computing)	32.7
Speech or language impairment	Communication disorder	18.9
Traumatic brain injury (TBI)	Brain injury that may affect learning, behavior, social skills, and language	0.4
Visual impairment	Low vision, blindness	0.4

*Statistics source: U.S. Department of Education, Office of Special Education Programs, Individuals With Disabilities Education Act (IDEA) database. Retrieved February 25, 2022, from https://data.ed.gov/dataset/idea-section618-data-products-state-level-data-files. See *Digest of Education Statistics 2021*, table 204.60.

Data from National Center for Education Statistics. (2022). Students With Disabilities. *Condition of Education*. U.S. Department of Education, Institute of Education Sciences. Retrieved from https://nces.ed.gov/programs/coe/indicator/cgg

motivation, anxiety level) that affect learning and performing skills for which teachers will also have to make accommodations to ensure success (Gagen & Getchell, 2004). Constraints can be in the form of structural or functional characteristics related to a child's fitness level, intellectual capabilities, social skills, or emotional well-being. All of these factors affect how a student interacts with the curriculum, instruction, and environment. Table 5.5 presents a template for planning how to adapt activities for all students in your classroom. If you know that a student has an individual constraint, you should consider how that constraint will interact with the environment, equipment, task or game rules, or your instructional methods. Knowing a student's constraints and how to adapt activities allows a physical educator to create a positive, inclusive environment and deliver instruction that allows all students to be successful.

Since there are such varying abilities and individual characteristics in physical education, how you choose to group students in a classroom can greatly affect the environment. To maximize the number of practice opportunities that students have in physical education, it is recommended that students work in small groups (SHAPE America, 2014). Very rarely should physical education teachers use full-sided games; students who are typically lower skilled can hide in the large setting and not have a chance to utilize the skills they are learning. Student grouping examples include

TABLE 5.5 Template for Adapting Activities for Student Constraints

Constraints	Interacts With Equipment, Task Rules, Environment, or Instruction	Modifications or Accommodations to Improve Performance Outcome
Autism: auditory sensitivity	Environment Instruction	Allow student to wear sound-reducing headphones in class; don't play music. Use visual cues for start and stop signals as opposed to a whistle or bell.
Limited coordination	Equipment Task rules	Increase surface area on manipulatives (e.g., larger ball, larger bat). Allow for more than one bounce or hit. Allow manipulatives to be stationary or slow moving.
Short attention span	Instruction	Provide brief instructional periods more frequently. Use visuals along with auditory instruction. Vary activities to prevent boredom.
Visual impairments	Equipment	Use beeper or bell ball in activities.

From J. Greenberg and J. LoBianco, *Organization and Administration of Physical Education,* 2nd ed. (Human Kinetics, 2026). Based on Gagen and Getchell (2004).

coed, single-gender, ability-based, and mixed-ability groupings. These grouping options have limitations and advantages. Some research indicates that single-gender groupings can greatly enhance physical activity levels and skill achievement of female students (Gabbei, 2004; Murphy et al., 2014). The nature of the activity often influences male and female students' motivation to participate, so alternating between coed and single-gender tasks depending on the activity may enhance performance and participation (Gabbei, 2004). Ability grouping can help both high- and low-achieving students reach higher levels of success by adjusting instruction to meet their ability level. Ability grouping has the potential to motivate students to personally improve more, but it can also be discouraging for low-achieving students in that they may feel segregated and of lesser importance than the skilled students in the class (Fletcher, 2008). Alternating between mixed-ability and ability-based groups has been shown to increase students' pleasure in physical education (Lentillon-Kaestner & Patelli, 2016). Physical educators will want to select the grouping strategy that most effectively supports learning and achievement for their student population, and this task may involve gathering student input.

Teachers have control over many factors that facilitate the delivery of quality instruction. Your content and pedagogical knowledge and the ability to create an inclusive environment can improve daily as you commit to learning and applying best practices. Other influential factors, such as class size, scheduling, facilities, and equipment, may not be within your control. While administrators, policies, and funding often dictate these factors, you do have the power to advocate for organizational change for the betterment of your program. Chapter 8 addresses how you can work to improve your equipment and facility situation. The next section addresses institutional factors that you have the potential to change through advocacy.

Institutional-Related Factors

As stated earlier, several institutional factors influence the quality of physical education independent of the teacher-related factors. Institutional factors are often determined by legislative policy, school board policy, or, in some cases, individual school policy. These factors are often identified as the amount of time allocated to physical education on a daily basis, weekly basis, semester basis, or annually; the size of the class as well as how the physical education classes are scheduled, including daily or block scheduling patterns; and the attitudes and beliefs of the decision makers regarding the purpose of physical education.

Time Allotted to Physical Education

State and district policy are the driving forces behind how much time is allotted to physical education. In states that have a law specifying the minimum number of minutes required, students spend more time in physical education—approximately 27 more minutes per week at the elementary level and 60 more minutes per week at the middle school level (Perna et al., 2012). A quality program offers at least 150 minutes per week (30 minutes a day) of physical education in elementary schools and at least 225 minutes per week (45 minutes a day) in middle schools and high schools (SHAPE America, 2015a). This amount of time is recommended so that students can participate in moderate-to-vigorous physical activity for at least 50 percent of physical education class time and have the opportunity to learn physical education concepts. However, only 8.3 percent of elementary schools, 6 percent of middle schools, and 4 percent of high schools require daily physical education or its time equivalent for the entire school year (36 weeks) for students in all grades in the school (Piekarz-Porter et al., 2021).

Why is so little time allotted to physical education in many districts? First, consider the ongoing struggle that physical education has had in showing its value and worth. Many administrators are still unaware of the various benefits of a quality physical education program. The main answer is that since standardized test scores in math and language arts are typically the only evidence used to determine whether a school appears to be succeeding, administrators often reduce time in curricular areas that are not tested. Such reductions have led to decreasing or eliminating physical education classes, recess, and other extracurricular physical activity opportunities during the school day. Nationwide, the percentage of high school students attending daily physical education classes all five days of the week decreased from 29.4 percent in 2013 to 25.9 percent in 2019 (CDC, 2021a). However, research indicates that reducing physical education time does not necessarily equate to greater academic achievement and standardized test scores (CDC, 2010; Ericsson, 2008; Sallis et al., 1999; Wilkins et al., 2003). In fact, a growing body of research shows the positive impact that physical activity has on academic performance through various mechanisms: physiological, cognitive, and emotional (Ardoy et al., 2014). Physical activity during the school day can prepare students to do cognitively challenging work (Hillman et al., 2009). Figure 5.2 shows how brain activity is enhanced through physical activity; it depicts brain activity during sitting and during walking. Time spent in physical education is not only

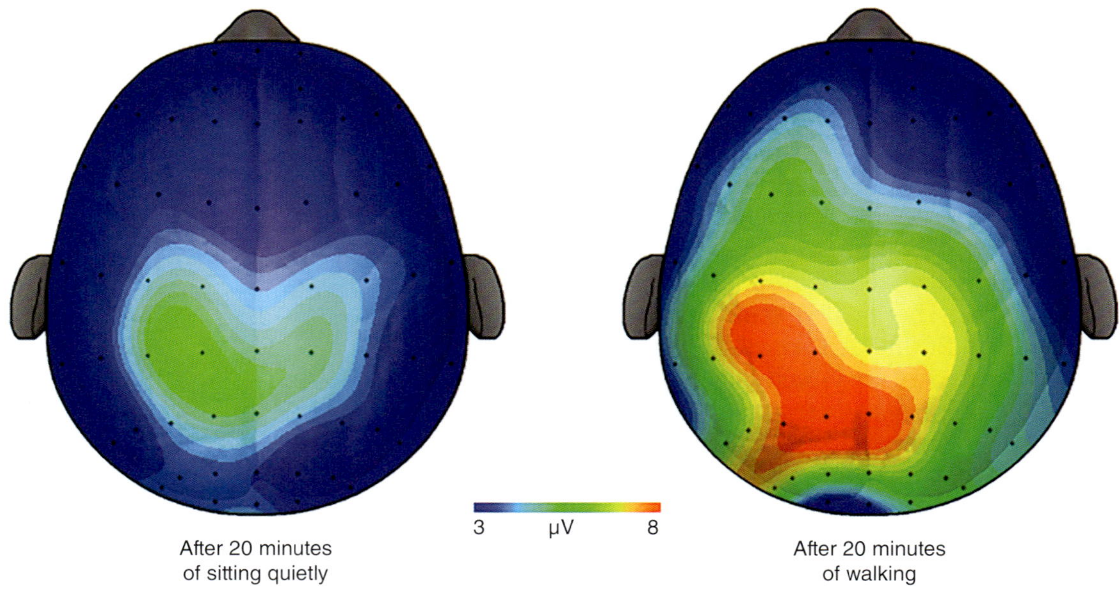

FIGURE 5.2 Brain activity: sitting versus walking.

Courtesy of Dr. Charles H. Hillman.

improving students' overall health status; it is also enhancing academic achievement.

If you are in a school district that has the need for more physical education minutes to deliver quality instruction, you can organize a committee to present policy changes to your school board and superintendent. However, before advocating for a greater quantity of physical education minutes, ensure that you can provide quality physical education. It will be difficult to convince administration of the need for more of something that is less than top quality. Table 5.6 provides you with a plan for collecting evidence that can be beneficial in a proposal for more physical education minutes. You should be able to use data to paint a picture of what physical education is like now and what it can be through increased instructional time.

TABLE 5.6 Advocating for Quality Physical Education: Data Collection

Data	Question(s) to Answer	Potential Data Sources
Obesity rates	What percentage of students are obese or overweight? How might obesity affect our students' ability to learn?	• The Youth Risk Behavior Surveillance System (YRBSS) (CDC, 2021a) • Resource article: Burkhalter & Hillman (2011) • NHANES (CDC, 2021b)
Physical activity rates	How many students are active 60 min a day?	• YRBSS (CDC, 2021a) • CDC, Healthy Schools Facts • National Survey of Children's Health (NSCH) (Child and Adolescent Health Measurement Initiative, n.d.)
Motor skill proficiency	What percentage of students are at grade level for motor skill milestones? How might our students' cognitive performance be enhanced through motor skills proficiency?	• PE Metrics (SHAPE America, 2019) • Standardized, grade-level motor skill assessments • Resource article: van der Fels et al. (2015)
Physical fitness performance	What percentage of students meet the healthy fitness zone for cardiorespiratory, muscular endurance, and flexibility standards? What percentage of students would be able to pass career-related fitness tests, such as the military, police force, or firefighting entrance requirements?	• FitnessGram • Career-related fitness assessments
Success stories	What do students in the current physical education program say about their experience? How are students benefiting?	• Student interviews • Parent interviews
Standards met	What outcomes are achieved through the current program? What grade-span learning indicators and intended outcomes are not achieved due to lack of time?	• Curriculum map • National standards and grade-span learning indicators • State standards and grade-span learning indicators and intended outcomes
Academic and health outcomes	How can students' health and academic outcomes be positively affected through increased physical education instruction?	• CDC data • Resource article: Trudeau & Shepard (2008) • Relevant books: *Brain Rules* by John Medina; *Sitting Kills, Moving Heals* by Joan Vernikos; *Spark* by John J. Ratey

Class Size

Class size has a direct impact on instruction. The number of students in a class affects the instructional strategies teachers use, how equipment and space are utilized, and how feedback is given. The recommended size of a physical education class is a maximum teacher-to-student ratio of 1:25 for elementary school, 1:30 for middle school, and 1:35 for high school because those numbers are relatively consistent with other subject areas (National Association for Sport and Physical Education [NASPE], 2006b). Unfortunately, the reality is that some teachers may average 40 to 70 students in their physical education classes (Hardman, 2004). Studies have shown that in physical education, high student-to-teacher ratios and large class sizes are associated with reduced student physical activity and a slower rate of learning (Burgeson et al., 2001). Students in large classes receive less individualized instruction and may have fewer practice opportunities, resulting in poorer achievement. In addition, large class sizes can inhibit proper supervision and effective management, which increases the likelihood of student injuries and potential negligence claims against teachers (Murphy & Beh, 2014). Adhering to recommended class sizes is a form of risk management for districts in that it can minimize future liability losses since teachers are able to more properly supervise students and deliver appropriate instruction.

Most states have at least one policy that limits the number of students that may be in a general education classroom. Regardless of the state policy, school districts can establish their own caps on class size as part of their contracts with teachers' unions, specific to grade-level configurations that vary between elementary, middle, and high schools. According to a 2016 School Health Policies and Practices Study (SHPPS) report, 25.9 percent of districts had adopted a policy specifying a maximum student-to-teacher ratio for physical education in elementary school, 25.0 percent of districts had adopted such a policy for physical education in middle school, and 30.5 percent of districts had adopted such a policy for physical education in high school (CDC, 2016, p. 18).

Class size policies work to ensure that physical education classes can provide a safe environment that maximizes learning efficiency. If class sizes are overwhelming and teachers are unable to receive assistance from building administration in lowering class sizes, then a potential action may be to solicit the assistance of the teachers' union in creating contract language for class size and teacher workload.

Class Scheduling

A teacher's capacity to deliver appropriate instruction can also be affected by class scheduling. In the elementary setting, students typically attend physical education during the classroom teacher's planning period, which drives the timing of when each grade has physical education. It is not uncommon for classes to come to physical education back-to-back with little time for the physical education teacher to reorganize for the next class; therefore, it is essential for the scheduling of the grade levels to facilitate a quick and smooth transition between classes. It is easier for the physical education teacher to transition quickly if classes are in ascending or descending chronological grade order. That way, the teacher can use similar equipment and facility organization. For example, it would be more efficient to transition between two kindergarten classes if the classes came to physical education one after the other, rather than to have a 5th grade class in between, when the equipment and lesson plan would have to be changed significantly to be developmentally appropriate. Furthermore, having a 1st grade class directly after the kindergarten class would be appropriate in that similar equipment could be used with some added locomotor skills or combinations of skills not used in the kindergarten class. Lastly, if substantial grade jumps in the schedule are necessary, it is most beneficial if they can take place after a break or planning period if possible. In other words, if it is essential that 5th grade attend physical education after the kindergarten classes, then a planning period should be scheduled in between or 5th grade should attend after lunch to allow the teacher time to make needed changes in equipment for the next lesson. This advice is not meant to minimize how difficult school scheduling can be; rather, it highlights how scheduling can affect a physical educator's ability to deliver quality instruction at the elementary level.

At the secondary level, class scheduling most affects instruction through block scheduling. Block scheduling is a system for scheduling classes so that students meet fewer times a week but for longer periods. In block scheduling, students have fewer total classes in a day and do not see each teacher every day of the week. Teachers must be prepared to deliver lessons upward of 90 minutes at a time, which requires a different organization scheme than a 40- to 50-minute lesson. A considerable amount of time can be wasted in a long period if teachers are unable to maintain consistent routines and establish effective transitions.

Although you may not always have control over having a block or traditional schedule, you will be able to control how you plan and deliver the instruction. A recommended strategy for organizing extended-period lessons is the three-part lesson design as shown in table 5.7, which is slightly modified for physical education to include an instant activity at the beginning of class. Following an established lesson design will help both the teacher and the students maximize learning and movement during an extended period.

Attitudes and Beliefs About Physical Education

Aside from the ability to deliver appropriate instruction, the most influential factor on instruction is the attitudes and beliefs that the district, community members, parents, and students have about physical education. In general, it is important for stakeholders to support and value physical education in order to make any positive changes to institutional factors that affect instruction and the delivery of quality physical education programs. Many of the beliefs about physical education affect the delivery of instruction in a district, who delivers the instruction, and the frequency of instruction. Districts may create and implement policies on minutes in physical education, class size, teacher certification, waivers, and online physical education based on their beliefs about the value of physical education. Some students may never be able to experience physical education or have a very limited experience because of district policies that inhibit the delivery of a quality physical education program.

Other Factors

In addition to the teacher-related factors and the institutional factors that influence quality instruction and the physical education environment, several other factors should be considered. These factors include the impact of certified physical education versus noncertified physical education teachers, exemptions and waivers, and the delivery of physical education through online opportunities.

Certified Versus Noncertified Physical Education Teachers

Through legislative mandates, states create and implement policies related to the requirements for teacher preparation programs, how to achieve teacher certification, and whether

TABLE 5.7 Three-Part Lesson Design for Physical Education Extended Period

Instant Activity (5-10 Min)	Fitness and skill drills
Step 1: Explanation (15-20 Min)	Daily objective(s) and agenda Connections to previous learning, review Teaching new concepts, skills, knowledge
Step 2: Application (40-45 Min)	Experiencing the concepts in guided practice Skill application in practice sessions Demonstrating understanding of the concepts through movement
Step 3: Synthesis (15-20 Min)	Assessment Re-teaching Closure

Based on Canady and Rettig (1995).

physical education needs to be taught by certified physical education teachers. Obtaining a teaching license or certification establishes that physical education teachers have completed state-mandated requirements that prepare them to effectively teach their subject. However, only 39 percent of states, including the District of Columbia, require K-12 physical education teachers to be state certified or licensed and endorsed to teach physical education (National Institutes of Health, 2021). Of greater concern is that only 23 percent of states require adapted physical education teachers to be certified, licensed, or credentialed.

Research has shown that students' experience in physical education is diminished when instruction is delivered by a generalist teacher and not a certified physical education teacher, and that certified physical education specialists can provide more and longer opportunities for students to meet physical activity guidelines compared with classroom teachers trained to teach physical education (DeCorby et al., 2005; McKenzie et al., 2001). Certified physical education teachers are prepared to deliver developmentally appropriate curriculum and instruction that meet the needs of diverse learners. Generalist teachers may often provide supervised play or haphazard lessons that do not follow an intentional scope and sequence due to a lack of preparation time and knowledge (DeCorby et al., 2005). Generalist teachers have not received the specialized training necessary to implement instruction that allows students to learn the knowledge and skills needed to obtain physical literacy, and they may find it difficult to plan lessons to support student learning. This lack of training is of greatest concern at the elementary level because that is the time for students to learn the fundamental motor skills necessary for lifelong health and fitness. Even if states do not have a policy that requires physical education to be taught by a certified physical education teacher, districts can create and implement their own policy. Establishing such a policy demonstrates the value that the district places on physical education. If the physical education program is to develop physically literate individuals, then it needs teachers who are trained to deliver that type of standards-based instruction. The evidence is unequivocal regarding the need for a continued effort to train physical education specialists as well as the need for schools to continue to employ them as the main teaching force who are designing and implementing health-enhancing physical education programs to the fullest extent (IOM, 2013, p. 226). Additionally, to stay updated on new instructional strategies and methods, all physical education teachers should attend professional development on a regular basis, as described in chapter 12.

In addition, many certified physical education teachers can assist in planning and providing before-, during-, and after-school physical activity programs. Physical education teachers can create a culture of health and wellness at their school by utilizing their expertise in many ways. You can see just how vast the opportunities are for a physical education teacher to make an impact on the health and well-being of students by looking at the Comprehensive School Physical Activity Program (CSPAP), as expressed in chapter 3.

Exemptions and Waivers

There are two types of physical education **waivers**: exemptions and substitutions. Thirty states have policies that allow student exemptions from physical education, and 31 states allow for substitutions (SHAPE America, 2016). *Exemption* means that the student is released from physical education class and any credit requirements attached to the class. Exemptions are typically based on religious beliefs, physical disability, health reasons, or early graduation. Unfortunately, physicians may excuse students from physical education based on a disability or medical condition instead of specifying what types of adaptations the child may need for that condition during physical activity (Lieberman & Houston-Wilson, 2025). As mentioned previously in the chapter, teachers can provide adapted physical education to students of varying abilities. It is possible that many exemptions are solely the result of miscommunication between parents, physicians, and teachers about what physical education is and what it can provide to the student. Since physical education is a legal obligation for students with disabilities, no student should be excused from physical education due to a medical condition unless it would be deemed life-threatening. Even if students cannot physically participate in activity, they may still be able to complete physical education cognitive tasks, so an exemption would not be necessary. In addition, most exemptions can be eliminated by having the physician submit to the school what the student *can* do rather than what the student can*not* do.

At the high school level, many districts offer substitutions to waive the physical education requirement so that students receive the necessary credits to graduate, but they don't have to take a physical education class to receive that credit. Common substitutions are Junior Reserve Officer Training (JROTC), cheerleading, band, chorus, and interscholastic or recreational sports. Districts may choose to allow substitutions because they believe that these experiences are equivalent to a physical education class. However, as table 5.8 shows, the goals of physical education are distinctly different from those of athletics and physical activity experiences. There really is no substitute for physical education, just as there is no substitute for learning in other content areas such as math, science, or language arts. In reality, the knowledge and skills taught in physical education are just as imperative for a successful future as those things taught in other subjects. If students can substitute a variety of unstandardized experiences for physical education, they may not have the opportunity to learn the knowledge and skills that can prevent them from acquiring chronic diseases and achieving lifelong health and fitness. Essentially, students are misled into thinking that such experiences are equivalent and that they will receive the same benefits from participating in athletics or band as they would from physical education. This false equivalency undermines the value of physical education, and allowing for substitutions means that students can opt out of physical education simply because this may be an easier route to earning credit. The learning accountability systems in common

TABLE 5.8 The Differences Between Physical Education, Physical Activity, and Athletics

Physical Education	Physical Activity	Athletics
• *Physical education* is defined as a planned, sequential program of curricula and instruction that helps students develop the knowledge, attitudes, motor skills, confidence, and self-management skills needed to adopt and maintain physically active and healthy lifestyles. • Physical education, like other content areas, is guided by national and state physical education standards and grade-span learning indicators and intended outcomes. • Physical education holds students accountable for learning how to develop healthy and active lifestyles that will increase their quality of life through improved emotional and social health and that will lower their risk for chronic diseases. • Teachers design instruction to support students of all abilities to reach their highest level of achievement.	• *Physical activity* is defined by the CDC as any bodily movement produced by skeletal muscles that results in energy expenditure. • CDC states that 60 min of physical activity is needed along with daily physical education. Physical activity may include recreational, fitness, and sport activities such as jumping rope, playing soccer, and lifting weights, as well as daily activities such as walking to the store, taking the stairs, or raking the leaves. • Good physical education teaches individuals to have the knowledge, skills, and confidence to enjoy a lifetime of physical activity. Physical activity and exercise are the application of what is learned in physical education class. • Children need time to learn and practice basic locomotor skills and knowledge so that they can apply proper technique and understanding outside of the classroom.	• *Athletics* is described as a diversion requiring physical exertion and competition, a contest between athletes. • While athletics participation is a valuable part of school life, athletics represents extracurricular activities that are not aligned to any national physical education standards and grade-span learning indicators. • Athletics typically focuses on becoming successful in one sport. Athletics provides sport-specific instruction, but the coach is not responsible for teaching any knowledge or skills outside of that sport. • Athletics holds students accountable for performing the sport at a high level. • Athletics does not promote equal participation by all students. Athletes who are less skilled tend to have fewer opportunities to participate and perform.

Adapted from Office of the Superintendent of Public Instruction (2013).

substitutions are often less rigorous, and students don't necessarily have to demonstrate any type of improvement or learning. They may simply have to show up and go through the motions. Since 2005, through the National Association for Sport and Physical Education (NASPE), SHAPE America and the American Heart Association have used stronger language than in the past, saying to states, "Do not allow" waivers and substitutions (NASPE, 2006a). The guidance document *The Essential Components of Physical Education* (ECPE) specifies that waivers and substitutions should be prohibited (SHAPE America, 2015a). Additionally, as an accountability measure, schools must have eliminated waivers and substitutions or cite progress toward elimination as documented in the Physical Education Program Checklist to support the ECPE (SHAPE America, 2015b). Perhaps the added accountability will be the turning point to achieve compliance.

If the knowledge and skills outlined in the National Physical Education Standards & Grade-Span Learning Indicators are of worth to students and society, then administrators need to safeguard that learning through policies that prohibit exemptions or substitutions.

Online Physical Education

Technology has brought vast changes to educational settings across all subject areas. From the Internet to ebooks to personal computer tablets and gaming devices, students have become saturated with technology. Even the youngest of children seem to have familiarity with technology. For college students, it has become the norm with distance education programs and online classes and degrees, especially during and after the emergence of the COVID-19 pandemic. The U.S. Department of Education (2023) defines online learning as "a course provided by an institution under which the institution provides instructional materials, by mail or electronic transmission, including examinations on the materials, to students who are separated from the instructors."

Safeguarding learning should also include policy and quality control for online physical education (OLPE). Prior to the onset of COVID-19, OLPE was a growing trend; 59 percent of states were allowing physical education credits to be earned through online courses (SHAPE America, 2016). Post COVID-19 OLPE has become more popular both as a necessity to deliver instruction and as a way to provide another option for students earning physical education credit (e.g., if they lack room in their schedule for face-to-face classes, need to make up credit, or are looking for an alternative to the traditional physical education class). Advantages to delivering physical education online include no space limitations, a flexible schedule, immediate feedback, and a personalized pace and learning experience. Disadvantages include less accountability for learning, technology barriers, and lack of social interaction. In addition, OLPE programs often focus more on cognitive development than increasing physical activity, which leads to the question whether this instructional method can appropriately meet the goals of physical education (Daum & Buschner, 2012).

A recommended strategy for utilizing OLPE in physical education programs is to use a hybrid or blended model of instruction (SHAPE America, 2017). This model requires some face-to-face instruction with a certified physical education teacher as well as instruction and assessment online. In this format, teachers could conduct physical fitness tests and motor skills testing (pre and post) in the face-to-face instruction and then students complete all other work online. Both synchronous and asynchronous delivery systems provide valuable learning opportunities for the delivery of online instruction. This model can provide an accountability piece so that students must demonstrate that they are achieving a health-enhancing level of fitness through their physical activity and that they are performing motor skill practice that leads to greater proficiency.

OLPE has the potential to be a successful tool in helping students learn physical education concepts if it adheres to certain criteria. First, it must be standards based and promote learning the grade-level content and skills. Second, it needs to utilize good instructional design that links content, instructional strategies, assessments, feedback mechanisms, and resources together in a way that allows students to demonstrate proficiency on the standards (Mohnsen, 2012). It may be easier to develop a course that aligns with the cognitive concepts of physical education, such as fitness foundations courses rather than team sports courses. Finally, OLPE needs to have a checklist of student prerequisites that outlines for students and parents what is necessary for success in the course, such as technology requirements, time management skills, and an adequate level of physical education knowledge and skill (SHAPE America, 2018). A more comprehensive view of OLPE can be found in chapter 9.

Policies related to waivers and online education work to improve the quality of instruction by ensuring that students receive a physical education experience that promotes physical literacy. If a student's only physical education experience is through an online course or participation on a sports team (or both), then the system has most likely failed to provide that student with a well-rounded education that leads to lifelong health and fitness habits. Using these options to ease scheduling burdens, alleviate potential credit deficiencies, or increase instructional time for other subjects may come at a cost to the student that materializes many years down the road.

Comprehensive School Physical Activity Program (CSPAP)

One of the most useful tools in changing attitudes and beliefs about physical education is the Comprehensive School Physical Activity Program (CSPAP) (see chapter 3). The program is a multicomponent approach that school districts and schools can use to help students meet the nationally recommended 60 minutes of physical activity each day and develop the knowledge, skills, and confidence to be physically active for a lifetime. This program emphasizes quality physical education as the foundation for a physically active lifestyle. It recommends using physical activity before, during, and after school; staff involvement; and family and community engagement to further help students be active and learn.

The CDC, in collaboration with SHAPE America, has developed a step-by-step guide for schools and school districts to develop, implement, and evaluate CSPAPs (SHAPE America, 2017). This guide provides tools for planning all aspects of a well-designed comprehensive physical education and physical activity program. Look in the References and Resources chapter 3 section for more information on using CSPAP to improve the quality of physical education in your program. Additional support materials for CSPAP can be found on the CDC website at www.cdc.gov/healthyschools/professional_development/e-learning/CSPAP/index.html.

Conclusion

Physical education is a comprehensive, progressive, and articulated program that aims to provide learners with quality PreK-12 instruction. The delivery of quality instruction is key to student achievement in obtaining the knowledge, skills, and attitudes necessary to become a physically literate individual. This chapter presented several instructional models to guide the delivery of a standards-based instructional program. Teachers and administrators need to work together to provide a positive learning experience for all students in physical education, ensuring that instruction is age and developmentally appropriate. Physical education may provide the only opportunity for many children to develop proficient motor skills; therefore, effective instructional strategies for motor skill acquisition are essential to enhance physically active lifestyles. A student's path to lifelong health and fitness becomes more promising through participation in high-quality physical education programs.

Although institutional situations may present challenges, with instruction delivered by certified physical education teachers, appropriate class sizes, and time allocations coordinated with class scheduling, most obstacles can be eliminated. Advocacy and quality programs can eliminate barriers to the delivery of high-quality instruction. The resources provided throughout this chapter, and listed at the back of the book, are intended to help you advocate for quality physical education that leads to physically literate individuals.

Review Questions

1. Explain how the Individuals with Disabilities Education Act (IDEA) affects physical education.
2. What instructional models may work best in a full-inclusion classroom that has 20 percent of students with an IEP? Explain why you would choose these models.
3. What data would you collect to advocate for more physical education minutes in your school district?
4. Summarize what is meant by *appropriate instruction* in physical education.
5. Write an example of a learning objective for the psychomotor, one for the affective, and one for the cognitive domains.
6. Fitness assessment is an important component of the overall instructional program. Differentiate between appropriate and inappropriate practices for fitness assessment.

» Visit HK*Propel* for reproducible forms.

CHAPTER 6

Teacher and Program Evaluation

Erin E. Centeio, Heather E. Erwin, and Jayne D. Greenberg

Photo by Marialys Vega, Crotalus Yearbook, Felix Varela Senior High

LEARNING OBJECTIVES

After reading this chapter, you will be able to do the following:

- Understand the purpose of teacher evaluations.
- Differentiate between teacher evaluation models.
- Identify how to assess teacher effectiveness.
- Align teacher evaluation to best practices.
- Explain the teacher observation and assessment process.
- Understand how to plan for teacher growth and professional development.
- Understand how to plan for and conduct program evaluation.

KEY CONCEPTS

observation
post-observation conference
program evaluation
scaffolding
teacher evaluation models

Effective teacher evaluation reflects the belief that everyone in a school plays a critical role in the education process. The overall purpose of teacher evaluation is to improve teaching practice and affect student outcomes. According to the National Education Association (NEA) Framework on Teacher Assessment and Evaluation,

> *The core purpose of teacher assessment and evaluation should be to strengthen the knowledge, skills, dispositions, and classroom practices of professional educators. Assessments are used to gather information, such as measuring performance or a skill and to offer feedback based on strengths and weaknesses to improve future performance. Evaluation, on the other hand, is used to document the level of achievement or performance that has been attained. This goal serves to promote student growth and learning. Comprehensive systems of continuous teacher education and professional growth help teachers master content, refine their teaching skills, critically analyze their own performance and their students' performance, and implement the changes needed to improve teaching and learning. (NEA, 2010, p.2)*

To better understand the relationship between student learning, the evaluation component, and assessment relating the student standards to teacher standards, the NEA further asserts that there is a relationship between student learning and teacher education and assessment. A concept map diagramming the relationship is shown in figure 6.1.

Research has shown that teacher **observation** alone provides only a few snapshots of a teacher's performance and that it is not an accurate predictor of a teacher's overall performance. According to Ennis (2014), the process of effective teaching is directly related to student learning of standards-based content. This claim is supported by Rink (2013), McKenzie and Lounsbery (2013), McKenzie and van der Mars (2015), and Lund and Veal (2013). Multiple measures should make up the evaluation to include student achievement data, student surveys, and teacher observations. Using a combination of measures can better tell the full story of a teacher's performance (Kane & Staiger, 2012, p. 26). This chapter will assist both physical education administrators and school site administrators in developing physical education teachers through observation and collection of student data. It will further provide administrators with the best practices

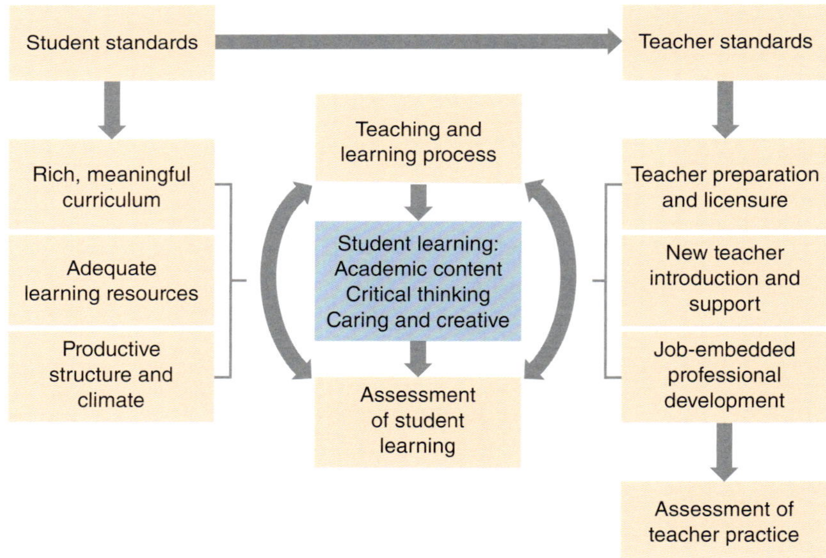

FIGURE 6.1 NEA concept map for a standards-based learning and assessment system.

Reprinted by permission from The National Education Association, *Teacher Assessment and Evaluation: The National Education Association's Framework for Transforming Education Systems to Support Effective Teaching and Improve Student Learning* (2010), 1. www.nea.org/assets/docs/HE/TeachrAssmntWhtPaperTransform10_2.pdf

and pedagogy related to a quality physical education class and reinforce the essentials of a quality physical education program as discussed in chapter 3.

Feedback from a combination of classroom observations and student data showing growth over the year can assist physical educators with the support they need to create a quality physical education program. In order to appropriately support teachers, it is important to establish clear expectations for each lesson and long-term goals aligned to the content. When ongoing evaluation of student learning is combined with formal and informal observations, teachers have the support necessary to plan more deliberately and facilitate learning in order to achieve desired student outcomes.

The assessment skills and strategies presented in this chapter will help you do the following:

- *Clarify expectations.* Create and outline clear performance expectations for teacher evaluation performance metrics. Develop supporting rubrics that are clear and aligned to best practices in teaching physical education.
- *Internalize the essentials of teacher evaluation.* Use an evaluation tool that reflects best practices in teaching specifically for physical education teaching and learning. Establish a formal process that includes observation, evaluation, and a post-observation conference.
- *Provide feedback.* Effectively communicate quality feedback in order to plan for and develop teacher growth. Provide feedback on strengths and areas for growth for effective teaching of physical education.
- *Drive professional development.* Using the teacher evaluation, collaborate with the teacher to determine a plan for professional growth.

Teacher Evaluation Models

Through various educational reforms, teacher evaluations and assessment have become a critical component for making policy decisions regarding tenure, merit pay, and professional growth; the most critical factor is teacher effectiveness in terms of student achievement gains. However, deciding on which instrument to use to evaluate teachers is not always easy. Many school districts form committees and make their decisions through collaborative efforts between the office of labor relations, teacher unions, administrators, and community interest groups. As a result, some school districts adopt research-based teacher evaluation models in their entirety, while others borrow components from a variety of models and develop the evaluation tool in-house to meet their individual needs as well as those in the best interest of the teachers. This section discusses a few of the **teacher evaluation models** most prevalent in the literature that have guided the teacher evaluation process.

Measures of Teaching Effectiveness (MET)

This model is named for the Measures of Teaching Effectiveness (MET) project (Kane et al., 2013). Funded through the Gates Foundation, the MET project attempted to determine whether it is possible to reliably measure teacher effectiveness; the conclusion was that it is possible. This model evaluates teachers through five measures: (1) students' gains in standardized testing; (2) recorded classroom sessions and teacher reflections afterward; (3) teachers' knowledge in the pedagogical content; (4) students' views of the classroom and instruction of the teacher; and (5) the teachers' own views on their working conditions and the support of the school. Through the work of the measurement and feedback systems, the quality of instruction will "ultimately lead to enhanced student success" (Kane et al., 2013).

Danielson Framework for Teaching

The Danielson Framework for Teaching, developed by Charlotte Danielson, an internationally recognized expert in the area of teacher effectiveness, is a research-based set of components of instruction, developed to determine effective teaching practices (see figure 6.2). The framework is composed of four domains of teaching responsibility, and it entails 22 components. The four domains include (1)

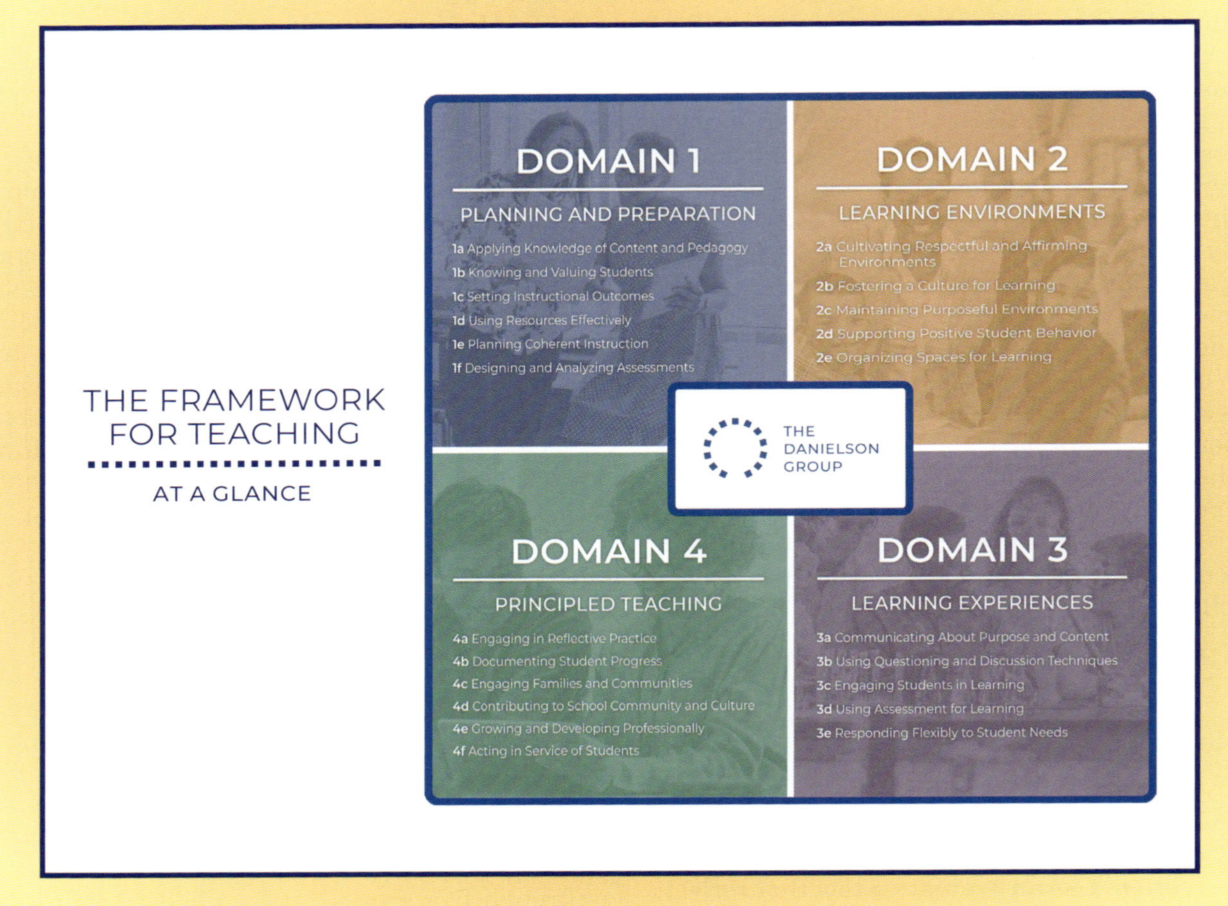

FIGURE 6.2 The Danielson Framework for Teaching.

planning and preparation, (2) learning environments, (3) learning experiences, and (4) principled teaching. The framework can serve as the foundation of a school district's "mentoring, coaching, professional development, and teacher evaluation processes, thus linking all those activities together and helping teachers become more thoughtful practitioners." Additional information can be found at https://danielsongroup.org/framework/.

In addition to the traditional Framework for Teaching, the Danielson Group has also created a Framework for Remote Teaching (https://danielsongroup.org/resources/framework-for-remote-teaching-2). As online classrooms and online schools become more available for students, teacher evaluation should not be set aside in the online environment. Utilizing a framework that is designed for in-person learning to evaluate online teaching is not a best practice. However, utilizing a framework that is designed for online teaching will help one understand the intricacies of online learning and guide the teacher evaluation process in the necessary way.

Classroom Assessment Scoring System (CLASS) Approach

The Classroom Assessment Scoring System (CLASS) approach (developed by Robert Pianta at the University of Virginia, Curry School Center for Advanced Study of Teaching and Learning) is an observational instrument that uses multiple dimensions of teaching that are connected to student achievement (see figure 6.3). It also evaluates teachers based on their behaviors and interactions with students.

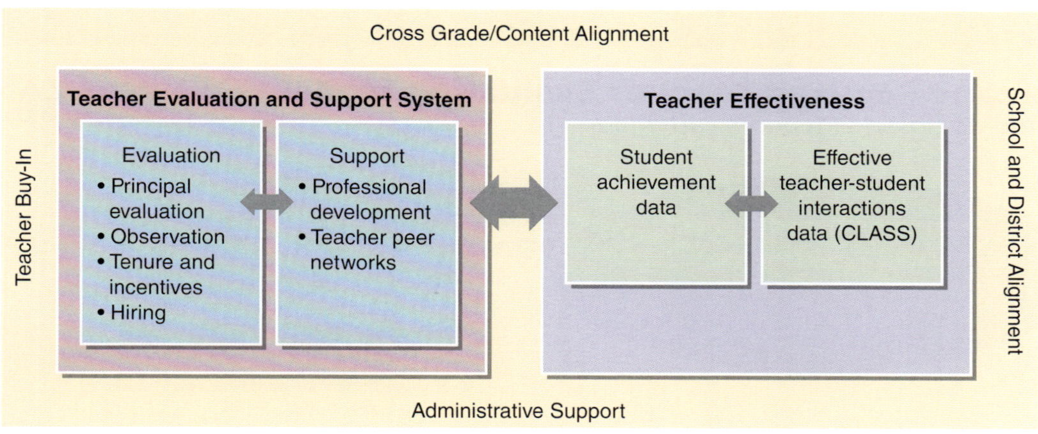

FIGURE 6.3 Classroom Assessment Scoring System (CLASS).
Reprinted by permission from Curry School of Education, Center for Advanced Study of Teaching and Learning, University of Virginia.

The three domains used for measurement are (1) emotional support, (2) classroom organization, and (3) instructional support.

CLASS is a research-based approach (with most of the research focused on early elementary assessment), and it is designed to provide valid and reliable data on teacher effectiveness through consecutive teacher observations. By using the CLASS approach, schools can create a common language across their grade levels in regard to teacher effectiveness; help teachers better understand how their actions and interactions impact student learning; provide a platform that can be used for all teachers within a school setting; and document improvements of teacher effectiveness (National Institutes of Health, n.d.). It is important to note that CLASS has partnered with myTeachstone, and it now uses a subscription model. The subscription allows for CLASS observation certification as well as access to many online resources and tools. It can be accessed at https://teachstone.com/myteachstone.

Value-Added Model (VAM)

A value-added model (VAM) is a form of teacher evaluation that takes into account the teacher's impact on student achievement independent of considerations such as school factors (class size, instructional time, resources), peer culture and family life, individual ability and student needs, and past experience. Through this approach, a statistical analysis is used to assess student test score gains to determine teacher effectiveness. Although it is more controversial than other traditional evaluation models, it does have merit if the VAM metrics can "accurately identify individual teachers' contributions to student learning and hence offer a credible measure of teacher 'effectiveness'" (Darling-Hammond, 2015, p. 132).

Marzano Focused Teacher Evaluation Model

Through an evolution of several tested models, the Marzano Focused Teacher Evaluation Model has been a widely accepted tool for evaluating teachers. This model identifies key elements divided into four domains: (1) standards-based planning, (2) standards-based instruction, (3) conditions for learning, and (4) professional responsibilities (see figure 6.4). Robert J. Marzano, a leading researcher in education, believes that in order for teachers to be effective, they need to set goals and check for understanding; provide positive feedback to students; and reteach what a student does not understand. Marzano further believes that students should be physically active and that simulation and games should be included in the delivery of instruction to increase students' interest, motivation, and information retention (Marzano, 2010). The model consists of five steps following the pre-conference session that the administrator has with the teacher:

1. Determine whether the teacher used the strategy correctly or incorrectly for the element observed.

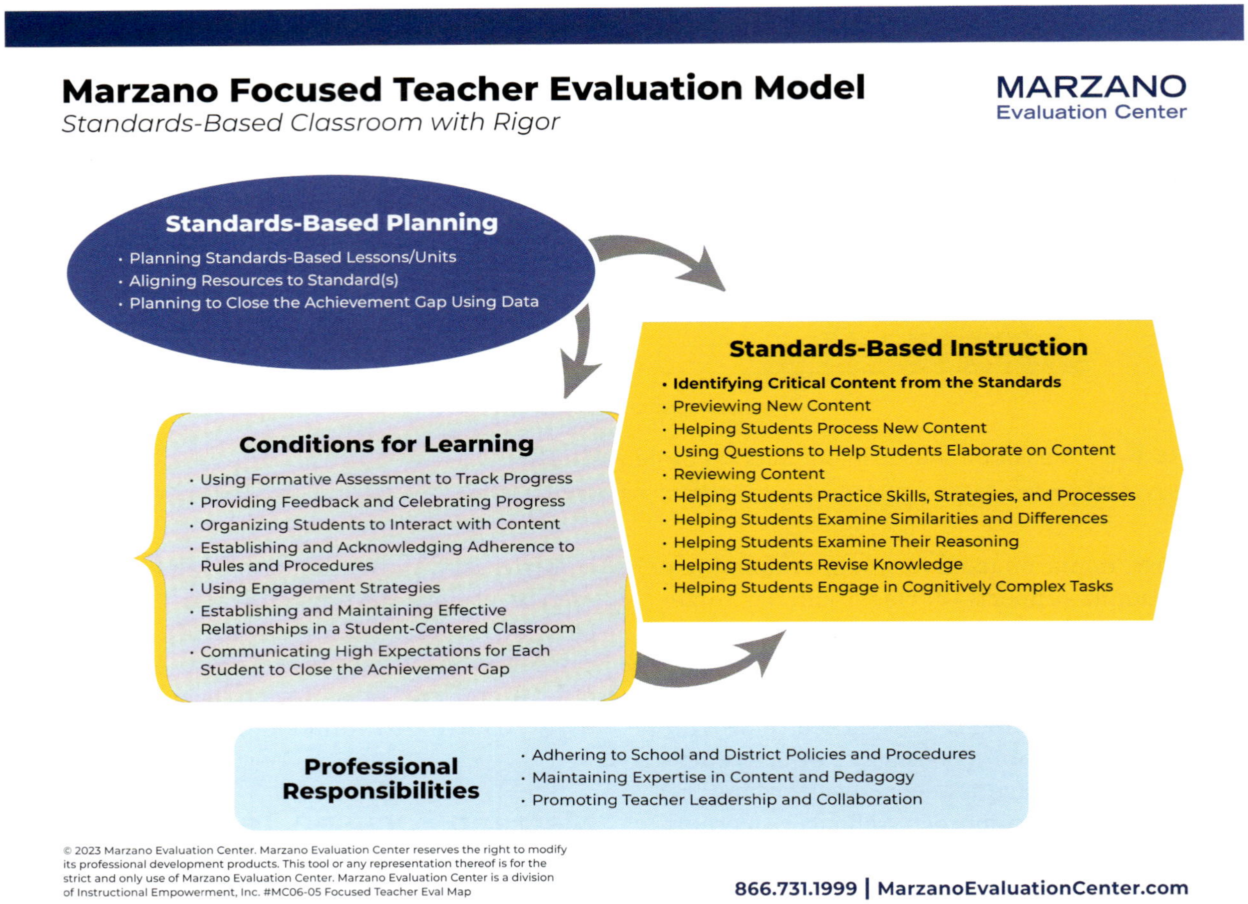
Marzano Focused Teacher Evaluation Model
Standards-Based Classroom with Rigor
MARZANO
Evaluation Center
Standards-Based Planning
• Planning Standards-Based Lessons/Units
• Aligning Resources to Standard(s)
• Planning to Close the Achievement Gap Using Data
Standards-Based Instruction
• Identifying Critical Content from the Standards
• Previewing New Content
• Helping Students Process New Content
• Using Questions to Help Students Elaborate on Content
• Reviewing Content
• Helping Students Practice Skills, Strategies, and Processes
• Helping Students Examine Similarities and Differences
• Helping Students Examine Their Reasoning
• Helping Students Revise Knowledge
• Helping Students Engage in Cognitively Complex Tasks
Conditions for Learning
• Using Formative Assessment to Track Progress
• Providing Feedback and Celebrating Progress
• Organizing Students to Interact with Content
• Establishing and Acknowledging Adherence to Rules and Procedures
• Using Engagement Strategies
• Establishing and Maintaining Effective Relationships in a Student-Centered Classroom
• Communicating High Expectations for Each Student to Close the Achievement Gap
Professional Responsibilities
• Adhering to School and District Policies and Procedures
• Maintaining Expertise in Content and Pedagogy
• Promoting Teacher Leadership and Collaboration
© 2023 Marzano Evaluation Center. Marzano Evaluation Center reserves the right to modify its professional development products. This tool or any representation thereof is for the strict and only use of Marzano Evaluation Center. Marzano Evaluation Center is a division of Instructional Empowerment, Inc. #MC06-05 Focused Teacher Eval Map
866.731.1999 | MarzanoEvaluationCenter.com

FIGURE 6.4 The Marzano Focused Teacher Evaluation Model is composed of 23 elements in four domains, or areas of expertise.

Marzano Evaluation Center (2023). The Marzano focused teacher evaluation model: A focused, scientific-behavioral evaluation model for standards-based classrooms (p. 6). Used with permission. Copyright 2023 by Marzano Evaluation Center, a division of Instructional Empowerment, Inc. MarzanoEvaluationCenter.com, 866-731-1999.

2. Document the technique the teacher used to monitor the student outcome.
3. Ensure that the teacher identified the percent of students who demonstrated achievement of the outcome.
4. List modifications the teacher made in order to help students reach the outcome.
5. Use student evidence to determine final scores for all elements observed in the lesson.

Although several models for teacher evaluation have been presented, it is generally up to each individual school district or school to determine which model best fits its philosophy, objectives, and needs. As educational reform is an ever-evolving topic of top educational and policy decision makers, school districts must also exercise the opportunity to evolve and modify selected models over time. The main concern is that districts adopt some form of evidence-based model for teacher evaluation. It will ensure that teachers receive feedback for continuous improvement, and it will help guide administrators in how to conduct fair and effective teaching evaluations.

Perception of Evaluation

Regardless of which framework your school district is using, the way teachers perceive the process is just as important as the process itself. While many people appreciate the process and look forward to the feedback, growth, and potential bonus and career mobility, others have a different perspective. The Network for Public Education (2016) commissioned a study and survey to learn more about the impact of teacher evaluation on the education profession. It surveyed almost 3,000 teachers and principals in 48 U.S. states and asked educators about the impact of evaluation on their work, their students, and the culture of their schools. In brief, the results reflected the following:

- An overall majority (83%) of principals and teachers reported that basing evaluations on student test scores negatively impacted their instruction and was neither a valid nor a reliable measure of their work.
- Concentrating on test scores is overwhelming for teachers; many reported that the focus takes away from time they could spend with students. A majority (66%) of teachers reported that they felt focusing on the test had a negative impact on their relationships with students.
- Over half of the respondents (52.08%) reported witnessing evidence of bias against veteran educators.
- Teachers (85%) reported that much of the high-quality professional development that is offered is not tied to their evaluations; moreover, when professional development is tied to the evaluation process, it essentially handcuffs them and undermines their sense of autonomy, leaving less room for real professional growth.

In order to prevent this type of negative perception from being pervasive in your school community, it is incumbent on district and school administration to implement successful educator reform by utilizing a highly collaborative process that is focused on well-defined actions and strategies. After studying systems change literature, Shakman and colleagues (2012) surmised that in support of successful district implementation, the literature suggests the following:

1. Strong leaders guide with a morally compelling vision.
2. Relationships are established across the district to gain the trust of key stakeholders.
3. Stakeholders engage in an iterative, collaborative change process with considerable involvement throughout the system.
4. Complex interrelationships of elements of a system are addressed by making appropriate shifts in organizational structure and processes.
5. Accountability and support structures are aligned.
6. Policymakers recognize that change takes place within a particular context and that implementation must be responsive to local needs and the specific environment.

Once the process is in place, administrators and teacher leaders should continue to promote the process with an emphasis on growth. Using a collaborative approach throughout, making the process less cumbersome with meetings and paperwork, and urging teachers to work together can help ensure a positive experience with desired outcomes. Educators want to be treated as professionals; *guiding* their development (versus *demanding* it) is essential to their participation in the process.

It should be noted that veteran teachers in physical education will likely share with evaluators that they have received little to no meaningful feedback in their entire career until recent reform measures were put in place. The reputation of physical education teachers as a whole has been demeaned by a misunderstanding of the purpose of physical education and the lack of meaningful, professional collaboration with administration.

Developing a Growth Mindset and Considerations for Evaluation

Over 30 years before the publication of this book, Dr. Carol Dweck (2007) coined the terms *fixed mindset* and *growth mindset*. The idea of mindset is related to people's understanding of where ability comes from. Recently, educators have used this idea as a tool to explore knowledge of student achievement and its improvement. A fixed mindset can be described as the belief that your abilities—and consequently, your successes and failures—are innate. A growth mindset can be characterized as the belief that success is based on learning, persistence, and hard work. People with a fixed mindset dread failure; they feel that it reflects badly on themselves as individuals. In contrast, people with a growth mindset embrace failure; they view it as an opportunity to learn and improve their abilities. However, mindset is not a permanent situation; it is possible and desirable to shift from a fixed mindset to a growth mindset.

Although most mindset studies related to education have been conducted with students, the results apply to teachers as well. If administrators help teachers shift from a fixed to a growth mindset, they can model it for students and everyone can benefit. The school setting provides multiple opportunities for teachers to try new things and make mistakes. It may be difficult for teachers to embrace, but it is essential for developing a growth mindset. A key principle of growth mindset is the willingness to try new approaches (Gerstein, 2014). As part of creating this opportunity, it is important to ask, *What will teachers and the school learn as part of the process?* The process—not whether there was success or failure—is what reflects the learning. Teachers should be given time to reflect on this approach, and administrators should urge them to take chances.

Evaluators providing feedback to teachers should be cognizant of these ideas. New approaches should be attempted and celebrated. While the language of the rubric selected by the school district is very important because it provides the criteria for an objective evaluation, evaluators must be flexible enough to recognize when teacher actions are reflecting a learning process, thus providing meaningful modeling for students. Supportive dialogue with the teacher around continuing to try new approaches and providing supporting strategies is necessary for promoting a growth mindset. Using rubrics with no flexibility can cause teachers to create cookie-cutter lessons and steer away from new, exciting, and innovative approaches to learning.

To better understand the importance of teacher evaluation, you must first examine what quality physical education is (as expanded on in chapter 3) as well as what to look for while performing observations. If you expect students enrolled in physical education to achieve performance expectations from a standards-based curriculum and grade-span learning indicators, then you need to ensure that the physical education teachers are delivering a quality physical education program. Through teacher evaluation, administrators can ensure that physical education teachers are delivering well-defined content, using age- and developmentally appropriate instructional practices, maintaining good class management, and providing for student assessment. Keep in mind that because evaluations are often seen as stressful and situations that produce anxiety, the role of the physical education administrator in the evaluation process should be perceived as that of a facilitator for improvement and support.

What Quality Physical Education Is

Quality physical education is discussed extensively in chapter 3. However, before diving into examples of student outcomes and classroom observations, it is important to review what a quality physical education program is and is what it is not. Physical education class is an academic subject aligned to established physical education standards (SHAPE America, 2025). It follows a curriculum with grade-span learning indicators and assessments. A quality physical education class is accessible to all students at all levels; it should not be tailored to highly skilled athletes. As stated in chapters 4 and 5, it comprises instruction in a range of skills, including sports skills, fitness and movement concepts, and social and cooperative skills that develop positive attitudes and behaviors for a lifetime of physical, mental, and emotional and social wellness. Furthermore, as stated in chapter 3, SHAPE America (2015a) defines these four essential components of quality physical education as follows: (1) policy and environment, (2) curriculum, (3) appropriate instruction, and (4) student assessment (see figure 3.6).

It is important for the physical education teacher not only to offer a wide variety of activities that appeal to all types of students but also to instruct in a way that leads all students to becoming physically literate. While divergent views exist regarding the definition of physical literacy as cited by Corbin (2016), the 2024 SHAPE America National Physical Education Standards define physical literacy as a journey. The new standards "consider psychomotor, cognitive, social, and affective learning domains essential to facilitating the physical literacy journey of PreK-12 learners, as an ongoing journey" (SHAPE America, 2025, p. 3).

What Physical Education Is Not

Often, thinking about physical education also brings other thoughts to mind. Typically, experience as a student or memories of a teacher in this area are the first associations people make. For some, these associations might be memories of playing kickball, choosing teams, playing traditional sports, or having time to socialize with friends. For others, past experiences may include being teased for being nonathletic, small in stature, or overweight; or being chosen last. Unfortunately, according to Cardinal and colleagues (2013), an ineffective physical education program can lead to negative associations regarding physical activity and reduced participation in regular physical activity later in life. Having students just play games or work out does not lead to physical literacy.

A lack of accountability, combined with the overall acceptance of physical education teachers functioning only as people leading physical activities and not as true educators, has been a detriment to the physical education profession. In conjunction with these factors, a de-emphasis on the importance of physical education on a larger scale has negatively affected physical education teachers as well as the students they serve. A common example of devaluing physical education is when the physical education teacher is asked to perform extra duties, such as security, coaching, taking on extra students, covering double classes, and performing other noninstructional duties. Administrators often value physical education teachers for performing the extra duties and do not hold them to a high standard in the classroom. They accept "busy, happy, good" as good teaching. This limited view puts physical education teachers in a difficult position. With the additional demands their administrator places on them, they often struggle to plan appropriate lessons while also keeping administrators satisfied, letting students simply play without truly engaging in physical literacy.

Physical education teachers who choose to keep their standards high in order to meet the needs of students often end up frustrated and unappreciated, and their position lacks opportunities for growth. Additionally, organizational stress factors such as work overload, lack of support, and isolation have been shown to be significant predictors of teacher burnout (Mazur & Lynch, 1989; Skaalvik & Skaalvik, 2020; Agyapong et al., 2022). For example, since physical education was added to ESSA (2016) as part of a well-rounded education, as an administrator or teacher, if you neglect to consider the *education* component of physical education, it is just physical activity and not physical education.

Establishing the Protocol for Teacher Observations

As with any type of evaluation of job performance, clear expectations and establishing a process for evaluation are important. As previously mentioned, the way the teacher perceives the evaluation process is paramount to the success of the district or school. Approaching all observations with a positive attitude is important. Teachers talk. Based on another teacher's experience, the evaluator may already have a reputation for being tough or unfair. Teachers should have a voice when creating the protocol, and they should be fully aware of what that protocol is prior to the start of the school year. Here are some things to consider when establishing the protocol:

- Set a time frame for observations. Make sure that it is long enough to collect evidence for each of the criteria in the rubric while ensuring that observation time has a base and a cap.
- Consider whether the observation takes place with or without notice to the teacher.
- Determine whether the observation can take place if the class has already started or whether it must occur at the beginning of the class.
- Create a clear time frame in which to complete the report and conference with the teacher.

- Determine a set time frame for the conference. Be sure to include time to discuss the evaluation as well as the professional development plan or next steps.
- Determine what types of lessons or class time are not observable; for example:
  - When students are taking a summative test (no evidence of instruction could be gathered)
  - When a culminating activity is taking place such that students are applying skills learned in a unit (Due to the lack of direct instruction, the observer would not have opportunities to collect evidence of direct instruction.)
  - At the beginning of the year or semester, when students are new to the class and routines and procedures are being established
- Determine the window for observations and the number of observations per year. It should apply to all teachers with no exceptions.

Before conducting official observations, it is recommended that administrators conduct walk-throughs. Walk-throughs are unofficial observations that are shorter than official observations and don't require the same protocols. Cervone and Martinez-Miller (2007) describe classroom walk-throughs as a tool to "drive a cycle of continuous improvement by focusing on the effects of instruction" (p. 1). Ginsberg and Murphy (2002) discuss these specific benefits:

- Administrators become more familiar with the school's curriculum and teachers' instructional practices.
- Administrators can gauge the climate of a school. (e.g., Are students engaged? Are cross-curricular concepts a part of everyday teaching? Are new teachers catching on?)
- A team atmosphere develops as teachers and administrators examine instruction and student motivation and achievement.
- Administrators establish themselves as campus leaders and instructional mentors, influencing teaching, learning, and ongoing school renewal.
- Students see that both administrators and teachers value instruction and learning.

Walk-throughs are particularly useful at the beginning of the year. They provide the teacher with valuable feedback that can be utilized when setting professional goals. It will also inform the process of setting measurable growth goals for students. Having a deeper understanding of what is happening in a classroom throughout the year allows the evaluator to notice teacher practices and student behaviors that are or are not unique to the snapshot of the official observation.

It is also good practice to have teachers perform self-assessments using the designated evaluation rubric prior to official evaluations. Teachers are usually aware of their greatest areas of strength and improvement. Self-assessments will give the evaluator a valuable opportunity to acknowledge those strengths, clarify misunderstandings, and support areas of growth through informal discussions.

Components of Teacher Evaluation

The components of teacher evaluation vary from district to district. Deciding what to weigh and how much it weighs is a controversial topic. Overall scores, however, often consist of student achievement data as well as teacher summative evaluation scores measuring instructional expertise, professionalism, and school and community participation. The following section provides examples of student achievement data in physical education and instructional expertise unique to physical education.

Student Achievement

A teacher's most important responsibility is to ensure that students learn and grow. In physical education, a teacher should develop students' understanding of movement concepts, fitness, lifetime sports, and nutrition in order for them to be physically literate for a lifetime. By using student work and appropriate assessments, physical education teachers can show their impact on student learning.

Effective teachers will choose several priority standards to focus on throughout the course;

the standards you choose will depend on the standards that your state follows. These priority standards measure depth of understanding of a variety of concepts during the course. Using priority standards gives students multiple opportunities to demonstrate understanding of a few key concepts. An example of a priority standard and outcome is one that focuses on exhibiting personal and social behavior that respects self and others.

An elementary school example for grade 5 might focus on accepting, recognizing, and actively involving others with both higher and lower skill abilities into physical activities and group projects. An appropriate assessment might be as follows: *I can accept and include all peers during physical education class.* The self-reflection or self-assessment, completed by each student, is an example of student achievement data reflecting the impact a physical education teacher has on student learning for a grade 5 class (see figure 6.5). As part of the instructional component of the lesson, the teacher will address acceptable and unacceptable examples of including others in group activities. Therefore, the assessment is a direct reflection of learning in the classroom.

An example for middle school physical education might be focusing on demonstrating competency in a variety of motor skills, as shown in figure 6.6. Specifically, it addresses that students demonstrate the mature form of forehand and backhand strokes with a short- or long-handled implement with power and accuracy in different game or activity settings. Appropriate assessment for the grade 8 Net and Wall Unit would be as follows: *An 8th grader should be able to observe a partner and determine whether that person is refining, practicing, or learning the cue listed.* This assessment can be measured with tennis, badminton, pickleball, or racquetball at the end of the Net and Wall Unit. Figure 6.6 provides an example of a rubric for assessing student performance for a pickleball skill.

Figure 6.7 presents an example in high school physical education. It focuses on similar concepts as middle school, instead demonstrating competency or refining activity-specific movement skills in one or more lifetime activities (outdoor pursuits, individual-performance activities, aquatics, net or wall games, or target games). An appropriate performance task aligned to the grade-level outcome would be for the teacher to assess students on their cues for kicking a soccer ball.

Instructional Expertise

School site administrators are responsible for observing all teachers throughout the year, including their physical education teachers.

FEEDBACK

Today I accepted and included all my peers during physical education.

Learning

Practicing

Refining

Provide an example: ______________________

FIGURE 6.5 Sample student achievement for elementary physical education teachers.

Adapted by permission from R.P. Pangrazi, *Dynamic Physical Education, ASAP* (Gopher Sport, 2023), http://dynamicpeasap.com.

Pickleball Peer Assessment

Observe your partner demonstrating the following skills. For each cue, indicate if they are Refining, Practicing, or Learning the cue.

Forehand	
	Opposite Side to Target
	Racquet Back
	Flat Paddle
	Follow through

R=Refining

P=Practicing

L=Learning

Backhand	
	Same Side to Target
	Racquet Back
	Flat Paddle
	Follow through

I can perform a pickleball forehand demonstrating three of four cues.

FIGURE 6.6 Sample pickleball peer assessment.

Adapted by permission from R.P. Pangrazi, *Dynamic Physical Education, ASAP* (Gopher Sport, 2023), http://dynamicpeasap.com.

During these observations, it is recommended that teachers be assessed using a content-neutral instructional rubric, which outlines the key instructional strategies that lead to increased student achievement and engagement. Using a content-neutral rubric allows for consistency across the observations; however, considerations of the content area should be applied. The chosen rubric then defines the instructional expertise expected and reflects the various levels within.

After each observation, the administrator provides specific feedback aligned to the rubric in areas of strength and identified growth that has taken place for each observation. As previously discussed, many districts have their own framework or rubric that is derived from other frameworks, such as the Danielson Framework for Teaching and the Marzano Focused Teacher Evaluation Model.

Essential Criteria: Alignment With Physical Education Best Practice

It is recommended that teachers' instructional expertise be assessed using a content-neutral rubric. For the purposes of this chapter,

FIGURE 6.7 Sample Student Achievement Data for High School Physical Education Teachers

STUDENT NAME	OPPOSITE FOOT BESIDE BALL	EYES ON BALL	INSIDE OF FOOT	FOLLOW-THROUGH TO TARGET	TOTAL
Student 1					0
Student 2					0
Student 3					0
Student 4					0
Student 5					0
Total for cues	0	0	0	0	

Developed by E.E. Centeio and H.E. Erwin

a combination of frameworks (District of Columbia Public Schools [DCPS] Teaching and Learning Framework, Essential Practices, the New Teacher Project Framework, the Danielson Framework for Teaching, and the Teacher Development and Evaluation Plan for Stillwater Schools) are narrowed down to these five components, which are used to clarify instructional expectations for excellent teaching:

1. A safe and inclusive learning environment
2. Engagement in rigorous, age-appropriate instruction
3. Leading a well-planned, objective-driven lesson aligned to age-appropriate content standards
4. Checking and responding to student evidence of learning
5. Developing higher-level understanding through effective questions and tasks

Using these five components is a practical approach that provides teachers and administrators a common language with which to discuss practice. They are each discussed next.

Component 1: A Safe and Inclusive Learning Environment

Teachers are expected to create a safe and inclusive learning environment. Safety practices in physical education include physical and emotional safety. Keeping students protected from physical danger is a priority. Inclusion is a state of being that enables all students to successfully participate, develop skills, and have a sense of belonging in a class. A safe and inclusive learning environment cannot exist without teachers providing high-quality, effective classroom management. Many of the practices listed next assume good classroom management. Without control of the class, safety and inclusion are difficult to achieve. In addition, an inclusive environment should be culturally responsive; it should respond to the particular needs of the students that are in each individual school and classroom.

Accommodating various needs in physical education can be challenging. Evaluators should work with teachers to make sure they have all the necessary training to support an inclusive environment. Specific practices for promoting a supportive and safe physical education learning community that is inclusive for all students may include these practices:

- *Include a specific written portion in the lesson plan that addresses physical safety.* This part of the plan should address safety with regard to space, equipment, self, and others.
- *Group students by ability level or randomly.* Use of grouping strategies that are random allows students to build their social skills and learn to work cooperatively with a variety of people. Grouping students by skill level allows students within their ability groups to challenge one another and themselves. Physical education teachers should never have students pick teams themselves, nor should students be grouped by gender. Picking teams does not contribute to an inclusive culture; often nonathletes and unpopular students get picked last. Grouping by gender is not the same as grouping by skill level, but as discussed in chapter 5, single-gender tasks may actually enhance performance and participation (Gabbei, 2004).
- *Use inclusive language during discussions to establish a community that engages all students.* For example, when teaching dance, the teacher might use gender-neutral language such as "partner," "leader," and "follower" instead of gender-specific language.
- *Implement lesson activities that are inclusive of all ability levels, such as challenges that are cooperative rather than competitive.* For example, a teacher might ask students to focus on how well they work together rather than have students see how fast they can complete an activity. When students try to complete an activity with speed, technique suffers and students often cheat to win.
- *Ensure that every physical education class engages all students in class.* The overall goal is for students to feel confident in their movement and to be physically active for a lifetime. Sometimes teachers need to find a balance between correcting students who are struggling and allowing them to enjoy themselves. Teachers should strategically respond to students who are struggling by using encouragement balanced with corrective feedback in order to avoid embarrassing or discouraging them. Additionally, preventing long lines, which create wait time for students, will help students engage in a given activity and obtain many opportunities for participation.

■ *Utilize space and equipment so that there are multiple opportunities for all students to engage in the lesson.* For example, a teacher might choose to divide students into multiple groups so that students can participate in differentiated lead-up games simultaneously; doing so will avoid having games in which students are waiting for their turns to participate. Another example is for a teacher to set up skill practice in pairs with a piece of equipment for each pair so that students get multiple opportunities to practice the skill.

Component 2: Engagement in Rigorous, Age-Appropriate Instruction

In physical education class, rigorous instruction is twofold; teachers should be addressing both the psychomotor and cognitive domains. Specific practices for promoting engagement in rigorous, age-appropriate instruction should be included in every class. Each lesson should be aligned to grade-span learning indicators described in the National Physical Education Standards (SHAPE America, 2025).

Lessons should help students make connections to how they can use the content they are learning in other areas and in their lives. Lessons should strive to consist of at least 50 percent moderate-to-vigorous physical activity (MVPA); however, depending on the focus of the lesson, it might not be possible. Increasing the amount of time spent in MVPA while participating in meaningful movement during physical education classes has the greatest potential for enabling students to increase their health benefits as well as their academic and social skills. Metabolic equivalents (METs) are commonly used to express the intensity of physical activities or the amount of effort required to perform an activity. The terms *moderate physical activity* and *vigorous physical activity* are related to intensity; they are defined as follows:

- *Moderate physical activity* refers to activities equivalent in intensity to brisk walking or bicycling.
- *Vigorous physical activity* produces large increases in breathing or heart rate, such as jogging, aerobic dance, or bicycling uphill.

Component 3: Leading a Well-Planned, Objective-Driven Lesson Aligned to Age-Appropriate Content Standards

Teachers should follow a prescribed scope and sequence and utilize approved curriculum (see the Program Evaluation section, later in this chapter, for more details). Creating clear objectives for every lesson should be required. Schools often have their own parameters regarding objectives. Some districts require an objective to be written and read to students, while other districts may accept an implied objective. The administration should establish this protocol.

Specific practices for facilitating a well-planned, objective-driven lesson in a physical education learning community may include the following:

■ *Consider all domains when designing a lesson.* Account for all three domains (psychomotor, cognitive, and affective). Specifically, all physical education lessons should contain psychomotor learning through skill acquisition, movement, games, and various movement patterns. Teachers should also consider cognitive development surrounding the acquisition of skills and movement patterns. Students can develop their understanding of skill acquisition through peer observation using cues to observe their partner and provide feedback. Through an understanding of the affective domain, as students gain an appreciation for learning a new skill, they develop certain behaviors and values that influence their skill attainment. All three domains are integral processes for achieving the content standards.

■ *Plan lessons that contain a logical progression.* For example, students go from stationary movement to movement between obstacles. Lessons should never progress from skills in isolation directly to using the skills with a complex movement. For example, students throw a disc to a stationary target using the backhand throw and then the flick; throw a disc to a moving target using the flick and the backhand throw; then throw a disc with a defender in place.

■ *Provide opportunities for students to practice strategy.* Examples include using a grid setup or small-sided games. For example, students learn how to create space to get open for a pass. Set up a grid (four cones) where students have one stationary passer, a partner, and a defender. Students work on change of direction and pace as well as nonverbal communication skills to get open within the three other points of the grid.

- *Create opportunities for students to be challenged within their levels.* For example, students may be asked to do as many push-ups as they can in two minutes rather than count repetitions.

Component 4: Checking and Responding to Student Evidence of Learning

Physical education teachers should be checking for understanding throughout the lesson. They should ask questions after delivering the objective, activating prior knowledge, giving directions, reviewing safety, and explaining technique. These typical portions of the lesson should be followed by verbal questioning or quick thumbs-up checks (quick and easy formative assessments that teachers use to gauge student understanding).

Physical education teachers should spend a lot of time observing students and providing hands-on correction for students as they break down the skills, then have students practice parts of skills; this practice of providing full support and gradually removing it as the student gains competence is known as **scaffolding**. Additionally, teachers should probe students to deepen understanding through more specific questions or have students push themselves to refine a skill, perhaps asking them to be more accurate or to flick their wrist more during a basketball shot. Scaffolding and probing are two particular areas in which evaluators have to be especially savvy when collecting evidence during physical education observations.

Specific practices to respond to evidence of student learning may include the following:

- *Choose not to immediately respond to evidence of student understanding.* For example, if feedback disrupts a game or activity, the teacher may gather information about student learning and respond later to allow for students to make their own corrections.

- *Break down physical skills into smaller components, and present them using specific student or teacher demonstrations in multiple ways.* For example, to respond to a student who is not lifting the opposite leg to skip, the teacher might model and use the cues "step and hop, step and hop," demonstrating for the student how to alternate legs.

- *Provide adequate opportunities for students to practice, reflect, and incorporate feedback.* Students need time to practice physical skills, reflect, and incorporate specific feedback for their growth and development through teacher feedback, peer evaluation, and self-evaluation. For example, students can use a simple rubric to evaluate their partners on their technique. The rubric should cover four or five things to look for and be scaffolded appropriately. Have students first look for one important component and then add other components of the skill for other students to observe. For practicing the underhand toss, a key component to look for is stepping with opposition. Other components are the swinging of the arm and the follow-through toward the target.

- *Utilize verbal questioning throughout physical education class.* This process often takes place as the teacher questions individual students while circulating, at the end of an explanation to the whole class, or at the end of the class during the closing or debriefing.

Component 5: Developing Higher-Level Understanding Through Effective Questions and Tasks

Evaluators may be less aware than they should be of instances when a task in physical education requires critical thinking. By nature, sport requires critical thinking for skill refinement and its subsequent application in games. Consider how the teacher presents the task to the student. If the teacher simply tells students to play—without a focus, or without taking time to strategize or refine—there will obviously be no clear objective for developing higher-level understanding, and credit should not be granted.

Specific practices for engaging students in meaningful cognitive work in a physical education learning classroom may include the following:

- *Plan lessons that emphasize cognitive development.* For example, a lesson on fitness should include engaging students in principles of fitness and fitness concepts so that they can apply those concepts to improve their own fitness or create a plan for themselves or someone else.
- *Ensure that lessons balance instruction and application through skill practice.* Lessons should lead to an application of the skill in a lead-up activity, or they should become more complex with movement.
- *Present students with more complexity within activities.* When students move from just practicing a skill to practicing the skill and having to observe and make decisions, the activity becomes more complex and strategic. Other sport concepts such as making space or moving into passing lanes (at the appropriate grade level) are more complex and also develop deeper understanding.
- *Ask students to respond to tasks in ways that also require cognitive engagement.* For example, a teacher could require students to devise an offensive strategy with their team, then have them explain what they did and why.
- *Make the lessons or tasks more challenging by including skills that require refinement or lesson extensions.* For example, a teacher could have students focus on accuracy by using a smaller target.

Teacher Observation

As with any assessment tool, it is important that when one is observing physical education teachers in an authentic setting, the evaluation tools selected are valid and reliable. The ability to effectively evaluate teachers is a process that involves properly and effectively training the evaluator on a variety of tools. Attention must be given to how the instruction is delivered and the context in which the instruction is delivered. A number of instruments can be used to conduct observations during physical education. One of the most common is the System for Observing Fitness Instruction Time (SOFIT) (McKenzie, 2015; McKenzie et al., 1991), which has been validated to collect observational data on student engagement and teacher interactions during physical education classes. With training, it can provide the administrator with information on teacher instruction and student activity levels.

Evaluators always improve with practice. However, considering that livelihoods and children's learning are at stake, it is important that evaluators work hard to improve quickly. High-quality observations should always be fair, accurate, and reflective of a teacher's performance, which in turn could provide valuable feedback to the teacher. While this chapter offers a variety of checklists for consideration (see figures 6.8 to 6.12), it is also in the best interest of the school district to offer calibration events for evaluators. Calibrating evaluations is a way of ensuring accuracy among one or more observers against a standard. It should be discussed and implemented if your school or district is using multiple observers for a single tool.

When performing the classroom observation of a physical education teacher, consider the following:

- Collect a variety of data points. Data points provide an unbiased approach to teacher feedback during the conference.
  - Be sure to time each component of the lesson (instant activity, introduction, main lesson, closure) and transition time in between.
  - Track student participation by identifying a few students to follow during the class.
  - Observe skill practice, and count the number of times a student gets to practice (e.g., number of throws, strikes).
  - Count the number of touches a student gets during a lead-up activity. For example, when students are playing a small-sided game of Ultimate Frisbee, count how many times a student touches the disc.
- Note verbal questions, responses, and whether the teacher gets a depth and range of understanding.
- Note follow-up questions, scaffolds, and probes. A scaffold in physical education

may be seen when a teacher asks a student to break down the skill into its parts and practice the parts independently. Probing in physical education may be seen when a teacher asks the student to refine a skill further.

- Note visual demonstrations, whether the skills were broken down by the teacher, and how many times they were demonstrated.
- Note any student–student interactions.
- Note whether students were offered a different-size ball or various types of implements; it should be credited as making the lesson more accessible for students.
- Ask students questions at appropriate times to ascertain if they understand what they are learning and why they are learning it, and ask any questions that could reflect their learning in the given lesson.

Physical Education Sample Observation Tools

Once the evaluation tool is selected and the observers have been trained on how to perform an evaluation in a physical education class setting, it is important for the observer to gain an understanding of what to look for in a quality physical education lesson. This section describes scenarios that are commonly observed and provides sample tools for use in those situations.

Management Strategies

The following skill practice scenario does not represent a best practice; nevertheless, it is a common occurrence in elementary physical education classes. This is often the case when students arrive to physical education class ready to participate.

- Students stand in four lines of five at the beginning of class in a designated area, indoor or outdoor space, waiting for attendance to be taken.
- A ball is given to a student at the beginning of each line.
- Students are told to practice dribbling down the court, or designated activity lines, and back, then give the ball to the next person in line.

In this scenario, it is important to consider overall management of students. The administrator conducting the observation could use a simple checklist to ensure appropriate delivery of content, time management, safety of students, and teacher placement during the lesson. Figure 6.8 provides a sample management strategies checklist for this situation.

Initially, the situation may seem to be appropriate because it appears that students are orderly and are following instructions. However, the observer may eventually note that students are getting restless waiting in line and seem to be racing and getting off task. Utilizing the management strategies checklist (figure 6.8) allows the observer to use the data to help tell the story of classroom management. It helps the observer understand what efficient and effective practices the teacher is implementing and what the teacher still needs to work on.

An appropriate solution to the skill practice problem just described is as follows:

- Have students dribble all at the same time in general space.
- Progress practice from stationary and waist-high to low and high dribbles.
- Have students practice with different hands.
- Add movement and obstacles, such as avoiding other students or changing direction around a cone.

Setting up skill practice in this way involves all students at once, so there is no start and finish; they are able to practice at their own pace the entire time, and the practice allows for progression to more complex and challenging tasks.

- Focus on the student actions more than the teacher actions.
- Consider that a teacher may have explained something, but if student actions demonstrate that they misunderstood the explanation, then it was not effective.

Off-Task Behaviors

If students are disengaged or off task, several reasons could explain the lack of participation. Most often, students are off task because they are unable to access the content in an

FIGURE 6.8 Management Strategies Checklist

Teacher ______________ Date ______________ Grade/Period ______________

Observer ______________ School ______________

✓ = observed   X = not observed   n/a = not applicable

- ☐ Starts activity quickly (less than 2 minutes).
- ☐ Ensures equipment and environment are safe.
- ☐ Ensures equipment is easily accessible.
- ☐ Establishes and reinforces stop and go signals.
- ☐ Clearly communicates and reinforces behavior rules and expectations.
- ☐ Quickly and consistently enforces consequences for inappropriate behavior.
- ☐ Gives directions clearly and briefly.
- ☐ Tells or demonstrates to students what to do before they get equipment.
- ☐ Effectively uses demonstrations.
- ☐ Observes class from the perimeter.
- ☐ Moves around class, and keeps students on task.
- ☐ Ensures transitions are planned and efficient.
- ☐ Speaks to students only when they are quiet and listening.
- ☐ Conducts a lesson closure (less than 2 minutes).

Comments:

appropriate way. Consider using a form to track on-task behavior (see figure 6.9).

Examples of common mistakes include the following:

- Skill practice is set up such that students must wait in line, resulting in much downtime.
- The application practice is set up so that it focuses on competition rather than skill acquisition.
- The application practice has a ratio that limits the number of opportunities to practice but requires high skill acquisition. For example, if a teacher has set up a traditional kickball game for students, for the majority of the game, most fielders won't have to do anything. Students will have limited opportunities to practice fielding. This type of traditional game does not promote skill acquisition; instead, it focuses on competition.

Using the form in figure 6.9, the observer can better understand how much time students are spending off task. The teacher could redesign the lesson to address the off-task behavior.

Teacher Movement

How the teacher moves during the class is important, especially in physical education. If a teacher stays in the same place most of the time, students who are positioned farther away tend to become more off task as time moves along. One tool for observing, tracking, and depicting the teacher's movement is a teacher movement map (see figure 6.10). Using this tool, administrators can help teachers understand their movement in the classroom and how they are reaching all of their students during a given lesson.

Teacher Verbal Behavior

When the focus is on behavior management and learning of skills and content, teacher feedback

FIGURE 6.9 On-Task Behavior

Teacher __________ Date __________ Grade/Period __________

School __________ Activity __________

This tool is to help you track behavior for students who are on task during any given class or activity. Every minute that you are observing the class, scan the room to observe student behavior. Then, record the total number of students who are on task and the total number of students who are off task at each time point during the activity. For example, at the 1-minute mark, scan and record. Then at the 2-minute mark, scan and record. Continue this until you have completed the entire class or activity that you are targeting, then calculate the percentage of students who were on task for the class or activity.

TIME	NUMBER OF STUDENTS ON TASK	NUMBER OF STUDENTS OFF TASK
1 minute		
2 minutes		
3 minutes		
4 minutes		
5 minutes		
6 minutes		
7 minutes		
8 minutes		
9 minutes		
10 minutes		
11 minutes		
12 minutes		
13 minutes		
14 minutes		
15 minutes		
Total		

Number of students on task = __________

Number of students off task = __________

$$\text{Percent of students on task} = \frac{\text{Total \# on task} \times 100}{(\text{Total \# on task} + \text{Total \# off task})}$$

From J. Greenberg and J. LoBianco, *Organization and Administration of Physical Education,* 2nd ed. (Human Kinetics, 2026). On-Task Behaviour Checklist developed by E.E. Centeio and H.E. Erwin.

is an important factor. Students often participate in the practice of skills without receiving specific feedback to help them improve. An observation tool for this situation is a chart for teacher verbal behavior (see figure 6.11).

Teacher Time Analysis

Maximizing the amount of time students are active and engaged is important in physical education; it is one of the few times during school when the psychomotor domain is engaged in the learning process. While there are no official recommendations for percentage of time students should be active during physical education, 50 percent of the time has often been accepted as an appropriate level. Using a time analysis tool (see figure 6.12) can help the observer track this information.

FIGURE 6.10 Teacher Movement Map

Teacher ______________________ Observer ______________________

Class ______________ Grade ______________ Date and time ______________

Lesson focus ____

Comments ____

Start time ______________ End time ______________ Duration of lesson ______________

Draw a line following the teacher around the teaching area.

If the teacher stays in one position for 30 seconds or more, place a dot there.

If the teacher stays there for 1 minute or more, draw a circle around the dot.

Comments:

From J. Greenberg and J. LoBianco, *Organization and Administration of Physical Education,* 2nd ed. (Human Kinetics, 2026). Developed by E.E. Centeio and H.E. Erwin.

Teacher Evaluation Report

Teacher evaluation reports are considered legal documents; they should be written in such a way that they could be presented in a court of law and justified. Evaluators should present the teacher with the report prior to the post-observation conference (see Post-Observation Conference, later in this chapter). Depending on the district's evaluation tool, the report could include not only the class observation but also a review of the instructional materials, the teacher's lesson plans, and student portfolios as examples. Evaluators should remember that this document is the *teacher's*—not the evaluator's—report. Copies of the report should be printed for the post-observation conference and also sent electronically. Teachers should be given ample time to read the report and prepare notes for the post-observation discussion. The way this discussion is handled is extremely important.

FIGURE 6.11 Teacher Verbal Behavior

Teacher ____________ Date ____________ Grade/Period ____________

School ____________ Activity ____________

DIRECTIONS:

The purpose of this observation form is to provide feedback to the teacher regarding their verbal behavior towards the students. Under the expectations communicated you should write what expectations the teacher gave the students in regards to behavior management.

The **feedback table** is intended to provide frequency counts (tally marks) counting the number of statements the teacher makes throughout the class period. The goal is to have more specific feedback than general.

- **Positive General** is a positive comment that is not specific. For example, great job or way to go.
- **Positive Specific** is a positive comment with more detail. For example, I really like how you stepped with opposition.
- **Corrective General** is a statement meant to change a behavior or action but is still vague. For example, stop talking, eyes on me, or be sure you are skipping.
- **Corrective Specific** is a redirection of behavior that is more specific in nature. For example, make sure you are stepping with opposition, make sure that you are following through, next time you should hold the ball with two hands over your head.

Teaching Cues: These are words or phrases that help describe the actions a person should take to perform a skill. Typically, a skill may use three or four cues. For example, when throwing the cues may be 1) make a "T," 2) step with opposition, 3) elbow high in "L shape," and 4) release and follow through.

EXPECTATIONS COMMUNICATED

1. ____________
2. ____________
3. ____________
4. ____________
5. ____________
6. ____________

FEEDBACK

POSITIVE GENERAL	CORRECTIVE GENERAL
POSITIVE SPECIFIC	**CORRECTIVE SPECIFIC**

Number positive ____________ Number general ____________

Number corrective ____________ Number specific ____________

(continued)

FIGURE 6.11 *(continued)*

TEACHING CUES:

1. ________________
2. ________________
3. ________________
4. ________________
5. ________________
6. ________________

From J. Greenberg and J. LoBianco, *Organization and Administration of Physical Education,* 2nd ed. (Human Kinetics, 2026). Developed by E.E. Centeio and H.E. Erwin.

FIGURE 6.12 Teacher Time Analysis

Teacher ________________ Observer ________________

Class ________________ Grade ________________ Date and time ________________

Lesson focus ________________

Start time ________________ End time ________________ Duration of lesson ________________

Total activity time (at least half of students active):

Percentage of time students were active (activity time ÷ total time × 100):

Comments:

From J. Greenberg and J. LoBianco, *Organization and Administration of Physical Education,* 2nd ed. (Human Kinetics, 2026). Developed by E.E. Centeio and H.E. Erwin.

The feedback included in the formal evaluation report should clearly communicate the following:

- Evidence from the observation aligned to a rubric for each of the scoring criteria.
- Evidence that explains what the teacher did well in addition to areas for improvement. If there are no obvious areas for improvement, the evaluator should highlight portions of the observation that were effective and explain why. This positive feedback can give teachers a better understanding of why something they did worked well, and it will inspire them to continue to use that strategy.
- Examples of ways the teacher can change the lesson activity or component of the lesson to improve. This feedback should be meaningful and content specific. In addition, the evaluator can provide resources.

A variety of walk-through documents exist for administrators to use for physical education. Figure 6.13 provides a sample data collection checklist that is beneficial in guiding evaluators through the observation process during a physical education class. Additional examples of walk-through documents are shown in figures 6.14, 6.15, and 6.16.

The reports should not only provide the feedback but also drive the professional development of the teachers. While it may seem obvious that teachers will do so independently, empowering teachers to reflect and make their

FIGURE 6.13 Sample Data Collection Checklist from DC Public Schools

TEACHER ACTIONS	OBSERVER COMMENTS
Do Now/Warm-Up is instant, engaging, and requires minimal prompting.	
Teacher states objective in a manner that emphasizes skill and concepts rather than playing a game. *(e.g., "We are going to work on invasion skills and strategies" instead of "We are going to play capture the flag.")*	
Vocabulary is introduced to students in context (in reference to skill or focus). *(e.g., Students learn about different pathways as they move in straight, zig-zag, and curved pathways.)*	
Equipment, activities, and expectations of skills are developmentally appropriate and aligned to standards and grade-span learning indicators. *(e.g., 2nd graders should not be playing volleyball, K students should not be learning hockey skills.)*	
Skill progression and scaffolding is evident in lesson plan and design. *(e.g., Skill isolation that progresses in complexity, small-sided games, and deliberate practice leading to game play.)*	
At least 50% of class is dedicated to moderate-to-vigorous physical activity (MVPA). (*Use heart-rate monitors to measure PA in all secondary classes.*)	
Use of technology (*e.g., presentation software, audio and video equipment, heart rate monitors*) is embedded into class procedures and lesson with little interruption.	
STUDENT ACTIONS	**OBSERVER COMMENTS**
Students draw comparisons and ties to content in their life.	
Students collaborate, cooperate, and show acceptance of all.	
Students reflect on relevance of activities and apply them to other units of study or life through exit tickets, think pair shares, etc.	
Students are engaged cognitively, stay involved, and are challenged with the content or activities.	
CLASSROOM ENVIRONMENT	**OBSERVER COMMENTS**
Evidence of agenda and specific learning objective	
Adequate equipment (size, type, amount) (*Each student has equipment or shares with a partner or small group as appropriate for activity.*)	
Presence of standards as well as purposeful and meaningful objectives	
General pictures promoting a healthy, fit lifestyle	
Data and word wall with images of lesson vocabulary and everyday classroom requests	

From J. Greenberg and J. LoBianco, *Organization and Administration of Physical Education,* 2nd ed. (Human Kinetics, 2026). Developed by Miriam Kenyon, DC Public Schools.

own choices about professional development is still recommended. The report for the teacher should describe the lesson from start to finish and include rubric language that is aligned with evidence collected from the observation. Here is an example of a summary of the lesson and rubric language for a well-planned, objective-driven lesson that is aligned to age-appropriate standards:

The lesson observed was a kindergarten lesson; it was aligned to the Kindergarten outcomes "2.2.8 Identifies the heart as a muscle that gets stronger with physical activity; 2.2.9 Recognizes that regular physical activity is good for health; and 2.2.10 Recognizes physiological changes in their body during physical activities" (SHAPE America, 2025).

FIGURE 6.14 Sample Physical Education Walk-Through Tool 1

Date: ____________ Teacher: ____________ Grade: ____________

Professional dress: Yes No

Rating: 5 = always; 4 = usually; 3 = sometimes; 0 = never; n/a = not apply

TEACHING BEHAVIOR	COMMENTS
Preparation ____Lesson plan is evident, appropriate, followed, and consistent with district curriculum. ____Appropriate activities are selected. ____State and national standards are addressed.	
Class Management ____Necessary equipment is ready and easily accessible. ____Teacher establishes a consistent stop signal and listening position for students. ____Teacher positions students so all can see and hear. ____Teacher avoids talking excessively (or not enough). ____Class is organized to maximize activity time (active at least 50% of the time). ____Addresses any behavior issues privately and efficiently. ____Ensures that students are on task. ____Allows students to be active a majority of the lesson time. ____Verbal interactions are easy to hear and clearly stated. ____Teacher is a catalyst for student motivation (shows enthusiasm).	
Instruction ____Introduces the skill (or activity) and purpose. ____Breaks skill (or activity) down into key points. ____Provides appropriate demonstration. ____Keeps bouts of instruction to no longer than 45 seconds. ____Ties instruction to objectives when appropriate.	
Practice Time ____Designs appropriate progressions if necessary. ____Clearly shows students how they are expected to practice. ____Assures that students are practicing correctly. ____Uses effective questioning skills. ____Uses cue words repeatedly.	
Providing Appropriate Feedback ____Circulates and gives specific feedback.	
Assessment ____Monitors student comprehension and subsequent performance, altering instruction when necessary. ____Utilizes formative and summative assessments when appropriate. ____Provides closure that summarizes the lesson and promotes learning.	

General Comments

From J. Greenberg and J. LoBianco, *Organization and Administration of Physical Education,* 2nd ed. (Human Kinetics, 2026). Developed by E.E. Centeio and H.E. Erwin.

FIGURE 6.15 Sample Physical Education Walk-Through Tool 2

WALK-THROUGH NAME	TEMPLATE
	4- part PE lesson
Board name	**School name**
Observer	**Subject**
Start date	**End date**
Grade level	

Page 1	
1. Learning targets posted • Visible to all students. • Written in student-friendly language. • Direct correlation to standard. • Current/Updated. • Referred to during lessons.	
2. Instant activity • Students engage in immediate activity upon entering the room. • Activity is rigorous. • Activity lasts 2 to 3 minutes. • Instruction is provided during student recovery.	
3. Fitness component • Is designed to enhance health-related fitness. • Promotes a lifetime of physical activity. • Includes 5 components of health-related fitness. • Includes FITT principle. • Exercise is varied. • Lasts 5 to 7 minutes. • Students are taught how to determine their personal workload.	
4. Lesson focus • Is designed to teach physical skill. • Contains learning experiences. • Uses repetition and refinement. • Lasts 15 to 25 minutes.	
5. Game play/Closure activity • Evaluates skills learned. • Reinforces skills learned. • Revisits prior or related skills. • Checks for understanding. • Uses skills developed in lesson focus. • Children enjoy the game or activity. • Lasts 5 to 7 minutes.	

From J. Greenberg and J. LoBianco, *Organization and Administration of Physical Education,* 2nd ed. (Human Kinetics, 2026). Developed by E.E. Centeio and H.E. Erwin.

FIGURE 6.16 Teacher Walk-Through Feedback Form

DIRECTIONS:

As the observer you should complete the general information at the top of the form before the lesson begins. It is also recommended that you have a pre-conference with the teacher to understand the lesson plan, objectives, and what you will be observing.

During the lesson, make observations and provide notes within the various categories. You should take notes on observations of both the student behavior as well as the teacher actions. Additionally, notes may be taken regarding meeting the objectives of the lesson. Another suggestion would be to have a post-conference with the teacher to discuss the form and provide positive feedback (praise) and areas for growth (polish).

Teacher email	
Observer	
Grade level	
Number of students	
Content or subject	
Time into class	
1. Student-friendly learning intention(s) is posted or evidenced and aligned to grade- or course-appropriate standard.	
Evidence Notes 1	
2. Student learning activity is aligned to a learning intention.	
Evidence Notes 2	
3. Success criteria is posted or evidenced.	
Evidence Notes 3	
4. Teachers actively use formative assessment to check for understanding and mastery of the content.	
Evidence Notes 4	
5. Students are asked to respond to higher-ordered questions designed to promote thinking and understanding.	
Evidence Notes 5	
6. Students are actively participating in an activity that promotes learning (e.g., speaking, writing, reading, discussing, Kagan activities, cooperative learning, etc).	
Evidence Notes 6	
7. The teacher consistently engages a diverse group of students. This could include but not be limited to ability, SES, race, culture, gender, etc.	
Evidence Notes 7	

8. Students engage with a grade-appropriate assignment or task that requires high level thinking.
Evidence Notes 8
9. Students demonstrate knowledge of and follow school and classroom rules and behavioral expectations.
Evidence Notes 9
10. Learners speak and interact respectfully with teacher(s) and each other.
Evidence Notes 10
11. Teachers and staff speak and interact respectfully with learner(s) and each other.
Evidence Notes 11
12. Teachers are effectively using technology tools and strategies to: • Design instructional lessons • Design resources • Design assignments • Design assessments • Engage students in learning • Give students timely feedback • Demonstrate and encourage good digital citizenship
Evidence Notes 12
13. Students are using technology to achieve and demonstrate their learning by: • Critically curating a variety of resources to construct knowledge • Producing creative artifacts using technology to demonstrate learning • Using technology to identify and solve real-world problems • Using digital tools to communicate and/or work collaboratively to support learning • Demonstrating good digital citizenship
Evidence Notes 13
14. Students receive specific, accurate, and timely feedback to improve understanding and/or revise work.
Evidence Notes 14
15. Do students have the opportunity to see themselves and a global society reflected in the curriculum, resources, and instructional delivery?
Evidence Notes 15
16. The teacher responds to specific learning needs through differentiation evidenced by one of the following methods: content, process, product, or learning style.
Evidence Notes 16

(continued)

FIGURE 6.16 *(continued)*

17. A high-yield instructional strategy (e.g., similarities and differences; summarizing and note taking; reinforcing effort; practice; non-linguistic representation; cooperative learning; objectives and feedback; generating and testing hypothesis; questions, cues, and advanced organizers; etc.) is evidenced during instruction.
Evidence Notes 17
18. The predominant classroom structure observed can be classified as:
Evidence Notes 18
Praise:
Polish:

From J. Greenberg and J. LoBianco, *Organization and Administration of Physical Education,* 2nd ed. (Human Kinetics, 2026). Developed by E.E. Centeio and H.E. Erwin.

- *The lesson was well organized; all parts of the lesson were connected to each other and aligned to the objective; and all parts significantly moved all students toward mastery of the objective. The lesson consisted of the following:*
  - *Review of previous lesson on moving the rope*
  - *Warm-up dance (feel your heart)*
  - *Locomotor movements around ropes*
  - *Stations: (1) Drawing a heart; (2) Tossing and catching; (3) Basketball; (4) Jump rope; (5) Kicking in a goal; (6) Creative movements*
- *The objective of the lesson was clear to students, and students understood the importance of the objective. The learning objective for the class was "Students will review three ways to move the rope and explain the job of their heart." Students were asked to focus on their heartbeat when exercising to see if it made the heart go faster or slower. Students were able to explain that the heart was moving blood throughout the body and that their heart was beating faster during exercise.*

From reading this sample report excerpt, it is clear what the various activities of the lesson were. The objective of the lesson and the lesson focus were aligned to an age-appropriate standard. In addition to clearly outlining the lesson, the report should include both evidence from each of the different rubric criteria and suggestions for improvement.

Here is an example in which the area of improvement was student engagement at stations; it includes the actionable feedback that could help the teacher increase engagement.

- *The teacher made the content accessible to most students by providing some visual demonstrations and offering clear explanations; however, some students needed additional demonstrating to help them access the content. Some students did not know what they were supposed to do at the station, and they stood around waiting for further instruction.*
- *In this case, the teacher could have checked for understanding with a range of students prior to release, had a student demonstrate, provided cue cards at each station, or provided additional demonstrations for students to ensure their readiness to practice independently.*

Based on this scenario for improving student engagement, scaffolded instruction is a widely accepted approach to move instruction from teacher-centered, whole-group instruction to student-centered learning based on collaboration and independent practice. The three phases of scaffolding, *I do, We do,* and *You do,* provide the students with an opportunity to gain new skills while accepting responsibility for completing the learning task. Table 6.1 provides the framework for accomplishing this goal.

TABLE 6.1 Mentoring Roles and Responsibilities

	Teacher	Student
I do it *Direct instruction*	• Provides direct instruction • Establishes goals and purpose • Models • Thinks aloud	• Actively listens • Takes notes • Asks for clarification
We do it *Guided instruction*	• Provides interactive instruction • Works with students • Checks, prompts, clues • Provides additional modeling • Meets with needs-based groups	• Asks and responds to questions • Works with teacher and classmates • Completes process alongside others
You do it independently *Independent practice*	• Provides feedback • Evaluates • Determines level of understanding	• Works alone • Relies on notes, activities, classroom learning to complete assignment • Takes full responsibility for outcome
You do it together *Collaborative learning*	• Moves among groups • Clarifies confusion • Provides support	• Works with classmates, shares outcome • Collaborates on authentic task • Consolidates learning • Completes process in small group • Looks to peers for clarification

Developed by Ellen Levy © E.L.Achieve/2007.

Post-Observation Conference

The **post-observation conference** is a critical component of the teacher evaluation process since it provides feedback to the teacher as to what was observed during the evaluation. It further offers an opportunity for the teacher to provide any additional information or clarification if there are questions on the outcome of the evaluation. Post-observation conferences should be viewed as a conversation between the physical education teacher and the administrator conducting the evaluation such that a continuous dialogue takes place regarding effective instruction, students' achievement, professional growth opportunities, and how to manage difficult class situations. There are varied approaches to the post-observation conference; in order to determine the best approach, consider the following:

- *Was the teacher nervous?* Observations often cause anxiety for teachers. Whether they are seasoned veterans or brand-new teachers, having someone watching them teach and taking notes during the class can be nerve-racking. If you notice that a teacher is nervous, it is helpful to begin the conference by mentioning something unrelated to the observation in order to build rapport. For example, asking if the teacher is excited about an upcoming event can shift attention to a more comfortable, neutral topic of discussion and help to ease her anxiety.
- *How did this lesson fare against other lessons observed? Did the teacher perform at the level where he had been, or did he improve?* If the teacher improved on aspects of the rubric that might have been an area for improvement in the past, consider starting with that. For example, you might say, "Last observation, your area for improvement was ensuring the classroom environment was safe and inclusive. During this observation, you used pairing and grouping strategies that engaged all students in a variety of ways to ensure they felt safe to engage in the content." Starting the conference by recognizing the teacher for a successful effort to improve helps foster a growth mindset, boosting confidence and motivation work toward future improvements.
- *Are there any areas of the lesson that may change your evaluation? Is this conference more of a discussion?* Remember, this part of the process is for the teacher's professional

development. Teachers are experts in their content area, so inviting them to discuss decisions made during the lesson can help them feel empowered and invested in the process.

- *Was this lesson below standard? Is this conversation going to be met with defensiveness?* If so, be sure to focus on the data and concrete examples that demonstrate the rating. For example, during the volleyball activity, there was 1 student in the middle of a circle of 30, passing to students one at a time. With the exception of the student in the middle, students got one opportunity to practice their underhand pass. The activity took five minutes, and students were idle for most of the activity. Reviewing this situation will keep the conversation on the facts and focused on the students.
- *What is the teacher's professional development area? Based on the observation, what is the most foundational component of teaching that the teacher needs to improve?* Identify some areas for improvement that could help the overall lesson. For example, if the environment wasn't safe and inclusive, it can change the engagement and therefore affect the entire lesson. If students have a lot of wait time, behavior issues might arise. Consider routines and procedures the teacher could implement to change how students engage in the lesson. Improving the procedure for practicing a skill can allow all students to have access to the content as well as feel challenged based on their individual level.

Most importantly, focus on what the students were doing. Remember that the number one reason for teaching is the students. No matter what the teacher did, focusing on what the students did is more important. Student actions show whether something was done effectively or not. Making sure that the teacher had an opportunity to reflect on the student actions can help the teacher plan for upcoming lessons.

The *professional growth plan*, which is developed following the post-observation conference, should consider what area to focus on in order for the teacher to make significant improvements. For example, if a teacher has poor classroom management such that students are idle for long periods, the teacher should focus on creating efficient routines and procedures to maximize learning time. The key is to ensure that the conversation involves an exchange of ideas and that the teacher takes an active role in developing the professional growth plan.

Coaching the Teacher

Depending on the outcome of the observation, the school site administrator can provide professional assistance and support to the physical education teacher or can solicit support and input from the physical education administrator. While the post-observation conference gives the administrator opportunities to coach teachers with regard to the lesson observed, there are opportunities throughout the year to help build their confidence and improve their skills. Conversations through open communication, professional development opportunities, and periodic follow-up can give you the opportunity to provide resources as needed.

Program Evaluation

In addition to evaluating individual teachers within a program, it is important to also evaluate the physical education program as a whole. This evaluation might occur at different levels depending on your situation (school level, district level, etc.). In order to help facilitate **program evaluation**, SHAPE America created a Physical Education Program Checklist (SHAPE America, 2015b). The checklist is aligned with the essential components of physical education and includes four areas: (1) Policy and Environment, (2) Curriculum, (3) Appropriate Instruction, and (4) Student Assessment. When conducting program evaluation, it is important to evaluate all four areas and not just focus on one particular area, such as curriculum. Evaluating and addressing all areas on a regular basis will ensure a quality physical education program.

Policy and Environment

The Policy and Environment portion of the checklist focuses on many policies that should be present at the district and state level. When a policy is well defined, it helps create an environment that is clearly defined for students in understanding what the intended outcomes are. It further assists the teacher in the delivery of instruction to students that is consistent

LEADERSHIP IN ACTION

The Importance of Teacher Evaluation

Kathleen Satterley, MA

Founder, The Champion Initiative Educational (TCI) Consulting

Teacher observation, evaluation, and professional development will always be an integral part of education. As you develop your evaluation skills, the most important consideration is your ability to be completely objective. Maintaining objectivity is a challenging and sometimes daunting task because you must conduct your entire evaluation process in a manner that is consistent from person to person.

Teacher evaluation should be highly collaborative and focused on development. Many observations should be conducted using a variety of methods. Therefore, observations should not be limited to just one method, such as classroom walk-throughs or formal evaluations. A combination of methods can be used, including peer observations, video recordings, and student feedback. This approach provides a more comprehensive view of the teacher's instructional practice, and it allows for more targeted feedback. Celebrating successes and identifying strengths can be just as important as addressing areas for improvement, and it can help to motivate teachers to continue to grow and develop in their practice.

Administrators should also recognize the many differences between a PE classroom and a traditional classroom. Without understanding how a PE teacher may require higher-level thinking through skill refinement and application of skills in game play, a non-PE administrator could miss these best practices in this setting. I would suggest here that the teacher or department chair be prepared to educate the evaluating administrator.

In my experience, these were some best practices that led me through over 1,000 K-12 and adapted physical education evaluations over a five-year period in our nation's capital:

- Understand the philosophy of the district, building, and PE program.
- Roll out rubrics and evaluation processes in a way that gives ownership to teachers.
- Teachers and evaluators should have a deep understanding of rubric expectations in the context of their content area. (See sample PE modified rubric.)
- Ask questions of the teacher and a sample of students during observation.
- Require objectives to be clearly stated or posted.
- Provide teachers with their report prior to the post-observation conference.
- Include actionable feedback in the report focusing on bite-size pieces with the greatest leverage.
- Instead of conducting a prescriptive feedback session, ask questions of your teachers that lead *them* to think through the new strategies required for improvement.
- Model feedback, allow them to practice, give more feedback, provide resources, and leverage mentor teachers.

While these best practices support objectivity, being cognizant of your own biases, judgments, and preconceived notions are equally important. As difficult as it may be, you must be honest with yourself about your own shortfalls in this area. Whether or not your school or district has rolled out the evaluation process well, you have the responsibility to provide the teacher with opportunities for growth. Hold them accountable, be patient, and take your own personal inventory.

across classes (SHAPE America, 2015b). Understanding these policies and how they align to best practices is important. Once this area is evaluated, determining strengths and weaknesses is fundamental to ensuring that one can begin working on advocating to change policies at various levels (school, district, and state). Minutes for physical education, not withholding physical activity as punishment, and physical education taught by certified teachers endorsed in physical education are some of the policies mentioned within the document. For example, the checklist asks programs to evaluate the number of minutes of physical education that are offered per week and that all students are included in physical education. Another policy focus is making sure that programs do not allow waivers, exemptions, and substitutions for physical education. Additional policies that schools are asked to consider include class size, physical activity as punishment, and having a certified physical education teacher.

Curriculum

Curriculum is the second area that should be analyzed within program evaluation. Having a written curriculum with proper scope and sequence is key to a quality program. Evaluating the overall curriculum at the school level is important for understanding the overall scope and sequence and understanding the experience that students have as they progress through the grade levels. It is important to evaluate a program even beyond the school walls and periodically engage in program evaluation at the district level. Doing so will allow teachers and administrators to understand the scope and sequence at a higher level. In addition to understanding how a student experiences physical education at a given school, there should also be an understanding of how they are meeting the standards and experiencing physical education from PreK through grade 12. Teachers within a district should be conducting program evaluations within their school at least every couple of years, and evaluations should be consistent with curriculum reviews in other subject areas. These evaluations must go beyond individual evaluations and teachers within a district; along with a district curriculum coordinator, they should be evaluating students' PreK-12 experience and creating expectations that every student will have a similar experience in physical education no matter what school they attend or how they track through the district.

In addition to the checklist items provided by SHAPE America (2015b), some tools are designed to help facilitate in-depth curricular analysis. One of these tools is called the Physical Education Curriculum Analysis Tool (PECAT) (CDC, 2019). The PECAT is one example of a tool that is designed for teachers, principals, and district coordinators to assess the physical education curriculum. Designed and published by the Centers for Disease Control and Prevention (CDC), the PECAT aims to help school districts and schools conduct a comprehensive analysis of their physical education curriculum based on the National Standards for Physical Education. According to the CDC (2019), the PECAT has four main functions:

1. Help schools and districts assess how closely their curriculum is aligned with national standards.
2. Help schools and districts analyze outcomes, content, and assessment components and how they align with standards and grade-span learning indicators.
3. Help schools and districts identify needed changes.
4. Help schools and districts develop their physical education curriculum.

Results from the PECAT can help school districts and individual schools "improve, develop, or select appropriate and effective curricula for delivering physical education. This, in turn, will improve the ability of schools to positively influence knowledge, motor skills, and physical activity behaviors among school-aged youth" (CDC, 2019, p. 1).

You can conduct the PECAT online at the CDC website (www.cdc.gov/healthyschools/pecat/index.htm); the site also provides a PDF version for download. It is not meant to be completed in isolation by one single person in the district. In fact, the CDC (2019) suggests that the PECAT be conducted using a comprehensive team that is composed of individuals from a curriculum committee, state education agency staff, higher education faculty, and physical education department representatives from all schools involved. The PECAT has three main parts: (1) Preliminary Review, (2) Standards Analysis, and (3) Curriculum Improvement Plan.

The Preliminary Review portion of the PECAT is meant to help the committee initially assess the overall curriculum that is being reviewed, before digging into how the curriculum aligns to the national standards. There are five worksheets to be completed in this section of the PECAT: Physical Education Curriculum Description, Accuracy Analysis, Acceptability Analysis, Feasibility Analysis, and Affordability Analysis. Each of these worksheets is meant to help the team better understand the current curriculum. The Description worksheet helps the team understand the original origins of the curriculum and what the curriculum entails. The Accuracy Analysis worksheet helps determine the accuracy of what is written in the current curriculum. The Acceptability Analysis worksheet looks at cultural norms within the school or district to determine how the curriculum aligns with the community in which it is intended to serve and to help better understand if it is developmentally appropriate. The Feasibility Analysis worksheet is meant to help determine if the curriculum and surrounding materials can be successfully implemented within the allotted time for physical education and within existing facilities. Finally, the Affordability Analysis worksheet is meant to forecast the costs of sustaining curriculum materials annually and to help you better understand the cost of implementation.

The second part of the PECAT is the Standards Analysis. This section is meant to help assess the curriculum based on the National Physical Education Standards. If a team is analyzing its own curriculum, this portion of the PECAT is essential. If a school or district is conducting the PECAT based on an evidence-based curriculum, then this section is not necessary. Currently, the PECAT is aligned to the SHAPE America National Standards that were originally published in 2013. The Standards Analysis section takes the team through each of the five standards for physical education. Within each standard, the provided worksheet helps the team analyze whether the curriculum includes content pertaining to the grade-level outcomes, physical education content (units, lessons, activities), and student assessments. Once the Standards Analysis at each grade band is conducted, the team is asked to complete a standards scorecard that rates each standard in the three areas.

The final part of the PECAT is the Curriculum Improvement Plan. In this section, the team is asked to analyze the data collected in Section 2: Standards Analysis. It is meant to begin with a general overview of recognizing strengths and weaknesses within the curriculum. Then, the teams are asked to complete a Curriculum Improvement Plan worksheet that helps them identify weaknesses that were found, provide recommendations on how to improve the weaknesses, and finally determine the necessary actions to move forward. After the plan is in place, schools are then encouraged to systematically enact their plan across the school and district.

Appropriate Instruction

Appropriate instruction is the third component that should be evaluated in an overall physical education program evaluation. This part of the evaluation can occur at both the district and school level by requiring lesson plans to be turned in and analyzed for documentation of instructional practices and deliberate-practice tasks. It would be best that districts and schools provide a template for teachers to complete that addresses all major components of appropriate instruction. Within the lesson plans, it is important to check for areas of appropriate instruction (e.g., making sure that teachers are including formative and summative assessments, providing evidence of student learning, including transitions within their instruction and activities, and providing differentiation of learning). Additionally, items mentioned previously within the teacher evaluation section (e.g., classroom management, time spent in physical activity, and inclusion of all students within a lesson) should also be included. Finally, programs should be evaluated to ensure that they are providing a physical education experience that is appropriate for all students (including making the necessary adaptations for students with special needs or disabilities).

Student Assessment

Student assessments can be used *for learning* or *of learning*. In other words, assessments should not just be used for grading. Sometimes, the purpose of the assessment is solely for the students to receive feedback and learn something about themselves (for learning); other times, the assessment is done to determine whether the student learned something (of learning). When conducting a student assessment according to the SHAPE America Physical Education Program Checklist, the first thing to consider is aligning the program and curriculum with standards-based physical education and grade-span learning indicators. No matter what standards (state or national) are being followed, ensuring that the assessments are aligned with standards is important. Another consideration is that assessment occurs across the three learning domains (cognitive, affective, and psychomotor). Ensuring that a variety of assessments are taking place is important for understanding the program in its entirety. In addition to having a variety of assessments that align to standards, it is also best practice to make sure that assessments are given and graded with fidelity across the program. Therefore, teachers should be using a protocol for administering the assessments, and they should be provided with common rubrics that are aligned with the objectives for their lessons. Finally, teachers should maintain constant communication with both the student and the parent or caregiver about the student's progress in the course.

Evaluating a physical education program is important; however, one of the most important components of the evaluation is using the data collected to inform decisions that are made for the future. It's important to not simply conduct an evaluation and let it sit. The data should be collected and analyzed, then stakeholders need to discuss how to use it to better the physical education experience for students. This discussion should occur at least once a year, and it should include teachers as well as school and district administrators. They should use the data collected during program evaluation to guide programmatic decisions for the future.

Conclusion

As educational reform continues to be an ongoing process, one of the most critical conversations among policy makers and educational leaders and administrators is how to improve student performance through teacher and program evaluation. Keep in mind that the purpose of teacher evaluation is to improve the delivery of instruction while promoting increases in student achievement. Physical education is no different when it comes to instructional practices that lead to student attainment of state and national physical education standards. Although several models for conducting teacher evaluation have been presented in this chapter, it is ultimately up to individual school districts to determine which model to incorporate, what components of published models to incorporate, and what types of evaluation systems districts are developing in-house to best measure teacher effectiveness—which ultimately leads to student achievement. The evaluation process should also be perceived in a positive mode by changing the mindset and culture; it should highlight growth potential while maintaining accountability for the delivery of instruction and student achievement. Additionally, program evaluation is meant to help see the bigger picture, allowing districts and schools to understand physical education beyond their individual instructors.

Review Questions

1. Why is teacher evaluation important to educational reforms?
2. Describe the various teacher evaluation models presented, and explain the differences between them.
3. What is the relationship between teacher evaluation and student performance?
4. What are some reliable strategies for assessing student achievement in physical education?
5. Explain the recommended protocols to consider when one is conducting a teacher observation.
6. What role does professional development play in individual teacher growth?
7. What are the four components that should be considered when conducting program evaluation?
8. What is the PECAT, and why is it important to use within a school or district?

CHAPTER 7

Event Planning, Special Programs, and Field Trips

Jayne D. Greenberg

Courtesy of the BikeSafe Program KiDZ Neuroscience Center, University of Miami Miller School of Medicine

LEARNING OBJECTIVES

After reading this chapter, you will be able to do the following:

- Identify the basic elements of event planning and management.
- Describe the roles and responsibilities of event planners.
- Develop a plan to design, implement, and evaluate a community event.
- Identify ways to collaborate with community stakeholders.
- Explain the importance of advocacy and marketing for your program.
- Identify programs to promote school-wide events and programs occurring before, during, or after school.

KEY CONCEPTS

budget management
elements of event management
event planning
field days
field trips
marketing events
public relations
special events
volunteer coordinator

In addition to curriculum development and instructional leadership responsibilities, as a physical education administrator, organizing and conducting **special events** and **field trips** within your school district or community serves several purposes. It allows you to expand learning opportunities for students, advocate for your programs, raise funds for your projects, and bring the community and parents together for a common cause. In addition, it helps you enhance team building among your senior-level administrators, school board members, colleagues, and—most important—the physical education teachers and students in your district. As you read this chapter, you will see that as a physical education administrator, your ability to conduct successful special events or programs, whether large or small, is contingent on your ability to successfully plan, implement, and evaluate your event and activities through a methodical process. It all begins with a vision and a purpose.

This chapter is divided into three sections to serve as a guide in developing and organizing events and special programs. The first section provides a road map for how to conduct community-wide events for the purpose of engaging your school community with members of the community at large. The second section discusses field trips. The third section presents ideas and guidance on how to use professional development opportunities to educate physical education teachers in conducting school-wide special events and programs at their individual sites. The final section examines the opportunities available to implement before- and after-school physical activity programs throughout the district by developing community-based partnerships.

Through your leadership and initiatives, which engage staff and motivate the community to support physical education programs through events, academic outreach, and special programs, you will be able to expand opportunities for teachers and students throughout your district.

Conducting Community-Wide Events

As an educational leader in your school district you also have a unique opportunity to become a respected leader in your community. In conducting community-wide events, you engage not only community members from all sectors of the community but also the parents of the students you serve through physical education programs. Collaborating with community stakeholders in conducting community-wide events provides you with an opportunity to advocate for your physical education programs, market your successes, and (in some cases) raise much-needed funds to enhance your programs.

Leadership Roles and Responsibilities

As with any other major undertaking, coordinating special events is a complex process that can be manageable provided there is strong leadership that has the capacity and skill set for decision making as well as the capacity to work in a collaborative environment. In many projects, the person designated as the event chair takes on the major responsibilities as well as selecting the committee who will fulfill the individual subcommittee responsibilities. The success of any leader is the ability to foster a shared vision that will motivate others to achieve the desired outcomes of the project or event. Although there are many different styles of leadership (delineated in chapter 1), the level of involvement of each subcommittee director or coordinator will, in essence, depend on the experience of the event team. In areas where the subcommittee director has little experience, the event chair will probably take a more hands-on approach to ensure a successful event. In subcommittees in which the director has vast experience, the leader may step back and allow that team member more control. Delegating responsibilities to experienced team members further builds morale, trust, and respect among the planning committee members. The ultimate goal is to develop collaborative relationships within the event team whereby the roles, responsibilities, and tasks are delineated and shared decision making becomes an accepted process toward achieving the goals. However, the event chair is always ultimately responsible for ensuring that the process is managed and the goals and objectives of the event are met. Flow of communication between the event chair and subcommittee directors should be a constant and continuous process from the initial planning meeting to the final post-event evaluation. The organizational flowchart shown in figure 7.1 provides an outline of the roles and responsibilities of each subcommittee chair—media and marketing, operations and logistics, administrative and finance, and client and special services—defining how each subcommittee fits into the **elements of event management** structure.

Key Elements of Event Planning

There are several components inherent in planning any special event that should be considered when developing your overall plan. The quality and experience of your planning committee and subcommittee directors should be considered when assigning project tasks. The following list of key elements comprises all major components that must be included as you develop the initial plan. Having a written plan for what you would like to accomplish is the first step in conceptualizing your thoughts and, more precisely, what you need to do. It will also serve as a guiding document in developing time lines and logistics. To ensure a successful event, you have to give yourself and your team advance time to work on the **event planning** stage to ensure that all details are addressed in a timely manner. Sufficient time for planning is a critical step in organizing effective and successful events. Meticulous attention to details, regardless of the size of the event, is also a necessary part of the planning process if the event is to be successful. See figure 7.2 for a sample pre-event planning checklist.

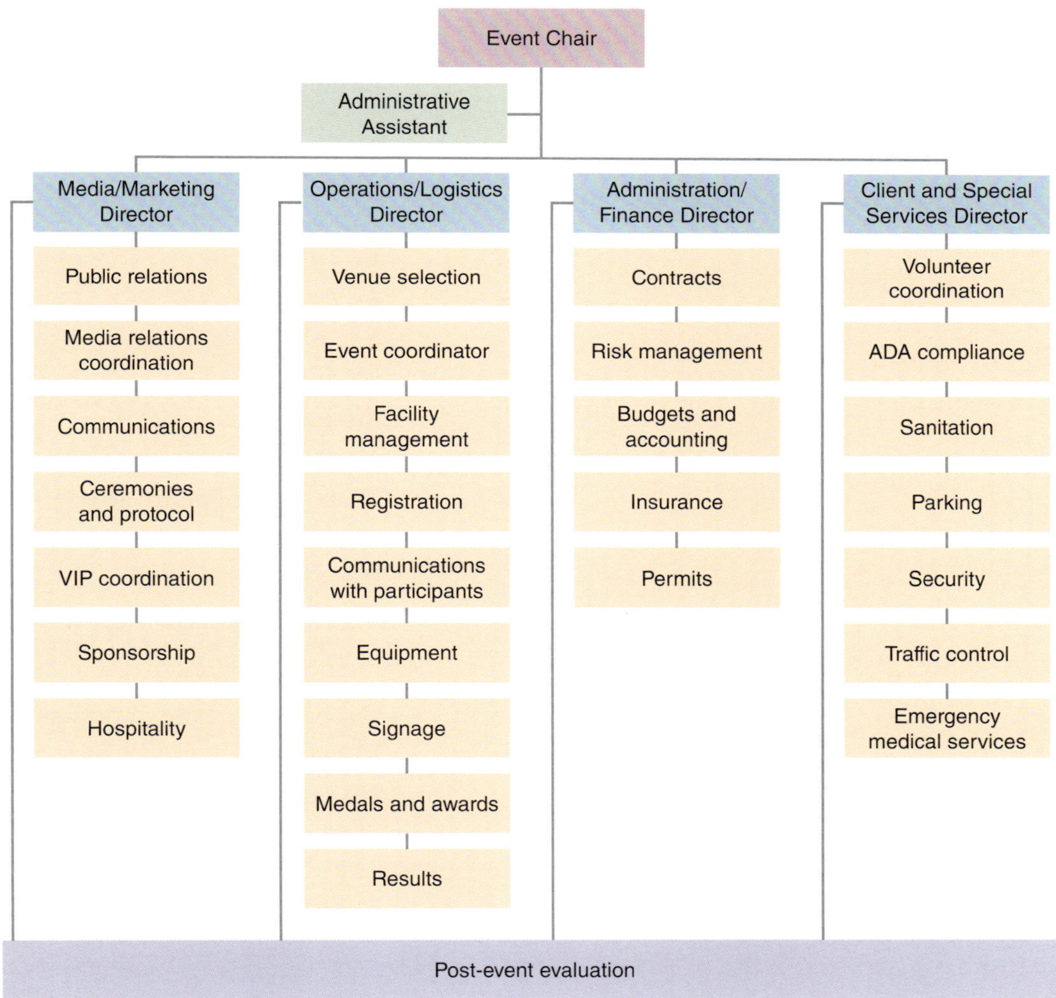

FIGURE 7.1 Leadership roles in event planning.

FIGURE 7.2 Pre-Event Planning Checklist

Event Name: ________________ Event Date: ________________

1. Preplanning
   - ☐ Objectives
   - ☐ Audience(s)
   - ☐ Messages
   - ☐ Costs
   - ☐ Dates
   - ☐ Location
2. Invitations
   - ☐ Phone call
   - ☐ Letter
   - ☐ Printed, informal
   - ☐ Printed, formal
   - ☐ RSVP return card
   - ☐ RSVP by phone
   - ☐ Reminder mailing
3. Program
   - ☐ Topics
   - ☐ Speakers
   - ☐ Speaker contacts
   - ☐ Speaker agreements, honoraria
   - ☐ Equipment needed
   - ☐ Biographies
   - ☐ Introductions
   - ☐ Hospitality
   - ☐ Transportation
   - ☐ Housing
   - ☐ Mementos
4. Facilities
   - ☐ Number of people
   - ☐ Auditorium-type seating
   - ☐ Conference room seating
   - ☐ Table shapes: O, U, V
   - ☐ Food service needed
   - ☐ Parking
   - ☐ Directional signs
   - ☐ Marquee sign(s)
5. Equipment
   - ☐ Lectern
   - ☐ Public address system
   - ☐ Microphone(s): lapel, neck, podium, table, floor
   - ☐ Raised platform
   - ☐ Projection screen
   - ☐ Projector
   - ☐ Slide advancer, pointer
   - ☐ Overhead projector
   - ☐ Video projector
   - ☐ Flip charts, markers
   - ☐ Extension cords
   - ☐ DVD player and monitor
   - ☐ Music player
   - ☐ Other: ________________
6. Publicity, promotion
   - ☐ Mailing lists
   - ☐ Promotional mailings
   - ☐ Posters, flyers
   - ☐ Advertising
   - ☐ Social media
   - ☐ Media contact
   - ☐ Media fact sheets
   - ☐ News releases
   - ☐ Talk show appearances
   - ☐ Press packets
   - ☐ Press room
   - ☐ Special phone lines for media
7. Photography, video
   - ☐ Type: slides, black and white, color
   - ☐ Video
   - ☐ Hiring of photographer or videographer
   - ☐ Shot list for photographer or videographer

8. Food, beverages
   - ☐ Menu selection
   - ☐ Caterers
   - ☐ Schedule
   - ☐ Type of service (buffet, seated)
   - ☐ Tables for 6, 8, 10
   - ☐ Head table
   - ☐ Place cards
   - ☐ Seating diagram
   - ☐ Beverages
   - ☐ Hospitality room service
9. Printed program
   - ☐ Agenda
   - ☐ Speakers' biographies and photos
   - ☐ Organizational information
   - ☐ Lists of officers, committees
   - ☐ Lists of contributors
   - ☐ Design, printing
   - ☐ Quantity
   - ☐ Distribution
10. Registration
   - ☐ Registration form
   - ☐ Bank account
   - ☐ Reporting system
   - ☐ Registration confirmation
   - ☐ On-site registration
     - ☐ Tables
     - ☐ Computers
     - ☐ Equipment
     - ☐ Personnel
     - ☐ Cash receipts
     - ☐ Programs
     - ☐ Name badges
     - ☐ Preregistration list
     - ☐ Ticket sales
     - ☐ Host identification
     - ☐ Signs
11. Transportation
   - ☐ For equipment
   - ☐ Lease or charter vehicles
   - ☐ To and from parking areas
   - ☐ For speakers and special guests
   - ☐ Between locations
   - ☐ Signs on vehicles
   - ☐ Schedules posted or published
12. Escorts and guides
   - ☐ For speakers
   - ☐ For special guests
   - ☐ For tours, exhibits, and so on
   - ☐ Aboard buses as needed
13. Decor
   - ☐ Selection of theme
   - ☐ Entrances and exits
   - ☐ Speaker platform
   - ☐ Head tables
   - ☐ Dining tables
   - ☐ Hospitality suite
14. Tickets
   - ☐ Prices
   - ☐ Advance sales
   - ☐ Printing
   - ☐ Distribution
   - ☐ Sales reports
   - ☐ Ticket and money control
   - ☐ Complimentary tickets
   - ☐ Press tickets
   - ☐ Sales at doors
   - ☐ Collection at events
15. Additional considerations
   - ☐ Bad weather planning
   - ☐ Exhibits, displays
   - ☐ Entertainment
   - ☐ Security
   - ☐ Technicians for equipment
   - ☐ Ambulance on stand-by
   - ☐ Police, traffic control, security
   - ☐ Valet parking

From J. Greenberg and J. LoBianco, *Organization and Administration of Physical Education,* 2nd ed. (Human Kinetics, 2026). Reprinted by permission from Charlene McWilliams, MBA, MSM. Sam Houston State University.

Within the literature there appears to be general consensus (Greenwell et al., 2014; Masteralexis et al., 2005; Watt, 2004) that the major elements involved in the organization of any special event can be categorized as shown in this list:

- Deciding on the purpose of the event
- Choosing the type of event
- Setting goals and objectives
- Planning the logistics
- Setting the budget
- Securing sponsorship
- Staffing for the event
- Securing a volunteer force
- Maintaining communications
- **Marketing events** and promoting them
- Media considerations
- Managing risk and contracts
- Providing awards
- Conducting post-event evaluation and follow-up

Purpose of the Event

The most fundamental question that any event organizer has to ask is *Why conduct this event?* To plan a successful event, purposeful goals and objectives must be clear and present. Hosting an event for the sake of hosting an event is not a sufficient reason, and it could have disastrous results. For example, if your purpose is to raise funds for your program, then you need to make sure you can secure enough corporate sponsors or participating members to yield a profit at the end of the event (see chapter 14). If your goal is to advocate for your program, then you need to make sure you have a strong marketing and media plan in place so that your messaging is clear and has a wide outreach. If your main objective is to build coherence and teamwork among faculty, parents, and community members, you need to ensure buy-in by the targeted groups so that you have participants on the day of the event. If your event is for charitable causes independent of your program, such as Jump Rope for Heart or Hoops for Heart, then you need to have the support and assistance of the affected organizations as well as school district administrative approval. Having a strong vision and purpose will help you decide what type of event will fulfill that need.

Type of Event

The type of event you choose to host will be contingent on the purpose of your event. You will also need to remain cognizant of the time, personnel, and funds you have for implementing the event. Hosting sport events is one of the most successful activities that school district personnel can conduct to raise funds for their programs. The scale of the event will be determined by the realistic plan and logistics that you and your committee develop. Some of the most popular sport events a physical education administrator can organize in the community are golf tournaments, 5K walks/runs, bowling tournaments, kickball tournaments, and softball tournaments; other popular events include creative activities such as family snowman building competition in the winter months. The interest and facilities in your community would in part dictate the type of tournament you can host.

The size of the tournament is further determined by your budget. For example, 5K walks/runs are extremely popular events to host because they include community members of all ages. Not only do they engage the youngest school-aged participants, but they also serve as a great intergenerational activity, bringing family members of all ages together to promote health and wellness. With respect to implementation, you could easily conduct your own 5K walk/run by partnering with a local park or university that already has a 5K route measured out for community use. Using an existing confined, safe route would not require street closures, making it the most cost-effective decision. Furthermore, you would have access to existing bathroom facilities and would not have to rent portable facilities. Using an existing route would require you to supply only what would be needed for logistical purposes: a registration table, a timing device, awards, refreshments, and postrace entertainment. If you choose to scale up and have a major event, it is strongly recommended that you contract with a professional company that manages races on a regular basis. In doing so, you would need either to secure a title sponsor and other corporate partners to make certain your event will be profitable or to ensure you will have large community participation whereby registration fees could cover a good portion of those contracted expenses. The advantage of contracting with companies that conduct 5Ks, 10Ks, half-marathons, or marathons is that they have the knowledge and skill to implement a large-scale event. Working with municipal departments for permitting, street closures, and security presence is common practice within their businesses. Other popular fundraising community events are health fairs, produce sales from school gardens, and sales of school gear and promotional items at middle and high school sport events.

As an example, consider that you are planning your first 5K community walk/run on a shoestring budget (which is what most school district programs operate on). Since this event will include the student and community population, you want to be certain that the event meets your purposes as well as ensure that it is fun for all involved. Assume that this walk/run is an advocacy event, and you want to promote the importance of being physically active throughout the calendar year. You begin the planning in late August to conduct the event prior to winter recess, allowing you approximately 12 weeks to solidify the plan. Based on that time line, and assuming that you are the event chair, where do you begin? Figure 7.3 should serve as a starting point.

If the goal of your special event is to raise awareness and advocate for your program, then consider partnering with your local professional sports teams or college and university sports teams. For example, you could have students representing several schools play a

FIGURE 7.3 How to Conduct a Community-Based 5K Walk/Run

PREPLANNING COMMITTEE MEETING

WEEK	MEDIA AND MARKETING DIRECTOR	OPERATIONS AND LOGISTICS DIRECTOR	ADMINISTRATION AND FINANCE DIRECTOR	SPECIAL SERVICES DIRECTOR
1		• Secure venue for 5K walk/run (county park).		
2	• Send out sponsorship requests. • Begin communications plan.	• Collaborate with county park management on logistics.	• Develop contracts, and submit permits for park. • Develop contracts for on-site vendors.	• Ensure ADA compliance.
3	• Design registration brochure. • Develop online registration website. • Advertise the event. • Coordinate public relations.	• Begin to monitor registration. • Work with marketing director for sharing logistics. • Create or obtain a map of 5K course. • Determine parking options.	• Secure insurance for event. • Have a risk management plan. • Have accounting procedures in place for registration.	• Coordinate volunteer registration. • Determine parking details and traffic flow.
4	• Communicate with weekly emails to race participants or more often as needed. • Determine VIP protocol, and develop invitation list.	• Order race bibs. • Order medals and awards for age-level finishers. • Order participation medals.	• Monitor contract status. • Contract with organization to have race bibs with chips for race results.	• Continue to monitor volunteer force. • Order sanitation facilities.
5	• Send out save-the-date communication to VIPs and media.	• Order sponsor signage. • Order event signage.	• Ensure all contracts are executed.	• Coordinate traffic control.

(continued)

FIGURE 7.3 *(continued)*

WEEK	MEDIA AND MARKETING DIRECTOR	OPERATIONS AND LOGISTICS DIRECTOR	ADMINISTRATION AND FINANCE DIRECTOR	SPECIAL SERVICES DIRECTOR
6	• Continue race promotion through all media outlets, and post on social media regularly.	• Order race shirts. • Order tents. • Order tables and chairs.	• Monitor registration. • Secure sponsorships. • Oversee accounting.	• Communicate with volunteers weekly or more frequently as needed.
7	• Continue race promotion through all media outlets. • Post on social media regularly.	• Monitor registration. • Communicate with park weekly or more frequently as needed.	• Monitor registration. • Secure sponsorships. • Oversee accounting.	• Schedule emergency medical services.
8	• Secure hospitality for VIP tent. • Secure post-event entertainment.	• Reserve barriers, timing equipment, and sound system.	• Monitor registration. • Secure sponsorships. • Oversee accounting. • Finalize food and drink sponsors.	• Communicate with volunteers.
9	• Continue race promotion through all media outlets.	• Monitor registration. • Monitor logistics.	• Monitor registration. • Secure sponsorships. • Oversee accounting.	• Develop volunteer schedule.
10	• Plan ceremonies and protocol.	• Monitor registration. • Monitor logistics.	• Monitor registration. • Secure sponsorships. • Oversee accounting.	• Communicate with volunteers.
11	• Print race day registration.	• Monitor registration. • Monitor logistics.	• Monitor registration. • Secure sponsorships. • Oversee accounting.	• Finalize logistics.
12	• Print final list of preregistered participants. • Contact local media.	• Perform race day coordination.	• Set up table for on-site registration.	• Set up volunteer check-in table.
Post-event evaluation				

mini basketball game during halftime at an NBA or college game. Another example would be to have schools adopt a mall and conduct rope-jumping demonstrations simultaneously at several malls across the community. Partnering with a local marathon is another great example of promoting your physical education program by having the students run their final mile in the actual marathon. For example, Kids Run Miami is a free county-wide program that invites all middle schools in Miami-Dade County to establish a consistent running program as a part of their physical education daily lesson plans in support of fitness education (figure 7.4). The goal of the program is to offer every child enrolled in Miami-Dade County middle schools an opportunity to run their first marathon (26.2 miles) and, in doing so, to promote a fit and healthy lifestyle while teaching children to create and fulfill goals. During this 15-week program, the kids must run a cumulative 25 miles leading up to the Final Mile event (1.2 miles), which is run on part of the same course, on the same day, and across the same finish line as the Life Time Miami Marathon & Half. Although the Final Mile is not timed, all participating kids receive shirts, race bibs, and medals along with having the unforgettable experience of running their first marathon. It becomes a huge media event with existing sponsorship, cheering crowds, and a feeling of self-efficacy when the student crosses the marathon finish line.

Other popular events that have proven to be hugely successful include a community-wide CPR Day, in which physical education teachers

FIGURE 7.4 Students participating in the Life Time Kids Run Miami, part of the Miami Marathon & Half.
Courtesy of Jake Butters.

certified in cardiopulmonary resuscitation (CPR) conduct hands-only training for registered community members in their school's gymnasiums on a given day; and a water safety awareness event prior to the summer months, such as the April Pool's Day event conducted annually by the National Basketball Association's (NBA's) Miami Heat. Countless events can be conducted when the physical education administrator develops partnerships and relationships with all facets of community-based organizations and businesses.

Conducting team-building events for district office personnel, school site administrators, or school board members at retreats is another way physical education administrators can use their talents while advocating for their programs. Since most retreats are off school site properties, events can be hosted at state parks, beaches, or other outdoor venues that offer a serene environment for people to relax and engage with staff members they might not get to interact with in the school environment. Project Adventure, a non-profit organization, uses adventure-based activities to advance the learning and development of students through experiential-based learning. Activities often include orienteering and geocaching in groups, Project Adventure teams, kayaking and canoeing, or seated brain teasers. The team-building process creates a culture of teamwork among employees that fosters better communication and understanding of each other's strengths, weaknesses, and interests; a shared vision; and a sense of connectedness. Planning for a nutritious breakfast or lunch catered either by an outside vendor or by the school district's department of food and nutrition is another way to subtly get the message across that sound nutritional habits and physical activity can promote health and wellness at all ages and that it's never too late to start. As a physical education department chairperson, you can implement the same types of team-building events through offering grade-level staff activities, serving covered dishes during holiday luncheons, and having school-based athletic and activity competitions to show support for the student-athletes.

Finally, charity-driven special events can be planned and implemented by the physical education administrator or physical education department chairperson. These events include nationally recognized events at the school level, such as Jump Rope for Heart activities, which help raise money for both the school and the American Heart Association. They could also include a No Uniform Day, for schools that require uniforms, to raise money for charitable organizations of your choice, such as the United Way, Ronald McDonald House Charities, children's hospitals, or cancer research organizations. Another option is to coordinate with organizers to offer special race fees to participate in community-based charity runs. Another type of event that can both advocate for your program and provide a service to your community is a Fresh Market Day, created to provide free produce from school gardens to families in need in your community.

Goals and Objectives

Whether you're planning a special event or writing a grant, a critical step in the development phase of any program or event is identifying the goals and objectives that you are expecting to achieve. As stated in chapter 14, clearly defined goals and objectives keep you focused on the purpose of the event and provide guidance throughout the planning and implementation process as well as the post-evaluation process. While goals are stated in relatively broad terms regarding what you would like to achieve as a result of project implementation, objectives are specific in scope. With well-defined objectives, adhering to your overall event plan assists you in staying on task; in addition, your plan provides a road map for attaining benchmarks and performance indicators that will be helpful in your final post-event evaluation. Through collaborative planning, objectives provide a clear vision for all stakeholders involved.

To structure your goals in a clear and precise manner, it is recommended that you follow the SMART principle for developing objectives. SMART goals and objectives should be written in simple terms and clearly define what you expect to accomplish. The type of objectives you write will be contingent on whether the goal is a long- or short-term one. For the purpose of event planning, examples are provided later. For the purpose of grant writing, please refer to chapter 14.

You may recall from chapter 3 that these SMART goals and objectives are defined in the following way:

***S**pecific*: Goals should be attainable, and they must be clearly defined and stated. They should answer the *who*, *what*, *where*, *when*, and *why* questions.

***M**easurable*: Goals should be stated in quantitative terms and must be measurable.

***A**chievable*: Goals should be set in challenging yet achievable and realistic terms.

***R**elevant*: Goals must be relevant to the purpose and to the needs of the project.

***T**ime-bound*: Goals must have time lines to determine progress toward meeting the end results of the event.

As an example, consider that you have chosen to conduct a community-based golf tournament to raise funds for your district's physical education program. A SMART goal might look something like this:

Overall goal: Conduct a community-wide golf tournament to raise money to provide physical education equipment for elementary schools in the Hometown school district.

Specific: Based on a survey of schools, it is determined that $10,000 is needed to fulfill the school's equipment needs.

Measurable: The amount raised through corporate sponsorship and registration fees can be measured on an ongoing basis through event accounting.

Achievable: Through a supportive corporate sponsor and an involved community, the amount is achievable.

Relevant: Through the efforts of the event subcommittee directors working collaboratively, raising $10,000 is a realistic goal.

Time-bound: Based on the time line of 9 months of planning (September through May), the goal of raising $10,000 is reasonable and achievable.

Setting SMART goals and objectives and adhering to your event plan bring you one step closer to ensuring a successful event. It is critically important for the leader to have constant communication with the event planning committee and subcommittee chairs to determine interim progress in meeting the goals and objectives. This communication effort will also provide immediate feedback to the event chairperson if additional support is needed in any specific subcommittees throughout the planning stages. Regularly scheduled meetings and conference calls will assist in monitoring the process every step of the way. The achievement of the goals and objectives will further lend support to conducting an extensive end-of-event evaluation.

Logistics Planning

During the initial planning meeting with key stakeholders, several logistical constructs need to be considered before the special event is finalized. These considerations include the date, location, duration of event, and proposed budget. Other logistical components such as the specified committees and subcommittees will need to be included as depicted in figure 7.1, but they will become more prominent as the event materializes and your subcommittee directors are in place.

After the type of event to host is determined, the next step is to decide on the date. When determining the date for your event, you need to take several factors into account. The first factor to consider is whether there are conflicting events or holidays that would affect participation. For example, if you are planning the 5K walk/run as shown in figure 7.2, are there any other large community events or races that are happening on that same date? If your proposed date conflicts with a well-established community walk/run (e.g., the Susan B. Komen event), you will probably not have a large turnout and may not reach your desired goals and objectives. You should also be aware of other existing events that bring groups of people together for social gatherings such as Super Bowls, NBA playoffs, World Cups, Grand Slams, and the World Series. Geographical weather conditions are another important factor when you are selecting a date. If you are planning an outdoor event, you also need to monitor weather conditions that are unique to certain times of the year. Consider heat and humidity; snow and precipitation; and other severe weather conditions such as thunderstorms, lightning, tornadoes, waterspouts, and dust storms.

The second logistical consideration is the location. To ensure widespread participation from community members, it would be best to select a centralized location so that no one in any geographic area of the community would need to travel too far; this idea holds true for both large, urban communities and rural communities. However, the availability of specific locations may also be contingent on the date your committee selects. For example, if you plan to hold a golf tournament, there may be one golf course that attracts more players than others, but it may not be available to host a tournament due to heavy member utilization. In this situation, you would need to explore other golf courses that would be able to host your tournament on the selected date, have the capacity to assist with tournament play, have ample parking for your participants, and can provide hospitality services for breakfast or lunch as well as a post-tournament reception area for the awards presentation. Negotiating the foursome fee would also be a consideration when selecting your venue.

The duration of the event is another logistical consideration that would also affect the date and location. For most runners, early morning races are preferred due to weather and road or traffic issues. In the 5K walk/run example, you should figure that you would need a location for a maximum of approximately four hours. If your run will start at 7:30 a.m., plan on setting up at approximately 5:30 a.m. to ensure that all troubleshooting can occur before the event and that everything is ready by the time the runners arrive. It should take no longer than one hour for the last walker to cross the finish line, so you can plan on having your awards presentation by 8:45. Runners and walkers can participate in post-event entertainment and consumption of snacks and beverages while waiting for the awards ceremony. The participants will begin to thin out by approximately 9:30 a.m., at which time cleanup can start (unless you have a full day of events planned and have contracted with the facility to do so).

Finally, your initial budget, sponsorship, and registration fees will further determine what you can include in your event. The full event planning committee needs to be involved in securing community and business partnerships and sponsorships. (Refer to chapter 14 for ideas and recommendations.) Most participants engaged in community-based events look forward to receiving their event T-shirt, participation medal, and participation goodie bags. These items should be a high priority when you determine what should be included in registration fees; however, your first option would always be to attempt to get them donated so you can increase your revenue margin. If additional funding becomes available, other activities could include a post-event bounce house and a face painting station (especially if young students are involved). Hospitality items such as food and beverages could be provided by your local farmers markets or supermarkets. Prizes and giveaways could be secured from community businesses, including passes to museums and other local attractions. School uniform vendors could provide deep discounts on race shirts and other incentives to schools for their participation levels.

Planning special events entails many different components and logistics, but it can be easily accomplished if you pay attention to details. Figures 7.1, 7.2, 7.3, and 7.5 can assist you in organizing and implementing all facets of your special events. Although it might seem overwhelming at first, the details are all manageable when the event planning committee works collaboratively to ensure a successful event for the participants as well as meeting the goals and objectives of the event.

Setting the Budget

When planning an event, you need to make certain that you have the funds readily available, you have the commitment of sponsors, or you are confident that participant registration fees will cover most of the needed funds. You should take a serious look at what you anticipate in revenue, what you anticipate in expenses, and what you have in contingency for unexpected expenses. Throughout the event planning process, the committee and subcommittee directors should continuously brainstorm on ways to secure additional funding sources, partners, and sponsors. Staying on budget through **budget management** procedures and controls will further assist you in implementing a successful event and meeting the goals and objectives of your plan.

One of the key subcommittee members is the administration and finance director. This team member should have skills in managing budgets; securing contracts and making sure income receipt is timely; and working with the media and marketing subcommittee director to secure sponsorships, business partnerships, and community donations. The finance director should report to the event chair on a regular basis regarding the budget status in case modifications need to be made to the event. If this is the first year you are hosting an event, it may take a little longer to develop relationships with potential or title sponsors. If this is your second year or beyond conducting the same event, then based on the success of the event in the previous year, you should have a revenue stream flowing.

Since in many cases the district physical education administrator is the event chairperson and the other leadership roles are filled by other school district personnel or volunteers from the business community, the cost of salaries will not be an issue; funding will be spent on the actual event. In some cases, budget items you will need to account for are the venue; contracts, permits, and insurance; printing; supplies and equipment; table, chair, and tent rentals; postage; food; event gear such as T-shirts; sound systems and entertainment; and awards. However, many of these items can take the form of in-kind services. For example, you can engage the school district's attorney's office to process contracts and permits; have the graphics department print invitations and event registration forms; and have schools provide tables, chairs, and portable sound systems. The event planning committee will still need to be vigilant in controlling and monitoring costs. For items that will need to be either purchased or rented, the district's office of procurement management could assist by putting those items out on bid (as identified in chapter 13) to ensure you are getting the best competitive pricing. Setting up a spreadsheet such as the worksheet in figure 7.5 will help you manage your funds.

Throughout the course of planning for the event, a series of budget controls should be put in place to monitor the budget throughout the process. Budget control is a necessary leadership responsibility to ensure that you do not overspend your budget and that all financial obligations are met. Always aim to stay within your working budget, but be alert to the fact that situations may arise that could cause you to expand your projected budget. Updating the budget worksheet periodically, or as new expenses and revenues become evident, will ensure checks and balances and provide for greater fiscal management.

Securing Sponsorship

After your budget is set and you monitor your expenses versus your revenues, it makes sense to secure as much sponsorship as possible so that you can conduct the type of event that you and your planning committee envisioned. It takes the entire team to reach out to their

LEADERSHIP IN ACTION

The Role of Partnership and Development in Advancing Physical Education, Physical Activity, and Fitness

Meredith Aronson

Director of Strategy and Partnerships, National Fitness Foundation

Over the past 30 years, U.S. childhood obesity rates tripled. According to the CDC in 2024, approximately one in five children and adolescents is obese while approximately one in six is overweight. Studies show that a lack of physical activity among kids can also lead to lower test scores, higher health care costs, and a greater likelihood of becoming overweight or obese into adulthood. It's clear that if we don't change the path we're on, this generation of children could live shorter lives than their parents.

We know we can't solve this problem alone. Everyone has a role to play, and it's our responsibility to continue to create opportunities for the next generation to be active, whether that's within the school walls or at home. In this endeavor, partnerships are instrumental. They enable different groups to come together regarding common goals and objectives. Schools are a perfect setting to find those synergies, particularly in an environment where health and education go hand in hand. Here are four partnership keys to success:

1. *Build trust with key stakeholders*. Partnerships aren't made overnight. It's important to establish relationships with these individuals so that you understand their motivations, challenges, and goals.
2. *Understand the common goals and objectives*. As you build a rapport with these individuals, think about how your interests and goals align.
3. *Leverage each other's strengths and insights*. The beauty of partnerships is that you can build upon each individual's or organization's strengths. When collaborating, ensure that each party has clearly defined roles and responsibilities.
4. *Adapt and grow together*. Alongside your teammates, work together to ensure you are meeting your goals and objectives. Continually reflect on and analyze how you can improve your work together. Partnerships must evolve and grow.

Through partnership and collaboration, any school or district can take simple steps toward improving the health and wellness of the students, which in turn increases the likelihood that these students will score better on exams, show up to class, and go on to graduate with great success. If health and education champions and agencies partner together, it's a winning situation for all.

community and to corporate businesses to garner additional fiscal support. Event sponsorship can come in many forms, from simply having a company name in the event print and media materials to full-out event naming rights, or title sponsorship. Sponsorship opportunities can also come through as in-kind contributions whereby a product, service, or merchandise (as opposed to monetary donations) is provided to assist with the event. Such services can include provision of food for the event, a portable stage on loan, and all print materials and banners without any exchange of cash. Securing the sponsorship from local businesses and organizations can not only defray the costs of the event but also serve to increase participation, which in turn will increase revenue from registration fees. As demonstrated in chapter 14, business partners and community sponsors obtain reciprocal benefits when supporting school district and community-based special events.

As a follow-up, once you have your final list of event sponsors secured, remember to keep them in the communication loop, invite them to the VIP reception area at the event, present them with recognition certificates or plaques at the event in front of all of the participants, send follow-up thank-you notes, and recognize them in all media interviews and post-event

FIGURE 7.5 Sample Event Planning Budget Worksheet

Name of event: ______________________________

Date of event: ______________ Location: ______________

EXPENSE	ESTIMATED COST PRE-EVENT	ACTUAL COST POST-EVENT
Venue fee		
Insurance		
Permits		
Rentals: tables and chairs		
Rentals: tents		
Rentals: sound system		
Contracts (race bibs and computerized results)		
Printing		
Postage		
Website development (online registration)		
Food and catering		
Signage		
Event T-shirts		
Post-event entertainment		
Other		
Total expenses		
REVENUE	**ESTIMATED COST PRE-EVENT**	**ACTUAL COST POST-EVENT**
Registration fees		
Vendor fees		
Sponsorships		
Corporate cash donations		
Other		
Total revenues		

newsletters and articles. These simple practices will help ensure that your sponsors become repeat donors for future events.

Staffing the Event

Since planning and coordinating special events is a complex process, staffing requires that you identify critical staff members before the event begins. The numbers of staff and volunteers needed will depend on the size and type of event. Keep in mind that as exhibited in figure 7.1, there are lead staff members and committee members already identified in the organizational chart who have key roles and responsibilities. Their presence at the event will be just as important; they will be ultimately responsible for overseeing the full event logistics and operations. It should also be understood during the planning sessions that you (the event chair) and your team (event co-chair, media and marketing director, operations director, administration and finance director, and client and special services director) will all have a role in identifying and recruiting personnel within their subcommittees to assist with the implementation of the special event. Having the right staff in place is a major part of ensuring that you conduct a successful event. Since this event is hosted by the local school district, most (if not all) staff members work in a voluntary role. Therefore, since budget for personnel will not be a factor, having enough qualified and trained personnel to staff the event is an important consideration.

Media and Marketing

Throughout the planning process, your media and marketing director, along with input from the event planning committee, will have ultimately developed a marketing plan that takes into account the type of event, the potential participants, the media and communications plan, and all **public relations** associated with the event. Branding your event to be theme based or securing a title for the event will also be the responsibility of the media and marketing team. Most of the marketing and media outreach will have taken place throughout the planning process, including sending out media releases, maintaining communication with sponsors and other personnel, and—most importantly—developing a website that will host the online registration forms and all event information. The website should be updated on a regular basis all the way through event day. Throughout the process, the operations and logistics director needs to be in constant communication with the media and marketing director to ensure that any updated logistical information that needs to reach the registered participants is sent out in a timely manner and posted immediately. Regular communications should be sent out weekly (or daily as the event approaches) to all registered participants and sponsors to continue to promote interest and generate excitement.

On event day, your major responsibility will be to ensure that you have enough trained staff to assist with the end product of your marketing plan. The media and marketing director should have staff available on-site early to greet the VIPs and media personalities as they check in at the registration table and to escort them to the VIP reception tent prior to the start of the event. At this time VIPs could be briefed on the run of show (what happens from the beginning of the event to the end of the event), the event logistics, and any lingering questions. During the pre-event meet and greet, select volunteers should alert the event chair as to who has arrived so that the chair and other key directors can personally meet them. Having an internal communication system during the event, whether by phone or using walkie-talkies, should be on your event checklist so that key players in the know can be alerted of all ongoing activities and incidents. During that initial meet and greet, television, radio, and print media reporters could conduct interviews while staff responsible for social media should be taking photographs and posting them on all social media outlets with the appropriate hashtags for corporate and partner sites. Having enough staff available to be assigned to select VIPs will only enhance the public relations efforts that have been generated.

Event Operations and Logistics

Event day is when it all comes together. All of the planning, logistics, preparation, and communications are ready to go. The morning of the event, the operations and logistics director needs to be the first one on-site to meet with key logistics staff and volunteers to make sure that they all know what their roles and responsibilities are, what the layout of the event will look like, where everything will be set up, and what to do if an emergency occurs. Event-day operations require the majority of on-site staff and volunteers to ensure that the event runs smoothly. In many cases unexpected situations arise, but if event staff are prepared to handle them calmly and quickly, making sure that the people who are making the decisions are notified immediately, then the occurrence will stay behind the scenes. All event staff members and volunteers should have in their possession a map of the logistics, a time line for the event, and a question-and-answer sheet, and they should be comfortable with knowing who to contact if they encounter a situation they are not sure how to handle. For example, for the 5K walk/run, they should be aware of where the on-site registration table is, where preregistered participants can pick up their T-shirt and bib if they have not already done so, where walk/run participants can store their personal items during the event, where the start and finish lines are, where spectators need to stand, what time the run will start, what time the awards ceremony will occur, where the restrooms or portable facilities are, and where to go for emergency assistance. Figure 7.6 provides a sample of the logistics map that should be posted on your website in advance of the event as well as in the hands of all staff and volunteers on the day of the event.

Staff and volunteers also need to know where they will be staged during the event so that all participants can identify them if they have questions or need assistance. Having staff and volunteers in identifiable T-shirts visible at key points can help participants with the logistics such as ensuring that they stay on the course route or know where to obtain emergency assistance. For example, volunteers and staff could be staged at key points along the route, setting up and picking up equipment, hanging banners for sponsor signage, assisting with on-site registration, assisting with the awards ceremony, having the medals in order for age-group winners, and monitoring awards for VIPs and other event giveaways. After the event, operations staff will also be responsible for making sure that all of the equipment and signage in their designated areas are collected and returned to a designated home base. This step will not only assist those assigned to the client and special services director for cleanup, it will also be useful for saving money on future events; many of the sponsor signs and banners can be reused, which will cut down on future budgetary needs.

Administration and Finance

Most of the work through the administration and finance director will be completed well in advance of the event. Contracts and permits will already have been signed and approved, event insurance will have been purchased, and sponsorship checks and event registration fees will have been deposited and accounted for. During event day, the primary responsibilities of staff will be to collect money at the on-site registration table and make sure that sponsor tables are strategically placed so that they get good traffic and visibility as well as stay clear of any obstruction of participant activity. The work of the finance director will resume after the event, when all accounts need to be

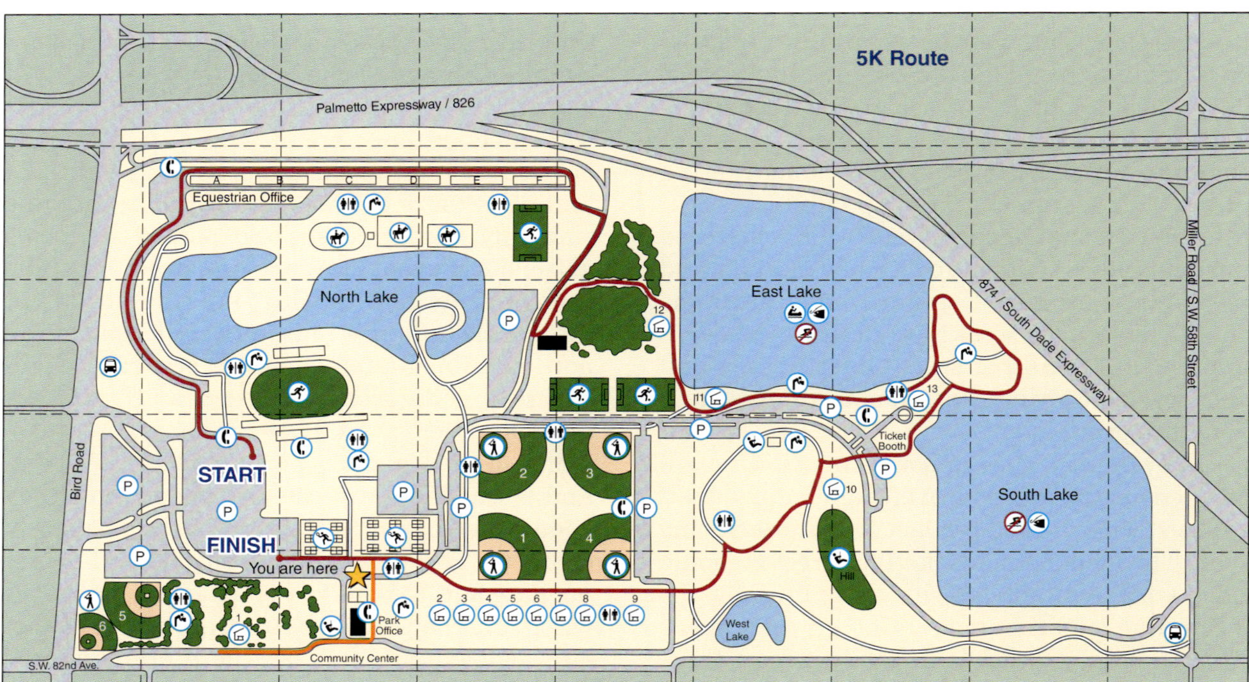

FIGURE 7.6 Sample 5K walk/run logistics map.
Courtesy of Miami-Dade County Parks, Recreation and Open Spaces Department.

balanced and closed out and all receipts need to be delivered to the sponsors.

Risk management concerns need to be addressed prior to the event as well as on event day to ensure that the potential for participant or spectator injury is eliminated or diminished to the extent possible. The obvious first step in risk management begins with the development of both the printed and online registration forms. Embedded in the registration form is a waiver of liability that must be signed by participants over the age of 18 and a parent or guardian for those under the age of 18. Certificates of insurance require that this policy be in place. Staff assigned to this subcommittee must also conduct an event-day walk-through on the morning of the event to ensure that no obstacles or hazards appear that were not there on a pre-event walk-through. Potential risks should be assessed well in advance of the start of the event. If any new hazards appear, such as downed branches from a thunderstorm the night before, then event staff needs to be notified immediately so it can be removed prior to the start of the event. Administrators employed by the venue being utilized, whether a park director or city manager, must also be involved in the risk management plan as well as the pre-event and event-day walk-through. Having them engaged will correct any foreseeable risks well in advance of the event. Other risk management issues to monitor for outdoor events include whether the venue has an alarm system and siren for possible lightning strikes, enough hydration stations and shady areas to help prevent heat illness, and a contingency plan for unexpected weather conditions. Appropriate advance planning and a vigilant staff during event-day operations should reduce the risk of any liability issues occurring. Remember: *Safety for all involved should always be the first and foremost concern of all event planners.*

Client and Special Services

Staff assigned to the client and special services director have a huge job, but they often get little recognition for the work that they perform. These responsibilities often include coordinating volunteers; ensuring Americans with Disabilities Act (ADA) compliance; and ensuring services needed on event day, such as sanitation accommodations, parking, security, traffic control, emergency medical services, and more.

From the initial day of planning through the event day, the special services director needs to work with the operations and logistics director to ensure that through carefully planned logistics, the event is accessible to all students and community members with disabilities. If not at the time of the first walk-through, then it gives the event planning team time to make the necessary accommodations so that all participants have equal access. Title III of the ADA, enacted in 1990, mandates that individuals with disabilities have equal access to public facilities and that they should be provided the opportunity to benefit from equal goods or services. A concerted effort needs to be exerted to ensure that there are no barriers in the built or natural environment that would prevent a person with disabilities from participating. Potential barriers include access to the venue, the walk/run course, restroom facilities, parking, and other designated areas such as food and beverage stations and medal presentation areas. (Chapter 5 presents additional information regarding physical education and physical activity programs for students with disabilities.) Staff assigned to assist any person with a disability should have undergone previous training and should alert the director immediately if any unforeseen situation occurs.

The second major area of responsibility is the securing and coordination of volunteers for the event. It is highly recommended that the **volunteer coordinator** secure more volunteers than may be needed, keeping in mind that they are generously volunteering their time but that not all volunteers always show up for an event. Additionally, as an event coordinator, you must be sensitive to the time requirements of volunteers on event day. A 5K walk/run usually lasts four hours. However, if you were conducting a golf tournament, it could last as long as eight hours from setup time to the end of the awards ceremony and the following meal reception. In that case, you would need to secure extra volunteers and assign them to shifts based on their personal schedule preferences and availability. Having access to a pool of committed volunteers that can be secured through school staff, health organizations, municipal organizations, local businesses, and community service clubs is a great starting place. Many of the sponsor organizations will also have their employees show up in force to volunteer in support of the event. Providing community service hours to high school clubs and athletic teams will further secure an ample number of volunteers for your district-coordinated event. Volunteers should get their event-day assignments during a pre-event kick-off meeting. Their roles and responsibilities should be clearly delineated. As the coordinator, you also have the responsibility of treating all volunteers with dignity and respect and making sure that they are recognized during the introduction at the event kickoff and thanked again at the awards ceremony. In doing so, you will garner your own database of volunteers for future events. It is further recommended that through budgeting you provide volunteers with uniquely designed T-shirts so that they can be readily identified if any participants or spectators need assistance.

Other volunteer staff that will be needed for event-day operations are those willing to assist with parking and foot traffic flow as well as be on call as floaters (people assigned to perform multiple duties as needed). It is highly recommended that these responsibilities be given to adult volunteers as opposed to school-aged volunteers. Emergency medical staff and security on-site would be ideally provided by the municipality in which the event is being conducted. Hopefully, with advance planning and coordination, these services will be provided as in-kind as part of the employee's regular duty hours.

Awards Ceremony and Presentation

The final act of the event-day activity is the awards ceremony and medal presentation. For the 5K walk/run, you would ensure that enough volunteer staff are posted at the finish line to see that all of the registered participants receive a participation medal. At the ceremony, you would begin by once again recognizing the event sponsors and would present them with a certificate or plaque that they can proudly display in their business or corporation to showcase their involvement. During this time, it would also be good to recognize and thank all of the volunteers for their hard work and dedication to making the event successful. Lastly, it would be an appropriate time to recognize your subcommittee directors; invite them to come up onstage or in front of the group to identify the age-group winners and award them with either a special place medal or a place trophy. The subcommittee directors who took the journey with you should be a part of the final recognition ceremony.

If goodie bags were not distributed during registration or at the time when race materials, shirts, and bibs were distributed, the time to give them out would be as the registered participants are leaving. Having a takeaway is a great reminder of how appreciated everyone is for participating and assisting you in reaching your event goals and objectives.

Once all of the participants have left the venue, then all hands on deck, staff, and volunteers need to clean up and collect all equipment. This effort gives the venue administration a sign of good faith that you respect their facility, and it will open up opportunities to continue a working relationship for future events.

Post-Event Duties and Evaluation

Although the event has successfully ended, your duties as the special event chairperson are not over. Once you gather your thoughts and are in your office the next day, the first line of action is to send out thank-you letters to all sponsors, subcommittee chairs, and committee members who assisted you in planning and implementing the event. If funding or sponsorship opportunities are available, hosting an invite-only thank-you reception or dinner would be appreciated by all. The media and marketing director should also send out a thank-you note to all registered participants with the race results included. Social media should continue posting photos and comments about the event. In addition, a photo library should be posted on the event website.

Within the first week after the event, the final formal duty would be to hold a post-event meeting with key stakeholders and subcommittee directors in order to receive authentic feedback on how they thought the event went—what they learned from the experience, what was successful, as well as what they would have done differently. It is extremely important to receive this type of feedback because it will be helpful in conducting future community-wide events or repeating the same event on an annual basis. At this time, it is also important to clean up your databases so that you can communicate with volunteers, event participants, and staff in the future. Having this information readily available will serve as a launching point for staffing needs and event growth. Document all comments so that you have them readily available for future reference in both hard copy and electronic files. Lastly, conducting a systemic formal evaluation will be your final responsibility in determining whether you met your goals and objectives.

Once you have secured verbal feedback from your planning committee and subcommittee chairs, it is recommended that you conduct an analysis of strengths, weaknesses, opportunities, and threats (SWOT analysis). A SWOT analysis is a useful technique for understanding your project's strengths and weaknesses as well as identifying available opportunities and threats in the planning and execution of your special event. Figure 7.7 shows the interaction of all four components of the analysis.

This process should be viewed in relation to your original goals and objectives for the purposes of improving on what you have initiated in your event plan. It could also assist in determining if you met the original goals and objectives of your event and the degree to which they were met. The results of your SWOT analysis should be used to modify your planning processes and management plan for future events, building on the successes of your present event.

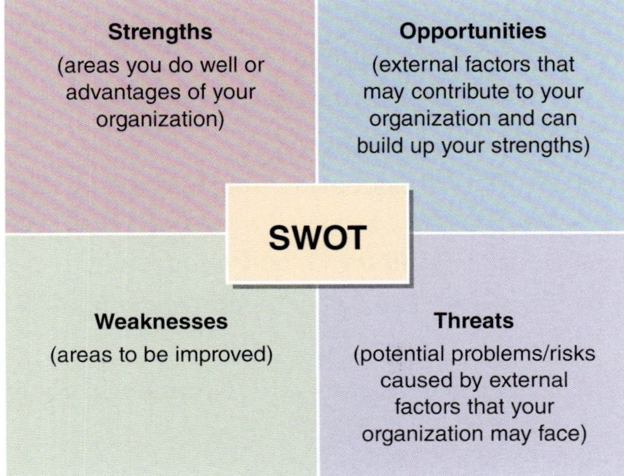

FIGURE 7.7 SWOT analysis.

Field Trips

Both teachers and students look forward to field trips. Although often viewed as a fun experience away from the school building for the day, when properly planned, these external events provide for an extension of the learning environment by offering many academic and social experiences for students. Keep in mind that whether the experience is planned by district-level administrators, physical education department chairpersons, or individual physical education teachers, there is a huge amount of responsibility in the planning and supervision of field trips, which includes ensuring that safety protocols are followed. Some of the benefits of field trips include the following:

- They offer an opportunity to reinforce the curriculum by providing experiential learning in real-world settings.
- They increase student engagement and motivation for learning and reinforcing concepts that are taught in the classroom.
- They enhance critical-thinking skills through active learning, active listening, asking questions, problem solving, and engaging in discussions regarding the activity.
- They promote social-emotional learning by allowing students to collaborate with their peers, make connections, and make lifetime positive memories.

Deciding whether or not to plan a field trip requires considering several factors, including time, resources, and rules and regulations. Here are some of the most important considerations for planning a field trip:

- Follow school and district protocols in the planning and approval process for all field trips. Every school and school district has a process in place, usually in the form of a field trip manual, which is approved annually by the school board.

- Consider all of the logistics, including parental permission; approved transportation; expenses incurred; and number of approved chaperones and volunteers (who are cleared through district screenings) that will be needed to meet student-to-adult ratios.
- Secure funding for students from disadvantaged communities who might need fiscal support to attend so that every child—independent of each family's economic status—has an opportunity to engage in all activities. Funds from school clubs or organizations that participate in fundraising activities can assist with providing financial support to students with demonstrated needs.
- Always plan a follow-up activity in class to ensure that students realized the academic impact of the field trip.

In addition to these considerations, specific protocols may exist for schools that participate in field trips outside the district's county. Finally, virtual field trips are a practical option that provides opportunities to explore educational and cultural experiences without the concern of planning off-site travel.

Conducting School-Wide Events

Once you (as the physical education administrator) have gained the skills and knowledge necessary to conduct a community-wide event to raise funds for your schools or to advocate for your physical education programs, the next step is to use your management and leadership skills to educate the physical education teachers on how to conduct their own school-wide events. The process is similar in planning and execution; it's just smaller in scope and nature.

From a district-wide perspective, early in the school year, consider focusing one of your professional service days or professional development opportunities on training teachers how to advocate for physical education and physical activity by conducting school site events for students, teachers, and parents. During this training, also consider providing support for teachers on how to write mini grants so that they can secure funding for their own programs. Information for grant writing can be found in chapter 14. Several community-based foundation grants, professional sports teams foundation grants, and hospital foundation and trust foundation grants are usually geographically based in the community where the schools are located.

Fuel Up to Play 60 FLAG in Schools is an example of how the National Football League (NFL), local professional sports leagues, and community-based organizations and foundations come together to support the implementation of flag football in the schools by offering professional development opportunities for physical education teachers and after-school leaders as well as by providing equipment through their grant-funded programs. Led by a partnership between the GENYOUth Foundation, SHAPE America, and USA Football, the program offers the opportunity to expand your physical activity offerings to students.

This example is not the only one; the list of nationally recognized mini grants available for teachers and school settings is endless. The following list includes some of the most popular resources for funding opportunities for physical education teachers:

- Dick's Sporting Goods
- Finish Line Youth Foundation
- GENYOUth Fuel Up to Play 60 NFL FLAG in Schools
- Fuel Up to Play 60 and Play 60—National Dairy Council and NFL
- Life Time Foundation
- Lowe's Foundation
- Nike School Innovative Fund
- NHL Floor Hockey
- PYFP—Presidential Youth Fitness Program
- Saucony Run for Good Foundation
- The First Tee—youth golf programs
- Under Armour Foundation
- USA Field Hockey—FUNdamental Field Hockey
- U.S. Soccer Foundation
- Women's Sports Foundation

Promotion of Nationally Recognized Events and Programs

The physical education administrator can also assist schools in promoting their physical education programs through nationally recognized events and programs. These major events take place annually, so setting time lines to plan, fund, and conduct an event is manageable. Since these opportunities would primarily be based at the school site, a great partner to work with would be your school's Parent–Teacher Association (PTA) or Parent–Teacher–Student Organization (PTSO). Parents are incredibly resourceful, have great imaginations and vision, and would be happy to assist. The school calendar of events for a sample of these activities could include the following:

- October: National and International Walk to School Day, http://kidzneurosciencecenter.com/walksafe
- February: American Heart Month, www.heart.org/HEARTORG
- May: National Physical Education and Sport Week, http://portal.shapeamerica.org/events/pesportweek/National-PE-and-Sport-Week.aspx
- May: National Physical Fitness and Sports Month, https://healthfinder.gov/NHO/MayToolkit.aspx
- May: Project ACES, http://lensaunders.com/aces/aces.html

See the Planning a Themed Activity sidebar for an example of how to plan a themed activity.

Another major program that is highly recommended for all schools across the United States is the I Can Do It! (ICDI) program for students with disabilities. ICDI is a health promotion program that partners with K-12 schools and school districts, colleges and universities, and community-based organizations to provide access and opportunities for children and adults with a disability to be healthy and active (U.S. Department of Health and Human Services, 2024). The program and resources are managed by the Administration for Community Living (ACL), U.S. Department of Health and Human Services. For more information on this program, see their website (www.acl.gov). Perfect for school settings, the ICDI program allows physical education teachers and other school support personnel to set and track weekly physical activity and nutrition goals enabling the student to receive the Presidential Active Lifestyle Award (PALA+). Anchors Away, a community-funded program to provide sailing and other water sports opportunities for students with disabilities in Miami-Dade County Public Schools (see figure 7.8), initialized by the Aventura Marketing Council, is another way students can earn their PALA+ Award through the ICDI program.

Promotion of School Site Events and Activities

Aside from nationally recognized advocacy programs, the physical education administrator can assist teachers in coming up with monthly theme-based activities that could recharge teachers and engage students, staff,

FIGURE 7.8 Anchors Away provides a sailing program as well as other water sports opportunities for students with disabilities in Miami-Dade County, Florida.

Aventura Marketing Council's Anchors Away foundation, photography by Andrew Goldstein.

Planning a Themed Activity

Issue

Celebrate holidays by making the experience fun, nutritional, and full of physical activity.

The Big Idea

To engage more student involvement in special projects, especially theme-based ones, activities should be fun and motivating. As students engage in these types of activities, especially around holidays, make sure that you provide activities that can be completed either individually or as a team. Being part of an activity further builds a sense of class unity and cooperation among students. Giving students the option to run individually or as a team will also spark interest and involvement. Begin with early planning, map out your course (depending on your grade level: elementary, middle, or high school), and build the excitement.

Implementation

Fitness

- Map out a 1K run (0.62 miles) for elementary school, 2K (1.2 miles) run for middle school, and 3K (1.8 miles) run for high school students.

Provide a nutritional meal after the run.

- Have samples of holiday food representing various cultures to enable students to taste foods that may be new to them.
- Show portion sizes and calorie counts.

Interdisciplinary

- Use math concepts in measuring out the course (can either be done by students or by the teacher).
- Work with cafeteria personnel in developing unique and nutritious menus.
- Include social studies lessons on cultures of the world.

Community

- Engage parents in soliciting food donations from local grocery stores.
- Contact your school's business partnerships to fund medals and participation giveaways.
- Have your school social and print media cover the event so that parents and community members at large can see what you do to advocate for your students' ability to lead healthy and happy lives through physical activity.

Takeaway

Conducting special events centered on physical activity generates excitement as students celebrate various holidays and traditions. It further engages the whole school community to be a part of something bigger than their own departments.

Results

- Students complete their designated distances (1K, 2K, or 3K).
- The event promotes cultural understanding.
- The event promotes team building and collaboration among students, staff, faculty, and administration.

and parents. Keep in mind that these special event activities, although most notably implemented in elementary schools, have the same motivational effect for middle and high school students. Figure 7.9 lists examples of monthly theme-based activities.

FIGURE 7.9 Theme-Based Activities for School Site Field Days and Activities

SEPTEMBER

Theme: Walking Workout

Activity: Students take laps around a track or field as they acclimate into fitness for the new school year.

Objective: Count steps; calculate resting heart rate (RHR).

OCTOBER

Theme: Pumpkin Patch Circuit Training

Activity: Students rotate through an obstacle course.

Objective: Choose creative activities that are fun and unique.

NOVEMBER

Theme: Turkey Trot

Activity: Students participate in a walk/roll/run at their grade-level distance: 1K (0.62 miles) for elementary school; 2K (1.2 miles) for middle school; 3K (1.8 miles) for high school.

Objective: Complete the distance.

DECEMBER

Theme: Gingerbread Relay

Activity: Teams of four take turns during a relay to pick up one item at a time to decorate their gingerbread cutout. The first team to use all of the items to complete their gingerbread cutout wins that round.

Objective: Practice teamwork and collaboration.

JANUARY

Theme: New Year's Resolution

Activity: Students write in journals.

Objective: Set goals, and develop a plan to achieve them.

FEBRUARY

Theme: Healthy Heart Month

Activity: Students in grades K-12 participate in school-wide CPR/AED training days.

Objective: Learn how to do hands-only CPR.

MARCH

Theme: Maximize Your Fitness through Rhythms and Dance

Activity: Students participate in either teacher- or student-led dance activities.

Objective: Explore more fun ways to be physically activity through dance.

APRIL

Theme: Pass the Egg

Activity: Partners move through an obstacle course passing a raw egg on a spoon between themselves. If the egg drops and breaks, then they start from the beginning. The team with the best time wins the activity. (*Note*: This activity should be done outdoors.)

Objective: Complete the course with a partner in the least amount of time.

MAY

Theme: Spring Into Fitness

Activity: Students in teams of five participate in a mile run and fitness assessment; they alternate between jogging, jumping, skipping, and hopping every time the whistle blows.

Objective: Complete the mile as a team, crossing the finish line at the same time.

The Administrator's Role in Elementary School Field Days

For students in elementary school, the annual **field day** reminds them that the end of the school year is near and that summer recess is around the corner. Field days have always been an important event for children of all ages. Although competition can be fun, the focus of the activities should be more on fun than on competition. When selecting activities to conduct, keep in mind that they should be age appropriate and should vary based on the grade level of the students. Field days should be safe and fun, and they should build lots of school spirt and excitement.

As a physical education administrator, you play an important role in assisting beginning physical education teachers in coordinating field days, from the planning to the grade-level organization to activities that are safe yet fun. As with conducting community-wide events, advance planning is critical to making the day a success. The physical education teacher needs to understand that the field day must be coordinated with the principal and conducted in collaboration with the classroom teachers.

The first decision is to select a date that does not conflict with any of the other activities that are going on at the school, taking into account the testing calendar, holidays, and other preplanned programs. Having buy-in from the whole school environment, including secretaries, custodians, and cafeteria managers, will add much-needed support in adjusting the school day when you have the event. Here are some of the considerations:

1. In the K-5 environment, will each grade level have their own field day, or will some grades be combined?
2. Will each grade level have their own day? Alternatively, will it be scheduled as half-day events with one grade level in the morning and another in the afternoon?
3. How many events do you plan to conduct during the field day?
4. Will all students take part in the activities, or will some have other responsibilities, including roles as spectators and cheering squads?
5. What types of activities will you have? Will they all be competitive?

6. Will everyone get a participation certificate? Will medals be awarded for event winners?
7. Will overall scores be kept so that there is a grade-level champion, or is the emphasis only on fun?
8. Have you coordinated with the cafeteria to have bag lunches for everyone, or will the classes work around their regularly scheduled lunchtimes?
9. Do you have enough equipment to set up several stations, or do you need time between each transition?

The second step for the physical education teacher is developing a communication plan in order to start getting community support or sponsors to purchase T-shirts, medals, ribbons, and any other supplies and equipment needed beyond what the teacher has in the supply room. The communication plan will also include a time line for classroom teacher and parent notifications. As you assist in selecting activities and begin to get a count of how many staff members will be needed, you can start assigning responsibilities to the volunteers who will assist you. The volunteers can be staff members, parents, college students, community members, and other approved school site volunteers. Volunteers can be assigned to monitor the same activity through the day so that the students rotate on a scheduled basis. Logistically, the volunteers can monitor their assigned activity stations and the equipment needs as well as keep track of scores or results for particular heats in each class. Examples of age and developmentally appropriate field day activities can be found online; they are posted on professional physical education organization websites.

Two more considerations involve safety and awards. For student safety, make sure that you set up plenty of hydration stations and that the school nurse is on-site to assist with any illnesses or injuries. For the safety of staff members who may not be used to being outdoors for extended periods, it is wise to suggest that they bring sunscreen and that they wear hats and light-colored clothing.

Awards leave a lasting impact on children of all ages. If you are giving out awards, they can be distributed at the end of the field day or immediately after each event. It is further recommended that the results of the event and the award recipients be announced on the morning announcements on the day immediately following the event. Make sure you have a script ready for the next day so the results can be included in the morning announcements.

Another important preparation is to always have a contingency plan in case of inclement weather. Lastly, just as with conducting community-wide events, after the field day, remember to send out thank-you notes and hold an end-of-event planning committee meeting to evaluate the implementation. Once beginning physical education teachers have conducted their first field day, they will be ready for the following year.

Before- and After-School Programs

Physical activity programs before or after school can benefit students not only by helping them meet their 60 minutes of daily physical activity as recommended by the Physical Activity Guidelines for Americans but also by helping to boost academic performance, as described in chapter 3. Providing opportunities for students to participate in a safe and supervised program is an additional asset for working parents who cannot always pick up their child from school when the bell rings. The physical education administrator can play a role in researching all of the available programs and providing the school with a selection of ideas from which to choose, as some programs may be fee based while others are offered at no cost to schools or families.

One of the most popular types of before- or after-school programs involves walking, biking, or rolling to and from school. Most parents are familiar with pedestrian and biking programs, but adding rolling to the options gives students in wheelchairs the same access to the fitness and social benefits of safe transport to and from school. These programs can also be a part of the International Walk to School Day and Bike to School Day when implemented district-wide.

LEADERSHIP IN ACTION

Inclusion and Leadership Through Special Olympics

Special Olympics

With sports as the foundation, Special Olympics' Unified Champion Schools program offers a combination of activities that equip young people with tools and training to create sport, classroom, and community experiences that reduce bullying and exclusion; promote healthy activity and interactions; combat stereotypes and stigma; eliminate hurtful language in schools; and engage young people in prosocial activities that lead to more inclusive and accepting attitudes, behaviors, and school climate.

The activities of the Unified Champion Schools program enhance a number of key educational initiatives in important and relevant ways. The initiatives listed next are frequently a part of school improvement plans and activities as school staff seek to increase student success. Data show that Unified Champion Schools programming can serve as a meaningful and effective intervention in support of the following:

- Core content and 21st-century skills
- A positive, caring, equitable school climate
- Positive behavior interventions and supports
- School connectedness
- Physical health and emotional well-being

One component of Unified Champion Schools is Special Olympics Unified Sports, which combines students with and without disabilities to participate in sports and physical activities together. In schools, this component can take the shape of an extracurricular athletics team, a fitness club, or a Unified Physical Education class.

Unified Physical Education in particular provides a unique opportunity for students with and without disabilities to come together through ongoing educational and physical activities, using the power of Special Olympics. The Unified Physical Education course is structured around the national physical education standards and grade-span learning indicators. Additionally, the class supports the development of leadership skills for all students as well as the empowerment of all students to foster an inclusive class and school-wide environment. Students in Unified Physical Education courses may have the opportunity to participate in competitions with other schools or attend Special Olympics events.

Special Olympics Unified Champion Schools programming follows the belief that full inclusion is the key to successful school-wide event planning and programs. It is a change strategy focused on the belief that different generations and abilities bring critical perspectives, skills, and relationships to the work that others do not. It is the belief that in order to achieve common goals, we all need to work together.

The following are noteworthy keys to inclusive event planning that can carry over into classroom activities as well:

- A goal is identified that neither adults nor young people can achieve on their own.
- Nurturing the development of effective, empowered young people is a strategy for achieving goals.
- Effective, empowered adults share decision-making authority, and they support and create space for young people to lead (because it is a good strategy to achieve goals, not because it is a nice thing to do).
- Youth and adults of different abilities form a team with differing and complementary skills, networks, perspectives, and opportunities to lead.
- Both youth and adults share responsibility and accountability for the work and for achieving goals.

Before-School Programs

Active Kids (formerly known as BOKS Kids), a free before-school program that promotes the powerful link between physical activity and increased academic performance, is a great example of how a community can come together to provide before-school activity (figure 7.10). Active Kids was a grassroots organization started by a group of moms at one school in 2010; it grew into a scalable, sustainable, and evidenced-based international program in over 12,000 schools, directly impacting over 1.7 million kids. The program empowers parents, teachers, and community volunteers to give kids a so-called body and brain boost that will set them up for a day of learning. The program typically runs two or three mornings a week, but the curriculum can be adapted for before, during, or after school. It is also used in many community-based organizations and in homes.

Organized intramural programs before or after school, contingent on the start of the school day, are another way to keep students engaged in physical activity. Although most intramural programs are sports based, the focus should be on all students participating and incorporating the skills they have acquired during physical education classes. The school should offer these programs to all students at no cost. Providing a marginal supplement to the physical education teacher to coordinate these activities should be a part of the school's annual budget for supplements.

After-School Programs

According to the America After 3PM report (After School Alliance, 2022), after-school hours are a critical time for youth, as many of them are unsupervised between the time the school bell rings for dismissal and the time that parents and caregivers return from work. Key findings from the report indicate that regardless of the type of community, the geographic location across the country, and political affiliation, parents agree that after-school programs provide for the healthy development of youth, including increased physical activity, the ability to be active in a safe and supervised environment, and the opportunity to engage with their peers, to name a few. The physical education administrator is uniquely positioned to assist in developing district-wide contracts to provide services at as many school sites as possible. Some programs are conducted at the school site by school site personnel, while others are conducted on the school site but run by external organizations. In contrast, other after-school programs require that the student be transported from the school site to their facility.

Some of the most popular after-school programs are the After-School All-Stars, Kids on the Move, 100 Mile Club/Billion Mile Race, Boys and Girls Clubs, Police Athletic League (PAL), YMCAs, Marathon Kids, and activities developed by CATCH, SPARK, and OPEN physical education activities program. Another popular after-school program is Kuul Play.

FIGURE 7.10 Active Kids running.

Photo courtesy of BOKS, an initiative of the Reebok Foundation.

Kuul Play is a digital educational program that is designed to bring the joy of movement to every child and develop their physical literacy, regardless of their background or ability. It especially engages all children who may not be drawn to sports and physical activity. As an easy plug-and-play solution that's aligned to physical education standards, it supports educators' ability to deliver inclusive, structured, quality physical literacy experiences to students in grades PreK through 6. Many other after-school programs are available in individual communities; the physical education administrator can assist schools in identifying them. Although several community-based programs are fee based, they do offer a wide variety of activities or sport-specific pursuits for students to choose from, such as karate or martial arts schools (figure 7.11).

Conclusion

As a physical education administrator, whether you conduct a special event to raise funds for your projects or to advocate for your physical education programs, it is hoped that after reading this chapter you will understand the processes and basic elements of event planning and management. Whether the event is community-wide or school site driven, the process is the same; only the scale is different. Having an understanding of the leadership positions and the roles and responsibilities of those involved in the planning phases, you can see that conducting special events comes down to a systematic process.

Working collaboratively with key stakeholders, such as key leaders, community businesses, and corporate partners, will help you ensure a successful event. Through a further understanding of the fundraising concepts and procedures outlined in chapter 14, securing sponsorship for special events becomes a more manageable process. Advocating for your programs and marketing your events will further elevate your role as a physical education administrator in the community to one as a community leader. Finally, the skill set you develop as an event planner will equip you as the physical education administrator to assist your schools in developing their own special events; field days; and before-, during-, and after-school programs.

FIGURE 7.11 Before- or after-school activity programs for *(a)* preschool, (*b*) elementary school, and *(c)* community-based activity programs for youth.

(a) Courtesy of Steve Anderson and Sonya Ottaway; *(b and c)* Photo courtesy of Tiffany Sanchez

Review Questions

1. Identify the basic elements of event planning.
2. Describe the key leadership positions in an organizational chart, and identify their roles and responsibilities.
3. What role does an understanding of risk management have in implementing special events?
4. Select a special event that you would like to implement, and describe the steps that you would consider during the planning phase.
5. What is the purpose of conducting a post-event evaluation? What can be learned from the evaluation?
6. How do you see your role as a physical education administrator in assisting schools with special projects or before- or after-school programs?

» **Visit HK*Propel* for reproducible forms.**

PART III

Facilities, Equipment, and Technology

CHAPTER 8

Facilities, Design Criteria, and Equipment

Jayne D. Greenberg

Courtesy of Annie Perez

LEARNING OBJECTIVES

After reading this chapter, you will be able to do the following:

- Identify the educational specifications required to design a physical education facility.
- Identify the major indoor and outdoor components that make up a physical education facility.
- Identify the role of the planning committee in designing a new facility.
- Identify the benefits of following sustainable design criteria for a new physical education facility.
- Explain the differences in surfaces for indoor and outdoor facilities.
- Explain safety and risk management considerations for a physical education facility.
- Identify the preferred list of equipment necessary to implement a quality physical education program.

KEY CONCEPTS

accessibility
design criteria
educational specifications
environmental design
risk management in facility design
sustainable design
universal design

Facilities, equipment, and supplies are important considerations for physical education administrators because in many circumstances, they determine the type of physical education program that school districts can implement. Planning and designing physical education facilities offers a unique opportunity to expand physical education programs, enhance physical activity levels, and provide opportunities for community utilization and after-school activities while meeting standards for sustainability and accessibility.

As a physical education administrator working with a team of construction and architectural personnel, you have the ability to provide expert input on the type of facility needed, the functional design of the facility, and the extended utilization of the facility. Indoor facilities (e.g., gymnasiums, locker rooms and showers, athletic training rooms, weight and fitness rooms, climbing walls, dance studios, and ancillary spaces) and outdoor facilities (e.g., courts, fields, playgrounds and play stations, shelters, and pools) make up the essential components of a well-rounded physical education program.

This chapter covers how to provide input and support to your district's construction and facilities team when designing or renovating existing schools while following all state educational specifications and addressing equity issues. Special consideration is directed toward planning and designing indoor and outdoor facilities that are age and grade-level appropriate while adhering to design standards for sustainability and **accessibility** to ensure that safety and equity are evident in all facilities. Additionally, many decisions are also influenced by existing laws and regulations, building codes, architectural designs, and of course, available resources. Issues of **risk management in facility design** regarding student safety concerns should be addressed early in the facility design phase.

Defining the Purpose of a Facility

In the PreK-12 educational setting, the decision to either build a new facility or renovate an existing facility will be made at a higher level once a need is established and funding is secured. Your role in working with the design team will be to determine what space is needed and how it will affect the program. Keep in mind that the purposes of physical activity spaces are multiple; uses could include physical education classes, physical activity sessions before or after school, and interscholastic athletics as well as community recreation and athletics. With so many diverse uses, it is important to give consideration to all possibilities when designing and building a facility.

Construction of a New Facility

The job of building physical education facilities such as a gymnasium or installing athletic fields and courts is not an individual effort; rather, it is a collaborative effort involving a wide array of personnel representing various job codes from the Offices of Capital Construction and Capital Improvements. All architectural and construction team personnel are needed to make sure the facility is planned, financed, constructed, and used effectively. The initial meetings involve everything pertaining to the master plan, from the site plan selection to the types of utilities needed to fulfill the intent of program utilization. Although most education facilities must follow (at a minimum) their state requirements for educational facilities or their state's guidance for educational specifications, a physical education administrator needs to consider all of the components in ensuring that a vision for the facility is brought to life in construction.

In the PreK-12 setting, construction this expensive is considered a separate budget item known as Capital Improvements. Financing and contributions may be gathered from state and local governments as well as portions of the local school system budget, from private donations, from bonds, and from usage fees. However, no funding will be secured or construction begun until a series of budget hearings has taken place. Each local educational agency (LEA) has a different format for conducting these meetings, but as a minimum, effective physical education administrators will attend and follow the process. If allowed, administrators may wish to testify or advocate about the potential benefits of any physical education facility.

Planning Facilities

The planning process for any facility for physical education needs to begin with the question *What purpose will this facility serve for our educational community?* A school, as the hub of the community, is more than simply a collection of classrooms, and it is utilized beyond the bell-to-bell times. The facility should ideally be a place that can be used for the good of the students and the community as a whole.

When considering both inside and outside physical activity spaces, it is important to do a needs assessment pertaining to the local community and its current spaces. Collecting responses from all stakeholders is important. Members of a community-based committee may include parents, recreation leaders, community planners, and advocacy groups.

In planning, the needs assessment should identify as many priority areas as possible. Data should be collected and analyzed to determine the overall needs of the school and community. Funding decisions and budget projections will be decided on later in the process after the master plan has been finalized. Along with priorities identified by surveying community stakeholders, additional questions should be asked that focus on community needs. Here are some examples:

- How can a maximum number of people access and use the facility?
- Are there underserved groups that could be provided with an opportunity with regard to both access and facility space?
- Do potential designs provide barriers for use? Are they universally designed?
- Are facility choices made to maximize usage, or are there local interests that supersede enrollment data?
- How will the spaces integrate with the rest of the community or school in both design and function?

Role of the Planning Committee

After the master plan has been developed, reviewed, revised, and finalized, it's time to coordinate the members of the design team. According to Sawyer (2013), the project planning committee consists of architects, facility consultants, program specialists, engineers, end users, and specialists with expertise in financial, acoustical, energy, illumination, managerial, and other specific areas.

Selecting the architectural firm to design the building and facility usually occurs through a bid process with precise specifications. The bids are developed in collaboration between the office of capital construction and the office of procurement management and then publicly advertised. Although physical education administrators may or may not be a part of the bid process, they will have a say in the design and layout of the activity courts and fields as well as the gymnasiums and the areas associated with physical education and athletic utilization. For example, architects may place athletic fields and courts on the site plan to fit the footprint of the space, but they may not have them in the correct orientation to address student safety and playability. In this type of situation, the knowledge of the physical education administrator plays a critical role in the field and court layouts.

Although this book focuses on organization and administration of physical education programs, shared facilities for athletic utilization must be considered during the design phase. It would be a travesty to design a track facility that is too short, making it impossible to sanction a home track and field competition.

Design Standards, Universal Design, and Sustainable Design

Construction and design standards are guiding documents developed for specific state, university, or school district construction projects. It is expected that all new or renovation projects follow the design standards as well as all state and federal requirements, which include factors such as Title IX for equity, universal design for inclusion and access, and sustainable design for environmental responsibility.

Title IX

Examining the design standards for physical education spaces requires a review of the laws and policies that may affect plans. For example, Title IX guidelines issued in the Education Amendments of 1972 clarify that school systems have a responsibility to provide comparable facilities and equipment to all students regardless of sex, which must be included in the design standards (U.S. Department of Education, 1972, 2024). Facilities include locker rooms and practice and competitive facilities as well as equipment and supplies. A prudent activity before construction planning begins, and again after a first draft is done, would be to consult with the local Title IX coordinator to make sure that all planned facilities and equipment purchases are consistent with Title IX guidance.

States, local municipalities, and local boards of education may have their own laws or policy affecting construction. A thorough search of applicable laws and permit requirements should be done prior to any project. Ignorance of a law will not be viewed favorably should an issue with facilities end up in the legal system.

Universal Design

Universal design is a concept that involves designing products and environments to be used for all abilities without the need for special accommodations. To address these concerns, seven principles of universal design were developed: 1) equitable use; 2) flexibility in use; 3) simple and intuitive use; 4) perceptible information; 5) tolerance for error; 6) low physical effort; and 7) size and space for approach and use (Lieberman, et al., 2021, p.4). The Americans with Disabilities Act (ADA) provides precise requirements and guidelines pertaining to the building of public facilities (U.S. Department of Justice, 1990). Spaces for physical education and physical activity in a school must meet the federal ADA accessibility guidelines. These guidelines are available online and in print from the federal government (www.ada.gov/). It is vital that the most recent guidelines be used in the planning and construction of all facilities. As noted in *ACSM's Health/Fitness Facility Standards and Guidelines, Fifth Edition* (Sanders, 2019, p. 78), several key elements must be addressed in designing and building physical education and physical activity facilities. They include the following:

- Elevation changes: *Any change in elevation in excess of 0.5 inch (1.27 cm) must have a ramp or lift, with a slope of 12 inches (30 cm) for every inch of elevation change. In cases of extreme changes in height, a mechanical lift or elevator can be used in place of a ramp.*
- Passageway width: *Doors, entryways, and exits must have a width of at least 36 inches (.91 m) to accommodate wheelchair access. Hallways and circulation passages need to have a width of at least 60 inches (1.5 m).*
- Height of switches and fountains: *These and other such items must be at a height that can be reached by a person in a wheelchair. They include light switches (15 to 48 inches [.38 to 1.2 m] above the floor); water fountains (no taller than 36 inches [91 cm]); fire extinguishers (no higher than 48 inches [1.2 m] above the floor); and automated external defibrillator (AED) devices (no higher than 48 inches [1.2 m] above the floor).*
- Signage: *Facilities must provide essential signage that can be viewed by persons with visual impairment, particularly signage on emergency exits and signage that identifies other key space locations.*
- Clear floor space: *Each piece of equipment must have an adjacent clear floor space of at least 30 inches by 48 inches (0.76 × 1.2 m).*

The United States Access Board, an independent federal agency, is devoted to accessibility for people with disabilities, and develops and maintains design criteria for the built environment, transit vehicles, telecommunication equipment, and electronic and information technology (U.S. Access Board, n.d.). The Board further provides guidance for the following:

- *Lockers*: If lockers are provided, at least 5 percent, but not less than one of each type (full, half, quarter, and so on) must be accessible. Accessible benches should be located adjacent to the accessible lockers.
- *Benches*: Accessible benches are required in dressing, fitting, and locker rooms. Benches must have a clear floor space positioned to allow people using wheelchairs or other mobility devices to approach parallel to the short end of a bench seat. Benches

must have seats that are a minimum of 20 inches (51 cm) to a maximum of 24 inches (61 cm) in depth and 42 inches (1 m) minimum in length. The seat height should be a minimum of 17 inches (43 cm) to a maximum of 19 inches (48 cm) above the finished floor.

Other issues that should be addressed are locker room, shower, and bathroom accessibility; ticket window height; accessible pathways to all indoor and outdoor facilities and courts; and areas for spectatorship including indoor and outdoor bleachers. A complete list of ADA Standards for Accessible Design can be found at www.ada.gov.

Sustainable Design

Sustainable design for fitness and athletic facilities is becoming more prevalent as more ecologically efficient and environmentally friendly design has become recognized as a necessity. Some features of a sustainable design in a fitness facility would include energy efficiency, with respect to lighting and HVAC systems, as well as water conservation systems, using low-flow faucets and showers. The research linking **environmental design** to enhanced health and increased physical activity is also getting the attention of design planners, leading to changes in building industry standards. Because the majority of people spend most waking hours indoors, more attention is focusing on the benefits of natural environments to positively affect physical, social, and mental health. Sustainable design is a broader concept that includes environmental design to improve the health and well-being.

As **design criteria** have evolved, several building certification programs relating directly to health and wellness have emerged. As physical education administrators work with the construction and planning team, emphasis should be placed on designing facilities that include sustainable design criteria toward improving the quality of air circulation, water quality, lighting, temperature control, and types of paint and flooring. As a leader in the industry, Fitwel (which stands for "facility innovations toward wellness environment leadership") was originally created by the U.S. Centers for Disease Control and Prevention (CDC) and the U.S. General Services Administration, and it aims to improve the health and well-being of building occupants and local communities. Although the CDC remains the research and evaluation partner for Fitwel, The Center for Active Design was selected as the licensed operator of Fitwel; it is charged with expanding Fitwel to the global market. However, *Active Design Guidelines* (Center for Active Design, 2010) further discusses the following resources and strategies:

- Building Research Establishment Environmental Assessment Method (BREEAM), a certification that specifies and measures sustainability performance (applies to buildings and neighborhoods)
- Fitwel certification, a certification platform committed to building health for all
- Leadership in Energy and Environmental Design (LEED), a program of the U.S. Green Building Council and a well-known certification system for green building (applies to buildings and neighborhoods)
- Leadership in Energy and Environmental Design (LEED) certification, which provides a framework for healthy, highly efficient, and cost-saving green buildings
- Living Building Challenge and Living Community Challenge (apply to buildings and communities), programs that aim to create a more sustainable built environment
- STAR Community Rating System (applies to cities and towns), which measures and manages sustainability outcomes
- Sustainable SITES Initiative, SITES rating system (applies to landscape design)
- WELL Building Standard (applies to buildings), emphasizing people's health and wellness at the center of the design

You are encouraged to examine closely all the resources listed; as an example, consider the WELL Building Standard. Its certification program focuses on the elements of building design and performance that address the health and well-being of individuals participating in fitness, sports, and recreational activities. Pioneered by Delos and administered by the International WELL Building Institute, WELL includes 102 features grouped into seven categories: air, water, nourishment, light,

Built Environment | Opportunity Zones

Typical aspects within the sports, fitness, and recreation macro-sector include a myriad of spaces designed to support individuals and teams along their journey to optimal health and performance—yet many are falling short. There are many opportunities to expand the existing WELL Building Standard® with a focus on elements that are specific to a sports, fitness, and recreation setting. Initial thinking specific to the built environment is provided below.

AIR

Excellent air quality is of critical importance to individuals who are breathing deeply during exercise or an athletic performance; minimization of bacteria, mold, and fumes from toxic cleaning supplies takes care of the respiratory system.

Group exercise studios
Cardio + weight zones
Aquatic centers
Indoor tracks
Climbing wall zones
Locker rooms
Training rooms

WATER

Hydration is critical to optimal performance in sports, fitness, and recreational activities; toxic chlorine and chloramines need to be removed from swimming pools and showers in order to maintain healthy skin and respiration.

Water fountains
Swimming pools
Athlete hydration stations
Showers

NOURISHMENT

Access to, and education about, foods that optimize athletic performance and overall physical fitness is a critical variable (e.g., low- to zero-sugar, organic, plant-focused, grass-fed meat diet).

Fitness center cafes
Athletic training cafes
Vending machines

LIGHT

Access to natural light, minimizing glare, and selection of lighting types that promote rather than deplete energy are all critical variables in sports, fitness, and recreation spaces.

Group exercise studios
Cardio + weight training zones
Enclosed sports arenas
Aquatic centers
Indoor tracks
Climbing wall zones

FITNESS

"Fitness" is the core focus in sports, fitness, and recreation spaces.

Group exercise studios
Cardio + weight training zones
Enclosed sports arenas
Aquatic centers
Indoor tracks
Climbing wall zones

COMFORT

Environments without proper ventilation are even more critical when individuals are exerting high energy, as they are put at greater risk for overheating; acoustical imbalances cause high levels of stress.

Music/overhead system levels and HVAC systems in all exercise and training zones, as well as enclosed sports arenas

MIND

Bringing nature indoors (biophilia), the addition of creative signage to promote awareness of health and performance promoting behaviors, and the addition of meditation zones all support the mental aspect of "physical training."

Building signage
Biophilia
Meditation zones

The Seven Concepts of the WELL Building Standard®

FIGURE 8.1 The seven concepts of the WELL Building Standard.

fitness, comfort, and mind (WELL Building Standard, n.d.) (see figure 8.1). Grounded in evidence-based medical and scientific studies on the impacts of the built environment on human health and wellness, the WELL Building Standard was extensively peer reviewed prior to its public release in October 2014.

Physical education administrators need to be knowledgeable about what sustainable options are available and are successfully implemented in existing facilities so that when they meet with the initial planning team, they will have the information readily available to discuss.

General Considerations for Physical Education Construction Projects

Regardless of the type of physical education setting—gymnasium, auxiliary gym, fitness center, field or outdoor courts, playground, or hardtop—several common factors will need to be part of the facilities plan, including the following:

- *Acoustics*: The ability of students to hear instruction and the need to minimize stress on the teacher's voice are both concerns during planning for how sound will flow in the gymnasium. Consult with the architect on your planning committee for ways to lower the background noise (measured in decibels) in the gymnasium. Facilities should be designed to maintain noise levels below 70 decibels (Tharrett & Peterson, 2012; Sanders 2019). Also consider the ability to install and place speakers (ideally wireless) that will allow sound to be broadcast both during the school day and during community events. Indoor speakers for gymnasiums should be selected based on quality and sound clarity. Classes conducted in the gymnasium are considered teaching stations, so sound systems should be included in the furniture, fixtures, and equipment (FF&E) during building or renovation of the gymnasium.

- *Floor*: Floor surfaces should match the activities being done in the area. Hardwood floors in the gymnasium will allow for participation for most major sports and activities. Floor markings should reflect the anticipated use of the facility and should align with the state educational specifications. Dance floors, for injury prevention as well as optimal performance, should be installed with two types of flooring. A sprung floor, also referred to as the subfloor, is one that absorbs shock and is considered best for dance, indoor sports, and physical education. The top layer of a sprung floor can be either hardwood or a vinyl surface known as a Marley floor. Vinyl surfaces can accommodate most styles of dance, and they can be used for fitness classes as well.

- *Walls*: Walls should have a nonabrasive surface free of protrusions that could cause impact injuries or minor injuries to students who brush against the wall during physical activity sessions. Smooth, flush walls will also prevent damage to equipment when the walls are used as teaching stations.

- *Hydration stations:* In both indoor and outdoor facilities, students should have the opportunity to hydrate frequently when engaged in physical activities, whether physical education, recess, athletics, or before- and after-school programs. Water fountains should be readily available in or near locker rooms, in hallways near physical education facilities, and in outdoor spaces.

- *Technology:* The types of devices used to share information are evolving constantly. Chalkboards and overhead screens have basically disappeared from construction, and it is impossible to predict what innovation will come next. Indoor physical activity spaces should enable projecting on a large screen or a flat, white wall. Additionally, physical education teachers should have the same capability as other teachers to use resources from the Internet and from other forms of media in teaching.

- *Risk management principles:* Managing the risk to student safety and to the liability of the school is the responsibility of the physical education administrator or department chairperson. When designing and purchasing equipment for a new facility, one needs to pay careful attention to the safety standards specified in current research and design guidelines. In addition, a standard set of rules for the facility is important so that the safety rules do not change as different groups occupy the space. Here are some factors to consider:

  - Maximum number of participants, spectators, or both
  - Allowable footwear for participants
  - Padding for walls and any protruding equipment
  - Visible and easily accessible first aid equipment
  - Well-marked and well-lit facilities and exits
  - Equipment that meets safety specifications (No homemade equipment should be present.)
  - Easy access to the local emergency management guide and documentation
  - Delivery of proper instruction
  - Utilization of common field spaces for various activities
  - Supervision at all times during classes and events sponsored by the school site

Managing risk also involves the constant supervision and safety checks of all facilities. Each day, staff should visually inspect facilities and report on any repairs that need to be made or clearing that needs to be completed. This inspection includes physical education outdoor fields and courts as well as any indoor physical education facilities as discussed throughout this chapter. It may be necessary to revise planned activities temporarily until an existing problem has been resolved. The same holds true for regular safety checks of all physical education equipment. Chapter 11 provides additional information on risk management and legal aspects.

Indoor Facilities

As a physical education administrator working with the planning and construction team, most of your recommendations will be based on two areas: (1) *indoor* courts and ancillary spaces, such as locker rooms, dance or aerobic rooms, wrestling rooms, weight rooms, fitness centers, athletic training rooms, office spaces, and storage; and (2) *outdoor* facilities, such as courts, fields, and storage. When designing the facilities, keep in mind that although physical education should be your first concern, many of the facilities will also be used for athletics and community-based programs and activities. Therefore, it is an integral part of the physical administrator's job to ensure that these facilities—indoor and outdoor—are both constructed and maintained in a way that promotes the ability of all students to become physically active.

Educational specifications (also called Ed Specs) are unique to each state and serve to ensure that the facility designed matches the curriculum function it is intended to house. They are part of the master plan and construction specifications that lend guidance to the overarching facility design. Most of the Ed Specs serve as guidance documents for both indoor and outdoor facilities at the elementary and middle school levels, as well as indoor ancillary spaces at the high school level. Design criteria for high school level activity spaces usually follow the National Federation of State High School Associations (NFHS) specifications for court and field competitions (2020).

Gymnasiums

Gymnasiums are often the largest of the indoor teaching and physical activity spaces in schools. When planning the gymnasium, consideration must be given to the number of teaching spaces that will be necessary to accommodate the expected enrollment of the school, the educational program, and the intended use or uses. At the secondary level, one must also pay attention to the need for and size of spectator seating for whole-school and athletic events that may be held in the gymnasium. Schools come in all configurations of grades. Accommodations must be made to facilitate physical education programs for all grade levels as well as to facilitate athletic competitions.

Elementary School Gymnasiums

Elementary school gymnasiums should be designed with the physical education instructional program in mind, taking into consideration large- and small-group games, dance, gymnastics, and fitness-related activities. The number of teaching spaces should be considered first and foremost in the gymnasium design. This number of teaching spaces would include a calculation involving the number of students per class, the number of grade-level classes per school, the number of physical education periods, the frequency of physical education, and the number of physical education teachers. The dimensions of the elementary gymnasium for grades PreK-5 should range from 3,500 to 5,000 square feet (1,067-1,524 m^2) for a single class and from 7,000 to 8,000 square feet (2,133-2,438 m^2) for two classes.

For both student safety and convenience, the indoor gymnasium should be adjacent to the physical education teacher's office as well as convenient to restrooms, water fountains, and storage. If multiple physical education classes will be using the facility simultaneously, a strong recommendation would be to install movable partitions or vinyl-mesh curtains to separate instructional spaces. Additionally, the gymnasium should be positioned within the school away from other instructional classrooms due to the noise factor inherent when children play.

The elementary gymnasium floor should be constructed of either hardwood or vinyl (synthetic floor coverings), and it should include appropriate markings for activity. The walls should be made of acoustic materials, such as concrete blocks, and have a smooth or flat surface so that they could be used for such

LEADERSHIP IN ACTION

Elementary Physical Education Equipment: It's Not About the Tool

Aaron Hart, MSEd

Executive Director, OPENPhysEd.org

Tools of the Trade

I've been teaching physical education for 20 years, and I've been a part of the physical education equipment industry for 15 years. This experience has given me interesting insight as both a consumer and a vendor. I had found it difficult to articulate my equipment philosophy until I had a conversation with Dr. Helena Beart, my colleague at SUNY Cortland. Dr. Beart is known for her passionate repetition of five simple words all physical educators should hear: "It's not about the tool!" These words have the power to solve any teacher's purchasing dilemmas.

In other words, as physical educators, our singular focus should remain on the instructional outcomes we've set for our students. Those outcomes may derive from the SHAPE America Grade-Span Learning Indicators; they may be based on 21st-century learning skills; or they may focus heavily on teaching personal and social responsibility. In the same way we intentionally grab a hammer to pound a nail, we should be intentional about the equipment we choose in order to teach the outcomes we're guiding our students toward.

Don't be charmed by the newest gadgets that grace the glossy pages of catalogs. Don't get caught up in blowing your budget on technology that works only to meet two or three outcomes. No matter how cool and enticing a new piece of equipment may be, it's important to remember that effective physical education programs can and do exist without that new and cool item.

With all those things considered, my advice for people looking for help managing their equipment budgets follows.

Stock Up on the Essentials

Certain types of equipment are foundational to our equipment rooms. For these essential items, buy the highest-quality equipment your school can afford. PE teachers need to be able to create boundaries, establish floor marks, group students, and manage starts and stops—all while providing space for students to travel safely, jump, dance, throw, catch, kick, receive, volley, and strike.

Know What the Essentials Are

Physical educators must be able to set up safe instructional environments by creating boundaries, establishing floor marks, effectively grouping students, and managing start and stop signals. Therefore, essentials to keep in stock include items such as cones, spot markers, task tents (or other display options), pinnies, and a drum or a whistle.

These management essentials help physical educators create space for students to safely travel, jump, dance, throw, catch, kick, receive, volley, and strike. A lot of these skills can be taught and practiced with bean bags, coated foam balls, pool noodles, and jump ropes.

That list may seem to make for a bare and very boring equipment room. However, the nine items listed in the preceding two paragraphs will supply a good teacher with all of the essential tools to be a great teacher.

Know When to Move Beyond the Essentials

If your equipment room is stocked with high-quality essentials and you still have money to work with, then it's time to have some fun. However, be sure that you're listening to the good words of Dr. Beart: *It's not about the tool!*

With student learning objectives clearly in focus, consider three categories of equipment that provide useful and effective tools for your toolbox:

1. *Original activity equipment*: This type of equipment brings trending activities into your teaching and can breathe fresh life into the units you offer. *Example*: Spikeball game sets

(continued)

Elementary Physical Education Equipment: It's Not About the Tool *(continued)*

2. *Motivational equipment*: This type of equipment takes the place of essential equipment, such as basic bean bags or foam balls, while increasing student fun and motivation. *Example*: U.S. Games critters

3. *Technology*: Many physical educators love their technology; they may even say they can't live without it. However, effective physical education did happen before Bluetooth music systems, group heart rate monitors, and LCD projectors. However, I do agree that technology can enhance the quality and effectiveness of your lessons. If you're lucky enough to have the budget for these items, and you're committed to using them as effective tools for teaching, then I say go for it. *Example*: Group heart rate monitoring systems

---

instructional activities as throwing and striking. Floor-to-ceiling height should be a minimum of 20 feet (6 m), with unobstructed space (free of all obstacles, including LED lights), with a preferred 24 feet (7.3 m) of clear space height. Lighting in the gymnasium should provide a minimum of 35 to 50 foot-candles of light, lights should be covered with protective grids, and a light switch should be placed at each point of entry. If natural light is recommended, then design considerations should focus on placement of the windows, how to protect against glare and direct sunlight, and the type of protective covering for the window. Climate control should also be included in the master plan, taking into account how the instructional space will be utilized and ensuring maximum air circulation. The gymnasium should include independent controls to provide for heating, ventilation, and air conditioning (HVAC).

Remembering that the gymnasium is the largest classroom, it should be equipped as such. There should be technology that would allow each teaching station to work identically; one tech setup for a space that is planned for two to four classes is not sufficient to provide equity in the learning environment. Sound systems should be installed that allow for clarity when instructions are provided; choosing a high-quality speaker system can help accomplish this goal. Ideally, wireless technology with multiple outlets and a variety of technology tools should be available.

If multipurpose spaces such as cafetoriums (cafeteria, auditorium, and gymnasium) or cafeteria–gymnasium shared facilities are in the design criteria, then careful consideration should be given to scheduling physical education classes around the lunch schedule or school-wide activities. In this design, breakfast or lunch tables should have the capacity to be folded quickly and moved to the perimeter of the area with ease.

All facilities, whether elementary or secondary, should also have buffer zones; a buffer zone is a 10-foot (3 m) safety zone between walls, bleachers, obstructions, and instructional spaces. Planners must take into account all of these key elements as well as consider the utilization needs both for the present and in the future.

Secondary School Gymnasiums

Although they are designed for instructional purposes, high school gymnasiums are additionally designed to meet the needs of interscholastic competition. In designing the educational facility layout, high school gymnasiums should be placed on the facility footprint to allow for close proximity to classrooms, locker rooms, storage spaces, athletic training rooms, wrestling rooms, dance studios, weight and fitness centers, and office spaces for the physical education and athletic directors. From the outside, gymnasiums should be near parking lots to allow for after-school and weekend activities and competitions. The gymnasium should have its own designated points of egress for use during events that are held outside of school hours to keep the facility safe and inaccessible to outsiders. An exit should be placed near the outside field and court space for ease of access to teaching stations and in order to facilitate quick transitions from indoor to outdoor facilities. Additionally, since the high school competitions usually take place both indoors and outdoors, the design should include access for emergency vehicles to enter the facility in case of injuries.

Secondary school gymnasiums (grades 6-12) should be constructed with square footage ranging from 7,000 to 22,000 (2,134 to 6,706 m^2), should be at least the size of two basketball courts, and they should be divisible into two private teaching stations large enough to handle two classes of typically 30 to 45 students. Careful consideration must be given to the predicted number of gymnasium teaching stations. Square footage of other parts of a gymnasium, such as foyers, bleachers, indoor ticket counters, and concessions, should not be counted as part of the instructional activity space. Designers of secondary school gymnasiums need to consider the amount of seating that is available for either athletics or school-wide programs. With regard to potential seating, space on the gymnasium floor occupied by folding chairs may or may not be practical.

The secondary gymnasium floor should be constructed of either hardwood or synthetic surfaces, and it should be lined properly for interscholastic competition before the recommended three coats of varnish are applied. Gymnasium floors should be installed with the appropriate standards rating according to each state's Ed Specs and by a certified installer. The floors should provide appropriate surface friction to allow for sliding, appropriate shock absorption, and adequate ball bounce. Since it is an expensive component in gymnasium construction, careful consideration should be given to flooring selection. In new construction, wooden gym floors should be properly sanded and coated. Then appropriate lines and markings per sport should be installed, followed by the school's logo, mascot, and any letters, such as the school's name or nickname. After all markings on the court are complete, it should be coated with the final finish. Make sure to leave at least three weeks of drying time in an environment controlled at 65 degrees prior to using the court. Court lines and markings are usually colored according to sport-specific guidelines, and the size of the lines and buffer areas is generally regulated by the governing body for competition. Additionally, since the gymnasium is used for other school-based activities, such as pep rallies, graduation practice, and other events that would call for chairs to be placed on the gym floor, another recommendation is to purchase gym floor covers that are easy to install and uninstall.

The walls should be made of acoustic materials, such as concrete blocks, and have a smooth or flat surface so that they could be used for such instructional activities as throwing and striking. Walls should be painted in a neutral color and with materials that make them easy to clean. It is further recommended that acoustic panels be strategically placed on the walls of the gymnasium to assist with the sound quality when instruction is being delivered in physical education classes or announcements are being made during athletic competition. If the gymnasium does not have a 10-foot (3 m) buffer zone at each end of the basketball courts, then padding should be attached to the walls to prevent a player from overrunning the court and hitting the wall. Floor-to-ceiling height should be a minimum of 24 feet (7.3 m), with unobstructed space free of obstacles and lights. The height of the ceiling for high schools is more critical if the gymnasium is used for basketball, volleyball, and badminton competition. Lighting in the gymnasium should provide a minimum of 35 to 50 foot-candles of light, lights should be covered with protective grids, and a light switch should be placed at each point of entry. If natural light is recommended, then design considerations should focus on the placement of the windows, how to protect against glare and direct sunlight, and the type of protective covering for the window. Windows should be placed high in the gymnasium with a north-to-south orientation to reduce the glare as much as possible. Climate control should also be included in the master plan, taking into account how the instructional space will be utilized and ensuring maximum air circulation. Independent controls should be in the gymnasium to provide for HVAC.

The type of fixed equipment should also be considered in the design of a gymnasium. Fixed equipment includes the type of suspended and retractable basketball backboards, floor plates for volleyball systems, floor plates and pockets for electrical and microphone systems, and scoreboards. Placement of suspended sound system speakers should also be considered during planning for instructional and athletic events. Many modern gymnasiums also install suspended gymnasium projectors and screens that drop down from the beams to add another instructional element to the gymnasium.

Gymnasium bleachers are another type of equipment to consider during facility planning. Spectator and student seating play an important role in gymnasium utilization. Telescopic and retractable bleachers that are electrically driven are preferred for high school gymnasiums. This type of equipment allows the instructor or coach to easily push in or pull out all or a part of the bleachers and move them flush against the wall to add more instructional space when needed. The type and size of the bleachers may be subject to local or state Ed Specs, but all should include footboards, seat boards, risers, and handrails (Sawyer, 2013). School site bleachers must also provide accessible seating to meet ADA requirements.

Locker Rooms

Designing the secondary school locker room is a very complex process; it involves areas for dressing, showers, restrooms, grooming, and office spaces. Changing facilities for individuals and teams are a necessity for spaces inside a physical education facility. In addition, the type of lockers that are installed must be a function of the locker room utilization. For example, if the locker room is used just for physical education, then the typical 12- by 12- by 15-inch (30 cm × 30 cm × 38 cm), six-tiered ventilated lockers will suffice; they will accommodate clothes, personal toiletries, books, and a backpack. If the locker room will have a dual purpose for athletics and physical education, then the size of the lockers will vary from 15 by 15 by 72 inches (38 cm × 38 cm × 180 cm) for football to 15 by 15 by 36 inches (38 cm × 38 cm × 91 cm) for sports such as tennis, basketball, and volleyball. For durability, the lockers should be heavy-duty, 14-gauge steel as a minimum, should be ventilated, and should have secure locking mechanisms. The size, type of material, and purpose will be a local decision based on need and budget. The minimum number of lockers needed for physical education will also be determined by the Ed Specs.

The design and layout of the lockers should allow for flow and supervision while also allowing for privacy. Hanging convex mirrors in the corners of the locker room can help the physical education teacher view blind spots from the office window. This view will allow for supervision without physically standing in the locker room at all times. Although shower areas have all too often become storage areas in locker rooms, students should be encouraged to shower after physical education. Designing showers with privacy and dressing areas will encourage students to take a shower after class. Maintaining proper water temperature of showers is also a point for consideration during the design phase. The appropriate number of toilets, including accessible facilities, will further be determined by the Ed Specs, which will account for the size of the locker room and student population utilization. Water fountains should be installed either in the locker room or directly outside of the locker room for hydration purposes.

In schools where square footage permits, secondary locker rooms often house team rooms that allow for private meetings and changing space for visiting athletic teams. The ideal high school facility will include male and female physical education locker rooms, as well as separate male and female athletic locker rooms with separate coaches' offices. The location of the athletic director's office should also be a consideration; the ideal location is in the main office, making it easy to collect money for insurance, obtain forms, and enable ready access to school counselors and administrators.

Office Space

In all schools, it is expected that an office for the physical education teacher, providing individual work stations and storage, be the same size and quality as those for all other staff. In most secondary schools, the physical education teachers share office space inside the locker rooms. If planned correctly, the locker room includes a separate bathroom and shower inside the office. This configuration keeps the teachers separate from the private areas of the students while allowing students access to their teachers for consultation or assistance. Furniture such as desks, bookshelves, and computers with Internet access, as well as first aid supplies, should also be in the physical education teacher's office.

Athletic Training Rooms

Due to increases in the number of interscholastic sports teams for all student-athletes, most high schools employ certified athletic trainers to provide the best possible health care to prevent, evaluate, treat, and rehabilitate injuries; therefore, they include athletic training rooms in their master plans. The athletic training room, either attached to the gymnasium or in an area with close proximity to the gymnasium, should be a minimum of 1,000 square feet (305 m^2). The room should be divided into several functional spaces, including an office for the athletic trainer to keep and store records, a taping area, a treatment area, a wet area, an exercise and rehabilitation area, and a supply area. Although most training rooms have a typical 10-foot (3 m) ceiling, attention should be paid to ensuring either that the doors are a minimum of 4 feet (1.2 m) wide or that double doors are installed with easy egress for emergency transport.

Flooring should have nonslip tiles or surfaces that can be easily cleaned and sanitized. In the wet areas of the room, floor drains should be installed near the whirlpools, ice machines, and sinks; and ground fault circuit interrupter (GFCI) electrical supply circuits should be installed for these types of equipment. Floors near the drains should be slightly sloped to avoid the pooling of water, minimizing the risk of fall-related injuries. Electrical outlets should be placed 3 feet (0.9 m) from the floor and approximately every 4 feet (1.2 m) apart. The athletic training room should also be designed with ACSM's temperature control standards for HVAC, ensuring proper ventilation and humidity control (Sanders, 2019).

Athletic training rooms should also be strategically placed near the gymnasiums and outdoor athletic facilities, have access to restrooms and locker rooms (for changing clothes and showering), have outside access for emergency vehicles, and be located on the ground floor of the school facility. Placing an athletic training room on the second floor of the building would impede access for athletes in need of assistance.

The office space for the athletic trainer should be secure but have a window so that a view of the treatment space is always available. The office should have Internet access, phone service, locking cabinets, a desk, and a chair.

Some of the basic equipment needs for maintaining an athletic training room are as follows.

Equipment

- Treatment tables (Recommended size is 78 inches [2 m] long, 30 inches [.76 m] high, and a combination of 24 inches [.61 m] and 30 inches [.76 m] wide. The tables should preferably have shelves and cabinets and be strong enough to hold student-athletes weighing up to 400 pounds [181 kg].)
- Taping tables
- Double sink with hot and cold water
- Ice machine with ice scooper
- Whirlpool
- Whirlpool table
- Hydrocollator with terry covers for hot packs
- Floor drains in wet area
- Washer and dryer
- Locking cabinets
- Refrigerator
- Movable cart

Supplies

- Hydration supplies, water bottles, and portable hydration stations
- Athletic training kits
- Gloves (latex-free), various sizes
- Immobilization braces, splints, slings, crutches, and boards
- Wheelchair
- Cold therapy packs, ice bags, and sprays
- Moist heat packs
- Athletic tape, elastic wraps, gauze, and appropriate scissors and tape cutters
- Bandages, gauze pads, cotton tips
- Biohazard bags
- Foam, moleskin
- Tape remover
- Analgesics
- Eyewash
- Mouth guards

- Disinfectant hand wash to prevent the spread of germs and bacteria
- Disinfectants for cleaning
- First aid kits
- Automated external defibrillator (AED)

The fully supplied and staffed athletic training room will be ready for student-athletes as needed. School budgets should ensure that the athletic training room be both restocked as supplies are needed and included in the school's annual supply budget.

Laundry Room

Although predominately used for athletics, laundry rooms are an integral part of any physical education facilities design. Although laundering is not a favorite part of the workday, having the ability to provide towels for aquatic programs, to clean loaner (school-owned) physical education uniforms, or to make provisions for students' showering needs after physical education makes for a cost-effective service for the program. The typical high school laundry room is approximately 200 square feet (61 m^2), and it is equipped with two front-loaded commercial washers and three commercial dryers. In addition, it is reinforced with concrete floors, it has appropriate plumbing capabilities, it has recessed floor drains, and it has a more powerful air ventilation system installed to offset the heat and humidity. The laundry room should also be equipped with shelving and locking cabinets to store detergents and other cleaning products, it should have folding tables and shelves for towels, and it should be located near the physical education and athletic locker rooms. The door should be wide enough for commercial-size laundry bins to fit through, and open rack shelving should be available for hanging uniforms or drying out damp equipment. If towels are dispensed through the laundry room, installing a Dutch door should be considered. Because this laundry equipment is heavy-grade commercial equipment, anyone assigned to provide laundry services at the school site should receive training from the manufacturer on correct use of the equipment.

Figure 8.2 is a sample rendition of what a high school could look like with all of the facilities discussed so far in place. In addition to the overall architectural designs such as the one shown in figure 8.2, many court and field layouts follow the competition criteria as set forth by the NFHS. Figure 8.3 shows the exact dimensions of a high school volleyball court that would be marked in the diagram shown in figure 8.2.

Dance and Aerobics Rooms

Although dance education is often housed in the fine arts department, it often occupies a shared facility with physical education, especially when aerobics, yoga, and Pilates classes are taught. However, with regard to design, the dance facility requirements often include special electrical, flooring, acoustics, and sound system needs. The ceilings are usually higher than in other locations, with unobstructed spaces.

A typical educational dance room is approximately 1,800 to 2,000 square feet (549-610 m^2) to accommodate a class of students all moving at the same time (figure 8.4). The room should be rectangular to enhance the acoustic environment, with a ceiling height of 16 feet (4.9 m) at a minimum. Sprung wood or resilient wood floors are the most desirable to prevent injury from constant movement, including repetitive jumps. The room should be well lit with LED lighting, within a 50 to 75 foot-candle range throughout. If fluorescent systems are still being used, they should have remote ballasts or type A quiet recessed ballasts.

Just as with all other physical activity indoor spaces, the HVAC system should be monitored for humidity capacity, ventilation, and air conditioning. Shatterproof mirrors should be installed on at least one wall, and electrical outlets should be placed on the perimeter walls along with ballet barre railings. It is further recommended that directional track lighting be installed to control for various lighting needs and that it be installed on a separate switch. If the dance room is built with windows, darkening curtains should be provided to handle the various lighting needs.

In a school that has a fine arts or performing arts program, dressing rooms, storage for dance costumes, and cabinets should be available in close proximity to the dance room. Sound systems and floor mats should also be included in the equipment list.

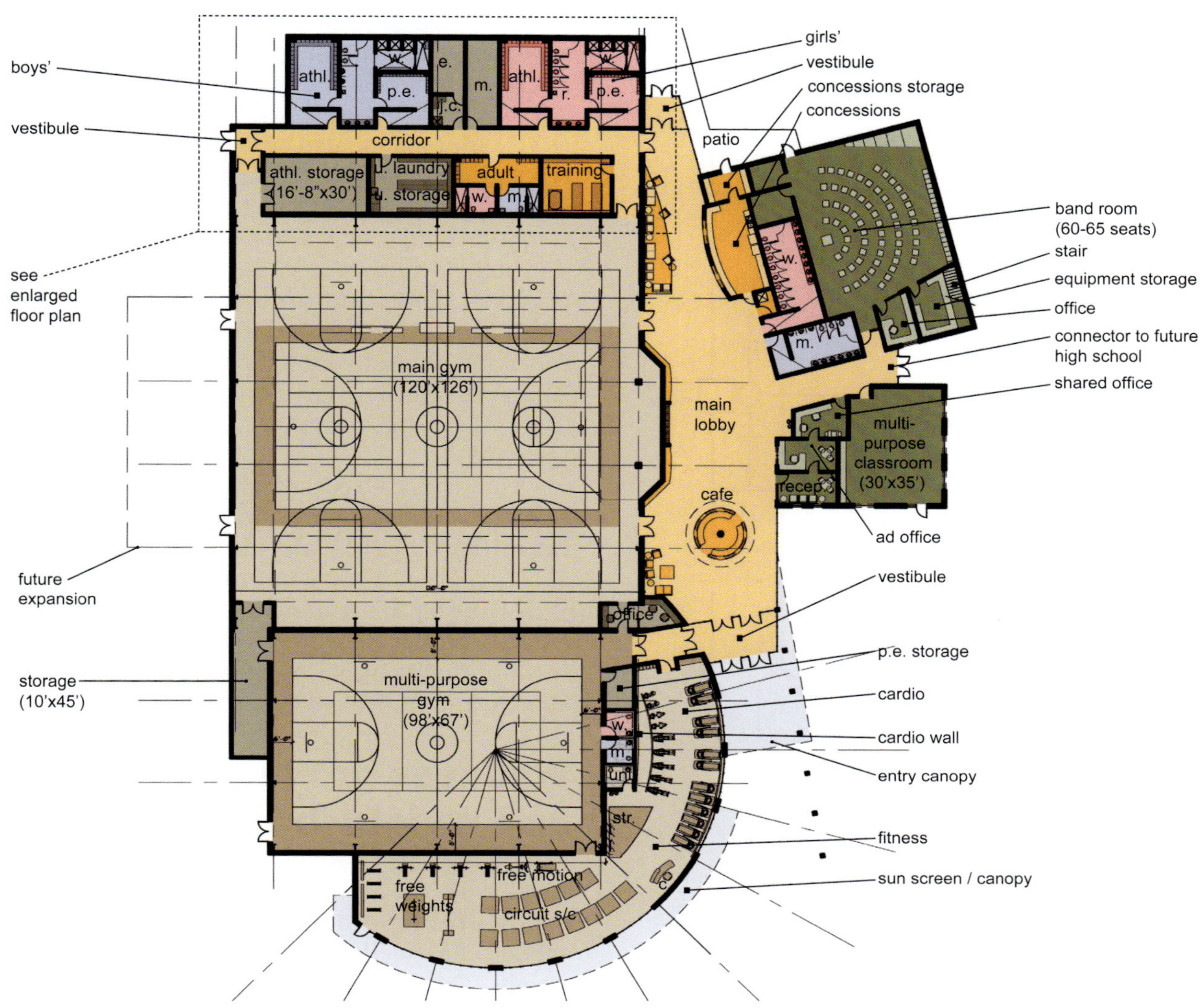

FIGURE 8.2 Sample rendition of a high school facility: Rehoboth Christian School, New Mexico.

Drawings courtesy of AMDG Architects in collaboration with LAM Architects.

Wrestling Rooms

Wrestling is an extremely popular class in physical education as well as a high school interscholastic sport. The key to safety in a wrestling room is supervision of the students at all times. It's important for the teacher and coach to appreciate that the actions inherent in wrestling include rolling, falling, lunging, pushing, and pulling.

In most high schools, the wrestling room would ideally measure 40 by 120 feet (12 × 37 m) and can accommodate three wrestling mats. However, when state Ed Specs for public schools revise square footage, the wrestling rooms are usually smaller and can accommodate only one wrestling mat; in most cases, they are 40 by 60 feet (12 × 18 m). This size results in competitions being held in the gymnasium or, if the gymnasium is being utilized by another seasonal sport, in high school cafeterias.

The NFHS (2020) rules state that a high school wrestling mat must be a minimum of 38 feet (11.6 m) on each side. This size will accommodate the 10-foot (3 m) inner circle and the 28-foot (8.5 m) wrestling area circle, and it will allow for the minimum 5-foot (1.5 m) safety area surrounding the wrestling area. However, it is recommended that there be a 10-foot (3 m) clearance between the edge of the wrestling mat and any obstruction, such as walls, benches, and scorer's or official's table.

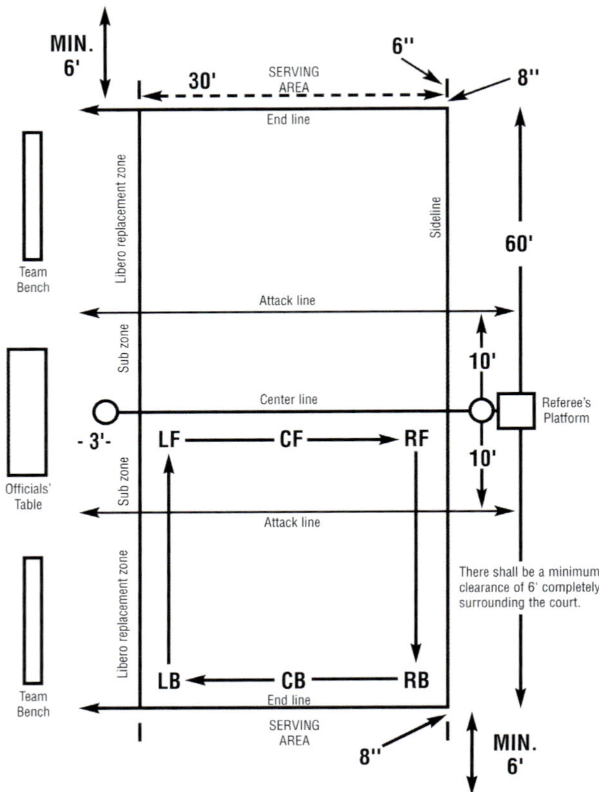

FIGURE 8.3 NFHS volleyball court layout.

Note: Except as specifically stated in the rules, information on field diagrams in this book should be viewed as suggestive only; it does not reflect NFHS requirements. The construction and layout of all courts and fields used for high school competition are subject to any controlling laws and building codes and to the sound judgment of the persons in charge of the facilities.

From J. Greenberg and J. LoBianco, *Organization and Administration of Physical Education,* 2nd ed. (Human Kinetics, 2026). Reprinted by permission from NFHS.

Additionally, the mat must be of uniform thickness, not more than 4 inches (10 cm) thick and not less than a mat size, with at least 1 inch (2.5 cm) foam covered with polyvinyl chloride (PVC). Mats must also be kept clean to prevent the spread of skin infections. Antimicrobial cleansers are the best way to keep mat surfaces free from dangerous molds, bacteria, fungi, and methicillin-resistant Staphylococcus aureus (MRSA). Clean and sanitize mats before and after practice and matches. Before mats are rolled up, all their sides should be cleaned. The American Society for Testing and Materials (ASTM) provides further standards for wrestling mats.

Other than the cost of wrestling mats, wrestling is a relatively inexpensive sport. Installing mirrors on two walls of a wrestling room is also an option in various state design criteria. Wrestling equipment includes wrestling shoes, singlets (uniforms), kneepads, head gear, scales (to monitor weight for weight classes), mat straps, and mat transport carts.

Wellness or Fitness Centers and Weight Training Rooms

Aside from the gymnasium, the two most commonly utilized indoor facilities in secondary schools are wellness or fitness centers and weight training rooms. The wellness or fitness center is an indoor facility where students use a variety of cardiorespiratory, strength, and

FIGURE 8.4 Dance studio.

Owngarden/iStock/Getty Images

flexibility equipment while working toward meeting their fitness goals. Weight training rooms focus more on strength and conditioning using weight machines, free weights, and other resistance training equipment. Both the wellness or fitness center and the weight training room provide additional opportunities for students to gain the skills and knowledge necessary to develop and maintain a lifelong appreciation of physical activity and fitness.

Wellness and Fitness Centers

As noted in chapter 4, fitness education plays a major role in the overall curriculum and instructional plan for the delivery of a comprehensive physical education program. The underlying premise of a fitness education model is that physical activity is essential to a healthy lifestyle and that students' understanding about fitness and behavior change is a result of engagement in a fitness education program (Institute of Medicine, 2013, p. 202). Through a well-designed fitness or wellness center, the Instructional Framework for Fitness Education in Physical Education (SHAPE America, 2012) can be implemented. Students have the opportunity to achieve the health-related components of fitness—cardiorespiratory, muscular strength and endurance, and flexibility—through activities that are challenging yet motivational.

Prior to approaching your administration for support in establishing a center, it is important to have a concrete, well-defined plan for its implementation. The plan should start with a clear statement articulating (1) why you want and need a center, (2) who will benefit from the center, (3) what will be included in the center, (4) where the center will be located, and (5) when the center can be ready for student use. As a physical education administrator or physical education department chairperson, presenting this information in writing in the form of a proposal will let the administration know how much thought you have put into planning and that you are ready to develop a center.

Securing an Area for the Wellness Center

Perhaps the hardest part of implementing a school site wellness center is finding the appropriate space within your existing facility. In times when schools are overcrowded and reduced class sizes are difficult to maintain, often space is not available for physical education and wellness needs. However, with a little creativity and innovative planning, most school site facilities can sacrifice space to implement wellness centers. The important thing to keep in mind when selecting an appropriate space is to determine whether the space is large enough to sustain a full class of students exercising and whether the space meets the building codes to ensure proper implementation of the program. The following are other factors to keep in mind: (1) Does the facility meet the requirements of the ADA? (2) Are the doorways wide enough to allow large pieces of fitness equipment to be placed in the center? (3) Does the space provide for appropriate ventilation for air flow and air quality? (4) Is the facility designed to meet the standards and requirements of your school district's risk management office?

Converting Unused Space

When searching for an area to set up your wellness center, it would be nice to have a freshly painted multipurpose room available; however, in existing or older buildings, it probably will not be the case. What might be offered as an alternative is a space that was once a wood shop or drafting room for a program that has been dropped, or an old storage area consisting of unused student desks, outdated electronic materials, and so-called computer graveyards; in this case, you will need to remodel it (figure 8.5). These areas are usually larger than an average-size classroom of approximately 1,000 square feet (305 m^2), and they provide open space to create your own wellness center layout.

Selecting Equipment

Once you have secured an appropriate space within your facility to meet the design criteria and educational specifications as mandated by building codes, and you have secured the funding necessary to staff and equip the wellness center, you are ready to start the process of selecting equipment. When you are selecting equipment for your wellness center, several factors come into play. First and foremost, since you are setting up a school-based wellness

FIGURE 8.5 Wellness center *(a)* before and *(b)* after remodel.

center, the equipment selected must be age appropriate to ensure that the students will be exercising in a safe environment void of any liability or risk factors. The age and physical size of the students will determine the type of equipment you purchase. Second, the equipment selected should be appropriate for the square footage of the wellness center to allow for proper flow and space utilization. Considerations should be made for setting up specific cardiorespiratory training, strength and resistance training, stretching and flexibility, and abdominal or core training areas or stations. The best way to begin this process is to contact reputable vendors to discuss what you are looking to do and the type of equipment you are looking to purchase, and work around their recommendations.

The types of equipment most commonly installed in wellness or fitness centers are cardiorespiratory and strength training equipment. In addition to the machines and free weights typically purchased, the physical education administrator should include a host of ancillary equipment, such as stability balls and resistance bands that can be set up as stations and enhance the fitness opportunities in the center.

Once you have made your final decisions, work with your office of procurement management to secure three bids. When possible, order directly through the manufacturer because you will usually get the best pricing and best service that way. Direct manufacturers can also be included as one of the three bids secured. Additionally, make sure your bids include service contracts and staff training. Coordinating delivery schedules will ensure that the equipment is delivered during the hours that the school is open.

Multisensory Equipment

In addition to strength and cardio equipment, the wellness center could best serve all age groups by offering multisensory fitness equipment. Equipment such as core fitness (figure 8.6) and SMARTfit (figure 8.7) shares the utilization of game play with video games to engage participation and motivation. However, instead of simply simulating play, SMARTfit engages players in multisensory kinesthetic experiences, including dynamic, integrated, multiplanar athletic movement. This engagement is in combination with tactile contact and resistance, using sport, fitness, or physical education equipment. The result is a powerful combination of cardio fitness, brain fitness, functional fitness, sport-specific training, and action-based learning in one system.

Cardiorespiratory Fitness Equipment

Cardiorespiratory fitness equipment is an integral component of any school-based program. The space and number of rooms available at your school site will also determine the type of equipment you select. If you have one

FIGURE 8.6 Core fitness multisensory activities.
Courtesy of SMARTfit Inc.

FIGURE 8.7 SMARTfit cardio fitness multisensory activities for youth.
Courtesy of SMARTfit Inc.

large wellness center and you are setting up a combination cardiorespiratory and strength training center, it is recommended that the ratio of cardio equipment to strength training equipment be 70:30; in other words, include 70 percent cardiorespiratory and 30 percent strength training equipment. The most popular types of cardio equipment are treadmills, stair steppers, upright and recumbent cycles, cross-trainers, spinning cycles, and rowers.

To allow for additional teaching stations, it is further recommended that the supplemental equipment listed in the next section be added to enhance programmatic results.

Ancillary Equipment

Aside from the traditional strength and cardiorespiratory equipment, to enhance the overall program you should consider adding stability balls, resistance bands, medicine and weighted balls, plyometric boxes, dumbbells, and kettlebells. For safety, all wellness centers should have an AED, and all personnel supervising the wellness center should be trained in cardiopulmonary resuscitation (CPR) and AED.

Strength and Conditioning

The strength training component focuses on the ability to select age-appropriate equipment for students and the available space. In schools where square footage is limited, it is recommended that the strength training component include the use of weighted bars, handheld weights, kettlebells, stability or physio balls, and resistance bands. For middle school centers, multistation pulley-weight systems with limited weight capacity are recommended, whereas high school and university or college centers use various equipment such as shoulder press, fixed pull-down, leg press, leg curl, leg extension, chest press, and dual adjustable pulley machines; abdominal crunch benches; and more. Note that the strength equipment used in the school wellness center is slightly different from the strength equipment that would be used in an athletic weight training room, since the weight equipment in the athletic training room will usually entail systems with a greater amount of weight.

Flow Space

As discussed previously, the layout of your wellness center should be designed to accommodate equipment addressing cardiorespiratory, strength, and flexibility training. In most cases, similar equipment is grouped together to allow for a better flow in circuit training. The amount and type of equipment selected and the layout of your wellness center are contingent on both the age of the student population being served and the size of the facility housing the center.

When designing the layout of your wellness center and selecting your equipment, regardless of the size of the facility, you should give careful consideration to ensuring that the needs and objectives of your program are met. However, the most important consideration in layout design is student safety. Fitness equipment is usually grouped and placed in areas based on function. For example, there should be a strength training area where all the weight training equipment can be accessed. This grouping allows students to comfortably rotate among equipment while concentrating on a specific area of training. One should follow the American College of Sports Medicine (ACSM) guidelines (Sanders, 2019) when determining equipment placement. Additionally, all equipment should be placed in activity areas in full accordance with the manufacturers' instructions, tolerances, and recommendations (Standard 4.1; National Strength and Conditioning Association [NSCA], 2017). Although the ADA does not provide design standards for exercise equipment, it does require an accessible route and transfer space equal to 30 by 48 inches (.76 × 1.2 m) for at least one of each type of equipment. The same recommendations would apply to cardiorespiratory equipment, such as treadmills, upright and recumbent cycles, stair steppers, and cross-trainers. For an example of grouping equipment by function with proper spacing, see figure 8.8.

The many reputable brands of fitness equipment to choose from include LifeFitness, Precor, Cybex, Matrix, Star Trac, Concept 2, and many others. Figures 8.9 through 8.11 show samples of wellness center layout designs for high school and middle schools from LifeFitness and Hammer Strength. These samples can assist you in designing your facility based on specific square footage and program needs.

Wellness Center Design Criteria

When designing a new facility for a wellness center (e.g., when the school is under construction), several other factors need to be considered. First, the door to the wellness center

FIGURE 8.8 Fitness equipment grouped by function with proper spacing.
Getty Images/Blend Images/Space Images

should be 4 feet (1.2 m) wide to ensure that the equipment will fit through it when delivered. Additionally, a door opening with a minimum of 36 inches (.91 m) is required for ADA compliance. Second, if possible, you should design the room with ceilings at a minimum height of 15 feet (4.6 m). Although a traditional 10-foot (3 m) ceiling would accommodate the center, having a higher ceiling would allow for adding more equipment, posting educational charts, and hanging a television for instructional media use and school announcements. Finally, you should aim to have the wellness center in an area that has open access to the gymnasium and dance or aerobics room. This location will allow a class to participate in a variety of activities in close proximity to the wellness center while still under the supervision of the physical education teacher.

Electricity

All fitness equipment will run on a standard 110-volt receptacle using American standards. Manufacturers follow international voltage standards by country for fitness equipment needs abroad. In designing centers, it is recommended that a minimum of two standard receptacles be placed on each wall, except the wall that will be used as the traverse climbing wall (if one is planned). Generally, treadmills are the only cardiorespiratory equipment requiring designated electrical receptacles. If select pieces of equipment will be grouped close together in one area of the room, then during construction, accommodations for running electrical lines should be considered so that enough outlets are placed appropriately to avoid the use of extension cords. During construction, it is highly recommended that as many receptacles as possible be installed, with 4 feet (1.2 m) between each one; doing so would allow for additional equipment placement in the future. Additionally, if the center will have a water cooler, make sure that a ground fault circuit interrupter (GFCI) outlet is installed. It would also be a good idea to have the water cooler placed on a wall away from where the data drops or routers will be installed for the computer stations.

LifeFitness

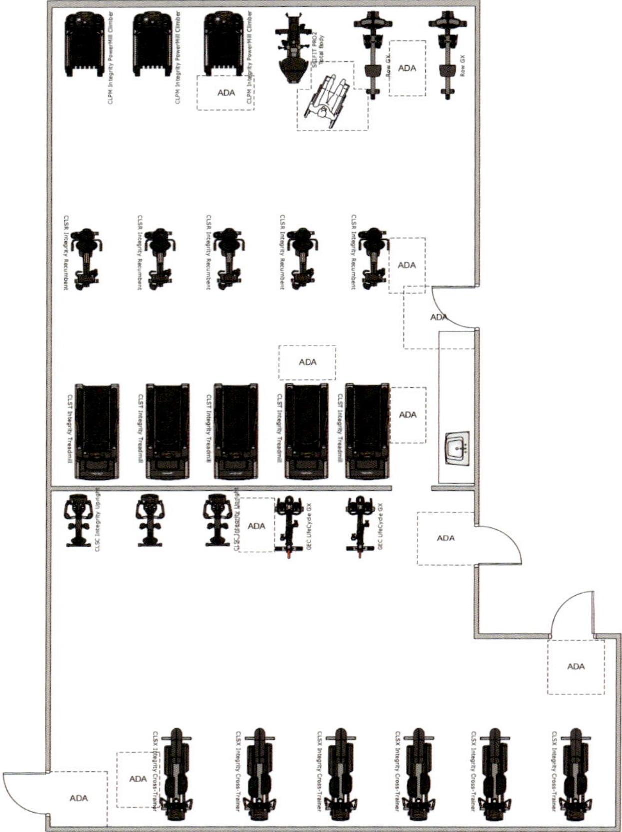

HAMMER STRENGTH®

Sales Contact:

Date:

Version:

Scale: 3/32" = 1'-0"

Disclaimer:

Floor plan dimensions are based on information provided by facility owner or its representatives and should be verified in the field. This drawing is NOT to be used as building document by any parties as layout provided is for equipment spacing purposes only.

Notes:

CEILING HEIGHT:

Recommended height is 9'-6"(2.89m) above finish floor for units with step-ups, pull-up bar(s) & rebounder. Units taller than 8'-0" (2.59m) may require additional clearance height.

EQUIPMENT STABILIZING:
SYNRGY & HAMMER STRENGTH

Units are either required or recommended (dependant on unit) to be bolted to a concrete subfloor. Please refer to product manual or contact customer service.

CARDIO SPACING:

*Treadmills – a minimum of 19.7 in (0.5 m) on each side and 78 in (2 m) from the rear to the nearest obstruction.

*Other Cardio equipment – a minimum of 19.7 in (0.5 m) on at least one side, and 19.7 in (0.5 m) behind or in front of the machine.

Additional Notes:

Electrical Legend:

STANDARD RECEPTACLE

DEDICATED RECEPTACLE

TV POWER RECEPTACLE

TV COAXIAL OUTLET

NETWORK OUTLET

*Symbol locations are approximate. Consult a qualified electrical professional to determine exact power placement.
*Reference Product Manual (s) and/or Life Fitness website for product specifications.

FIGURE 8.9 Middle school and high school cardio room.

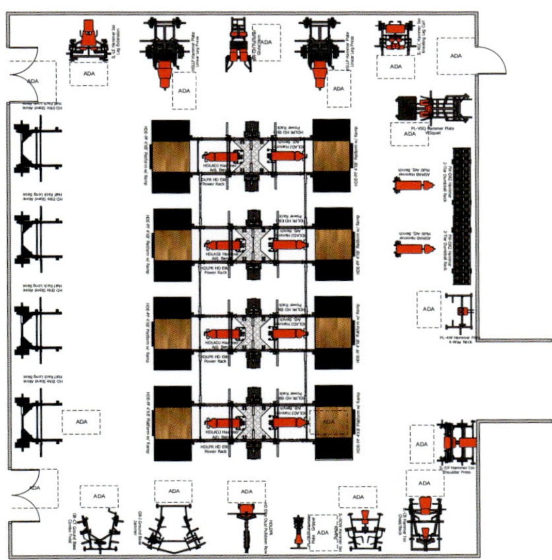

FIGURE 8.10 High school weight room.

From J. Greenberg and J. LoBianco, *Organization and Administration of Physical Education,* 2nd ed. (Human Kinetics, 2026). The right to use the copyrighted and trademarked material referenced herein granted by Brunswick Corporation. All right reserved.

Aside from the need for standard electrical outlets, school site wellness centers should also have electrical wiring for emergency fire alarm systems and emergency communication systems, including public-address (PA) systems and an emergency call button to the main office (to allow immediate communication with the main office in case of an emergency).

Other electrical factors to be aware of include the need for a quality air-conditioning system, with the average temperature for the wellness center kept at 72 degrees Fahrenheit (23.9 °C). As the wellness center reaches capacity with students exercising from moderate to vigorous intensity, so do the humidity and heat levels in the room. Without proper ventilation and an appropriate air source, students may succumb to a variety of heat illnesses. When at capacity, it is recommended by the American College of Sports Medicine (ACSM) (Sanders, 2019) that the wellness center temperature be adjusted to between 68 and 72 degrees Fahrenheit.

LifeFitness

Sales Contact:

Date:

Version: 1

Scale:

Disclaimer:
Floor plan dimensions are based on information provided by facility owner or its representatives and should be verified in the field. This drawing is NOT to be used as building document by any parties as layout provided is for equipment spacing purposes only.

Notes:
CEILING HEIGHT:
Recommended height is 9'-6"(2.89m) above finish floor for units with step-ups, pull-up bar(s) & rebounder. Units taller than 8'-0" (2.59m) may require additional clearance height.

EQUIPMENT STABILIZING:
SYNRGY & HAMMER STRENGTH
Units are either required or recommended (dependant on unit) to be bolted to a concrete subfloor. Please refer to product manual or contact customer service.

CARDIO SPACING:
*Treadmills – a minimum of 19.7 in (0.5 m) on each side and 78 in (2 m) from the rear to the nearest obstruction.
*Other Cardio equipment – a minimum of 19.7 in (0.5 m) on at least one side, and 19.7 in (0.5 m) behind or in front of the machine.

Additional Notes:

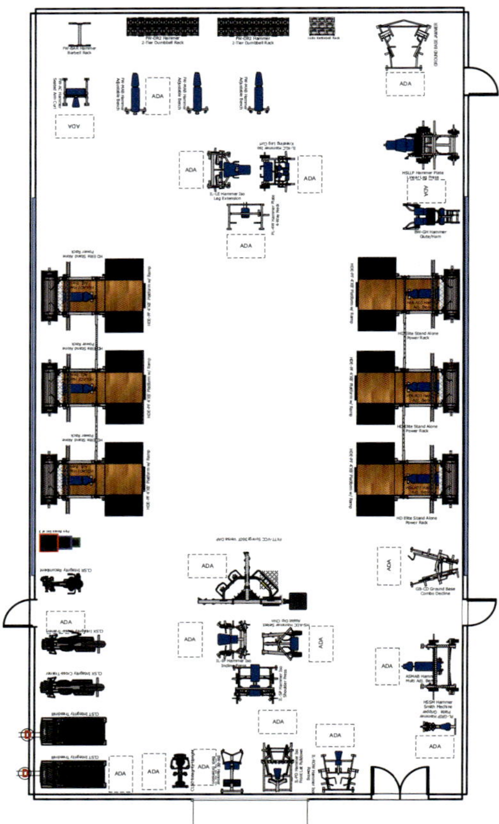

HAMMER STRENGTH®

Electrical Legend:
STANDARD RECEPTACLE
DEDICATED RECEPTACLE
TV POWER RECEPTACLE
TV COAXIAL OUTLET
NETWORK OUTLET

*Symbol locations are approximate. Consult a qualified electrical professional to determine exact power placement.
*Reference Product Manual (s) and/or Life Fitness website for product specifications.

FIGURE 8.11 High school cardio and weight room combination.

From J. Greenberg and J. LoBianco, *Organization and Administration of Physical Education,* 2nd ed. (Human Kinetics, 2026). The right to use the copyrighted and trademarked material referenced herein granted by Brunswick Corporation. All right reserved.

Data Center Drops and Routers

Electronic record keeping and student fitness assessment are critical components of any wellness program. The ability to perform pre- and posttests to monitor improvement in students' fitness levels or biometric measures will determine the program's effectiveness. In the area of the wellness center where the teacher's desk, biometric fitness assessment equipment, and student computer stations will be placed, it is important to ensure that a data center is dropped. It will allow for Internet access, Wi-Fi, phone lines, wireless routers, and closed circuit television. Once the room is constructed, it will be more difficult to retrofit the rooms to allow for proper technology infrastructure. Additionally, ensure that an intercom or emergency system is also available near the data drop center.

Water Coolers and Hydration Stations

Students' ability to continually hydrate during their exercise time is critical to their performance as well as health needs. Make sure that there are provisions for installing a water cooler either in the center (if it is large enough) or immediately outside the room in an accessible area. If your wellness center does not allow for installation of a water cooler, then accommodations should be made; students can bring in their own water bottles, or a suitable area can house a large water container, with cups set on a tabletop or rolling cart.

Flooring

Proper flooring provides many kinds of protection in the wellness center. Adding rubberized flooring, whether placing protective mats under the fitness equipment or covering the entire center surface, protects the life of the equipment by preventing dust from entering the belts and mechanical parts as well as by reducing noise and vibrations while the equipment is in use. Protective flooring further absorbs shocks and noise of heavy free weights and gym equipment while it protects the surface of the original floor. When selecting a protective surface for your wellness center, be sure to select matting that has an overall thickness between 3/8 and 1/2 inch (0.95 cm and 1.27 cm) and a slip coefficient of friction of .85 dry and .95 wet. It will assist in avoiding injuries if the surface gets wet due to perspiration or spilled beverages. Whether you choose mats, tiles, or rolled rubber, flooring can help keep your exercise area quiet and comfortable.

Storage of Equipment and Educational Materials

As an educational facility, the wellness center should also dedicate an area for instructional materials such as a locking file cabinet to store individual student portfolios, instructional hard copy materials, backup computer software, and equipment manuals, or it should have a separate room for larger pieces of equipment such as mobile device storing and charging carts if mobile devices are being used by students.

Maintenance, Setup, and Upkeep of the Wellness Center

As noted throughout this chapter, fitness equipment maintenance is important for keeping your wellness center up and running. Nothing is more discouraging to students who enter the center expecting to be on task with their planned exercise routine only to find out that the piece of equipment they plan to work out on is in disrepair. Although it is inevitable that fitness equipment will eventually break down due to heavy usage, there are several steps you can take to extend the life of the equipment and reduce the amount of downtime. These steps include purchasing the right kind of equipment, incorporating a preventive maintenance program, and contracting for planned maintenance.

Although heavy commercial-grade fitness equipment is more costly than light commercial-grade equipment or home use fitness equipment, the durability, warranty, and overall maintenance provisions far outweigh its initial cost. Purchasing name-brand, heavy commercial-grade fitness equipment from a reputable manufacturer or vendor will minimize downtime and ensure quality service and training of your staff.

Once the fitness equipment arrives at your site, the first thing you should do before signing off on the receipt is to make sure it is in working order. If the equipment arrives by delivery service, have it placed in the area of the center where you want it, keeping in mind that heavy pieces of equipment will be difficult to move at a later time and that moving equipment incorrectly could prove damaging or throw off the calibration. Equipment should also be professionally installed on dedicated electrical circuits. While the delivery service is still on-site, contact the vendor to set up a date and time when personnel can come to the site to test the equipment and train your staff on its use, especially if it has computerized settings. This step is critical to the overall maintenance of equipment because you and your staff will ultimately be responsible for providing instruction and supervision to all students and staff using it, including the settings, functions, and workout levels. Certified vendors have the capacity to train your staff not only on how to use the equipment but also how to perform daily maintenance.

Preventive maintenance on a regular basis will keep the equipment in proper working condition and avert any safety issues. See table 8.1 for common maintenance practices. If not identified, a worn cable on a piece of strength equipment can snap or a loose belt on a treadmill can jerk, which could cause injury to a student or faculty member working out. Keeping students and staff safe and injury free by establishing a preventive maintenance program further reduces your wellness center's liability owing to neglect.

Although manufacturers provide specific maintenance tips for particular pieces of equipment, a general standard is to simply wipe down equipment after each use and vacuum daily to keep dust and dirt away from moving parts; this task will help reduce friction and heat that can cause motors to wear out prematurely. Removing sweat, dust, and dirt will help the electronics and upholstery last longer. For cleaning the exterior of a piece of equipment, ask the manufacturer what should be used. In most cases, it will probably be an antibacterial type of wipe; liquid mixtures could leak into the machine and cause electronics to short.

Outdoor Facilities

Outdoor facilities for physical education must also be planned with multiple uses in mind so that the community can have access to courts and fields when school is not in session. Unlike indoor facilities, outdoor facilities require the installation of irrigation and drainage systems, court and field orientation, access to emergency vehicles, placement of fences and gates, and a variety of turf and court surfaces. Regardless of whether you are planning for indoor or outdoor facilities, the physical education curricular needs should be identified early during the design phase and well before construction begins.

Elementary School

The major spaces for elementary school physical education programs involve the hardtop or courts, covered shelters, open field space, and primary grade school playgrounds. The elementary hardtop is the area most commonly used for physical education because the class usually begins with lining up the students for attendance, followed by activity-specific warm-up exercises, the scheduled activity, and then lesson closure. The outdoor hard surface area is usually constructed with asphalt or a synthetic product, similar to tennis court facilities, such that it is appropriate for outdoor physical education instruction and allows for greater durability and a reduction in injuries. The hard court usually includes fixed play equipment such as basketball poles and backboards, as well as less-structured spaces for portable equipment and innovative games. Multicolored court striping is most commonly used for courts including basketball, volleyball, four square, and hopscotch, as well as markings for managerial tasks. Additionally, for aesthetic and educational purposes, markings should be used for both physical education instruction and recess times. Common configurations of lines include large and small circles, four square courts, a map of the United States, and local state and artistic representations of the community. The elementary hard court could also include sleeves with removable poles for outdoor volleyball, tennis, or badminton.

TABLE 8.1 Common Preventive Maintenance Practices for Resistance and Cardiorespiratory Equipment

Equipment	Daily	Weekly	Monthly	As Needed
RESISTANCE EQUIPMENT				
Variable-resistance, selectorized resistance, and alternate resistance equipment	Clean frames with mild soap and water. Clean upholstery with mild soap and water.	Check all cables and bolts, and tighten as needed. Check moving parts, and adjust as needed.	Lubricate guide rods with lightweight oil.	Repair or replace pads. Replace cables if needed.
Free-weight benches	Clean frames with mild soap and water. Clean upholstery with mild soap and water.	Check all cables and bolts, and tighten as needed. Check moving parts, and adjust as needed.		Repair or replace pads. Replace cables if needed.
Dumbbells and bars	Clean dumbbells and all bar handles (plus any free eight attachment handles) daily with an antimicrobial solution on a damp cloth or an antimicrobial wipe.	Check all screws and bolts, and tighten as needed.	Use lightweight oil on cloth to remove any rust.	Repair or replace broken bars and dumbbells.
CARDIORESPIRATORY EQUIPMENT				
Bikes	Clean off control panel with dry cloth. Clean off handles with mild antibacterial soap and damp cloth. Clean off seats with mild antibacterial soap and damp cloth.	Check equipment diagnostics through control panel for any potential troubles. Check all screws and bolts, and tighten as needed.	Remove bike housing, and clean out dust and lint that may have collected.	Refer to manufacturer's guidelines.
Elliptical trainers	Clean off control panel with dry cloth. Clean off handles with mild antibacterial soap and damp cloth. Clean off foot pedals with damp cloth.	Check equipment diagnostics through control panel for any potential troubles. Check all screws and bolts, and tighten as needed.	Remove elliptical housing, and clean out dust and lint that may have collected.	Refer to manufacturer's guidelines.
Treadmills	Clean off control panels with dry cloth. Clean off housing with mild antibacterial soap and damp cloth.	Check equipment diagnostics through control panel for any potential troubles. Check all screws and bolts, and tighten as needed.	Clean belt using a damp cloth. Check belt and deck surface, and lubricate as needed and per manufacturer's specifications.	Replace belt, if needed. Refer to manufacturer's guidelines.

Adapted from Sanders (2019).

For elementary schools that do not have gymnasiums, outdoor covered shelters have recently become a preference for protecting students from the elements, rain, and heat during physical education. These shelters can be either stand-alone models (not connected to the school building) or attached to the building with easy access to the physical education storage room and teachers' office.

Aside from the hard court and covered shelter, the field becomes the main physical education teaching station for large-group games and a variety of sports activities. The majority of the activities are marked off using cones and imaginary boundary lines to designate safe playing spaces where no line markings exist. In some cases, elementary school physical education teachers use chalk and a field marker to provide temporary lines for various seasonal sports and field day activities. Any portable equipment that is used for sport events, such as soccer goals that are not anchored down, must be moved to a secure location at the end of the school day because it could become a hazard during unsupervised after-school play.

Since the physical education field is the largest outdoor teaching space, physical education teachers should rotate the teaching areas so that the grass in any one area does not get worn down. There may be times when the irrigation system is not working or is not used regularly, and rotation will help to preserve the grass. Outdoor areas should also be located away from classrooms; should have clearly defined boundaries; and should be away from parking lots, streets, and other openly accessible areas where safety could be a concern. All physical education spaces should be in close proximity to hydration stations and restrooms.

Elementary physical education teachers may be assigned office space inside the school building, or they can set up a remote office in the outdoor equipment storage area so that their personal items are safe and away from instruction and the elements. Physical education teachers should always be in close proximity to their students to ensure supervision at all times.

Playgrounds

Elementary school playgrounds serve dual purposes; one is for physical education, and the other is for recess and before- and after-school time. Playgrounds not only serve as a place and time for children to be physically active; they also serve to foster a child's social, emotional, and intellectual development. Through physical development, the child can master skills such as climbing, swinging, and balancing; through social and emotional development, a child learns the skills of communicating, sharing, taking turns, cooperation, and enhanced levels of self-esteem; through intellectual development, the child can master the skills of problem solving, develop better control over attention and memory, and become able to use cognitive abilities to attain goals.

Many professional vendors can assist with the design of a playground while addressing your school's needs and budget. All playgrounds should be designed to be inclusive for all students and meet ADA requirements. When properly installed, playgrounds should be inspected and should meet all requirements set forth by the Consumer Product Safety Commission (CPSC) and the American National Standards Institute (ANSI), which have created a standardized document and training system for certification of playground safety inspectors. These regulations are in force across the United States, and they provide a basis for safe playground installation and maintenance practices. The American Society for Testing and Materials (ASTM) provides a performance specification that deals with specific requirements regarding issues such as playground layout, use zones, and various test criteria for determining playground safety. See figure 8.12 for an example of an inclusive elementary school playground.

FIGURE 8.12 Inclusive elementary school playground.

Photo Courtesy of Landscape Structures

LEADERSHIP IN ACTION

10 Equipment and Inventory Organization Tips

Jessica Shawley, MEd, NBCT

SHAPE America Teacher of the Year, Lewiston High School, Idaho

I love the opportunity to organize and update my program's inventory and equipment space. An organized space helps my daily teaching flow be more efficient, which helps reduce stress and sets my lessons up for success. An up-to-date inventory helps guide my planning for the current year and beyond. You do not need to stress about being an organization expert; work to the best of your ability with what you have. You'll become more efficient each year as you dial in a process that works for you. Here are my 10 tips for equipment and inventory organization.

1. Organize by Type

I group most of my items by type. For example, all fitness equipment is in a specific section of our storage room; it is organized by type (bands, jump ropes, dumbbells, etc.). General multi-use items are also together; they typically include cones, spots, pinnies, and other go-to daily-use items. I have what I call a *curriculum corner* area where task cards, station signs, nutrition and curriculum education materials, pencils, markers, and other teacher supplies are located.

2. Organize by Usage

As in our homes, frequently used items are more accessible; less frequently used items are in the back corner, and may take a few moments more to find when you need them. I like to use an in-season and out-of-season system. Equipment for the upcoming unit is placed up front, typically in collapsible, wheeled storage carts. The equipment I just finished using is put away in the back or on shelves.

3. Take Notes

It is essential to reflect on the end of each unit regarding the learning experience, what you would improve on the next time you teach it, and the condition the equipment and materials are in. I note what will be needed the next time I teach that unit, what needs fixing, and what needs to be purchased. You don't want the unit to come up next year and be short on equipment or have a broken item that is still unfixed, affecting your ability to provide meaningful opportunities for students. These reflections are especially critical if you share your equipment with others. There's nothing worse than preparing for a unit and finding damaged or missing equipment that someone forgot to document correctly, leaving another colleague scrambling last minute to make things work. Put in work orders for broken equipment immediately because they take time to get completed. In addition, keep a running list of items that need purchasing so that your end-of-year purchasing can run more smoothly.

I like having a whiteboard or notepad and pencil in the equipment room for everyone to make notes. I take a picture of the note or notes and email it to myself so that when I return to my office, I can take action on items as needed and transfer purchasing needs to our purchasing wish list, in our shared online inventory sheet.

4. Use Labels

I label *everything*. I use deluxe vinyl floor tape for labeling all tubs, boxes, larger items, and so on. Every piece of equipment is marked with "LHS PE" and the year we received it using a black permanent marker. The year helps me know how old something is and reminds me when to add it to the replacement rotation list. It also lets me know whether an item is holding up to the expectation of use or we have to find another option that will last longer.

Note: Sometimes you get what you pay for. Therefore, consider how long you want something to last as well as the warranties and customer service each vendor offers. For example, if I know a company's warranty that offers an unconditional, 100 percent satisfaction guarantee is the real deal, and if I know their customer

(continued)

Ten Equipment and Inventory Organization Tips *(continued)*

service team is exceptional, I am more confident in purchasing its products. Knowing their items will last longer provides peace of mind and helps budget funding to be used efficiently.

5. Think: Portability

One of the most significant aids in our storage room is having the ability to wheel equipment around the room so that we can change between units quickly. I like how I can take my wheeled carts and equipment racks into the gym so that students can help with setup and have a choice in equipment selection; it also keeps them from going in and out of the storage room without supervision. One of our department's rules is that students are only allowed in the storage room with permission. To save space, look for wheeled carts that are collapsible.

6. Color-Code

Purchasing equipment in rainbow colors helps with organizing teams and stations. It helps with clean-up; students can be in charge of their team or color and be responsible for returning all of their team's equipment. Color coding has made my lessons run more smoothly, and I recommend it whenever possible.

7. Look for Storage Options

I always look for deals on storage items such as tubs, shelving, boxes, collapsible carts, wheeled carts, milk crates, wall hooks, and utility hooks to help maximize our storage. I also keep an ear open for old utility or AV wheeled carts that teachers no longer need so that I can use them for various needs. They make great technology charging stations for tablets and computers.

8. Charge and Store Technology

An important thing to keep in mind is where you will organize, secure, and charge all technology and devices. Have specific charging and technology areas within your storage room or teacher's office. You will need multiport power strips for charging multiple devices simultaneously. Find crates, tubs, or shelving that allows you to secure, store, and charge the technology daily.

9. Designate Utility, Supply, and Repair Areas

Our storage rooms and teacher offices have a specific utility area for supplies and repairs. Our supply shelf stores containers with zip ties, cords, carabiners, clips, rope, hook-and-loop closure strips, adhesive strips, replacement batteries, extra-strength glue, and random pieces of equipment that may come in handy later. We also have multiple tool kits that enable us to tighten loose parts and make simple fixes when necessary. You never know what you need, so a utility area is handy. The inflator is also in this area. A repair area is where broken or damaged items reside or where new things go that need inflation or labeling before officially going into storage.

10. Keep an Electronic Inventory

Our department uses an electronic inventory in the form of a spreadsheet file shared on a team drive. This document keeps a detailed record of everything. Equipment is organized by type or category, and each storage space has a separate tab; for example, there is a tab for the main gym, one for the small gym, one for the weight room, and one for the wrestling room. The spreadsheet also includes a tab for our list of items to purchase and a wish list of things we'd like to enhance our program. We complete inventory checks at the midpoint of the year and again near the end of the year so that we can finalize purchasing needs before we leave for the summer.

Playgrounds should be designed for age-appropriate utilization. For security reasons, they should be enclosed, especially if they are primary-age playgrounds. Students should never be left alone while on the playground, and adult supervision should be present at all times. Students can also take responsibility for ensuring safe play spaces by following the rules set by the physical education teacher and using playground equipment for its intended purpose.

According to the Centers for Disease Control and Prevention (CDC, 2016), more than 200,000 playground-related injuries require a visit to the emergency room each year; most of the injuries involve broken bones, concussions, and traumatic brain injuries (TBIs). The National Safety Council and the U.S. CPSC (2015) identify the following problems that imperil playground safety, and they provide the following recommendations:

- *Improper protective surfaces*: Fall surfaces should be made of wood chips, mulch, wood fibers, sand, pea gravel, shredded tires, or rubber mats, and they should be at least 12 inches (30 cm) deep.
- *Inadequate use zone*: The area under and around play equipment where a child might fall should be a minimum of 6 feet (1.8 m) in all directions.
- *Protrusion hazards:* Beware of hardware that is capable of impaling or cutting a child (bolts, hooks, rungs, etc.) or catching strings or items of clothing. Children should never wear sweatshirts with drawstrings at the playground.
- *Head entrapment hazards*: No openings that measure between 3.5 and 9 inches (10 and 23 cm) should be present.
- *Overcrowded play area*: Swings should be set far enough away from other equipment that children won't be hit by a moving swing.
- *Trip hazards:* These are objects like rocks or tree stumps, which should be removed.
- *Lack of supervision*: Children under age 4 shouldn't play on climbing equipment or horizontal ladders.
- *Age-inappropriate activities*: Spring-loaded seesaws are best for young children. Avoid adjustable seesaws with chains because children can crush their hands under the chains. A traditional seesaw should not hit the ground. Whirls or roundabouts are best for school-aged children.
- *Lack of maintenance*: Metal or wooden swing seats should be replaced with soft seats, and equipment should not be split or splintered.
- *Sharp edges*: Sharp edges on equipment should be avoided.
- *Platforms with no guardrails*: All platforms should have guardrails.

For additional information on playground safety, the U.S. CPSC's publication, *Public Playground Safety Handbook*, can be found at www.cpsc.gov/s3fs-public/325.pdf.

Secondary Schools

Secondary school hardtop facilities generally serve multiple purposes, and they are used for physical education instruction and community recreation rather than for athletic competition. In general, the hardtop is usually marked with lines to accommodate a minimum of four basketball courts with goals, and it is also lined for volleyball play. As with the elementary school hardtop, metal sleeves are inserted into the court for removable poles, which can accommodate volleyball, badminton, and tennis. Both elementary and secondary schools can use portable poles that can be moved to the grass area for additional teaching stations. If the school does not have an indoor facility to store the portable poles in, it is recommended (for safety purposes) that they be moved to an area away from the playing surface and chained together.

Tennis Courts

Tennis courts at the high school level, although used for physical education instruction, are usually designed as stand-alone facilities for high school interscholastic competition. The court is usually composed of either asphalt or concrete; depending on the design criteria, it either is installed with a drainage system or is sloped to expel excess water. The base is then heavily coated with a synthetic surface coating system to add multiple layers of cushioning and leveling capabilities. After the court is cured and all surfaces have dried, it can be properly lined. Although the playing surface on most tennis courts is either green or red, the color selection is completely up to the school. The number of courts installed depends on the size of the area that has been designated for tennis during the planning phase. A regulation tennis court for doubles play is 60 by 120 feet (18 × 36.6 m), measured from fence to fence. The actual size of the court is 36 by 78 feet (11 × 23.7 m) with an additional 21 feet (6.4 m) between the court and the fence (backstop) for the service line. The poles securing the net should be 3 feet (0.9 m) from the sideline, and there should be a minimum of 12 feet (3.7 m) between each court.

The fences surrounding the tennis courts are usually 10 feet (3 m) high, and they are constructed with either galvanized chain link or vinyl-coated chain link. Additionally, many schools add nylon mesh netting to the chain-link fence both to serve as a windscreen and to provide privacy during match play. The mesh netting also assists with visibility by increasing the contrast of tennis balls against the screen backdrop. Tennis courts should always be constructed with a north-to-south orientation to avoid having the players look into the sun in the morning and late afternoon. It is highly recommended that a professional contractor with experience install the tennis courts to ensure that the slopes, drainage, and surfaces are properly constructed. For physical education instruction, as long as the student is dressed properly and is wearing the appropriate athletic shoes, the only equipment needed includes tennis rackets and optic yellow tennis balls (for greater visibility). Since pressurized balls out of the can are best for competition, the physical education teacher can work closely with the tennis coach to secure used balls after a competition.

Field Areas

Before any athletic field is designed, it must be properly planned. The planning phase involves ensuring that the initial field is level, that plans for irrigation and drainage are made with the venue location in mind, and that accommodations are made for fence and gate installation. Ensure that electricity for scoring, scoreboards, and potential lighting is installed; determine the location for permanent or movable bleachers; and determine space for foot traffic and sidewalks. Uniform building code standards will specify the required dimensions, seating capacity, guardrails, and gaps between footboards and seat boards. Bleachers must also be constructed and installed according to ADA requirements, as with the gymnasium bleacher seating. The type of surface (natural grass, turf, or a hybrid material) must also be considered at this time. Now that the footprints for physical education and athletic facilities are established, the next step is to determine the location of each venue, taking orientation into consideration.

A school should plan for utilization of multiple fields with adjacent parking along with access and proximity to the gymnasium doors. These fields will be used for a variety of school and community events, and they need to be laid out to maximize the convenience of participants. All fields intended for use in athletics should maintain the size and layout required by state and local athletic policy. Community recreation groups may also have specific needs and requests related to the planning of a facility.

Turf Considerations

Of all of the aspects of facilities discussed in this chapter, the one that is most difficult to maintain is the turf, or natural grass that grows on the majority of physical education and athletic fields. Maintaining physical education fields is a major programmatic priority for safe, playable spaces. Natural grass is the most cost-effective surface; therefore, whether you choose Bermuda grass for warm-weather climates or Kentucky bluegrass for cold-weather fields, the grass planted should be maintained on a regular basis. Setting maintenance schedules for mowing, fertilizing, overseeding, and aerating the field will assist in maintaining the quality of playing fields. To avoid overuse on specific areas of the field, physical education teachers should rotate activities to prevent wearing down grassy areas. Proper irrigation and drainage for your fields should be a part of the initial planning process. Landscape professionals and your district's office of facilities management will be available to assist you in selection of the appropriate type of grass for your specific geographic environment.

If installing synthetic turf surfaces is an option, it is highly recommended that a committee be convened to explore the various types of surfaces as well as to weigh the pros and cons of each surface. Other decisions might involve having natural grass in some areas of the physical education field and a synthetic turf in some of the athletic fields (e.g., for football, soccer, and field hockey). Although a hybrid model is a favorable solution, it may also be cost prohibitive.

Track and Field

The track facility is another multipurpose facility that is commonly used for physical education, athletics, and community activities. The design of most track and field facilities includes the running track, which should be a 400-meter oval track with eight lanes; a high-jump pad; a long-jump runway and pit; a pole vault runway and landing pad in two directions; shot put and discus pads; and a triple-jump runway and pit. The track should also be constructed in a north-to-south orientation, and the strength of wind speeds and the sun should be taken into consideration for all events. The types of landing pads and cage requirements are spelled out in the NFHS's *Court and Field Diagram Guide* (2020). This publication provides all of the requirements for installing a competition-ready venue. If the specifications are not adhered to, the school may not be able to host an interscholastic track and field meet because the function would not be sanctioned. It is during the design phase that the planning committee meets to determine the location of components of a track and field program. In many cases, the planners must work around the football field goals as well as drainage systems to ensure student safety.

The next issue for consideration is the type of running surface to be installed for the running area. An important choice in planning a track is the type of surface. Since there are many options to choose from, the selection made by the school district or individual school will be based on financial resources, type of usage, location, and maintenance capability.

In past years, school district track surfaces were either cinder, clay, or asphalt. More recently, synthetic materials that are environmentally friendly and user-friendly have been developed. A surface known as solid polyurethane is made by casting polyurethane and rubber granules. The porous surface track consists of a base mat composed of black granules and a binder, covered by a porous layer coated in a texture spray. Although several options are available, it is highly recommended that after the initial track surface has been laid, it should be flooded with water so that low points or areas of water pooling can be identified. Once the contractor fixes the low spots, it is time to have the top coats installed. This process will help preserve the life of the coating and prevent surface cracking. Track lanes can also be painted in a variety of colors; whichever is chosen, check for the UV status of the paint, which will allow the paint to hold its color longer. Installation of the track should also include appropriate lane markings and an inside curb if required by regulations.

Figure 8.13 shows a rendition of a proposed track and field layout by the NFHS. It is highly recommended that these standards be utilized when designing any athletic facility for high school competition. For exact dimensions and requirements for all track and field facilities and events, please refer to the *Court and Field Diagram Guide* (NFHS, 2020).

Equipment needed for the track and field instructional program, as well as for athletic competition, includes the following: starting blocks; hurdles; a long-jump takeoff board; a triple-jump takeoff board; high-jump standards and a crossbar; 24-inch (61 cm) high-jump mats consisting of foam rubber or shock-absorbing materials; pole vault standards and a crossbar; a pole vault landing surface a minimum of 19 feet, 8 inches (6 m) wide; a landing surface in the back of the vaulting box 16 feet, 5 inches (5 m) deep; a fiberglass or carbon fiber flexible pole; a discus cage; a discus metal, wood, or plastic band throwing circle; a men's 3-pound 9-ounce (1.6 kg) discus; a women's 2.2-pound (0.99 kg) discus; a shot put cage with an aluminum toe or stop board; a men's 12-pound (5.4 kg) shot and women's 8.8-pound (4 kg) shot; and various carts to transport the equipment. Additional equipment and supplies can be purchased contingent on the activities being implemented.

Soccer Fields

In many cases, depending on the size of the field space at individual high schools, the soccer field is marked within the inside of the track, since the soccer field is 100 yards (91.4 m) long and 60

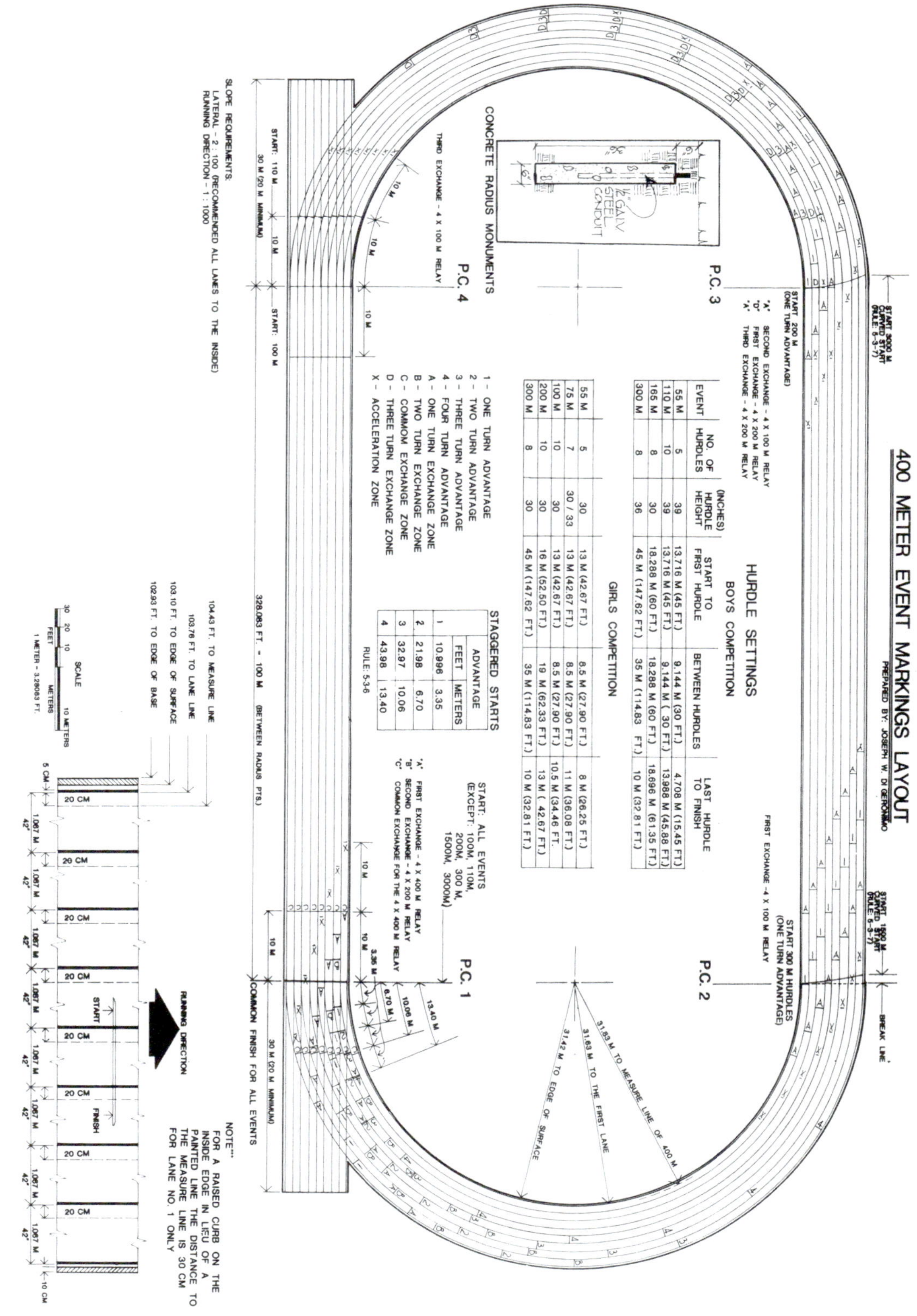
400 METER EVENT MARKINGS LAYOUT
PREPARED BY: JOSEPH W. DI GERONIMO
HURDLE SETTINGS
BOYS COMPETITION
EVENT | NO. OF HURDLES | (INCHES) HURDLE HEIGHT | START TO FIRST HURDLE | BETWEEN HURDLES | LAST HURDLE TO FINISH
55 M | 5 | 39 | 13.716 M (45 FT.) | 9.144 M (30 FT.) | 4.708 M (15.45 FT.)
110 M | 10 | 39 | 13.716 M (45 FT.) | 9.144 M (30 FT.) | 13.988 M (45.88 FT.)
165 M | 8 | 30 | 18.288 M (60 FT.) | 18.288 M (60 FT.) | 18.696 M (61.35 FT.)
300 M | 8 | 36 | 45 M (147.62 FT.) | 35 M (114.83 FT.) | 10 M (32.81 FT.)
GIRLS COMPETITION
55 M | 5 | 30 | 13 M (42.67 FT.) | 8.5 M (27.90 FT.) | 8 M (26.25 FT.)
75 M | 7 | 30 / 33 | 13 M (42.67 FT.) | 8.5 M (27.90 FT.) | 11 M (36.08 FT.)
100 M | 10 | 30 | 13 M (42.67 FT.) | 8.5 M (27.90 FT.) | 10.5 M (34.46 FT.)
200 M | 10 | 30 | 16 M (52.50 FT.) | 19 M (62.33 FT.) | 13 M (42.67 FT.)
300 M | 8 | 30 | 45 M (147.62 FT.) | 35 M (114.83 FT.) | 10 M (32.81 FT.)
STAGGERED STARTS
ADVANTAGE
FEET | METERS
1 | 10.996 | 3.35
2 | 21.98 | 6.70
3 | 32.97 | 10.06
4 | 43.98 | 13.40
RULE: 5-3-6
1 - ONE TURN ADVANTAGE
2 - TWO TURN ADVANTAGE
3 - THREE TURN ADVANTAGE
4 - FOUR TURN ADVANTAGE
A - ONE TURN EXCHANGE ZONE
B - TWO TURN EXCHANGE ZONE
C - COMMOM EXCHANGE ZONE
D - THREE TURN EXCHANGE ZONE
X - ACCELERATION ZONE
START: ALL EVENTS
(EXCEPT: 100M, 110M, 200M, 300 M, 1500M, 3000M)
P.C. 1
P.C. 2
P.C. 3
P.C. 4
CONCRETE RADIUS MONUMENTS
328.083 FT. - 100 M (BETWEEN RADIUS PTS.)
COMMON FINISH FOR ALL EVENTS
RUNNING DIRECTION
SLOPE REQUIREMENTS:
LATERAL - 2 : 100 (RECOMMENDED ALL LANES TO THE INSIDE)
RUNNING DIRECTION - 1 : 1000
NOTE:
FOR A RAISED CURB ON THE INSIDE EDGE IN LIEU OF A PAINTED LINE THE DISTANCE TO THE MEASURE LINE IS 30 CM FOR LANE NO. 1 ONLY
36.83 M TO MEASURE LINE OF 400 M
31.63 M TO THE FIRST LANE
31.42 M TO EDGE OF SURFACE
104.43 FT. TO MEASURE LINE
103.76 FT. TO LANE LINE
103.10 FT. TO EDGE OF SURFACE
102.93 FT. TO EDGE OF BASE
SCALE
1 METER - 3.28083 FT.

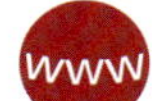

FIGURE 8.13 NFHS track and field construction diagram.

Note: Except as specifically stated in the rules, information on field diagrams in this book is suggestive only; it does not reflect NFHS requirements. The construction and layout of all courts and fields used for high school competition are subject to any controlling laws and building codes and to the sound judgment of the persons in charge of the facilities.

From J. Greenberg and J. LoBianco, *Organization and Administration of Physical Education,* 2nd ed. (Human Kinetics, 2026). Reprinted by permission from National Federation of High Schools.

yards (54.9 m) wide. Aside from the outer field markings, other markings include the midfield line; the center circle should be drawn with a 10-foot (3 m) radius, the penalty area should be a rectangle box 44 yards (40 m) wide by 18 yards (16.5 m) deep, the goal area inside the penalty area should be 20 yards (18.2 m) wide by 6 yards deep (5.5 m), and a 1-yard (0.9 m) quarter circle should be marked on each corner of the field for a corner kick. The soccer goals have a width of 8 yards (7.3 m) between the posts and a height of 8 feet (2.4 m) from the lower edge of the crossbar to the ground. Since the soccer goals are removable, it is recommended that they be secured per vendor specifications to ensure safety concerns are addressed. The *Court and Field Diagram Guide* (NFHS, 2020) should be used as a reference when designing the soccer field.

Football Fields

If your school district is fortunate enough to have the funding and space to build a football stadium or separate football field on school sites, it would be the preferred option. However, as with soccer fields, the football field is often designed within the inner space of the track and field facility. As to design, the football field should be 360 feet (110 m) long by 160 feet (49 m) wide. The end zone should be 10 yards (9.1 m) deep, and the field should be marked with 10-yard line markers. Team benches should be placed along a restraining line between the 30-yard (27.4 m) line markers. The goalpost should be a total of 30 feet (9.1 m) high, with the football goal crossbar 10 feet (3 m) high and 23 feet, 4 inches (7.1 m) wide. Football goalposts should be installed according to the vendor specifications to ensure safety. The *Court and Field Diagram Guide* (NFHS, 2020) should be used as a reference when designing the football field.

Baseball and Softball Fields

Along with track and field and tennis, baseball and softball fields are two commonly installed facilities in secondary school athletic fields. The construction of baseball and softball fields should adhere to the *Court and Field Diagram Guide* (NFHS, 2020) (see figures 8.14 and 8.15). However, when designing these fields, careful attention needs to be paid to the types of bases and anchors for the bases, pitcher's mound, backstop, dugouts, and batting cages or practice areas. Spectator seating and pedestrian flow are also major considerations for field design.

To minimize sun interference for the players, especially the batter and the pitcher, the field should be oriented so that the setting sun is generally at a right angle to the imaginary line between home plate, the pitching rubber, and second base, and should run east-northeast (NFHS, 2025). Since baseball and softball fields have the same recommended orientation and the games take place during the same season, facilities planning could be challenging. Baseball is not recommended for physical education; however, equipment needed for a softball instructional unit would include bats, gloves, bases, a pitcher's rubber, soft training softballs, a batting helmet, a catcher's mask and helmet, and a portable backstop (if a grassy area is being used as opposed to the softball field).

Storage

One thing that any physical education teacher or coach will attest to is that you can never have enough storage space. Following the requirements in Ed Specs documents, space should be provided both inside and outside of the building to allow for the permanent storage of all equipment and the temporary storage of equipment used for a particular unit or activity. Storage space is an often overlooked component in the design of physical education and sports facilities. Temperature-controlled indoor storage should be provided to maintain the quality of equipment as well as athletic uniforms and gear. For outside storage of large equipment such as pole vault poles, standards, and crossbars as well as select football equipment, storage with a roll-up external door would best be suited for ease of transport. Additional storage for both outdoors and indoors should consist of shelving; portable carts; hooks to hang mats and equipment; and any variety of crates, canisters, or other such devices used to store equipment. If space is available, separate storage facilities should be planned for both the school and outside groups to allow all users a private space to secure their equipment.

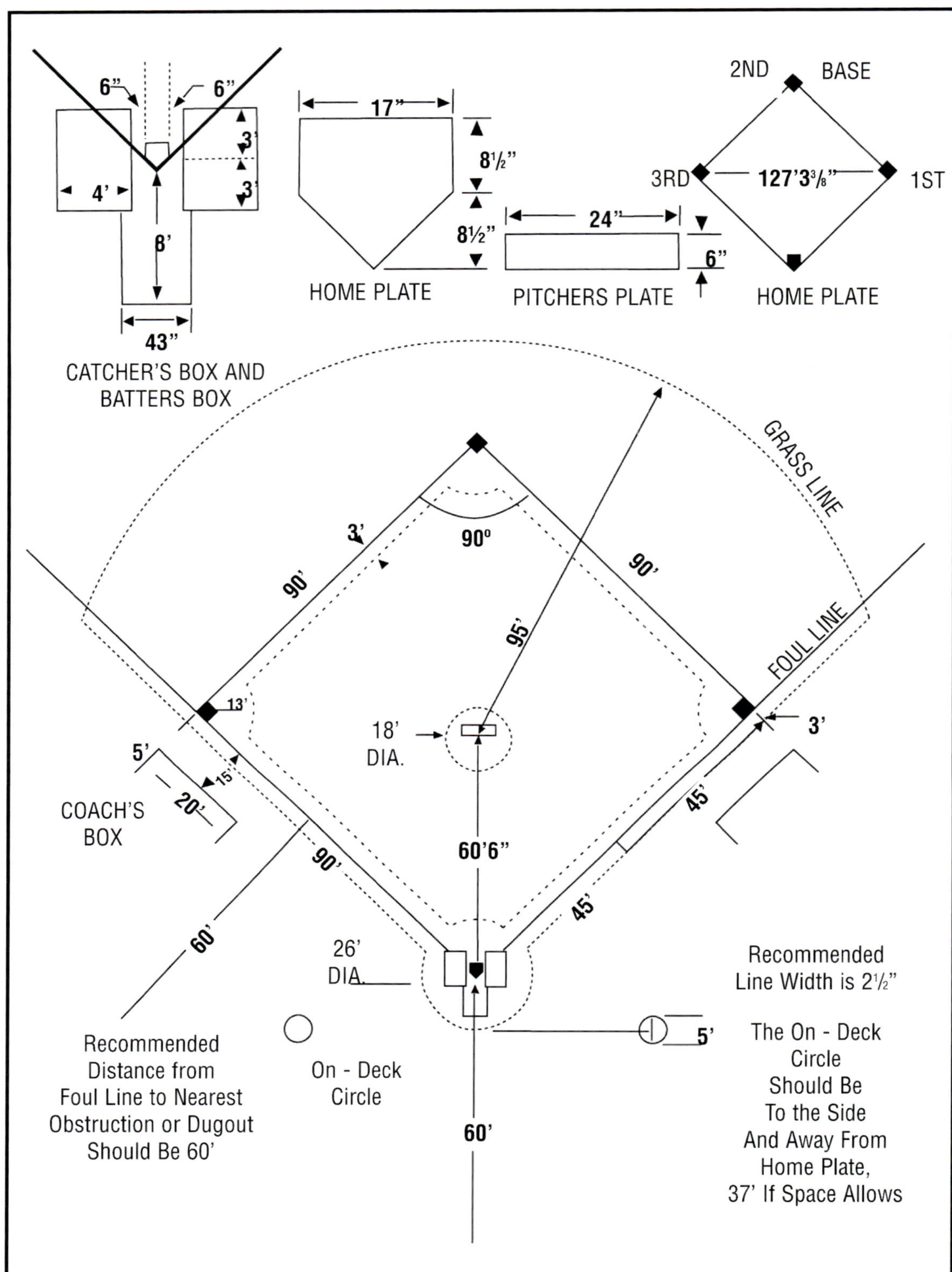

FIGURE 8.14 NFHS baseball field construction diagram.

Note: Except as specifically stated in the rules, information on field diagrams in this book is suggestive only; it does not reflect NFHS requirements. The construction and layout of all courts and fields used for high school competition are subject to any controlling laws and building codes, and to the sound judgment of the persons in charge of the facilities.

From J. Greenberg and J. LoBianco, *Organization and Administration of Physical Education,* 2nd ed. (Human Kinetics, 2026). Reprinted by permission from National Federation of High Schools.

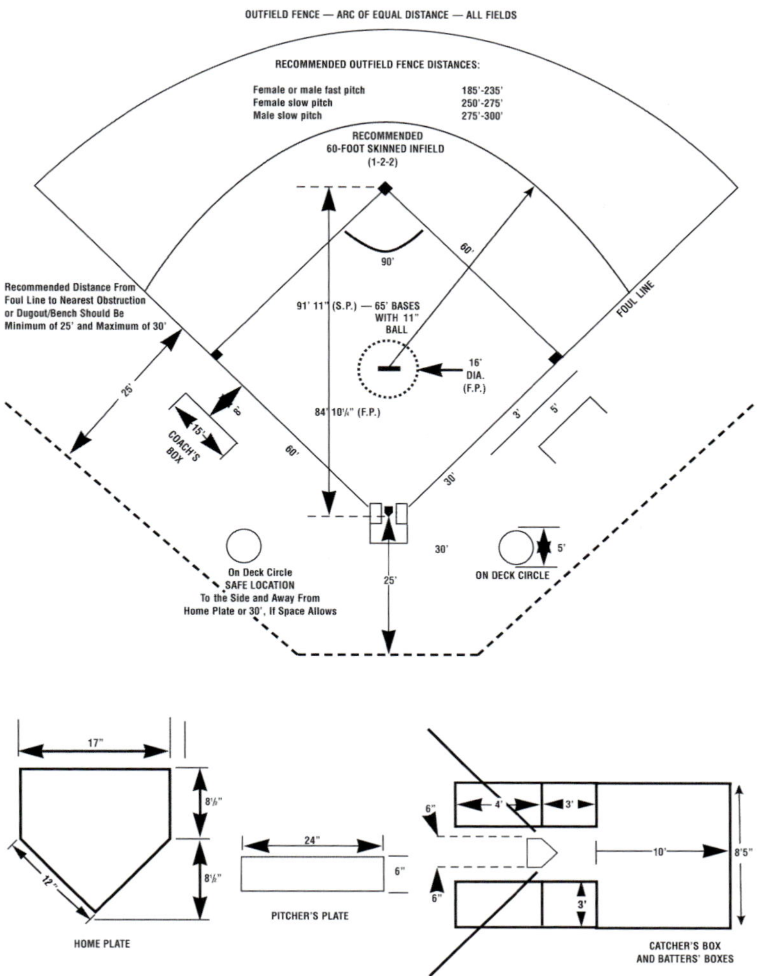

FIGURE 8.15 NFHS softball field construction diagram.

Note: Except as specifically stated in the rules, information on field diagrams in this book is suggestive only; it does not reflect NFHS requirements. The construction and layout of all courts and fields used for high school competition are subject to any controlling laws and building codes, and to the sound judgment of the persons in charge of the facilities.

From J. Greenberg and J. LoBianco, *Organization and Administration of Physical Education,* 2nd ed. (Human Kinetics, 2026). Reprinted by permission from National Federation of High Schools.

Physical Education Preferred Equipment

Equipment selected for physical education should be age and developmentally appropriate and selected to align with the instructional program. As with all curriculum areas, school site budgets should provide that all physical education equipment be kept in working order and that it be replaced if there are concerns about compromising the safety of students. Prior to ordering any physical education equipment or supplies, whether for elementary or secondary school, it is highly recommended that you complete an inventory assessment to determine exactly what you have in storage and exactly what you need in order to run your program. This assessment will ensure that your budget will be spent wisely on the type of equipment you need to run your program for the upcoming school year.

Tables 8.2-8.5 show recommended equipment lists for grades K-5, 6-8, 9-12, and

TABLE 8.2 Equipment Recommendations for K-5 Physical Education Outcomes

Standard 1: Demonstrates competency in a variety of motor skills and movement patterns

LOCOMOTOR AND NONLOCOMOTOR	
Locomotor: Hopping, Galloping, Running, Sliding, Skipping, Leaping, Jogging, Running, Dance, Combinations	
• Lines in gymnasium • Cones • Polyspots • Directional arrows • Floor tape	
Nonlocomotor: Balance, Weight Transfer, Rolling, Curling or Stretching, Twisting, Bending, Combinations	
• Physical activity books • Balance beam • Yoga mats • Tumbling mats	
MANIPULATIVE	
Underhand Throw, Overhand Throw, Passing With Hands, Catching	
Throw/catch • Foam skin balls: 5", 6.3", 8.25" • Fleece/yarn balls • Velcro mitts • Scoops/wiffle balls • Tail balls • Footballs: mini or junior/size 3 • Bean bags • Bowling balls • Frisbees • Squish or bump balls/Tumble-n-Ball • Grab balls/sticks	Targets • Bean bag targets • Buckets • Bowling pins • Nets • Rebounders • Floor tape/visual targets • Frisbee targets
Dribbling/Ball Control With Hands	
Bounce/catch and dribbling: • Playground balls: 8.5" • Basketballs: Mini, Junior, Intermediate • Bounceable foam/grip balls: 6" or 8" • Oversized ball: 30" or 40" • Mesh bungee dribble aid	
Dribbling/Ball Control With Feet, Passing/Receiving With Feet, Dribbling in Combination, Kicking	
• Soccer balls: Size 3 (under 8), Size 4 (8-12) • Foam soccer balls • Tether soccer ball • Soccer nets or cones for goals • Poly spots for kicking (home base or spot to land for oppositional step)	

Volley Underhand and Overhead

- Balloons (latex free, if possible)
- Beach balls
- Soft touch volleyballs
- Oversized volleyballs
- Volleyball nets
- Portable gym standards
- Hula hoops or spike ball/round nets
- Bounceable balls

Striking Short Implement and Long Implement, in Combination With Locomotor

Short implement

- BoundaLoons
- Lollipop paddles
- Scoops
- Fluff balls/yarn balls
- Nerf tennis balls
- Wiffle balls

Long implement

- BadaLoons
- Badminton or Speedminton racquets
- Youth tennis racquets: 21" (K-3), 24" (4-6)
- Bats: 27.5" jumbo bats, 29" foam bats, 30" plastic bats
- Floor hockey sticks: 30" or 36" foam or soft
- Blade sticks

Striking accessories

- Batting tee
- Mesh bag and jump rope combination (to hang ball from basketball hoop)
- Baseball gloves: 11" or 12"; right and left
- Portable tennis nets
- Portable badminton nets
- Over-the-cone net strips
- Fluff balls
- Shuttlecocks/birdies: standard, slow speed, and oversized
- Nerf tennis balls
- Wiffleballs or Softie softballs
- Hockey pucks or balls

Jumping Rope

- Short jump ropes: 7', 8', 9', a few 10'
- Hula hoops
- Floor lines, floor tape
- Long jump ropes: 14'
- Jump bands
- Chinese jump ropes

Programs must include equipment that helps students of all abilities learn, build skills, and feel successful in each lesson and instructional unit, including adaptive physical education students.

Examples include providing equipment that is softer, larger, and/or lighter. Equipment should assist with skill development and game play adaptation.

Look to equipment vendors for a wide selection of adapted PE equipment ideas.

Adapted by permission from SHAPE America, *SHAPE America Guidelines for Facilities, Equipment, Instructional Materials & Technology in K-12 Physical Education.*

adapted physical education developed by SHAPE America (2022), through their position statement "Guidelines for Facilities, Equipment, Instructional Materials and Technology in K-12 Physical Education." The full equipment lists can be found on SHAPE America's website. Additionally, vendors such as US Games, Gopher Sport, BSN Sports, S&S Worldwide, School Specialty, Flaghouse, and Palos Sports provide recommended equipment lists based on their individual lesson plans and curricula.

TABLE 8.3 Equipment Recommendations for 6-8 Middle School Outcomes

Standard 1: Underhand serving, overhand striking, forehand, backhand, weight transfer, volley, two hand volley.

Standard 2: Creating space through variation. Using tactics and shots.

NET AND WALL GAMES

General
- Skill development signs for activities
- Wheeled equipment carts for activities
- Storage bags
- Cones and spots for boundaries

Net system notes
- Use the same nets in pickleball and badminton.
- If you do not have standard nets or courts, use mini nets, tether-based net systems, ropes over cones, portable net systems or wheeled standard nets.
- In volleyball, use standard nets or try small-sided game play using pickleball or badminton nets for smaller courts.

Badminton
- Rackets
- Shuttlecocks/birdies: standard, slow speed, and oversize.
- Net system of choice.

Round net (*Name brand: Spikeball)
- Hula hoops with 3.5" - 5" playground or high-bounce rubber ball of choice.
- Spikeball net game set

Pickleball
- Paddles, wooden, plastic
- Balls: pickleballs, wiffle balls, and foam high bounce (standard and oversize)
- Net system of choice

Table tennis
- Paddles
- Balls: regular and slower play
- Tabletop barriers

Tennis
- Rackets
- Balls: regular, foam, slow bounce
- Net system of choice

Volleyball
- Volleyballs: standard and soft-play
- Volleyballs: oversize/training and jumbo/biggie
- Net system of choice

Adapted by permission from SHAPE America, *SHAPE America Guidelines for Facilities, Equipment, Instructional Materials & Technology in K-12 Physical Education.*

TABLE 8.4 Equipment Recommendations for 9-12 High School Outcomes

Standard 5: Recognizes the value of physical activity for health, enjoyment, challenge, self-expression and/or social interaction.

HEALTH

- Physical activity posters
- Nutrition posters
- Mindfulness/stress management/wellness/emoji posters

CHALLENGE

- Lifetime wellness activities: *Equipment is optional based on district curriculum, availability, and regional interest/opportunities.
- Outdoor education activities: snowshoes, skiing, biking, skating, Razor scooters, spin boards, rollerblades/skates, skateboards, slacklining, balance boards
- Traverse climbing wall
- Growth mindset posters
- Teamwork posters

SELF-EXPRESSION AND ENJOYMENT

- Field day equipment
- Cardio drumming: stability balls and drumsticks
- Creative movement/dance music activities
- Portable sound system

SOCIAL INTERACTION

- Sport education activities
- Cooperative activities and equipment

Adapted by permission from SHAPE America, *SHAPE America Guidelines for Facilities, Equipment, Instructional Materials & Technology in K-12 Physical Education.*

TABLE 8.5 Adapted Physical Education Equipment

Item Name	Purpose	Often Sold As	Recommend
Foam discs	Soft catching of the Frisbee	1 set of 6	2 sets
Velcro catch sets	Catching	1 set of 2	6 sets
Batting tee insert	Striking support	1	1
Gymnic GrabBall	Catching	1 set of 6	6
Poly spots	Assist with stations or squad spots (tape student faces to the poly spot to help with assigned seats)	1 set of 12	1
Slow motion soccer ball	Kicking support	1	1
Volleyball trainers	Volleying	1 set of 6	1

Adapted by permission from SHAPE America, *SHAPE America Guidelines for Facilities, Equipment, Instructional Materials & Technology in K-12 Physical Education.*

Shared Facilities

Although it would be ideal for each school to have its own facilities, it's often the case that school districts have to participate in shared facilities utilization agreements when space or funding is not available. In some cases, the school district holds ownership of a facility that is utilized by the schools; in other scenarios, an individual school has to rent the facility from a community or private organization for an agreed-upon amount.

Some of the most common shared facilities are football stadiums, swimming and diving pools, ice hockey rinks, and baseball or softball fields for tournament play. In cases where a school is built next to a municipal park, there may be a shared-land agreement for utilization during the school day. This type of agreement becomes a necessity in circumstances when a school is built on a smaller parcel of land with limited outdoor space or facilities.

Conclusion

The intent in this chapter was to assist physical education administrators and physical education department chairpersons in developing the knowledge and skills involved in planning physical education facilities, both at the elementary level and at the secondary level. Although there are common factors to consider, such as flooring, lighting, and acoustical design, facilities at the elementary level are primarily designed for developing motor skills and motor movement, whereas facilities at the secondary level serve both the physical education instructional program and the high school interscholastic program.

Regardless of the level, all facilities, whether indoor or outdoor, should be designed according to ADA standards, utilizing universal and sustainable design criteria. This compliance will ensure, to the extent possible, that all students have access to all programs and facilities in an inclusive and environmentally friendly facility.

In support of fitness education, the chapter has discussed the development of wellness centers and strength and conditioning rooms, and it has provided sample layouts. The chapter further covered samples of athletic fields and courts seen in most secondary school facility designs, along with equipment for each sport identified. In most cases, sports such as football, soccer, lacrosse, and field hockey are played within the inside of the track with appropriate competition lines drawn. Where funding is available, aquatic centers are also part of the athletic facility design; they are used for both physical education and swimming, diving, and water polo instruction and competition. Combative and martial arts can be conducted within the wrestling room or other open spaces with appropriate flooring.

This chapter aimed help you feel more comfortable when asked to participate in facility planning and design meetings. It is recommended that the design planning team and the physical education administrator refer to the NFHS's *Court and Field Diagram Guide* (2020) for assistance.

Review Questions

1. Detail the type of support that different members of a facilities planning team will provide.
2. Identify what ADA components should be considered when one is designing physical education facilities.
3. Why is sustainable design being considered for physical education facilities, and what are the components of the WELL Building Standard?
4. List several factors to consider in developing a risk management strategy.
5. Design a wellness center to be housed in a predetermined space. What should be included?
6. Compare the storage and locker room needs of physical education classes and athletic teams.

» Visit HK*Propel* for reproducible forms.

CHAPTER 9

Technology in Physical Education

David N. Daum, Tyler Goad, and Jayne D. Greenberg

Photo courtesy of Michelina "Mickey" Witte

LEARNING OBJECTIVES

After reading this chapter, you will be able to do the following:

- Identify skills and knowledge needed for successful technology integration.
- Describe the benefits of using educational technology.
- Identify strategies to overcome the digital divide.
- Discuss appropriate and inappropriate uses of educational technology.
- Describe the basic infrastructure needed to use technology in the school setting.
- Discuss the role of technology in the delivery of physical education instruction.

KEY CONCEPTS

instructional technology
learning management system (LMS)
planning for technology integration
stages of technology adoption
technology infrastructure

Educational institutions, as dynamic organizations, have witnessed the transformation of both teaching and learning through the use of technology. This transformation was perhaps no more evident than during early spring of 2020, when the emergence of the COVID-19 pandemic in the United States led to the requirement that students stay home to learn remotely. During this time, educational institutions saw the accelerated use of educational technology by teachers and students. The world went from offering education predominantly in a face-to-face mode to almost fully online in a matter of weeks. Even before the time of this pandemic, technology had become a crucial component of a thriving 21st-century physical education learning environment. Within physical education, often people have a visceral reaction to the integration of technology within the learning environment. The dynamic of using technology to enhance educational experiences is at times in direct conflict with the basic nature of being physically active and removed from screens and devices. Conversely, when properly applied, technology in physical education can be a tool to increase learning opportunities and promote physically active lifestyles.

This chapter focuses on how to successfully integrate technology into the physical education curriculum to increase student learning and engagement while promoting lifetime physical activity. Before any teacher can implement technology into the classroom, the physical education administrator should have a thorough understanding of the technologies available, have the ability of the school district's infrastructure to implement the technology, and complete the vetting process with senior staff to ensure that the technology or technology platform is compatible and consistent with the district's goals and objectives. First, the chapter provides context in understanding why educational technology is important, introducing frameworks that will help you understand the foundational skills and knowledge required for successful technology integration. Next, the chapter addresses experiences that teachers and students have with technology, including a discussion about equity and the digital divide.

After setting the stage with the context of understanding educational technology, the chapter dives into technology specific to physical education by addressing teaching practices. Additionally, an overview of the infrastructure needed and how to fund educational technology are presented. Then, the chapter reviews a wide range of commonly used technological tools as well as some innovative tools by addressing what the tools are, how they can be managed, and how to use these tools for assessment. The chapter concludes with a discussion on how to stay current with technology and how to take advantage of digital professional development opportunities.

As is demonstrated throughout this chapter, when implemented thoughtfully, technology can enhance students' ability to meet learning outcomes and improve teacher efficiency in the physical education setting. Furthermore, technology can help increase interest and engagement in physical activities that transcend what happens in the physical education classroom.

Why Use Technology in Education?

Technology in the modern classroom has evolved greatly from the inception of electronic devices such as handheld calculators and the first personal computers to current devices such as tablets, cell phones, artificial intelligence (AI), and virtual reality (VR). Educational technology is a multibillion-dollar industry that includes hardware, software, professional development, and technology support. Every U.S. district and school has integrated technology into the classroom at different rates and levels; some schools have one device per student (known as 1:1), while other schools have fewer devices allowing students to share devices.

The benefits of technology use in the classroom have been heavily researched since the 1990s. There are many evidence-based reasons to integrate technology into the classroom. When technology is implemented properly (a concept discussed later on in this chapter), it can lead to significant gains in student achievement as well as boost engagement, particularly for underserved students (Zielezinski &

Darling-Hammond, 2016). Some of the benefits of using technology in the classroom include the following:

- Increased content knowledge
- Improved writing skills
- Increased engagement and desire to participate
- Increased ownership of learning
- Alternative opportunities to demonstrate knowledge
- Promotion of independence and collaboration
- Increased student behavior and motivation
- Allowing for self-pacing and independent learning

Conversely, there are ongoing concerns about student safety and privacy with the myriad of applications and websites that schools and districts use for learning, grading, behavior management, testing, and much more. The physical educator may be concerned about screen time and its influence on social skills, physical activity, sedentary behavior, and obesity. Moreover, there is a growing societal concern about digital addiction, which the medical community identifies as a mental disorder that can have detrimental impacts on the growth and development of children (Christakis, 2019). Evidence suggests that these concerns are valid, but only in cases of extreme exposure.

As with any pedagogical tool, concept, or theory, the *why* to implement must be defined by each individual teacher; it is based on the teacher's own philosophies about the teaching and learning process. While there is ample evidence to suggest that integrating technology into the learning environment can be beneficial to students, the value of the technology will be defined by the quality of learning experiences a teacher provides.

The U.S. Department of Education conducts periodic reports on issues related to schools through the National Center on Educational Statistics (NCES). One such report specifically addressed educational technology in public schools. The most recent report, published in 2021, came from the 2019-2020 academic year, which was prior to the start of the COVID-19 pandemic (Gray & Lewis, 2021). Reliable data have not yet described what school technology looks like in the era after COVID-19. However, key findings from the 2021 report include the following:

- 45 percent of schools had a computer for each student.
- 34 percent of schools let students carry a computer for the entire school day.
- 15 percent of schools let students take school-provided computers home.
- 15 percent of schools let students check out computers on a short-term basis.
- Over 80 percent of schools rated the quality of their hardware (computers) and software as good or very good.
- 64 percent of schools said their Internet connections in teaching and learning areas of the school were very reliable.
- 52 percent of schools reported having issues with connectivity when large numbers of students were online.
- About half of schools provided moderate (about 40%) or high (about 10%) levels of professional development on how to use computers or software, or how to use technology for teaching and learning.
- 18 percent of schools said their teachers were sufficiently trained in how to use technology and used technology for teaching.
- Over 90 percent of schools strongly agreed or somewhat agreed that educational technology assists students to be more independent and self-directed, helps students engage in more active learning, and allows students to learn at their own pace.

Based on these data, an interesting dichotomy is presented. Before the COVID-19 pandemic, schools were still a long way away from being able to have one device per student throughout the school day. Schools seem to have access to quality hardware and software, but their Internet connection may not be fully reliable. Schools provide professional development to their teachers, but it is not enough. However, despite the issues, there is very strong support for educational technology in schools.

Technology Frameworks

The two frameworks discussed in this section, the stages of technology adoption and the Technological Pedagogical Content Knowledge (TPACK) model, provide a foundation for understanding the complexity of integrating technology in education. It is easy to say, "I will be a teacher who integrates technology in my teaching." However, research and practice have proven that this task is not simple. The frameworks underpinning this chapter describe the skills and knowledge that teachers need to have for a more meaningful and impactful educational technology learning experience.

Stages of Technology Adoption

The **stages of technology adoption**, conceptualized by Anne Russell (1995), describes six distinct stages an adult goes through when learning to use new technology. You, the technology adopter, can enter at any stage, which depends on your comfort level with prior uses of technology. It is important to understand your own context before trying to implement any technology into the classroom. When reviewing the six stages (figure 9.1), note that it isn't until Stage Five where the technology is actually implemented in the classroom. Stages One through Four are necessary building blocks to gain awareness of and confidence in using the technology before implementing it with students.

Consider this scenario: A teacher goes to a physical education conference and attends a session on heart rate monitors. He has never used the technology before, and he is interested in learning more. He thinks to himself, "This is really cool; I love the way these presenters have implemented this into their own classrooms." This teacher goes back to his school and maps out how the heart rate monitors can supplement instruction in a current health-related fitness unit. Still riding the technology high from the conference, he convinces the principal to purchase a class set, which costs about $8,000. The company the teacher purchased the heart rate monitors from provides a one-hour tutorial on how to set up and use the heart rate monitors.

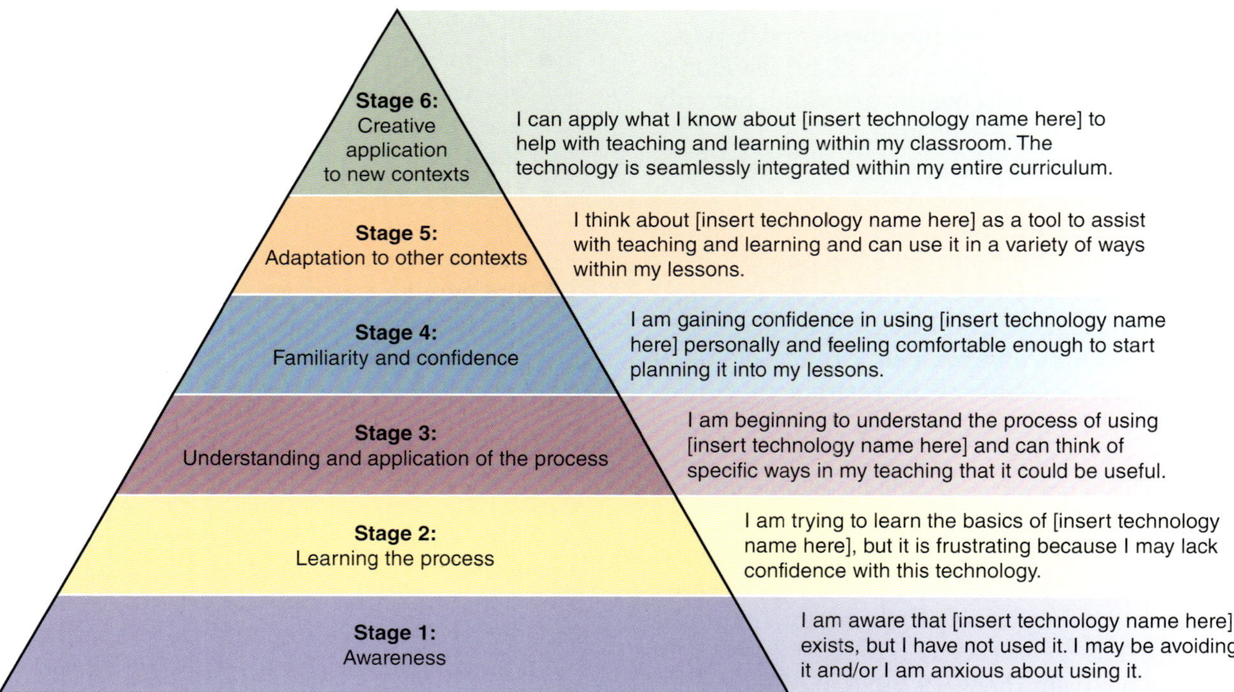

FIGURE 9.1 The stages of technology adoption.
Adapted from Russell (1995).

After the brief training, the teacher feels good and plans to use them in his next lesson. The lesson goes horribly, and the teacher and students run into many unexpected problems with the technology; consequently, everyone is frustrated. The teacher thinks to himself, "Well, I tried it; it didn't work," and the heart rate monitors go into the closet, never to be used again.

Unfortunately, such scenarios are more common than you may think; high percentages of software go unused by teachers, essentially wasting billions of dollars annually (Davis, 2019). This teacher entered his heart rate monitor journey at Stage Two, knowing very little and having very little practice at using the technology personally (and certainly not with students). This teacher should have considered a better adoption plan, such as seeking out teachers who have implemented heart rate monitors successfully, to gain more knowledge about the product (Stage Three). He could have tried out the heart rate monitors on his own and then with a small group of students to learn how the technology works (Stage Four). Once this teacher had gained greater confidence, then he could have started thinking about what specific learning outcomes this technology could assist with, and when and how he would implement this technology into his classroom (Stage Five).

Ultimately, teachers are responsible for doing their due diligence and ensuring they have the knowledge and skills to manage any new pedagogical tool. Throughout this chapter, you are provided with tips and considerations for technology adoption and implementation. It is also important for teachers to conduct a self-assessment regarding their relationship with technology and at what stage of technology adoption they are. Later in this chapter, the Technology for Instructional Use section discusses a variety of technologies; for each one you review, consider at what stage you are.

TPACK Model

The Technological Pedagogical Content Knowledge (TPACK) model, originally called TPCK and described by Mishra and Koehler (2006), expands on the work by Shulman (1986) that describes the complexity of skills required of teachers. Shulman (1986) initially described the interaction between content knowledge (CK) and pedagogical knowledge (PK). CK is the knowledge required to be an expert in any given subject area, such as the knowledge about how the body functions and rules of different sports and activities. PK is the knowledge about pedagogy required to teach, such as setting up an effective learning environment and how to interact with students. CK and PK overlap in pedagogical content knowledge (PCK), where an educator combines knowledge of content and pedagogy to deliver lessons. Mishra and Koehler (2006) added a third overlapping construct they called technological knowledge (TK). TK is knowledge about technology, such as knowing about and how to use heart rate monitors and QR codes. Figure 9.2 displays the interactive processes between CK, PK, and TK, which forms the TPACK model. TPACK is a way of describing how technology, pedagogy, and content fit together to enable learning.

In terms of the physical educator, Physical Education Teacher Education (PETE) programs tend to focus on the PK and CK, while TK has lagged behind. In terms of developing technological skills required for teaching, TK is not

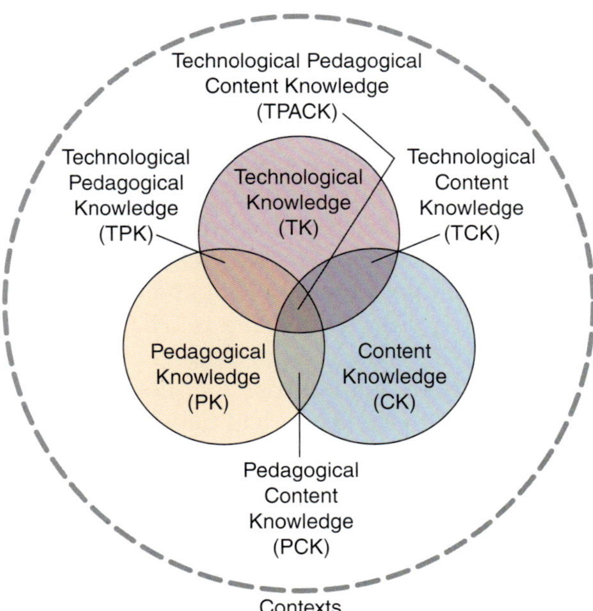

FIGURE 9.2 The Technological Pedagogical Content Knowledge (TPACK) model.

Permission granted from Dr. Matthew Koehler at https://tpack.org.

always well supported in schools; the next section discusses this issue. For successful integration of educational technology, a teacher must use a combination of PK, CK, and TK.

Understanding Teachers and Students

So far, this chapter has described the context of technology for teachers and students. Equally important is understanding the relationship that teachers and students have with technology and how it influences their views about technology. Teachers and students have similarities in their relationships and views, but they also have drastically different stories to tell regarding their motivations for and barriers to using technology.

Teachers

The story of a teacher's relationship with educational technology doesn't start with the moment she becomes a teacher. For all teachers, it starts when they are students in PreK-12 schools and continues into pre-service and in-service teacher education programs. This *apprenticeship of observation*, as described by Dan Lortie (1975), is where teachers have spent thousands of hours in schools observing and evaluating education in action. These observations influence conceptions about the role of technology in education. Beliefs that pre-service teachers hold early in their training will influence the level of educational technology they use when they begin teaching (Liu, 2012). Ultimately, the role that technology plays in teachers' classrooms directly relates to their beliefs about teaching and learning. Simply put, if a teacher sees the value of using educational technology in her pedagogy, then she will use technology; if she cannot align her pedagogical beliefs with educational technology, then it is not likely that she will use it.

Teachers will use technology in the classroom in two ways. The first is a teacher-centered approach to using technology for administrative or institutional tasks related to teaching. This approach could include a wide variety of tasks, such as communicating with parents, colleagues, and administrators, and developing lesson materials. The second way is to use a student-centered approach to support the learning process and achieve educational goals. Both teacher-centered and student-centered technology uses are important in the 21st century classroom not only to manage teaching tasks but also to incorporate technology into the classroom. However, teachers who hold constructivist and student-centered beliefs are more likely to not only use technology in the classroom but also use it as a means to develop higher-order thinking and problem-solving skills (Becker, 2000; Ertmer & Glazewski, 2015; Tondeur, et al., 2016).

The main barriers to teachers incorporating digital technologies into the classroom include lack of resources, lack of technical support, lack of time, and pressure to cover many different topics and assignments. Secondary barriers that have been noted (although to a much lesser extent) include lack of technical knowledge, lack of training, and resistance by colleagues or administrators to incorporating technology in the classroom (Purcell et al., 2013). However, these barriers are not necessarily deterrents or predictors of a teacher's use or nonuse of technology. They simply describe the barriers that teachers may need to overcome. As previously stated, the amount that educators will use technology for teacher- and student-centered tasks is directly related to their pedagogical beliefs.

Students

When teachers are thinking about incorporating technology into their lessons, a key consideration is the difference between students accessing and using technology for personal use, and accessing and using it for educational purposes. There is no denying the fact that today's society by and large uses technology for personal uses more than previous generations have ever had to manage. As technology evolves, so does society's engagement with it.

A Pew Research Center study (Vogels et al., 2022) comparing teens' (ages 13-17) use of social media and technology compared results from 2014-2015 and then again in 2022. The results indicated that websites and applications such as Facebook and Twitter that were once heavily popular saw declines, whereas YouTube, TikTok, Instagram, and Snapchat were the most widely used. Additionally, this report found that in 2022, 90 percent of teens had access to a desktop or laptop computer, while 95 percent of teens had access to a smartphone. The percentage of access to smartphones did not drastically change based on demographics such as gender, race, age, or socioeconomic status. However, access to desktop or laptop computers is influenced by socioeconomic status. Understanding who your students are, what technologies they use, and what technologies they have access to is an important consideration when planning for **technology integration** in your classroom.

Equity and Addressing the Digital Divide

Narrowing the digital divide is a critical element of technological educational equity. Two of the biggest barriers to overcome are access to a stable Internet connection and access to devices suited for educational purposes. A study by Stelitano and colleagues (2020) found that 20 percent of students struggle to have access to adequate Internet and devices; this issue disproportionately affects economically disadvantaged students (Garcia & Weiss, 2020).

Schools play a major role in addressing the inequities inherent in the digital divide by providing high-speed Wi-Fi throughout the schools as well as providing access to devices for all students. To address the digital divide, schools and teachers can do the following:

- *Offer options.* Ensure assignments and tasks have nontechnology options, or put students in groups where only one device is needed.
- *Allow time.* Provide enough time in class to complete any assignments requiring use of technology.
- *Manage access to devices.* Develop checkout procedures for technology required for school assignments.
- *Provide resources.* Learn about free Wi-Fi hot spots and about free and reduced-cost technology; be sure to share this information with students. Work with the information technology department to identify resources.

When considering using technology in education with traditionally underserved and underresourced students, it goes beyond the question of what technology to use. A teacher must understand how to use technology in a meaningful way. Teaching strategies for underserved populations include the following (Zielezinski & Darling-Hammond, 2016):

- Focusing on learning activities that develop higher-order thinking skills
- Connecting to culturally relevant and community-relevant content in learning activities
- Providing opportunities for choice (e.g., choosing which technology to use and how to use that technology)

When using digital technologies, especially the Internet, students will need training on not only how to use the technology but also on how to navigate potentially being exposed to negative content online. For example, according to a Pew Research Center report (Duggan, 2017), Black and Hispanic people experience harassment at much higher rates than White people. Therefore, teachers must be careful when using Internet resources such as video and social media platforms that allow users to publicly comment or view public comments. Resources such as ViewPure (www.viewpure.com) allow teachers to take YouTube videos and play them without ads to better control access to noneducational content.

Technology in Physical Education

SHAPE America promotes the use of technology in physical education to enhance teaching and learning. SHAPE America's guidance documents "Appropriate Use of Technology in Physical Education" (2023) and "Guidelines of Facilities, Equipment, Instructional Materials & Technology" (2022) provide educators with resources in what types of technology may be useful and also in what supplies assist with the storage and protection of technology. Physical educators are generally technologically literate, and teachers who have greater technology literacy use technology more frequently in their lessons (Kretschmann, 2012). Physical educators use technology for teacher-centered uses such as preparation for lessons and connecting on social media to learn new ideas (Krause et al., 2017). Physical educators also use technology for student-centered instruction with technology such as using images, activity monitors, and mobile applications (Kretschmann, 2015; Krause, et al., 2017). As discussed later in this chapter, mobile applications are used by physical educators to plan lessons, manage time, perform assessments, provide feedback, collect and manage class data, contact students and parents, and promote their programs (Yu et al., 2018).

Inappropriate Uses of Technology in Physical Education

The use of technology is exciting and engaging for administrators, teachers, and students. When using technology, physical educators must deliver instruction with appropriate practices to ensure that technology is an essential tool for both teachers and students in the learning environment. Much of the remaining parts of this chapter will discuss the many ways technology can be appropriately implemented in physical education. However, as with any new teaching strategy or tool, missteps are possible. This list represents the most common issues relating to inappropriate application of technology in a physical education environment:

- *Noncompliance with state law or district policy*: States and school districts may have laws or policies about the types of technology, websites, or applications a teacher may or may not use. For example, the district may have a list of approved websites and applications teachers can use. Teachers are responsible for ensuring that whatever technology they are considering to use is in compliance with any laws or policies that may regulate technology use in educational settings.
- *Replacing sound teaching practices with technology*: When technology becomes a tool to replace the teacher instead of enhance learning, it has been misused. A common example is when an educator finds a video and lets it do all the instruction without any discussion or teacher intervention. A video can be a great resource, but it should never replace the teacher.
- *Picking the technology first*: Using the appropriate backward design principles, physical educators should consider using national standards and grade-span learning indicators first as opposed to selecting the technology and then planning around it. If backward design concepts are efficiently applied, then student learning will be first. There is nothing wrong with researching a variety of technologies and using creativity to think about how it might fit within the physical education class, but picking the technology first can lead to deviating far from the learning goals for students.
- *Using technology just for fun*: Incorporating any technology can bring a specific wow factor to a teaching setting. There is nothing wrong with fun, and it can have a positive impact on student engagement and student learning. However, when a teacher is planning to incorporate technology in a physical education setting, the first consideration is to always ensure the technology allows the educator to do things that could not otherwise be done without the technology. It is easy to get excited about a new tool or resource, but the foundation of a highly effective physical education class is ensuring a well-planned, developmentally appropriate lesson.
- *The novelty effect*: The novelty effect is a well-researched phenomenon; it describes the ebb and flow of user engagement. When implementing a new tool, engagement is high at the beginning because of the excitement of the new stimulus; however, excitement and engagement decline as the initial effect wears off. This decline can lead to dissatisfaction and ultimately to abandonment of a tool because it is not having the desired effect. Be sure to account for the novelty effect by ensuring the technology is pedagogically relevant,

keeping the technology relevant to the context of the task, and ensuring that students connect the importance of using the technology to their learning.

- *Not accounting for training*: Teachers should not assume students know how to use technology as it applies to the lesson, even if it is a technology they may use on a daily basis. For example, students are asked to record a partner on their phone, then watch that video and complete a peer evaluation rubric. The teacher should not only provide instructions on how to capture quality video but also provide instructions on how to record, pause, rewind, and use slow-motion or other tools that may be useful in the context of the lesson. Students also need instruction on how to delete video once the task is completed.

Technology can add an exciting and dynamic element to any lesson; however, excitement alone is not enough to justify integrating technology. Using technology in the classroom requires teachers to shift their teaching practices as well as change their classroom habits. Teachers may need to be more vigilant about new off-task behaviors. When using technology, students may seem to be on task while they are in fact watching and listening to music videos, playing games, or using search engines. Some districts offer classroom management software that allows the teacher to control student devices and monitor what they are viewing. While these tools may be offered, the teacher still needs to remain attentive and continuously monitor student activity.

Planning for Technology Integration

For a physical educator who wants to begin integrating technology as a teaching and learning tool into programs, the first question is likely to be *Where do I begin?* Understanding the frameworks outlined earlier in this chapter as well as one's own philosophy toward technology in physical education are good first steps. It is important to acknowledge that technology can never take the place of the personal touch physical educators have on student learning. Technology should complement a teacher's ability to convey instruction and enable students to show growth toward attaining grade-span learning indicators. Teachers should focus on their ability to use sound teaching practices before emphasizing the use of technology in their instructional units.

Technology Infrastructure in Schools

So far, this chapter has highlighted the importance of technology in developing the 21st-century learner and educational environments; this section focuses on gaining an understanding of the infrastructure necessary to use technology for teaching and learning. Some of the concepts and practices related to **technology infrastructure** are common knowledge, but most will require technical assistance by the district technology department.

Current school environments likely have the infrastructure to support existing and new technologies. Common infrastructure includes access to secure Internet and Wi-Fi throughout various learning spaces, a work computer or laptop, and learning management systems and other productivity software. However, older and underfunded schools may need to be retrofitted with new wiring and servers to enable access to the same technological opportunities. Decisions about the type of educational learning systems a teacher may plan to implement, the number of devices being used, and the type of connectivity needed will further determine infrastructure needs.

The National Education Technology Plan, developed by the U.S. Department of Education, Office of Educational Technology (2017), "sets a national vision and plan for learning enabled by technology through building on the work of leading education researchers; district, school, and higher education leaders; classroom teachers; developers; entrepreneurs; and nonprofit organizations" (p. 3). The National Education Technology Plan serves as both a guide and a resource for ensuring equity and accessibility while transforming education through the use of technology. The plan of implementation takes a systems approach by addressing how the education stakeholders (leaders, teachers, faculty, and other educators; researchers; policymakers;

funders; technology developers; community members and organizations; and learners and their families) need to collaborate to realize the full benefits of technology.

According to the U.S. Department of Education National Education Technology Plan (2017, p. 69), the essential components of supporting transformational learning experiences include the following:

- *Ubiquitous connectivity*: Persistent access to high-speed Internet in and out of school
- *Powerful learning devices*: Access to mobile devices (e.g., tablets, phones, and notebook computers) that connect learners and educators to the vast resources of the Internet and facilitate communication and collaboration
- *High-quality digital learning content*: Digital learning content and tools that can be used to design and deliver engaging and relevant learning experiences
- *Responsible use policies (RUPs)*: Guidelines to safeguard students and ensure that the infrastructure is used to support learning (Districts with Internet connectivity and device access also should have policies in place to promote responsible use and protect student privacy.)

School districts should further plan (through fiscal and human resources) for managing, monitoring, and providing maintenance and periodic updates to the network infrastructure. Considerations include licensing fees for digital learning content, firewall protection, backup and recovery plans, expansion for network capability, insurance for devices, technical support, and the like. Figure 9.3 demonstrates the infrastructure and coordination needed to

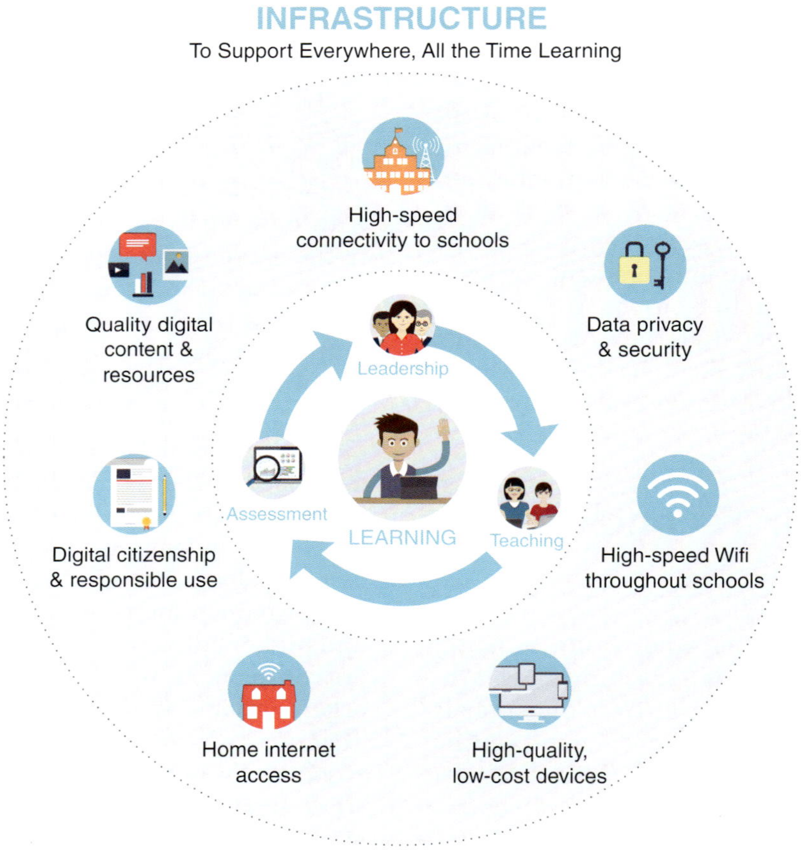

FIGURE 9.3 The U.S. Department of Education's 2017 Technology Infrastructure Plan.

Reprinted from United States Department of Education, *Reimagining the Role of Technology in Education: 2017 National Education Technology Plan Update*. (Office of Educational Technology, 2017), https://tech.ed.gov/netp/introduction/.

support a learning environment where technology integration is set up to succeed.

Preparing for Implementation

A teacher should understand the district's vision for technology as a teaching and learning tool in the classroom, field, or gymnasium. As a physical education administrator, you should first become acquainted with the district or school technology leader or coordinator to gain a fuller understanding of available technologies. Next, determine what types of **instructional technology** (online software, programs and resources) are available. These steps will help you to work with teachers in understanding what resources in terms of technology, technological assistance, and financial support are available.

The following questions are helpful for teachers investigating the available technology:

- What type of technology is available at the school (e.g., interactive boards, desktop computers, audio system, mirroring devices, mobile devices)?
- Are there mobile devices (e.g., laptops, tablets) that can be checked out by teachers or students for instructional use in the classroom or at home?
- What is the wireless capability at the school? Does it reach all teaching spaces? Are there bandwidth issues?
- How are other teachers integrating technology in their classrooms?
- What instructional online programs, software, tools, and resources are available in your district (e.g., Flip Grid, Edmondo, EdPuzzle, Kahoot, Rack Performance, Team Builder)?
- What professional development is offered on technology integration in the classroom?

As cited earlier in the chapter, schools tend to have access to devices, software, and wireless Internet; however, it is important to understand the context of the school. Also, regarding professional development, remember that only 18 percent of schools said their teachers are sufficiently trained in how to use technology and use technology for teaching (Gray & Lewis, 2021). It is important to understand professional development a teacher may have access to. If there are no local professional development opportunities, it will be necessary to seek funds from the school or district to support external professional development.

Lesson Planning

Once an educator is aware of what technology is available, it is important to identify what the instructional goals are. Guiding students in attaining grade-span learning indicators of a developmentally appropriate lesson is the crux of what a physical educator does. Everything that occurs within the educational setting is centered on standards, grade-span learning indicators and outcomes, and student learning; technology is no exception to this rule. Using the backward mapping design (outlined in chapter 4), grade-span learning indicators and standards are determined first.

Understanding by Design (UbD), as presented by Wiggins and McTighe (2005), is an educational planning approach involving these three phases of design: (1) Identify the desired outcomes; (2) determine the acceptable criteria for evaluating students' progress; and (3) plan instructional methodologies. During the first phase, identifying the desired outcomes, a physical educator can rely on the standards and grade-span learning indicators as a guide. During the second phase, determining the acceptable criteria for evaluating students' progress and planning instructional methodologies, technology will begin to be a part of preparing for assessment purposes, as discussed in detail later in this chapter. During the last phase (planning instructional methodologies), pedagogical determinations will be made. After evaluating the grade-span learning indicators, outcomes, and standards, the educator may begin to see what pieces of technology can complement student learning naturally.

As identified earlier in the chapter, teachers should plan with regard to any state or local laws or policy when it comes to educational technology. Another tool to assist in the planning process, specifically around technology, is a group of technology standards. Physical educators may also use the technology standards developed by the International Society for Technology in Education (ISTE) (www.iste.org/iste-standards). These standards were designed to help students, educators, educational leaders, and educational coaches to effectively use technology in schools. The fact that each of these four groups of users has its own benchmarks is a sign of the complexity of using technology in schools.

Understanding the 21st-Century Learner

Throughout the educational literature it is clear that as we develop educational administrative leaders, teachers, and students for the 21st century, we come to a realization that although educational outcomes continue to focus on student achievement in terms of attainment of national and state standards, how we deliver instruction and develop the skills necessary for 21st-century learners has evolved. To address this direction and focus, in 2002, the National Education Association established the Partnership for 21st Century Skills (P21) to develop what has since become known as the *Framework for 21st Century Learning* (figure 9.4). Through the efforts of leaders from a variety of sectors, four specific skills emerged as the most important, known as the "Four Cs": *critical thinking, communication, collaboration,* and *creativity.* It has since become the challenge for educators as to how to incorporate this into the learning environment.

Critical thinking as one of the components cuts across all subject areas in that students today need to become active problem solvers and able to develop analytical abilities and other thought processes. Through physical

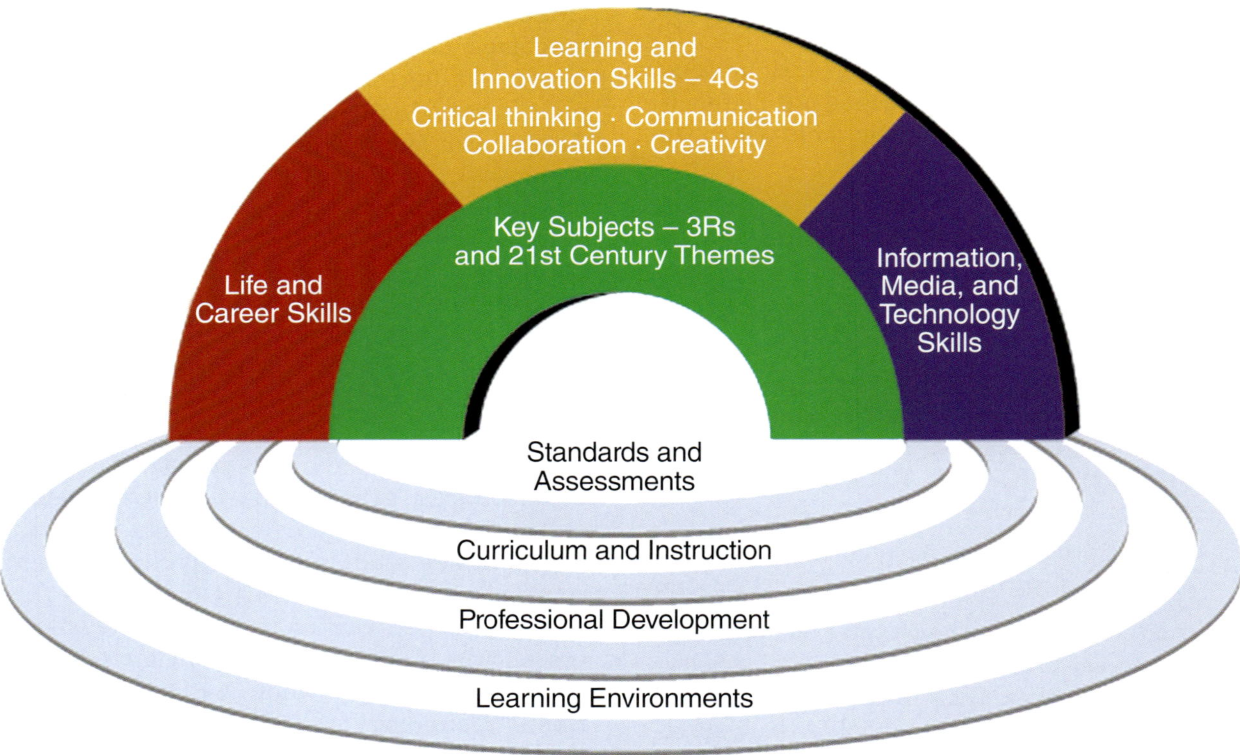

FIGURE 9.4 Partnership for 21st Century Skills (P21): Framework for 21st Century Learning.

education, students can learn to use a systems approach in attempting to solve problems such as childhood obesity and physical inactivity by synthesizing and interpreting research related to the issue.

Communication through technological advances has also grown from the basic modes of reading, writing, and speaking to a more global perspective of how to communicate through linguistically and culturally effective means, such as effective listening and empathy. As discussed in chapter 1, as the United States is becoming more multicultural, learning these skills in the K-12 setting will become necessary in effective physical education. Learning sports and dances introduced by peers from other cultures in authentic gymnasium and field settings enables the students of today to become more globally educated as well as develop emotional and social values.

The physical education learning environment further supports and embraces the need for *collaboration* among all learners. Through sports, games, and physical activity, students are provided with the opportunity to work effectively by acknowledging the contributions that each member of the team can make, and they can learn the importance of teamwork to become successful. Showing respect for others is also a valuable skill on the playing field and through class projects.

And lastly, the importance of *creativity* and *innovation* cannot be understated in any subject area. The ability to create new ideas and ways of delivering instruction, such as apps and learning systems, a variety of digital resources, such as e-books and online educational forums, for achieving learning outcomes and providing opportunities to students in an open and creative learning environment have great impact on socialization, leadership, and interpersonal skill development. This is seen throughout the chapter as we discuss innovations in physical education such as geocaching, coding, and robotics.

This framework provides the district physical education administrator an opportunity to enhance learning in a physical education environment. Physical education teachers and students must develop critical thinking and problem-solving skills, as well as the ability to be innovative and collaborative. They also must know how to access information, technology, and media. These skills can be successfully integrated within a physical education environment in the overall development of 21st-century learners.

A challenge for educators is determining how to incorporate the Four Cs into the learning environment; in terms of this chapter, a further challenge is determining how technology can assist in facilitating the Four Cs. Later in this chapter, where specific technologies are addressed, the Four Cs are presented as an overall instructional approach when planning to integrate technology into lessons.

Implementation Strategies

When transitioning the learning environment to one that incorporates technology, it is important to note that any technology applied in the classroom will require planning and management strategies for effective and successful implementation. The following list includes recommendations for teachers implementing technology in general into the classroom; additional ideas for specific types of technology are discussed later in this chapter.

- *Try paper and pencil first.* Sometimes the old-school way is the best way to get started. Think of this method as the way to work out some of the issues prior to integrating technology. For example, have students create a table to track their running times on paper before using a spreadsheet or use a paper version of a rubric before digitizing it.
- *Teach one class at a time.* Try new teaching methods with one class at a time; use one class to work out the issues before implementing new methods across all classes. Be upfront with the class; tell them what is happening—including *why*—and acknowledge that this approach is an experiment. For classes that did not get the initial exposure, let them know that they will get their turn.
- *Use one technology at a time.* As with the prior two points, trying one new thing at a time will allow the teacher and students time to troubleshoot any issues.
- *Use technology at your level.* Consider the stages of technology adoption discussed earlier in this chapter. Remember that

being at least at Stage Five with the technology will lead to greater success. If a teacher is not at least at Stage Five, it is best to wait until he is adequately prepared before implementing any technology with students.

- *Scaffold technology experiences.* Scaffolding learning experiences is a key characteristic of any quality education program. How a teacher scaffolds technology is no different. When using a spreadsheet, provide students with a template (instead of having them create their own). Once they get proficient in using the technology, then maybe they can create on their own.
- *Have a device management plan.* Communicate with other teachers who use the same technology, and establish common use protocols or incorporate lessons on digital citizenship. Management transitions should look similar to those for other equipment. Just as physical educators use the first few classes or weeks on routines in management, they should do so with technology devices. Consider implementing a checkout system for pedometers, heart rate monitors, wearable technology, or other similar devices. Develop a plan that covers procedures for proper device care and effective use (e.g., no food or drinks around devices), when to charge devices (e.g., during a planning period or a lunch break), the correct way to shut down devices, and the like.
- *Allow for technology support.* Technology, like anything else, sometimes fails; therefore, it is essential to be proactive in learning how to troubleshoot in order to minimize distractions that may impede instruction and to maximize instructional time. The teacher should become familiar with troubleshooting tips, such as resetting the wireless connection on mobile devices in the case of a lost connection during instruction, or calibrating interactive boards. The teacher may not be able to solve all issues; it may be necessary to decide that it is best to turn the technology off for the day rather than spend too much class time troubleshooting.
- *Know your district's bring your own device (BYOD) plan.* Become familiar with the school district's bring your own device (BYOD) and acceptable use policies to which students and employees must adhere. The technology coordinator or school site technician can verify this information.

Needless to say, having a good technology implementation plan is paramount to reducing the issues that may arise. It is impossible to eliminate all issues, but as with behavior management strategies, it is best to develop a tool chest filled with a variety of tools in the hopes that the teacher has at least one strategy that will work at any moment.

Funding Technology

The U.S. federal government supports schools in the purchase and support of educational technology through Title IV, Part A of the Every Student Succeeds Act (ESSA), specifically a group of funds known as Student Support and Academic Enrichment grants. Title IV, Part A was authorized at $1.21 billion in the fiscal year 2020 (Congress, 2015). After the COVID-19 pandemic emerged, multiple economic stimulus bills pumped over $190 billion into schools; some of that funding was earmarked to support educational technology (Center for Education Policy Research, 2024). In addition to federal funding, there is likely state and local funding support available to teachers, schools, and districts; however, it takes research and an understanding of school budgets to find out where the money is, how it is being spent, and how to gain access to it. It is in every educator's best interest to gain an understanding of how their school is funded and how money is allocated. It is the responsibility of the physical education administrator to know this information and how to share it with their teachers to ensure that if additional funds are allocated then they could receive a part of this funding for their programs.

The ESSA recognizes physical education as part of a well-rounded education (Jones & Workman, 2016). Therefore, physical education should be treated with the same expectations as other subject areas within public schools, and physical education teachers should have

LEADERSHIP IN ACTION

Integrating Technology in K-12 Health and Physical Education: Enhancing Learning and Adapting to Changing Times

Brian Devore, MS

Professional Development Manager, Online Physical Education Network (OPEN)

In recent years, the field of education has witnessed a rapid integration of technology across various subjects, and health and physical education (HPE) classes in K-12 schools are no exception. Let's explore the significance of technology in K-12 HPE classes, particularly considering the impact of the COVID-19 pandemic, the growing role of artificial intelligence (AI), and the importance of school social media policies for teachers and staff. By leveraging technology, educators can enhance student engagement, provide personalized learning experiences, and adapt to the evolving needs of students.

The COVID-19 pandemic forced a dramatic shift in educational practices, compelling schools to adapt to remote and hybrid learning models. In HPE, technology played a crucial role in maintaining student engagement and promoting physical activity even when students were confined to their homes. Online platforms and video conferencing tools enabled educators to deliver virtual lessons, demonstrate exercises, and provide personalized feedback to students. Additionally, wearable fitness trackers and mobile applications allowed students to track their progress, set goals, and participate in gamified challenges, fostering motivation and accountability. Many of these tools that were implemented during school closures remain in use in today's face-to-face environment.

AI has emerged as a powerful tool for enhancing HPE in K-12 settings. AI-powered applications can provide personalized exercise routines based on individual fitness levels and goals. Virtual reality (VR) and augmented reality (AR) technologies enable students to explore interactive simulations, expanding their understanding of anatomy, nutrition, and injury prevention. AI algorithms can analyze student data to identify trends and patterns, assisting educators in tailoring instructional strategies and interventions to meet students' specific needs. While AI brings numerous benefits, ethical considerations surrounding data privacy, algorithm bias, and equitable access must be carefully addressed. Students could potentially use AI to create answers for an assignment without really knowing the content of which teachers are asking them to prove mastery. In addition, teachers could potentially use this technology to write lesson plans for HPE classes. While this shortcut seems to streamline a long-standing teacher responsibility, it may not consider the needs of individual learners or other critical components of a particular class. AI will continue to evolve over the years, and educators will have to keep up with its evolution to understand the value and limitations of using it.

The proliferation of social media has necessitated the establishment of clear policies for teachers and staff members in K-12 schools. Social media platforms provide opportunities for educators to share resources, communicate with students and parents, and foster a sense of community. However, maintaining professional boundaries and ensuring student privacy and safety are critical concerns. School policies should provide guidelines on appropriate online behavior, including refraining from sharing identifiable student information and maintaining a respectful and inclusive online environment. Training programs can empower educators to navigate the complexities of social media, promoting responsible digital citizenship and safeguarding the well-being of all stakeholders.

In conclusion, technology has become an indispensable asset in K-12 HPE classes, especially in the face of the COVID-19 pandemic. It has facilitated remote learning, personalized instruction, and student engagement, transcending the traditional boundaries of the classroom. As AI continues to advance, its potential for enhancing HPE holds great promise. At the same time, the evolving landscape of social media requires thoughtful policy development and teacher training to ensure ethical and responsible use. By leveraging technology effectively, educators can create immersive and inclusive learning experiences, empowering students to lead healthier lives both inside and outside the classroom.

the same resources available to them as any other educators trying to integrate technology into the learning process. Understanding the research related to student achievement using educational technology provides an enormous opportunity for physical educators to make the case for and expand the use of technology in physical education. By having an understanding of school budgets and knowing how money is allocated, educators have the ability to make an impact on their subject area learning environments through enhanced funding for technology and professional development.

However, being part of a well-rounded education without taking advantage of the opportunity is not enough. Physical educators should advocate and share with district colleagues and administrators the importance of integrating technology into physical education classrooms. The ability to advocate for technology in physical education could range from sharing what is done to explaining what a teacher would like to do (and why) in the physical education environment. This information can be shared by communicating with other teachers and administrators at the school or by providing brief presentations at district-level meetings, school board events, or Parent-Teacher Association (PTA) meetings. This advocacy can help gain allies and, in turn, financial resources to help purchase and support the technology a teacher wishes to have to enhance teaching and learning.

Technology for Instructional Use

As outlined earlier in the chapter, the 21st-century teacher must use technology for teacher-centered or student-centered purposes. School districts are focusing especially on student-centered approaches that incorporate technology, making the management of a variety of technologies in a physical education environment a priority. When incorporating technology into the learning environment, it takes careful planning to set up the equipment and monitor its use. Depending on the piece of equipment selected for instructional purposes, different strategies can be used to effectively manage the teaching and learning opportunities.

The Four Cs (critical thinking, communication, collaboration, and creativity) were identified earlier in the chapter as part of the Framework for 21st Century Learning. In the sections that follow, a case can be made that each of the technologies described can be used in a way to meet most—if not all—of these Four Cs. The degree to which the technology can meet the Four Cs will depend on how the teacher utilizes the technology. For example, to foster communication and collaboration, the teacher must use the technology in a way that puts students in a position to work together, such as in pairs or small groups. For a technology to foster critical thinking and creativity, the teacher should consider incorporating technology that allows students to create and share information. This approach can facilitate content inspired creation; for example, having students use mobile fitness applications gives them the opportunity to create personalized workouts from the library of exercises and movements built into the application and then share it with other students.

The following sections discuss a wide range of technologies in terms of why and how to use each technology, how to manage the technology, and how to use the technology for assessment purposes. The sections are organized in order of technologies that are easiest to implement and most widely used, to technologies that may require greater technological comfort (consider Stages One through Six of the stages of technology adoption).

Interactive Boards and Projectors

Every physical education environment should include a variety of 21st-century technologies, and an interactive board or projector is essential. Both technologies have become common fixtures in gymnasiums. They offer instructors an easy and effective way to display content to the students to enhance their cognitive knowledge related to the content. Presentation slides are an outstanding way to display visuals on a projector. Various apps, programs, and websites give you the opportunity to display teaching content to students. In fact, presentation slides allow you to view virtually all of the digital visuals you create for your students. Task cards, videos, GIFs, infographics, presentation programs (e.g., PowerPoint, Keynote, Google Slide, Prezi, etc.), and many more visuals can be displayed using presentation slides. As outlined in the following paragraphs, interactive boards and projectors require different infrastructure and training, but they can be utilized in similar ways.

The most usual placement for a projector is on a rolling cart with the visual to be displayed on a wall-mounted screen. The more ideal option is to mount the projector on the ceiling. Through new construction or renovation, many schools are mounting projectors on the gymnasium ceiling along with drop-down screens for use not only during class but also during school assemblies. Using this technology eliminates the need for the physical education teacher to roll in a cart with a projector that would require a portable screen and an extension cord (which would be a tripping hazard), ensuring that the technology is permanent. The physical educator should work alongside the maintenance department and technology department to ensure that both departments understand the specific needs of the gymnasium. For example, not only the projector will need to be installed; connections to the current sound system as well as additional High-Definition Multimedia Interface (HDMI) and other outlets also need to be installed. Protocols must be put in place for replacing damaged equipment or bulbs. Coordination between departments is needed to get the proper equipment in the specific school to reach the overhead-mounted projector.

While projectors allow students to see visuals from any space in the gymnasium, interactive boards take this a step further with interactive features provided by the incorporation of a touch screen and onboard computer. Schools that have classrooms or a gymnasium equipped with an interactive board can open avenues for students to actively participate in whole-group or small-group projects and interactive lessons as well as to interact with digital media and simulations, enhancing their learning experiences. Interactive boards also include tools such as polling, quizzes, and predeveloped lessons, and they allow for dynamic and interactive presentations. One example is a mobile game app called CDC HEADS UP: Rocket Blades, which was developed by 3-2-1 Blast Off!, the Centers for Disease Control and Prevention's Center for Injury and Violence Prevention, to educate youth on how to prevent, identify, and recover from concussions (CDC, n.d.).

Wearable Physical Activity Tracking Technology

Wearable devices, such as heart rate monitors, pedometers, and fitness trackers are valuable tools for accountability and instantaneous feedback in physical education. These devices record and measure different dimensions of fitness such as heart rate, energy expenditure, moderate-to-vigorous physical activity (MVPA), and movement (steps, distance, speed). When selecting a wearable device for a program, consider not only the educator's stage of technology adoption but also what features and functions best meet curricular goals, the school setting, and students' needs.

Additionally, it is important to consider the accompanying management software when selecting a wearable device for use in a school setting. It is important to ensure the software can manage and aggregate data collected for each class of students. While the software will collect and aggregate health-related fitness data, the physical education teacher will need to be a content expert (CK from the TPACK model) to teach students about how to interpret the results and what those results mean to them personally. This software will enable teachers to use the data for assessment, improve their instructional practice, help guide students in reaching their personal goals, and provide information that can be shared with parents and administration to advocate for your program.

Incorporating wearable devices will require effective management for successful implementation. An adequate and secure storage system should be designated for wearable technology devices to be locked up and accounted for. Usually the physical education teacher's office or a secure cabinet in the gymnasium serves as a safe place. The storage system should also allow for quick student access to the devices during class distribution. The physical education teacher should set up guidelines regarding how students should use and manage wearable technology. Numbering each device and developing a daily checkout system or routine for where to pick up a device, where to return a device, and how to wear the tracker safely and efficiently are crucial for student success and for the longevity of devices.

These devices are not limited to monitoring physical education class participation; they can also be used in a more holistic approach to help students become more self-aware and control their emotions. While emotional regulation is a complex process that involves a multitude of factors, heart rate monitors allow students to make the connection between what is happening in their bodies and how they are feeling. Using the strategies taught in class to help self-regulate (e.g., mindfulness exercises, social support, and healthy lifestyle habits) in tandem with heart rate tracking technology can support students' emotional well-being. Additionally, introducing students to wearable technology allows them to learn how to incorporate such technology into their daily lives, ensuring that physical activity becomes a sustainable part of their lifelong routine.

QR Codes

Quick-response (QR) codes are prevalent in education settings because of the technology's relative ease of use and wide range of application. Use of QR codes increased after the onset of the COVID-19 pandemic; educators leveraged the scanning features of QR codes to digitally display and distribute information to students that would typically have been on paper. QR codes allow students to access web-based classroom materials quickly when they scan a code using a device such as a smartphone, tablet, or computer. This simple, effective technology allows students to take ownership of their own learning while it frees up time from direct instruction because task-related materials can be transferred to QR codes. For example, a physical education teacher could set up a fitness circuit by linking each station's step-by-step video instructions and exercise examples to QR codes. This approach would allow students to explore the movements for themselves while freeing up the teacher to give more individual feedback as students complete the activity.

The QR codes are scanned by the integrated camera on most mobile devices or by downloading any free QR code reader app. QR codes can be made through accessing a variety of apps, downloading a free code generator from a website, or using the built-in QR creator feature in the Chrome web browser. Once QR codes are created, they can be downloaded and reused for as long as the uniform resource locator (URL) link to the QR code is live. After the code is downloaded, it can either be displayed on the gymnasium's interactive board or projector screen or be printed and laminated for students to scan at specific times or stations.

Beyond using QR codes as an instructional tool as just outlined, it can be linked to quizzes such as those managed in form creators (e.g., Google Forms). The students scan the QR code, allowing for quick dissemination of an exit slip without the management of paper and pencil. An example of an innovative use of QR codes, implemented in Miami-Dade County Public Schools in 2014, showcases the possibilities of this technology. The district's Technology Based Indoor Fitness Trail for Recess was implemented district-wide in Miami-Dade County Public Schools with funding from the CDC Community Transformation Grant (CTG) Program. The program was implemented at 216 elementary schools in the district. With a tablet in hand, students walk along an indoor fitness trail to locate QR codes strategically placed at designated locations (figure 9.5). Once the QR code is located, the group leader scans that code, which links to an age-appropriate 90-second exercise video. Overall, this program has empowered both teachers and students to engage in more physical activity. This concept can be useful when weather conditions prohibit going outside for recess or when classroom teachers are looking for more innovative ways to motivate students to be physically active during recess.

Geocaching

Geocaching is another technology-based activity that is fun, innovative, and challenging. Originally developed as an outdoor activity known as letterboxing and later as global scavenger hunts for hidden caches, it provides students with an opportunity to use Global Positioning System (GPS) technology. Mobile GPS devices or smartphones can be used to find hidden objects at specific coordinates set up or

FIGURE 9.5 QR codes for Technology-Based Indoor Fitness Trail for Recess
Courtesy of JAM School Program.

identified by the instructor. These geocaches often include puzzles or riddles; students work in groups to find and solve them. Geocaching can be used as a part of an adventure education unit to teach students about the local environment and outdoor pursuits opportunities. All in all, geocaching presents a great opportunity for combining physical activity with GPS technology and problem-solving skills to create an engaging educational experience for students in physical education. For teachers who are still becoming comfortable with GPS technology, depending on their stage of technology adoption they can do similar activities with a map and compass.

To set up a geocaching lesson, an instructor will first have to determine what geocaching locations are suitable for their students and school. Preexisting geolocation at parks, nature trials, or nearby outdoor locations can be used. However, if it is not feasible for a school to use one of these locations because of distance or school policy, a physical education teacher can create a geocache location on the school grounds. Some apps (e.g., Munzee) allow a user to add a number of locations for free. To create geocache locations, a teacher can record the latitude and longitude coordinates from the GPS devices to be used in the activity. Then, the teacher can create a description of the geocache for each of the way points, providing information about each location's significance or unique features. This approach allows a teacher to create challenges, problem-solving puzzles, or questions related to the location's appearance or history for the students to work through. These challenges should align with the learning objectives and provide students with the opportunity to demonstrate their knowledge and skill. It's important to note that when creating geocaches, teachers should keep them far enough apart to prevent overlap and confusion, which could lead to students becoming stagnant as they wait their turn.

In order to use GPS technology in physical education, students will first have to be educated on how to use the GPS mobile device or a smartphone app for the geocaching activity. Consider training students on how to input coordinates, read maps, and interpret GPS coordinates to find the hidden geocaches. Additionally, safety guidelines emphasizing the importance of respecting nature, private property, and being mindful of their surroundings while participating in geocaching should be covered.

As students move through the predetermined geocache locations, they can document their experience through reflective journaling or a task sheet to complete while participating in the activity. Another method of recording student geocaching is to link an online form creator to QR codes that students can scan when they find a cache. The linked form can contain questions for students to answer (e.g., puzzles, riddles, content review questions), instructions for completing a task, or coordinates for the next location, or it can simply be a place for students to input their names to indicate they have found the location. The benefit of using QR codes linked to an online form is that it allows the teacher to track the students from the form with the information being uploaded to a spreadsheet in real time. This way, the teacher can monitor students' progress from a more centralized location.

An effective use of geocaching in physical education was implemented in Miami-Dade County Public Schools. In this activity, students used a GPS unit (figure 9.6), and they were provided with GPS locations organized by station (figure 9.7). Once they found the coordinate, or waypoint, they had to locate an exercise card at each station and do the exercise as a group before breaking into teams again to find the next set of coordinates (figure 9.8). What made this program unique was that the students were tracked with a drone equipped with an action camera so that they could have a recorded video of their activity (figure 9.9). Since this activity was tied to many other academic standards, especially science, technology, engineering, and math (STEM), it was conducted during the school day as a physical education field trip. Geocaching should be promoted as a family-friendly and lifelong physical activity; teachers can encourage students and their caregivers to download the GPS app and take this activity outside of school hours.

FIGURE 9.6 GPS unit.

FIGURE 9.7 Geocaching: Satellite Points, Oleta River State Park

Station 1	N 25′54.710′ W 080′07.758′
Station 2	N 25′54.637′ W 080′07.796′
Station 3	N 25′54.533″ W 080′07.802′
Station 4	N 25′54.479′ W 080′07.796′
Station 5	N 25′54.427′ W 080′07.858′
Station 6	N 25′54.353′ W 080′07.917′
Station 7	N 25′54.473″ W 080′07.912′
Station 8	N 25′54.411′ W 080′07.944″
Station 9	N 25′54.568′ W 080′08.012′

GIFs

Graphics Interchange Format (GIF) is a file format that supports animation and static images. GIFs are popular on social media and in text messages. Benefits of GIF use in physical education include the following:

- Animations can provide a visual example for a motor skill or concept being taught.
- GIF use can provide a looping visual example of a motor skill or provide tactical concepts from multiple angles.
- GIFs offer quick bursts of information that can be easily learned through repetition, supporting microlearning.
- The ability to change GIF speed to slow motion supports learning of concepts.
- The visual format allows teachers to direct learners' attention to focus on specific movement elements or cues.
- The technology engages students with a format they are accustomed to seeing and using.
- The small file size and compatibility with the majority of devices and software make it a convenient choice.

FIGURE 9.8 Students *(a)* searching for satellite points and *(b)* doing a group exercise at the station.

Having the ability to create GIFs using mobile or web applications provides the physical education teacher with another avenue to repeatedly demonstrate specific movement patterns or skill concepts. This technology can function as a tool to help a teacher attend to students in more than one place at a time; for example, a teacher can have a GIF display on the gymnasium's smartboard or projector while he walks around and gives individual feedback to students. Another example is for a teacher to generate GIFs as QR codes for station work, where she has instruction and premade visual demonstrations for students to learn from whether or not they are near her. This use of technology enables students to gain a better understanding while maximizing class time.

FIGURE 9.9 Students being tracked by a drone.

A variety of websites, apps, and programs allow for the creation of GIFs. Research has shown that students in physical education who participate in GIF creation and self-assess their performance have shown increased performance compared to those who participate in a traditional skill breakdown (Chaker, 2018). Many of these programs are free of charge; however, for more complex GIFs, an educator will need to pay for more advanced software. Doing an Internet search for "free GIF maker" is a good starting point. Depending on how an instructor plans to use GIFs in the physical education course, finding software that allows for the creation of GIFs from premade videos (e.g., from YouTube or MP4 files) or new, user-created GIFs may be preferable. For example, if a physical education teacher wants to demonstrate proper throwing technique in a football unit, they may want to use software that allows them to generate a GIF from a highlight video (e.g., from YouTube). However, if the goal of the lesson is for students to create GIFs that target specific muscle groups, then they would need software (e.g., ImgPlay) that allows them to directly capture GIFs.

If the physical education teacher plans to have students create their own GIFs in or outside of the classroom, preclass videos providing an overview of how to use the GIF software would be advisable. These short preclass videos should cover the basic features and functions of the GIF software that you plan on using for your lesson. General topics to cover include how to access the software, how to record the GIF, and basic editing features (trims/cuts, cropping, inserting text, playback speed, saving, and uploading). These short preclass overview videos can be accompanied by a short quiz to ensure students are ready to use the software to create GIFs in class.

The obvious strength of GIF use in physical education lies in its ability to visually demonstrate motor skill and movement concepts that are broken down to discrete steps. However, this technology tool can also be used as a creative means to assess learning. Examples of creative and effective GIF use for assessment include the following:

- A student submits a GIF to the instructor in the middle of the unit. During the second half of the unit, the student practice time is spent focused on her individualized plan for improvement. She submits a second GIF at the end of the unit that includes evidence of progress toward a specific goal.
- Students can create GIFs that break down the steps in performing a skill or movement concept. For example, students can be assigned tactical problems (e.g., creating open space) to address and create GIFs demonstrating their understanding of the movement or tactics (e.g., pick and roll) associated with those concepts.
- Students create GIFs that target assigned muscle groups to assess their knowledge of anatomy and physiology.
- The teacher posts GIFs on the gymnasium's smartboard or projector and has students identify the critical skill elements or cues being demonstrated.
- Using a so-called jigsaw instructional approach, students can be tasked with creating GIFs covering one or two eight-count measures of a line dance to assess their ability to count music. Those GIFs can then be displayed with the other student-created GIF line dance segments as a visual cue while the class performs the line dance routine.
- Students can create GIFs that identify safety issues and measures needed for participation in physical activity.

Exergaming and Active Gaming

Exergaming, also known as active gaming, which utilizes technology in the form of games and fitness equipment, has become hugely popular as a way of engaging and motivating youth and adults to become physically active. (See the section in chapter 8 devoted to the use of technology predominantly implemented in school-site wellness centers.) From the earliest version of wired *Dance Dance Revolution* to the more technologically integrated game bikes and multisensory fitness equipment, active gaming and technology have a perpetual place in all conversations related to technology and physical activity.

Mobile exergaming is similar to console-based exergaming (e.g., Xbox Kinect, Nintendo Wii, PlayStation VR) in that it requires kinesthetic movement by the player to progress through the game. However, there are evident barriers to the widespread adoption of console-based exergaming in physical education due to additional costs (e.g., video game consoles, peripheral devices, and user subscriptions) in combination with the relatively short life cycles of the hardware used to run exergames (devices tend to have less than a 5-year life cycle). The use of smartphones and mobile exergaming applications presents an alternative that has the potential to alleviate those challenges so that instructors can keep up with the rapidly changing hardware and software.

When selecting mobile exergames to incorporate into physical education, an instructor should consider the following:

- Mobile exergaming applications that align with the unit and lesson outcomes
- Incorporating gamification principles (story-driven, incremental complexity, tracking system, rewards, collecting)
- Multiplatform games (e.g., iOS, Android, Google Play)
- Tracking of fitness activity (distance, speed, steps)

Exergames contain gamification features designed to engage students in cardiovascular fitness that blend well with any physical education curriculum. Giving students the opportunity to select the exergame they want to participate in gives them a voice and a choice for what, where, and how they get active. For example, a student wanting to increase their cardiovascular endurance may choose to use Zombie Run. This application combines elements of a run tracking app with a zombie apocalypse narrative to create an immersive experience that can be used for interval training. As students progress through the storyline, they will encounter periodic zombie chases where they will need to increase their speed to escape and progress through the mission. Students can set the level of their pace in relation to the story based on their current level of fitness. The application gives students audio cues and uses GPS tracking to monitor their running distance, speed, and route. After the lesson is completed, students can review their workout pace, calories burned, and total distance covered. If aligned properly with lesson outcomes, mobile exergaming can be a tool to accommodate students in a unique and immersive way.

Video Analysis

Video analysis is an effective and practical tool that is used in a variety of physical education classrooms. Video analysis allows a physical educator to visually break down a skill into its critical elements, assists with authentic assessments, and, most importantly, provides immediate and accurate feedback to students. A variety of apps, websites, and programs have been designed for this purpose (e.g., OnForm, Hudl Technique, CoachView, CoachNow, Dartfish). The following are specific ways to incorporate video into the classroom:

- Show a quick tutorial about a specific learning task.
- Show a specific skill being performed to give students a visual guide. It can include a variety of demonstrations, such as a whole-part-whole demonstration, a focus on a specific element of the skill, a slow-motion version of the skill, and views from multiple angles.
- Use video as an anticipatory set while students are waiting to enter the physical education classroom.
- Use visuals in the form of a video to meet the needs of a variety of learners with a variety of learning styles.
- Use it as an assessment tool to evaluate student performance. Either the teacher can watch and evaluate, or students can work in pairs or small groups to evaluate videos of each other performing specific skills. It is important to include a rubric with cues and common errors to help guide the peer evaluation.
- Review a gameplay video to address tactical problems.

When deciding on what software to use, physical educators should consider basic features such as drawing markups, slow motion, file sharing, and side-by-side video comparisons as well as more advanced features such as voiceover recording feedback, auto capture detection, video delay, and skeleton tracking. In addition, they may choose to use teaching platforms that allow them to organize, sync, and send group and individual messages across devices. The more advanced features may be more important for educators who use online and blended learning models.

Video analysis through software and mobile applications is a technology tool that can be universally applied to informal and formal assessment for the majority of content in physical education. Whether it is a video of a skill performance or a student describing cognitive or affective content, video is very versatile. An example of how video can be used for assessment (beyond examples already listed) is to have the students record a skill, then analyze the recording of the skill at the beginning, middle, and end of a unit. With each iteration of the assessment, the students could be tasked with analyzing their performance in relation to the critical skill elements using a criteria checklist or skill rubric, then they could set goals for improvement to work on until the next video is completed.

Additionally, students can analyze gameplay situations and tactics with this technology to demonstrate an understanding of sport tactics and strategy. To manage this task, the teacher can have one group of students participate in gameplay while another group (the off group) records the performance. While the off group is recording and analyzing gameplay, the teacher can visit with and review the clips with them, or the teacher can provide prompts or tasks for the off group to address while they are analyzing the gameplay footage. This assignment can also be extended to addressing the affective domain by having students point out appropriate behavior and fair play that occurs during the game.

Mobile Devices: Laptops, Tablets, and Smartphones

The use of mobile devices can be a powerful tool for individualizing learning based on academic needs and student interest. Mobile apps provide an array of instructional tools and resources that can facilitate creating a more student-centered lesson or unit. As of 2017, there were over 165,000 mobile fitness apps that focus on a wide range of fitness activities, from weight training to table tennis (Kesiraju & Vogels, 2017). App choice depends on what needs to be accomplished within a PreK-12 grade classroom, but more importantly, any app must be approved by the school, district, or state.

When designing a course or learning activity, physical educators and districts must not fall into an app trap. It is essential that the physical educator view the content of the mobile application in detail before assigning it for instructional purposes (e.g., ensuring it is developmentally appropriate and contains correct demonstrations). This attention will not only prevent injuries to students, it will also avoid the risk of teacher negligence. Teachers should follow these guidelines when using mobile devices and applications:

- Leverage multimedia (e.g., images, video, audio, augmented reality) that can supplement demonstrations of skill cues or tactical concepts performed live in a traditional PE lesson or before class (Goad et al., 2019). If used as a flipped learning approach, this technology has the potential to serve as a gateway to independent student behavior while allowing for more in-class activity time.
- Use mobile fitness apps to help students create a personalized workout from the catalog of exercises built in the app and move at their own pace or to help them choose a particular way to meet the learning outcomes.
- Provide students with the opportunity to dive deeper into topics that are interesting to them through digital tools, learning resources, and gamification skills. There are ways to engage students with content using tools such as discussion boards, journals, and social media to foster interaction and real-time communication among students. This opportunity provides students with a platform to create, share, discuss, and collaborate within a learning environment that is tailored to their personal health and fitness goals and interests both inside and outside of the classroom.

As mentioned earlier, new apps are always being developed. Physical education teachers who use apps will need to make it a priority to be aware of the latest apps that are available and can be leveraged to increase student growth, engagement, and teacher productivity. As mentioned earlier, any new app must be vetted by the existing protocols at the school, district, or state. Consistently advocating for this technology in physical education and reminding districts and IT departments that apps should reflect the use of technology in all subject areas will help ensure that physical education students can access a variety of apps; consequently, this access will lead to a wider range of learning opportunities.

Finding the right balance between instruction, practice, personalized attention, and modern technology is crucial for student engagement through mobile devices. No two districts or class environments are alike, and the decision to implement mobile devices is a school-to-school decision unless mandated by the district. Some schools have a one-to-one student-to-device ratio, while others have class sets of devices or bring your own device (BYOD) policies. The key to successful implementation is to have management strategies and routines in place that account for the unique context and setting in which the mobile devices will be used. Refer to Implementation Strategies, earlier in this chapter, for recommendations on management strategies.

Utilizing multiple mobile devices in a physical education setting allows opportunities for assessment. Assessments can include formative and summative assessments using a cloud-based platform that enables the teacher to create forms or quizzes. They can also consist of video or image-based movement analysis assessments. In addition, available technologies allow teachers using one device to assess the whole classroom within seconds. An example of this technology is a cloud-based platform, such as Plickers, a tool that can quickly assess a student's knowledge through multiple-choice questions. During the question-and-answer session, students hold up a card with their answer and the teacher scans the card with a mobile device. This tool provides immediate feedback to the students and teachers using real-time formative assessment data.

Innovative Uses of Technology

Teachers who have experience successfully and creatively implementing (Stage Six of the technology adoption model) the technology previously mentioned in this chapter may consider using currently emerging technologies that are not yet commonly integrated in physical education or education in general. In late 2022 and early 2023, artificial intelligence (AI) technology such as ChatGPT became a widely discussed topic in education. Such disruptive technology requires teachers to determine how they and their students might use it—appropriately or inappropriately—and provide appropriate guidance. This section briefly describes innovative uses of technology, and it explores the possibilities for integrating emerging technologies in a meaningful way.

Drones

Uncrewed aerial vehicles, commonly known as drones, are small remote control aircraft used for recreation, for professional applications, and—perhaps less commonly known—for educational applications. Typically, drones have onboard smart software and GPS that stabilize flight, allowing for an integrated video camera to capture high-quality footage. This technology allows teachers and students to view the activities from an aerial perspective, giving them a view of the whole court or field. This type of perspective provides the opportunity for novel feedback related to gameplay and tactics.

Drones with video-recording capabilities vary greatly in price; nevertheless, they can become costly to obtain when upgraded features such as range, flying time, windspeed resistance, integrated GPS, camera resolution and quality, and internal memory storage are considered. However, when purchasing big-ticket items, especially when it comes to technology, making the case that this device can be used for more than one purpose is important. For example, the drone can also be used as an advocacy tool for the school when taking footage from a field day or school pep assembly to share with the community and parents.

The ability of drones to remain in flight, hovering in predetermined locations without the need for the teacher to provide constant monitoring or remote controlling, makes this technology manageable in a physical education setting. When selecting a drone to be used for filming sport-related activities outdoors, those that are equipped with GPS are a good choice because they often have hovering functionality built in. In addition, battery life is an essential consideration in terms of practical usability and price. Entry-level drones can have battery life that will keep them in flight for around 10 minutes and will cost around $300, while higher-end models can last 40 or more minutes of flight and cost more than $1,200. Consider also that it is possible to have multiple batteries charged and ready to go; therefore, even if an entry-level drone is purchased, purchasing multiple batteries is advised. Therefore, flight time and batteries that are easily swapped out are key features to consider for a teacher purchasing a drone for use in physical education.

The videos captured with drone cameras are typically higher-resolution images, which creates large file sizes. For students to have access to the videos for review or assessment, they can be uploaded to any cloud-based service (e.g., Microsoft OneDrive or Google Drive) used by the school. Then, students can review the videos by sharing a link using the school's learning management system (LMS). It is essential for teachers to ensure they have a file-sharing plan to take full advantage of this technology.

As mentioned previously, a drone's ability to capture high-quality aerial footage makes it a tool that can be used for student analysis and reflection of tactics. Small-sided games would work best for keeping all students in view and to simulate gamelike situations more often. For example, in an Ultimate Frisbee flag football unit, a drone can be used to record an aerial view of the students while on offense or defense. (*Note:* Using a high-visibility Frisbee, such as a bright orange one, ensures the disc is easier to see on the video.) In this example, each team can be given the same scripted plays to implement, after which the footage can be loaded onto a cloud-based drive. Then, students can be tasked with analyzing and reflecting by picking out various video segments that supplement their written statements. The assessment prompts could include the following:

- Pick out two plays that were successful, and identify what type of coverage the defense was running.
- What plays were successful against team X's defense? Why was each play successful?
- Find a clip of someone on offense who found open space.
- Find a situation where the defense was successful, and describe why it was successful.

Robotics and Coding: STEM-PE

Robotics and coding may not have an immediate connection to physical education. Robotics certainly has obvious applications in math and science classes. In physical education, it has enormous potential to both motivate and engage young children to become physically active (figure 9.10). STEM-PE was rolled out at the 2017 Shape America National Convention & Expo during the 50 Million Strong by 2029 advocacy session. For example, the NAO (pronounced "now") robot, named JAI, is a humanoid robot that can perform humanlike movements such as those shown in figure 9.11. For students, it provides an opportunity to learn programming or coding to create various movements and to learn anatomical analysis of motor skills. Robotics, coding, and STEM connections have the potential to strengthen interdisciplinary connections with other educators at the school site, and they may also influence how others perceive what is possible in physical education.

Virtual and Augmented Reality

Much like robotics and coding, virtual reality (VR) and augmented reality (AR) have the potential to significantly enhance physical education by providing interactive and immersive learning experiences. The inherent ability of VR and AR to create simulated environments of different sport venues has the potential to simulate environments such as baseball diamonds, soccer pitches, basketball courts, swimming pools, and the like. This technology would allow for students to practice and experience different activities without leaving the classroom. Pair with this capability the potential for immersive skill lessons where students can learn proper technique while receiving feedback on their performance to refine their skills, and you get a recipe for game-changing innovation.

The gamification aspects provided by VR and AR technologies are another intriguing element with potential applications for physical education. Similar to exergames in physical education, the gamification aspect (e.g., interactive challenges, rewards, competition, etc.) for VR/AR technologies is leveraged in a physical education setting to enhance student motivation and attitudes toward physical activity. Additionally, the immersive atmosphere provided by VR and AR games can distract players from high levels of physical exertion while playing.

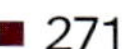

FIGURE 9.10 A robot motivates young children to engage in physical activity as the class leader.

For example, popular exergames such as *Beat Saber*, a VR rhythm game, are good examples of exergames utilizing this technology that are immersive and incorporate many gamification features.

VR and AR could be used to set up virtual field trips to explore ideas within venues not readily accessible to students. For example, if you want your students to experience hiking in the outdoors, a virtual trip to the woods would not meet these expectations. However, if you want the students to be aware of various flora and fauna or safety issues related to hiking before they embark on an actual hike,

FIGURE 9.11 JAI, the NAO robot in programmed physical activity moves.

it would be a good (purposeful) use of a virtual trip. This technology is growing rapidly, and it is becoming more accessible with a wider range of applications in the learning environment.

Artificial Intelligence

One of the more notable technological developments in recent years is the advent of conversational artificial intelligence (AI), such as ChatGPT. This type of technology has the potential to cause a large paradigm shift for physical education teachers. It's important to examine the potential benefits and challenges associated with integrating AI technology into education.

AI has the potential to revolutionize education by enhancing the learning experience for students. It can provide immediate access to information, answer questions, and engage in meaningful conversations with learners. This technology can serve as an in-the-moment tutor, promoting personalized learning and adaptive instructions. Students can receive instant feedback, guidance, and support, fostering independent thinking and problem-solving skills. Moreover, AI can help bridge knowledge gaps, ensuring that students have access to comprehensive information regardless of their geographical location or school resources.

Specifically, AI can assist in disseminating accurate and up-to-date health and physical activity information, which can be used to help students make informed decisions about their well-being. It can provide personalized advice based on individual needs, promoting health habits and preventive measures. For instance, AI can assist students in pursuing and achieving self-prescribed SMART goals. A student with a SMART goal related to nutrition can input the parameters into AI software and have it create a seven-day meal plan in relation to that goal. After that point, the student can take it further by having AI make a grocery shopping list based on a previously generated meal plan that includes portion amounts to purchase in order to make each of the meals.

While AI offers exciting possibilities, it also raises important questions and concerns. One major challenge is ensuring the accuracy and reliability of the information provided by AI software. Conversational AI may not always possess the contextual understanding or discernment necessary to distinguish between accurate and misleading information. Educators must be cautious in selecting and vetting reliable sources of information for integration into AI systems. Furthermore, the integration of AI should complement—not replace—human interaction in education. While AI can provide an initial response and information, it cannot replace the role of educators in facilitating meaningful discussion, building relationships, and fostering critical-thinking skills.

When considering AI, a teacher must also consider ethics. It is crucial to address privacy concerns, ensure data security, and ensure that the use of AI does not compromise student privacy rights. Transparent guidelines and regulations should be established to ensure ethical implementation and protect students' well-being. As with all other technologies discussed in this chapter, teachers should work with the school technology specialist and adhere to any school, district, and state policies regarding technology.

Similar to the introduction of digital calculators, which was disruptive to math education, AI will affect every subject area in some capacity. AI and machine learning are new resources in education. They have the potential to revolutionize education by providing immediate access to information, personalizing instruction and feedback, and increasing student engagement. By leveraging the strengths of AI while acknowledging its limitations, teachers can harness its potential to create a more dynamic and effective physical education environment, benefiting students in their pursuit of knowledge and well-being.

Adapted Physical Education and Assistive Technology

As discussed in chapter 4, teaching a variety of learners within an inclusive physical education classroom is critical for ensuring that there is equitable opportunity to receive instruction in all areas of the curriculum. The use of technology (or assistive technology, where warranted) serves to ensure that the specific needs of all students with disabilities are met with appropriate accommodations and strategies that are designed to deliver developmentally

FIGURE 9.12 Electronic joystick used in the Anchors Away Sailing Program in Miami, Florida.
Aventura Marketing Council's Anchors Away Foundation, photography by Andrew Goldstein.

appropriate instruction. Various programs and applications can help to increase the level of success of all students within a physical education classroom.

Consider the VR and AI technology discussed in the previous section. VR and AI have the potential to accommodate select students with disabilities with the modified environment to meet their needs, enabling them to participate and benefit from physical education. Applications exist that help students communicate and participate with educational assistants and teachers alike. Researching and identifying applications to meet the needs of students with varying disabilities will further ensure a thriving learning environment, which will also lead to socialization and integration within the class setting.

A physical educator should research and identify a variety of resources available for a specific student's learning needs. Reaching out to the special education department within a school district can also assist in this process. Figure 9.12 shows an example of how technology can be used to assist students with disabilities. An electronic joystick similar to the one on an electric wheelchair, added to each of the Access Dinghies in the Anchors Away Sailing Program for students with disabilities, enables students to go sailing in an inclusive environment.

Teaching With Learning Management Systems (LMSs)

Learning management systems (LMS) have become ubiquitous in secondary schools, especially since the COVID-19 pandemic. The integration of contemporary LMSs (e.g., Google Classroom, Schoology, Canvas, Blackboard, etc.) provides teachers with a platform to efficiently distribute course content, integrate external online resources, post assignments, deliver quizzes, create discussion boards, and provide student feedback. Although a wide variety of LMSs are available and many school districts have adopted this technology since 2020 (the onset of the COVID-19 pandemic), they all have similar features and functions to support both face-to-face and online learning. Some examples of how to incorporate LMS features into your own classroom include the following:

- *Assessment*: Built-in assessment features in LMS applications (e.g., assignment submissions, discussion boards, quizzes, etc.) allow teachers to digitally provide instant feedback to students and their parents or guardians. This feedback can consist of student assessments as well as behavioral feedback. Some LMSs allow for question randomization to discourage cheating, and some offer automated grading to reduce grading burden. Additionally, through LMSs, secure fitness data can be shared, and parents or guardians can check on a student's homework assignments.
- *Promoting student interactions*: The integration of web-based video and audio discussion tools (e.g., Flip, Seesaw, Kaltura, etc.) into LMSs presents opportunities for teachers to facilitate meaningful learner–content interactions.
- *Advocacy and family engagement*: The announcements feature embedded in most LMSs represents a tool for teachers to easily share information with students and their parents or guardians. For example, this LMS tool can be used to promote your program by sharing class updates, sharing student experiences, promoting physical activity, encouraging family-based activities, and, above all, reinforcing the *why* behind your program.
- *Content organization*: LMS course modules provide a centralized platform for instructors to organize course content in a single location that students can access anytime and anywhere. This feature assists instructors in effectively managing the flow of the course, and it helps reduce the administrative hassles associated with maintaining content and assessments in multiple places.
- *Facilitating flipped and blended learning*: Leveraging assessment and content delivery features of the LMS allows instructors to prime and engage students with content prior to class to preserve in-class time for physical activity and skill development.

The degree to which educators utilize a LMS will likely be connected not only to their stage of technology adoption but also to the extent that other teachers use this resource. The greater the expectation at the school site for LMS use, the easier it will be to use the wide range of tools an LMS has to offer.

Blended Learning

Blended learning and flipped learning are innovative instructional strategies. Although they are often used synonymously, they are different strategies. *Blended learning* involves face-to-face instruction along with some online (web-based) learning, which is made possible with the integration of an LMS. *Flipped learning* is a type of blended learning that flips the traditional learning model by having students learn content outside of class and then apply it in class. In flipped learning, students often watch videos or read articles before class, and then use class time to work on projects that apply the concepts they learned. Blended learning allows students to work at their own pace and work both outside of and during classroom time. Research has identified benefits of blended learning within classroom-based subjects for students in regard to improvement in their preparation for class and knowledge of subject matter and opportunities for skill application (Wang, 2016). In the realm of physical education, the integration of blended learning has shown positive effects on student motivation and learning outcomes (Osterlie & Kjelaas, 2019). Additionally, it extends the time students spend engaging in moderate-to-vigorous physical activity (MVPA) and practicing skills, surpassing the levels achieved through direct instruction (Killian & Woods, 2018). Moreover, evidence suggests that flipped learning facilitates greater interaction between students and their teachers (Chen, 2016). As a result, blended learning has proven to be a viable educational approach. When incorporating this method of delivery in physical education, educators should consider the following strategies:

1. *Unit pre-assessment*: Gauge students' knowledge and understanding of cognitive, affective, and psychomotor content related to an upcoming unit by having

them complete a pre-assessment. The teacher can then analyze the results and design a unit that better meets the needs of where the students are.

2. *Anticipatory set*: Prime students with foundational content (e.g., skill demonstration videos, game strategy, or key vocabulary) that would typically be given through direct instructional approaches, by using LMS modules prior to class. For example, for a lesson on the components of health-related fitness, all of the activities and learning objectives are loaded and ready for students to access through the school's LMS. Students would view these short (less than 5 minutes) videos prior to class to prepare for in-class activities. Consequently, the students would now be entering class with prior knowledge of learning goals and expectations and preserving in-class time for activity.
3. *More in-class physical activity time*: Focus in-class time on student application of skills and knowledge through activities and gameplay. This focus can facilitate content-inspired creation; for example, students can put together yoga flows, based on their current ability level, to use in class.
4. *Choice and a voice*: Through creative and active learning opportunities, students can relate content to their own personal goals and interests. For example, if the objective of the lesson is for students to stay in their target heart rate zone for a set amount of time, they can choose from a set of activities provided by the teacher that facilitates their meeting that objective. Allowing students to have autonomy over their learning has been found to be an effective strategy for motivating and engaging students in physical education (Gray et al., 2019).
5. *Embracing student-directed autonomous physical activity*: Implementing progressive movement or activity goals to be completed outside of class time can encourage self-directed learning and provide exposure to different physical activities. Leveraging modern technologies identified earlier in this chapter can help students establish links with the subject matter through experiential learning.

Blended and flipped learning, much like the integration of an LMS, will both depend on a teacher's comfort with and philosophy toward technology. Research has demonstrated multiple benefits of blended learning that takes advantage of available technology.

Online Physical Education (OLPE)

Fully online and virtual programs existed before the 2000s. However, online programs became more prevalent after the COVID-19 pandemic; preexisting programs were able to assist face-to-face educators who were shifting to a fully virtual mode. Online physical education (OLPE) presents a unique set of challenges in translating traditional physical education to a digital space, all while meeting the same benchmarks, curriculum, and assessment standards of traditional courses. The delivery of OLPE courses has been met with some skepticism and viewed by some as an oxymoron due to the inability to conceptualize effective instruction and evaluation of physical activity in an online setting. Online education is available in every state, and at least 31 states have rules or legislation allowing physical education credits to be taken online (SHAPE America, 2016). This section addresses the entirety of designing an OLPE program due to the overall complexity. In addition, it is important to acknowledge that online education before and after the onset of the COVID-19 pandemic still serves a relatively small percentage of the overall K-12 student population. However, this section discusses the basics for getting started because online learning is a reality in many districts.

There are two ways an OLPE program becomes available to students. The first is when a school district contracts with an existing virtual school to access its OLPE courses. The second way is when the school district develops its own online or virtual school or classes in order to maintain full-time equivalent (FTE) or student funding. The choice to purchase a preexisting curriculum or develop one from scratch is typically a decision made by the school district; it will likely come down to two factors: time and money.

Whether a program is purchased from a vendor or is developed from scratch, it is important for physical education teachers to ensure that it is based on standards and is in line with the overall philosophy of physical education at the school or district. It is important to have an OLPE course with high expectations so that it does not turn into simply an alternative for students who failed face-to-face classes or something that is perceived as easy. Student accountability and participation are a must in any physical education class; this requirement applies equally to in-person and online classes. The following sections describe considerations for designing or screening an OLPE course. Additionally, SHAPE America's (2020) *Guidelines for K-12 Online Physical Education* provides a good resource to get started and begin to conceptualize how OLPE can be used to address all content standards within physical education.

Course Setup

During the development stage, teachers need to have a thorough understanding of the tools necessary to run a successful OLPE course. Setting up an OLPE course requires an instructor to use the school district's LMS as the platform to deliver course content, deliver assignments, and engage students. Many school districts already have the proper infrastructure set up for an OLPE course. However, it can't be understated how important it is that a physical education instructor teaching an online course needs to have a thorough understanding of their school district's LMS features and functions when developing and delivering an OLPE course.

Accountability in the Online Environment

The question most physical education teachers have is how to successfully monitor progress in an online course as students are growing in their knowledge of physical education and also participating regularly in physical activity.

Assessing the psychomotor domain in an online setting is challenging, but it can be done. The use of video analysis software can be beneficial. For example, delivering a fitness unit remotely, the use of a video discussion and sharing app (e.g., Flip, formerly known as Flipgrid) provides students with a platform to demonstrate correct movement patterns of a self-selected exercise related to their own personal goals. Wearable devices can track student fitness and activity levels and allow for students to submit their daily physical activity data to the instructor. The application of VR and AR technologies in an OLPE setting presents another tool that could greatly enhance the interaction between students and the content.

In addition to wearable devices and video analysis software applications, online learning tools should be integrated into the LMS that allow students to demonstrate their comprehension of cognitive content. One example is using presentation software (e.g., Google Slides) to create wellness portfolio templates for students to track their own health and wellness journey. This type of digital portfolio is where students can place their work for the physical education instructor to view and assess to determine whether they are making positive gains toward achieving the course standards and expected outcomes or they need additional support. This type of student project can also be used as a tool for an OLPE class to assess the affective domain, such as determining the extent to which students value physical education. Teachers can make this determination by assessing the types of products that students develop and place in their portfolio, such as required course assignments, reflection journals, photos, videos, and any other original material to document their progress.

Student Socialization

Student socialization is another concern often cited as lacking in OLPE (Daum & Buschner, 2012; Williams, 2014). However, some of these concerns can be addressed with the built-in features of a LMS (discussion boards, video feedback, wikis, and messaging) in tandem with creative course design and assignments. For example, students in an OLPE can be divided into small groups based on similar fitness and wellness goals they have identified at the beginning of the course. This grouping approach would provide the opportunity for OLPE students who have similar fitness and wellness interests and goals to collaborate and interact with each other. Placing students in small groups with similar interests related to the content helps foster meaningful interaction and potentially reduces the social isolation many OLPE students experience.

While there is no one-for-one substitute for in-person socialization, another tool at the disposal of the OLPE teacher includes the social media features that are integrated into many popular mobile fitness applications. Research has shown that the socialization features of mobile fitness applications contribute to students viewing the health and fitness activities they participate in more positively (Lu & Turner, 2013). These features contribute to an additional creative and familiar platform that students can use; they can explore and share web-based fitness resources while creating a more socially interactive atmosphere in an OLPE course.

Keeping Up With Technology

Technology is extremely difficult to keep up with; new technologies are constantly released, which challenges schools to keep up both cognitively and financially with the latest trends. When it comes to big purchases and technology for physical education, teachers should carefully evaluate any device or software. Here are some considerations for educators to get the most for the money:

- *Evaluate the capabilities of technology in relation to the needs of the physical education department.* Research competitors in the market to determine availability of similar features or functions on similar products and to determine which product best suits the needs of the school and students.
- *Find out whether the device or software allows for and currently receives periodic updates.* If updates are provided, it means that the product will remain current if a license is purchased.
- *Evaluate the company.* If the technology is from a startup company or an unknown company, chances are that it could be discontinued. However, some of the best new educational technologies come from startups. Carefully evaluate each situation individually.
- *Determine what type of professional development support is available through the company or even with the school district.* Professional development will help you stay current and use the technology effectively.

In terms of keeping up with the latest trends in educational technology, it is important to be an educated consumer. Additionally, it is critical for future physical educators to consider how the technology may enable them to measure the impact of their instructional practices and student achievement in their schools. When used effectively, technology used for assessment purposes can help drive a teacher's instruction and enhance student learning in regard to lesson outcomes if managed properly.

Once instructors have a strong knowledge base regarding the resources available for technology within physical education, they should look at the implementation process as a continuum (see figure 9.13). They can select

FIGURE 9.13 How to keep up with using technology.

Developed by Colin Brooks.

a resource, incorporate this resource into their daily life, share it with others, reevaluate the relevance of the resource, then start the process over again.

Professionals must immerse themselves in current best practices to understand modern technology practices. Therefore, physical educators need to participate in a variety of professional development opportunities, including attending in-person professional development, reading current journal articles, attending webinars, listening to podcasts, taking LMS courses, and many more. It is also suggested that teachers keep up with technology trends by communicating with those in the field who themselves are setting the technology trends.

Continuing Professional Development

Many of the professional development programs that are currently offered to teachers fail to provide the kind of ongoing support teachers need to make effective use of educational technology; as a result, few teachers are in a position to integrate new technologies into their classroom practices. Teachers may attend a one-day workshop and return to school the following day, not knowing how or having no time to integrate what they learned into their curricula. To be successful in their endeavors to learn and implement new technologies, teachers need hands-on learning rooted in their own curricula that will enable them to translate training into practice.

Like many educators, physical education teachers juggle a number of diverse and time-consuming responsibilities, and scheduling time for ongoing professional development or productive interaction with colleagues can be extremely difficult. Educators need to be able to participate in professional development courses whenever and wherever it is convenient for them—before or after school, during a free planning period in the classroom, or at home on the weekends. Digital professional development presents one avenue in which teachers could fill this gap at any time or place.

Digital professional development is continually becoming more prevalent in the world of physical education. Webinars, podcasts, blogs, and online professional learning communities (e.g., state SHAPE organizations) are all examples of digital professional development opportunities. Most digital professional development is an example of practitioner-to-practitioner or peer-to-peer professional development. Although there is no substitute for face-to-face professional development, the capacity to provide more frequent and timely professional development becomes an attractive option when flexibility is needed to accommodate the varied schedules and needs of teachers. Digital media and resources have dramatically increased the accessibility of professional development for physical education professionals everywhere.

Webinars

Webinars are an excellent tool for physical education professionals for further developing their teaching skills and content. Webinars are web-based presentations that are either live or recorded. Webinars vary in how they are conducted; some encourage high levels of participation on the part of attendees, whereas others do not have a high level of engagement (by design) and are mainly for sharing information or new instructional techniques. Some webinars are free, and others range from a nominal fee to higher costs. You can access a variety of physical education webinars through national associations and organizations as well as through groups or individuals who specialize in digital professional development.

Podcasts

Podcasts are a remarkable tool for professional development that can be accessed anywhere someone can listen to the audio. Professionals from all over the world are sharing professional development in this manner. Podcasts can be listened to by professionals while commuting to work, while engaging in physical activity, and during class preparation times. Podcasts specific to the topics of physical education can be found by searching in any podcast app. There are many high-quality podcasts by individuals, organizations, and national associations that are specific to physical education. The benefit of podcasts for physical education professionals is that they can select the particular content they would like to hear and when they would like to hear it. Furthermore, professionals will enjoy listening to peers who they respect as quality practitioners.

Websites

When navigating the Internet, it is important to find quality resources. With countless physical education websites available, choosing the right ones can be overwhelming. To narrow the search and find innovative websites, physical education teachers should consider the *why* behind each website. Furthermore, instructors should take time to explore a variety of websites that they would like to learn from in order to grow. The key to finding relevant content on websites is to be specific in the search parameters. For example, if a teacher is seeking out resources related to standards-based physical education, it is essential to specify the state and grade level.

Professional organizations such as SHAPE America and state affiliates can offer quality resources; however, there are many other websites to consider. Websites that have quality physical education content will include the following characteristics:

- Connections to standards
- Information about who developed the website and why this source is reliable
- Frequent updates
- Ways to connect with the website owner and other users of the website

In addition to using these guidelines, the physical education teachers can consult with other colleagues in their district or professional colleagues that they know in other school districts. Physical education administrators can also encourage teachers to continue to explore and communicate their findings.

Conclusion

Changes in education and in society are inevitable, and technology has placed new demands on the teaching profession. While the demands are high, technology in a physical education setting is essential for the growth and development of 21st-century students as well as of physical education teachers. Innovative technology in education often promises to make work in classrooms more efficient, stress-free, and interactive. However, the simple adoption of technology itself does not equate to optimal and effective integration methods.

Although this chapter has presented many examples, it is important to note that endless opportunities are available to incorporate technology into a physical education program. To successfully facilitate the development and use of technology, the physical education teacher must invest in learning, stay current, and understand best practices using technology. A key component to the implementation of technology is investment and support at the district level—which the physical educator must advocate for. Physical education, like all subjects, requires equal access to technology. Advocating for these investments, including understanding what to advocate for, is essential if a physical educator is to garner resources that ensure appropriate student learning while using technology.

The use of technology in a physical education setting can provide professional development and professional growth opportunities. One of the silver linings of the COVID-19 pandemic is that physical educators and students now have more experience and training with online technologies. This experience has prepared some to transition toward a more effective and favorable approach to delivering content, assessments, and activities through active learning methodologies. The lessons learned from this experience have the potential to make the profession more meaningful for students by focusing on the cultivation of 21st-century skills, such as problem-solving, interpersonal communication, leadership, and creativity. By engaging students in personally relevant content, physical educators can encourage them to stay active and healthy throughout their lives.

Review Questions

1. According to the stages of technology adoption described by Anne Russell, why is it important for a teacher to consider their own context and gain awareness and confidence with a new technology before implementing it in the classroom? Provide an example from the scenario to support your answer.
2. Why is it important for teachers to develop and integrate their technological knowledge (TK) alongside their pedagogical knowledge (PK) and content knowledge (CK)? Provide examples to illustrate your answer.
3. What are some of the benefits of integrating technology into the classroom? Provide examples to support your answer.
4. What are some concerns and considerations that teachers should be mindful of when implementing technology in the classroom?
5. Explain the influence of teachers' prior experiences and beliefs on their use of educational technology in the classroom. How does the *apprenticeship of observation* concept by Dan Lortie relate to teachers' perceptions and adoption of technology?
6. Identify some common barriers that teachers face in incorporating digital technologies, and explain how these barriers are related to pedagogical beliefs.
7. Explain the significance of addressing the digital divide in educational equity, and discuss the challenges faced by students, particularly those from low-income backgrounds, in accessing stable Internet connections and suitable devices for educational purposes.
8. How do the backward mapping design and Understanding by Design (UbD) approaches assist physical educators in integrating technology into their instructional planning?
9. What steps can physical educators take to advocate for and access funding for technology resources and professional development in their classrooms?
10. What strategies would you develop to advocate for the use of technology in physical education?

PART IV

Communication, Legal Issues, and Human Resources

CHAPTER 10

Communications, Internal and External Public Relations, and Advocacy

Jayne D. Greenberg and Carly Wright

Courtesy of SHAPE America

LEARNING OBJECTIVES

After reading this chapter, you will be able to do the following:

- Describe the characteristics of effective communication.
- Explain the importance of communication and how to communicate in various ways.
- Identify the various models of communication.
- Discuss how to communicate with administrators, teachers, and the media.
- Describe the essential attributes of an effective advocate.
- Identify the various legislative funding opportunities available to the profession.

KEY CONCEPTS

active listening
advocacy
effective communication
Every Student Succeeds Act (ESSA)
formal and informal communication
horizontal communication
lobbying
nonverbal communication
public relations
verbal communication
vertical communication
well-rounded education

A crucial skill that transcends all levels of leadership, management, and administration is the ability to effectively communicate. Whether communication takes a verbal, written, or electronic form or it occurs through social media, it is essential that physical education administrators develop the skills to effectively tell people what they want them to understand and do as well as what action they need to take based on that communication.

Within an organization, **formal and informal communication** occur both internally and externally, and they involve many stakeholders; in a school district, these stakeholders include students, teachers, parents, community members, and educational policymakers. Formal communication within an organization is usually considered an official exchange of information between individuals with an established set of protocols, following a chain of command, and with the information documented. Informal communication can entail casual conversation, messages between coworkers, or the sharing of personal news. Whether you are communicating through formal or informal channels, your message must be clear and concise as well as be understood by recipients in order to ensure that the intended outcome is attained.

One of the most significant contributions instructional leaders can make to their programs—and to the profession as a whole—is to be advocates for the work that teachers do and for the impact their work has on students. This particular skill set requires that administrators be knowledgeable about the issues, trends, and needs in the field and that they be able to successfully communicate these factors to a variety of stakeholders and decision makers at the local, state, and federal levels.

This chapter explores the characteristics of effective communication and active listening, barriers to effective communication, and ways of tying it all together. In addition, it highlights the importance of public relations and advocacy efforts as they relate to securing funding and support for physical education programs as well as to overall respect for the profession and subject area. Understanding the unique role an administrator plays as a communicator and advocate can go a long way toward improving the instructional program; moreover, it can facilitate a better understanding of the contribution that physical education makes to the overarching goals of the larger academic program.

Effective Communication

Since communication is the way one interacts with others on a regular basis, **effective communication**, in simple terms, is a process in which there is an exchange of ideas initiated by one person who sends a message to another person (or groups of people) so that the information being shared is received and understood by the target audience. Since every administrative function involves communication, when messaging or information is communicated effectively, it helps in establishing rapport among those involved; feedback can be immediate, and the intended results can be achieved. In an attempt to explain the human process involved in communication, several models of communication have been developed. They fall into three categories: the linear model, the transactional model, and the interactive model.

Developed by Shannon and Weaver (1949) and based on early radio technology (figure 10.1), the *linear model* was the earliest model of communication. The developers of this model believed that communication is the process of sending and receiving information. Their model was based on four parts of communication: the *sender*, who encodes the idea in word selection; the *message*, the outcome of the encoded words; the *channel*, the medium by which the message is transmitted; and the *receiver*, who decodes the message into meaningful information (Lunenburg, 2010). *Noise*, originally identified as the static on phone lines, can refer to any signal that interferes with the message as it is

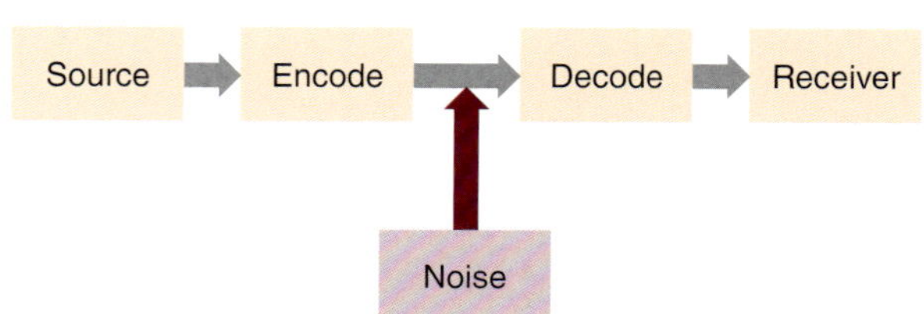

FIGURE 10.1 Shannon and Weaver's linear model of communication.

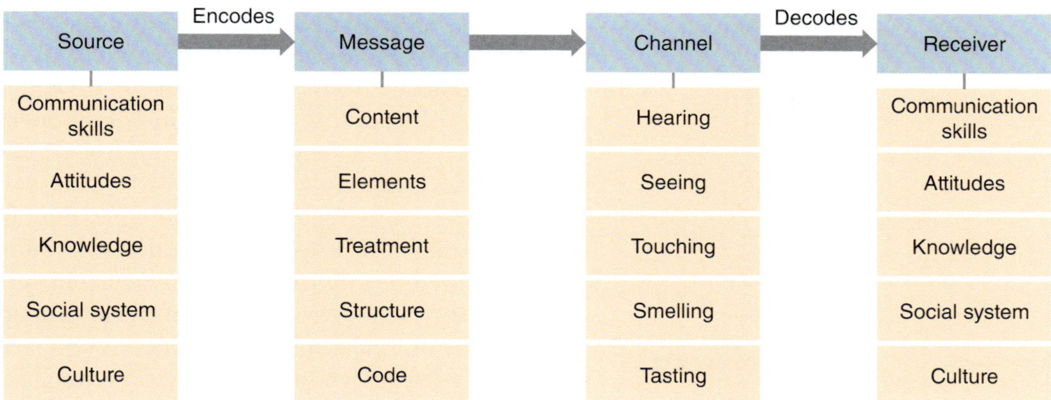

FIGURE 10.2 Berlo's SMCR model of communication.

Reprinted from D. Berlo, *The Process of Communication: An Introduction to Theory and Practice* (Holt, Rinehart and Winston, 1960).

being sent. A fifth part of communication that comes into play in later models is feedback, which provides the basis for understanding between the sender and receiver through response mechanisms.

Berlo (1960) expanded on the linear model, creating the sender–message–channel–receiver (SMCR) model of communication (figure 10.2). The SMCR model was based on one-way communication in which the sender sends the message and the receiver receives it. In the linear model, there is no interaction and no feedback, and the message flows in a straight line from the sender to the receiver. This type of model works best when the end goal is sending out mass communication. The defined set of components of the linear model involves the sender, who sends out the message after encoding it for the receiver to understand it, and the receiver, who decodes the message into understandable language.

Barnlund (1970; cited in Mortensen, 2007) proposed a *transactional model* of communication with the understanding that individuals are simultaneously engaging in the sending and receiving of messages in a reciprocal manner (figure 10.3). The sender and the receiver play an equally important role in the communication process. The transactional model is used predominantly for interpersonal communication where simultaneous feedback occurs. Nonverbal feedback, such as body language and gestures, is considered feedback in this model.

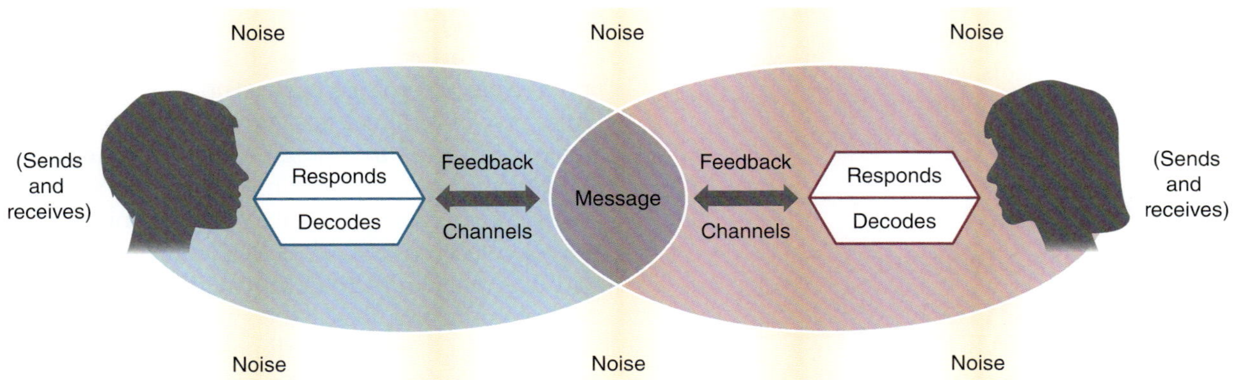

FIGURE 10.3 Barnlund's transactional model of communication.

Reprinted from D. Barnlund, "A Transactional Model of Communication," in *Foundations of Communication Theory*, edited by K.K. Sereno and C.D. Mortenson (Harper, 1970), 83-102.

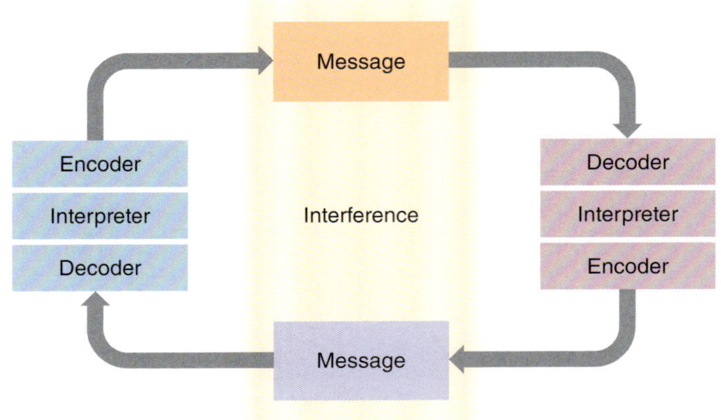

FIGURE 10.4 The Schramm model of communication.
Courtesy of Tsilatipac, Wikimedia Commons.

The *interactional model* (also known as the convergence model) is used for new modes of communication, such as the Internet; however, it is often slower with regard to feedback. Schramm (1954) asserted that the sender and receiver take turns playing the role of encoder and decoder when communicating (figure 10.4). Throughout the communication process, both the sender and receiver can exchange their ideas and views.

It is important to note that each of these models of communication is beneficial in various situations. They each provide an understanding of how people communicate and the processes involved in effective communication; this understanding enables administrators to communicate better with both their superiors and their subordinates. However, regardless of the model, effective communication between the person sending the message and the person or persons receiving the message is the key element. In addition, communication flows in many directions depending on the context of the message and the intended recipients.

Direction and Flow of Organizational Communication

As a physical education administrator, your lines of communication are both vertical and horizontal. **Vertical communication** involves the flow of information both upward and downward throughout the educational institution or school district with the primary purpose to advise, inform, or direct. *Upward communication* allows you the opportunity to transmit information through senior levels of management starting with your immediate supervising administrator and, depending on the level of importance, up to the superintendent. The advantage of upward communication is that it keeps everyone in the loop of activities, events, and especially of situations that might have negative consequences or outcomes. *Downward communication*, on the other hand, gives you the opportunity to effectively and efficiently communicate with your subordinates, school site physical education department chairpersons, or teachers on important changes to policies or procedures that would have immediate impact on those involved. For example, if new state legislation were enacted prior to the start of the school year, such as requiring cardiopulmonary resuscitation (CPR) instruction in physical education, then immediate professional development and training would need to occur for physical education teachers to implement the new legislation. The timeliness of the release of this information would be critical if the physical education classes were taught on a semester basis, and some students may be enrolled only during the first semester.

Horizontal communication is the exchange of information between colleagues, departments, or divisions that are on the same level in the organization. Within school districts, this communication allows for seamless collaboration on assignments, projects, or programs. For example, a physical education supervisor could work with a supervisor from the office of early childhood to develop programs to ensure both students in the voluntary pre-kindergarten (VPK) or preschool programs that are housed at the school site and students in the primary grades are getting their age-appropriate required number of physical activity minutes daily. Although vertical and horizontal communication can take a variety of forms, vertical communication tends to be more formal and will pass through several channels before reaching the highest level in the chain of command.

Diagonal communication is the exchange of information that cuts across different levels and functions in an organization. An example of diagonal communication in an educational setting would be for the associate superintendent to request a specific report or information from a principal without going through the assistant superintendent over curriculum or the subject area administrator over that topic.

Informal lines of communication, known as *grapevine communication*, are usually verbal; here, information is transmitted quickly between employees and serves both organizational and social needs of those involved. The benefits are that employees are kept involved on organizational matters. However, the information shared may not always be factual, and it often can give rise to unsubstantiated rumors (Lunenburg & Ornstein, 2011). Once there is understanding on how communication flows, the elements of effective communication should be mastered.

Elements of Effective Communication

In this chapter, the terms *organizations* and *educational institutions* are not referring to brick-and-mortar structures or abstract entities; they are referring to organizations that involve people and the series of networks and interactions that occur among them. The ability to effectively communicate begins with three basic skills: **verbal communication**, the ability to speak; **written communication**, the ability to transmit messages in writing; and **nonverbal communication**, the ability to understand body language, facial expressions, and gestures. Another key skill involved in effective communication is active listening.

The school district office, in both large and small school environments, is usually the hub of all communication sent to schools, administrators, teachers, and staff. Communicating during the workday is one of the most commonplace daily activities. Whether with respect to face-to-face, email, social media, or phone, effective administrators are also good communicators. The ability to communicate effectively is about being genuine as well as about the written and spoken word. Being able to communicate well allows you to inspire, motivate, and guide others. All communications should be clear and concise, and the tone should be business-like yet sincere and welcoming. Messages should be appropriate for your target audience, and they should be specific and purposeful. Additionally, communications should be relayed in a timely manner so that you can get information out quickly as well as stay ahead of any difficult or negative issues that are either pending or occurring; in other words, sooner is better. Moreover, if you don't communicate clearly, trust and respect can easily break down.

According to Stoner and colleagues (2006, p. 94), for administrators to be effective with various education stakeholders, to set the foundation for providing effective and meaningful communication they should consider following the "10 Commandments of Good Communication":

1. *Seek to clarify ideas before communicating.*
2. *Examine the true purpose of each communication.*
3. *Consider the total physical and human setting.*
4. *Consult with others, when appropriate, in planning communications.*
5. *Be mindful of the overtones as well as the basic content of the message.*
6. *Take the opportunity, when it arises, to convey something helpful or of value to the receiver.*
7. *Follow up on communication.*
8. *Communicate for tomorrow as well as today.*
9. *Be sure that actions support communications.*
10. *Seek not only to be understood but to understand (be a good listener).*

Methods of Communication

As previously stated, communication generally consists of three types: verbal, written, and nonverbal. Each type, when used effectively, proves to be valuable when conveying information or requests or when responding to specific situations.

Verbal Communication

Verbal communication can occur face-to-face; over the phone; through in-person presentations; through various video conferencing, chat, and messaging apps (e.g., Zoom, Teams, Skype, FaceTime); in live webinars; or using other modes of technology. Real-time verbal communication is one of the most powerful modes of communication because it allows you to exchange ideas and information immediately. It also provides an opportunity for the sender to provide clarification if the intent of the message is misunderstood, and it allows for interaction to occur naturally. Verbal communication involves the ability to speak clearly and articulate your thoughts so that your message is easily understood. Emphasis on words and phrases of importance is appealing and interesting to listeners. Spoken words should be in their standard form, not jargon or slang.

When conversing face-to-face, you have the ability to maintain eye contact and observe body language as the conversation progresses. It's important to keep in mind that conversations can have carryover effects; they stay in the memory of the person receiving the message. In verbal exchanges, consider your use of inflections and intonations, which can reflect your intentions as well as affect the meaning of your words. For presentations, such as during professional development workshops or conferences, it is important to have planned well in advance. In addition to making sure you checked for technical, grammatical, spelling, or other types of mishaps before a presentation, during a presentation it is also essential that you remain sensitive to who your audience is. You also must have a level of content expertise and know your topic well enough to engage in conversation during question-and-answer periods.

Since telephone conversations figure most prominently among the conversations people engage in on a regular basis, as a district administrator it is imperative that you ensure that your phones are answered promptly or go to voicemail after four or five rings. Make certain that whoever in your office answers calls is courteous and practices appropriate phone etiquette. When answering the phone in a business environment, such as the district office, it is important that you offer a greeting and identify yourself; address the caller by name once it has been established; be cognizant of your tone of voice; and speak clearly and slowly when providing information such as mailing addresses, emails, or phone numbers. It is also important to the caller that you avoid any interruptions unless the matter is urgent; if you do need to put the caller on hold, make sure that the call does not get dropped. Lastly, at the end of calls, secure feedback from callers to establish that they were satisfied with your response; finish up with a friendly closure that not only leaves callers with a good impression but also lets them know that they can reach out to you in the future if needed.

If you have a secretary or an administrative assistant, make certain that phone messages are kept in a log so that you can respond to them immediately; in addition, keep a written log of callers' names, phone numbers, content of calls and responses, and the date calls were received and returned. See figure 10.5 for a sample log. This system is especially crucial when communicating with parents. For example, if your

WWW **FIGURE 10.5** Sample Phone Log

DATE OF CONTACT	TIME OF CONTACT	CALLER'S NAME	DISCUSSION	PHONE NUMBER	ACTION REQUESTED (E.G., RETURN CALL, WILL CALL BACK, WANTS A MEETING, WILL STOP BY)	COMMENTS

personal responsibilities require you to be out of the office frequently or you are attending a conference, your secretary can communicate with you on a regular basis during scheduled times or can electronically send your phone log at the end of the workday. All calls should be returned ideally within 24 hours and certainly within no more than 48 hours, unless extenuating circumstances prevail.

Written Communication

Written communication occurs in the form of emails, letters, reports, newsletters, and memoranda, among other types of documents. It is the most commonly used method of communication, the purpose being to convey information through what you put on paper or on a screen. Written communication, such as memoranda, requires an administrator to have good command of the English language, and documents should be checked for spelling and grammar before they are finalized. Written communication should focus on clarity, the use of appropriate language, and the style of business writing commonly used in your district. If the topic is difficult or sensitive, it is recommended that a proofreader look it over for contextual understanding and grammatical errors before it is sent up the channels. This could save a lot of time making revisions and could avoid embarrassment. Written communication is usually used when the information needs to be permanent, as would be the case with district policy, grant reports, or responses to external communications received by the district office. In instances when face-to-face encounters may be difficult, exchanging information in writing might be the most appropriate method.

Internal and External Communication

Most organizations have specific policies for *internal* and *external communication* that every administrator is expected to follow. This becomes increasingly critical if the communication deals with important district policies, specific employee professional standards situations, and other privacy issues. It is up to the administrator to have the integrity to ensure that any communication marked "For internal use only" or "Confidential" stay in-house unless otherwise directed by senior staff to send to a third party. At no time should internal communication be shared with anyone other than the intended recipients. Aside from direct email communication, memoranda are the most common form of internal communication, whereas letters are most commonly used for external communication. However, both memoranda and letters, once signed, can be transmitted electronically by email. The earlier method of interoffice communication involved creating massive numbers of paper copies sent through interoffice mail. Electronic transmittal provides the opportunity to receive the communication more expediently, provides evidence that the communication has been received by the appropriate recipient, is more ecologically sound, and is a huge cost-saving measure.

Internal Communication Internal communication occurs between and among people within your organization or school district for the purpose of sharing business-related information. Since internal communication is monitored by the school district, sending jokes or other inappropriate materials not related to the school district could have severe negative consequences. Internal communication can occur electronically, in print, face-to-face, within departmental office workspaces at the district office, or in school settings. The most common form of internal communication for policy and informational issues is the memorandum. Every organization has its own format for internal memoranda (memos), but in most cases it is similar to the one shown next. A memo should be one page, if possible, and never more than two pages. Memos most commonly use a format like the following:

- To:
- From:
- Subject:
- Date:
- [Body]
- Memorandum number:
- cc:
- Attachments:

The parts of the memo include the introduction or purpose; the body, which provides an explanation of the issue or problem; and the conclusion or closing segment, which requests

 **FIGURE 10.6** Sample Internal Memorandum

MEMORANDUM

DATE ___________________

SCHOOL YEAR/# ________

TO: Elementary school principals

FROM: Dr. YYY, supervisor, Office of Physical Education

SUBJECT: W.H.A.L.E. TALES WATER SAFETY PROGRAM AT XXX LOCAL POOL

XYZ Public Schools has partnered with the American Red Cross AND XXX Parks and Recreation Department to kick off the W.H.A.L.E. (Water Habits Are Learned Early) Tales water safety educational program. The purpose of this program is to ensure that children in grades K-5 adhere to the safety rules of participating in activities in and around water. Important water safety tips and lessons will be provided by community experts.

The program will take place at XXX Pool, Address, on Saturday, DATE, and Sunday, DATE, from 10:00 a.m. to 4:00 p.m. Discount coupons are currently being delivered to your school that will enable one child to enter free with each paid adult admission of $1.00. The $1.00 donation will provide snacks and a beverage to all in attendance at the event. Please deliver these coupons to every student at your school.

Thank you for your continued support as we desperately put forth efforts to reduce the number of actual and near drownings in our ABC community. If additional information is requested, please contact me at (XXX) XXX-XXXX.

YYY: abc (From: typist initials)

Attachment (possible flyer)

cc: Rank Order 1
Rank Order 2
Rank Order 3

a response from the reader and specifies a due date for the response. Figure 10.6 provides an example of an internal memo.

As a district-level administrator, it is extremely important that you follow district protocol in the chain of command. One of the first things senior-level administrators read after looking at the subject line is the carbon copy (cc) list. It is essential that after you decide who should be copied on the memo, the recipients be listed in rank order by title, with the person holding the highest title listed first. If more than one administrator on the cc list has the same title or rank, then the one you report to goes first and the others are listed in alphabetical order.

External Communication External communication occurs between someone within your organization or school district and a person or persons outside of the organization, such as parents, vendors, business and community members, or university professors. Using external communications for public relations is viewed positively because it connects the school district with the community and keeps people informed on what is happening within the school district. These notifications can occur by way of press releases, public or community bulletin boards, and newsletters sent home to parents, to name a few.

However, depending on the situation, such as when you are contacted by a parent or community member to address a particular situation, the best way to communicate is usually with a letter so that there will be a record of your response and it can be cataloged. As with any business letter, this type of formal communication should use the proper format, including the following components:

- *The heading:* Return address and date
- *The inside address:* Recipient information
- *The greeting:* A salutation (e.g., "Dear Ms. XXX," "Dear Dr. YYY,")
- *The body:* The content of the letter, beginning with why you are writing
- *The complimentary close:* A polite closing (e.g., "Sincerely," "Cordially,")
- *The signature line:* The sender's name and title, if appropriate

When the response letter is being sent on behalf of the school district for official school district business, it should be on the district's letterhead. Also, depending on the type of response and who the recipient is, it may at some point need to be approved and signed by a senior staff member. District letterhead should be used only for official school district business and not for personal correspondence unrelated to the district.

There are also situations in which someone outside of the community sends the district office an email that requires immediate action. Unlike a standard letter that has a return address or phone contact information, your response would have to be sent back via email as well. Figure 10.7 provides an example of a response to an email.

FIGURE 10.7 How to Respond to an Email Communication

Parent@XYZ.EDU

Ms. XXX

Email Address Line 1

Dear Ms. XXX:

I am responding to your recent correspondence regarding childhood obesity and the recommendation to increase the high school physical education graduation requirement. I applaud your efforts to address an issue that is negatively affecting young people in the nation. I share your concern about the obesity epidemic and its impact on both student health and academic achievement. You are to be commended for your work in this important area.

We are very proud of our physical education programs in ABC Public Schools and the difference the physical education teachers are making in helping students to adopt healthy lifestyles. We agree that all students should engage in daily physical education; however, with current budget restraints, it is not possible at this time to require all high school students to take four years of physical education. It is on our future radar, and both the superintendent and senior staff are supportive of your recommendation.

Thank you again for your interest in the students of ABC Public Schools. I wish you much success with your research projects and with your efforts to reduce childhood obesity.

Sincerely,

ABCDEF

Physical education supervisor

ABD:fd

L345

cc: Associate Superintendent 1
Associate Superintendent 2

Email and Social Media Communication

Email is the most common form of communication in the workplace. It's fast and easy to use, it quickly connects you with all of your stakeholders and contacts, and it serves as a storage site for tasks and information previously addressed. However, it is critical that administrators respect the power of this form of communication as a written record of their daily work and conversations with others. Email puts everything in writing, and those historical records can be accessed by districts and schools in the event of a need for their legal use. According to Romkema (2023, para. 2), the following 10 tips should be followed for effective email communication:

1. Be clear and specific! Keep them concise, short and to the point.
2. Be prompt and respond to important email. Even if you can't respond to the actual message immediately, at least let the person know you are in receipt of it.
3. Use the subject line to clearly state what your email is about. This will assist in sorting out and organizing emails in terms of importance.
4. Add important directional words to the subject line when an email needs special attention. Words like "response needed" or "urgent" assist in relaying what is expected and by when.
5. Be restrained about forwarding jokes and other non-work-related material. Keep work emails about work.
6. Include one main topic per email and limit the number of questions and requests. Although you may have numerous things to ask or say, keeping the email focused on one topic will ensure that all of your questions are answered.
7. Decide carefully who should be cc'd on email. Carefully decide whether to respond back to the sender or to all on the email.
8. If you have concerns and need clarification, pick up the phone. For clarification purposes, if there is a misunderstanding message in your email, it may be best to pick up the phone and call. Trying to resolve a conflict through emails is not advisable and the situation could worsen.
9. Minimize your use of ALL CAPS or bold to highlight words. These visual cues can often be misunderstood by some recipients.
10. Include an email "signature" on all of your emails. It is important to have a signature line with all of your contact information clearly and easily accessible.

Although it is a relatively new method of communicating official school business to persons both inside and outside of the school district, social media has become a widely accepted mode of electronic communication. As professionals, educational administrators spend more time in transit between work and home and at off-site meetings, and they need quick answers to questions. As with email, when used as a quick response mechanism, social media has become more common in all professional settings. As social media has become more commonplace in the general professional realm, the number of teacher and school social media accounts has increased. As communication continues to move from face-to-face interactions to technological platforms, people may lose the ability to interact effectively through human contact; people don't get a good sense of others' feelings, and body language and eye contact are missing.

However, these platforms allow administrators and teachers to share information with interested stakeholders, such as parents or guardians and funders, on a variety of activities and events. They also allow for the development of private groups so that only the people in those groups have access. When using social media, it is important to follow an ethical protocol, including keeping the posted information factual and not posting personal comments or judgmental statements or comments about students, colleagues, senior staff, or the school district that could be interpreted negatively.

Nonverbal Communication

Nonverbal communication is commonly used but often underestimated. It is characterized by the use of gestures, facial expressions, eye contact, body movements, sitting posture, other types of body language, and even an individual's proximity to another person when communicating. Because nonverbal communication involves expressing messages through gestures and body language, it can be more powerful than verbal or written communication. Communicating this way without words can send various signals at once. It is an equally important method of communication to using words, especially when the nonverbal signal indicates disinterest, boredom, or some type of discord.

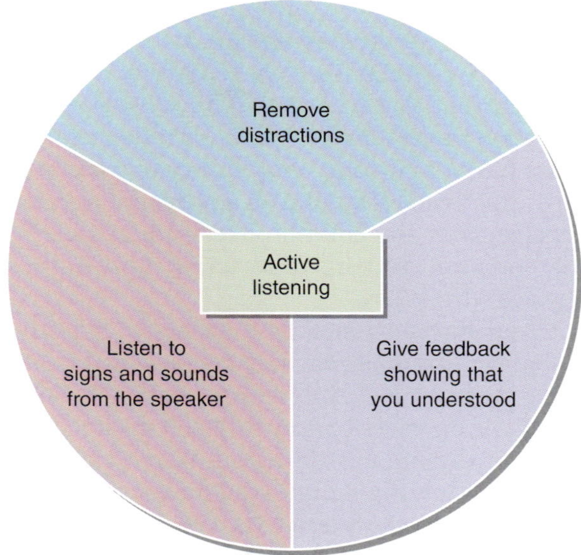

FIGURE 10.8 Active listening.

Active Listening

Communication, whether verbal or nonverbal, sets the tone of your interactions. As discussed in the previous sections, verbal communication is represented by your personal tone and voice; nonverbal communication, such as facial expressions, posture, eye contact, and gestures, also sends messages. Another essential component of both verbal and nonverbal communication is the need for the listener to block out any distractions and to focus on listening actively.

Active listening, popularized by the work of Carl Rogers and Richard Farson (1957), is another skill that is necessary in order for communication to be effective. It requires you as the listener to be fully focused on what the other person is saying and respond through the use of body language, such as eye contact, to convey to the speaker that you are listening. Asking questions and responding to what is being said by recapping the conversation also confirms that you have been paying attention. Active listening additionally involves understanding the other person's feelings and views without passing judgment (see figure 10.8).

According to Coursera.org (2023), these seven active listening techniques can help school administrators become more active listeners when listening for total meaning:

1. Focus on the intent and purpose of the conversation.
2. Pay attention to body language.
3. Give encouraging verbal cues.
4. Clarify and paraphrase information.
5. Ask questions.
6. Refrain from judgment.
7. Summarize, share, and reflect.

As an administrator, active listening gives you the opportunity to fully understand what the speaker is saying while ensuring that accurate information and ideas are being exchanged. This level of attention further ensures that there is no misunderstanding about what is being said and that feedback, whether verbal or nonverbal, is a part of the conversation. Active listening is also a key to overcoming barriers to effective communication.

Barriers to Effective Communication

In a perfect world, everyone would communicate in a civil manner with full understanding of and sensitivity to the feelings of both the sender and receiver. However, it is unfortunately not the reality, and there are times when communication breaks down. In the educational environment as well as other organizational settings, the complexity of each of these entities, coupled with a changing and diverse workplace, lends itself to occasional misunderstanding and misinterpretation of what is being communicated.

However, to work effectively toward goal attainment, strategies need to be put in place to assist in overcoming these barriers to communication. According to the University of Waterloo Centre for Teaching Excellence (n.d.), these barriers inhibit your ability to communicate effectively: focusing on a personal agenda, experiencing information overload, criticizing the speaker, getting distracted, and having physical difficulty.

Other barriers include barriers to effective verbal communication, such as lacking clarity, using stereotypes, and jumping to conclusions, as well as barriers to accurate perception, such as generalizing, assuming similar interpretations, and having a distorted focus.

Although these barriers are real, it's possible to overcome many of them by listening actively, using simple language for clarity, eliminating physical and emotional noise, giving constructive feedback, and learning how to be sensitive to cultural and linguistic differences.

Tying It Together for the Physical Education Administrator

Understanding the communication process is a skill that is required by every administrator at every level. For the physical education administrator, it is extremely important in that most of the job is spent communicating with a variety of stakeholders, including parents, community members, teachers, and senior staff. The type of communication will be contingent on each individual situation and setting.

When providing information to teachers, administrators need to know how to write an informational and persuasive memo or email so that the teacher understands what is requested or required. Providing teachers with technical support and assistance in implementing current national physical education standards and grade-span learning indicators can take the form of a written document with the essential supportive documents attached. Asking teachers to participate in events outside of their contractual workday is a difficult task, but relaying the importance of advocating for their programs needs to be a priority. Keep in mind that if you ask teachers to participate outside of school hours, the expectation is that you will be there as well. That commitment sends a very strong message of respect and support.

Verbal communication is another critical competence for all administrators in that presenting at meetings and conducting professional development sessions make up a large part of the job. Correlating communication skills with management skills (discussed in chapter 2) is essential to effective leaders and managers. When speaking on the phone or meeting with parents or guardians in your office, active listening is probably one of the most important skills to master. Although your first instinct may be that the teacher is right, you need to listen carefully to the parents' or guardians' perspective in order to make a valid decision on next steps. Parents and guardians want to be heard, and you need to be willing to listen and to be open-minded regarding the next steps. Irate parents or guardians leaving your office will require additional action on your part because they will go up the chain of command. Most issues can be resolved through good channels of effective communication.

The need to address a teacher who is going through the professional standards process for some type of negative behavior is another situation that requires both written and verbal communication. Because the teachers' union will usually be involved in this process, keep your immediate supervisor in the loop. In addition, you should work closely with your office of professional standards for proper wording of notifications because this type of communication could lead to litigious action. During the teacher meeting, it is critical that you keep your emotions in check and just give the teacher an opportunity to be heard. Since the written report will go in the teacher's permanent file, it would be advantageous to have staff in the office of professional standards review it before you call the teacher back in to sign it. The full investigation will for the most part take place outside of your office, and you may not know the results until the case has been closed.

On a more positive note, there are many new and exciting ways to use your communication skills when providing information to the public about the exceptional programs and activities that are occurring in physical education.

Knowing how to work with the community and secure recognition and publicity for your programs is discussed in the next section.

Public Relations

As with most organizations both large and small, public perception is critical in defining a school district's image in the community. Although the bottom line in an educational setting is student achievement and not generation of profits, **public relations** is important in securing funds for educational systems. Therefore, the superintendent, cabinet, office of communications, district-level administrators, school site administrators, and teachers all need to take a major role in promoting programs and opportunities for students, as well as in engaging in community activities and events, so that the general public is aware of the positive activities going on in their local schools. Schools *need* public support to achieve their goals and objectives, and the immediate community whose children attend the local schools wants to know what is going on. This effort in promotion is especially important when a public vote is scheduled to secure general obligation bonds.

According to Jensen and Overman (2003, pp. 152-153), the purpose of school public relations is to inform the public of the work and accomplishments of the school and school district; establish confidence in the schools; rally adequate support for educational programs; develop awareness of the importance of education; improve the partnership that should exist among the schools, the students, the parents or guardians, and other members of the public; and correct any misunderstanding regarding the aims and activities of the schools. The National School Public Relations Association (NSPRA, n.d., para. 1) further asserts that "educational public relations programs assist in interpreting public attitudes, identify and help shape policies and procedures in the public interest, and carry on involvement and information activities which earn public understanding and support."

Public relations efforts can occur between employees and departments within the school district or through external channels such as print and live media (television and radio) as well as verbal and written communication, interviews, speaking at public meetings, and the release of annual reports. The visibility of school district leadership is perhaps one of the best public relations tools, as leaders provide factual updates and make presentations at professional organization and community meetings such as those of the Chamber of Commerce and civic and Rotary clubs. They also give media interviews and speak to political and legislative entities, foundations and charitable organizations, and watchdog groups. Since members of these organizations do attend school board meetings, it is important to provide the public with pertinent information well in advance. The goal is to be *pro*active, not *re*active. Public relations efforts can also be supported through the use of social media since social media comments can be posted around the clock.

Engaging with local health and activity organizations is just as important for the physical education administrator in order to establish a public relations image as well as a coalition of support. These organizations would include local parks and recreation departments, hospitals, county and federally qualified health care providers and departments, Police Athletic League, YMCAs, and other community-based organizations. The following are some of the promotional activities the physical education administrator should participate in:

- Sharing the results of overall fitness assessments of the student population
- Taking part in open house activities and public demonstrations such as Jump Rope for Heart activities at a local mall
- Engaging teachers, schools, and students in community service activities such as assisting in community fitness events and 5K runs
- Developing web pages to host activities from schools across the district

For physical educators, conveying the importance of physical education in relation to the health, fitness, and academic performance of students, and showcasing how your programs are meeting the standards and the needs of youth, will further lead to community support and potential outside funding for your programs. Having a solid public relations and marketing plan will provide significant support for your programs. With such a plan available, you can share your district's program successes more readily to garner community and administrative support. Since district-level public relations and marketing plans require senior staff approval, it is highly recommended that meetings occur on a regular basis with your chief communications officer or the office of communications and public relations staff to help you develop your plan and to guide you through the district process. A good rule of thumb is to engage their assistance, support, and approval before conducting any public media events.

Communicating With the Media

In most school districts, large and small, staff in the office of communications are usually charged with notifying the media about special events, developing the press releases, and being spokespersons for the school district to address both positive and negative incidents. Maintaining a positive and transparent relationship with the local media reflects positively on your programs.

As the district physical education administrator, on occasion you will receive calls from the local media to get your opinion on a national physical education announcement or to discuss highlighting one of your programs. As tempting as it would be to proceed immediately with the interview, the correct protocol would be to contact staff in the office of communications to get permission and to inform them of the context of the requested interview. Although agreeing to such an interview may seem harmless, there could be unintended negative consequences that are not immediately apparent. Administrators in the office of communications will converse with you and guide you through the process. If it is the first time you are doing an interview, or if you think that it might touch on something controversial, it would be appropriate for you to ask your district personnel to be on the phone with you during the interview. Not only would the district staff appreciate being part of the conversation, they also could intervene if the conversation does not go as planned, which would save you from having to clean up any unforeseen issues later.

Developing a Public Service Announcement (PSA)

Another opportunity that the media could assist you with is the development of public service announcements (PSAs). PSAs are messages that are developed in collaboration with the media and serve to disseminate information free of charge. All media outlets need a certain number of PSAs released annually, so plan ahead in working with your district staff to take advantage of the opportunity. Some of the most recent PSAs that have attracted local and national attention have dealt with obesity, smoking, and texting while driving as national health concerns. Since PSAs are on air for only a short time (usually 30 seconds), your message should be concise, have a narrow focus, and have impact. Because PSAs are topic specific, the district physical education administrator can provide content information to the communications director, but the office of communications would prepare the PSA itself. Once it is approved by all appropriate offices and the administrative chain of command, the PSA is released to the media outlet.

Developing a Press Release

A press release is essentially an official announcement to the news media for the purpose of getting media attention regarding specific issues, programs, or events. The ability to develop a press release will garner additional public support for your program.

According to James (2010), developing a well-written press release is the most cost-effective, quickest, and easiest way to get free publicity for your program. Since reporters receive many press releases on a daily basis for community-based organizations, universities, and school district and sports clubs, many of them go unread, leaving programs unrecognized. To ensure that a press release catches the eye of the reporter, James provides these five rules to increase the odds of the press actually making contact with you:

- Rule #1: Use the press release as a sales tool. Communicate an inviting message.

- Rule #2: Have a newsworthy story.
- Rule #3: Write it like a reporter would write it. Stick to the facts without any jargon.
- Rule #4: Provide some good quotes.
- Rule #5: Contact your top outlets personally.

As a school district administrator, you will have help from the staff in the office of communications in developing the press release and in sending it out to various media markets. Usually school districts have a protocol regarding how to interact with the media, and it would be advantageous to become knowledgeable about the process, policy, and procedure. Your first draft will usually answer the *who, what, when, where,* and *why* questions. Then the narrative is developed from the factual information provided. The essential points included in a press release, which should be no longer than one page, are as follows:

1. *The headline*: The wording should be strong enough to grab attention.
2. *The summary*: This section should be between one and four sentences.
3. *The lead paragraph*: This paragraph provides concise information about the event.
4. *The body*: In this section, you tell your story.
5. *Boilerplate*: This section provides information about your organization.
6. *Contact information*: This section provides information about whom to contact for additional details.

In formatting the press release, the top line should read "FOR IMMEDIATE RELEASE" with the date below it, and the text should be written in terms that average readers would understand. Technical terms may be a bit confusing for the person making the decision as to whether your event is newsworthy. For accepted media events, a staff member from the office of communications is usually on hand to meet with the on-site reporter and photographer prior to the start of the event. This pre-event conversation will give you an opportunity to very briefly explain the run of show and a bit more about the project or program receiving the press. Figure 10.9 is an example of a press release from the U.S. Department of Health and Human Services (HHS) announcing the Physical Activity Guidelines for Americans Midcourse Report: Implementation Strategies for Older Adults.

Advocacy

In the context of administration in physical education, **advocacy** is a way of getting public support for a particular cause or policy to bring about systemic change. Physical educators have had a long history of advocating for everything from funding programs to mandating minutes of instructional time during the school day. To be a good advocate, you must be knowledgeable on what you are trying to educate decision makers about, be able to build and secure a strong base of support, and be willing to mobilize people to support the cause. For many years, SHAPE America, as the nation's top organization for health and physical educators, has led the charge in advocating for health and physical education as well as helped states and districts through the development of tools to assist and train those ready to become advocates. The organization's website contains valuable information for physical educators and administrators who want to learn about advocacy; see www.shapeamerica.org/advocacy/default.aspx.

Advocacy Versus Lobbying

As an administrator at the district level, it is paramount for you to understand the difference between advocacy and lobbying, because advocating for your programs may be permissible, whereas **lobbying** in an official capacity may be against your district's policies. Although at the grassroots level it may be difficult to differentiate between the two, there are very distinct differences.

Advocacy usually involves educating policymakers or the public about the impact of a policy or legislation on your area of interest, such as physical education and health education programs; lobbying, on the other hand, is an attempt to influence a politician on a particular piece of legislation. When participating in advocacy, you may be educating your audience about your programs, how they affect students,

FIGURE 10.9 Sample Press Release

FOR IMMEDIATE RELEASE

June 27, 2023

Contact: HHS Press Office

202-690-6343

media@hhs.gov

HHS Releases Physical Activity Guidelines for Americans Midcourse Report: Implementation Strategies for Older Adults

Report will share evidence-based strategies for increasing physical activity among older adults.

Today, the U.S. Department of Health and Human Services (HHS) released a report showcasing evidence-based interventions to support physical activity among adults ages 65 years and older.

By the year 2030, one in every five Americans will be age 65 or over. More than 85 percent of older adults currently have at least one chronic health condition. The growing population of older adults can gain substantial health benefits and prevent or manage chronic disease by engaging in physical activity.

The *Physical Activity Guidelines for Americans Midcourse Report: Implementation Strategies for Older Adults* extends the work of the *Physical Activity Guidelines for Americans, Second Edition* and provides details on how to help older adults achieve the recommended 150 minutes or more of moderate-intensity aerobic physical activity and two days of muscle-strengthening physical activity each week.

"The immediate and long-term health benefits of engaging in regular physical activity are well documented. This is why it is so important for all Americans, including older Americans, to stay physically active," said HHS Secretary Xavier Becerra. "The Biden-Harris administration is committed to improving the health of all Americans, no matter their age. This report will help us support older adults in living physically active lives."

The *Physical Activity Guidelines for Americans, Second Edition*, which serves as the primary, authoritative voice of the federal government for evidence-based guidance on physical activity, fitness, and health for Americans, is reviewed by experts every five years to evaluate a specific topic of importance. This iteration focuses on adults aged 65 and older.

"The mindset that physical activity is an individual responsibility is shifting, and progress to ensuring all Americans have the opportunity to be physically active requires a united effort. Everyone has a role to play," said Admiral Rachel Levine, M.D., Assistant Secretary for Health. "The *Midcourse Report* lays the foundation for a coordinated and cross-sectoral approach to make being active the easy and enjoyable choice for older adults."

The *Midcourse Report* identifies strategies that policymakers; exercise and health professionals; clinicians; gerontologists; built environment professionals; local, state, territorial, and Tribal leaders; and others working with older adults can use in key settings to increase physical activity. It reinforces the message that physical activity can begin or restart at any age. Collaboration among these professionals is key to planning and implementing these strategies to connect older adults with safe opportunities to be physically active.

You can read the full *Midcourse Report* at Health.gov. For more information on the Guidelines and supporting materials, please visit https://health.gov/our-work/nutrition-physical-activity/physical-activity-guidelines.

Move Your Way resources for providers and older adults are also available to support the activities listed in the *Midcourse Report*. Move Your Way is the promotional campaign for the Guidelines.

The HHS Office of Disease Prevention and Health Promotion encourages all Americans to lead healthy and active lives. We accomplish this by establishing and promoting national public health priorities; translating science into policy, guidance, and tools; and working to improve health literacy and equitable access to clear and actionable health information.

U.S. Department of Health and Human Services

---

and why they are important; you may even be asking for general support for your work, teachers, and programs. When you are asking policymakers or the public to support or oppose a specific piece of legislation or policy, the activity becomes lobbying.

The two types of lobbying are direct lobbying and grassroots lobbying. *Direct lobbying* involves direct communication with a member of the legislative body, their staff, or another government official who has a say in the legislation, with the intent of influencing specific legislation at the local, state, or federal level. *Grassroots lobbying* involves asking the general public to take action on a specific policy or legislation, and it encourages people to contact their legislator in mobilizing around an issue (Internal Revenue Service, 2016).

There is no limit to the number of advocacy efforts you can participate in, and teachers usually have a bit more latitude as long as any political activity is conducted outside of the normal contractually negotiated work hours. However, as an administrator, there may be some restrictions you might want to seek clarification on before engaging in such activities.

Advocating for the Profession

In an administrator's daily work, issues regularly come to light that will require the need to advocate for funding, for appropriate class sizes, for facilities, or for additional staffing. It is essential that leaders know every facet of the deficiencies they are fighting or of the successes they are promoting in their program and then prepare their pitch with the right message for the right audience (see figure 10.10). The circumstances under which an administrator advocates may be planned or frequently encountered situations, but often they emerge spontaneously. It is always good practice to have your finger on the pulse of the issues at all times. It's also helpful to script speeches and practice delivering them with someone in person. Advocacy should become a consistent part of your daily practice so that when a specific call to action arises, you have already built relationships with key stakeholders and garnered necessary support for your cause.

Target Audiences

It is important to note that there is no limit on who our audiences are. Promoting the health and wellness of children in a school setting means that everyone is a stakeholder. Often, however, key stakeholders are physical education teachers, administrative colleagues or principals, superintendents, boards of education, state departments of education, legislators, parents, and students. When advocating for the profession, you will not always get what you are asking for right away. Not getting to the goal in the first interaction is not a failure. A win comes when you are regularly moving someone forward, engaging the person in conversation, and getting them to listen to your point of view. See it as a long-term undertaking. Promoting your needs is about moving your target audience along the advocacy continuum (figure 10.11). You first need to know where they are on the continuum; for example, are they already supporting you (champion), or are they completely against you (opponent)? Every time you interact with them, your goal should be to move them one step further along on the continuum.

Strategies for Success

One strategy that has proven successful among administrators is promoting the great things that are happening with the program and staff when things are going well and spreading the good news about those events and accomplishments. If you wait for an emergency, such as the cutting of teachers or losing funds, it appears to decision makers that you are reacting to a single crisis. Rather, you should be educating

LEADERSHIP IN ACTION

Advocacy in Physical Education

Mario Reyna

Director, Society for Health and Physical Educators (SHAPE America) Southern District

After 40 years in the field of health and physical education, including 20 years in administration, when asked, "What are the major factors affecting our profession?" I rate the lack of advocacy at the top. Education is valued by standardized testing in the core subjects, with fitness testing and social-emotional learning at the bottom of accountability. It is not uncommon that fitness scores are not valued to the same level of core subject results. Health and physical education coordinators play a vital role in providing leadership in the field of health and physical education. Besides standardized testing, additional challenges include budget cuts and reductions in minutes of physical education.

I have realized that strong public relations and marketing of my physical education programs has led to a culture of wellness in McAllen ISD and our community. A nonnegotiable factor for me is that sharing success stories through advocacy should be mandatory for all physical education leaders. The secret to a successful advocacy plan is to begin with proclamations from the board of trustees. Such proclamations bring buy-in by key decision makers such as the board of trustees, superintendent, and central office administrators. Once you have this group on your side, even reluctant principals will follow. Because of strong advocacy, our physical education programs have attained state and national recognition, which creates a culture where the community wants to be part of our program. Committee members included district leaders, city leaders, and local media. In our first pep rally, approximately 5,000 students and parents attended. This event is now an annual pep rally that brings everyone together in the fight against childhood obesity.

It all begins with a decision to make a change. Start at the top; get buy-in from key stakeholders, and go from there. Your students will be the beneficiaries.

FIGURE 10.10 Prepare Your Pitch

To develop the right message for the right audience, ask the following questions:

- What do you want or need to advocate for right now?
- Who is your target audience?
- Why is it important to advocate for this cause?
- What is your risk?
- When will you follow up?

From *Physical Activity Leader Training Guide,* SHAPE America.

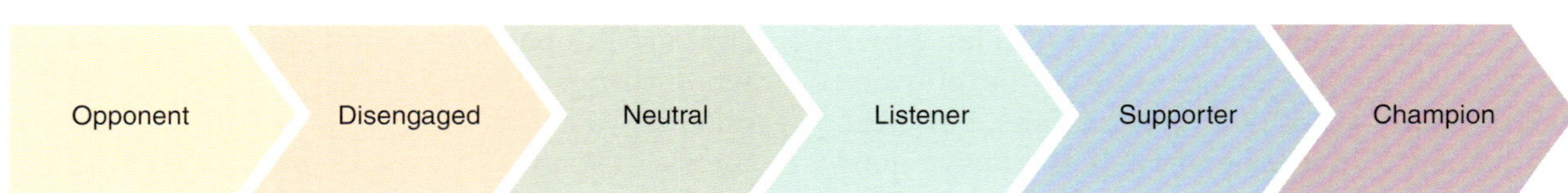

FIGURE 10.11 The advocacy continuum.

them regularly about the reasons any potential future cuts in funding or staffing are detrimental to students and about the benefits that your programs provide to the entire school community.

In addition, empowering physical education teachers to be advocates or teacher leaders is an essential strategy in supporting your district's students. It is the staff in the classroom and gymnasium that can make the best case for why physical education is essential because they have a front-row seat as to its impact on the daily lives of the children they serve. Successful administrators must set the tone for that leadership among the teachers they supervise. Figure 10.12 provides some strategies for successful advocacy efforts.

Advocacy at the State or Federal Level

In 2015, Congress passed the education law known as the **Every Student Succeeds Act (ESSA)**. This law identifies school health and physical education as part of a student's **well-rounded education** along with other subjects such as art, music, civics, and science (Jones & Workman, 2016). The passage of this law marks the first time physical education was placed on a level playing field with other subject areas, due to many years of advocacy at the national level. This federal education legislation provides increased access to funds for physical education programs, and it allows states and school districts to set their own priorities for funding and accountability. The physical education administrator has an important role in knowing the intricacies of the law, the details of local allocations at the state level, and where to advocate locally for funding to support the physical education program.

Under the ESSA, all 50 states and the District of Columbia have been required to develop their own plans for accountability and implementation. This requirement means that physical educators in every state must advocate within their own education system to help influence the changes they hope to see.

Members of Congress have an obligation to their constituents to act on issues that are important to them. Regular communication with your elected officials is essential in keeping physical education on the minds of legislators. Throughout the year, members of Congress return home from Washington, DC, to their state and district offices to meet with constituents about key issues in their state. When members of Congress know that their constituents care about physical education, they vote accordingly.

Understanding the ESSA to Advocate for Funding

The ESSA is composed of separate programs, called Titles, which have significance for the physical education profession. Understanding these funding streams can assist administrators in planning their communication and advocacy plan for their local needs. The most significant parts of the law that affect physical education are Titles I, II, and IV.

Title I provides financial assistance to local educational agencies (LEAs) and schools with high numbers or high percentages of children from low-income families to help ensure that all children meet challenging state academic standards. Schools enrolling at least 40 percent of children from low-income families are eligible to use Title I funds for school-wide programs designed to upgrade their entire educational program to improve achievement for all students, particularly the lowest-achieving students. Title I schools with less than the 40 percent school-wide threshold or those that choose not to operate a school-wide program can

FIGURE 10.12 Successful Advocacy Strategies

Be knowledgeable about your content and its impact on students' health, growth, academic achievement, and self-confidence.

Be brave. Have the moral courage to speak in front of a crowd, at a board meeting, or to an administrative colleague in a stairwell.

Know your audience and what their specific needs are, and speak to how their profession fulfills those needs (for example, a principal at the elementary level may have an annual goal of decreasing chronic absenteeism).

offer so-called targeted assistance programs, in which the school identifies students who are failing, or most at risk of failing, to meet the state's challenging academic achievement standards. Physical education leaders can build a case for programming around meeting state physical education standards of instruction in these specific schools in order to provide students with a well-rounded education.

Title II funds increase student academic achievement through strategies such as improving the quality and effectiveness of teachers, principals, and other school leaders and increasing the number of teachers, principals, and other school leaders who are effective at improving student academic achievement in schools.

These funds must be spent on evidence-based instructional practices, and they are meant to support teacher and principal recruitment and leadership. Title II funds can also be allocated for resources that have an impact on reduction of class size. Professional development for physical educators is covered under Title II, and local physical education administrators should be advocating for this funding in order to plan for in-service programs and attendance at local, regional, and national physical education conferences.

Title IV is the most significant part of ESSA for physical education. In *Part A of Title IV*, the law authorizes activities in these three broad areas:

1. Providing students with a well-rounded education (e.g., counseling, STEM, music and arts, civics, International Baccalaureate [IB] and Advanced Placement [AP], health, physical education)
2. Supporting safe and healthy students (e.g., mental health, drug and violence prevention, training on trauma-informed practices, health and physical education)
3. Supporting the effective use of technology (e.g., professional development, blended learning, and purchase of devices)

Title IV, Part B provides funding for after-school and summer programs for low-income schools, including programs that focus on nutrition and physical activity with an emphasis on partnering with community organizations to deliver this programming to students. Advocacy on the federal level is essential in helping to keep up support at the national level for physical education so that Congress supports the funding necessary to benefit the most states, schools, and physical education programs possible. For more information on the ESSA, visit the U.S. Department of Education web page at www2.ed.gov/policy/elsec/leg/essa/index.html.

Meetings With Stakeholders

When meeting with stakeholders in your work as an administrator, it is important to strategize the message and be specific about what you are asking for. Prior to any meeting, be sure to put together a team, decide who should be at the meeting, identify the decision maker you should be meeting with, and come up with talking points that are audience specific. Most important, if you have a specific idea or concept you will be asking support for, be prepared to come with a possible solution.

The following are some recommended steps that you should take when meeting with decision makers. The more prepared you are, the more positive the outcome will be.

1. Introduce yourself and each meeting attendee, offer credentials, and exchange business cards.
2. Share the importance and the benefits of health and physical education programs to students—health, academic achievement, behavior, and so on.
3. Share personal stories about health and physical education from your state or school district or school. Use local or state-specific information or data to personalize the messaging.
4. Share highlights of the ESSA. Health and physical education are included in the definition of a well-rounded education, which makes your content area eligible for Title I, Title II, and Title IV funding and support.
5. Be knowledgeable about Title IV, Part A funding. States, school districts, and schools can use this funding to support well-rounded education, safe and healthy student programs, and effective uses of

technology—all of which encompass physical education. It's critical to advocate for appropriation of funds for Title IV, Part A at the federal level, physical education as a funding priority at the state level, and spending of funds on physical education at the school district and school level.

6. Make specific asks for decision makers to support physical education.
7. Close the meeting, thank stakeholders, and offer to follow up.

Conclusion

The ability to effectively communicate is a key skill that is critical at every level of administration. Communication can be viewed as the transmission of information or ideas from one person to another. This chapter has referred to several models to explain how information is received and understood. For the physical education administrator, understanding the flow and the direction in which communication travels, whether vertically or horizontally, is beneficial for understanding the types of communication that occur within the school district at each level as well as the types of internal and external communications.

Effective communication can be verbal, written, or nonverbal, and being sensitive to the information trail will assist in ensuring understanding of messages sent. However, regardless of the mode of communication, both the sender and receiver should be courteous, concise, and equally attentive as listeners and speakers. Becoming skillful in active listening will also allow you to be empathetic to the needs of others while addressing situations that could be negative in nature.

The physical education administrator as an effective communicator has the responsibility of putting those skills to use through communication with teachers, parents, community members, policymakers, and senior staff. Maintaining good community public relations will inform the community of the strengths of your programs as well as the opportunities their children have when they enroll in physical education. Promoting both the health and academic benefits of regular physical activity is critical for wide support. Becoming an advocate for physical education and knowing how to promote physical education through cause-driven action or education legislation are advantageous in securing local support. Administrators should also be knowledgeable about ways to secure state and federal support.

Review Questions

1. What are the essential components of effective communication?
2. Describe the directionality in communication and when it is used.
3. Differentiate between internal and external communication.
4. Explain the differences between advocacy and lobbying.
5. Describe the relationship between public relations and program funding.
6. What is the importance of the fact that the ESSA covers physical education?

» Visit HK*Propel* for reproducible forms.

CHAPTER 11

Legal Issues and Loss Prevention in Physical Education

John O. Spengler and Jayne D. Greenberg

webdata/fotolia.com

LEARNING OBJECTIVES

After reading this chapter, you will be able to do the following:

- Explain the applicability of constitutional law to physical education practice.
- Describe the manner in which federal and state legislation influence physical education policies and procedures.
- Identify loss-prevention strategies designed to avoid or prevent injury or liability in physical education programs.
- Understand laws intended to prevent harassment and bullying in a physical education setting.
- Identify supervisory and instructional practices specific to teacher and student behaviors that might give rise to liability.
- Understand the elements of negligence in the context of liability in physical education.

KEY CONCEPTS

bullying
gender issues
harassment
liability
mitigation
negligence
sexual harassment
sovereign immunity
statutory law

A critical aspect of any administrative position is familiarity with legal issues that guide the actions of educational leaders and staff. This chapter provides an overview of legal issues in physical education instruction and supervision. The issues addressed in this chapter will serve as a starting point in understanding professional educational responsibilities, behaviors, and practices in light of liability and loss prevention. The laws of each state differ to some degree; in legal matters, they often determine the outcome of legal disputes.

As a practical matter, most schools or school districts have loss-prevention policies and procedures that specify obtaining the advice of qualified legal counsel, and prudent physical education administrators follow those guidelines. This chapter is not intended to provide legal advice, because only an attorney licensed to practice law in your state can provide that level of consultation. Instead, it provides an overview of legal issues relevant to physical education, and it acts as a starting point to understanding the legal responsibilities of educators and educational administrators.

Constitutional Law

Laws that affect the daily work of physical education administrators and teachers come from a variety of sources. This section examines how the Bill of Rights provides for individual freedoms and how statutes, case law, and administrative rulings affect education in general and physical education in particular.

As you begin to understand how the U.S. legal system affects educational policy and the basic rights of all citizens, it is important to understand the rights that all individuals have under the law. The first 10 amendments to the U.S. Constitution are called the Bill of Rights. The Bill of Rights, by ensuring a variety of rights to individuals, circumscribes how school employees and districts may address certain types of student behavior. It begins with the 1st amendment concerning freedom of speech and of religion.

First Amendment: Freedom of Speech for Teachers

Two important and sometimes conflicting constitutional rights are the right to express an opinion and the right to believe and worship as you please. These two 1st amendment rights are central to the political and social structure of the United States. The first part of the 1st amendment declares, "Congress shall make no law respecting an establishment of religion, or prohibiting the free exercise thereof" (U.S. Const. amend. I).

This rather simple and important amendment has two significant aspects:

1. The government cannot embrace or establish a specific religion. This aspect has been further expanded to mean that there must be a separation between church and state.
2. The government cannot interfere with a person's practice of religious beliefs. This aspect is generally referred to as the free exercise part of the 1st amendment.

The second part of the 1st amendment adds, "Congress shall make no law . . . abridging the freedom of speech or of the press . . ." (U.S. Const. amend. I). Freedom of speech is synonymous with freedom of expression. One may express personal opinions about policy, political figures, and so forth, without breaking a federal or state law.

The courts have determined that people's freedom to say whatever they wish has some limitations. Expressing damaging and inaccurate information (defamatory statements) about another, advocating the violent overthrow of government, and shouting "Fire!" in a crowded theater certainly run counter to good order in society. There must be some reasonable limits to the right to express oneself.

Teachers, like everyone else, possess fundamental rights. These rights include freedom from discrimination, freedom of speech, and academic freedom, albeit with reasonable limitations. The issue of teachers' free speech rights has been historically debated, particularly under the 1st amendment of the U.S. Constitution, which safeguards free speech for all citizens, including educators. However, as public employees, teachers' speech rights within educational settings are not absolute (Findlaw.com, 2024).

In the 1969 landmark case *Tinker v. Des Moines* (U.S. Courts, 1969), the Supreme Court ruled that students retain their constitutional rights while in school; however, school authorities can restrict speech that disrupts learning or violates the rights of others. This principle also applies to teachers, significantly shaping education law.

When fulfilling their responsibilities in the classroom, teachers must consider the age, maturity, and grade level of their students. Courts use these factors to determine the extent of academic freedom teachers should enjoy. Additionally, school administrators bear the responsibility of maintaining an effective, respectful, and inclusive learning environment.

Fourth Amendment: Searches, Seizures, and Locker Privacy

Sometimes it is necessary to search a student or to search a student's locker or property. Such searches can and do prevent senseless tragedies. However, the 4th amendment to the U.S. Constitution provides freedom from unreasonable search and seizure. While there is more latitude to search on school property and at school-related functions in order to protect the safety of students, determining whether or not a search is permissible is often difficult. Questions often arise in determining where to draw the line between a search that is reasonable and a search that is not reasonable.

In the case of *New Jersey v. T.L.O.* (U.S. Courts, 1985), the U.S. Supreme Court ruled that the 4th amendment does apply to students in public schools. The court also ruled that warrants are not needed in school searches but that a search must be based on reasonable suspicion. The court went on to establish this two-pronged test by which to determine whether a public school search satisfies the standard of reasonable suspicion:

1. *The search is justified at its inception*; in other words, there are reasonable grounds for suspecting that the search will reveal evidence that the student has violated or is violating the law or school rules.
2. *The search is reasonably related in scope to the circumstances that justified the search*; in other words, the measures used to conduct the search are reasonably related to the objectives of the search and that the search is not excessively intrusive in light of the student's age and sex and the nature of the offense.

The first prong of the test appears relatively straightforward. Those conducting the search must have reasonable suspicion at the time the search begins. If there is no reasonable suspicion at the time the search begins, the search is not permissible whether or not the search reveals drugs, weapons, or other contraband. The more difficult question is What are *reasonable grounds* for suspecting that the evidence will reveal the student has violated or is violating the law or school rules? The cases that have construed this question offer some guidance, but each is very fact specific. The following facts have all been found to constitute reasonable suspicion to justify a search by school officials:

- A report by two students to school personnel that a third student possessed a gun: *Commonwealth v. Carey* (1990)
- A search of a student's property for stolen property when searches of the property of the remaining students in the classroom did not disclose the stolen property: *DesRoches v. Caprio* (1997)
- An experienced drug counselor's observation of a student with dilated pupils who appeared distracted, warranting a blood test: *Bridgeman v. New Trier H.S. District No. 203* (1997)
- An anonymous call that a student would be bringing drugs to school coupled with the reputation of that student as a drug dealer: *State of New Hampshire v. Drake* (1995)

On the other hand, in the following examples, facts have been ruled insufficient to support a reasonable suspicion to search:

- The smell of marijuana in a school hallway is not enough to search all handbags and pockets of students in the hallway; see *Burnham v. West* (1987).
- Four students together, one with money in hand, one with a hand in a pocket, will not justify a search; see *A.S. v. State of Florida* (1997).

The California courts have used the phrase *articulable facts* as necessary to support a search. It is a helpful test. You must be able to explain what, in particular, about the situation gives you a reason to believe there is a need to search.

The cases referenced all searches of concern by school officials. Searches by police or law enforcement personnel require probable cause, a higher standard, or a warrant. Additionally, any search must be conducted carefully. School officials should not conduct a search without another school official present. Additionally, while a search may be impermissible from the perspective of possible criminal consequences, the search may be permissible both for school disciplinary purposes (e.g., suspension) and for the safety of the school. If in doubt, it is best to contact local law enforcement for guidance or the attorney associated with the local school district, if one is available.

Fifth Amendment: Due Process

The 5th amendment addresses due process more broadly as well as the right not to incriminate oneself. It means that it is the responsibility of the government to prove its case, and a criminal defendant has no obligation to provide information. The 5th amendment provides the following:

> *No person shall be held to answer for a capital, or otherwise infamous crime, unless on a presentment or indictment of a Grand Jury, except in cases arising in the land or naval forces, or in the Militia, when in actual service in time of War or public danger; nor shall any person be subject for the same offence to be twice put in jeopardy of life or limb; nor shall be compelled in any criminal case to be a witness against himself, nor be deprived of life, liberty, or property, without due process of law; nor shall private property be taken for public use, without just compensation (U.S. Const. amend. V).*

Most Americans are familiar with the result of *Miranda v. Arizona* (Justia, 1966); it is from this case that the reading of Miranda rights originated. You are likely familiar with television shows, where prior to questioning suspects, the police or another government interrogator reads the suspects their rights so they know they have a right to remain silent and that anything said may be used in court against them. This warning reflects the 5th amendment safeguard against self-incrimination, and the right to due process.

In the school setting, however, there are circumstances in which Miranda warnings to students are not required. Supreme Court cases such as *J.D.B. v. North Carolina* (2011), *Roper v. Simmons* (2005), and *Graham v. Florida* (2010), have held that factors such as the student's age, the student's mental or emotional frame of mind, whether the student is in police or school custody, and whether the student is assisting law enforcement are considerations in whether Miranda warnings are required. However, some states require due process Miranda warnings for all students. It should be remembered that, as a general rule, there are fewer safeguards for students facing school district disciplinary consequences than for those facing judicial consequences.

Tenth Amendment: State's Authority for Public Education

The 10th amendment to the U.S. Constitution "reserves to the States, or to the people, any powers not delegated to the United States" (U.S. Const. amend. X). Since education is not a power delegated to the United States, each state controls its own system of public education. However, each state's system of education must be in accord with the remainder of the U.S. Constitution, and to the extent that receipt of federal funds may be involved, programs must be implemented in accordance with any federal funding requirements. Therefore, the 10th amendment, by exclusion, provides each state has the authority to establish, and has established, its own system of public schools.

Statutory Law

In addition to constitutional law, **statutory laws** (laws that are enacted by a state or federal legislative body) have an important bearing on the work of physical education teachers and administrators. Statutes play a role in determining the parameters in which a particular educational program may operate, and they may serve to clarify liability for schools.

Federal statutes relevant to education are found in the U.S. Code, while state statutes are contained in individual state codes. Additionally, local units of government, including counties, municipalities, and local boards of education, may have the authority in some states to regulate education or certain aspects of education. Local laws, rules, and regulations have a variety of names, such as *codes*, *ordinances*, *resolutions*, and *board policy*.

The federal government and each state have one or more agencies responsible for administering public education. For the federal government, it is the U.S. Department of Education. Both the U.S. Department of Education and each state education agency have the authority to promulgate rules or regulations. Federal regulations appear in the Code of Federal Regulations, frequently referred to as the C.F.R.

In some states, regulations are adopted by an administrative agency, such as a department of education; in others, regulations are adopted by a state board of education or other entities with a mission that is relevant to education. These regulations, or codes, regulate certain activities and procedures in public education, and they are often codified in state statutes. For example, Florida's law on physical education (Florida State Statute 1003.455) provides the parameters in which a particular educational program may operate. The law requires 150 minutes of physical education each week for students in grades K through 5. A minimum of 30 consecutive minutes is required on any day physical education instruction is provided. Some state statutes might serve other functions, such as clarifying liability or placing limitations on liability for schools.

Case Law

When someone brings a lawsuit, it may result in a trial and, in some cases, an appeal from the decision in the trial court. This situation can happen in both federal and state courts. When the case is finalized, it is then published and is available to the public. Published cases, also called published decisions, may then act as precedent for future cases, where future decisions rely on the findings and holdings of prior cases (court decisions).

Most cases don't make it past settlement, or trial (entry-level) court, and therefore don't result in published decisions. Prior to trial, information is gathered (a process called discovery) and settlements are negotiated; depending on the type of case, certain governmental action may be involved. For example, in special education cases, which are largely determined by federal law due to issues of disability, a local state administrative agency may first hold a hearing, the outcome of which may result in an appeal to federal district court. Each state has one or more federal district courts. If one side is not satisfied with the outcome, the case may go from there to the federal court of appeals. The final recourse for appeal is the U.S. Supreme Court, which is very selective about the cases it chooses to hear. The flowchart in figure 11.1 illustrates an example of the special education case law appeals process.

Each state has a similar appeal structure, starting with the trial courts, leading to the state courts of appeal, and ultimately and in rare cases, ending up in the U.S. Supreme Court. In every case, the decision of the court is binding on the litigants in that case. As mentioned earlier, cases decided upon by appellate court judges result in published decisions that often have precedent setting value and create the law on particular issues. However, it is important to know that the laws of various states often differ, therefore case law often has precedent setting value for its jurisdiction. Additionally, the law of one county or judicial circuit may not be binding on a different county or judicial circuit. However, a court may still look to a decision from another jurisdiction; one court

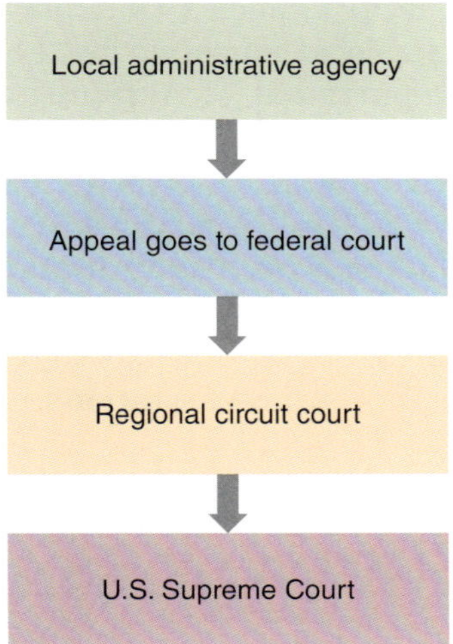

FIGURE 11.1 Special education case law appeals process.

may be interested in learning what decision another court reached on a similar set of facts and why the other court reached that decision.

Case law is important to physical education administrators because it serves as a basis for informing programmatic issues and expected behaviors of physical education teachers and it informs those teachers who need assistance. In the case of special education, for example, many physical education teachers may not be familiar with the legal requirements of implementing a quality physical education program for students with disabilities who are enrolled either in an adapted physical education class or in an inclusive physical education class, as outlined by statute (the Individuals with Disabilities Education Act [IDEA]; see chapter 5). The provisions of this statute, and many others, are further defined by case law. It is through the facts and holdings of legal cases that administrators can better inform teachers of the requirements of the legislation through professional development opportunities designed to address individual student activity needs.

Administrative Rulings

In some states, cases are decided through an administrative decision-making process. Administrative rulings or regulations differ from case law in that case laws are established by the courts through judicial rulings, whereas administrative rulings are concerned with the enactment and enforcement of the rules.

Finally, there are a number of other federal, state, and local agencies that play a role in administering local education law. For example, the U.S. Department of Agriculture (USDA) implements the school lunch program. Other agencies have authority over the execution of building codes, fire inspections, health codes, and local law enforcement. All play a role in various aspects of school administration, and each has rules and regulations that need to be followed in appropriate situations.

Liability in Physical Education

A primary responsibility of a physical education administrator is to ensure that programs and teachers stay within the laws that govern the rights of all students enrolled in physical education and that the programs are conducted in a safe and educationally sound manner. Despite the best intentions, a school district or physical education teacher may become the subject of a lawsuit. Physical education teachers are at greater risk of personal injury lawsuits than classroom teachers because their students are engaged in physical activity, which carries with it the risk of injury. There is no guarantee that a teacher and school administration won't be sued, but there are ways to limit liability and the associated risk of loss.

According to Spengler, Anderson, Connaughton, and Baker (2016, p. 57), two of the most important issues to address with respect to supervision and the delivery of instruction involve (1) properly matching participants when choosing sides for participation and (2) teaching sport progression to ensure safety and using specific, or close (arm's-length), supervision for high-risk activities.

It is paramount that students engage in physical activity within an effective, developmentally appropriate, and age-appropriate physical education program that is standards-based and aligned to grade-span learning indicators. Despite good intentions and efforts to maintain a safe environment, accidents sometimes happen. Therefore, it is the responsibility of both teachers and administrators to provide for adequate supervision of physical education programs and activities. In addition to supervising students when on the playing field or in the gymnasium, physical education teachers should also be aware of unsafe student behaviors in other areas such as locker rooms, spill-out areas where they are waiting for class to begin or for the dismissal bell, and designated supervisory areas where they go between class periods (e.g., the entrance door to the locker room and the adjacent hallway).

School Versus Individual Liability

Historically, the government (including local schools and school districts) could not be sued. Schools, but not individuals such as teachers, were protected under the doctrine of **sovereign immunity**. However, this doctrine has been eroded over time, and most states and the federal government have enacted statutes called

Tort Claims Acts to permit legal action against governmental entities, including schools and districts in certain situations. *Tort* is an umbrella term for legal claims where a wrong has been committed; it includes claims such as negligence and intentional torts. Therefore, a Tort Claims statute might clarify liability for a school but not provide immunity should they commit a wrong (e.g., failing to provide a safe facility).

Negligence in Physical Education

By virtue of the nature of physical education, where students are physically active in moderate-to-vigorous physical activity (MVPA), there is a higher likelihood of injury compared to that in other subject areas. Physical education, fitness, and sports programs sometimes place participants at relatively high risk of injury; activities involve moving, sometimes at high speed, possibly using implements, and in a confined area that could be inherently risky. When injury does occur and a lawsuit results, the administrator and teacher are sure to come under scrutiny. **Liability** is a legal responsibility. **Negligence** is carelessness, where someone has done something (or failed to do something) and that action (or lack of it) results in injury to another. Overall, the responsibility of an administrator or teacher is to act as a reasonably prudent person would under the same or similar circumstances.

Four Required Elements of Negligence (Duty of Care, Breach, Cause, Harm)

For the legal claim of negligence to be successful, four elements must be met. The first is *duty of care*. A duty is established by the nature of the relationship between the parties involved, such as the relationship between student and teacher or between athlete and coach. The duty the teacher owes to the student varies with the degree of responsibility inherent in the relationship. With the duty, or relationship, established, what follows is the nature of that duty—the duty, responsibility, or standard of care owed to another person. It might be determined by school policy, case precedent, statutes, industry standard or practice, or rules or regulations, or it may be determined by other sources with relevance to physical education, sport, and activities that occur in the school setting.

The second element is *breach of duty*. Once a duty has been established, it must next be shown that it was breached. Typically, the standard of care determines whether a duty was breached. For example, if school policy requires teachers and other school personnel to immediately call 911 in the event of a suspected head injury, and there is a substantial delay or failure to call, then the standard set forth in the school policy has been breached. The standard of care in physical education litigation often arises in the context of instruction (e.g., skill development and lead-up activities), supervision, age appropriateness, emergency care, facilities and equipment, and other facets of physical activity curriculum and programming. When an educator or education administrator fails to meet the standard, a breach occurs. Therefore, it is incumbent on both teachers and supervisors to (1) understand the applicable guidelines and standards, and (2) adhere to them.

The third element, *causation*, is a legal concept that logically follows duty and breach of duty. In most simple terms, it asks the question *Did the failure to meet the standard of care—breach of duty—result in harm to another?* Put another way, *Did the breach of duty cause the injury?* If there is a close, causal connection, such as where a physical education teacher fails to provide padding in a high-traffic area where a collision injury is likely and foreseeable, then causation would likely exist in the form of *proximate cause*. Causation is often most evident where a negligent act, or failure to act, was the precise cause of the injury. Causation can become more difficult to ascertain when there are intervening factors, such as subsequent circumstances or injuries that occur after the initial injury. For this reason, causation is specific to the facts and circumstances surrounding each individual case.

The fourth element of negligence is *injury*. A breach of duty must cause harm or damage for negligence liability to occur. The type of injury can be physical, mental, or emotional. In cases where harm occurs, the student and the student's family (in this case, the plaintiffs) may seek financial damages for the present injury as well as future physical or emotional suffering connected to that injury. As teachers, coaches, and administrators know, it is impossible to have a mistake-free professional life given the nature of those professions. Fortunately, most mistakes that might technically be defined as a breach of duty don't result in an injury. In physical education classes and activity programs, limiting mistakes, learning from them when they do occur, and taking proactive steps through training and preparation are important for maintaining a reasonable level of safety and protecting students from reasonably foreseeable risks.

Types of Negligence

A prudent physical education administrator or physical education teacher takes great pride in providing safe programs and curricula for students. Unfortunately, even with the best intentions, teachers and administrators often find themselves subject to litigation when a student is injured in a physical education environment. When this litigation occurs, various defenses can be raised to address the plaintiff's claims. Types of defenses to negligence include assumption of risk, contributory and comparative negligence, and act of God.

Assumption of Risk *Assumption of risk* is a legal defense that a school might employ in a lawsuit when a student is injured in an activity in which they voluntarily participate, and where the risks are known and understood. There are two types of assumption of risk: express and implied. *Express assumption of risk* occurs when the participant actively acknowledges they assume the risks of an activity upon full disclosure of the risks. The participant could acknowledge willingness to participate in an activity either by reading and signing a participation agreement or waiver, or by providing a verbal acknowledgment. When schools provide paperwork addressing the risks of participation, students acknowledge acceptance of the risk through their signature or, in the case of minors, through a parent's or a legal guardian's signature. *Implied assumption of risk* exists when a student, through past experience, knowledge, or learning, is made aware of the risks in a particular activity. For example, if a high school gymnast, who has participated in the sport from an early age, is injured in beginning gymnastics class during physical education and sues, it might be argued in defense that the student assumed the risk based on experience as a gymnast.

Comparative Fault and Contributory Negligence *Comparative fault* apportions damages according to the degree to which each party (plaintiff and defendant) is at fault. In comparing fault, various states either have a pure comparative fault system or they modify the concept. A pure comparative fault system is one in which plaintiffs recover some damages no matter their own degree of fault. For example, in its purest form, even if a plaintiff is 90 percent at fault, then the plaintiff still recovers 10 percent of the financial award for damages incurred. However, some jurisdictions require the defendant to be more at fault than the plaintiff before financial recovery is available to the plaintiff. These states are called modified rule jurisdictions because they have modified the concept of comparative fault to prevent plaintiffs from recovering if they are more at fault than the defendant. For example, if it is determined that the plaintiff is 51 percent responsible for harm to the defendant, then the plaintiff is barred from recovering any damages.

Contributory negligence is a defense to negligence that places blame on the conduct of the plaintiff. It is an absolute defense that precludes recovery for the plaintiff if established. The theory provides that plaintiffs may not recover if their own negligence, or carelessness, is the proximate cause of their own injuries. It shifts the blame totally from the defendant to the plaintiff, even if the plaintiff's own negligence was slight. Due to the harsh results for plaintiffs, only a few states have retained contributory negligence as a defense.

Act of God *Act of God* refers to unpredictable environmental conditions (e.g., dangerous weather events) that, due to their nature, cannot be fully protected against. For example, if a physical education teacher is implementing a golf lesson outside on a sunny day with a storm occurring a safe distance away, and an errant bolt of lightning arcs across the sky and strikes a student, this incident would likely be considered an act of God. It is an unexpected and unforeseen act of nature. With advances in technology and improved ability to predict dangerous weather conditions, this defense is often less protective. However, weather prediction is not foolproof, and unforeseen and unpredictable weather events such as fast-moving storms and tornadoes do occur. It is the duty of the physical education teacher to exercise caution when dangerous weather events are foreseeable; in this case, the teacher should move students to a safe location.

Loss Prevention in Physical Education

Loss-prevention measures are those taken to reduce or prevent the risk of loss due to personal injury. In this context, the term *loss* refers to loss of physical or emotional well-being due to injury, and the loss of school resources due to resultant litigation. When seeking to reduce loss, focus areas should include supervision and instruction, facilities and equipment, signage, and emergency care.

Supervision and Instruction

Both teachers and administrators should work collaboratively to make certain that students are properly and adequately supervised from the time the bell rings at the start of the class period to the time students are dismissed from physical education class. The importance of proper supervision in physical education cannot be overemphasized; many personal injury lawsuits in physical education are attributed to lack of supervision. Supervisory and instructional responsibilities include properly matching participants with certified physical education teachers. The *James v. Jackson* (Findlaw, 2005) case study is an example of negligence during physical education when a substitute art teacher was hired to teach the physical education class.

Matching

The terms *matching* and *mismatching* refer to how students are grouped in pairs or teams during participation in physical activity. One area in which courts are likely to find liability for negligence is when students who are injured were found to be mismatched with others by size, physical capability, or other characteristics. It is not possible to get a perfect match, and nothing prohibits encouraging students to pick their own partner; however, a teacher must be mindful of the likelihood of injury when students are mismatched and change the pairings as appropriate. When students are grouped according to age, skill level, physical size, experience, and cognitive abilities and understand the risks associated with an activity, it improves the safety of the experience and lessens the probability of injury and subsequent litigation. However, if students are mismatched according to the factors just mentioned, then a breach of the duty of care

Case Study: *James v. Jackson*

Darrell James, a 16-year-old student, collapsed during a physical education class while playing basketball. He experienced a headache and seizure, and he was pronounced dead upon arrival at the medical center. The class, conducted by a substitute teacher, was taking place in the gymnasium, which lacked air conditioning and had an indoor temperature of 90 degrees Fahrenheit (32 °C). The class played basketball for 20 minutes before any rest period was taken or water breaks were given. James weighed 327 pounds (148 kg).

Through a series of court filings and appeals, the courts ruled that the defendants failed to exercise reasonable care and supervision over the decedent, considering the age and environmental circumstances. Several other breaches were determined in this case: an unqualified substitute teacher, a poorly ventilated gymnasium, lack of water breaks, participation in the activity by the substitute teacher, and not monitoring the participation of an at-risk student.

may occur, resulting in unnecessary injury and loss. To reduce the possibility of injury in a physical education setting, it is important to group students appropriately.

In addition, coaches and physical educators should not participate in team sports and activities with younger students where it would hinder proper supervision or would increase the risk of injury to participants. The case of *Prejean v. East Baton Rouge Parish School Board* (1999) provides a good example. In *Prejean*, an elementary school student experienced multiple leg fractures following a fall during a school-sponsored extracurricular football game in which the coach participated. The size and weight of the coach contributed to the injuries of the student.

Mismatching can occur at any grade level, but it is especially likely at the middle school level. At the middle school level, students can be at varying stages in adolescence, and there are typically more variations in body sizes. To reduce the risk of liability, a prudent physical education instructor should pair students of similar size and ability.

Age- and Grade-Level Developmentally Appropriate Instruction

Another essential component of supervision and instruction is age appropriateness. It is important for teachers to consider age-appropriate instruction as well as developmental levels to deliver quality instruction for their students. Age doesn't always match a student's level of maturity and development, so teachers should account for individual differences when assessing progression to higher instructional levels. In addition, individual student learning outcomes should be assessed to best determine the appropriate level of instruction and progression. Developing a curriculum map (discussed in chapter 4) will assist in the development of horizontal and vertical instruction. Age-appropriate instruction should take into consideration the learning environment, the use of instructional strategies, the curriculum content, and the assessment to determine student progress and attainment of the standards. SHAPE America (2025) provides National

Case Study: *Size Difference*

Negligence

In New York, a court found negligence when students in lacrosse drill pairings were mismatched. The case was *Tepper v. City of New Rochelle* (1988). A 260-pound (118 kg) senior with three years of lacrosse experience collided with the plaintiff as they both dashed for a ball, causing the two to fall. The plaintiff, who weighed a mere 130 pounds (59 kg) and had no lacrosse experience, broke his arm as a result.

No Negligence

Similarly, in New Jersey, a court paid close attention to skill level and other characteristics in finding no liability when a female student was paired with a male student during touch football (*Snyder v. Morristown School District*, 1990). In this case, the plaintiff was injured while playing a coeducational touch football game in physical education class. She alleged that the defendant "was negligent in conducting the activity outside during inclement weather and on a wet, muddy playing field, and in directing a game where the boys were quicker, stronger and of different weight than the girls" (para.1). Following a nonjury trial, the trial court granted judgment to the defendant school district, dismissing the complaint. The plaintiff appealed, and according to the appeals court, "a school district has a duty to exercise the same degree of care toward its students as would a reasonably prudent parent under comparable circumstances to adequately supervise athletic activities and to assign pupils to exercises which are within their abilities" (para. 2). Applying this well-settled principle to the facts of the case, the appeals court concluded that the school district "did not breach its duty of care by conducting the PE class outside on this occasion and in directing a coeducational game of touch football" (para. 4).

Standards and Grade-Span Learning Indicators for K-12 Physical Education, which is an excellent guide to determine general age- and developmental-appropriate instruction. Additional recommendations for age-appropriate instruction are presented in chapter 5.

Lesson Plans

Age- and developmentally appropriate instruction, coupled with sequential lesson planning, can help with loss-prevention efforts (the avoidance of injury and litigation). When students move from the mastery of one skill to another sequentially and according to a pre-determined plan, accidents and injuries may be avoided or reduced. Students, through reasonable progression, can understand how certain skills build as well as learn the importance of mastery of lower-level skills prior to taking on more difficult, higher-skilled activities. A poorly planned lesson, however, may be inadequate in teaching students the skills necessary to avoid injury. Additionally, effective sequentially designed lesson plans take into account the various characteristics of each student, including students who have an Individualized Education Program (IEP) or a 504 plan for accommodations.

Training

Another important issue for teachers, with the support of administration, is training. From the standpoint of loss prevention, it is important that teachers be properly trained to instruct a given activity, understand the use of equipment, and understand key safety issues specific to the activities they teach. The instructor must also be aware of the suitability of the space for an activity, the condition of the equipment, and any challenges particular to a specific student. In addition to certification as a physical education teacher, additional opportunities for training (offered in-house or through outside organizations) might serve to improve the safety of programs and activities. Examples include certifications for lifeguards, playground safety, rock climbing, wilderness medicine, scuba, and other high-risk activities. With so many potential instructional responsibilities that have an element of risk, teachers should be aware of the regulations, guidelines, or requirements for instruction in the activities they teach.

Substitute Teachers

The proper training and monitoring of substitute teachers when a certified physical educator is absent is also of great importance. Substitute teachers are an essential support service for schools, but they can only contribute effectively with proper lesson planning. Substitute teachers might not hold physical education certifications. When the primary teacher is absent, appropriate substitute lesson planning is critical for the safety of students. Administrators should provide oversight of up-to-date substitute teacher plans that address activities appropriate for a substitute teacher who may not necessarily be certified in physical education. Also, they should guide physical education teachers in planning substitute activities that are safe, and age- and developmentally appropriate, given that most substitutes lack the training of certified instructors and lack an understanding of individual student strengths and weaknesses. Additionally, administrators are responsible for developing, implementing, and communicating policies and procedures that are important to the everyday work of teachers and staff.

Punishment

Another important issue relevant to instruction and supervision is the appropriateness of punishment. When students are at school, teachers assume the role of parents by being *in loco parentis* (Latin for "in place of the parent") in both supervision and discipline. Establishing sound classroom management protocols that are clearly communicated to the students will greatly assist in reducing student off-task behavior. However, there will be occasions when appropriate punishment is necessary to ensure the student learning environment is safe and free from constant distractions. Having clear rules and consequences provides transparency and consistency in school, and it can contribute to establishing a safe and organized culture. Teachers and administrators should exercise caution when addressing punishment as a means to correct unwanted behavior. Battery (unwanted and unwelcome touching) and negligence are legal claims that have been brought by students and their families when physical punishment has resulted in physical or emotional injury.

LEADERSHIP IN ACTION

The Importance of Supervision in Physical Education to Avoid Legal Issues

Felicia Ceaser-White, MS

K-12 Curriculum Manager of Health and Physical Education K-12, Houston Independent School District

Supervision in physical education class is critical to ensuring the safety and well-being of students at different developmental stages. Younger students may require closer supervision than older students due to their limited physical abilities and lack of experience in following safety protocols. Proper supervision of students is critically important for first and foremost, the safety of students; and second, to prevent lawsuits as a result of inadequate supervision. As a district-level administrator, my job is also to ensure that physical education teachers are aware of the district policies and safety protocols as well as exercise the proper level of care to reduce legal liability and avoid all types of injuries caused by negligent behavior. Examples of age-appropriate supervision in physical education class include the following:

- *For elementary school students*: Physical education teachers should provide direct and constant supervision during activities, ensuring that the curriculum and equipment are age appropriate, students are following safety protocols, and students are safe and receive high-quality instruction at their individual developmental stages.
- *For middle school students*: Physical education teachers should provide close supervision and instruction on proper equipment usage and safety protocols while still allowing students the opportunity to develop independence and decision-making skills. The locker room, gymnasium, hard court, and other instruction areas should be supervised at all times as well.
- *For high school students*: Physical education teachers should provide guidance and oversight while also allowing a broader range of independence and decision-making opportunities as students display greater physical abilities and maturity. As with the middle school students, the locker room, gymnasium, hard court, and other instruction areas should be supervised at all times as well.

Teachers should adjust their supervision practices to meet the needs of their students and the expectations of the student code of conduct. Supervision is crucial to ensure student safety, prevent injuries, and maintain an appropriate learning environment. Teachers and other staff members should be present and attentive during the class to monitor students' behavior, provide instruction, and address any safety concerns that may arise.

In the outdoor environment, supervision during physical education class is paramount to ensure student safety, promote appropriate behavior, and provide proper instruction. Supervision in the outdoor space during physical education class is important for these reasons:

- *Safety*: Outdoor spaces can present various safety hazards, such as uneven terrain, obstacles, insects, and inclement weather conditions. A supervisor can help prevent accidents and injuries by ensuring that students are using equipment correctly and following safety procedures.
- *Behavior*: Outdoor spaces can provide several opportunities for students to engage in inappropriate behavior, such as bullying or horseplay. A supervisor can help prevent such behavior by promoting a positive and respectful learning environment, physical fitness, safety, and well-being among students within an inclusive learning environment.
- *Exposure to the elements*: Exposure to extreme hot or cold temperatures, sun, or wind can be harmful to students' health. A supervisor can ensure that students are taking appropriate precautions and that activities are adjusted to accommodate weather conditions.

Working in a unique environment where injuries can occur in physical education, the physical education teacher plays an influential role in promoting safety and well-being for all students within an inclusive learning environment.

Although some teachers and coaches use exercise as punishment, believing that it assists in refocusing students' attention while eliminating bad behavior and poor attitudes (Rosenthal et al., 2010), exercise should not be used as punishment. One of the many reasons for refraining from this practice is the fact that exercise in the form of physical exertion can be considered corporal punishment, which can have dangerous outcomes and legal consequences (Sawyer et al., 2003).

After determining that student behavior modification is needed, one should consider alternatives to using exercise as punishment in physical education. Preferred options are strategies that solicit assistance from the school's administrative or counseling staff, and contact with parents or guardians.

Aggressive Student Behavior

Related to punishment, addressing violent and aggressive behavior in students is another issue for administrators and physical education teachers to prepare for. Every school has a legal duty of care to keep children safe. This duty includes addressing students' aggressive behavior. When a school is aware of a student's tendency toward violence, the school has a legal duty to take action before something happens. If the appropriate action is not taken and the student harms others, the school may be liable. With the all-too-common occurrence of school shootings, many schools have taken additional precautions to keep schools safe from violent behavior of students, or those coming from outside the school, by hiring additional security and implementing structural safety measures. From a supervisory standpoint, teachers and staff must now be extra aware, and they must be diligent in addressing and reporting aggressive behaviors that might portend heightened acts of violence. School administrators can address this issue in professional development sessions or meetings on school safety. The *Hall v. Jones* case study provides an example of the expectations of teacher supervision at all times during class. It also provides an example of how the judicial process works and expected timelines for state agent immunity, a legal concept that protects public employees from lawsuits when they act within their authority as state agents.

Facilities and Equipment

In addition to people, teachers, and administrators, the physical characteristics of the school's physical education facilities and equipment are important to loss-prevention efforts. While facilities are critical to the proper functioning of a physical education program, they may pose both noticeable and hidden hazards. Therefore, physical education facilities and instructional spaces should be inspected on a regular basis and evaluated for damage or hazards before the start of any activity. For example, if a rainstorm just passed through and you are planning an activity on the outside hard court, you need to determine whether the sitting water would allow you to conduct the activity or it might present a slip-and-fall hazard. The same would hold true if you were using the indoor gymnasium and you knew that one of the floorboards had lifted and buckled, causing a trip hazard. All facilities—from the outside fields and courts to indoor facilities such as gymnasiums, swimming pools, weight-training

Case Study: *Hall v. Jones*

Hall, a physical education student, was injured when he got into a fight with another student. The severe injury occurred when a third student engaged in the incident, which resulted in a serious head injury to Hall. Jones, the physical education teacher, was on the other side of the gymnasium delivering a message to another teacher. Hall's parent alleged negligence and wantonness because the teacher had breached his duty to responsibly supervise the boys for an extended period. Although the teacher had state agent immunity, he had failed to file within the generally accepted time frame of 42 days.

rooms, fitness centers, dance studios, and wrestling rooms—should be inspected on a regular schedule; they should be inspected more often if a work order for repairs has been submitted and service is still pending. Another important regular practice is having an outside expert perform a baseline inspection to address areas of greatest risk and most pressing concerns and to inform management and staff of safety recommendations. It is essential that facilities be maintained to provide a safe environment. Monitoring and inspecting physical education facilities prior to student use is a responsibility of the physical education teacher. The physical education administrator should discuss these types of situations at the professional development meeting for the opening of schools.

Additionally, physical educators need to ensure that the equipment selected for student use is appropriate for the age and physical maturity level of the students, is in proper working condition, is without defect, and hasn't been modified for use in a manner that might increase the risk of injury. Types of equipment used in physical education classes that require periodic inspection are wide ranging; they include everything from helmets and straps on face masks in softball, to resistance bands, collars on barbells, and cables on weight machines. When possible, equipment should be repaired; however, any equipment that is in complete disrepair (e.g., having structural faults, cracks, or broken handles) should be discarded. When schools and teachers distribute defective equipment or they modify equipment in-house, and use of that equipment results in injury to a student, the potential for liability is increased. In addition, equipment should meet the applicable safety guidelines and voluntary standards put forth by such organizations as the American Society for Testing and Materials (ASTM), the Consumer Product Safety Commission (CPSC), the American National Standards Institute (ANSI), and others. Equipment must also be used as intended, and it must be properly maintained according to manufacturer's recommendations. Chapter 8 provides additional information on types of age-appropriate equipment.

Facility Safety Signage

Signage is a critical safety feature in all schools. Signs warn of potential hazards and dangerous conditions, and they provide informational direction on issues such as the location of automated external defibrillators (AEDs) and emergency phones, exit access, and ADA accessible features.

Warning, Rules, and Informational Signage

The wide variety of sport and recreational facilities and activities that occur on the typical school campus lead to many types of warning signage in the educational environment. Examples include warnings of foul balls entering a baseball spectator seating area; warnings of dangerous wildlife near rivers or ponds in southern climates; warnings inherent to swimming and diving; and those relevant to courts and gymnasiums, climbing walls, and others. Rules signage is important for playgrounds and play areas, aquatics facilities, courts and ball fields, and most places where they have application. Informational signage is often found where relevant to the location of AEDs or first aid kits, severe weather protocol for lightning and tornadic events, ADA accessibility, and emergencies such as fire and electrical events.

Fire and Safety Signage

Signage regulations relating to fire and other safety issues are established at either the state or local level. However, there are national standards in place that state and local governments may (and often do) use to establish local requirements. The National Fire Protection Association (NFPA) is a national voluntary association that develops and proposes standards related to fire, electrical, and building safety. The association has also developed a series of standard fire and emergency symbols. (For more information see their website at www.nfpa.org.) Fire codes for very large spaces, such as main gymnasiums, often have large maximum capacities (the number of persons permitted in the space). Fire code facility capacities are not indicators of safe class size, and they should never be used to determine

FIGURE 11.2 Appropriate fire exit signage.

appropriate class sizes. Figure 11.2 shows appropriate fire exit signage.

ADA Signage Requirements

The Americans with Disabilities Act (ADA) regulates signage requirements to protect people with disabilities (U.S. Department of Justice, 2004). ADA signs are required in order to make buildings accessible to people with visual disabilities. The thrust of these regulations is to ensure that signs are large and legible and that all symbols used are standard. Figure 11.3 shows examples of accessible bathroom and stairwell signage with appropriate braille lettering under the words.

Advertising Signage

A different concern related to signs is the sale of advertising space on school playing fields and in school facilities. In difficult economic times, advertising revenue can provide funds to support athletic and other activities. The sale or lease of advertising space is not without pitfalls. Schools and districts must be careful to comply with any bidding requirements. Contracts will need to include provisions for installation, maintenance, and removal of signs. Signs may be permanent, temporary, or electronic; each type will present its own set of issues. Probably the thorniest issues relate to the content on the signs; these issues relate to the extent to which the district may be seen as promoting or sponsoring the advertiser, contact information included in the advertising, and potential for the signs to cause distraction.

Additionally, advertisements may not include prohibited speech, and schools may reasonably regulate hate speech. However, balancing 1st amendment issues can be particularly challenging in the school advertising context. Schools may restrict or prohibit advertisements for alcohol, tobacco, firearms, or other dangerous or regulated products or activities.

Emergency Medical Care

An important responsibility of school administrators, teachers, and staff is to provide reasonable emergency medical care through a practiced and coherent emergency action plan (EAP) when a student is injured on

FIGURE 11.3 ADA bathroom and stairway signage with braille lettering.

school grounds or while in a physical education class. The failure to act, or act reasonably under the circumstances, not only may worsen the condition of the injured student but may result in liability for the teacher and the school. For example, suppose a student in a physical education class falls and hits her head on the floor during a basketball unit. She reports dizziness, but the teacher just has her sit out without following up, filing a report, or contacting the school nurse or a parent or guardian. Suppose that the parent or guardian doesn't arrive until after school, only to find the child's condition has significantly worsened over time. The lag in time to treatment caused the child to endure lasting brain damage. In this scenario, the conduct of the teachers, administration, and staff might be considered to have risen above negligence to what constitutes willful or reckless conduct, removing immunity protections for the school and its employees. Procedures for responding to medical emergencies are an integral component of school safety policy. It is important that EAPs are communicated to all teachers and staff in the physical education program, and they should be practiced regularly in collaboration with local emergency medical services. From a loss-prevention standpoint, an EAP is an important **mitigation** strategy; it is intended to mitigate injuries (keep them from getting worse).

Strategies for Avoiding Legal Liability in Physical Education

There are many strategies to reduce or prevent injuries and liability in physical education. Carpenter (2008) recommends identifying possible risks, evaluating these risks, and then managing these risks through preventive strategies. In negligence lawsuits, lawyers often use an expert witness, a person who is deemed to have expertise in a particular subject area that is relevant to the case. Expert witnesses can serve to inform attorneys and courts of safety and prevention issues relevant to physical education.

In the 1990s, a group of expert witnesses were asked the key issues they addressed in physical education personal injury cases. Their responses, outlined by Gray (1995, pp. 19-21), edited, and provided next in the form of 16 questions, are still instructive; they provide important guidance to physical education teachers and administrators to this day. Physical education instructors should ask themselves the following:

1. *Does the activity or drill have a legitimate educational or athletic objective or purpose?*
2. *Is the activity or drill inherently dangerous?*
3. *Are participants appropriately grouped or matched?*
4. *Is the activity or drill appropriate for the readiness level (age, ability, maturity, psychological, etc.) of the participants?*
5. *Have the participants been appropriately warned about the inherent risks of an activity and told how to guard against injury as a result of those risks?*
6. *Have the participants been provided appropriate feedback related to proper skill or activity execution so as to prevent injury?*
7. *Is the teacher or coach providing correct instruction?*
8. *Have all necessary physical skills been taught prior to the student's participation in the activity?*
9. *Have all necessary progressions been provided so that the participant can master essential simple to complex skills?*
10. *Have all necessary safety rules been developed, communicated, and consistently enforced?*
11. *Has the teacher or coach adequately anticipated the hazards involved in the activity and taken the necessary steps to provide for the participant's safety to a reasonable degree?*
12. *Are the participants being properly supervised?*
13. *Is equipment adequate, safe, and proper?*
14. *Is the design and condition of the facility safe and proper?*
15. *Do the potential likelihood and potential severity of injury outweigh the*

teacher's or coach's reason for conducting the activity a certain way?

16. *Have any participants been pressured, coerced, or forced to perform an activity against their reluctance to do so?*

These questions provide a good checklist for administrators and teachers to use as a loss-prevention tool.

In addition to the previous list, other considerations relevant to loss prevention include the following:

- Ensuring that instructors have the appropriate training for each particular activity
- Ensuring suitability of the activity space and the condition of the equipment
- Following all regulations, guidelines, and requirements for instruction in the particular activity or the use of equipment
- Paying close attention to the needs of each student
- Understanding the general legal requirements related to important issues such as harassment, special education, discrimination, and accessibility
- Understanding and following appropriate protocol if an accident or injury does occur

Following this guidance will serve as a starting point for creating a safe learning environment while minimizing the potential of liability. Student safety should always be the first and foremost concern of all educators and administrators.

Proper physical education administrative support for newly hired teachers will also provide critical assistance in the avoidance of injuries to students. The physical education administrator, along with the school site administrator, should review all safety protocols with the newly hired teacher and provide ongoing support through in-person site visits or email communication. In addition to safety protocols, the administrator should review the curriculum that the teacher plans to implement to ensure that it is age- and developmentally appropriate, and that locker room and activity spaces are supervised at all times. In addition to specific safety protocols for sports, physical educators also need to be cognizant of ensuring student safety during traditional games and play activities at all levels. Safety precautions include setting up cones for directionality to avoid any head-to-head collisions during tag games or foot races, establishing traveling directionality on a horizontal ladder, and making sure that all equipment is in safe working order. Inspecting playing fields for broken glass and other debris after weekend utilization is another recommendation to avoid any unintentional injury to students.

How the physical education teacher delivers the instruction in the lesson plans also ensures that students understand how their physical education instruction affects their learning outcomes. They will acquire the knowledge, skills, attitudes, and values needed for a lifetime of health and wellness. Teacher job descriptions typically emphasize the importance of understanding well-developed sequential lesson plans. These teacher-developed unit plans and daily lesson plans are considered legal artifacts;

Case Study: *Moore v. Willis Independent School District*

In the case of *Moore v. Willis Independent School District* (2000) (cited in Sawyer et al., 2003, p. 12), exercise was used as punishment. Moore, an 8th grade student, was talking to another student during roll call in physical education. As punishment, the physical education teacher required the student to do 100 squat thrusts and then participate in weightlifting for 20 to 25 minutes. As a result of the excessive exercise used as punishment, the student was diagnosed with degenerative skeletal muscle disease and renal failure. Following a series of court filings that initially included violations of the 1st, 5th, and 14th (the right to due process of law and equal protection of the law) amendments, Title IX violations, and state-law claims of negligence and intentional infliction of emotional distress against the teacher, it was ultimately determined that the teacher was entitled to "official immunity from the state-law claims" (Findlaw, 2000, para. 6). Through a series of appeals, the case was remanded to be decided in state court on the state-law claims.

they must be aligned to standards, offering age- and skill-appropriate outcomes.

As teachers develop unit plans, along with ancillary study guides for students, they must put the date on the document, specifying when it was developed, when it was updated, and when it was distributed to the students. This documentation will validate that if any instructional documents are requested, those documents were actually the ones distributed to students.

In the role as administrator, it is an imperative duty to collect and review teacher lesson plans for these characteristics. Teachers must be expected to write, review, and update their plans regularly in order to ensure safety and maintain quality instruction. It is the administrator's responsibility to provide feedback and keep lesson plan artifacts on file during formal observation periods.

Bullying, Harassment, and Sexual Harassment

The terms *bullying* and *harassment* are often used interchangeably. While there are some similarities in the behaviors, the main distinction between the two is that there is no federal law that applies to bullying, but harassment constitutes prohibited, illegal behavior. Bullying by definition is "the repetitive, intentional hurting of one person or group by another person or group where the relationship involves an imbalance of power. Bullying can be physical, verbal or psychological. It can happen face-to-face or online" (Anti-Bullying Alliance, p.1). Harassment as defined by the U.S. Department of Education (2012, para. 4) is defined as "threatening, harmful or humiliating conduct based on race, color, national origin, sex or disability. Harassment may result in a hostile environment that interferes or limits a student's ability to participate in or benefit from the services, activities or opportunities offered by a school." Harassment related to other protected categories such as race, religion, or national ancestry is also illegal.

Bullying and harassment by adults or children is never acceptable in school settings. Bullying and harassment are forms of aggression in which an individual intimidates, harasses, and torments someone to gain power over the person. Consequences for such behavior differ depend on various factors, including whether the actor or actors are children or adults, and the severity of the behavior. According to stopbullying.gov, **bullying** by youth "is unwanted, aggressive behavior among school aged children that involves a real or perceived power imbalance. The behavior is repeated, or has the potential to be repeated, over time. Both kids who are bullied and who bully others may have serious, lasting problems" (para. 1). Table 11.1 indicates the percentage of U.S. students who reported being bullied in the 2021-2022 school year, organized by selected student and school characteristics and represents the prevalence of bullying in schools across the United States. It is important to note that bullying affects students in all grade levels, across all genders, races, religions, national ancestry, communities, and public and private schools.

Harassment, or harassing conduct, may take many forms, including verbal acts and name-calling; graphic and written statements, which may include use of cell phones or the Internet; and conduct that may be physically threatening, harmful, or humiliating. Harassment does not have to include intent to harm, be directed at a specific target, or involve repeated incidents. Harassment creates a hostile environment when the conduct is sufficiently severe, pervasive, or persistent to interfere with or limit a student's ability to participate in or benefit from the services, activities, or opportunities offered by a school. When such harassment is based on race, color, national origin, sex, or disability, it violates the civil rights laws that the Office for Civil Rights enforces. Unfortunately, name-calling and derision are sometimes a part of organized sports. They have no place in school sports, in locker rooms, in physical education classes, or on athletic fields. Respect is an essential part of competing honorably; it should be taught, modeled, and nurtured by physical education staff members.

Strauss (2012) states that the importance of distinguishing between bullying behavior and harassment has to do with the tendency to put many behaviors in the bullying category. The reality is that bullying is bad behavior, but

TABLE 11.1 Percentage of U.S. Students Ages 12-18 Who Reported Being Bullied at School During the 2021-2022 School Year

Student and School Characteristics	Percentage of Students
Total	19.2
SEX	
Male	16.7
Female	21.8
RACE/ETHNICITY	
White	21.6
Black	17.0
Hispanic	21.6
Asian	9.0
Two or more races	30.1
GRADE	
6th	26.9
7th	26.3
8th	25.1
9th	17.7
10th	15.8
11th	10.4
12th	14.8
SCHOOL LOCALE	
City	19.0
Suburban	16.8
Town	23.4
Rural	14.8
CONTROL OF SCHOOL	
Public	20.0
Private	14.5

Source: National Center for Educational Statistics (2023). Table 230.40. Percentage of students ages 12-18 who reported being bullied during school during the school year, by selected student and school characteristics: Selected school years, 2004-05 through 2021-22

harassment is against the law. *Sexual harassment* (discussed in detail later in this section) is defined as unwanted behavior or harassment that is sexual in nature. The common thread in bullying and harassment is that they are unwanted and often persistent and the intent is to "cause hurt, humiliation, belittlement, isolation, and discrimination" (Stephens & Hallas, 2006, p. 1).

It is important to understand the difference between bullying and harassment because each has different consequences for the unwanted behavior as designated by each school district's code of student conduct. Physical education teachers should immediately report these types of behaviors to the school site administrator, who should take immediate action to diffuse these situations before they escalate further.

Bullying by Adults

Administrators, teachers, staff, and school district central office personnel are not immune to bullying by adults. In addition, these individuals may feel bullied by parents and even students. It is important for employers to be aware of laws and penalties regarding failing to protect employees from bullying and harassment in the workplace. However, when adults bully students in the education setting, immediate intervention and action must take place.

A bullying teacher can be characterized as one who uses the imbalance of power to intentionally harm students physically, emotionally, or socially. According to Parsons (2005), bullying behaviors by teachers can include the following:

- Verbal abuse *through the use of sexist, racist, cultural, socioeconomic, ability-related, or homophobic stereotyping and labeling*
- Physical abuse, *such as shaking, pushing, pinching, pulling the hair or ears, slapping with a ruler, and throwing things*
- Psychological abuse, *such as yelling, using sarcasm, ripping up work, setting student against student, and making threats*
- Professional abuse, *such as unfair marking; applying penalties selectively; using inappropriate disciplinary methods; inducing failure by setting inappropriate standards; lying to colleagues, parents, or superiors about a student's behavior; denying students equal access to lessons, resources, or remediation; and intimidating parents who, through language, culture, or socioeconomic status, are cut off from a complaint process (p. 39)*

Schools must have the same zero tolerance for teachers who bully students as they do for students who bully other students. When observed, these actions must immediately be reported to the appropriate administrator or agency.

Bullying by Students

Sometimes it is difficult to tell when a student is being harassed or bullied. Furthermore, at times, it can be difficult to identify students who may be engaging in bullying behavior. According to stopbullying.gov (n.d.), during the 2021-2022 school year, about 19 percent of U.S. students aged 12 to 18 experienced bullying, and about 21% of those students were cyberbullied. Since bullying and cyberbullying (bullying via the Internet through multiple forms of technology including instant messaging, online chat rooms, email, blogs, social networking websites, and texting) (Juvonen & Gross, 2008) have become prevalent negative behaviors, it is important to open the channels of communication with students and create an environment in which students feel comfortable sharing concerns with adults. To assist in identifying students who may be engaged in bullying behavior, stopbullying.gov recommends that educators look for these indicators in students:

- Getting into physical or verbal fights
- Having friends who bully others
- Becoming increasingly aggressive
- Getting sent to the principal's office or to detention frequently
- Having unexplained extra money or new belongings
- Blaming others for their problems
- Not accepting responsibility for their actions
- Being competitive and worrying about their reputation or popularity

When a student who is being bullied cannot overcome the emotional stress caused by the bully, horrific acts such as these can result. The severity of the impact of bullying by students can be seen in the following examples. Tragically, student bullying is one cause of suicide. In September 2014, a middle school student in a district north of Orlando, Florida, shot himself in the school bathroom because "the hopelessness was overwhelming," his mother reported (Reuters). Three weeks before her 14th birthday, a student in Dardenne Prairie, Missouri, hanged herself following repeated cyberbullying by an adult posing as a student. Six teenagers were charged in Massachusetts following the suicide of one of their classmates after she had been bullied. The New Jersey Anti-Bullying Bill of Rights Act was created immediately after the suicide of a Rutgers freshman who had been harassed by his roommate.

In July 2017, the family of a 12-year-old New Jersey girl who committed suicide sued her school district for not stepping in to address the problem of cyberbullying. An attorney for the family filed a notice of intent to sue the school district for negligence. The girl took her own life in June 2017 after months of bullying by several of her classmates both in person and through social media. Some of the messages were vile and malicious. For months, she was told she was a loser and that she had no friends; finally, someone told her, "Why don't you kill yourself?" Search the Internet for any state, and you will find a news report of a child or teen suicide or attempted suicide directly related to bullying.

Every state and most territories have either laws or policies that address student bullying. Most have both. When anti-bullying is addressed in state legislation, the law typically requires a school to report, document, and investigate a bullying incident within a specific time frame.

All educators, administrators, students, and school site personnel should address bullying, feel free to report it, and take appropriate action to intervene. The primary role of physical educators and administrators is to make sure that students not only *feel* safe but *are* safe. In many jurisdictions, the law requires school employees with information about student harassment or bullying by an adult, to report that information to the appropriate authorities—either a child welfare agency, the police, or both. Administrators need to take all allegations seriously, and they must take appropriate and immediate action.

Adult-to-Adult Harassment

As stated earlier, adults in the school environment are not immune to harassment. Having clear policies in place, including known reporting protocols along with ongoing professional development to educate people on the topic, are good preventive strategies. School site personnel who assume the role of a bully while harassing other staff members have a negative impact on teacher morale and collegiality. The site or district administrator has an obligation to ensure that interventions are in place to address harassment. Collaboration and respect among educational professionals should be the norm, and this expectation must be communicated to all educational employees.

In New Jersey, the state's anti-bullying statute, which might appear to be applicable only to students, has been held by the State Commissioner of Education to apply to adult behavior as well (*K.T., on behalf of minor children, K.H. and T.D. v. Board of Education, Township of Deerfield*) (Commissioner's Decision, July 30, 2013). Examples of bullying behavior by adults include public humiliation, excessive screaming, teasing, taunting, use of derogatory names or name-calling, pushing, and hitting. A significant portion of adult bullying behavior comes in the form of sexual harassment.

Adult-to-Student Harassment

Too often, school districts are ill-prepared to handle harassment cases between a teacher and a student. The recommendation is to have proper protocols in place, including trained individuals to handle an investigation of any reports of harassment. As discussed in the gender issues section later in this chapter, without these provisions in place, schools are open to Title IX violations. The same reporting procedures should be followed when students are bullied by teachers.

Sexual Harassment

Sexual harassment is words or conduct of a sexual nature that have the effect of creating an embarrassing, hostile, or uncomfortable environment. Sexual harassment does not need to include sexual advances. Sexual harassment may include making comments about gender or sexual orientation, touching or grabbing, forcing someone to engage in any kind of sexual physical conduct, and telling sexually explicit stories or jokes or showing sexually explicit material of any kind. It is imperative that administrators act responsibly to follow up on any reported behaviors brought to their attention by staff, parents, and students. Failure to act (*act* means investigating and then putting incidents in writing and including them in a teacher's personnel file) can be construed as negligence on the part of the administrator or principal. Disciplinary action, tenure charges, or both can be brought against the staff member depending on the severity of the action.

The U.S. Department of Education (2015) Office for Civil Rights provides the following guidance concerning sexual harassment in schools. The following are the compliance standards:

1. *To take prompt and effective action to stop the harassment, to prevent further victimization, and when appropriate, to provide redress to the victim.*
2. *To establish, publish, and distribute to students, parents, staff, and faculty a sex discrimination policy and grievance procedure for students to know how and to whom to report complaints.*
3. *To name a school employee as the coordinator/administrator of Title IX standards and regulations and to coordinate investigations and other required steps when responding to a complaint of discrimination.*
4. *To educate students about sexual harassment including the policy and grievance procedures.*
5. *To ensure that all employees who are aware of harassment recognize their obligation to report the behavior to the appropriate school official who can correct the behavior.*
6. *If harassment is out in the open and pervasive, the school should know it is occurring and conduct an investigation.*
7. *To conduct a fair and impartial investigation of sexual harassment complaints and any observations of potential harassment.*
8. *To provide information regarding the outcome of the investigation to all parties involved.*

Sexual harassment in any form should not be tolerated by any adult or student, especially in an educational setting. All allegations of sexual harassment must be immediately reported to school administrators and to the proper law enforcement agency.

School District Responsibility

Failure by a school district or its employees to act when confronted with issues of harassment or bullying is a basis for liability. The U.S. Department of Education, Office of Civil Rights (2010a), issued a detailed "Dear Colleague" letter outlining the specific steps districts must take to address harassment or bullying when that harassment or bullying may also constitute a violation of federal law. See www2.ed.gov/about/offices/list/ocr/letters/colleague-201010.pdf.

These statutes include Title VI of the Civil Rights Act of 1964 (Title VI), which prohibits discrimination on the basis of race, color, or national origin; Title IX of the Education Amendments of 1972 (Title IX), which prohibits discrimination on the basis of sex; Section 504 of the Rehabilitation Act of 1973 (Section 504); and Title II of the Americans with Disabilities Act of 1990 (Title II). Section 504 and Title II prohibit discrimination on the basis of disability.

Sawyer and colleagues (2010, p. 52) provide useful risk-management tips to avoid negligence cases through preventive strategies related to bullying by students. These strategies include the following:

1. A strict, zero-tolerance anti-bully and harassment policy should be developed and communicated to all stakeholders.
2. Students, teachers, coaches, parents, and administrators should all be educated on the dangers of bullying and other forms of harassment.
3. Athletes and participants should be required to sign a contract stating that they have read and understand the anti-bullying policy and that they agree to refrain from engaging in any bullying behavior.
4. Strong disciplinary and corrective measures should be taken for known cases of bullying.
5. Ensure proper supervision of physical education classes, recess, and after-school or weekend sport activities.

6. Establish an easy-to-implement reporting system for bullying as well as a protocol for conducting a fair investigation of reported bullying behavior.
7. Be aware of anti-bullying statutes that may exist in your state, and make sure to comply with such legislation.
8. Keep a thorough record of reported instances of bullying and of the action taken.
9. Evaluate the school's or organization's anti-bullying practices and their effectiveness.

A school is responsible for addressing harassment incidents it knows about or reasonably should have known about. In some situations, harassment may be in plain sight, widespread, or well known to students and staff, such as harassment occurring in hallways, during academic or physical education classes, during extracurricular activities, at recess, on a school bus, or through graffiti in public areas. In these cases, the obvious signs of the harassment are sufficient to put the school on notice. In other situations, the school may become aware of misconduct, triggering an investigation that could lead to the discovery of additional incidents that, taken together, may constitute a hostile environment. In all cases, schools should have well-publicized policies prohibiting harassment and procedures for reporting and resolving complaints that will alert the school to incidents of harassment.

When responding to harassment, a school must take immediate and appropriate action to investigate or otherwise determine what occurred. The specific steps in a school's investigation will vary depending upon the nature of the allegations, the source of the complaint, the age of the student or students involved, the size and administrative structure of the school, and other factors. In all cases, however, the inquiry should be prompt, thorough, and impartial.

If an investigation reveals that discriminatory harassment has occurred, a school must take prompt and effective steps reasonably calculated to end the harassment, eliminate any hostile environment and its effects, and prevent the harassment from recurring. These duties are a school's responsibility even if the misconduct is covered by an anti-bullying policy, and regardless of whether a student has complained, asked the school to take action, or identified the harassment as a form of discrimination.

Appropriate steps to end harassment may include separating the accused harasser and the target, providing counseling for the target or the harasser or both, or taking disciplinary action against the harasser. These steps should not penalize the student who was harassed. For example, any separation of the target from an alleged harasser should be designed to minimize the burden on the target's educational program (e.g., not require the target to change her class schedule).

In addition, depending on the extent of the harassment, the school may need to provide training or other interventions not only for the perpetrators but also for the larger school community to ensure that all students, their families, and school staff can recognize harassment if it recurs and know how to respond. A school also may be required to provide additional services to the student who was harassed in order to address the effects of the harassment, particularly if the school initially delays in responding or responds inappropriately or inadequately to information about harassment.

An effective response may also need to include the issuance of new policies against harassment and new procedures by which students, parents, and employees may report allegations of harassment (or wide dissemination of existing policies and procedures), as well as wide distribution of the contact information for the district's Title IX and Section 504/Title II coordinators.

Finally, a school should take steps to stop further harassment and prevent any retaliation against the person who made the complaint (or was the subject of the harassment) or against those who provided information as witnesses. At a minimum, the school's responsibilities include making sure that harassed students and their families know how to report any subsequent problems, conducting follow-up inquiries to see if there have been any new incidents or any instances of retaliation, and responding promptly and appropriately to address continuing or new problems.

Gender Issues

SHAPE America replaced the term *physical literacy* with the term *physical literacy journey* (2025, p. 3). These standards "consider psychomotor, cognitive, social, and affective learning domains essential to facilitating the physical literacy journey of PreK-12 learners, as an ongoing journey" (SHAPE America, 2025, p. 3). To achieve that goal, administrators must ensure that physical education programs are designed and implemented so that all children are provided with the opportunity to improve their physical health and well-being, as well as their psychological and social well-being. The playing fields, gymnasiums, and classrooms must foster an environment of equity and inclusion where all students feel safe and respected. Addressing **gender issues** in physical education requires deliberate action on the part of the physical education teacher; moreover, it requires the physical education administrator to develop meaningful and appropriate policies and practices.

Title IX

In June of 1972, Title IX of the Education Amendments Act of 1972 was enacted by Congress. It includes this provision:

> *No person in the United States shall, on the basis of sex, be excluded from participation in, be denied the benefits of, or be subjected to discrimination under any education program or activity receiving Federal financial assistance.*

Since public school districts receive federal funds for a variety of programs or services, including funds for special education, school lunches, and assistance for low-income students, public school districts are required to comply with the requirements of Title IX when it comes to participation in programs and activities (U.S. Department of Education, 2024). The regulations to support Title IX of the Education Amendments Act of 1972 are set forth at 34 C.F.R. Part 106.

Title IX addresses a variety of situations related to discrimination in education, including comparable educational opportunities, the right to equal treatment, and sexual violence. This chapter focuses on the two areas the physical education teacher is most likely to encounter. First, Title IX prohibits sexual and gender-based harassment, including harassment and bullying based on gender and sex stereotypes. Individual states may define harassment and bullying more broadly than does federal law. In those situations, the broader prohibitions will apply. Second, Title IX requires schools to provide equal access to athletic opportunities and benefits at all levels.

In April 2010, the U.S. Department of Education (2010b) Office for Civil Rights (OCR) issued a Dear Colleague letter that provides policy guidance for school personnel on implementing Title IX of the Education Act of 1972. The OCR is responsible for enforcing Title IX. A parent or student who feels aggrieved by an alleged violation of Title IX has the right to file a complaint with the OCR, and OCR will conduct a detailed investigation.

Physical education teachers should be mindful of Title IX in their lesson planning and ensure that there are no groupings in classes that are strictly one gender. This situation can be avoided by pre-testing students on their level of ability and grouping them based on their movement competencies (rather than assuming, e.g., that all boys are stronger than girls or that boys are more athletic, in general, than girls). Additional guidance on the role that Title IX plays in physical education with regard to facilities can be found in chapter 8.

Transgender Legal Issues in Physical Education

Today, more students are identifying as transgender, and they are doing so at an earlier age. The implications for physical educators addressing gender issues stretch from safe spaces to change clothes to other issues that may arise in the restrooms, locker rooms, and gymnasiums. The first obligation that teachers have is to know their students. Ensuring that each student feels safe both physically and emotionally is a foundational need prior to any instruction. In general, students and their parents or guardians will determine what is in the best interest of the students when it comes to where they will change clothes and to what extent they want other students involved in knowing about their transgender status. In younger grades, this determination will most likely involve the classroom teacher. Although these decisions are driven by students and their parents or guardians, the school's administrator and physical education teacher should be included in the conversation. This involvement will ensure a safe environment for all students. The role of the physical educator is to provide a safe space for all students, which includes preventing bullying, intimidation, and harassment.

If a transgender student chooses to change in the locker room associated with that person's gender identity, then accommodations also must be made for other students who are uncomfortable in this situation. California was the first state to develop a statute for transgender students in schools that involved locker room and bathroom issues as well as sports (California AB 1266 [2013]). It is imperative that administrators communicate with and educate teachers on sensitivities to gender identity and gender bias when planning for physical activities in their classes. For example, when explaining and discussing activities in the classroom, teachers should be mindful of the pronouns they use to refer to gender and refrain from using phrases such as "boys and girls" or "ladies and gentlemen" because doing so may cause unintended embarrassment and feelings of exclusion or nonbelonging for the transgender student.

Block (2014) suggested that physical educators are in an ideal position to address the negative views toward lesbian, gay, bisexual, transgender, and queer or questioning (LGBTQ) students that can lead to negative psychosocial and health outcomes. A teacher may choose to ignore the fact that a student is lesbian, gay, bisexual, transgender, queer, or questioning simply because he is not familiar with LGBTQ issues. Barber and Krane (2007) reminded teachers that their inaction or silence toward students who are LGBTQ can send a strong message to them and their classmates that the teacher either does not care about or does not support them. Additionally nonbinary youth (someone who does not identify as male or female) in schools are more likely to report feeling unhappy and isolated and to report depressive symptoms compared to cisgender youth (Eisenberg et al., 2017). They also feel unsafe in certain physical environments such as bathrooms and locker rooms (Kelley et al., 2022).

It is paramount that physical educators help youth connect to their inner selves and their classmates. From a legal standpoint, teachers are expected to act in ways that garner support and understanding for all children. To ignore the struggles, questions, and needs of LGBTQ students is an invitation for negligent behavior on the part of the adult. The question remains, What should reasonable teachers do or what should they have done to prevent unfortunate circumstances around LGBTQ incidents in schools? Resources such as the Centers for Disease Control and Prevention (CDC) website (www.cdc.gov/healthyyouth/safe-supportive-environments/lgbtq_youth.htm) and the Gay, Lesbian and Straight Education Network (GLSEN) website (http://glsen.org/educate/resources) have information for educators on inclusion and respect. Teachers must also be made aware of the potential bullying implications for these young people and take steps to educate themselves and their students. Another helpful resource is stopbullying.gov.

Conclusion

Physical education administrators, department chairpersons, and teachers have both a moral and a legal obligation to protect students from physical and psychological harm during the time they are engaged in physical education, whether on the playing field, in the gymnasium, or in the locker room. Loss-prevention efforts can be enhanced by understanding the legal and safety issues relevant to physical education programs and facilities, and by implementing strategies designed to prevent and reduce the likelihood of harm to everyone involved.

This chapter has discussed constitutional issues, and the role of legislation and case law in understanding the legal protections and rights afforded to both students and adults in the school environment. Physical education programs and activities which, by their nature, involve an element of risk, open the potential for injury and litigation. Therefore, it is important for physical education administrators and teachers to understand not only the risks inherent in their work but also the interplay of law, management, and loss prevention. From the standpoint of liability and injury prevention, a key takeaway is that it is the responsibility of the physical education teacher to act as a reasonable person would under the circumstances. This standard of behavior requires physical educators to be aware of the applicable safety guidelines, rules, and standards; to follow school policy; and to act in compliance with the standard of care. Maintaining safe facilities and equipment, providing proper supervision and instruction, and caring for students in the event of a medical emergency are all important loss-prevention measures. Physical educators must also be aware of—and work to prevent—bullying, harassment, and sexual harassment; they must work to ensure the rights and dignity of all students are protected at all times. In addition, all school districts should have safety procedures in place for their physical education programs, developed and produced with the assistance of the district's attorney's office, district's office of safety, or office of risk management.

Review Questions

1. Provide an example of a constitutional amendment and its applicability to physical education.
2. Describe the elements of negligence, and explain each in the context of physical education practice.
3. Explain the importance of supervision and instruction from the standpoint of loss prevention, and describe best practices to avoid student injury and liability.
4. Describe several strategies to prevent bullying and harassment in physical education.
5. What is the responsibility of the administrator when a physical education class has a substitute teacher?
6. What laws govern sexual harassment and discrimination based on gender, and how do they apply to physical education?

CHAPTER 12

Human Capital Management

Lauren O'Mara and Jayne D. Greenberg

skynesher/E+/Getty Images

LEARNING OBJECTIVES

After reading this chapter, you will be able to do the following:

- Describe how human capital management affects the recruiting, selection, and hiring of teachers.
- Identify factors that impact teacher shortages.
- Apply appropriate interviewing techniques.
- Describe the role of professional development in supporting teachers.
- Explain labor relations and collective bargaining.

KEY CONCEPTS

alternative certification programs
behavior-based interviewing (BBI)
collective bargaining
human capital management
interest-based bargaining
labor unions
professional development
proposal bargaining
selecting candidates
situational interview

Recruiting, developing, and retaining talent are key to the success of any organization; physical education is no exception. In reading this chapter, you will gain an understanding of human capital management systems, gain practical insights into identifying and **selecting candidates**, understand the importance of professional development and performance management, and learn about the role of labor unions in the teaching profession.

For decades, the term *human resources* was used to refer to the department within an organization that was responsible for employee transactions related to hiring and firing. While human resources is still a part of any organization, the term **human capital management** is used to refer to the larger effort of an organization to invest in its human talent to benefit the business.

Milanowski and Kimball (2010) define human capital as "the productive skills and technical knowledge of workers. It includes the individuals' knowledge, skills, and abilities and the values and motivation they have to apply their skills to the organization's goals" (p. 70). Kearns (2005) adds that human capital management is "the total development of human potential expressed as organizational value" (p. 14). When organizations are focused on the value that employees' skills and abilities can bring, they recognize the need to invest in and cultivate this human capital to better the organization. Therefore, by making strategic human capital decisions, an organization is investing in its own success.

School systems, by nature, are human-centric organizations that rely heavily on people to accomplish their goals. A school system's output, student achievement, is achieved only through the work of its teachers; as such, it is impossible to run a school district without human capital. In education, human capital management is about investing in teacher, support staff, and administrator talent to improve student outcomes. To achieve that goal, school systems must recruit and screen talent strategically as well as differentiate support to maximize the talents of every employee.

Recruiting Talent

Researchers agree that teacher quality is the most important factor in determining student outcomes and that strong teachers are the cornerstone of a successful school. Studies have shown that every teacher selection decision can significantly affect the quality of the education a student receives. In fact, of the many factors that play into student performance, teacher quality is the most important and can significantly outweigh other factors, including socioeconomic levels, class size, and school and classroom context (Gordon et al., 2006). According to Curtis and Wurtzel (2010), "The best way school systems can accelerate student learning is to ensure that every teacher in every classroom is effective" (p. 4).

Despite this understanding, administrators still struggle to identify and recruit the best teachers. Frequent teacher turnover due to both personal choice and normal attrition require that schools and districts engage in consistent, strategic teacher recruitment. This strategic recruitment can be difficult especially when other staffing challenges are taken into account. However, it's important to remember that the purpose of teacher recruitment is "not to hire just to fill a position, but rather to acquire the number and type of people necessary for the present and future success of the school district" (Rebore, 2001, p. 78; Konoske-Graf et al., 2016; Nyhus, 2024).

As a physical education administrator, your first step in building a strong recruiting program is identifying your district's or school's hiring challenges. According to the National School Boards Association (2016), although the shortage of teachers is often considered a hindrance to school staffing, the shortage is not related to the overall number of teaching candidates. Rather, teacher shortages tend to be subject specific and focused on hard-to-staff areas such as science, math, special education, and bilingual education. For some school systems, geographic location leads to staffing difficulty. For example, it is often difficult to attract experienced teachers to underperforming urban schools because of high workloads and accountability challenges, while rural schools may face challenges due to geographic isolation and lower salary schedules.

To identify your district's or school's hiring challenges, there are a number of questions you can ask; consider the following:

- Where do most of your teachers come from?
- Where are your teachers going when they leave, and why are they leaving?
- Do you have any teacher shortages? If so, in what areas are you having difficulty staffing (subject area, school type, or geographic locations)?
- What resources can you use to identify candidates (e.g., college and university partnerships, local businesses, advertising efforts)?
- What incentives do teachers have to come to work in your district? How can you leverage these incentives to attract more highly qualified teachers?
- What messages do you want candidates to get about your school and district? Are you relaying these messages effectively?
- Are you able to gauge the success of your current recruiting efforts? If so, what's working and what's not?
- Which recruiting activities are housed at schools versus at the central office? How can you maximize the effectiveness of these activities?
- How can you leverage connections of current staff to identify new staff members?

After you've identified your hiring challenges, you are ready to develop your recruitment program. A strong recruitment program should be strategic and targeted to fill anticipated district and school needs. For example, if your district is struggling to find physical education teachers who are willing to teach in high-needs urban schools, recruitment should focus on exposing candidates to these vacancies and selling the benefits of working in these schools.

Additionally, a holistic recruitment program involves engaging diverse candidates from all areas of the recruiting market. Strategic partnerships with institutions of higher education can help to ensure that your recruiting pools include education majors as well as noneducation majors and potential career changers from other industries who can bring invaluable knowledge to the teaching profession. Research by Boyd and colleagues (2004) suggests that "most public school teachers take their first public school teaching job very close to their hometowns or where they attended college" (p. 118), a fact that underscores the importance of establishing partnerships with local colleges and universities.

Often, traditional teacher preparation programs do not provide enough candidates to fill certain teaching vacancies, or schools may be looking for teachers with professional backgrounds who do not have an education degree. For this reason, many district recruitment programs also choose to target alternative certification candidates. **Alternative certification programs** target professionals who have subject matter knowledge and skills but who lack a formal teaching education. While the quality of alternative certification programs varies, they can be effective at recruiting ethnically diverse teaching candidates as well as teachers in high-needs subject areas (Barth, et al., 2016). Because most new alternatively certified teachers lack formal teaching experience, schools and districts should have systems in place to provide support and training to these teachers in the first few years of their career.

Finally, because school systems are often competing for the most qualified teachers, it's important to ensure that your school system has established a brand and a presence that will help to attract talent. This effort includes the creation of a recruiting presence that goes beyond schools of education. It should include an online presence with clear branding to get applicants interested in your organization. The best branding solutions include testimonials from teachers about why your school system is a great place to work, and they provide clear outlines of hiring process expectations as well as information on the benefits of employment. As a physical education administrator, it is critically important to market your programs to secure and retain innovative physical education teachers.

Screening and Hiring Processes

Even the strongest recruiting programs are of little importance without sound hiring practices. It's important to look at hiring practices to determine whether they are helping or hindering schools in hiring the most qualified teachers. According to The New Teacher Project (2012a), "schools with strong instructional cultures use a rigorous hiring and orientation process to set teacher expectations" (p. 6).

Hiring new teachers can be an exciting process for many administrators because it provides an opportunity to bring new and innovative ideas into the school. Aside from the required credentials involving teacher certification and cleared background checks, you (the administrator) have the opportunity to review potential candidates' professional portfolios and ask them to discuss

- their content knowledge,
- innovative lesson planning ideas,
- what assessment strategies they use for formative assessments,
- how they plan to engage students in the learning process,
- how they will use technology in their instructional strategies,
- how they would work with diverse learners in the class, and
- what their behavior management strategies are.

During the interview process, you will also be able to assess the candidate's communication skills and interpersonal skills; these skills are critical in education, and they cannot be assessed by simply viewing an application and résumé. Many school systems rely on antiquated hiring processes that focus on credentials rather than face-to-face interviews and behavioral and performance tasks (Liu & Johnson, 2006; Papay & Qazilbash, 2021) for initial screening.

Common hiring pitfalls include the following:

- *Delayed hiring*: Districts may wait until the end of the school year or the middle of the summer to begin teacher hiring for the following year. These delays may be related to budgetary concerns or delayed notice of upcoming teacher vacancies. They can be detrimental to educational programs because they can result in limited ability to hire top candidates. It is advisable for physical education administrators to begin the hiring process as soon as possible, even if staffing levels are not finalized, in order to secure the strongest physical education teachers for each position. It is especially critical for hard-to-staff areas or positions requiring a specific skill set. One way to mitigate this delay is to implement time lines on notification requirements for exiting teachers and find ways to ensure that transfer provisions of teachers' unions do not create challenges that delay the hiring of new teachers.
- *Lack of rigor and limited data in the hiring process*: As mentioned previously, the interview and hiring process for teachers is often limited to a review of paper-based credentials. This cursory review does little to ensure that a teacher is a good fit for a school or school system and can also result in hiring of candidates who lack a clear understanding of what's expected at the school site. Alternative interview methods include behavior-based interviews, sample teaching lessons, and multistep interview panels for all applicants. Furthermore, some districts also include data-based assessments of applicants' qualifications, which include additional review of qualifications, personality inventories, and student achievement data.
- *Insufficient training of hiring managers:* When hiring takes place at the school level, it is often difficult to ensure that principals and other hiring managers are fully versed in the intricacies of the hiring process. Quality training on hiring practices and expectations, as well as what to look for in potential teaching candidates, can mitigate this problem. In addition, many districts choose to implement a central, district-based initial screening process to ensure uniform hiring standards and to assist principals in sorting through the candidate pool.

Case studies of school systems with strong hiring processes reveal a number of similarities. First, strong hiring managers start with the end in mind by defining the ideal teacher. This task includes not only creation of a realistic and accurate job description but also the exercise of identifying the qualities of teachers who have been successful in similar school environments and codifying these expectations. Having a strong vision of the ideal candidate can help hiring managers to approach the hiring process with a keen eye aligned to the school's and district's vision, culture, and expectations.

Second, effective hiring managers have a strong recruitment pipeline and they use this pipeline to engage and hire candidates throughout the course of the year. As mentioned previously, recruiting efforts should focus on both traditional and nontraditional methods, and it should target high-needs areas. To effectively engage applicants and ensure that top contenders are not lost in the crowd, recruiters should take a high-touch approach, which includes ensuring consistent two-way communication through email, text message, and phone calls to help guide candidates through the hiring process. Candidates should also know who to contact when they have questions or concerns in the hiring process. Face-to-face interviews are also important to allow candidates to connect a face to your school or district. In the past, many face-to-face interviews occurred at teaching fairs or state and national conventions; however, most schools and districts are now moving to virtual video interviews (using platforms such as Zoom, Google Meet, or Microsoft Teams) or in-person interviews at the school site.

Third, schools and school systems that excel at hiring have established hiring processes, and they use these processes to set candidate expectations. A set hiring process is important because it not only ensures that hiring managers are able to accurately assess each applicant's fit with the organization but also helps candidates to develop an understanding of the organization's culture and expectations. To assist applicants in navigating the hiring process, it's advisable to have guidelines that clearly explain the steps of the process as well as what an applicant can expect. These explanations may be laid out on your organization's website and reiterated to candidates via emails and conversations during the hiring process. A rigorous hiring process can also be a deterrent for applicants who may eventually self-select out of the hiring process.

Finally, strong school systems dedicate time to reflect on and make adjustments to the hiring process. This reflection time includes analyzing data to determine which recruiting efforts were most effective, and determining where hires are coming from and why certain applicants do not choose to join the school or district. One method of making this determination is to analyze recruiting data on where applicants matriculated and which teacher preparation programs are providing the most effective and skilled teachers. Many schools and districts also survey candidates who ultimately choose not to join the organization to better understand areas where they can improve. This information can be used to improve hiring systems and processes moving forward. It can also be used to review staffing needs and ensure that recruitment processes are aligned to meet those needs.

Job Descriptions

At the district level, a number of steps can be taken to assist principals and hiring managers in identifying and hiring teachers. First is the creation of accurate, meaningful job descriptions. In many school systems, job descriptions or minimum qualifications (or both) are set by state or district policy. That being said, having up-to-date job descriptions can help a district not only to recruit and screen the most qualified candidates but also to attract candidates. An accurate job description can also help applicants to gauge fit (how they fit in to the job, and how the job fits them) early on, reducing turnover related to unrealistic expectations.

A job description should accurately reflect the duties and responsibilities of the teacher and clearly outline the key tasks, activities, and competencies required. The job description should also outline minimum qualifications, including college degree, certification, years of relevant experience, and the like

LEADERSHIP IN ACTION

Candid Thoughts on What Today's Physical Education Teacher Must Possess to Land the Job

Jayne D. Greenberg, EdD

First Impressions

When I'm asked to interview new candidates for a physical education teaching position, there are two things that I look for before getting to the meat of the curriculum: first, passion and compassion in their heart; and second, energy in their soul. Today's teachers need to understand that whether they teach in an urban, suburban, or rural setting, and regardless of the students' socioeconomic status or their demographic background, all their students need to be treated equally and with the expectation that all students can—and will—succeed. When candidates can show me these qualities, they pique my interest.

Skill Sets

Today's beginning teachers in any field must possess skill sets that are independent of their ability to deliver the curriculum. With educational budgets barely supporting subjects included in the standardized testing process, new teachers now need to know how to fund their programs, and they must show that they are willing to do so—whether it is through writing mini grants, establishing community partnerships, securing sponsorships, or implementing creative fundraising. This skill is essential to building and expanding quality physical education programs.

The second essential skill set is the ability to market the program. An applicant must understand that advocacy is a huge part of securing parental and community support. We can no longer be the best-kept secret when incredible things are happening in physical education. Teachers need to be proud of their accomplishments and those of their students.

Third, applicants need to be technology savvy. They need to be proficient in using business technology, such as word-processing and spreadsheet programs (e.g., Microsoft Word and Excel); management technology, such as the use of Gradebooks; instructional technology, such as the use of apps, instructional programs, and Learning Management Systems (LMSs); social media, such as X and Facebook; and mobile devices, such as tablets and wearables for fitness and assessment. In today's educational environment, teachers also need to know how to conduct online physical education (OPE) and use artificial intelligence (AI) and virtual reality (VR) effectively. I look for the recent college graduate to teach me something new every time I interview!

Curriculum Knowledge

It should be a given that every candidate holds at least the minimum knowledge of the state standards and SHAPE America's National Standards for Physical Education and Grade-Span Learning Indicators, but I don't take it for granted. I do ask the standard types of questions, such as what candidates consider to be the components of a quality physical education program; how they would implement a developmentally appropriate curriculum; what their plan for inclusion is; what their comfort level is in working with students with disabilities; how they would assess students; and what their philosophy is on physical activity throughout the school's environment, including before, during, and after school.

New teachers also need to explain their classroom management system and plans for addressing off-task behaviors. Finally, new teachers need to know that they can no longer work in a silo within the school setting. They have to get to know the rest of the school faculty and staff, and they have to become a part of the vision and mission of the school. Once they do that, they get more buy-in from the rest of the staff, and the physical education program becomes embedded in the school culture.

The Last Question

I usually end all interviews by asking one question: "Will you teach for 30 years; or will you teach for 1 year, 30 times?" I look for that innovative teacher who can evolve with new ideas and new programs and keep moving the program forward. The expectation is also that the physical education teacher will be a role model for the students, dressing professionally as well as living a healthy and active lifestyle. The teacher further sets the tone for good behavior by showing respect for all students, displaying sporting behavior, and engaging all students in all activities.

I end the interview by telling prospective teachers that every day they come to work they are building their own legacy. Be the teacher you want your students to remember 30 years from now so that when they are asked who their favorite teacher in school was, they will respond, "It was my physical education teacher."

(see figure 12.1). For physical education teacher or coach positions, job descriptions should denote whether supervision of, or participation in, additional extracurricular activities or tasks is a part of the required job responsibilities. Given the pivotal role that technology now plays in education for both students and teachers, it is also important to consider adding computer skills and other technology competencies to job descriptions.

Teacher Certification

The merits of teacher certification have been hotly debated among education researchers for several years. This topic is especially relevant as state agencies and school districts work to address teacher shortages while also seeking to diversify their workforce, being cognizant of the increasingly linguistically and racially diverse population (Stovall et al., 2024). Some argue that teacher certification requirements do not affect student achievement but rather make it more challenging for qualified applicants to enter the teaching profession (Ballou & Podgursky, 2000; Wilson et al., 2001). While exploring alternatives to traditional teacher certification, states such as New Hampshire are considering legislative bills (Reaching Higher NH, 2024) stating that teacher quality is the most powerful indicator of student achievement within the school; high-quality preparatory programs help future teachers build the skills and knowledge necessary to effectively serve their students; and uncertified teachers leave the profession at a higher rate than certified teachers (Haj-Broussard et al., 2016; Redding and Smith, 2016). Approximately 30 percent of uncertified teachers leave the profession within a five-year span (compared to 15 percent of certified teachers). Researchers further support the benefits of alternative certification programs for teachers, viewing them as viable means of recruiting, training, and certifying those who have a bachelor's degree and a desire to enter the field of teaching (Karge & McCabe, 2014; Bowen, 2013). Meanwhile, other scholars believe that teaching credentials are directly related to enhanced student outcomes. Linda Darling-Hammond (2000) found that the percentage of teachers with both a subject matter major and a full state certification was positively associated with a state's reading and mathematics scores on the National Assessment of Educational Progress (NAEP). Others, such as Teachers of Tomorrow (2023), argue that having teaching credentials signifies that the teacher possesses the essential knowledge, skills, and professional ethics to effectively educate and support students and further demonstrates the teacher's commitment to meeting the standards and expectations of the overall educational system.

From 2001 to 2015, the federal No Child Left Behind Act (Jones & Workman, 2016) required that all teachers of core subject areas be highly qualified. To meet this standard, a teacher was required to hold at least a bachelor's degree, obtain full state teaching certification, and demonstrate knowledge in the core academic subjects taught. While the theory behind employing highly qualified teachers defined in this way seemed sound, research showed that having a highly qualified teacher did not necessarily increase student achievement (Remer, 2017). In 2015, the federal government passed the Every Student Succeeds Act (Jones & Workman, 2016). With the shift to ESSA, each state is now permitted to develop their own criteria for effective teaching. Any

FIGURE 12.1 Physical Education Teacher Job Description

SCHOOL DISTRICT OF SOUTH ORANGE AND MAPLEWOOD

525 ACADEMY STREET. MAPLEWOOD, NJ 07040

JOB DESCRIPTION

POSITION TITLE	TEACHER
Requirements	☐ New Jersey Instructional Certificate or eligibility ☐ Teaching experience preferred, but not required ☐ Demonstrated knowledge in subject area ☐ Familiarity with use of technology as an instructional tool ☐ Strong interpersonal and communication skills ☐ Required criminal history background check ☐ Proof of U.S. citizenship or legal resident alien status
Reports to	Principal
Job goals	Provide instructional leadership in the classroom in accordance with the course of study and curriculum approved by the board of education.

PRIMARY RESPONSIBILITIES

1. Implements instruction to meet the individual needs, interests, and abilities of students.
2. Creates a classroom environment that is conducive to learning and appropriate to the maturity and interests of students.
3. Guides the learning process toward the achievement of curriculum goals and objectives.
4. Employs instructional methods and available materials that are appropriate for meeting stated objectives.
5. Assesses the performance of students on a continuing basis, and provides progress reports as required.
6. Identifies students who require additional support services, and partners with other providers to ensure that these supports are implemented.
7. Communicates with colleagues, students, and parents.
8. Maintains high expectations for student performance and behavior.
9. Engages in professional development activities, which enhances instructional practices.
10. Participates in appropriate building and district meetings.
11. Strives to maintain and improve professional competence.
12. Performs other related duties as assigned.

TERMS OF EMPLOYMENT 10 Months

Salary per SOMEA Agreement

teacher who meets these state requirements is eligible to teach in that state. The ESSA also allows each state to set its own criteria for teacher effectiveness. As a physical education administrator, it's important to ensure that you not only understand your state's teaching requirements but also design a thoughtful interview process that assesses whether or not a teaching candidate has the knowledge, skills, and mindset to be an asset to your physical education program.

To ensure that your school or district is in compliance with state regulations, it is important to understand your state's certification requirements and to put measures in place to make certain that prospective applicants meet these requirements. It is also advisable to have experts on staff who are well versed in the intricacies of state certification and who can assist in guiding applicants through the certification process. For information on your state's certification requirements, contact your state department of education. For physical education teachers transferring from out of state, your state department of education will help to determine whether reciprocity is allowable or additional certification requirements are warranted.

Interviewing Applicants

Interviews not only function as an excellent way to gauge the fit of a prospective teaching applicant, they also provide an opportunity for district-level administrators or principals to promote their school and help talent understand why they would want to work at that school. To maximize time and resources, interviews typically take place after an initial review of an applicant's qualifications (which may take place at either the school or the district office level). Interviews can take many forms, including phone interviews, face-to-face (digital or in-person) interviews, or experiential interviews in which the applicant completes a sample teaching lesson or exercise.

Selection and interview panel composition may vary by school and district; however, the International Labour Organization (2012, p. 21) suggests that, whenever possible, they "be composed of several members, respecting principles of diversity (a balance of men and women from different ethnic, religious and language backgrounds that reflect the country's or local area's diversity)." Including teachers, department heads, parents, and community leaders in interviews can also help to improve transparency and strengthen school–community ties.

When preparing to facilitate an interview, it's important to have a strong vision of what skills, attitudes, and qualifications make up an ideal teacher in your school and district. In addition, be sure to think about how to maximize interview time and ask the most pertinent questions, especially if applicants have already been prescreened. As hiring manager, consider the following:

- *What skills should the applicant possess?* Consider not only hard skills (e.g., technical knowledge, relevant experience, and teaching skills) but also soft skills (e.g., attitude, motivation, and beliefs about student learning and potential).
- *What do you already know about the applicant from the initial screening process?* Asking questions that are easily answered by looking at a candidate's résumé and application packet is not the best use of your limited interview time. Instead, take time to ask about what's not on paper, such as how the candidate has dealt with previous challenges or details about previous experiences that may be relevant to a new position.
- *How will you assess the applicant's responses?* To ensure that you are able to accurately assess a candidate or compare the responses of various candidates (or do both), the interviewer or interview team should determine in advance what acceptable responses entail. One way to do so is to develop a rubric or grading scale that can be used to assess each applicant in various areas (e.g., teaching skills, classroom management, pedagogy, attitude). This rubric should include criteria that define what is included in the ideal applicant response, which will help interviewers sort and compare applicant responses.
- *Should performance tasks be a part of the interview?* Some principals and hiring managers like to include performance tasks such as creating a lesson plan, teaching a sample lesson, or analyzing student data as a part of the interview process. If you plan to include a

performance task, be sure to think through the task in advance as well as create a rubric or anchor response to help interviewers evaluate the candidates accurately.

Once you know what you're looking for, consider how you will gauge whether or not an applicant meets these qualifications. The best way to gain insight into an applicant's working style and personality is through carefully crafted interview questions. Hiring managers are free to ask applicants questions about their roles and responsibilities at past jobs, and they can ask about preferences pertaining to work and working style, job knowledge, qualifications, and work experiences. However, labor regulations restrict employers from asking applicants about their age, race, sex, national origin, religion, sexual orientation, marital status, disability status, health status, or any other job-irrelevant factor (U.S. Equal Employment Opportunity Commission, n.d.).

As a general rule, the information obtained and questions asked in the pre-employment process should be limited to items that are essential in determining whether or not the applicant is qualified for this job. Conversation or inquiries related to race, sex, national origin, religion, disability, sexual orientation, marital status, or age can be used as evidence of an employer's intent to discriminate against an applicant. Although making small talk is a normal part of any interview and can help make an applicant feel comfortable, hiring managers need to be sensitive to the fact that small talk can sometimes lead to compromising scenarios. For example, if you notice that an applicant has listed on her résumé that she is a member of a church that is near your home, it's not advisable to ask about whether she knows your neighbor who also attends the church. This line of questioning could be used against the employer in a future discrimination suit because the information is not relevant to the job and could indicate the employer's intent to discriminate based on religion.

There are various types of interview questions; the two most common are behavioral and situational. **Behavior-based interviewing (BBI)** involves asking questions that require the candidate to discuss past experiences and problems. According to Clement (2008), "The premise of BBI is that a person who can describe previous experiences with a particular topic is equipped to deal with that topic in the classroom" (p. 45). To use this technique, ask questions that begin with phrases such as "Tell me about a time when . . ." or "Describe a situation where . . . ," making sure that questions focus on addressing skills that you think are important in the classroom.

Situational interview questions, on the other hand, present the applicant with a realistic job scenario and ask how the applicant would respond. The premise of this technique is that people's intentions and stated actions are often closely related to their actual behaviors. Situational interview questions typically present a fictional (but realistic) situation and then ask, "What would you do in this situation?" or "How would you handle this situation?"

Regardless of the questioning technique you use, it can be useful to be prepared with probing questions to dig deeper into initial responses. These questions will help you to gain deeper insight into and provide clarification regarding a candidate's responses. Sample probing questions include the following:

- Who was involved?
- Why do you believe ______ occurred?
- How did you respond to the situation?
- Why did you choose to take that course of action?
- What was the outcome?
- What was your role in this initiative?
- What, if anything, would you have done differently in this situation?

To assist physical education administrators and principals in selecting interview questions, please refer to SHAPE America's (2015) Administrator's guidance document, "Suggested Interview Questions for Prospective Physical Education Teachers."

Equity and Diversity in Hiring

Equal Employment Opportunity (EEO) laws prohibit specific types of job discrimination. These laws protect employees and job applicants from discrimination on the basis of race, color, religion, sex (including pregnancy), national origin, age (40 or older), disability, or genetic information. These laws extend not only to hiring but also to job advertisements, recruitment, background checks, job referrals, job assignment and promotion, discipline and discharge, and employment references. They also prohibit employers from retaliating against a person "because he or she complained about discrimination, filed a charge of discrimination, or participated in an employment discrimination investigation or lawsuit" (U.S. Equal Employment Opportunity Commission, n.d., Reasonability Accommodation & Religion Section).

With regard to job advertisements and recruitment, it is illegal for an employer to publish any advertisement or target recruitment efforts in a way that may discriminate based on the aforementioned categories or that may discourage certain applicants from applying for the position. For example, a school district should not post an advertisement seeking "highly motivated new college graduates to begin an exciting career in teaching" because this advertisement could discourage older applicants from applying to the position. In addition, if your school or district uses a referral process to attract new employees, it's important to make sure that all groups still have access to jobs. For example, if your current workforce is composed of a majority of Caucasian employees and your recruitment strategy is limited to employee referrals, the school or district may be in violation of the law if most new hires are also Caucasian.

Schools and districts must also be aware of discrimination in the hiring process. As mentioned previously, to ensure equity in hiring, the pre-employment process should focus only on obtaining information that is critical to determining whether or not an applicant is qualified for the job. Additionally, the application process should be open to any qualified applicant, regardless of race, color, religion, sex (including pregnancy), national origin, age (40 or older), or disability status. If, at any point in the application process, a job applicant with a disability needs an accommodation (such as additional time to complete a performance task, large print, or a sign language interpreter), the employer must provide the accommodation as long as the request "does not cause the employer significant difficulty or expense" (U.S. Equal Employment Opportunity Commission, n.d.).

Once an employee has been hired, it remains illegal for the school or district to discriminate on the basis of race, color, religion, sex, national origin, age, or disability status when it comes to assignment and promotion. For example, in the school setting, administrators may not give preference or consideration to sex when making teaching assignments. Therefore, a school that assigns only male teachers to teach physical education (when there are qualified female applicants) may be in violation of the law. It is also illegal for an employer to give a negative or false reference for an employee on the basis of these same factors.

Discipline and termination of employees are also situations in which it is important to be mindful of potential discrimination. For example, if two teachers are caught stealing equipment from the weight room after school, their subsequent discipline cannot be differentiated based on their race, color, religion, sex, national origin, age, or disability status. Furthermore, although layoff and termination procedures for educators are typically set forth in a collective bargaining agreement, these determinations cannot be discriminatory.

Onboarding and Orientation

Once you are prepared to make an offer of employment to a physical education candidate, it's important to engage in the *due diligence* process; that is, employers are responsible for taking reasonable steps to ensure that prospective hires are qualified to teach and work with children. Although specific requirements vary by state and by school system, this process typically involves identity confirmation, fingerprinting and a background check, proof of right to work, proof of education and teaching credentials, previous employment history confirmation, and reference checks. To avoid discrimination, the due diligence process in a school or district should be preestablished, and it must be the same for all employees. To avoid legal issues and ensure the safety of students, potential employees should not report to work until the due diligence process is complete.

After completion of onboarding requirements (typically at the district level), the responsibility shifts to the principal or direct manager to help the employee make a smooth transition to the school site. Some school systems have formal programs that address new teacher induction on a large scale; however, principals who are able to actively manage the orientation process are more likely to see positive impacts on new-hire retention and development (Milanowski & Kimball, 2010).

Focusing on this support early on is critical because research suggests that job satisfaction in the teaching profession is currently at a 50-year low (Kraft & Lyon, 2022). Furthermore, 68 percent of school system leaders report that the COVID-19 pandemic resulted in a shortage of teachers in their district, which underlines the importance of ensuring that new teachers feel welcomed and supported as they enter the profession (Schwartz & Diliberti, 2022). Researchers agree that the most successful schools are those with stable staff populations; therefore, it is incumbent on the physical education administrator and principal to provide support and assistance to new hires in order to positively affect retention.

Providing this support can take many forms, including the following:

- Assisting in the new employee's socialization by introducing them to colleagues
- Clearly expressing job and performance expectations
- Providing on-the-job training or assisting the employee in identifying off-site or online training opportunities
- Facilitating opportunities to collaborate with and learn from high-performing veteran teachers and identifying potential mentorship opportunities
- Providing guidance and emotional support to the new teacher

Induction, Training, and Mentoring for Teacher Retention

In an effort to retain beginning teachers, induction, training, and mentoring programs have been a successful strategy (Woods, 2016). In a review of lessons learned from new teachers, Public Agenda (2008) found that new teachers felt that their education programs did not prepare them for the realities of the classroom, particularly with regard to issues including diversity and teaching students with special needs. Similarly, the organization found that alternatively certified teachers overwhelmingly agreed that the support they received from other teachers and mentors was inadequate (Public Agenda, 2007). According to the American Federation of Teachers (AFT) (2017), educators further reported that they experienced more stress on the job, worked more hours than their regularly scheduled hours, needed additional resources, and were less enthusiastic now than at the beginning of their careers. Nonetheless, an international survey of teachers in 48 countries found that, in schools and districts with a strong focus on induction and mentoring teachers' job satisfaction was significantly higher (OECD, 2019). Perhaps the reason for these gaps is that teaching is an art that must be learned on the job and therefore, to be adequately prepared, novice teachers must spend time in the classroom learning this art.

New teacher induction can help to address these gaps through job-embedded professional learning opportunities. Induction programs that incorporate mentoring by an experienced teacher can occur on the district level, school level, or department level. According to the Alliance for Excellent Education (2007), "Comprehensive induction is a combination of mentoring, professional development and support, and formal assessments for new teachers during at least their first two years of teaching" (p. 12). Of the more than 250,000 teachers surveyed by the Organization for Economic Cooperation and Development (OECD) in 2018, only 38 percent participated in induction activities in their first teaching role despite evidence that shows that teachers who do participate in these activities tend to feel more confident in their teaching abilities and more satisfied with their job. In addition, while principals surveyed noted that mentoring was an important element of teacher effectiveness, only 22 percent of novice teachers reported having an assigned mentor (OECD, 2019). The physical education administrator can play an integral role in this process through regularly scheduled check-in calls, school site visits, or assigning a peer mentor to assist new teachers in their first year of teaching (or longer, if necessary).

Research shows that well-crafted new teacher induction programs can have a positive impact on teacher retention, teacher quality, and student performance. For example, in the Chicago Public Schools, novice elementary school teachers who received strong mentoring were 25 percent more likely to remain in the same school, and beginning high school teachers who received support were 50 percent more likely to remain in their schools than their colleagues who received little or no support (Maciejewski, 2007). Furthermore, one California school district went from a 75 percent turnover rate to an 87 percent retention rate after the first three years of implementing a new teacher induction program. The district also saw significant increases in student achievement after launching the program (Maciejewski, 2007).

Although many schools and districts have an initial orientation program, only 1 percent of beginning teachers receive the ongoing support necessary to adequately guide them through their initial years of teaching (Ingersoll & Smith, 2004). A strong induction program should be tailored to meet the needs of new teachers while also considering the needs of the school. To create an induction program, first consider why teachers are leaving your school or district. Joiner and Edwards (2008) list the following common reasons for teacher departure:

- Lack of instructional or emotional support
- Feelings of isolation
- Unclear or unrealistic expectations of classroom environment
- Inadequate professional development
- Lack of support or induction program
- Lack of formative observations or feedback
- Ineffective school climate and culture
- Life circumstances (relocation, raising children, cost of living, etc.)

While some factors, such as life circumstances, are hard to mitigate, induction programs should address as many of the remaining elements as possible. To do so, comprehensive induction programs include a number of interconnected elements, including the following:

- *Ongoing professional development*: Sessions and meetings should be timed to coincide with new teachers' needs and should address the skills and knowledge necessary to affect student outcomes. It includes both curricular sessions to deepen content knowledge and teaching skills sessions to address needs such as classroom management and teaching diverse learners.

- *Mentoring*: Mentoring for new teachers should be structured to meet teachers' needs by providing coaching and modeling from an experienced teacher working in the same subject area or grade level. Mentors should be carefully selected to ensure that they have the skills and content knowledge to guide novice teachers through classroom observations, feedback, lesson planning, and data analysis. Training for mentors is also essential to help them develop the skills to assess new teachers and to model successful teaching practices in an understandable manner. Many proven induction programs provide mentors with incentives such as stipends or release time to spend with their mentees.

- *Consistent collaborative planning*: According to the National Staff Development Council, "When opportunities for collaboration are present in a school's culture, teachers are typically more satisfied with their work, more actively involved in the schools, and work more productively toward school goals" (Killion, 2007, p. 144). Regularly scheduled common planning time can help novice teachers learn how to develop effective lesson plans, structure class time, assess student outcomes, and interpret student achievement data. It can also help to ensure that new teachers are armed with strong lesson plans and can gain insight from experienced teachers on how to implement these plans effectively. Common planning is most effective when collaborative groups are made up of teachers with similar subject area or grade-level teaching assignments.

- *Networking with other new teachers*: Often, new teachers feel isolated as they are confined to their own classrooms during the school day. As such, teachers have limited time and opportunity to interact with their colleagues both professionally and socially. By creating a space for networking with other new teachers, induction programs can help to engage new teachers in a community of peers, making the profession more collaborative and allowing teachers to develop a professional identity. One thing to consider when creating networking opportunities as a part of a district or school induction program is that they are often most effective when facilitated by third parties (as opposed to a school or district administrator). This situation allows teachers to openly voice concerns and frustrations without worrying about their employment status (Alliance for Excellent Education, 2007).

- *Classroom observation and feedback*: Classroom observations for new teachers can be formal or informal, and they can be conducted by a principal or administrator or by a peer teacher. Feedback on these observations can be used to identify the teacher's areas of strength and areas for growth as well as to help new teachers reflect and improve on their practice. It can also be useful to dedicate time for novice teachers to observe more experienced teachers' classrooms.
- *Meaningful, standards-based evaluation*: One of the main goals of any induction program should be to evaluate whether or not teachers are meeting school and district expectations and provide opportunities for improvement. Inevitably, some new teachers will be less effective than others in the classroom. Through the evaluation process, induction programs should provide support and assistance to new teachers to arm them with the skills necessary to demonstrate teaching competence. This evaluation should be tied to clearly defined teacher quality standards that are transparent to novice teachers. Many school systems and teacher groups support the use of summative evaluation in new teacher induction programs as a means of maintaining teacher quality.

Ingersoll and Smith (2004) analyzed elements of induction programs to determine which had the greatest effect on teacher retention. They found that having a mentor from the same subject area, collaborative and consistent planning time with other teachers on the same grade level and subject, and participating in networking activities with other beginning teachers were most effective at retaining new teachers. In addition, they found that the more induction activities a school or district used, the more successful the program was.

Professional Development

While induction programs address the needs of novice teachers, ongoing **professional development** is essential for all teachers, regardless of experience level. Professional development is also an investment in a school's human capital and academic success. According to Stein and Curtis (2010), school and district administrators lead student learning

> *[by] creating, through the process of human capital development, the conditions for a community of adults to continually build the knowledge and skills that most effectively generate student learning. It is an ongoing process of building structures and opportunities for teachers to collaborate, to improve practice, and to create a culture of continuous learning and improvement. The goal is not just to ensure that all individual teachers in the school are effective; it is to create a school environment where learning—for children and adults—is fostered, developed, and celebrated. (p.91)*

Providing and facilitating ongoing professional development for teachers at all stages in their careers requires significant planning, knowledge, and leadership on the part of the physical education administrator. Professional development can further assist educators in "improving their professional knowledge, competence, skill, and effectiveness . . . leading to an active learning environment that allows participants to master specific learning objectives" (CDC, 2017, p. 1). As stated in chapter 9, professional development can take many forms, from face-to-face or virtual meetings to webinars and online courses. As instructional leaders, administrators are charged with not only creating professional development opportunities but also creating and sustaining a positive culture of collaboration at the school site. According to Fink and Markholt (2011), the

LEADERSHIP IN ACTION

Learning Can Never End for a Great Teacher

Georgi Roberts

Director, Health and Physical Education, Fort Worth Independent School District, Texas

Focused, tiered professional development has been a key to all successes that have occurred in the Fort Worth Independent School District (FWISD) in our health and physical education (HPE) programs. The HPE department supports about 350 teachers and paraprofessionals, and they come from a variety of backgrounds and experience. This includes traditional university training, alternative certification, and physical education (PE) teachers who left the classroom for PE. Historically our turnover averaged 10 to 15 percent a year. As we move through the 21st century, this number is increasing; consequently, good candidates may become difficult to find. Schools may be forced to hire teachers *before* they have had significant training in the discipline. It is critical that we provide a way for our teachers to both learn and keep up with the changes in science, pedagogy, and new research. How better than quality professional development?

We have always planned our training calendar scope and sequence over a three-to-five-year span; we review topics and priorities regularly throughout that time, then modify as needed to reflect new state or district mandates, revised curriculum, or needs that come to light as we work day-to-day with our teachers. Some training lasts six hours, with our total cadre of teachers in attendance; some sessions consist of two or three teachers shadowing a master teacher; and some entail bringing in an expert to observe a teacher in their classroom, then provide a follow-up with a conversation about positives and negatives. The overarching consideration is how any training we do will improve our students' learning.

Each summer, before our veteran teachers return for the fall term, new teachers have two days of training totally focused on their needs. These sessions are for those who are just out of university, those who are new to our district, and those who are changing grade levels or disciplines. We work hard in advance to try to know exactly who our audience will be and how to directly provide what they need. New teachers leave after the two days with the practical tools to start off on the right foot, two weeks of lesson plans, increased confidence, and a knowledge that they have support. The group consists of about 35 to 40 teachers, and this time not only allows my department to really develop relationships with the new teachers but for the group to establish their own peer group as they grow as teachers.

These sessions are followed by two days with all our teachers. I give my State of Health and PE Address to set the goals and agenda for the year, talk about successes, and finally circle back to why it's important that our students are learning and our role in that learning. Following my address, there are multiple sessions to better address the individual needs of the attendees. As best we can, we tier the smaller presentations so that teachers can select them based on their needs. At this point, the new can feel very comfortable with the veterans as the so-called New Teacher Academy provided some background information as well as familiar faces.

Throughout the balance of the school year, we work on more focused needs. We do small-group activities with our first- and second-year teachers in high school health or our brand-new elementary PE teachers. These activities can include observing a model lesson provided by the department and providing a sub so that a new teacher can spend time observing a master teacher. We also try to include state and local conferences in our long-term planning; the consideration is always balancing value with cost and time. For teachers who have demonstrated a certain level of mastery, their attendance at a large conference can ultimately provide the district with a local expert—who can then provide the training to the entire group!

We always strive to hire teachers with a strong background in science and pedagogy and from a good university program that includes student teaching. However, regardless of their preparation, all teachers need to keep up with advances in the science and evolution of their field, and they need to stay active learners. Who better to provide this than the district? We know our students and facilities, we create our own curriculum, and we must support our teachers in their growth.

following characterize powerful professional development:

- It focuses on standards-based teaching and learning that is relevant to a particular subject area and focused on engaging all students.
- It is embedded in the context and needs of the school.
- It balances individual and school priorities and needs.
- It utilizes strong principles of adult learning.
- It supports and reinforces the roles and responsibilities of teachers and administrators.
- It engages learners in a peer-based, collaborative infrastructure whenever possible.

Yoon and colleagues (2007) assert that there is a strong link between professional development, teacher learning and practice, and student achievement. Figure 12.2 shows the impact that professional development has on student achievement (Cohen & Hill, 2000; Fishman et al., 2003; Garet et al., 2001; Guskey & Sparks, 2004; Kennedy, 1998; Loucks-Horsley & Matsumoto, 1999), through three steps: (1) Professional development enhances teacher knowledge and skills; (2) better knowledge and skills improve classroom teaching; and (3) improved teaching raises student achievement.

Teacher professional development can be delivered in a variety of formats, such as through in-person or online workshops, study groups, or professional learning communities, group or independent study, and through self-directed learning modules. The most effective professional development is timely, targeted toward teacher needs, engaging, and content driven. Unfortunately, teacher professional development is frequently delivered out of context, and it is not connected to a teacher's personal growth plan or classroom needs, making it difficult for teachers to put their learning into practice. For that reason, continuous, coherent, job-embedded professional development is most likely to positively affect both teacher and student learning.

Just as teachers differentiate instruction to meet individual student needs, administrators should differentiate professional development to meet each teacher's needs. In physical education, these opportunities can focus on how to deliver instruction in large classes, how to work in a fully inclusive classroom, and how to deliver instruction to meet the needs of diverse learners. While professional development can focus on many areas, common goals include expanding a teacher's content knowledge, sharing best practices in small-group settings, and managing student behavior.

Performance Management

Performance management is the ongoing cycle of communication about professional responsibilities that occurs throughout the year between a teacher and a site administrator. The performance management process includes planning, monitoring and feedback, and assessment. The purpose of performance management is to improve both teacher outcomes and

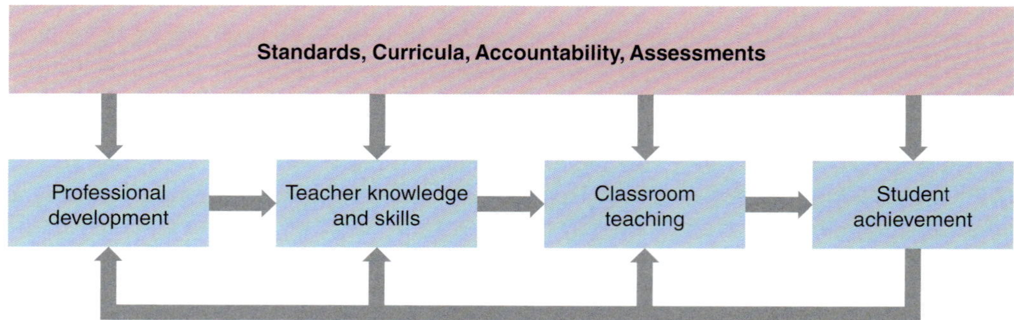

FIGURE 12.2 Logic model of the impact of professional development on student achievement.

Reprinted by permission from National Academies of Sciences, Engineering, and Medicine, *Educating the Student Body: Taking Physical Activity and Physical Education to School,* (National Academies Press, 2013), 230, www.nap.edu/read/18314/chapter/7#230.

professional growth as well as to improve the organizational effectiveness of the school or district.

In the planning stage, the teacher and administrator take time to set clear expectations and goals for the upcoming evaluation cycle. Involving teachers in the planning process will help gain buy-in and build trust between teachers and administrators. During this stage, all parties should take time to discuss and agree on goals that will be mutually beneficial, and they should develop a plan to meet these goals. Professional growth goals should be based primarily on student performance results, but they may also include data-based instructional strategies and professional behaviors (Curtis & Wurtzel, 2008). To ensure fair evaluation of attainment, goals should be measurable, verifiable, and achievable, and data systems should be in place to track progress toward goals. Planning conversations and documents should also include specific steps and actions that the employee will take to reach his goals. Ideally, the planning document should be a working document that is referred to, discussed, and updated frequently rather than a document that is completed and filed away until the end of the year.

Progress monitoring in the classroom, gymnasium, or field setting should take place on the part of both the administrator and the teacher. Throughout the year, teachers should engage in regular self-reflection and frequent data analysis to gauge progress. The administrator's role in the monitoring process is to ensure employee success through coaching and ongoing feedback. It entails conducting classroom observations and facilitating check-in conversations to discuss student data. Consistent assessment of teacher progress allows for revisions to goals if necessary and, in the case of unsatisfactory performance, allows the administrator to provide additional assistance or a plan to address performance prior to the end of the performance management cycle.

The final stage in any performance management process is assessment. The assessment phase serves multiple purposes. First, it provides a teacher with a summative evaluation of her performance for that school year or cycle. Evaluation ratings can be useful when comparing an individual's performance over time or comparing performance among a group of teachers. To ensure fair application of performance ratings, it's critical for your school and district to have a well-designed and vetted evaluation system or rubric that clearly differentiates the levels of performance and related behaviors and outcomes. Second, the assessment process provides a reflection point that allows for career management. Performance outcomes during the assessment phase may result in additional opportunities, recognition, or rewards for high-performing teachers. Alternatively, the evaluation phase may also be a time to consider redirection or dismissal for low-performing teachers or additional targeted support for struggling teachers. Depending on guidelines outlined in teacher contracts, summative performance evaluations may have bearing on salary increases and other personnel actions.

If school systems are unable to utilize performance management systems to recognize outstanding teachers, they are also unable to prioritize the retention of these teachers and leverage their skills to improve human capital and student outcomes throughout the district. At the same time, failing to dismiss low-performing teachers can cause resentment and frustration among teachers. To avoid this result, school systems not only need to take performance management seriously by creating meaningful performance management standards and holding administrators accountable for their implementation, they also need to take the time to identify and capitalize on high-performing teacher talent.

Working With Labor Unions

In 1935, the United States Congress passed the National Labor Relations Act (NLRA). The NLRA afforded certain groups of employees the right to organize and bargain collectively in order to safeguard "from injury, impairment, or interruption, and [promote] the flow of commerce by removing certain recognized sources of industrial strife and unrest by encouraging practices fundamental to the friendly adjustment of industrial disputes arising out of differences as to wages, hours, or other working conditions, and by restoring equality of bargaining power between employers and employees" (para. 1). Teachers in all 50 states have the right to unionize; however, not all states allow unions to negotiate terms of employment on behalf of their members. Currently, 34 states and the District of Columbia legally guarantee some bargaining rights for K-12 teachers while 6 states prohibit collective bargaining. For education support professionals, 31 states and the District of Columbia allow for the legal rights to bargain, while 7 states prohibit collective bargaining (National Education Association, 2022). Given these numbers, it's likely that many aspiring administrators will need to deal with **labor unions** at some point in their careers. Therefore, it's important to understand the collective bargaining process as well as the role of unions and collective bargaining agreements.

Collective Bargaining Process

Collective bargaining is the process by which a group of employees with common interests (typically represented by a union) negotiate a binding written contract with an employer. The purpose of the collective bargaining process is to provide an organized forum for labor unions and management to work together to solve problems and improve working conditions. In a nonbargaining environment, employment is at will. In other words, the employee agrees to work for an unspecified amount of time under set conditions. These agreements are maintained either through employee–management relationships or employer-created handbooks and policies that can change upon a shift in management or employer need. In a collective bargaining relationship, on the other hand, agreements on wages, hours, and working conditions are written into a binding contract that is intended to outlast union and management turnover.

In public education, collective bargaining shapes a significant amount of policy including resource allocation, assignment of teachers to schools and classes, teacher evaluation, teaching conditions and requirements, and teacher tenure. Although collective bargaining takes place at the school district or charter management organization level, it is governed by state collective bargaining laws that outline which topics are mandatory (must be bargained), which topics are permissive (may be bargained), and which topics are prohibited (cannot be bargained).

Throughout the collective bargaining process, teachers and support professionals are represented by labor unions. Members of the labor unions (teachers and support professionals) elect leaders or representatives to present their interests and needs in collective bargaining negotiations with the employer (typically, a school district, school board, or charter management organization). The collective bargaining process in education typically begins with extensive preparation on both sides. First, the union and management meet separately to identify and prioritize issues and review the existing collective bargaining agreement (sometimes called a *union contract* or *contract*) to determine the need for changes or updates.

Next, the parties meet to begin negotiations. Two styles of bargaining can take place: proposal bargaining and interest-based bargaining. In **proposal bargaining**, both sides draft desired changes to the collective bargaining agreement and present them to the other side during negotiations. There may be multiple iterations of each proposal as the bargaining teams engage in discussions and attempt to come to consensus. The final agreed-upon proposals are then incorporated into the updated contract.

In **interest-based bargaining**, both the union and management begin by identifying high-priority issues. During negotiations, the parties discuss why these issues are important, and they identify options to either resolve them or accommodate each other's interests. Once both sides agree on to how to address these interests, a smaller group meets to draft the contract language that will incorporate the interests.

After management and the union agree on contract updates and changes, they sign a tentative agreement. This agreement is then presented to both the union membership and the management's governing board (in education, it is typically the school board) for ratification. On the union side, ratification typically takes place by secret ballot after union leadership has explained the changes to and reasoning behind the tentative contract agreement to union members. A majority vote determines whether the contract is ratified or rejected. If the tentative agreement is rejected by either side, the parties return to the bargaining table to continue negotiations.

If, at any point, negotiations break down and the parties are unable to reach agreement, either party may choose to go to impasse. Impasse options vary by state; they may include mediation, arbitration, fact finding, or strike. In mediation, a neutral party is brought in to facilitate negotiations between labor and management. Arbitration also involves a neutral party; however, in this instance, an arbitration hearing is held to analyze arguments and information from both parties. The result is a formal binding decision from the arbitrator that settles the dispute. Fact finding is similar to arbitration in that a hearing is held; however, the outcome of this hearing is not binding, and it can be accepted or rejected by labor and management. The final option, strike, is carried out by the union, and it occurs when union members withhold services and refuse to work in an effort to pressure management into an agreement.

Collective Bargaining Agreements

In states where collective bargaining is permitted, collective bargaining agreements or contracts are the binding documents that govern hours, wages, and working conditions. In education, compensation and benefits, grievance procedure, employee security, and rules governing employee actions on the job are standard elements of collective bargaining agreements. While it's impossible to address specific details of every district's labor contract in this chapter, some elements of these agreements merit discussion for their potential impact on administrative functions.

First and foremost, it's important for any administrator to remember that the collective bargaining agreement lays out the requirements that must be followed when it comes to working conditions. It includes assignment of teachers, working hours, teacher planning periods, professional development or in-service dates, and job duties, among other topics. For that reason, it's important for all administrators to be well versed in their district's union contract to avoid grievance.

Tenure for teachers is another common element of many collective bargaining agreements. When teachers receive tenure, they are given a contract that essentially guarantees employment for a given period. Typically, it is very difficult to terminate a tenured teacher unless there is an instance of severe misconduct. While tenure details and requirements are often set in state statute, the process by which teachers receive tenure is often a function of the school system. Nevertheless, few school systems set up rigorous tenure review processes (Curtis, 2010).

Ideally, tenure should be awarded only after a rigorous review process that considers a teacher's performance against established teaching standards as well as student outcomes. For this process to be effective, however, it must not only take into account performance against standards but must also hold principals and other leaders accountable for their oversight of the process (by tracking the data of their tenure recommendations and including these data in administrator evaluations). Ensuring that the tenure process is both a high-stakes and a high-rigor process can help to ensure teacher quality moving forward.

Teacher termination procedures are also included in collective bargaining agreements. Termination for teachers typically falls into one of two categories: reduction in force or termination for cause. A reduction in force (RIF) usually occurs when a school district is under economic stress or is facing budget shortfalls and the district elects to eliminate some jobs in order to reduce the pressure on the budget. RIF policies and processes are outlined in collective bargaining agreements, and they frequently require the termination of less-experienced teachers first. Employees who have lost their job as a result of a RIF are usually eligible for recall, meaning that they may be offered jobs if positions become available in the future.

Termination for cause, on the other hand, occurs when there is wrongdoing or misconduct on the part of the employee. If there is an allegation of employee misconduct, administrators should alert the appropriate authorities (district or outside agency) and follow established procedures. Typically, the district's central office will assist school-based administrators in carrying out the termination process to ensure that all procedures and laws are followed. Employees may also be terminated for cause based on performance. When documenting teacher performance, it's important not only to follow district procedures but also to be thorough and accurate in your documentation because employees will be afforded due process before any action is taken.

Conclusion

As you have learned throughout this chapter, human capital management extends beyond the traditional hiring, firing, and compensation functions managed by district human resources departments. Strategic and systemic human capital development requires both physical education administrators and school site administrators to simultaneously be hiring managers, leaders of learning, and talent developers. By holding teachers accountable for their role in student outcomes and identifying and assessing against well-articulated performance metrics, administrators can have a direct impact on improving human capital and, in turn, improving student achievement. Providing support for teachers, whether newly hired to the profession or veterans of the system, is an ongoing responsibility of the physical education administrator.

Review Questions

1. What factors should you consider when hiring physical education teachers for your district?
2. What steps would you incorporate to ensure that a beginning teacher receives the support necessary to be successful?
3. Describe the key components of conducting quality professional development.
4. Given the impact of collective bargaining and labor unions, how would you provide assistance to a teacher who is having problems delivering instruction?
5. As a physical education administrator, what advice would you give your newly hired physical education teachers at their first orientation meeting?

» Visit HK*Propel* for reproducible forms.

PART V

Financial Management

CHAPTER 13

Fiscal Management

Jayne D. Greenberg

Courtesy of Grant Wentzel

LEARNING OBJECTIVES

After reading this chapter, you will be able to do the following:

- Discuss the importance of efficient financial management.
- Identify the components of budget control.
- Identify various types of budgets.
- Develop an understanding of the purchase order process.
- Explain the audit process.

KEY CONCEPTS

auditing processes
bid process
financial management
procurement processes
purchase orders
purchase requisitions

Managing and understanding financial challenges, processes, and responsibilities cuts across all aspects of education. Although funding revenues vary, school district budgets are often driven by allocation, contractual obligations, district-wide policies, and school-based programs and initiatives. One of the major responsibilities of all school districts is to ensure that they operate in a fiscally sound manner in monitoring both revenue and expenditures. The major objective of any office of procurement management or budget office is to be able to secure the best products, materials, and services at the most competitive prices while following federal, individual state, and local statutes and policies. The office of procurement management can assist you in selecting products, processing purchase orders, and tracking payment to vendors to ensure that all district **procurement processes** (the act of acquiring and paying for goods and services) are followed. As a physical education administrator, you not only have the responsibility of working within the fixed boundaries of your district's allocated funding; you also have to exert carefully honed leadership skills to determine how to achieve your strategic objectives while staying within your budget. In doing so, preparing the line-item budget, controlling expenditures throughout the school year, and managing finances reflected in the end-of-year reporting are critical administrative skills. To use budgets effectively, you need to know how they are built, how they work, and how they are evaluated.

Understanding District Budgets

Budgets in essence are guidelines indicating how an organization or a program within that organization intends to allocate its fiscal resources to achieve its objectives. Overall, school district budgets, through appropriate processes, serve as a means for district leadership to justify the collection and expenditure of public funds, which predominantly come from local, state, and federal sources. Whereas some funding structures offer flexibility in spending, federal funds such as those provided under Title I, the Individuals with Disabilities Education Act [IDEA], the Workforce Investment Act, and the Carl D. Perkins Vocational and Technical Education Act (which are often distributed through the states as entitlement funds) have strict requirements and are subject to annual audits. For example, in Florida, state funding for K-12 education is further based on a legislatively approved formula focusing on student enrollment (full-time equivalent [FTE]), local property taxes, varying educational program costs, varying costs of living, and varying costs for equivalent educational programs due to sparsity and dispersion of the student population (Florida Department of Education, 2023). Since each state has its own funding formula, it is recommended that you review the policies in the state where you secured your administrative position.

District budgets range from multimillions to multibillions of dollars; therefore, managing school districts is a Herculean job. In school districts, whether large or small, the chief financial officer (CFO), a member of the superintendent's cabinet, oversees the office of procurement management and holds the ultimate responsibility to ensure that the school district is prudent in managing its funds. Through the reporting chain of command, the CFO reports directly to the superintendent of schools. The CFO plans, organizes, assigns, directs, and reviews the financial services functions of the district, and participates in the planning and implementation of policies and programs. CFOs further advise other district administrative staff and school board members on finance-related issues pertaining to laws governing fiscal obligations, collective bargaining, and maintenance of financial records. Depending on the size of the school district, several administrative and staff positions are allocated to the office of procurement management to ensure that all policies and procedures are followed when district budgets are expended. Under the CFO is usually a chief procurement officer, an assistant superintendent, or an administrative director who oversees the daily operations of the office, ensuring that staff are aware of purchasing statutes, regulations, and board policies. The person in position works closely with the CFO as well as staff in preparing competitive procurement specifications, establishing vendor lists, overseeing the bid process, and resolving issues. This position further oversees budget controls and purchasing analysts.

The buyers have direct responsibility for the purchase of goods and services and assist with the development and revision of specifications for competitive procurements. The buyer is usually the direct line of contact for the physical education administrator for assistance in processing purchase requisitions and suggested vendors for quotes and bids. The clerical support staff assist the buyers in processing purchase requisitions into purchase orders and distributing them to the vendors and specific departments.

Since all purchasing through school districts is processed through offices of procurement management, it is in the best interest of the physical education administrator to become familiar with purchasing staff, who can greatly assist in securing quotes and bids and moving purchase requisitions along in the **purchase order** process.

Procurement staff personnel also serve as resources for managing grants and other funded projects. As a physical education administrator who is tasked with tracking all of your purchase orders as part of the ordering process, you will probably have more immediate contact with clerical support staff who can provide more immediate assistance and information than a higher-level administrator.

The Budget Process

Once you have received your annual budget from your district's office of procurement management, you need to determine how you are going to expend the funds and how you are going to distribute those funds using your budget worksheet based on the budget categories. As you begin to plan your district's physical education program, you need to identify what programs you need funding for, how much financial support each program will need in order to operate within the annual budget period, how you are going to distribute those funds, and what categories of funding you need for each program. For example, if you were implementing a new curriculum project for the upcoming school year, you would not need to allocate bus transportation funding to that program, but you would need to consider substitute days to bring in a cadre of physical education teachers to write the curriculum and resource materials. On the other hand, if you were expanding your water sports program, you would need to include bus transportation funding for students to attend the marine facilities.

Once you have successfully balanced your budget on your worksheet, it is recommended that you work with staff from the district's office of procurement management to ensure that you have properly identified the correct budget categories and the correct object and function codes (discussed in the Budget Categories and Approaches section) so that funds are properly and appropriately expended. As a physical education administrator, being fiscally responsible for developing and managing your budget is a major professional responsibility that involves careful consideration and constant monitoring.

Planning the Budget

When planning your overall annual budget, you should put careful thought into what your actual needs are based on your program goals, strategic plan, and objectives while providing a little wiggle room for unexpected emergencies. Since budgets are prepared in the spring prior to the start of the new year and reviewed at a higher level before being finalized, as a physical education administrator you should ensure that your budget is an accurate and thoughtful account of your needs for the upcoming school year. A good starting point would be to look at the previous year's budget at the start of the fiscal year and determine what your budget looks like at the close of the present year. This process would serve as an accurate indicator of your fiscal needs throughout the school year. As a practical hint, if you have an excess of funds in the present school year's budget in any of your line items, it would be difficult for you to request an increase in the following year's budget. Spending your present funds on necessary personnel, equipment, field trip transportation, professional development, substitute coverage, and supply needs is a part the responsible fiscal management process. By the close of the fiscal year, all or most of the funds should have been expended to show that your budget request for the upcoming school year is justified.

If you are supervising several different programs, it is recommended that you secure a separate funding program number for each. For example, you should have a separate funding program number for programs such as physical education, health education, driver education, Special Olympics, and adapted physical education. Doing so allows you to more carefully monitor the needs of each program and plan your budgets accordingly as well as justify increases or decreases in program fiscal needs. Since your budgets should be monitored on a regular basis, it is also recommended that you have the flexibility to perform budget transfers between line

FIGURE 13.1 Sample District Physical Education Budget

DISTRICT PHYSICAL EDUCATION BUDGET								ORIGINAL BUDGET
FUND	OBJECT		WORK LOCATION	PROGRAM		FUNCTION		$
1000	5144	Teacher	7602	4307	Physical Education	5102	Basic Instruction	350,000.00
1000	5210	Retirement	7602	4307	Physical Education	5102	Basic Instruction	60,000.00
1000	5210	Retirement	7602	4307	Physical Education	5103	Basic Instruction	
1000	5220	Social Security	7602	4307	Physical Education	5102	Basic Instruction	
1000	5221	Medicare	7602	4307	Physical Education	5102	Basic Instruction	
1000	5232	Distr. of Emp. Med. Ins.	7602	4307	Physical Education	5102	Basic Instruction	40,000.00
1000	5243	W/C and LIAB Distr. of	7602	4307	Physical Education	5102	Basic Instruction	
1000	5246	Vista Distr. of Char.	7602	4307	Physical Education	5102	Basic Instruction	
Result								450,000.00
1000	5149	Temporary Instructor	7602	4307	Physical Education	5103	Basic Instruction	40,000.00
1000	5399	Printing/ Duplicating	7602	4307	Physical Education	6300	Instr. and Curriculum Development SV	500.00
1000	5510	Supplies	7602	4307	Physical Education	5102	Basic Instruction	10,000
1000	5510	Supplies	7602	4307	Physical Education	6300	Instr. and Curriculum Development SV	10,000
Result								500.00
1000	5332	Field Trips	7602	4307	Physical Education	6300	Instr. and Curriculum Development SV	15,000.00
1000	5332	Field Trips	7602	4307	Physical Education	7800	Pupil Transportation Services	10,000.00
1000	5350	Repairs and Maintenance	7602	4307	Physical Education	8100	Maintenance of Plant	10,000.00
1000	5360	Rentals	7602	4307	Physical Education	6300	Instr. and Curriculum Development SV	5,000.00
1000	5390	Other Purchased Serv.	7602	4307	Physical Education	6300	Instr. and Curriculum Development SV	50,000.00
1000	5640	Furniture, Fixtures	7602	4307	Physical Education	6300	Instr. and Curriculum Development SV	20,000.00
Result								110,000.00
Overall Result								560,500.00

items throughout the year to adjust for varying programmatic needs. Monitor your time lines, and ensure that when budget submissions are requested, you meet the important deadline. Doing so will also give you an opportunity to appeal your requested budget if parts of it are denied or reduced. Figure 13.1 provides an example of what a district physical education budget might look like at the beginning of the school year. You can see how spending could be monitored throughout the year to ensure that funds are either spent as initially planned or transferred based on changing needs throughout the school year; it also serves as a starting point for subsequent years. The following sections describe each component of the budget.

	YTD TRANSFERS AND ADJUSTMENT	CURRENT BUDGET	YTD ENCUMBRANCE	YTD EXPENDITURES	AVAILABLE BALANCE	PERCENT BUDGET REMAINING	ADJUSTED BALANCE
	$	$	$	$	$		$

As a physical education district administrator, your budget will reflect what you plan to do for the upcoming school year, what you presently have, and what you presently need. Your decisions will be centralized as you chart out the school year and determine the number of professional development days you will need substitute coverage for; the number of field trips you plan for special events (see chapter 7); and other supplies, equipment, and services you project. As a physical education department chairperson, your budget will be more localized in that you would look at the immediate needs of your school site programs. Regardless of the location of services, the needs assessment will be similar.

Budget Categories and Approaches

In most school districts across the United States, revenues and expenditures are placed into a general fund through which most of the district's financial transactions flow for general, unrestricted purposes. However, other dedicated funds, specifically for compliance with state or federal mandates, are also placed in the general fund. Since district funds are audited for accountability, budget items are uniquely categorized using a standardized code structure. These code structures and categories are commonly known as objects, functions, and funds; they are used to set up budgets as well as expend budgets through purchase orders. This section focuses on understanding how to develop budgets using the code structure, as well as various types of budgetary planning approaches.

Object Classification

One of the most traditional types of budget categories used in school districts, and the one most easily understood, is the object classification budget. The first thing to understand is that most state budgets use standardized object codes to classify general fund revenues and expenditures. The district chart of accounts is developed in alignment with each state reporting system for the purpose of collecting, organizing, analyzing, and displaying financial information. This budget classification is based on the areas of expenses in uniform groupings or categories. The most commonly grouped object codes are as follows:

- Personnel Services, Salaries
- Personnel Services, Employee Benefits
- Purchased Professional and Technical Services
- Purchased Property Services
- Other Purchased Services
- Supplies
- Property
- Other Objects
- Other Financing Uses

Figure 13.1 and table 13.1 depict how the object codes are used to identify the most commonly used budget items in a school district physical education program.

Function

The function describes the activities for which a service or material is acquired. The functions of the local educational agency (LEA) are classified into five broad areas:

1. Instruction
2. Support Services
3. Operation of Noninstructional Services
4. Facilities Acquisition, Construction, and Improvement Services
5. Other Financing Uses

Functions consist of activities that have somewhat the same general operational objectives. For example, the subfunctions (the first major subdivision of a function) of the function Support Services consist of such areas as transportation, pupil personnel services, administration, and so on. The function for Instruction is broken down by program (e.g., Regular, Special, Vocational). Construction of the functional coding structure beyond the subfunction classification is based on the principle that the classification of activities should be combinable, comparable, relatable, and mutually exclusive (Pennsylvania Office of the Budget, School Finance Unit, 2017).

TABLE 13.1 Sample Function and Object Codes

Frequently Used Program Function Codes	
510000—Basic Instruction	720000—Indirect Cost
610000—Student Services	771000—Evaluation
620000—Instructional Media Services	780000—Pupil Transportation Services
630000—Instructional and Curriculum Development	910000—Community Service
640000—Instructional Staff Training	

Frequently Used Program Object Codes		
514900—Substitute Teacher	Requires Fringe Benefits	539900—Printing and Duplicating
513600—In-Service Reimbursement		551000—Supplies
515000—Hourly Employee		552000—Textbooks
531000—Professional and Technical		553000—Periodicals
533000—Travel, In County		561200—Library Books
533100—Travel, Out of County		562000 - AV Materials
533200—Field Trips (Function 780000)		564000—Furniture, Fixtures, Equipment, and Computers
536000—Rental		569000—Software
539000—Other Purchased Services		579200—Indirect Cost (if grant funded)

As seen in figure 13.1 and table 13.1, object codes identify the sources of revenue and classify expenditures in terms of what services and goods are being purchased. Function codes identify the activity or services for which funds are spent.

Line-Item Budget

The line-item budget is similar to the object classification system in that they are most commonly used and relatively easy to set up (see figure 13.2). In essence, each individual item in the budget is set up on its own line for proposed expenses by department or cost center. Line-item budgets are often referred to as the *historical approach* since school site administrators often base their expenditure requests on historical expenditure and revenue data (National Center for Educational Statistics, 2003).

Whether you are an administrator overseeing a department or writing grants, you probably will need to learn the skills for developing line-item budgets. The greatest advantage of the line-item budget is the high degree of control that administrators have in monitoring their budgets and preparing financial reports since they can see every expenditure throughout the school year. By having immediate access to your budget, you can readily monitor your spending, determine which line items still have funds available for spending, and see which line items need additional funds that may require a transfer of funds from other line items.

Incremental Budgeting

Incremental budgeting is the process of using the previous year's budget and adding given incremental amounts to the following year's budget. These amounts are usually stated in across-the-board percentages as an increase or even possibly a decrease. In well-funded years, incremental budgeting allows you to plan for future program growth; for example, you may expect to have a 5 percent growth over the previous year's budget, so you can plan for it. However, in years when funding is challenging, you may be asked to provide a budget with an across-the-board 5 percent decrease in funding. When this situation occurs, you need to seriously evaluate the strengths and weaknesses of your programs and decide where you could cut funds without negatively affecting services to physical education teachers and, consequently, services to students.

FIGURE 13.2 Sample Line-Item Budget for Grant Funding

Main Street School, Anytown, USA

BUDGET SUMMARY: YEAR 1					
ITEM	**# OF PERSONNEL**	**# OF UNITS**	**TYPE OF UNIT**	**UNIT COST**	**ITEM TOTAL**
Substitute Days—Teachers	40	1	Days	$100.00	$4,000.00
Schools—Teacher Training	15	1	Days	$100.00	$1,500.00
			Subtotal for Training		$7,500.00
BUS TRANSPORTATION					
ITEM	**SCHOOLS**	**# OF UNITS**	**TYPE OF UNIT**	**UNIT COST**	**ITEM TOTAL**
Accessible Bus Transportation		55	each	$160.00	$8,800.00
			Subtotal Bus Transportation		$8,800.00
RECREATION EQUIPMENT					
ITEM		**UNITS**	**TYPE OF UNIT**	**UNIT COST**	**ITEM TOTAL**
All-Terrain Wheelchair		1	each	$2,300.00	$2,300.00
Power Soccer Chair Guard		10	each	$116.00	$1,160.00
Quickie All Sport Wheelchair		1	each	$1,950.00	$1,950.00
Assorted Equipment (volleyballs, basketballs, tennis balls and rackets, etc.)			each	$400.00	$400.00
			Subtotal Recreation Equipment		$5,810.00
EVALUATION					
ITEM					
Statistician					$2,000.00
PRINTING AND DUPLICATING SERVICES					
Printing Newsletters (2/year)		500	each	2	$2,000.00
			Subtotal Printing Services		$2,000.00
Indirect costs	3.50%				$890.00
Total grant funding					$25,000.00

Although each type of budget has advantages and disadvantages, through incremental budgeting there is usually equity across programming as departments are seen as being treated similarly. The disadvantage of this approach is that budgets are funded without a careful analysis of program effectiveness, often leading to wasteful spending and ensuring that all funds are spent regardless of need, enabling the budget to be maintained the following year. Budgetary slack—another disadvantage of incremental budgeting—involves overestimating budgeted expenses, again ensuring future funding.

Planning, Programming, Budgeting, and Evaluation System (PPBES)

Another approach, although more complex, to developing a budget is commonly known as the planning, programming, budgeting, and evaluation system (PPBES). Originally developed in the 1960s, this system uses an interactive and coordinated approach between components to develop the budget.

During the *planning* process, programmatic goals and objectives are carefully analyzed to determine their effectiveness in meeting the school district's as well as students' needs. At this time, goals and objectives can be revised based on the needs assessment, and they can be used to further establish policies and standards for continuous evaluation. The *programming* phase explores the actual programs and activities that will be used to carry out the specified goals and objectives. Resources are then allocated to the specific activities that are selected to attain the desired performance outcomes. *Budgeting* follows the planning and programming phases; it is directly related to the programs and activities that will be implemented to meet the desired outcomes. Finally, the *evaluation system* examines the outcomes of planning, programming, and budgeting in terms of the effectiveness of expected outcomes. Since the evaluation is ongoing, formative processes and monitoring systems are reviewed throughout the budget period. Figure 13.3 depicts the PPBES model.

The advantage of using the PPBES for budget development is that through a systems approach, attention is given to all aspects during the budget preparation with both process and product evaluations ongoing. It is also advantageous for long-range planning. The drawback is that it requires personnel trained in budget management; moreover, it is more complex due to the interactive processes. This approach becomes more problematic when changes occur in long-term goals and difficulties in cost data analyses occur.

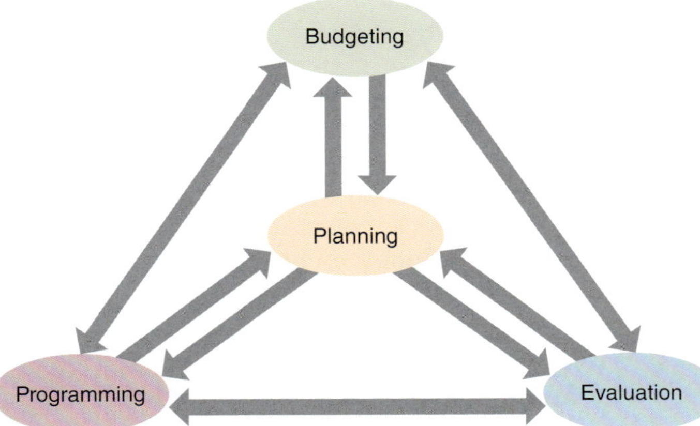

FIGURE 13.3 Planning, programming, budgeting, and evaluation system (PPBES).
Wisconsin Department of Public Instruction (1979, p. 3)

Zero-Based Budget

The basic premise behind zero-based budgeting (ZBB) is that all program activities and services must be justified during the budget development process for each new budget to be approved. It differs from incremental budgeting in that the previous year's budget is not the base for the following year's budget; instead, the base is the organization's or department's goals and objectives. A physical education administrator's annual allocated budget is based on the identified goals and objectives for the upcoming school year. For example, if you decide to expand programs for students with disabilities to attend more outside activities, then you would justify asking for additional funds for bus transportation. Through the ZBB approach, all programs and activities undergo a thorough review to determine whether future budgeting is necessitated. This approach gives the physical education district administrator the opportunity to fund new and innovative programs while, after careful analysis, closing or ending programs that may no longer need funding or are no longer effective. In essence, the greatest advantage of ZBB is that resources can be used where they will be most effective and have the greatest impact on program decisions. Such would be the case in bringing a new physical education program to schools in that once the initial equipment had been purchased, it would not need to be included in the following year's budget.

Capital Budget

For many school districts, capital expenditures represent the largest disbursement of funds. Capital budgets in school districts are usually long-term budgets, and they involve allocating funds for such projects as land acquisition, building new schools and facilities, renovations or additions, new technology infrastructure, and equipment needs. Purchasing administrators play a number of roles in capital budgeting, including assisting with requests for capital expenditures, serving on capital budget evaluation committees, and leading teams to acquire capital assets.

When a capital budget plan is developed for multiple fiscal years, it is usually developed

LEADERSHIP IN ACTION

The Importance of Managing Budgets

Artie Kamiya, MAT

Executive Director, North Carolina Society of Health and Physical Educators (NC SHAPE)

In times when budgetary constraints place a burden on developing and implementing new programs and curricula, district-level physical education administrators have a personal responsibility for managing their budgets regardless of whether the funding source is federal, state, local, or grant funds. It is up to the administrator to be knowledgeable about fiscal revenues and funding sources, as well as the budgetary policies and procedures for spending those funds.

Throughout my career, I have had the opportunity to work at a variety of administrative levels—as a senior administrator with Wake County Public Schools, a section chief for the North Carolina Department of Public Instruction, the president of a physical education publishing company, and the executive director of a statewide nonprofit. At each level, correctly managing funding streams was one of the more critical elements that kept me up at night; in other words, the fiscal responsibilities of an administrator can never be underrated or ignored.

For example, how you manage grant funds in particular will, in many cases, determine whether you receive additional grant funding for future applications. Your understanding of the district's bidding and ordering processes will determine how much lead time you will need. While it may be reasonable to assume that the funding agency or your district or school office can turn around needed purchases in a few weeks, you may be unexpectedly surprised by the length of time actually required to secure bids in advance of ordering equipment and supplies.

In managing budgets, you need to begin by planning what you intend to do with the funds you have and ensuring that they meet the goals and objectives of your program. Can staff T-shirts be purchased by grant funds? How about healthy snacks for meetings? In all cases, you'll need to know the answers to these three questions: What can be authorized? How will I keep track of expenses? What are my safeguards for never exceeding my available funds? By knowing the answers to these three planning questions, you'll greatly reduce the chances of having an audit exception.

---

through committee (as stated in chapter 8), and it involves several levels of administration and community members. Once the plan is finalized, it is presented to the school board for final approval. This is a rigorous process as it involves large sums of money and establishing community trust and confidence.

Expenditure of Funds: Purchasing Process

The bid process is an ongoing process; it occurs throughout the school year as new equipment or services are needed. Depending on the spending threshold established by each school district, in some cases the bid process should be completed before the purchasing process begins. Once the district budget is developed and approved, you have the obligation to be fiscally responsible in expending the funds throughout the school year. Whether your budget is composed of public funds or grant funding, being accountable for every dollar spent requires knowledge of the purchasing as well as the **auditing processes** and procedures.

Requisition Process

The requisition process is the first step in the request to spend funds before the actual purchase order is finalized and sent to the vendor. A **purchase requisition** is an internal document that the physical education administrator develops for the department, requesting the office of procurement management to initiate a purchase order. The request is usually electronically generated through each school district's automated system for the purchase of supplies, services, equipment, or any other item that you have requested in your budget.

As seen in figure 13.4, the purchase order requisition form should include these elements:

1. Specific information regarding billing, purchasing, and shipping

FIGURE 13.4 Sample Purchase Order Requisition

Bill to: Union School District
123 Main Street, Suite 100
Any Town, USA 12345

Purchase Order # ____________

Purchased from: ____________ Ship to: ____________

Date of order	Shipment method	Terms	FOB

ITEM NO.	QUANTITY	DESCRIPTION OF ITEMS (SPECIFIC COLOR, SIZE)	UNIT PRICE		TOTAL AMOUNT	
Total amount						

Funding structure:

FUND	FUNCTION	OBJECT	PROGRAM	AMOUNT

Authorized by: ____________ Date: ____________

Approved by: ____________ Date: ____________

FM 1234 Rev. 2018

2. The date on which the purchase request is finalized
3. The shipment method
4. The terms of payment, delivery date
5. The free on board (FOB) shipping point (customer takes receipt of goods) upon delivery
6. The item number, if from a catalog
7. The quantity
8. The description of the item (including size and color)
9. The unit price
10. The total or extended price
11. The funding structure
12. The signature approvals
13. The date processed

Since the actual purchase order is a legally binding document (discussed next), it is always best to get a quote from the vendor, and either attach the actual quote to the purchase requisition or place the quote number on the purchase requisition. Doing so ensures that you will be charged for the exact amount negotiated. As a point of reference, when securing quotes, be sure to ask for freight or shipping charges in advance as well as make sure that no sales taxes are included in the order (most school districts are tax exempt).

Purchase Orders

The purchase order is where the buying actually occurs, but only after the purchasing requisition has been finalized through the approval process. It is the responsibility of the physical education administrator to ensure that all authorized personnel sign off on a purchase order. Additionally, depending on individual school district policies, several levels of signatures may be required and contingent on the spending thresholds previously determined through school board approval. Large-ticket items for district-wide purchases exceeding threshold amounts (e.g., $50,000) may also need school board approval prior to the processing of orders. Violating these procedures could result in unauthorized purchases, which then would become the obligation of the school district.

A purchase order is actually a legally binding document between you (the buyer) and the vendor. The purchase order, the most commonly utilized method for procuring goods and services, once approved, serves as a binding commitment for the vendor to deliver goods and services and for the district to remit payment to the vendor after the item or items and an invoice are received by the district. As a rule of thumb, *only* the office of procurement management should send the approved purchase order to the vendor. This protocol will avoid any confusion or duplication of orders in the purchasing process. The physical education administrator can maintain communication with the vendor once the purchase order is processed but should not be involved in sending the purchase order to the vendor.

A purchase order further serves as an important accounting document because it contains information on the expenditure to be made and the account funding structure to be charged. Once issued, the purchase order encumbers funds, which serves as an expenditure control mechanism, and it can easily be tracked electronically (as exhibited in figure 13.1). Additionally, the purchase order is utilized in the accounts payable process; it documents that an order has been received and accepted by the user and that payment can be made to the vendor.

Invoice

Once the purchase order has been received by the vendor and the vendor delivers the purchased goods to the school, make sure that the school provides your office with a signed receipt of goods. This document will validate that the equipment was delivered in good working order or that acceptable services were provided. Since the vendor will send your office an invoice immediately after the goods are delivered, it is critically important to have that receipt of goods in hand before approving payment. Receiving goods online through the electronic automated system communicates with your office of procurement management that it is appropriate to process payment. In some cases, vendors may send you an invoice immediately upon receipt of the purchase order; however, it is highly recommended that you do not approve payment until everything is delivered and services are provided. Never offer to pay for goods or services in advance.

Open Purchase Orders

Used in district administrative offices, an open purchase order is usually permitted when services are rendered several times during the school year and a contract exists between the vendor and the administrative office for a set amount of funds payable monthly using the same purchase order number. For example, your district warehouse may store physical education equipment or stadium or facility rentals for program utilization throughout the school year. In this case, the owner of the warehouse might charge a $300 monthly fee, which would be payable each month and charged to the same funding structure using the same purchase order number. By using an open purchase order, you have to go out on bid only once a year rather than monthly, and the cost is secured throughout the year.

Purchasing Card (P-Card)

A purchasing card (P-Card) is in essence a commercial credit card provided to higher-level district administrators for ease of purchasing items under a certain threshold (usually under $1000), which is decided by the school board. The advantage of using a P-Card is that purchases can be made immediately without going through the formal purchase order process; however, the P-Card can be used only by the administrator whose name is on the card. Since you, the cardholder, are ultimately responsible for all purchases made using the P-Card, it is highly recommended that you do not share the number or card with anyone because it might result in unauthorized expenditures. Although there is a good amount of purchasing flexibility with using a P-Card, the district administrator is still bound to using district-approved vendors for certain supplies and following all district purchasing policies and procedures. It is also extremely important to track expenditures when using a P-Card to ensure that funds exist in the funding structure that the P-Card will be charged against. Additionally, as a district-level administrator, whether you take your P-Card to a business for an immediate purchase or secure the goods over the phone, make sure to provide either a tax-exempt form to the vendor or the tax-exempt number verbally.

Working With Vendors

In school districts across the United States, apart from personnel salaries, a large portion of a school district's institutional budget goes toward purchasing goods and essential services to operate the school district. These goods and services can range from purchasing equipment and textbooks to contracting for cleaning, maintenance, evaluation, and psychological services. In many school districts, the office of procurement management maintains a list of authorized vendors to select services and goods from; this allows those vendors who have officially registered as vendors with the school district to secure purchase requisitions. Vendors seeking to conduct business with the school district can apply to become a vendor any time during the school year, but they must reapply annually. To do business with a vendor that has not preregistered with the district, the administrator must either request that the seller become a vendor or secure a sole source letter stating why this is the only vendor these goods or services can be purchased from. To avoid any legal issues with the purchasing process, it is recommended that you ask for assistance if you are uncertain about working with a particular vendor.

Aside from the formal process of working with vendors, the ability to develop and maintain effective relationships with vendors will assist in maintaining clearly defined outcomes and accountability. It is important to note that working with vendors is a business engagement and that a collaborative and respectful relationship should be maintained.

Selecting Vendors

Since doing business with school districts can provide lucrative opportunities for vendors, contractors, and consultants, most school districts develop their own policies and procedures for persons, organizations, or businesses aspiring to become approved vendors. However, regardless of the school district, the one common denominator among districts is that before you as the administrator can do business with any vendor or consultant, the person or organization *must* submit a vendor application to the school district and be approved. Once the vendor is on the approved list, other district-specific requirements may be involved in selecting from the list, but at least there is a large pool to choose from.

For many physical education administrators, selected vendors often come from within the profession, and administrators probably have the opportunity to meet with their representatives in the district office or at state or national conventions. However, it is a good idea to explore online and paper catalogs for selected products because many items are also available through other subject area vendors and educational catalogs. Products that support health education and social, mental, and emotional health are examples of such items.

School districts may also hold threshold amounts that you can spend with any one vendor. If purchasing consumable supplies, such as balls, jump ropes, and hula hoops, you may be capped at $5,000 for any one vendor and will need to split your order between a couple of vendors. When purchasing more expensive equipment, such as treadmills, cycles, and weight room equipment, your spending threshold would be higher; however, the equipment would have to go out on bid or off another district or state contract.

Other than personal relationships, it is advantageous to look at the number of years a vendor has been in service, personnel who can answer questions, product lines, prices, and, most importantly, customer service reputation. When selecting consultants, it is also helpful to ask for references to ensure not only that the services can be delivered but also that they can be delivered in a timely manner and meet high standards. In particular, it would be important if you were hiring an evaluator or statistician for a grant- or community-funded project. Ensuring that the contractor can deliver the statistical analysis as well as complete the interim and final evaluations in a form that is ready for submission to the funding agency will lend great support to your project as well as your credibility as a grant manager.

Sole Source Vendor

Although the rules for securing vendors are clear and explicit, there are times when the only option is a sole source vendor. A sole source vendor is a company that has exclusivity in selling a particular product, whether it was developed by that vendor or is so distinctive that no other vendor carries the exact same product or another that meets the specifications. One example of a sole source product is the HOPSports Mini Training System; HOPSports, Inc. is the sole source for manufacturing and distributing the system. When a sole source vendor is selected, a formal letter must be submitted by the vendor explaining what the product is and why it is the only vendor for the product. The sole source letter must be submitted to the office of procurement management along with the purchase requisition before the purchase order is completed. In other instances, a sole source vendor can be utilized when a particular product has item specifications so distinctive that no other similar product meets those specifications. For example, this situation can occur when purchasing treadmills or other cardiorespiratory equipment. Although several manufacturers sell similar products, each one offers unique electronic components.

Vendor Gifts and Relations

As stated earlier, one of the criteria for selecting a vendor may be based on the personal relationships that you develop with the management, a representative, or the company itself. Although it can be tempting, school district employees cannot accept anything of value from a vendor, such as personal gifts or gratuities, because they may be seen as influencing the purchasing process. Although the acceptance of gifts varies by state statutes and municipalities, to avoid problems that could have serious consequences, school district employees should not accept personal gifts from vendors or contractors.

Conflict of Interest

Conflict of interest is another legal topic worth discussion in relation to selecting a vendor. Since public school employees are governed by a code of ethics for public officers and employees and by other statutes in the education code, as an administrator you must pay careful attention to how you choose to do business with a vendor. These statutes include prohibitions against accepting gifts, rewards, promise of future employment, favor, or service based on an understanding that official actions or judgment could be influenced by such a gift (Fla. Stat. § 112.313[2] [2024]). Many states, such as Florida, have state statutes that spell out provisions for conflicts of interest:

> *As a public officer or employee, you may not work for or contract with a business entity or agency that (1) is regulated by or doing business with your own entity, (2) would create a frequently recurring conflict between your private interests and your public duties, or (3) would impede the discharge of your public duties. (Fla. Stat. § 112.313[7][a])*

> *Public officers and procurement employees may not, on behalf of their agency, purchase or lease from their own, their spouse's, or their child's business. Public officers and procurement employees may not sell or lease from their own, their spouse's, or their child's business to their agency. (Fla. Stat. § 112.313[3])*

Other school district policies have been developed by Neola (formerly known as North East Ohio Learning Associates), an organization that provides guidance to states and school districts in developing board bylaws and policies, as well as administrative guidelines and procedures, which have been adopted districtwide. The following are examples of such policies (Miami-Dade County Public Schools 2011).

A conflict of interest shall exist upon use by an employee of the authority of his/her office or the use of any confidential information received through his/her employment for the private pecuniary benefit of the employee, or the employee's immediate family or a business with which the employee or a member of the employee's immediate family has employment or ownership worth $5000 or more, either directly or indirectly, without disclosure to the appropriate District official.

A. Financial Interest. Except as authorized in any collective bargaining agreement, an employee shall not engage, or have any interest, financial or otherwise, direct or indirect, in any business, transaction or professional entity, either as a director, officer, partner, trustee, employee, or manager in that entity, which conflicts with or impairs the proper discharge of official duties or which could bring disfavor or disrespect upon the employee or the District. Any provision of this code which requires disclosure to District officials will be satisfied by the filing of a financial disclosure statement in the form required of members of the Board.

B. Financial Conflict. An employee who has a financial conflict of interest because of a relationship with a business, governmental agency or not for profit institution must recuse himself/herself from any decision concerning that entity including any decision to contract or not to contract with the entity and the administration of the contract. The reason for such recusal must be stated in writing and filed with the Superintendent and the Board Attorney prior to or at the time of the action requiring the recusal.

Vendor and Contractor Evaluation

An administrator with purchasing responsibilities is prudent with regard to evaluating vendors and contractors. This process lends credence to the effectiveness of the purchasing function. At the end of each school year, vendors should be evaluated on their ability to deliver products in a timely manner, on customer support, and on the quality of their products or services. Contractors should also be evaluated at the end of the fiscal year on the quality of their services, the effectiveness of their services in contributing to the success of the program, and the personal relationships they develop with the district and school site personnel involved in the program. For example, say you are managing a grant and secure the services of an outside contractor to perform the evaluation of your grant data, and the evaluator fails to meet the grant-required deadline or the evaluation is not completed. You would want to make sure that those services are not rendered by that contractor in the future by any other district office. The benefit of formally evaluating vendors and contractors is to provide information to the office of procurement management (and, in some cases, the office of grants administration) so that there is a database of the quality of services performed. This database provides an opportunity for future informed decisions to be made when future services are needed.

Bid Process

For most purchases made by local school district offices, the bidding process is not a requirement. However, when the amount of the purchase exceeds a certain threshold determined by the school board, the office of procurement management will send out a bid. The intent of the bid is to provide for open and honest competition through which the district can secure the best-quality items for the best prices. Since the **bid process** is a legal process, all bids are advertised by the office of procurement management; bidders submit their bids in a sealed envelope, and submitted bids are opened at the time and place designated in the advertisement.

As a physical education administrator, you play a vital role in assisting staff in the office of procurement management by providing the exact specifications for the equipment or services that you are looking to purchase. For example, if you are designing a new weight room for a senior high school, you will identify the type of equipment, the weight load, and any ancillary equipment you are seeking to purchase and then provide the specifications for all equipment. The procurement staff will then put the information in a bid format and usually ask you to review it one more time. Once the bids are secured and the equipment is purchased, you cannot change your mind, so take your time when working on equipment specifications.

Quotes

As seen throughout this chapter, every school district sets its own local policies for dollar amount thresholds when developing purchase requisitions, so the physical education administrator should become familiar with all local and state requirements. In many districts, the threshold may be up to $1,000 before you need to solicit quotes or go out on bid; in others, it may be capped at $500. A quote differs from a bid based on the amount of funds you are expending. A bid may require a formal process, whereas a quote may fall under your responsibility to contact three vendors—one usually a minority vendor—and then purchase the equipment based on the best price. A quote still requires that you submit exact product or service specifications to the vendor. Once you place your purchase order, you will be required to attach the three quotes to the requisition, so make sure you keep a hard copy of the vendor responses. Securing three quotes for purchasing goods is a common practice in all educational settings. It is applicable whether you are a school district administrator or a school site administrator.

Another issue to be cognizant of is that most school districts operate their offices of procurement management such that they are fair and equitable in selecting vendors for goods and services. To ensure that you follow these guidelines, it is highly recommended (if not required by your school district) that when you reach the purchasing threshold and need to secure three quotes, you make sure one of the three falls under the category of minority vendor, woman-owned business, or a business owned by one or more persons with a disability. Doing so will ensure that diversity and inclusion exist in an equitable environment where potential vendors can seek to secure business with the school district.

When sending out a request for quotes, be as transparent and specific as possible to avoid any appearance of favoritism or conflict of interest. For example, if you are ordering basketballs for indoor use, be specific about the size of the ball in terms of centimeters or inches, the material (whether leather or rubber), its purpose (indoor use), and its sizing (youth sizes or regulation sizes for men or women). Once you receive your three quotes, review each independently to ensure that they meet the exact specifications that you requested, then place your order based on the best price and whether the vendor can meet your required terms for delivery.

For time-saving purposes, it would be beneficial for you to meet with personnel from the office of procurement management to see whether the quotes can be held for the length of the school year or not. If not, then every time you need to order the same equipment, you will have to send out for quotes again.

Competitive Bids

Competitive bidding aims to obtain goods and services at the lowest prices by stimulating competition among vendors through open and transparent advertising. An invitation to bid on select products or services is almost always initiated by staff from the office of procurement management, with the assistance of the physical education administrator in setting the specifications for the needed products or services. Once the specifications are set, then the formal bid request is sent out to initiate the formal competitive sealed bidding process. Each school district has on its procurement website instructions to vendors on how to submit a bid, and it is up to the vendors to know and follow those guidelines. The invitation to bid usually consists of detailed, specific instructions to bidders, specifications for each line item, and how the bids will be advertised. A reasonable time and date deadline is always assigned to the bid.

A major advantage of the competitive process is that many vendors will include services that may go beyond the specifications. For example, for fitness equipment, some vendors may include a warranty of up to three years on parts and services while others may only include one year. For the physical education administrator who is concerned about future maintenance costs, this result of competition is a valuable perk.

School districts, based on their policies, may have open competitive bid practices where the sealed bids are open to full view of any interested party that wants to witness the bid opening. In closed competitive bidding, the bids are opened in front of only authorized personnel. Once the bid is awarded to the selected vendor, the contracts must be developed and approved before services can commence.

Catalog Bids

Catalog bids are also sent out through the office of procurement management; in this case, vendors agree to provide a percent discount on items purchased through their catalog. These items also have a dollar amount threshold set by each school district, and they are usually for incidental and miscellaneous purchases. Most items on catalog bids fall under instructional and general supplies; examples include office supplies, art and music supplies, maintenance supplies, miscellaneous instructional supplies, science equipment and supplies, and physical education and athletic supplies. These items can be purchased throughout the year as needed, and the vendor is held to those prices.

Audits

As part of the **financial management** process, it's not unusual for your program or office budgets to be audited on an annual basis. An audit is an objective examination and evaluation of the financial statements of an organization or of a department within an organization to ensure compliance with spending policies. Most audits are conducted by an independent auditor hired within a school district or an outside company contracted to conduct an audit. In addition to internal budgets, you may have a federal grant or receive funding under various entitlement programs, such as IDEA, which will also require audit reviews.

If you do get notification that your program is being audited, the first thing you need to do is to alert your senior-level administrator that your program is being audited and then comply with all requests. If it is a grant audit, it would also be beneficial to notify your office of grants administration that a particular grant is being audited since those administrative personnel have extensive experience and could serve as an excellent resource to assist you through the process.

Although most financial transactions are conducted electronically, it would be a good time to start requesting hard copies of all of your purchase orders and expenditures under a specific program. Your secretary probably has copies of all purchase requisitions and purchase orders filed in folders and notebooks according to program numbers since this is one of the secretary's responsibilities. The job of the auditor is not to catch you doing something wrong, but rather to make sure that the financial records and expenditures are in compliance with district, state, or federal guidelines. If you follow all of the procurement policies and procedures outlined in this chapter, then the audit, although a time-consuming process, will produce positive results and will show that you as the physical education administrator follow district procurement protocols and can effectively manage budgets.

Travel and Meal Reimbursement

The last type of budget issue to be addressed is reimbursement for travel and meals to select functions, meetings, and conferences. If you are fortunate enough to have a district travel budget or a travel budget included in a grant, you will be asked to complete the anticipated travel budget in advance of your trip and submit it along with your request for professional leave or temporary duty. Upon return, you will once again be required to submit the appropriate paperwork with all original receipts. Make sure to get pre-travel approval through your administrative reporting chain; otherwise, the request for reimbursement may not be approved. The difficult part of the process is that unless you have a district requisition that pays for your airfare and conference registration fees in advance, you will probably have to carry airfare, hotel, meals, taxi or shuttle, and other incidental expenses on your personal credit card until the school district processes your request for reimbursement. Figure 13.5 provides a sample form for request for travel reimbursement.

www

FIGURE 13.5 Sample Out-of-County Travel Reimbursement Form

Request for Travel Out of County Travel Reimbursement
XYZ School District

Employee name: ____________ Title: ____________ Employee number: ____________

Employee work location name: ____________ WL# ________ Date of request: ____________

Departure date: ____________ Return date: ____________ No. of days requested: ____________

Reimbursement for Incurred Expenses:

The travel expense form must be submitted within 5 business days after travel is complete. All original receipts, conference/meeting programs, and agenda must be submitted with this request for reimbursement.

DESCRIPTION OF EXPENSES	REQUISITION #	ACTUAL EXPENSE	DUE EMPLOYEE
A. Transportation			
1. Air carrier (must have 3 quotes attached) = $ ____________		$	$
2. Private vehicle: ____________ miles @ ____________ rate		$	$
3. Rental car (must be approved in advance)		$	$
4. Taxi, tolls, parking, rideshare service, shuttle, etc. (attach original receipts)		$	$
B. Per diem option ____________ days Dates: ____________ X @ XYZ $ per day = $ ____________		$	$
C. Hotel # of nights ____________ @ $ ____________ nightly rate + $ ____________ taxes Hotel parking: $ ____________		$ $	$ $
D. Incidental expenses: $ ____________ (provide original receipts)		$	$
E. Conference registration fees: Attached documentation must include agenda, breakout sessions attended, copy of paid registration, sessions/events that included meals		$	$
Total			$

Charge to:

FUND	WORK LOCATION	OBJECT	PROGRAM	FUNCTION	CHARGE LOCATION

Authorization:

Supervisor of charge location	Signature	Title	Date
Superintendent of designee	Signature	Title	Date

After Travel

I hereby certify that these expenses were incurred by me while on official business for XYZ School District and request reimbursement for the above amount.

Name of employee requesting reimbursement	Signature	Title	Date

FM 1234 Revised 9/18

Conclusion

Financial management is a major administrative responsibility for the district-level physical education administrator. This chapter has discussed many aspects of financial management to increase understanding of the expectations, policies, and procedures that are common to most school districts as well as those that are specific to individual district requirements. Each school district's office of procurement management posts a procurement manual on its website that provides the most comprehensive guidance for school district and school site personnel as well as for vendors or for anyone looking to do business with the school district. The office of procurement management further sets the tone for operating within a code of ethics for all procurement transactions.

Understanding how district-level budgets are funded and developed is the first step in comprehending the procurement process. The processes involved—from planning the budget to developing purchase requisitions to the final approval of purchase orders—reflects how goods and services are approved and contracted within the school district. Practicing prudent financial management will ensure that all expenditures are conducted in compliance with spending policies and that they will hold up to both internal and external audits.

Review Questions

1. Identify each of the most commonly used budgets, and describe how each is developed.
2. Financial management is a key administrative skill. Explain the importance of financial management when one is developing and overseeing a physical education district budget.
3. Describe the differences between a purchase requisition and a purchase order.
4. Describe the difference between securing quotes and securing competitive bids.
5. Define what a conflict of interest is in the procurement process and how it can be avoided.
6. What is the purpose of a programmatic audit, and what information might the auditor request?

» Visit HK*Propel* for reproducible forms.

CHAPTER 14

Grant Writing and Outside Funding

Jayne D. Greenberg

Photo courtesy of the Loppet Foundation

LEARNING OBJECTIVES

After reading this chapter, you will be able to do the following:

- Identify ways to secure existing dollars, or local funding.
- Discuss strategies to develop a business partnership plan.
- Develop a presentation package to access corporate donations.
- Explain outside funding through fundraising measures.
- Describe the basics of grant writing.
- Discuss how to secure funding through federal, foundation, and local grants.

KEY CONCEPTS

business partnerships
corporate sponsorship
discretionary funding
fundraising procedures
grant-writing process

In times when the overall student population is growing and legislative dollars for public education are shrinking, many constraints (e.g., funding and hiring certified teachers) are placed on all programs, especially when public demands that school resources be spent on increasing student standardized test scores, reducing class size, and instituting tougher academic standards take precedence. These issues were further compounded by the COVID-19 pandemic, when schools were closed and many students experienced an academic slide; these students did not have access to technology to perform online learning, found it difficult to learn in the online environment, or did not have a parent or caregiver available to ensure that they were online during the designated at-home school hours. As an unintended consequence, physical education is often the hardest hit by budget cuts. When you are facing difficult financial times, nontraditional funding sources are vital to helping you achieve restructuring and modernization of your physical education programs. Financial opportunities are available if you spend time and exert a lot of effort in finding them. Those who hold the purse strings for many funding opportunities are eager to see students become active and healthy adults who have the skills to be successful in college and in their careers. Fully funded and effective physical education programs can help students achieve these outcomes.

This chapter moves from the simplest to the more complex methods of securing funds for your program, school, or school district. First, it examines where funds already exist from local sources; then, it moves on to community, business, and corporate sponsorships; and finally, it covers the basics of grant writing. The guidelines presented here will help you put your own innovative ideas into action and secure the funds you need to enhance your school's physical education programs, projects, and activities and fulfill your overall objective of developing individuals through their physical literacy journey.

Securing Local Funding: Dipping Into Discretionary Accounts

Individual school districts at the local level, called local educational agencies (LEAs), receive money from their respective state departments of education, in a proportionate manner, based on several evolving factors. Although state funding for PreK-12 education varies from state to state, it is generally distributed according to a per-pupil spending formula, but with weighted differential factors. These weighted factors include the number of students with disabilities, the number of students of low socioeconomic status, and the number of students who speak English as a second language. Other factors vary from state to state.

Local school districts further receive additional funds through the collection of property taxes when local governments collect taxes from residential and commercial properties. Therefore, the dollars generated by student FTE (full-time equivalent) are placed in the principal's discretionary account. The discretionary account is money that the principal can spend as long as the money spent benefits students and meets the state statutes for mandatory academic programming, current operations, or capital outlay and maintenance. Many school districts have also become creative and have placed additional school funding opportunities for items such as additional teacher pay and school safety through referenda on voter election ballots.

Once funding for mandatory educational programming is allocated, principals have the authority to disseminate funds as they see appropriate. The dissemination of these dollars is usually based on two program categories: (1) programs that support the strategic plan, goals, and objectives of both the individual school and the school district; and (2) programs that bring recognition and accolades to the school. Although physical education programs usually fall into the latter category, with the legislative focus on wellness policies in alignment with the National School Lunch Program and the School Breakfast Program, funded by the U.S. Department of Agriculture (USDA), they can no longer be eliminated from supporting the goals and objectives of the school district. Support can be further generated through provisions in the Every Student Succeeds Act (ESSA), making funding available through entitlements such as Title I, Title II, and Title IV (Jones & Workman, 2016).

So, how do you tap into the **discretionary funding** pot of gold? The best way is to show how your program supports the educational goals of the school and the needs of the students. Using scientific evidence to show how increasing student fitness levels supports an increase in academic performance would link your program to the goals and objectives of the school or to the strategic alignment of the school district. To become a part of the solution means becoming a contributing part of the school improvement plan (SIP) or school advisory committee (SAC). Although meetings are often held after school (and, in many cases, they interfere in part with your interscholastic practice schedule or intramural or after-school activity program), it is critical that you initiate creative coverage to ensure your attendance at these meetings. Having a member of your school's wellness council, or the school's comprehensive health committee, also hold a seat on the SIP or SAC committee will further lend support to securing funding for your programs. Today's principals look for programs that support the total school environment in a collaborative manner, not programs that work in silos. Creating a healthy school environment affects all members of the school environment.

Utilizing this strategy, you not only maintain high visibility for your program or department but also get to participate in the inner workings of the decision-making process. The key is sharing this concept with other members of your school and community, enabling them to buy in to the need. Inviting print, broadcasting, and mass media to your school to publicize your program will further add value to your efforts and engage new advocates to support future efforts. Social media also will quickly get the message out. Once you visibly associate yourself and the program with the school's mission and goals, financial support will be a necessity rather than a luxury.

Tagging Onto Existing Programs

Another strategy for securing local funds is to connect your program with another school-based program whose funding is provided under a different structure. For example, in a traditional school setting, students enrolled in alternative education or exceptional student education (ESE) programs usually take physical education with the general population. However, keep in mind that the FTE discussed earlier is significantly higher for students enrolled in alternative education and ESE programs than for students enrolled in the general educational program. Therefore, because every student enrolled in your programs has equal access to all your equipment (especially as the education system moves toward full inclusion, ensuring educational equity), you could request that alternative education or ESE dollars fund a specific piece of equipment; for example, you could request funds for upper-body ergometers for nonambulatory students to enhance their cardiorespiratory fitness. However, because of auditing issues, be certain that the equipment requested through these funds will be used by students as designated in the request.

Aligning with the digital convergence occurring in schools nationwide (as discussed in chapter 9) is another strategy worth exploring. With respect to technology, it is advisable to work closely with other faculty members or the instructional technology department across disciplines to ensure that students enrolled in physical education have access to the latest software and hardware. Since technology is constantly evolving, it is critical to your programs to ensure that the mobile devices needed on the field or in the gymnasiums stay on the procurement radar. A common way to accomplish this task as a physical education teacher is by coordinating your assignments with those of other faculty members. Say, for example, that the career or technical education teacher is providing presentation software lessons (e.g., using PowerPoint, Prezi, Google slides, Visme, or Keynote). Working closely with that teacher provides an opportunity for your students to develop their physical education and fitness education electronic portfolios. In a win-win situation, the career or technical education teacher accomplishes her instructional objectives by delivering the mechanics of the use of the software, and you accomplish your instructional objectives by having the students exposed to technology while adding physical education content to their business education applications. Similar lessons could be coordinated in science classes if heart rate monitors or activity trackers are purchased through funding generated by the National Science Foundation (NSF) for studying such topics as cardiac output in a physiology or biology class. In health classes, nutrition software might be purchased with entitlement dollars; this software could also be loaded onto the school's bank of computers through the purchase site licenses with district funds.

Parent–Teacher Association (PTA) Projects

At the elementary school level in particular, one of the most highly respected organizations that works closely with the schools is the parent–teacher association (PTA) or parent–teacher–student association (PTSA). Guided by the mission of supporting and speaking on behalf of children and youth in the schools and community, assisting parents or guardians in developing skills they need to protect and raise their children, and encouraging parent or guardian and public involvement in the public schools of this nation, members of the PTA and PTSA play an integral role in the overall development of educational programs and health issues of all students.

Because of their high profile of involvement, it is not surprising that educators often turn to the PTA or PTSA to assist in raising funds for individual school projects. After all, isn't it the parents you see selling paper and pencils before school in the school bookstore, selling physical education uniforms before and after school, selling wrapping paper prior to the holiday season, and selling food items? However, the real working capital of a PTA or PTSA lies not in its treasury but in its members' energy, resourcefulness, and determination to promote the well-being of children and youth. The local PTA or PTSA usually sponsors one major annual fundraising project for a specific educational purpose. Justifying to the parents your specific need in physical education is one way of getting on their calendar of fundraising activities. In addition, knowing the members of your PTA or PTSA could prove to be beneficial for securing funds from the community. Many members of the PTA or PTSA either work in local area businesses or know someone of influence in your community. Networking through the PTA or PTSA is one of the best vehicles for getting your needs known. The amount of funding can range from supporting a simple addition to the gardens on school property to supporting the complete replacement of grass with artificial turf.

Simply put, local money is often made available, through various sources, to accomplish all your existing instructional objectives as well as a few new initiatives. You just need to show that what you do contributes to the overall mission of the school and has a direct impact on all students. On a final note, don't forget to give public recognition to your school, parent group, supervisor, or principal for helping with everything you do. That acknowledgment goes a long way.

Education Foundations

Another type of locally based source of revenue is a school district foundation. Education foundations are private, nonprofit 501(c)(3) tax-exempt charitable organizations. Although these foundations have a board of directors separate from the local school boards, their primary function is to work in partnership with the local school district. Since they qualify as charitable organizations, they can collect tax-deductible donations that can be used to support educational programs, student needs, and requests from teachers and administrators. In many cases, school district foundations are the ones that host large-scale events, such as community 5K runs or VIP galas, to raise funds for programs and activities that are not funded through the normal operating budget yet directly benefit students and staff in the local school district. Through these types of activities, educational foundations give the community the opportunity to be a part of the educational system.

Community foundations such as the Children's Trust (www.thechildrenstrust.org) and the Health Foundation of South Florida (www.hfsf.org) are just two examples of local foundations in Miami, Florida, that serve the needs of the community to ensure health and wellness for all. At the national level, the Robert Wood Johnson Foundation (www.rwjf.org) focuses on developing a culture of health, and the Foundation for the National Institutes of Health (www.fnih.org) provides funding for local projects. One can find other funding sources through self-inquiry, or several large school districts with grants administration offices can lend assistance. The Foundation Center and Gold Star, now known as Candid (https://candid.org), or any general search engine will be of great assistance.

Securing and Developing Business Partnerships

Now that you have begun to conceptualize how relatively simple it is to secure local funding, it's time to venture out into the business world. The local business community, whether large or small, urban, suburban, or rural, has a vested interest in the operation of the schools for two primary reasons: The members of the business community are predominantly parents of children who attend the schools, and the graduates will be the next generation of employees for that business community. As tax-paying members of the community, nobody knows better than the business community the financial constraints placed on educational institutions. Knowing the importance of quality education across the board, many community businesses have come forward to provide both financial and human resources to public education.

By definition, partnerships achieve mutually agreed-upon goals and objectives by matching community resources to identified needs of the school system or individual schools, and by matching school resources to the identified needs of a particular partner, such as a business, university, or community group. The long-term purpose of developing partnerships is to provide greater awareness and understanding of the needs and resources of the schools and community; to provide ongoing dialogue between schools and the community; and to work together to improve and enhance educational programs responsive to the needs of the students, the community, and society.

Because of the financial responsibilities involved, securing a business partner becomes a formal process that often requires a memorandum of understanding (MOU) or letter of understanding (LOU). Although not as formal as a grant application, it begins with identifying a need and ends with an evaluation. But before signing on any dotted line, make sure you process the MOU or LOU through the proper chain of command and that your school district attorneys review the agreement. Doing so will ensure both that all language is in keeping with the mandated state statutes and that there are no potentially embarrassing legal issues following implementation. As with any other community-based partnership, this partnership process should also follow the guidelines set by your school system pertaining to entering contractual agreement.

Once you decide that your funding needs can be accomplished by securing a local **business partnership**, it is recommended that you follow the process shown in figure 14.1. You must have a solid, well-thought-out plan before approaching a potential funder.

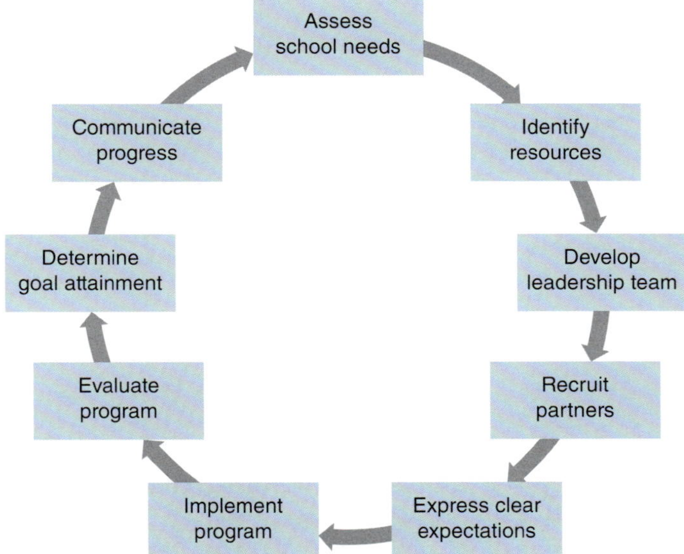

FIGURE 14.1 The school–community partnership process.

LEADERSHIP IN ACTION

Importance of Community Partnerships

Brett Fuller, MS

Curriculum Specialist for Health and Physical Education; Milwaukee Public Schools

David Nelson, PhD, MS

Department of Family and Community Medicine; Medical College of Wisconsin

Issue

Students need more than schools alone for support.

The Big Idea

Working with partners to support schools and not just for their benefit is essential to impact student achievement positively.

Implementation

Early in my career as an administrator of health and physical education, I discovered that many individuals and agencies wanted to impact students within our schools. However, many potential partners did not ask about the district's needs. Instead, many had their own ideas of what we needed. One partner in particular, the Medical College of Wisconsin, always asks, "What do we need?" first. This partnership has continued for over 15 years; since it began, it has expanded to include more like-minded agencies and individuals. As a result, we have successfully written grants for our district and also new partners. Even when there is no grant funding to support projects, we continue working together. This example underscores several principles of community engagement, including building trust, bidirectional learning, and developing partnerships with a long-term vision. When the partnership is about what *we* can accomplish *together*, the experience is more prosperous for *all* involved.

Takeaway

Developing long-standing collaborative partnerships make a difference in student achievement and being able to find resources to support student achievement successfully.

Results

Several years ago, we applied for a large grant to develop a new system to support physical education and connect to after-school programming. As part of the grant process, we presented to the granting authority. The chair of the committee told us that, on paper, she was going to vote No to our grant application. After witnessing firsthand the depth of our partnership and the genuine collaboration we modeled together, she had changed her vote to Yes. Due to our collaborative partnership, we can find additional support for our students.

The first step in developing your potential business partnership is to *identify your needs*. In essence, you must ask what is lacking in your educational program that you want to fund. For example, if you decide you want to install a wellness or fitness center in a particular school, ask yourself why you need a wellness center. What difference will it make for students, the school, and the community? Where is the deficiency, and what program can be implemented to correct it? Test your concept by asking yourself some relevant questions, such as these: Can you defend the program for which you are seeking funding? How many students will the program affect? What is the importance of implementing this program? Why should Corporation X fund this program? Keep in mind that all of your responses must have equal value or a return on investment (ROI) for the corporation.

Additionally, funding programs through corporate sponsorship is a reciprocal process.

While you are seeking funds for your programs, the businesses are asking themselves, "What's in it for us?" Once you have done a complete needs assessment analysis, you're ready to formalize your thoughts. After carefully thinking out your proposal, develop it formally on paper. Ask a colleague who is not familiar with your program to read it over and determine if your request is clear. Now that the proposal is ready for distribution, you're ready to progress to the next stage of the process—*identifying resources.*

Identifying the business that might be interested in funding your project can take some thought and some time. One good resource is the business listing offered through your local chamber of commerce. This directory describes local businesses and the types of service they provide. After identifying several businesses you might approach, or any of the educational foundations mentioned previously, do your homework. Learn about the company or organization, the types of activities it is already involved with in the community, and the types of services it is willing to provide for you.

If you are looking for fitness equipment, you might be restricted to an exercise equipment facility that will give you a significant discount or lend you equipment for a year. For example, a local fitness vendor in the Miami area became interested in working with Miami-Dade County Public Schools after learning about the Fit-Tech (fitness rooms with technology-based fitness equipment) centers that were opening in several of the middle schools. Knowing that the school system was securing funding to place high-tech fitness equipment in the schools, the vendor saw a golden opportunity to provide a variety of services to the schools. The most basic benefit it provided, naturally, was a significant discount for bulk purchases. In return, the vendor was granted permission to place its logo on the base of the equipment. As an extended service, any child or parent who visited that particular vendor and made mention of the equipment at that particular school was given a 25 percent discount on any purchase. This type of agreement not only helps the schools but also helps members of the community by making an investment in community wellness.

You might also establish a close working relationship with the fitness and health clubs in your community. All commercial fitness clubs must refurbish their equipment every three to five years; it rapidly becomes outdated, especially with extended usage and the advent of virtual reality (VR) equipment. Many fitness or health clubs would rather donate their old equipment to schools, take the tax write-off, and purchase new equipment. It is a win-win situation for all parties involved as long as the fitness equipment is in working order. To avoid future repair expenses, it would be a good idea to have the facility commit to five years of in-kind repairs in case the equipment falls into disrepair. Keeping students safe is the number one priority.

The next step in securing a business partner is the actual recruitment process. There are several ways to contact a potential business partner, depending on your comfort zone and level of experience. Regardless of how you proceed, be sure to develop a comprehensive plan of action before making a corporate contact. For your own credibility, make sure that all your "t's" are crossed and all your "i's" dotted. Strategies could include making a direct phone call, mailing a proposal on your school's letterhead with a request for a meeting, and asking a friend or neighbor within the company to present the concept to the manager and feel out the response.

It is critical that the proposal be well written and on your district's or school's letterhead. It tells the potential partner that your request already has the support of your school system and supervisor. In addition, remember to get permission from your administrator before you pursue a business partner. It would be embarrassing for you and the school, or school district, if you were to receive support and then found out that for one reason or another it was in conflict with the school system or in violation of procurement regulations. Once you get the approval, draft your introductory letter. Figure 14.2 will get you started on how to make the initial contact.

Designing and implementing the program are the next steps in the process. It simply means sitting down with all the players involved to determine the best strategy and develop a plan with specific schedules and responsibilities of project personnel. Issues that might arise include how to involve members of the business in the program, how to properly publicize the program, and which specific activities will be utilized to fully implement the program.

FIGURE 14.2 Sample Letter to Recruit a Business Partner

DISTRICT/SCHOOL LETTERHEAD

Date

Prospective Business Partner

Address

City, State Zip

Dear ____________________:

The purpose of this letter is to introduce you to [SCHOOL NAME], and to invite you to take part in an innovative and exciting new program known as [PROGRAM TITLE]. As a proactive business in the community, I am certain that you will be interested in learning more about this program as well as about how we could work together in a collaborative manner to improve the educational opportunities of our students.

[SCHOOL NAME] is composed of [SCHOOL DEMOGRAPHICS] for a total enrollment of [NUMBER OF STUDENTS]. [In this section you would describe your program as well as the void that will be filled through implementation of your program.]

I am enclosing a copy of the formal proposal for your review. I will follow up with a phone call within the week to arrange a meeting with you. If additional information is requested, please contact me at [SCHOOL PHONE NUMBER].

I look forward to meeting with you in the near future.

Sincerely,

[YOUR NAME]

[YOUR TITLE]

Communicate with your business partners on a regular basis to keep them updated on the status of the program, and invite your business partners to the opening of the program. The invitation gives the business partner a feeling of being a part of the program rather than strictly being a funding source. Having a sense of ownership will help to ensure future funding requests pertaining to your ideas and potential projects or programs. Remember, when a business partnership is formed, the school, business, and community all benefit.

Potential Benefits to Schools

- Additional personnel to enhance educational programs for students through a cadre of volunteers and mentors from the business community before, during, or after school
- Utilization of business perspectives to enhance the present curriculum
- Assistance in rewarding students for outstanding achievements

Potential Benefits to Businesses

- Satisfaction in becoming an active participant in the education of children
- Opportunities to motivate students, increase their awareness of career opportunities, and develop a more educated workforce
- Enhanced corporate image in the community
- Tax benefits from both financial and in-kind contributions

Potential Benefits to the Community

- Establishment of an ongoing dialogue between the schools and the community

- Increased awareness and understanding of the needs and resources of the schools and community

After the partnership is established between the school and business community and the program has been implemented, it is time for evaluation. At the conclusion of your initial year, perform a formal evaluation of your program. If an increase in fitness test scores was the culminating outcome of your program, did the involvement of the business partner help fulfill that objective? Did your business partner get the recognition that was deserved? Was your partner mentioned in all your school newsletters? Did you invite a representative of the company to all your functions? Was your partner recognized at your end-of-the-year awards ceremony? Always solicit feedback from your business partners so you can get their perspective as well. Since they have ownership in the program being implemented, they have to feel that they are a sustainable part of the program.

If all of these criteria were satisfied, congratulations on the successful implementation of your program. If not, then go back and make the necessary corrections and revisions. If after the first year of implementation you honestly feel that the program was successful in making an impact on the lives of your students, then move forward and expand the program.

Expanding a program can include adding more business partners but giving the new partners a different responsibility. This approach will ensure that the first corporation is not offended by the participation of another company in the project. After all is said and done, don't forget to formally thank your business partners. You can do so at a PTA or PTSA meeting, at an end-of-the-year awards ceremony, at a chamber of commerce luncheon, in your school newsletter, or simply with a formal thank-you letter. The letter shown in figure 14.3 will serve as a template to get you started. Of special note, it is great protocol to thank business partners who actually funded the program, but most of your communication

FIGURE 14.3 Sample Business Partner Thank-You Letter

DISTRICT/SCHOOL LETTERHEAD

Date

[Business Liaison], [Liaison Title]

[Name of Business]

[Business Address]

[City], [State] [Zip]

Dear [Business Partner]:

Welcome to the rank of a distinguished community leader who has become a partner to [SCHOOL NAME]. It is through partnership efforts such as yours that we can strengthen both our school and community.

I am especially grateful for your commitment to the students of [SCHOOL NAME]. Your partnership activities outlined in the proposal will contribute greatly to the success of our student population. Your ongoing efforts will only make the link stronger between the public and private sector and our community.

I look forward to a long and positive working relationship with you.

Sincerely,

[PRINCIPAL NAME]

[PRINCIPAL]

will be with their secretary. A personal handwritten note to the secretary will go a long way as well.

Business partnerships have become a viable way to fund educational programs when state allocations can no longer fully subsidize programs and principals' budgets are stretched to the limit. Physical education administrators may become involved in requesting local business support when the support is used for all schools in the district. Public involvement in support of primary and secondary education has, through proven programs, yielded many benefits to both the educational and business communities. Students benefit from the enriched school program, and business partners reap the intangible benefits of satisfaction derived from community involvement and helping young children succeed.

Corporate Donations and Sponsorship

Corporate sponsorships differ from business partnerships in that they are usually associated with a particular project or event and in many cases are housed in a corporate budget through event marketing or cause marketing. Corporate sponsors usually list their foundation's giving guidelines on their corporate websites, in sections on community involvement or community giving. Once you have identified a corporation, you will have to search through its site to find the specific funding guidelines. Corporations usually highlight their areas of interest, and they often mention past grants given to similar organizations, funding criteria, and guidelines for submitting an application.

In a manner less formal than in a contractual business partnership, many local corporations are willing to assist with school-wide projects through donations or sponsorships. This opportunity lends itself to having one major business or several small ones contribute to the implementation of your physical education or physical activity project. Just as in the business proposal, the process begins by developing a comprehensive plan of action before approaching a potential corporate sponsor. Once your plan is conceptualized, the next step involves developing a formal letter. It can be less sophisticated than a comprehensive proposal, but it should carefully lay out your plan. Always make sure that before making the initial contact, you acquire support and approval from your principal, district supervisor, or superintendent if necessary. Having the name of a contact person will greatly enhance the probability that your request will be taken seriously. The initial contact is usually made in a one- to two-page formal letter, followed up with a phone call shortly thereafter. Once you have an appointment with a member of the corporation, you're on your way. Through corporate sponsorships, leveraging personal relationships is of utmost importance. You should also consider brand marketing when approaching corporations for sponsorship. For example, approaching an alcoholic beverage or tobacco company to sponsor your district's 5K walk/run to promote wellness may not be in the best interest of either party.

Prior to your meeting, develop a corporate presentation packet for distribution. The corporate presentation packet should include a letter introducing you and providing your contact information, some information on the school district, and what you are asking from the recipient. A short proposal should also be included to introduce the project more fully along with a marketing plan on how the corporation will be recognized for its contribution. These materials should all be presented in a professional folder. It's also up to you to have a prepared, established agenda so that you can cover all your points efficiently and effectively during the meeting. Continuous and constant communication, along with a thank-you card, is essential after the initial meeting.

If your plan is successful and your funding request is granted, then you need to become an advocate for the company that is supporting you. The chief executive officer (CEO) or designee probably funded your project based on something he saw in your presentation. You must become the company's best public relations person in the community. You can accomplish that goal by mentioning the corporation in all of your publications and interviews as well as by using its logo in appropriate places. When corporations donate materials or actual dollars to educational institutions, they usually request a simple letter of receipt on official letterhead for tax purposes. It is critical that you maintain a positive relationship with corporate sponsors throughout the school year. In this type of relationship, the corporation becomes an active part of the local school, and the students and faculty become more supportive of the businesses in their community.

In addition to funding for projects or programs, corporate donations can also be secured through signage agreements. In this scenario, local corporations provide informative banners that can be hung around the gymnasium or on fencing surrounding the playing field. The school gets money, and the corporation benefits from the advertising that can be seen by parents and community members. Because a fiscal agreement is in place, it often requires a MOU or LOU as well.

Branding and merchandising is another innovative way to work with local businesses and corporations. Through contractual agreements, corporations can have their logos placed on physical education uniforms in exchange for funding opportunities. School gear can also be sold in local stores to promote school spirit while a portion of the sales goes back to the school or school district (depending on how the contract is written). This type of fundraising is similar to that commonly used in athletics, but it can also be utilized to support physical education programs. As a district physical education administrator, you are also positioned to negotiate large-scale contracts with corporations to service all of the schools in your district, with the support and assistance of your legal department. For example, you might work with beverage or food companies that would install scoreboards with their signage in all of your physical education fields in exchange for an agreement to sell their products in vending machines or at school-wide events. This arrangement could essentially bring in large sums of money for your programs, which in turn could provide much-needed equipment to schools. Always keep in mind that many of these agreements will require school board approval, so make sure that you report your activities to your chain of command so that they can provide guidance through the process.

It will save you time to remember that corporate sponsors usually list their foundation's "giving" guidelines on their corporate websites, in sections on community involvement or community giving. You will have to search through corporate sponsors' sites to find the specific funding guidelines. They highlight their areas of interest and mention past grants given to similar organizations. Search their websites further to find their funding criteria, guidelines, and application deadlines for each focused area of giving. Examples of corporate sponsorships at the local level can be found for Costco, Target, and Lowe's, to name just a few.

A good starting place is to visit the branch near your school or district office, introduce yourself to the manager or assistant manager, and talk about your program. Besides generating a future pool of volunteers for your school or schools or your cause, the location's affiliation with the program and school will help your cause when you are applying for larger sums of money from the corporate foundation.

Fundraising

The last component of securing outside funding prior to discussing how to write and secure grants is just basic fundraising opportunities. Many types of fundraising opportunities are available for your engagement depending on your interests and planning time. They can include hosting 5K walk/runs or other special events (discussed in chapter 7), hosting competitions such as a high school bodybuilding competition, or hosting a gala with a silent auction of donated items, to name a few. The truth is that grant writing alone will not meet all of your fundraising needs; in the meantime, you need to serve your students while securing funds for your projects and programs.

Fundraising activities can be conducted by both school-recognized groups (e.g., clubs or athletic teams) and school-related organizations (e.g., PTAs and booster clubs). The major difference between the two groups lies strictly in the accounting procedures. For example, the Florida State Board Regulations require that all financial transactions related to student activities and conducted by school-recognized groups be recorded in the internal funds of the school (Florida Department of Education, 2023). School-related organizations, such as athletic booster clubs, usually handle their finances outside the school, and they make gifts or donations to the school as they choose. State board regulations vary by state, so check your own state regulations for various accounting practices. As with any activity driven by the school or school district, all fundraising efforts must ensure that you are following the **fundraising procedures** required by your school district.

The second most important factor in the planning stage is selecting a company with which to work. When making your selection, you need to take into account such factors as how long the company has been in business, whether the company guarantees its products, whether it will give the school credit for (or buy back) unsold items, and whether it will assist you in your kick-off. It is also a good idea to make sure that the company is not in conflict with the goals of your program. For example, although selling candy makes money, it is not a good example of a fundraising activity for a physical education or physical activity program because encouraging consumption of high-sugar, low-nutrient snacks doesn't align with program goals. After you have identified your fundraising activity, you have to realize that you can't do it all alone—nor should. You need to secure volunteers, or supporters who see the same needs and want to help accomplish your agency's or project's mission. In other words, you need a team.

In order to build a successful fundraising team, you must first identify exactly what work needs to be done and which roles need to be filled. Therefore, you need to assess your fundraising strategy and make decisions about expanding programs that are working or scaling down programs that haven't been as productive, as well as determining how to incorporate new programs. You should develop an overall fundraising strategy that will guide your fundraising team. Write up a short description for each position you will need on your team. You may already have friends or associates who are working on some of these ideas, but if you are serious about looking for funding for your cause or programs, you have to create a team. Start by highlighting the major tasks involved in creating a fundraising team.

Select your team players carefully. Instead of looking for individuals who are already serving on boards and committees all the time (their time might be restricted due to other commitments), find individuals who are relatively new to volunteering yet believe in the cause or in the project you are proposing to do.

Through a traditional fundraising strategy, after your selection of team members is made, the actual planning of the fundraiser begins. Several strategies exist to make fundraising a manageable activity rather than a burdensome one; they include these steps:

1. *Form a committee, and divide the workload.* Appointing a cochair or several committee chairpersons to assist will ease your tensions. For example, one committee chairperson can assist you in the accounting, another can be in charge of inventory control, and a third can assist in the distribution of the items.
2. *Motivate your volunteers.* Include students in the decisions made in the early stages of organization. Provide incentives, prizes, and a means of tracking sales.
3. *Establish a financial goal.* Know exactly how much you will need for your project, how large your target sales audience is, and how much time you need to allot for sales. Attention to these numbers will help you keep realistic fundraising goals.
4. *Choose a quality product to sell.* If you are going to put time and effort into organizing a fundraiser, be certain that the product you choose to sell is a product that people are willing to buy. People won't pay for inferior or poor-quality merchandise. Keeping the customers satisfied will ensure repeat customers if you decide to do a second or an annual fundraiser.
5. *Set specific beginning and ending dates.* It will assist you in pacing your activity. Include target deadlines so that you can monitor the success of your efforts. A successful fundraising campaign will get you started in securing the funds you need to begin the first stage of implementing your program. If additional dollars are required to fully implement your program, then perhaps a corporate donation, or sponsorship, is what you need to explore.

In more recent times, nontraditional online fundraising strategies have become the norm rather than the exception. For example, crowdfunding and fundraising websites such as GoFundMe, GoGetFunding, and others offer a variety of ideas and categories for setting up your online fundraising page. Crowdfunding essentially is the ability to raise small amounts of money for a designated goal from a large number of people, usually through the Internet. The strength of crowdfunding is based on three simple elements: common cause, crowdfunding platform, and people. The benefits of setting up your own crowdfunding page are that it is more efficient than traditional fundraising, it builds social validation, you can secure loyal advocates, and it amplifies your marketing and media exposure.

Securing Funding Through Grants

Now that you have mastered the less formal means of securing funding for your program, you're ready to move on to a more sophisticated means of securing dollars—grant writing—a process more complicated than securing existing or local funds. This section gives you a basic understanding of the steps involved in how to search for funding, identify grant opportunities, and develop the planning process for establishing a viable project for submittal as a successful grant proposal. Keep in mind that grant writing is simply a question-and-answer process. The funder asks you what it is that you want the money for, and you clearly and specifically explain what you will do with the money once you receive it. In other words, grant writing is similar to developing a business partnership proposal in that it follows a set procedure.

What Is a Grant?

Grants are nonrepayable funds or products disbursed by one party (the grantmaker), usually a governmental department, corporation, foundation, or trust, to a recipient organization, which often—but not always—is a nonprofit entity, an educational institution, or even a for-profit business or an individual. Grant writing is not a difficult process, but it is a time-consuming one, and it requires much work on the part of the writer. If you can follow instructions, you can write a grant. However, keep in mind that the real work begins once a grant is funded. Accountability through programmatic reporting and budget utilization is inherent from the time the award is announced until the end of the grant period. Maintaining that level of accountability is incredibly important to your reputation as a grant recipient, so be ready to give detailed accounting statements regarding where every penny was spent as well as how the outcomes of the project were achieved. This practice not only will establish you as a respectable and credible grant manager but also will become a necessity if your grant gets audited.

Searching for and Identifying Grant Opportunities

The initial stage of grant writing requires finding a funding source that is interested in funding your type of idea. You might contact local or civic organizations, local or national foundations, and state or governmental agencies. Locally, mini grants for educators are usually made available through public education funds; chambers of commerce; area franchises such as local fast-food chains; and service organizations such as the Rotary, Lions, and Kiwanis clubs. Foundations, such as the Phi Delta Kappa Educational Foundation, and various health foundations and hospital trusts, are also potential funding sources for educators.

Grants vary based on the types of funding sources as well as the amounts funded. Individual school systems offer grant opportunities through entitlement programs such as Safe and Drug Free Schools and block grants, such as Title IV, Title V, and Title VI, as well as through department of education discretionary grants, as in the case of 21st Century Community Learning Centers. All of these funding sources provide an opportunity to fund physical education and physical activity programs as long as they are tied in to the overall objectives of the educational program. Federal grants, although extremely competitive, can be located through sources such as the *Federal Register*, the Catalog of Federal Domestic Assistance (CFDA), *Education Week*, and *Grantsmanship Magazine*, and they are disseminated through such agencies as the U.S. Department of Education's National Diffusion Network, the Department of

Health and Human Services (HHS), the Centers for Disease Control and Prevention (CDC), and the National Institutes of Health (NIH). Additionally, requests for proposals (RFPs) can be located online through various websites such as the CDC (www.cdc.gov), U.S. Department of Education (www.ed.gov), NIH (www.grants.nih.gov), and Federal Grants (www.grants.gov). Over the years, the Foundation Center library of resources has been one of the leading sources of viable information about philanthropy worldwide and the best primary site for researching funders and funding opportunities. In 2019, the Foundation Center's tools on foundations merged with GoldStar's tools on nonprofits to form a new nonprofit entity, Candid.

Using your preferred search engine, you will be able to do preliminary searches and look up possible funders. The following list names specific websites that will help you find current grant opportunities, initial guidelines, and funder websites. You can also visit these websites to gather the information you need in order to prepare your request:

https://candid.org

www.grants.gov

www.federalgrants.com

Become familiar with how search engines work, and start writing down all program areas and categories that your project could fall under; examples include Pre K-12 education; STEM education; after-school activities to include literacy, technology, arts, and culture; sports and fitness; and nutrition and school garden programs. Several professional sports organizations and foundations are also sources of available funding. Read through past awards issued; funders can be very selective as to the types of awards they will issue and causes they will support. It will give you a closer look at some of the initiatives they are willing to fund. Also, keep in mind that grants come in all sizes. Whether it's a $1 million-plus grant or a small activation grant like those awarded by some national organizations, the process is the same.

However, before beginning the search or writing process, be absolutely clear about what you want to achieve through your project, and ascertain exactly what funding agencies are looking to fund. Reading the grant application carefully will usually tell you exactly what kinds of projects they wish to fund and what their priorities for funding entail. Educational grants in particular usually target specific types of students such as at-risk students, exceptional education students (ESE), limited English proficient (LEP) students, underserved populations, and minority populations, as well as particular types of programs, such as academic achievement, physical activity before or after school (or both), and health and wellness offerings. In many instances, specific geographic locations are also targeted. It cannot be stressed enough how important it is to *read the grant application several times*, highlighting the important grant submission requirements. If you do not do so, you may miss an important deadline; for example, if submitting a letter of intent (submitted to the grant funder to express interest in applying for the grant notice of funding opportunity) is a requirement for submission, you need to know about that requirement as soon as possible. Figure 14.4 shows specific tips for writing federal grants. Before you begin writing any grant, consider these tips:

- Read the complete RFP before doing anything; then read it again!
- Follow the guidelines on the grant application precisely.
- Write in language that is understood by all; avoid using educational jargon, slang, or initials.
- Develop a concept or idea that is unique and innovative.
- Organize your thoughts before writing so there is a logical flow.
- Ensure that your thoughts and ideas are clearly presented.
- Keep your writing concise so that the reviewer understands what you are trying to say.
- Align your grant with the review criteria.
- Give yourself ample time to write, review, and rewrite the application; grants cannot be written in one or two days.

If you feel that your idea falls into a certain area of interest, then begin conceptualizing your proposal. If you feel that your idea is

FIGURE 14.4 Tips for Writing Federal Grants

FORMATTING AND WRITING TIPS

- Write clear headings.
- Use subheadings, short paragraphs, and other techniques to make the application as easy to navigate as possible. Be specific and informative, and avoid redundancies.
- Bookmark major sections.
- Use diagrams, figures, and tables, and include appropriate legends, to assist the reviewers to understand complex information. These aids should complement the text and be appropriately inserted.
- Make sure the figures and labels are readable in the size they will appear in the application.
- Use bullets and numbered lists for effective organization. In addition, use indents and bold print to emphasize and differentiate text.
- Utilize white space effectively.

EFFECTIVE WRITING STYLE

- Write a clear topic sentence for each paragraph with one main point or idea. This approach is key for readability.
- Make your points as direct as possible; avoid jargon or excessive language.
- Write simple and clear sentences; keep each one to about 20 words or less.
- Be consistent with terms, references, and writing style.
- Use the active (rather than passive) voice. For example, write, "We will develop an experiment," instead of "An experiment will be developed."
- Spell out all acronyms on first reference.
- Include enough background information to enable an intelligent reader to understand your proposed work.
- Support your idea with collaborators who have expertise that benefits the project.

EDITING

- Have zero tolerance for typographical errors, misspellings, grammatical mistakes, and sloppy formatting.
- A sloppy or disorganized application may lead the reviewers to conclude that your research may be conducted in the same manner.
- Remember the details! Follow all format requirements, such as font size, margins, and spacing.
- If more than one investigator is contributing to the writing, it would be helpful to have one editor to ensure that the application has a consistent writing style.

Adapted from NIH Grants and Funding, https://grants.nih.gov/grants/how-to-apply-application-guide.html.

outside of the parameters of the funding interests, then you will need to determine whether you could modify your proposal enough to meet the agency's requirements or you need to find another funding source. Once you are certain that you have found a match between your idea and a funding source, you're ready to begin writing the proposal.

The grant application or RFP will set forth specific guidelines and instructions to follow such as what font to use, the size of the font, the line spacing, the number of pages or words,

FIGURE 14.5 First Step: Conceptualizing Your Grant-Writing Process

Focus on where you are and where you want to go.

1. What are your needs? Does your idea address an important problem?
2. What are your strengths?
3. What are your weaknesses?
4. What do you want to accomplish?
5. What steps will you take to achieve your vision?

and sometimes even the number of characters allowed, which is particularly true in the case of Internet or online submittals. Your request for funds must be presented in a tight package; be ready to show the need for funding, and make a strong argument for why your project or program is deserving of the funds you are requesting as well as how it will be ready to deliver on time and within budget. Also, bear in mind that you must be able to highlight or identify the uniqueness of your program. Answer these questions: What makes your program stand out as different from services offered by other providers? What are the services or benefits of your program that no one else in your targeted community is providing?

How do you do all of this? By submitting a well-thought-out written proposal that follows the guidelines provided by the funder and answers all of the questions the funder has highlighted in the RFP.

Step-by-Step Process

Your project or program should be designed using a step-by-step process that will fill in all of the gaps before you begin writing. Your plan should carefully detail all of the project's needs, tools, and activities along with a plan of action for reporting program evaluations and outcomes. This process includes preparing a well-thought-out budget, with justifications for all of the necessary components, as well as a plan of action for how you will seek continuation of funding should your project be ongoing and require multiple years of funding. By creating a draft proposal outline, you will be able to seek and successfully apply for multiple funding sources as well as be ready to meet deadlines without any serious complications. Regardless of the type of grant you are applying for, all grant applications or proposals have basically the same format: Title of Project, Abstract, Proposal Narrative, Statement of the Problem, Related Research, Objectives, Project Design, Procedures or Activities, Program Evaluation, and Budget Narrative.

As you begin, the absolute first steps should be to conceptualize your **grant-writing process** according to what you are trying to achieve (figure 14.5). It should be based on either a formal or an informal needs assessment. You need to determine what the project should accomplish, what the needs of the stakeholders (teachers, students, staff, etc.) are, and, most importantly, whether you have buy-in. It would be a devastating mistake to spend several weeks or months writing a multimillion dollar grant only to find that the personnel you are writing this for do not want to be a part of the process. Securing letters of support from principals and teachers in advance of submitting the grant application will help ensure that once funded, the program objectives will be implemented.

Following the conceptualizing phase, the next steps should be based on how to put all of it together (figure 14.6). In particular, who will be on your proposal writing team, and what are their individual strengths? Writing grants, federal grants in particular, can be a cumbersome process. It would only strengthen the grant application to secure a team who has expertise in specific components of grant proposals. Figure 14.6 sets forth some of the areas of expertise to consider.

Once you secure your committed team, it is recommended that you take a day and have a brainstorming session to discuss what innovative ideas you could put forward, how this

FIGURE 14.6 Second Step: Putting Thoughts Together

Develop a team, and distribute areas of responsibility to all members based on individual strengths.

- Equipment (working with vendors)
- Curriculum writing
- Editing
- Budget

project could make a difference in the lives of students, and what makes your proposal unique such that it would get the attention of the reviewers. This section will also give all team members an opportunity to put their ideas on the table so that everyone can come to consensus on what the final proposal will look like.

With all players in place, the writing process is ready to start. Keep in mind that as previously mentioned, writing a grant proposal may appear to be complicated, but it is really a question-and-answer process. Based on most grant proposals, the Project Narrative will usually require responses to questions broken down into specific sections with headings such as Need for the Project, Significance, Quality of the Project Design, Adequacy of Resources, Quality of the Management Plan, Quality of the Project Evaluation, and Budget Narrative. Under each section heading, embedded in the RFP will also be a list of specific questions or bullet points that the writer is expected to address in the proposal submission. Many RFPs also have Absolute, Competitive, and Invitational Priorities. These sections are important to note because some are a must-include and others will earn extra points when the proposal is being scored. It is in this connection that it is critically important to read each section a couple of times and highlight the important concepts to be addressed. Another important consideration is developing a grant checklist. This way you can ensure that all of the requirements, forms, and materials for the appendix are included in your final grant submission.

Also note that some subsections are weighted differently in points assigned toward the total proposal scoring by the reviewer. All RFPs and notices of funding opportunity (NOFOs) provide information on how the proposal is scored, the process of securing reviewers to score the proposals, and usually how many points are provided for each section of the grant proposal. However, a good rule of thumb to follow, where possible, would be to decide how many pages you should write for each section of the proposal based on the percentage of points assigned. For example, if the proposal page limit is 20 double-spaced typed pages and the section is worth 25 points based on a total possible score of 100 points, then that section should be approximately 5 pages in length. In this situation, using tables and charts would enable you to insert a lot of information in a small amount of space. For example, in looking at the requirements for need for the project (seen later in figure 14.8), if you were to write it all out in narrative form, it would take up more than the recommended number of pages. Placing components into tables and graphs would enable you get the big picture across while conserving space. Conversely, if a grant assigns a certain number of pages to a section and you write less than the designated number of pages, you cannot give your extra pages to another section.

Proposal Development

A proposal should reflect thoughtful planning by an applicant seeking funds from a grant-making agency with which to provide or improve services to a constituency (students, teachers, families, etc.). Aside from showing that there is a need for your program, as the lead writer you must also be able to support the premise that your project will lead to sustainable systemic change. After all, the granting agency wants to ensure that the programmatic impact will remain intact long after the grant funding has expired. The amount of time you spend conceptualizing your project will be reflected in the final grant proposal submitted.

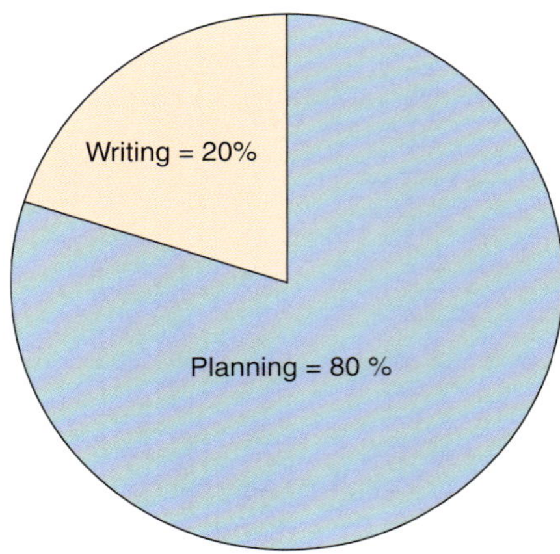

FIGURE 14.7 The 80:20 guideline for grant writing.

The formula to follow is the 80:20 guideline (figure 14.7). Planning equals 80 percent of your time and effort, while writing equals 20 percent of your effort. Program planning and design will take up 80 percent of your time as you do your research, create program design, clearly establish and document collaborative partnerships, and explain how you will evaluate the program's efforts and actual results, all while developing a precise final budget—and down to the last penny. The actual writing of the grant application may take only 20 percent of your time and effort as you put your detailed plan down on paper to show the funder what you will do with the money you are requesting. If well conducted, the project design strategy and planning phase will simplify the writing stage.

Needs Statement

The needs statement (or problem statement) is a more detailed justification and rationale piece that explains your request for funds; see figure 14.8 for a sample needs statement titled Need for the Project. It should start with an introductory section explaining what the problem is, its root cause, and how your project addresses these issues. In essence, you justify what you propose to do with the funds you are requesting in order to solve the particular problem. The needs statement is critical in getting across why your project or program is deserving of funds. Not only can a well-crafted needs statement convince funders of the importance of an issue or program, but it can also ensure that your project, program, and school have a clear understanding of the link between the issue and its mission of securing the intended program outcomes. Be ready to describe *who* you will be serving by using specific local demographics—facts and figures, not generalities. List your sources for information and the latest year the information was captured while making sure you have the most recent and accurate numbers available. Clearly describe *what* services you are proposing in order to solve a problem or improve the circumstances or conditions addressed. If you are using a best practice model (a program that has had evidence-based results), provide citations and reference sources. *Where* will you be providing these services? Describe the geographic scope of the project and the general conditions in the community (a useful tool for searching area demographics is your school's zip code). What are the area's poverty levels, educational levels, and median household income? How many single-parent households are there? These facts are good indicators of low economic development within the community. Begin to tie in to what your proposed program will do to solve the given problem.

FIGURE 14.8 Need for the Project (25 Points)

- The needs assessment is based on local, specific data on the target population.
- Begin with local data, then support it with national data.
- Conduct a survey, and gather data on the following:
  - Fitness data (FitnessGram, President's Council on Sports, Fitness & Nutrition)
  - Level of obesity (body mass index [BMI])
  - Daily participation in physical activity and physical education
  - Demographics (ethnicity, gender, socioeconomic status, Title I)

This section is where many physical education grants make note of fitness scores, results of the School Health Index, and so on. You need to show that you have a need that can be addressed only through additional outside funding and support.

Tables 14.1 and 14.2, respectively, answer questions on fitness data and demographics.

Significance of the Project

The Significance of the Project section for the most part will determine the likelihood that the project will result in systemic change or improvement. As seen in figure 14.9, much of it will be determined by (1) the commitment from the school administrators who support the curricular changes; (2) the dedication of the physical education teachers who are committed to improving the instructional program; (3) ongoing professional development and continuous support for teachers to guide them through the process; and (4) most importantly, collaboration with school health staff, food services staff, and local community organizations that can provide resources to support systemic change.

Quality of the Project Design

The next most common section in all RFPs is usually titled Quality of the Project Design. This section looks at the extent to which the proposed project is designed to build capacity and yield results that will extend beyond the period of financial assistance. It's also in this section that the grant writer has the opportunity to fully explain the primary project outcome goals and how those goals will be achieved through proposed project activities. Your project's goals, objectives, deliverables, and outcomes also need to be aligned with the funder's priorities.

Goals and Objectives and Methodology Next is your section titled Goals and Objectives, which is a step-by-step explanation of what you expect to accomplish, followed by a thorough description of the methods as well as the approach and design your project will involve. If you are incorporating a best practice model (a standard that is known to produce good outcomes if followed), you will need to provide references and explain the success rate.

TABLE 14.1 FitnessGram: Health-Related Fitness Test District Summary Report

Grade Level	Number of Students Tested	Number of Students Meeting 6 Standards	Number of Students Meeting 5 Standards	Total	Percentage of Award Recipients on 5/6 Items
Elementary	59,144	19,393	19,740	39,133	66%/33%
K-8 centers	7,138	2,381	2,162	4,543	64%/30%
Middle school	30,962	9,915	9,394	19,309	62%/30%
High school	35,596	8,195	11,573	19,768	56%/23%
Total	132,840	39,884	42,869	82,743	62%/32%

TABLE 14.2 Student Membership in Programs

Grade	White Non-Hispanic		African American Non-Hispanic		Hispanic		Asian/Indian Multiracial		Total
	Number	%	Number	%	Number	%	Number	%	Number
PreK-5	12,783	8	39,075	24	109,221	66	3,397	2	164,476
6-8	6,814	8	19,501	24	54,171	66	1,307	2	81,793
9-12	9,465	9	25,164	24	67,323	65	1,724	2	103,676
Total	29,062	8.3	83,740	23.9	230,715	65.9	6,428	1.9	349,945

FIGURE 14.9 Significance of the Project (25 Points)

- What is the likelihood that the project will result in systemic change?
- What promising new strategies will be developed?
- What will be the magnitude of results in teaching and student achievement?
- What are the planned sequential strategies and activities?

Your goals, objectives, methods, and approach and design should all be measurable; in other words, the strategies and actions you will be taking will produce positive results that can be measured by percentages of growth, performance, and overall improvement at the end of the funding period. A schedule should include the number of activities and the length of time you will be providing services. It should also detail the hours, days, and number of weeks when these activities will be offered and the number of people within the targeted population that will be served during the proposed funding period. What monitoring tools and assessments do you propose to use in order to assess student progress and outcome measures? Who will be collecting the data, how often will it be collected, and when will you be testing and gathering information to monitor ongoing progress?

Depending on the number of sections an RFP has, this section will also include the objectives of the project and how they align with the outcome goals (see figure 14.10).

When developing the objectives for your project, using the SMART principle is recommended to ensure that the goals and objectives are focused and provide a clear picture of the expected outcomes of your project. Figure 14.11 details SMART objectives.

Adequacy of the Management Plan In some RFPs, the Quality of the Project Design section also includes the adequacy of the management plan, which looks at how the applicant plans to manage and achieve the objectives of the proposed project on time and within budget, including clearly defined responsibilities, time lines, and milestones for accomplishing project tasks. The management plan can also be displayed in a table such as table 14.3 with the recommended headings.

Some funders may also request that you submit a Logic Model, Flowchart, or Organizational Chart section. Many CDC grant applications ask for information in these forms. A logic model, like a flowchart, helps to show the process you will be using to reach your goals and objectives. An example of a logic model can be seen in figure 14.12.

Program Evaluation

The final major heading of any grant proposal is the Quality of the Project Evaluation. The evaluation piece is important because it demonstrates to your prospective funder

FIGURE 14.10 Quality of the Project Design (25 Points)

- Quality of the applicant's plan to help students make progress toward meeting national, state, and local standards for physical education, including linkage between proposed activities and state standards
- Reflects a sustained program of training
- Reflects up-to-date knowledge from field of research and effective practice
- Reflects extent to which goals, objectives, and outcomes are clearly specified and measurable
- Reflects methods and time lines
  - What activities are you going to implement?
  - Which project personnel will accomplish which tasks?
  - When will activities be accomplished?

FIGURE 14.11 SMART Objectives

Specific: Your proposal should clearly identify *who* the targeted population you plan on serving is. *What* are some of the compelling needs affecting this population? What is the specific service you are proposing in order to meet these needs? *When* and *where* will you provide these services? How will you provide the services? What other sources of funding are you considering as matching funds?

Measurable: How will you assess the effect or quality of your program? What measuring tools will you use to track and quantify your program's outcomes at the end of the funding period?

Achievable: Is this project practical within the school setting or particular facility or place you are planning on using? What conditions exist that may impede your progress?

Relevant: Can your goals and objectives be achieved within the time frame you have identified, and have you calculated correctly the number of people and staff necessary to implement the program successfully?

Time-bound: Is the time you are allotting adequate to meet your goals and objectives? Will you be able to deliver the results you are expecting within the time frame stated? Consider the various components of the project and what specific costs you will incur in providing the services you are proposing.

how you will be monitoring and assessing the progress you hope to achieve with the funding. You need to identify what evaluation methodology and assessment tools will be used for evaluation purposes (e.g., pre- and post-testing results, individual student achievement and proficiency in subject matter, improved interaction between parents and children) and identify the major investigator who will be doing the evaluation. In some cases, you may have to use an outside evaluator; this addition becomes part of your overall budget.

Evaluations can be either process or product evaluations. A process evaluation, or formative evaluation, looks at the procedures carried out throughout the duration of the grant contract. It is a way to determine whether the process of the project was beneficial in achieving the objectives or whether changes need to be made. A product evaluation, or summative evaluation, is used to determine whether or not your project achieved its objectives. Additionally, data could be collected through either quantitative analyses or qualitative analyses. Quantitative analyses usually require data collection that is subjected to empirical research through statistical analyses, such as comparing pre- and post-test data. Qualitative data collection could involve focus groups from which opinions are collected to determine changes based on programmatic implementation.

Although not always a requirement, it is strongly recommended that the grant team use an outside evaluator to perform the data analysis. Not only are external statisticians objective in their final analyses, but given that they are conducting the analysis, they should also be able to write the evaluation section in the proposal. A statistician could also be asked to write the final evaluation report that would be submitted to the funder either annually during a multiyear grant-funded period or at the end

TABLE 14.3 Sample Management Plan

Objective	Activity	Outcome	Person Responsible	Time Line Milestone
Teachers will receive instruction in administering project assessment tests.	Hands-on introduction to BMI testing, 3-day physical activity recall, using pedometers, FitnessGram testing, and Youth Risk Behavior Surveillance System (YRBSS) fruit and vegetable consumption assessment	Teachers will be able to administer the baseline tests.	Evaluation team, statisticians	October-November 2024

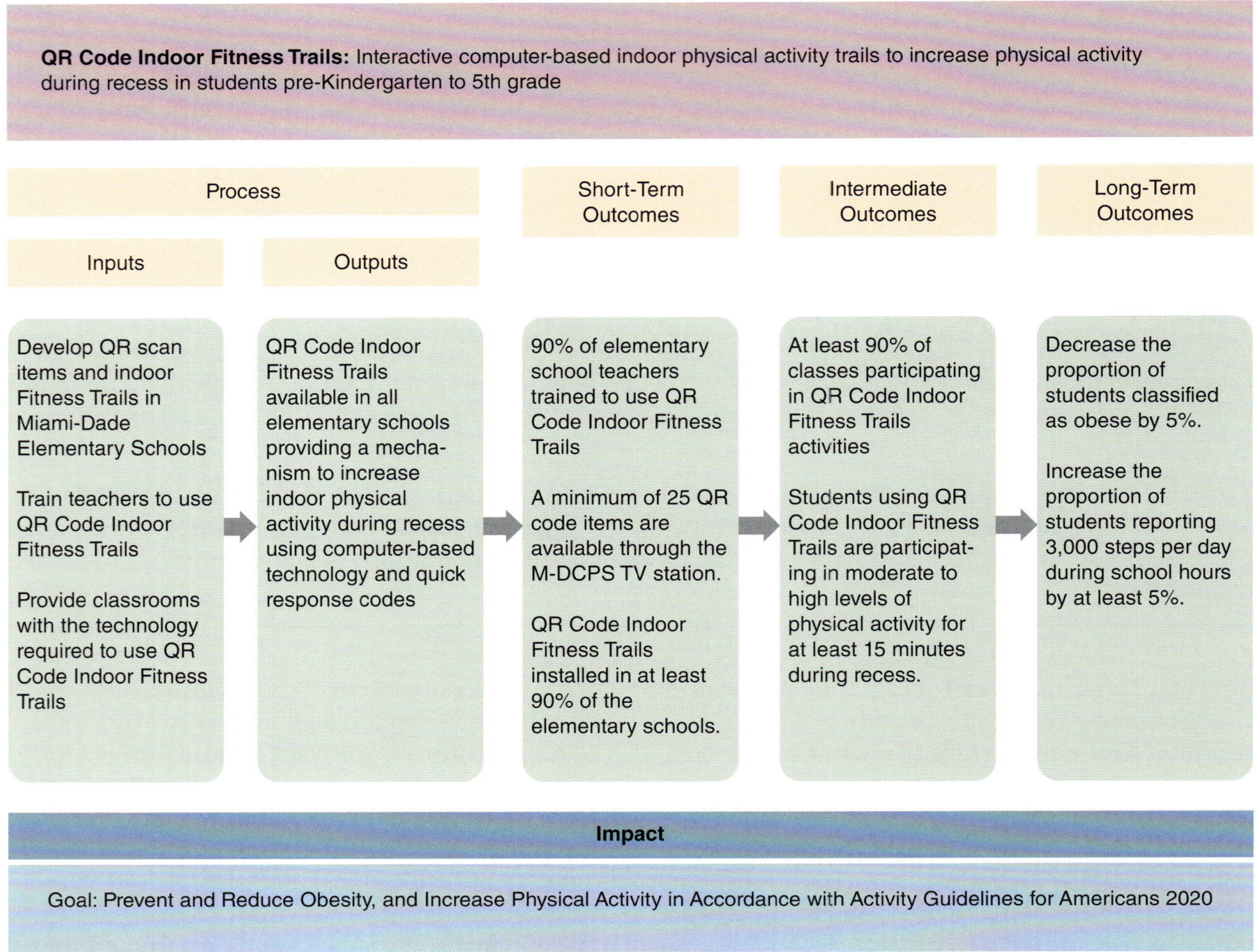

FIGURE 14.12 Sample logic model.

of the grant-funded period. When developing the overall grant budget, keep in mind that many university statisticians work as outside contractors to perform statistical analyses independent of contracting with a university. Using their services is a huge cost-saving move that would leave more funds available to directly affect your program implementation. Some recommended points to consider when developing your program evaluation are shown in figure 14.13.

Essentially, the program evaluation amounts to capturing the information necessary to provide proof that the program works and that the

FIGURE 14.13 Program Evaluation Process (25 Points)

- Consider the extent to which objective measures are related to intended outcomes.
- Consider production of quantitative and qualitative data.
- Consider periodic assessment of progress toward achieving intended outcomes.
- Regarding process evaluation, is your program being properly implemented?
- If possible, partner with a university to perform the evaluation of your project.
- Have university faculty write the evaluation section of your proposal.
- Budget to pay evaluation personnel to perform these duties. Contracts should be directly negotiated.

funder made a worthwhile investment in your project. You want to show the funding agent that you are carefully monitoring your work and the use of the funds.

Budget Development and Budget Narrative

Finally, although this section is not usually counted in relation to the proposal page limit, you should carefully develop the budget narrative. Use values as close to actual as possible, and tie them to the goals and objectives of your project. Reviewers often review the budget before they even look at your narrative piece; the budget is a major piece of your proposal. In developing your project design, make a list using the cost of activities as a basis for your budget (see figure 14.14). Creating this list will give you a clearer picture of what you need in order to provide the services and obtain the results you want. What supplies will you need, how many, and how much will they cost? What personnel or staff will you be needing, including program directors and actual service providers? You must calculate salaries for full-time, hourly, or stipends, and include fringe benefit costs and allowable travel expenses. Does the funder require a dollar match for the amount of funds you are requesting, and can the match be met by in-kind contributions?

You can use the sample budget worksheet, figure 14.15, to build your program's budget. When working out your preliminary budget, make sure to cover all of the line items that appear in the left column. Before listing these, make sure to reference the funder's parameters for funding cost allowable under funding priorities. Some funders may pay only for staff time and educational materials to be used by staff and clients of the program, and may refuse to pay for travel costs or equipment. When in doubt, always contact the funder if possible.

Continuation Funding

In many cases, funders ask how you plan to continue providing the services, program, or both once their funding is finished. Funders are very clear that their award may be a onetime donation, and they want to see what your development strategies are before committing

FIGURE 14.14 Planning for Your Budget

- Determine your budget based on your plan.
    - Determine what equipment will be purchased.
    - Identify vendors.
    - Get quotes in advance and follow your districts procurement bid process.
    - Determine quantities.
    - Negotiate with vendors.
    - Ensure they are approved vendors for your school system.
- Equipment
- Supplies
- Technology (computers)
- Personnel (contractual, not full-time; i.e., consultants, statisticians)
- Fringe benefits
- Indirect costs
- Develop the spreadsheet.
- Write the budget narrative, and explanation describing every line item in your actual budget.
- Matching funds with in-kind contributions (e.g.,10%, 25%)

When working out a preliminary budget, make sure to cover all of the line items that may appear on the sample worksheet (figure 14.15).

FIGURE 14.15 Sample Budget Worksheet

Budget Summary Page 1—Year 1

PROFESSIONAL DEVELOPMENT: TEACHER TRAINING					
ITEM	**# OF PERSONNEL**	**# OF UNITS**	**TYPE OF UNITS**	**UNIT COST**	**ITEM TOTAL**
Substitute Days—Teachers—Prof. dev.					
Substitute Days—Outdoor Physical Activity					
Full Inclusion Program					
Fringe Benefits					
Teacher Stipends—Prof. Dev.					
Summer Institute 4 Days					
Fringe Benefits					
			Subtotal for Training		$

CONTRACTED SERVICES AND PERSONNEL (CONSULTANTS/CLINICIANS/STATISTICIANS/ PROJECT MANAGER)					
ITEM	**# OF PERSONNEL**	**# OF UNITS**	**TYPE OF UNIT**	**UNIT COST**	**ITEM TOTAL**
Project Manager 100% Time	1	1	Salary		
Fringe Benefits					
Principal Consultant/Curriculum Coord.	1	1	Contract		
Principal Quantitative Statistician	1	1	Contract		
Principal Quantitative Statistician	1	1	Contract		
On-Site Curriculum Consultants	2	2	Contract		
University Clinicians Date Input	2	2	Contract		
Secretarial Part-Time	1	1	Hourly		
Fringe Benefits					
Dietitian and Physician Speakers			Contract		
			Personnel Subtotal		$

FITNESS EQUIPMENT					
ITEM	**SCHOOLS**	**# OF UNITS**	**TYPE OF UNIT**	**UNIT COST**	**ITEM TOTAL**
List all types of equipment under FF&E	6	3	18 Units		
	6	2	12 Units		
	6	3	18 Units		
	6	2	12 Units		
	6	1	Sets of 8		
Estimated Shipping Cost 10%					
			Subtotal Fitness Equipment		$

FITNESS ASSESSMENT/EVALUATION EQUIPMENT					
ITEM	**SCHOOLS**	**UNITS**	**TYPE OF UNIT**	**UNIT COST**	**ITEM TOTAL**
Scale	6	1	each		
Pedometers	6	300	each		
Shipping and Handling 10%					
		Subtotal Assessment/Evaluation Equipment			$

Budget Summary Page 2—Active Schools! Healthy Students!—Year 1

CURRICULUM MATERIALS				
ITEM	**SCHOOLS**	**UNITS**	**UNIT COST**	**ITEM TOTAL**
List all curriculum materials.	103	1		
	103	1		
	103	1		
	103	1		
	59	50		
Shipping	59	1		
		Subtotal Curriculum		$0.00
TECHNOLOGY				
ITEM	**SCHOOLS**	**UNITS**	**UNIT COST**	**ITEM TOTAL**
Desktop Computer	6	1	$1,000.00	$6,000.00
Printer	6	1	$400.00	$2,400.00
		Subtotal Technology		$8,400.00
PHYSICAL EDUCATION SUPPLIES TO SUPPORT CURRICULUM				
ITEM	**SCHOOLS**	**UNITS**	**UNIT COST**	**ITEM TOTAL**
List all supplies not FF&E.	103	1		
	6	1		
	6	9		
	6	1		
	6	10		
			Subtotal	$0.00
TRAVEL				
	# UNITS	**TYPE**	**UNIT COST**	**ITEM TOTAL**
Mandated Orientation Meeting—DC	2	each		
Airfare for 2 Mandated Grant Conferences	2	each		
Hotel for 2 Mandated Conferences	4	each		
Stipend—2 people/2 trips/2 days each/meals	4	day		
Ground Transportation/Parking	6	each		
			Subtotal Travel	$0.00
STUDENT BUS TRANSPORTATION				
Student Field Trips to Activities	60	Bus	$300	
Indirect Federal Negotiated Cost	3.77%			
		Grand Total Budget Request		$750,227.35

their dollars. These types of questions can also be addressed as part of your sustainability plan. How do you plan to continue the project after the grant dollars are expended and the funding period ends?

Final Touches

Now that you have your proposal written, it's time to write the abstract. The abstract is the last piece written, but it is the first thing read. The abstract usually consists of a one-page summary, typically ranging from 150 to 250 words, which essentially summarizes the entire proposal. The abstract includes the purpose of your project, a brief description of the project, the results expected, the time frame, and the total amount of funds requested. In pre-applications, the abstract becomes the introductory piece. If grant reviewers do not see what they are looking for in your abstract, they may not read further. Take your time, and write the best piece you can.

Attachments and Appendixes

Last but not least, many grant proposals require specific attachments, assurances, and appendixes. These items usually include organizational charts; logic models; a listing of the board of directors; copies of the nonprofit's 501(c)(3) Internal Revenue Service (IRS) exemption determination letter; résumés or curricula vitae (CVs) of the project director, division heads, coordinator, and teachers involved in the project; and any memoranda of understanding or letters of support from participating partners or collaborators. Figure 14.16 shows a sample letter of support. The guidelines will tell you what documents and how many of each are required. The funder may also request this information on dissemination: How do you plan to share your project's activities, outcomes, and final reports with colleagues and other professionals in the field? Funders want to know this information as well as what methods you will be incorporating, such as webinars, presentations at conferences, or reports published in journals or periodicals.

Final Review and Proofreading

Once you complete the writing process, it's recommended that you have several people read your proposal; they will each have a fresh set of eyes, and they will also be able to see if an outsider understands what you are saying

FIGURE 14.16 Sample Letter of Support

Dear Superintendent:

On behalf of the [organization], I am pleased to support your district's application to the U.S. Department of Health and Human Services, Centers for Disease Control and Prevention (CDC), [specific grant] application.

The [organization] is committed to partnering with, and fully supports, the school district's efforts to form a community coalition to prevent chronic diseases and health disparities in your community by engaging your youth populations in school site and community programs, which will lead to a healthy weight, increased physical activity, and better nutritional programs. We can assist these efforts by supporting district elementary and middle schools in their efforts to make physical activity opportunities available before, during, and after school.

The [organization] fully endorses [school district name] efforts to create an environment that promotes and protects the health of your diverse community in seeking external funding to continue their efforts in bringing education and prevention initiatives to reduce the health disparities in your population.

Sincerely,

[Signature]

[Print Name]

[Print Title (e.g., CEO/President/Manager)]

and asking for. Often people concentrate so much on writing that they don't see their own errors. Proofread your final proposal carefully to ensure that there are no typos or grammatical errors.

Next, go through the RFP checklist to ensure that you have included all of the required sections and adhered to the formatting requirements, which include margins, font style and size, and line spacing. Since the abstract is usually submitted separately from the project narrative, ensure that it is developed and submitted as its own entity if the uploading instructions stipulate that format. Have all of the federal forms and assurances completed and signed, on hard copy or electronically, as well as letters of support, and make sure that your proposal is within the designated page limit. Excessive pages may not be uploaded, and grant reviewers are not required to read any more than the number of pages designated.

Triple-check to make sure that you followed instructions carefully. Keep in mind that you will still need to provide digital versions and proof of your school's or agency's IRS tax I.D. number, state I.D. number, or the IRS nonprofit 501(c)(3) status of any partnering or collaborating agency involved in the services or program you are planning.

Now that you have all of the grant components in place, remember that the only way to guarantee that your proposal will not be funded is to fail to submit it in a timely manner. Grant deadlines are held firm to the date and time of day when the submission must be completed. Online submissions can pose a problem if you wait until the last minute to submit, such as at 4:59 p.m. at the close of the business day. Remember that other organizations may be trying to submit their applications all at the same time. In this circumstance, downloading may become difficult because the funder's website may slow down or get tied up. Always give yourself an extra day or two prior to the deadline date if possible. You are advised to work with your grants administration office to ensure that they have an account with the correct platform necessary to upload your grant into the federal grant system.

When working on an online application, it is usually best to print out the application and guidelines along with all of the questions the funder requires you to answer, in order to work out your draft answers in Word document format. Using the program's word count tools will help you edit and fine-tune your answers; then, all you have to do is copy and paste directly onto the online application form. Always print out a copy of your completed online application form for backup. Besides providing proof of submission, it will greatly assist if there is a glitch in the electronic transmission and you need to send a hard copy. It will help you prepare for your next funding request if you keep hard copy files of your work.

Once you feel confident that you and your team have checked everything, go ahead and hit that Submit button!

Conclusion

This chapter aimed to help you, as a physical education administrator, school site department chairperson, or university graduate or undergraduate student, feel more comfortable taking the lead in securing funds for your school district, school, or individual programs through either local or alternative funding strategies. The chapter presented the step-by-step approach to securing funds, from the simplest form of fundraising to the more complex form of grant proposal writing. Money is available to fund your programs and projects if you approach the task in a systematic and deliberate manner.

As you venture out into the corporate world, accept the challenge with the knowledge that the business community is behind you. Corporate or business partnerships and sponsorships are readily available in local communities because business community members also have young relatives who attend local schools and will be honored to be asked to assist in program development. Don't hesitate to make securing funds a group or team project. It becomes less burdensome when you have a support group to assist you in developing proposals. Additional assistance can always be secured from the community relations or grants administration office in your school system or university. There is a pot of gold out there just waiting to be tapped. Go ahead and go after your share!

Review Questions

1. How do school districts or local educational agencies receive the bulk of their funding?
2. What strategies would you develop when seeking a corporate sponsorship?
3. How does fundraising differ from community partnerships or grant writing?
4. What are the processes involved in developing a grant proposal?
5. Identify a project that you would like to see funded, and develop a business proposal to submit to a community corporate sponsor.

» **Visit HK*Propel* for reproducible forms.**

PART VI

Meeting Social Issues and Challenges

CHAPTER 15

Social and Emotional Learning and Physical Education Content, Pedagogy, and Practices

Cara D. Grant

Photo courtesy of FCC USA, SEL Program

LEARNING OBJECTIVES

After reading this chapter, you will be able to do the following:

- Explain the history and core competencies of social and emotional learning (SEL).
- Analyze the effects of trauma and adverse childhood experiences on SEL.
- Connect SEL with physical education practices and pedagogy.
- Evaluate various SEL programs and the importance of equity in their implementation.
- Identify barriers and successes for implementing SEL through case studies.
- Link SEL competencies with family and community partnerships.

KEY CONCEPTS

adverse childhood experiences (ACEs)
culturally responsive teaching
equity
model-based practices (MBPs)
relationship skills
responsible decision making
self-awareness
self-management
social awareness
trauma

The personal and social development of students in physical education have been paramount in fostering the cognitive, psychomotor, and affective domains of learning. Physical education is a content area with natural connections to social and emotional learning (SEL) in authentic learning situations. SEL in isolation can be skewed to a single narrative or voice and omit groups of people. In the post–COVID-19 world, students entered school with trauma and more **adverse childhood experiences (ACEs)** than ever before. The ability for the United States to identify all forms of discrimination as a public health issue has further elevated the need for schools to explicitly teach equity in combination with SEL with a culturally responsive approach (Centers for Disease Control and Prevention [CDC], 2021; American Public Health Association [APHA], 2022a and 2022b). In this chapter, you will have the opportunity to explore the history of SEL, SEL competencies, connections to ACEs and trauma, examples of SEL programs, and equity in physical education. In addition, **culturally responsive teaching** incorporates students' cultural identities and lived experiences into the classroom as tools for effective instruction (Will and Najarro, 2022).

History of Social and Emotional Learning (SEL)

The evolving origin and definition of SEL varies; however, this core truth remains the same: SEL involves fostering the development of critical life skills for students to aid their personal development and academic success. SEL includes the goal of a holistic curriculum in which students receive a balance of educational experiences from physical education, arts, math, science, moral judgment, and character. In the 1960s, James Comer of Yale University piloted the Comer School Development program and elevated SEL in U.S. schools. Comer's aim was to demonstrate that childhood experiences at home and at school needed to align to shape psychosocial development and influence positive academic achievement (Comer, 1988). His work focused on predominantly African American elementary schools with poor and low achievement data in New Haven, Connecticut. This work went on to lead the way for further work in SEL through the development of a framework to infuse SEL in schools (Catalano et al., 1998). It elevated emotional competence as "identifying and labeling feelings, expressing feelings, assessing the intensity of feelings, managing feelings, delaying gratification, controlling impulses, and reducing stress" (chapter 2, para. 12). In 1994, the Collaborative for Academic, Social, and Emotional Learning (CASEL) was created as a hub to bring together researchers, educators, and others to learn and grow SEL. As a result of the development of CASEL, the Association for Supervision and Curriculum Development (Elias, et al. 1997) published a resource to define SEL and practices in the field of education; it was called *Promoting Social and Emotional Learning: Guidelines for Educators*. Through general exploration and fostering, Daniel Goleman (1994) propelled the idea of SEL through the book *Emotional Intelligence: Why It Can Matter More Than IQ*. Goleman explained that character can be taught and is vital for human development. Since this time, many educational organizations and researchers have taken hold of SEL with the goal to develop life skills for students linked to character and self-regulation.

Defining Social and Emotional Learning (SEL)

The definition of social and emotional learning (SEL) has evolved over time. Many different organizations seek to develop and foster students' social and emotional learning from PreK through high school experiences. Since 1994, CASEL is one of the most widely known resources for SEL in PreK-12 education. CASEL defines SEL as skills students integrate through attitudes and behaviors as they navigate and deal effectively and ethically through daily challenges and tasks (CASEL et al., 2019). Further, SEL links to positive well-being and mental health; it helps to build the foundation for students through learning of lifelong skills to regulate emotions, work well with others, and develop positive self-esteem, which helps to prevent long-term mental health concerns. SEL also refers to "the process through which individuals learn and apply a set of social, emotional, behavioral, and character skills required to succeed in schooling, the workplace, relationships, and citizenship" (Jones et al., 2017. p.12). The process through which children and adults acquire and effectively apply the knowledge, attitudes, and skills necessary to understand and manage emotions, set and achieve positive goals, feel and show empathy for others, establish and maintain positive relationships, and make responsible decisions is another framing for SEL (Ford, 2020). The Committee for Children (2011) links SEL as a process for developing interpersonal skills, self-control, and self-awareness for use in school, work, and life as demonstrated in the Second Step Program. EVERFI (2022), an organization that develops digital student resources (discussed later in the chapter), terms SEL as social and emotional development, and it links resources to the development of skills such as resilience, self-awareness, conflict resolution, leadership, and empathy.

CASEL SEL Framework Overview

Most programs researched, made reference to, or cited CASEL as the governing organization to endorse SEL. Examples of these programs include Second Step, Paths, Edumotion/Catch, Playworks, Character Strong, EVERFI, and Quaver. Within these programs, there is a direct naming of the five basic SEL skills, or CASEL core competencies, of self-awareness, self-management, social awareness, relationship skills, and responsible decision making (CASEL, 2020); they are referred to as the CASEL Wheel (depicted in figure 15.1), and they are described as follows:

- *Self-awareness* is linked to identifying your own emotions, how accurately you perceive yourself, recognizing your strengths, self-confidence, and self-efficacy. Someone who is self-aware would take these individual reflections and use them to recognize and acknowledge personal thoughts, emotions, and values and how they may influence behaviors and actions (CASEL, 2020). A person who has self-awareness knows her strengths and limitations, with a well-grounded sense of confidence, optimism, and a growth mindset.
- *Self-management* extends from self-awareness into regulation of behaviors and actions. It includes impulse control, how one manages stress, self-discipline, self-motivation, goal setting, and organizational skills. A person who demonstrates self-management effectively manages stress, controls impulses, and motivates himself to set and achieve goals.
- *Social awareness* further links analyzing influences from family, community, and friends, and the ability to empathize with others or take on a different perspective than your own. It includes looking at various cultures and cultural norms that may be the same or different from your own to view different perspectives, appreciate and accept diversity, empathize with others, and foster respect for others. A person who exhibits social awareness understands the perspectives of others and empathizes with them, including those from diverse backgrounds and cultures.
- *Relationship skills* are fostered through interpersonal communication skill development. Within relationship skills, how does one create and sustain culturally diverse healthy relationships? Examples may include navigating conflict, cooperating, responding to peer pressure, accessing help, and teamwork. A person who has healthy relationship skills communicates clearly, listens well, cooperates with others, resists inappropriate social pressure, negotiates conflict constructively, and seeks and offers help when needed.
- *Responsible decision making* links the ability of an individual to make social and personal interactions and behavior choices with ethical standards, safety, laws, procedures, and social norms. A cycle of responsible decision making may be presented through

  1. identifying a problem;
  2. analyzing the situation (peer pressure, community, school, family influences);
  3. looking to solve a problem;
  4. evaluating the decision;
  5. reflecting on the decision made and the effects of the decision; and
  6. identifying the ethical responsibility.

  A person who demonstrates responsible decision making makes constructive choices

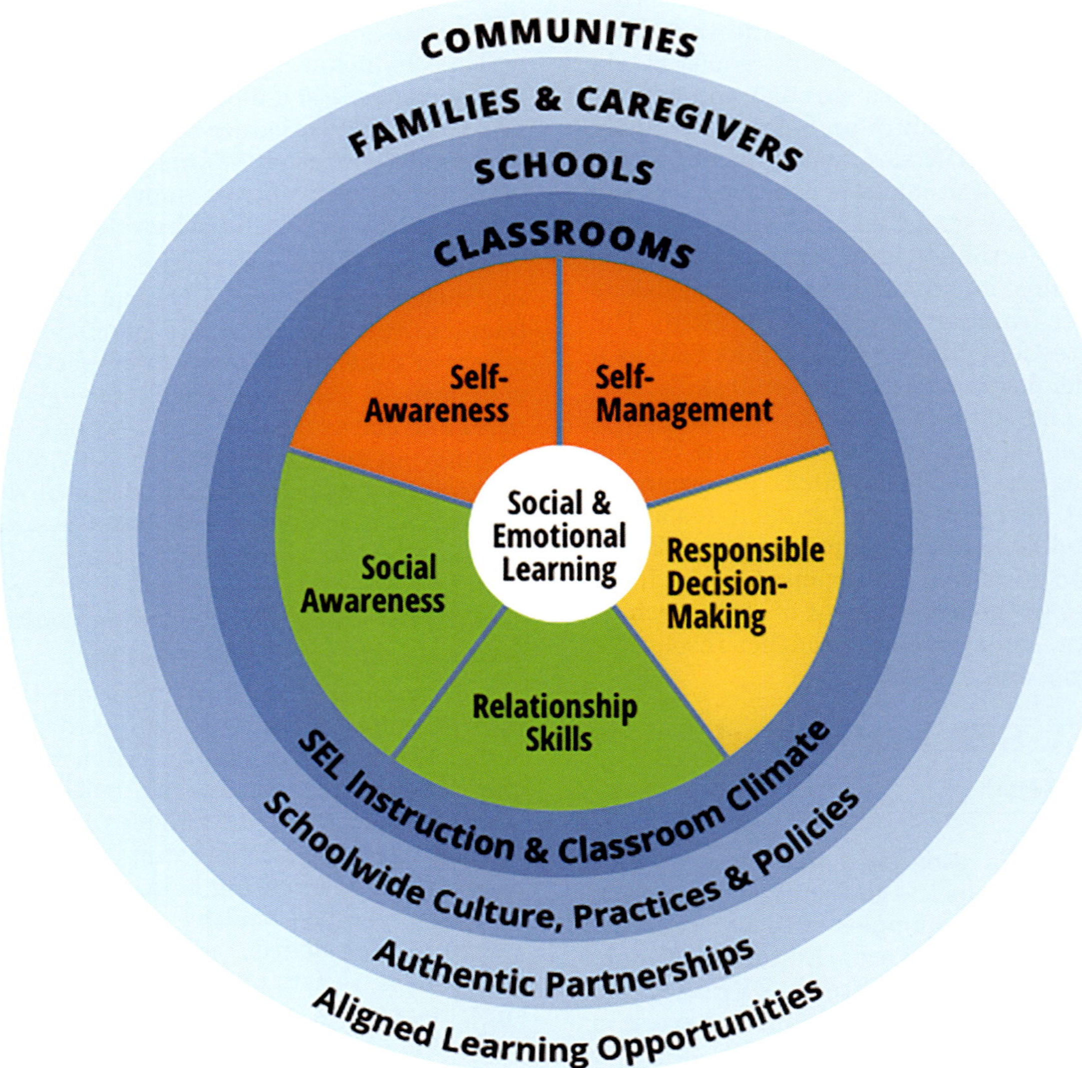

FIGURE 15.1 The CASEL Wheel.

about personal behavior and social interactions based on ethical standards, safety, and social norms.

SEL, Adverse Childhood Experiences (ACEs), and Trauma

Trauma is a serious and pervasive issue. The Substance Abuse and Mental Health Services Administration (SAMHSA, 2024, para. 1) defines "individual trauma as an event or circumstance resulting in physical harm, emotional harm, and/or life-threatening harm." Such an event can have sustaining adverse effects on an individual's mental health, physical health, emotional health, social well-being, and spiritual well-being. Trauma is felt by everyone regardless of sexual orientation, ethnicity, race, socioeconomic status, gender, or age. An example of a common trauma is the effect of the COVID-19 pandemic, which shut down schools; displaced individuals; and caused emotional harm, sickness, and possible changes in health and well-being. Prior to the COVID-19 pandemic, schools were combating childhood trauma or **adverse childhood experiences (ACEs)** to support students using SEL strategies and programs. Nearly 35 million children in the United States have experienced at least one event that could lead to childhood trauma (National Survey of Children's Health [NSCH], 2011). ACEs are potentially traumatic events that occur in childhood (0-17 years); they may include experiencing violence, abuse, or neglect; witnessing violence in the home; and having a family member who attempts or dies by suicide (National Child Traumatic Stress Network [NCTSN], 2019). The lasting impact of childhood trauma can increase the risk for psychological problems, behavioral difficulties, emotional problems (e.g., depression or post-traumatic stress disorder [PTSD]), substance use, low occupational attainment or academic failure, social maladjustment, and poor medical health (National Association of School Psychologists [NASP], 2015). Because students spend the majority of their day in school buildings in which caring adults are available and trained to help them, schools can mitigate the impact of trauma. Schools can help by establishing routines, providing a safe place to share concerns, being sensitive to cues in the environment that may trigger a traumatic response, and providing additional supports or wraparound services (e.g., small-group counseling, restorative practices, mindfulness classes, mentoring, or linking to health care services) (NASP, 2015).

There are evidence-based SEL programs and interventions to develop skills and promote positive outcomes in academic growth, behavior, and youth development in education (Corcoran et al., 2018; Durlak et al., 2011; Kopershock et al., 2016; Taylor et al., 2017). The National Center for Injury Prevention in the CDC has developed guidance for strategies and resources to prevent ACEs, including explicit instruction for skill-based learning to help youth handle stress, resolve conflicts, and manage emotions; these skills help reduce further risk behaviors or victimization (CDC, National Center for Injury Prevention and Control, Division of Violence Prevention, 2019). Three different approaches are presented to reduce ACEs and connect with SEL competencies and practices; they are described as follows:

1. The first approach embedded in SEL is to enhance and develop interpersonal skills as a universal school-wide strategy. Examples of evidence-based programs include Life Skills Training, the Good Behavior Game, and Promoting Alternative THinking Strategies (PATHS). These programs have systematic reviews as evidence to reduce peer violence in schools. In addition, they have data to demonstrate reductions in risky behaviors such as alcohol, tobacco, and drug use; reduced depression and anxiety; delinquency; reduced suicidal ideation and attempts; and reduced criminal activity. SEL is also linked to improved academic success in schools (Center for the Study and Prevention of Violence, 2019).
2. The second example focuses on safe dating and healthy relationship skills to address intimate partner relationships; these skills help to reduce violence and increase caring and respectful relationships. When students experience or witness violence in the home, engage in early sexual activity, or display aggression toward peers, they are at higher risk of experiencing adverse outcomes throughout their lifetime. Evidence-based programs that could be considered include Dating Matters, Safe Dates, and the Fourth R. In addition, Dating Matters and Safe Dates are linked to peer violence prevention.
3. The last approach links families and parents to foster development of problem-solving skills, healthy relationship behaviors, communication, and monitoring. The Incredible Years and Strengthening Families 10-14 are further examples of evidence-based programs that reduce youth behavior problems, substance use, fighting, stress, and depression, and increase family conflict resolution practices. Preventing ACEs and reducing trauma are linked to the SEL competencies; they include universal school programs to support development of students' self-awareness, self-management, social awareness, relationship skills, and responsible decision making.

Explicit trauma-informed practices that can be used in a school environment and physical education teaching space are vital to sustaining and fostering SEL. The National Association of School Psychologists (NASP, 2015) provides these four steps for building trauma-informed practices in schools:

1. Have each school create an environment where all students have a trusted adult and feel connected to the school.
2. Have each school promote mindfulness and emotional regulation strategies and provide the space for students to communicate when they need to access the strategies during class time. Examples of mindfulness and emotional regulation strategies in SEL are found in various lessons and programs. These strategies help students identify (self-awareness) emotions and feelings as well as regulate needs so that they can handle emotions that are not aligned for successful learning (self-management) and they can make decisions to act on the acknowledged emotions to advocate for coping mechanisms. Examples include walking around the teaching space to focus and clear negative emotions and practicing belly breathing to help reduce the heart rate.
3. Have each school teach strategies to help students develop resiliency and active coping to learn how to respond when bad things happen by learning to resist being traumatized and retraumatized.
4. Have each school create an environment where staff and students have a growth mindset. This mindset includes believing that everyone can be a strong leader, and everyone can work through and apply SEL competencies to their lives. All students have the potential to be leaders and to guide their individual and community actions.

Connecting SEL and Physical Education

Physical education, by virtue of its curriculum, programs, and class settings, continues to be aligned with the work of SEL competencies. From PreK through high school physical education learning experiences, students navigate communication, decision making, goal setting, and identifying emotions and feelings in physical activity settings to then decide on appropriate progressions. In addition, students experience various physical activity opportunities to correlate the value of movement with the positive feelings it releases within the body. Movement is a coping mechanism for working through adversity, celebrating successes, and generally managing stress. Within physical education, the goal is to help students identify a preferred movement practice or tool kit for now and in the future to maintain regular physical activity. This goal directly relates to the five CASEL core competencies (self-awareness, self-management, social awareness, relationship skills, and responsible decision making). Physical education is a perfect conduit for developing students' SEL skills and confidence in various settings, including during individual tasks, paired tasks, and tasks within small groups or teams. Development of SEL competencies permits students to be engaged in learning as well as to transfer their knowledge, skills, and confidence to other settings in school, in the community, and with peers.

Physical education content directly aligns with the five CASEL core competencies and related skills (SHAPE America, 2019, para. 1). Effective physical education programs provide opportunities for students to become competent movers, leading to lifelong physical activity engagement, as well as "practice the social and emotional skills and behaviors that help them succeed in life." These SEL skills include the five CASEL core competencies (CASEL, 2024). The next five sections guide you through incorporating each of the CASEL core competencies in physical education classes.

Self-Awareness

Self-awareness: The ability to understand your emotions, thoughts, and values and how they influence you (CASEL, 2020).

Topics: identifying emotions; accurate self-perception; recognizing strengths; linking feelings, values, and thoughts; examining prejudices and biases; having a growth mindset; developing interests and a sense of purpose; identifying personal, cultural, and linguistic assets (CASEL, 2020)

Content and concepts within physical education link directly to the CASEL core competency of self-awareness. Within the physical education teaching experiences, students receive explicit instruction on personal and social behavior linked to respect for self and others. Examples of instructional content topics may include unpacking differences of perceived self with those idealized images of elite athletes and others portrayed in media. By having students reflect on how they perceive themselves in contrast to cultural norms exhibited in media, students can practice identifying emotions. In addition, students can identify an accurate self-perception by appreciating and accepting differences from themselves and those in the media.

One of the major goals in physical education is to help students make connections between identifying emotions and recognizing how they feel before, during, or after participating in physical activities. Self-awareness through identifying physical activities that are enjoyable for students to complete is an example of identifying emotions in the physical education teaching space. In physical education, students experience identifying positive mental and emotional aspects of participating in various physical activities. Physical education teachers foster the development of proficiency in movement, which leads to comfort and competency in transfer of skills across modified games, to facilitate student recognition of linking enjoyment with movement. In physical education, teachers help students understand why picking a preferred movement activity correlates to enjoyment. Physical education instructional practices facilitate opportunities for students to identify self-expression through movement and discuss this awareness with peers.

Developing an accurate self-perception is facilitated in the physical education classroom through teaching challenge-based tasks. For example, the teacher can have students identify proficiency levels to acknowledge when a movement task is difficult or challenging. From there, students can take the challenge identified and develop a positive way to cope. To complete the process, the teacher can foster a reflection during which the students identify the effort put forward in the task. Students can also identify a physical education task progression that modifies the task to simplify it and work toward the grade-level expectation. In addition, students can find ways to develop an accurate self-perception through corrective feedback provided by the teacher, peers, and assessments to inform movement performance. This feedback leads to coaching students into recognizing their strengths and current ability to develop a plan to overcome the challenge or growth area identified, as shown in table 15.1.

Self-Management

Self-management: The ability to regulate and manage one's emotions, thoughts, and behaviors positively in various situations, and to set and achieve goals.

Topics: managing one's emotions; identifying and using stress-management strategies; exhibiting and practicing self-discipline and self-motivation; setting personal and collective goals; using planning and organizational skills; showing the courage to take initiative; demonstrating personal and collective agency (CASEL, 2020)

Physical education content, concepts, and topics include the ability to develop students' self-management skills. Organizational and planning skills are built on the self-awareness component to identify present levels of performance, then take that data to build out a plan for maintaining or exceeding present levels. Physical education teachers facilitate self-management and planning through using skill and tactic rubrics and assessments, and they coach students to improve performance on given content.

Connecting the biological response to movement as a positive stress management strategy is a critical undertaking within the physical education context. Physical education teachers foster and help students make connections with unpacking positive and negative stress on the body and identify ways to deal with these results. Physical education teachers can connect mindfulness, guided visualization, mental imagery, relaxation techniques, deep breathing, aerobic exercise, and meditation as strategies to cope with stress. In physical education classes, teachers provide opportunities for exploring different stress-relieving practices that are grounded more with flexibility and stretching movements (e.g., yoga, meditation, and mindful

TABLE 15.1 Self-Awareness in Physical Education Class: Lesson Considerations

Teacher Will Do the Following:	Students Will Do the Following:
Provide opportunities for students to reflect on personal performance in a variety of skills, concepts, and tactics.	Engage in various movement tasks and settings to analyze personal abilities and create *goals*.
Provide an opportunity for students to link the effects of exercise with the body's responses—health, enjoyment, endorphin release.	Reflect on *self-perception and emotions* linked with physical activity, and make connections to the body's response to various movement tasks.
Develop tasks that engage students with peers in pairs, small-side modified games, and tasks.	Investigate working with a variety of students from various *cultural backgrounds and ability levels*.
Create opportunities for students to collect personal data (skill or fitness goals), reflect, and build goals for maintenance or improvement.	Work to reflect on self and not peers to identify personal goals within skills, tactics, and fitness levels to *recognize strengths* and build *self-confidence*.
Facilitate goal development and provide feedback to monitor and coach students in the development of SMART goals.	Develop SMART goals that are specific, measurable, achievable, relevant, and time-bound with the assistance of their teacher to ensure that the goals are related to the class objectives.
Provide feedback to help students set *realistic goals* and model a *growth mindset* in working towards achieving the goal.	Develop and modify their goals with the support from their teacher to ensure that they are realistic and are open to trying new ideas and activities in order to achieve their stated goals.
Foster a class climate and environment that encourages self-efficacy for all students. *Self-efficacy*—An individual's belief in their ability and motivation to execute a particular task, skill, or behavior (Bandura, 1997).	Demonstrate and communicate motivation, ability, and drive to carry out and attempt physical education tasks.
Develop instructional practices and content that includes a variety of personal and social identities so all students are seen and feel included in the class.	Engage and reflect on *different identities* of others to build team and social connection with others.
Create opportunities for students to identify personal, cultural, and linguistic assets through instructional practices, content, and pedagogy.	Engage in learning about others' *personal, cultural, and linguistic assets* (e.g., students who identify with a community approach versus those who work through an individualistic approach).
Facilitate tasks that allow students to demonstrate *honesty and integrity*.	Engage in self-monitoring and peer monitoring of modified games (e.g., using the role of referee, coach, or umpire).
Provide opportunities for students to identify feelings, values, and thoughts through creating explicit time or identifying the teachable moment to unpack emotions and values.	Use specified time to reflect on *feelings, values, and thoughts* in physical education. During a teachable moment, work to reflect on self-awareness and communicate their feelings, values, and thoughts with others.
Create opportunities for students to examine prejudice and bias. *Prejudice* is a negative bias toward a group of people (Paluck et al., 2021). *Bias* is our ability to think that some ideas, thoughts, or people are better than others, leading to unequal treatment (Haffar et al., 2019).	Reflect on assumptions based on preexisting norms and biases within student knowledge and ability group in team, paired, or individual physical education tasks.
Develop multiple and varied opportunities for students to engage in physical education tasks and activities to develop lifelong *interests* and a *sense of purpose*. Help students self-select physical activities for enjoyment and self-expression.	Reflect and identify activities to do after school and on weekends. Explore physical activities for lifelong fitness and personal enjoyment.

From J. Greenberg and J. LoBianco, *Organization and Administration of Physical Education*, 2nd ed. (Human Kinetics, 2026). Developed by Cara D. Grant, Montgomery County Public Schools.

breathing) with the goal of equipping students to apply a strategy when they experience stress.

Self-motivation is a critical attribute in physical education classes; it enables students to set goals and actively work toward achieving those goals. Fostering interpersonal communication while working on a team or individually is driven through the teacher's prompting and facilitation. However, a large component is driven by student self-motivation to attend to and carry out physical activity tasks and movement outside of the instructional day. Physical education teachers foster and develop concepts, which include acknowledging and positively encouraging students to engage actively in class with limited or no teacher prompting. Self-motivation links with physical activity or movement outside of the instructional day, and it is supported by the *Physical Activity Guidelines for Americans, Second edition* (U.S. Department of Health and Human Services [HHS], 2018) for children ages 6 through 17 years to complete 60 minutes or more of moderate-to-vigorous physical activity (MVPA) daily.

Self-motivation connects with the topic of goal setting in the physical education space as students identify how much movement they complete daily. For example, students can collect present physical activity minutes to see whether they are meeting the minimum of 60 minutes per day. Students can take this data and identify a goal through designing and implementing a physical activity program. Physical education teachers can take it even further by having students reflect on the type of physical activity completed and how it links with health-related fitness components. Students can then design a program to enhance areas of growth and maintain areas where they are meeting the goal in specified health-related fitness components.

Self-awareness, evaluation, and designing goals are also closely aligned with SEL competencies, and they extend to self-discipline and self-management of implementing their plan, as seen in table 15.2. Students may have specified time within the physical education class to develop their plan, create specific activities to enhance performance, and receive feedback. Self-discipline in physical education may also include general practices, routines, and structures that are expected of the students, and they could entail working for an extended period individually, in pairs, or in small groups. Self-discipline is also illustrated through respect by following rules and etiquette while participating in modified games and activities. One example is refereeing a small-sided game while playing it or resolving conflict in a respectful manner. Self-discipline is exhibited in the physical education setting through practicing and observing safety procedures with equipment, peers, and space.

Social Awareness

Social awareness: The ability to understand diverse perspectives and empathize with others who have a different culture or background from your own.

Topics: taking others' perspectives; recognizing strengths in others; demonstrating empathy and compassion; showing concern for the feelings of others; understanding and expressing gratitude; identifying diverse social norms, including unjust ones; recognizing situational demands and opportunities; understanding the influences of organization or systems on behavior (CASEL, 2020)

Physical education class lends itself to practicing social awareness and subtopics in many ways, especially given that the majority of the context for learning is engaging with peers in pairs or small groups. For example, in forming small groups or teams, physical education classes are developed heterogeneously or with mixed-ability groups, unlike other courses that may have prerequisites or structures for advanced classes. This flexibility provides a natural opportunity for students to work in teams with mixed levels of ability. As a result, the teacher must develop structures and functions that align with social awareness and empathy for students with different ability levels. Norms, routines, and structures are put into place to build a climate in which all students have access to the physical education content regardless of ability. To this end, teachers facilitate numerous opportunities to elevate peer leaders and engage students in multiple grouping practices throughout the instructional time. Fostering team development involves teaching physical education students to accept, recognize, and involve all students in their teams with higher or lower skill abilities; this approach, in turn, fosters empathy.

TABLE 15.2 Self-Management in Physical Education Class: Lesson Considerations

Teacher Will Do the Following:	Students Will Do the Following:
Create opportunities for students to practice personal and social responsibility that demonstrates respect for self and others (impulse control).	Explore various physical education learning tasks to model personal and social responsibility for • Self: attending to tasks, asking questions when they do not understand, and practicing effective communication skills. • Others: helping classmates when they do not understand, providing learning cues for skills and tactics, and helping to record and provide feedback.
Provide opportunities for students to demonstrate the knowledge and skills to achieve and maintain a health-enhancing level of physical activity and fitness (stress management).	Explore various activities provided by the teacher to identify ways to manage stress.
Create opportunities for students to explore and practice self-discipline through individual, paired, and team pursuits (self-discipline).	Practice exhibiting self-discipline and self-motivation within various physical education settings (transitions; individual, paired, and small-sided games). Demonstrate personal and collective agency through leading and following in various physical education settings.
Foster and empower students to complete and carry out various physical education learning tasks (self-motivation).	Exhibit self-discipline and self-motivation within various physical education learning tasks.
Use different instructional models to empower students within the class setting.	Show the courage to take initiative; for example, implementing sport education in these roles: • Leading team warm-ups • Referee/official • Coach • Equipment manager
Develop opportunities for students to formally and informally reflect on various tasks to set goals (goal setting).	Set personal and collective goals, and use planning and organizational skills. For example, they reflect on modified games to implement a new strategy, or they set an objective to reduce scoring or to increase attacks on the goal.
Provide students with opportunities to apply knowledge of concepts, principles, strategies, and tactics related to movement and performance (organizational skills).	Actively engage in and explore various learning situations to apply knowledge of concepts, principles, strategies, and tactics.
Provide students with self-assessment opportunities to reflect on managing one's emotions.	Manage emotions and actions while participating in individual and group activities.

From J. Greenberg and J. LoBianco, *Organization and Administration of Physical Education,* 2nd ed. (Human Kinetics, 2026). Developed by Cara D. Grant, Montgomery County Public Schools.

Appreciating and accepting diversity is evidenced in the physical education classroom through acknowledging differences and teaching peers to provide encouragement and feedback regardless of ability level, socioeconomic background, gender, or culture. Physical education teachers develop structures and practices for applying acceptance of diversity through teaching cultural diversity norms and engaging students in cooperative and collaborative movement tasks. Through empathy, appreciating diversity, and accepting diversity, fostering a respect for others in the physical education class becomes paramount.

Students practice social awareness through monitoring and encouraging peers to attend to the physical education task. In addition, peers can coach and facilitate bringing students away from unethical behavior during physical activity through practicing conflict resolution and communication practices. Individually, social awareness and respect for others is exhibited by students when they model and follow the routines, procedures, and practices set forth by the physical education teacher. Students can exhibit social awareness and respect during planning and reflection for physical education. For example, students are playing a modified game and request a time-out to reflect on and change game strategy. Students show respect for others through following the request for a time-out. The teams show respect for others by listening to the ideas of the team and coming to agreement on what changes they need to make in the game to enhance overall performance. Social awareness is an overall component in the physical education classroom because students are expected to work with others in a common space. It may entail individually working in a fitness room and following procedures on transitions between equipment. It may look like small-sided games or a team dynamic warm-up routine. More examples of social awareness are found in table 15.3.

TABLE 15.3 Social Awareness in a Physical Education Class: Lesson Considerations

Teacher Will Do the Following:	Students Will Do the Following:
Create learning tasks that include reflection on various perspectives (perspective taking).	Take others' perspectives within the physical education class setting (individual, paired, team) to support and provide feedback for peers.
Develop opportunities for students to reflect, identify, and support students and community from different cultures and backgrounds (appreciating and accepting diversity).	Reflect and acknowledge that diversity is a value and not a deficit.
Create norms, routines, procedures and practices for students to practice respect for others.	Work collaboratively with the teacher and peers to establish and apply routines, practices, and procedures.
Identify opportunities for students to recognize strengths in others.	Select and uplift peers for various tasks and contributions in the physical education setting (e.g., cognitive, affective, psychomotor outcomes).
Teach concepts that help students develop empathy, compassion, sporting behavior, and ethics within modified games, individual pursuits, paired activities, and small-group activities.	Reflect on their role in supporting others to become physically literate through showing empathy and compassion for students with different ability levels and prior content knowledge in physical education.
Create opportunities for students to show concern for the feelings of others.	Acknowledge classmates' feelings and emotions to create a sense of belonging and teamwork. Identify when a disagreement or conflict arises, and work to develop an outcome that both sides of the conflict agree on.
Develop situations for students to reflect on gratitude, and express gratitude to others.	Identify and acknowledge peers for work being done on a team, and celebrate successes.
Foster ways for students to identify and unpack diverse social norms, including unjust ones (e.g., race, gender, sexual identity, ability).	Be open to reviewing stereotypes and bias around different groups of people based on race, gender, ability, and sexual identity to include all students in the physical education setting. An example of acting based on a stereotype is determining whether a person is able to be physically active or competitive in a game situation based only on assumptions drawn from the person's appearance and not from observing the person play.
Foster opportunities for students to recognize situational demands and opportunities.	Review different conditions for learning to see situational demands.
Assist students with identifying factors on the influences of organizations or systems on behavior.	Consider how the class environment, games, and tasks lead to how peers respond to physical education tasks, such as completing a fitness test individually versus practicing fitness-based components in a small team event.

From J. Greenberg and J. LoBianco, *Organization and Administration of Physical Education,* 2nd ed. (Human Kinetics, 2026). Developed by Cara D. Grant, Montgomery County Public Schools.

Relationship Skills

Relationship skills: The ability to create and maintain supportive and healthy relationships including navigating diverse settings, individuals, and groups.

Topics: communicating effectively; developing positive relationships; demonstrating cultural competency; practicing teamwork and collaborative problem solving; resolving conflicts constructively; resisting negative social pressure; showing leadership in groups; seeking or offering support and help when needed; standing up for the rights of others (CASEL, 2020)

Physical education learning environments and instructional practice include numerous opportunities for students to develop relationship skills. Students often are grouped or paired with other students, and they are provided tasks that are challenges to work through. Oftentimes, student groups can be culturally diverse, have different ability levels, and have language needs. Specifically, students are taught to use communication skills and strategies to help team and group dynamics. Challenges, tasks, and modified games created and explored during physical education class permit students to practice social engagement and teamwork. Within these settings, students are taught ways to encourage peers and provide constructive feedback toward the learning objective. They are taught to correct negative dialogue or put-downs as a way to enhance social engagement and practice positive communication strategies; examples are shown in table 15.4.

Responsible Decision Making

Responsible decision making: The ability to make constructive and caring choices about social interactions and personal behaviors across diverse situations.

Topics: demonstrating curiosity and open-mindedness; identifying solutions for personal and social problems; learning to make a reasoned judgment after analyzing information, data, and facts; anticipating and evaluating the consequences of one's actions; recognizing how critical thinking skills are useful in and out of school settings; reflecting on one's role to promote personal, family, and community well-being; evaluating personal, interpersonal, community, and institutional impacts (CASEL 2020)

Numerous opportunities are provided to investigate and apply responsible decision making in physical education classes, which includes the ability to analyze situations, solve problems, practice reflection, and exhibit ethical responsibility in diverse physical education learning environments. Students have the opportunity to decide and apply various movement concepts and strategies within modified game situations. Furthermore, students are able to analyze the physical education construct for learning and make adjustments to the strategy used. These decisions and reflections help to maintain safety for self, others, and community. Students are entrenched in opportunities to solve problems in physical education, which include understanding the type of skill to use in various situations. For example, students identify, recognize and apply a particular skill, such as throwing, volleying, or striking, within different games and sports categories. Students then have the opportunity to apply various strategies and tactics to analyze errors in gameplay within various tactical games categories (e.g., net wall, striking and fielding, invasion games, and target games).

Physical education teachers further provide opportunities for students to look at individual fitness assessment data. Students may predict their fitness level in various health-related fitness components, collect the data, analyze the results of the scores, and set a goal, as well as develop a fitness plan through a skill-related fitness approach. This approach is intertwined with the topic of reflecting. Every step of the way, students must reflect on the data, the skills, the environment, and the impact of life choices on health and fitness; this task includes student reflection on personal and social behaviors and how they connect with physical activity.

Physical education teachers provide students with opportunities to investigate and apply ethical responsibility. Rules, routines, and practices are taught or codeveloped in class, and

TABLE 15.4 Relationship Skills in a Physical Education Class: Lesson Considerations

Teacher Will Do the Following:	Students Will Do the Following:
Provide instruction on various interpersonal communication strategies and techniques, and model them for the class.	Use communication (verbal and nonverbal) effectively in paired, small-group, and whole-class (introduction and closure) settings.
Foster opportunities for social engagement of students.	Engage in various physical education tasks with others.
Provide instruction on effective relationship building in a physical education setting (peer feedback, encouragement, critical feedback, and support).	Develop positive relationships through paired and small-group interactions.
Create conditions to foster teamwork in multiple and varied ways. For example, the teacher may have one team for positive behavioral interventions and supports (PBIS) team points; paired team challenges; and small teams playing modified games.	Participate in activities that provide opportunities to practice teamwork and communication skills.
Provide instruction and create conditions to practice cultural competence in physical education. *Cultural competence* is when a person has the capacity to value diversity; conduct a personal assessment; unpack differences from their culture and that of others; acquire and institutionalize cultural knowledge; and adapt to diversity within the cultural contexts of the communities they are in (Cross et al., 1989).	Demonstrate cultural competence in physical education class through the following: • Acknowledging, appreciating, and accepting differences between self and others • Identifying cultural norms within self • Comparing differences in cultural norms with self and others • Considering institution, sport, and education cultural norms • Adapting and respecting cultural differences in the physical education class and school
Develop conditions for students to solve problems in modified game situations.	Practice teamwork and collaborative problem solving.
Provide instruction on various ways to practice effective interpersonal communication skills to resolve conflicts with empathy and compassion.	Resolve conflicts constructively.
Review norms, procedures, and ground rules to identify productive on-task and uplifting practices.	Resist negative social pressures that distract from the learning outcome and go against established norms, procedures, and ground rules.
Develop and modify conditions for fostering different relationships (e.g., various grouping and regrouping strategies of students).	Show leadership and followership in various groups.
Establish practices that affirm students to seek out support and critical feedback toward the learning outcome.	Seek or offer support and help when needed.
Foster a positive classroom environment that encourages all students to treat each other with dignity and respect.	Stand up for the rights of others.

From J. Greenberg and J. LoBianco, *Organization and Administration of Physical Education,* 2nd ed. (Human Kinetics, 2026). Developed by Cara D. Grant, Montgomery County Public Schools.

TABLE 15.5 Responsible Decision Making in a Physical Education Class: Lesson Considerations

Teacher Will Do the Following:	Students Will Do the Following:
Create various problems for students to identify and solve in game situations.	Identify tactical problems in various game settings. Identify problems in individual or fitness-based settings.
Develop situations for students to analyze in multiple and varied ways (e.g., health-related fitness, personal and social responsibility, and movement skills and concepts).	Demonstrate curiosity and open-mindedness to analyze situations in multiple and varied learning conditions and physical education grade-span learning indicators.
Identify physical education situations to solve problems.	Identify solutions for personal and social problems linked to well-being.
Provide opportunities for students to evaluate personal, interpersonal, community, and institutional impacts.	Anticipate and evaluate the consequences of their actions.
Create norms, routines, and practices that infuse student and peer reflection throughout the physical education class.	Practice reflection in multiple and varied learning tasks.
Provide instruction on empowering students to be advocates for well-being.	Reflect on one's role to promote personal, family, and community well-being; and make decisions on how to advocate for well-being.
Develop instructional opportunities to foster critical thinking skills, and help students connect transfer of these skills inside and outside of school.	Recognize how critical thinking skills are useful both inside and outside of school. For example, they notice peer and family influence on well-being choices (e.g., nutrition, physical activity, mental health practices).
Create and demonstrate ethical responsibility for students in physical education.	Learn to make a reasoned judgment after analyzing information, data, and facts.
Provide skill-specific feedback, and give direction to help students analyze and solve problems.	Utilize feedback to improve skills and performance.

From J. Greenberg and J. LoBianco, *Organization and Administration of Physical Education,* 2nd ed. (Human Kinetics, 2026). Developed by Cara D. Grant, Montgomery County Public Schools.

they are carried out both independently and with teacher facilitation. Students are taught to provide critique and critical feedback for self and peers to maintain adherence to rules, routines, and practices in a variety of modified game settings. Teachers can facilitate practice of these skills by assigning student roles as a referee or official as well as by having students collectively officiate the game; this way, all students are actively participating in the context if learning physically (see table 15.5). Collectively, ethical responsibility is exhibited through the active engagement of respect for self, peers, and others in a variety of physical education settings.

In summary, students engage in SEL competencies in physical education in multiple ways. The SEL competencies are skills that transfer across physical education content and context for learning whether within individual, paired, or small-group modified game-based learning situations. Students practice skills in physical education to develop social and interpersonal skills, cognitive regulation, emotional processes, character, and mindset (Jones & Doolittle, 2017). Eleven associated variables that have historically appeared in the physical education and sport literature align with national standards, and they could also be considered as SEL skills and outcomes; they include the following: work ethic; control and management; goal setting; decision making; problem solving; responsibility; leadership; cooperation; meeting people and making friends; communication; and prosocial behavior (Dyson et al., 2020). SEL skills and outcomes complement each other, and they connect across the learning opportunities in physical education.

LEADERSHIP IN ACTION

SEL in Physical Education

Aaron Hart, MS

Vice President, Curriculum and Program Engagement, Varsity Brands

SEL was formalized as an educational model in the mid-1990s when a group of researchers, educators, and child advocates gathered to discuss the fragmented school-based initiatives that had formed with a focus on developing the general social and psychological needs of school-aged children. It was at this gathering that the Collaborative for Academic, Social, and Emotional Learning (CASEL) was formed.

To be clear, the work of fostering the social and emotional needs of children didn't start there. Humans have focused on this work for thousands of years, and many of the findings of researchers and practitioners may seem natural and obvious. However, what may seem natural and obvious doesn't always make it into our schools.

Also happening in the mid-1990s, Don Hellison (1995) published his foundational book, *Teaching Personal and Social Responsibility Through Physical Activity*, and NASPE (1995) released the first edition set of seven *National Standards for Physical Education*. Both works highlighted the power of physical education to develop and strengthen students' social and emotional learning and potential. NASPE's published book was given the title *Moving Into the Future*. It's hard to imagine that the outcomes committee at that time would have known how important the inclusion of SEL would become.

To date, hundreds of circulated works have focused on various ways for developing and fostering SEL for our students. Many of those publications agree that SEL is the process through which all people acquire and apply knowledge, skills, and attitudes within these five broad domains (CASEL, 2003):

- Self-awareness
- Self-management
- Social awareness
- Relationship skills
- Responsible decision making

In current physical education classrooms, which are filled with students who are experiencing ongoing trauma from the COVID-19 pandemic and are struggling with mental health, the primary challenge for teachers has nothing to do with a lack of research or publications. The primary challenge for physical educators is how to sort through it all and find a place to start.

It's with this challenge in mind that OPEN (Hart, 2020) published *The OPEN Priority Learning Outcomes for Social and Emotional Learning*. This document places the focus on creating a physical education learning environment that establishes and maintains three essential components: safety, empowerment, and healing.

Understanding that these three components are critical for SEL to take root, physical educators can become laser focused on planning for success by unpacking each component as follows:

- *Safety—Establish a safe learning environment by building trust.* What are you doing to establish trust with each of your students? What are you doing to help students trust each other?
- *Empowerment—Establish an empowering learning environment by cultivating optimism.* What are you doing to demonstrate for your students that the work they're doing in your classroom today will make their lives better tomorrow? How are you connecting what they're learning to their everyday lives?
- *Healing—Establish a healing environment by being consistent.* Every hurt (physical or emotional) requires a healing environment maintained over time. How are you planning lessons so that they are consistently reinforcing trust and optimism? Are you providing tools and systems for your students to rebuild trust and regain optimism when a setback happens?

While these three core components can give educators clear and simple focal points for planning and teaching, the work of building trust, cultivating optimism, and staying consistent for weeks, months, and years is not easy. Teachers are most likely working through their own traumas and very real professional and personal challenges. Because of this challenge, administrators would benefit from asking the previously listed questions with respect to the type of working environment they're cultivating for their faculty and staff.

Model-Based Practices in Physical Education

Model-based practices (MBPs) have been posited as fundamental tools to help students accomplish SEL outcomes (Jacobs & Wright, 2014). In current research, there are limited connections between physical education and SEL (Dyson et al., 2020). However, there is a correlation within various physical education instructional models: cooperative learning model, Teaching Personal and Social Responsibility (TPSR) model, Tactical Games Model (TGM) or teaching games for understanding (TGfU) model, and outdoor and adventure education (OAE) models (Fernandez-Rio & Iglesias, 2022; Dyson et al., 2020). The previous (2013) conditions and grade-level outcomes and the current (2024) grade-span learning indicators in physical education show an overlap with the SEL content. This overlap is observable through cognitive, affective, and psychomotor outcomes that provide students with multiple ways to identify, explore, and create SEL practices for self and others. Gagnon (2016) affirmed that physical education is a content area in which teachers can foster emotional well-being and build healthy, positive social and emotional experiences. Ciotto and Gagnon (2018) further confirmed that physical education includes and aligns with helping students foster SEL through developing goals, establishing healthy relationships through physical education conditions for learning, reflecting on personal and social needs and responsibilities, and identifying and managing emotions.

Model-based practices are a pedagogical approach that fuses together the teacher's instructional style with student needs (Casey, 2016). The Sport Education Model (SEM) is the most widely studied approach that connects to developing student self-efficacy and to TPSR aligned with SEL competencies (Evangelio Caballero et al., 2018). SEM and SEL have direct overlap and connection in numerous components such as teamwork, equity, peer support and mentoring, empathy, problem solving, decision making, and leadership (Bessa et al., 2019). The TPSR model provides students with opportunities to model self-control; to exhibit responsibility for self and others; to experience structured levels of accountability; and to practice conflict resolution skills; these skills and practices directly align with SEL content and competencies (Dyson et al., 2020). Structures in the TPSR model lend themselves to fostering student development of self-control, self-awareness, goal setting, self-motivation, self-direction, empathy, and knowing consequences of one's actions in physical education classes. TPSR encompasses most of the SEL competencies and outcomes, with limitations on cultural diversity and differences linked therein.

Cooperative Learning

Cooperative learning is a model-based practice used in physical education that has explicit connections with SEL. These connections are evidenced through the opportunity for students to work together and a heightened focus on social interactions in the physical education setting. Social awareness and relationship skills are focal points of cooperative learning. Teaching cooperative learning is connected to elevating social perceptions of gender and sexism, leading to positive shifts in relationships; for example, one study reported girls feeling more valued and included by boys (Dyson et al., 2020). The cooperative learning model provides numerous opportunities for students to reflect on self and others while working toward a common goal aligned with SEL. As a result, the cooperative learning model in physical education and SEL content are connected through self-awareness, social perceptions, reflection, recognizing and naming emotions, communication, decision making, and goal setting.

Outdoor and Adventure Education (OAE)

Outdoor and adventure education (OAE) models present model-based practices that link opportunities for students to engage in challenges with practicing SEL skills and competencies. These skills and competencies include the core competencies of self-awareness, self-management, social awareness, relationship skills, and responsible decision making to solve problems and challenges focusing on the affective domain (Sutherland & Legge, 2016). Outdoor education links skill development and problem solving in the natural environment. Adventure education focuses highly on individual development or small group development. Adventure education can be outside in the natural environment or inside within a controlled environment (Timken & McNamee, 2012). The context and conditions for learning in OAE continue to provide students with opportunities to practice and expand SEL skills (Ee & Ong, 2014; Price, 2019). Lubans and colleagues (2011) identified that many studies confirm the connection of OAE to social and emotional well-being and to personal and social development.

Tactical Games or Teaching Games for Understanding

The Tactical Games Model (TGM), or teaching games for understanding (TGfU) model, has received less research aligning with SEL skills and competencies than the TPSR, cooperative learning, and OAE models. TGfU teaches sports through modifications, developing opportunities for all students to experience and play games. Game appreciation is taught through all three domains (psychomotor, cognitive, and affective) (Mitchell et al., 2021). TGfU explicitly teaches decision making through how the conditions of the modified game are set up. For example, the students reflect, identify, and select skills and concepts to create space or attack the goal. Learner appreciation fostering an SEL connection was added to the most recent framework for TGfU (2021). The social construct of gameplay is accentuated to elevate SEL competencies, including cultural competence and respecting diverse ability levels. Game appreciation instruction provides students with opportunities to learn how the game is played, its rules, and the etiquette involved in playing it (Mitchell et al., 2021). Learner appreciation focuses most explicitly on the SEL skills and competencies of self-awareness, self-management, social awareness, relationship skills, problem solving, and responsible decision making (Mitchell et al., 2021).

Teaching Personal and Social Responsibility, Cooperative Learning, Sport Education, and Teaching Games for Understanding

TPSR, cooperative learning, SEM, and TGfU infuse model-based practices focusing on combining instructional models where student needs are considered to address SEL skills and competencies. The learner profile drives the need for physical education teachers to know who the students are from an SEL focal point. Students leverage SEL practices within physical education learning environments to build personal and social connections and critically employ communication, goal setting, and decision making. SEL can be integrated in model-based practices through explicit planning and fidelity of implementation. There are common errors that drive focus away from physical education instructional outcomes infused with SEL instruction that lend practitioners to focus on too much in too little time (Fernandez-Rio & Iglesias, 2022). Having a learner-centered approach, in addition to matching with national, state, and local physical education outcomes and grade-span learning indicators, will assist in mitigating disruption to implementing SEL in physical education.

Sample SEL Educational Programs

There are numerous programs that identify and link SEL skills, content, and competencies within curricula. Some include Character Strong, EVERFI, Paths, Playworks, Second Step, Quaver SEL, SEL Catch Journeys, and Leader in Me. Most of these resources have used CASEL as a vetting source for validation of SEL alignment. As previously mentioned, CASEL provides an online program guide for educators, administrators, community members, or homes to research and select for use. Freestanding lessons, organizational strategies, integration of SEL, and teaching practices are included (CASEL, 2022c). The

CASEL program guide includes administrator support, coaching, technical assistance, professional learning communities (PLCs), an online resource library, self-report tools for implementation, observation tools, and tools for measuring student success. The CASEL program guide includes significant evaluation outcomes desired, including the following:

1. Improved academic performance
2. Reduced emotional stress
3. Improved identity development and agency
4. Reduced problem behaviors
5. Improved school climate
6. Improved school connectedness
7. Improved social behaviors
8. Improved teaching practices
9. Improved other SEL skills and attitudes

There are training offerings included within the CASEL program guide. The training offerings include on-site in-person training, virtual training, off-site training, and a train the trainer model. When determining which evidence-based program is right for your needs, these three steps could provide assistance in your selection:

Step 1: Determine your SEL team and goals.

Step 2: Connect your needs to CASEL metrics.

Step 3: Identify and compare SEL programs.

From there, reach out to each program to learn about cost and alignment to goals identified. Not all programs listed meet full outcomes as cited under the program type (SELect and Promising designations, SEL-Supportive program). SELect designates that all five CASEL core competencies are addressed and supported in the program. Promising designation identifies programs that address at least two of the core competencies. SEL-Supportive programs are those that meet some of the core competencies for teachers or students, but they do not meet all of them; therefore, they could be supplemental SEL programs. The following programs are a sample from the highest level of SEL evidence-based programs meeting all of the core competencies.

Leader in Me

The Leader in Me (LIM) program is a CASEL SELect program that is developed by Franklin Covey Education. Resources are vetted through CASEL programming in grades K through 6 and are most effective in grades K through 5. Additional programs that are not listed on the CASEL program inventory are available for high school. Students engage in strategies surrounding bias and youth action projects while unpacking Covey's (2022) Seven Habits:

Habit 1: Be proactive

Habit 2: Begin with the end in mind

Habit 3: Put first things first

Habit 4: Think win-win

Habit 5: Seek first to understand, then to be understood

Habit 6: Synergize

Habit 7: Sharpen the saw

The LIM program approach includes freestanding lessons, organizational strategies, and teaching practices. The significant evaluation outcomes identified are reduced problem behaviors. Student characteristics identified include Black/African American, Hispanic/Latinx, and low income. The school characteristics identified are rural, urban, suburban, and Southeast.

Mindful Practices and Class Catalyst: An Integrated SEL Approach

Mindful Practices and Class Catalyst: An Integrated SEL Approach (Class Catalyst) is a CASEL SELect program developed by Mindful Practices, LLC with programming for students in grades PreK through 12. The Class Catalyst program approach includes freestanding lessons. The significant evaluation outcomes identified are improved school connectedness and improved other SEL skills and attitudes. Student characteristics identified include Black/African American, White, and low income. The school characteristics identified are suburban and Midwest.

Promoting Alternative THinking Strategies (PATHS)

Promoting Alternative THinking Strategies (PATHS) is a CASEL SELect program focused on students in grades PreK through 6, with effectiveness in PreK and grades 1 through 3. PATHS provides youth action projects as the conduit for learning SEL. The PATHS program approach includes freestanding lessons. The significant evaluation outcomes identified are reduced problem behaviors, improved school climate, improved school connectedness, improved social behaviors, improved academic performance, and improved other SEL skills and attitudes. Student characteristics identified include Black/African American, Hispanic/Latinx, White, and low income. The school characteristics identified are urban, suburban, Northeast, Southeast, and West.

EduGuide

EduGuide is a SELect CASEL program that includes lessons for grades 4 through 12, and is most effective in grades 5 through 7. The EduGuide program approach includes freestanding lessons and organizational strategies. The significant evaluation outcomes identified are improved academic performance and reduced behavior problems. Student characteristics identified include Hispanic/Latinx and low income. The school characteristics identified are urban, suburban, Northeast, Southwest, and West.

Facing History and Ourselves

Facing History and Ourselves is a CASEL SELect program that integrates SEL lessons in social studies. The program is best suited for grades 7 through 10, but it is accessible for grades 6 through 12. Facing History and Ourselves includes SEL strategies for students to engage with context, bias, and youth action projects. The Facing History and Ourselves program approach includes integration of SEL and teaching practices. The significant evaluation outcomes identified are improved identity development and agency, reduced problem behaviors, improved school climate, improved social behaviors, improved teaching practices, and improved other SEL skills and attitudes. Student characteristics identified include Black/African American, Hispanic/Latinx, White, multiracial/other, and low income. The school characteristics identified are urban, Northeast, Southwest, Midwest, and West.

Second Step

Second Step is a unique program including three freestanding programs:

- *Second Step: Early Learning Curriculum (Promising).* Second Step: Early Learning Curriculum is a Promising CASEL program offered by the Committee for Children, and it is included due to the SELect designation of the other two Second Step SEL programs. The Second Step: Early Learning Curriculum program approach includes freestanding lessons. The significant evaluation outcomes identified are improved other SEL skills and attitudes. Student characteristics identified include Black/African American, Hispanic/Latinx, White, and low income. The school characteristics identified are Northeast.
- *Second Step: Elementary (SELect).* Second Step: Elementary is a CASEL SELect program offered by the Committee for Children. The Second Step: Elementary program approach includes freestanding lessons. The significant evaluation outcomes identified are reduced emotional distress, reduced problem behaviors, improved social behaviors, and improved other SEL skills and attitudes. Student characteristics identified include Black/African American, Hispanic/Latinx, White, multiracial/other, and low income. The school characteristics identified are rural, urban, Southwest, West, and non-U.S. location.
- *Second Step Middle School Curriculum (SELect).* Second Step: Middle School Curriculum is a CASEL SELect program developed by the Committee for Children. The Second Step: Middle School Curriculum program approach includes freestanding lessons. The significant evaluation outcomes identified are reduced problem behaviors. Student characteristics identified include Black/African American, Hispanic/Latinx, White, multiracial/other, and low income. The school characteristic identified is Midwest.

Sample SEL Programs Not Listed in CASEL Program Guide

Even though CASEL has become known as the authority vetting SEL programming and resources, numerous non-CASEL-affiliated curricula are adding to the body of resources to develop SEL in PreK through high school settings. They are summarized next.

Health.Moves.Minds. (HMM)

Health.Moves.Minds. (HMM) is a PreK through high school SEL program that includes lesson materials and fundraising opportunities for schools. It is the only explicit physical education SEL program identified, and it is the only one aligned to national standards and grade-span learning indicators for K-12 physical education. HMM was created and is managed by SHAPE America. It contains program free resources for teachers and schools to sign up and access SEL lessons. In addition, through this program, schools can also fundraise for a charity, for local and national SHAPE affiliates, or for their schools. Lessons include various SEL units by theme, aligning to CASEL core competencies. Lessons are tiered, with grades K-5, 6-8, and 9-12 available.

Figure 15.2 provides a sample HMM lesson, titled Gratitude Walking Warm-Up and Cool-Down, for grades 3 through 5. HMM lessons include mini lessons to engage students in SEL competencies through movement practices sharing lesson objectives, equipment needed, essential question (related to objective), CASEL Core SEL Competency, National Standards and Grade-Span Learning Indicators for K-12 Physical Education, Lesson Overview, Definitions of academic language, activity progressions, team champion tip, modifications, differentiation, and checks for understanding.

Character Strong

Character Strong is a PreK through high school research-based SEL curriculum. The goal of this program is to address SEL from a holistic or Whole Child approach with vertically aligned lessons that link character and SEL together. A *holistic approach* is defined as shaping the school culture through classrooms, staff, families, the playground, and community. High-leverage skills identified in Character Strong include the following: courage, kindness, perseverance, responsibility, honesty, cooperation, respect, creativity, gratitude, and empathy. This program is presently in 50 states and 21 countries. Character Strong includes plug-and-play lessons with comprehensive slide decks. Implementation support is available, and minimal to no supplies are needed to implement this program. To support implementation of Character Strong, there are implementation calendars, pre- and post-assessments, family letters, an implementation road map, and alignment guides for both CASEL and the American School Counselor Association (ASCA).

EVERFI

EVERFI is an organization that develops digital student resources that are free for K-12 teachers. Their products are aligned to content curriculum standards and CASEL core competencies. The SEL curriculum lessons are linked with compassion, character, and mental wellness, which are also branded as emotional intelligence development for the classroom. EVERFI cites the Committee for Children in linking the need for SEL development and programs to develop positive social behaviors in students, as shown in figure 15.3. EVERFI includes 26 free lesson modules and resources online. The lesson topics include understanding compassion; understanding self; practicing compassion; self-management; social awareness; responsible decision making; identifying bullying; relationships and leadership; resilience and courage; compassion and empathy; mistakes and self-care; emotions and mindfulness; digital safety and privacy; screen time versus offline time; evaluating digital resources; the science behind mental health; overcoming stigmas; effective coping mechanisms; and seeking help and supporting others. The lessons are grounded in Whole Child Education, which prioritizes the full scope of a child's developmental needs to ensure that every child reaches their fullest potential, combined with the Substance Abuse and Mental Health Services (SAMHSA) Dimensions of Wellness—emotional, physical, intellectual, spiritual, environmental, financial, occupational, and social. Reports and assessments accompany the digital SEL lessons.

Being Mindful, Being Kind

The key message throughout these lessons is that being mindful of our own feelings and being mindful of how we treat others can help us be kinder. Additionally, taking care of our minds and bodies makes us healthy. Students will also begin to learn basic mindfulness strategies. Alternatively, you can replace the word mindfulness with self-awareness throughout the lessons. It's also important to note, the lesson plans may need to be adjusted by the teacher to accommodate the unique attributes and diversity of individual classes and students.

Lesson Name: Gratitude Walking Warmup/Cooldown

Unit Name: Mindfulness

Grade Level: 3-5

Lesson Length: 10 minutes

Before beginning, teachers should offer accommodations specifically mentioned in a student's IEP to support their ability to participate in the mini-lesson. A sample list of common accommodations and modifications to aid you in selecting appropriate supports for students can be found under "Additional Resources" here.

Lesson Objective(s):

Students will be able to define gratitude. Students will be able to identify things they are thankful for.

Equipment Needed:

- Mindfulness music (optional)
- Letter cards for T-H-A-N-K-S
- Bulletin board paper

Essential Question (related to objective):

What is gratitude?

CASEL Core SEL Competency:

Social awareness

- Understanding and expressing gratitude

National Standards and Grade-Level Outcomes for K-12 Physical Education:

Standard 3: The physically literate individual demonstrates the knowledge and skills to achieve and maintain a health-enhancing level of physical activity and fitness.

- S3.E4.3 Recognizes the importance of warmup and cooldown relative to vigorous physical activity.
- S3.E4.4 Demonstrates warmup and cooldown relative to the cardiorespiratory fitness assessment.
- S3.E4.5 Identifies the need for warmup and cooldown relative to various physical activities.

Lesson Overview:

Teachers will introduce the concept of gratitude. Students will walk around the perimeter of the instructional area and think about things they are thankful for. Students will end by writing something they are thankful for on the Gratitude Wall. This activity is good for a warmup or closing activity of an already existing lesson.

FIGURE 15.2 Sample HMM lesson for grades 3 through 5: Gratitude Walking Warm-Up and Cool-Down (p. 1 of 9 shown).

FIGURE 15.3 Examples in Physical Education That Align With SEL

Elementary School

- Beginning to learn how to make decisions for the benefit of personal fitness and health
- Working well independently, cooperatively, and safely
- Identifying activities that bring confidence and challenge

Middle School

- Positive communication with peers in small- and large-group activities
- Learning how to develop and implement a plan for personal fitness and health
- Beginning to make decisions about implementing FITT (frequency, intensity, time, and type) independently
- Identifying the importance of positive social interaction in physical activities

High School

- Analyzing personalized physical activity plans and designing appropriate goals
- Assuming leadership roles in group settings while positively communicating with all classmates
- Identifying and evaluating the opportunity for positive social interaction
- Examining moral and ethical conduct
- Applying strategies for stress management

Playworks

Playworks is a unique program that leverages recess, the power of play, with CASEL core competencies. SEL competencies are linked within the recess environment through fostering self-awareness, self-management, social awareness, relationship skills, and responsible decision making. This connection is embodied through training recess aids and staff to help students solve problems, make decisions, take turns, share ideas, and listen to other students. Playworks uses a train the trainer model to equip staff in supporting and monitoring recess to develop routines and practices connected to SEL competencies. Free online resources are available around the power of play, group management, game facilitation, indoor recess design, and youth leadership to support implementation. Recess is a great physical activity opportunity and an extension of the physical education program. Recess serves as a way for students to identify movement activities, gain from the effects of exercise, and practice SEL skills for self and with others.

QuaverED

QuaverEd offers a PreK through grade 5 SEL curriculum. The curriculum is comprehensive and highly structured. There is flexibility for the teachers to integrate SEL into their classes. The SEL lessons are designed to meet a variety of learning needs. QuaverEd SEL lessons include catchy songs to engage students. They have a variety of interactive online activities. The characters in the module represent diverse populations and ability groups. The scope of the QuaverEd SEL curriculum is a complete school year, intertwining character education and SEL with over 250 lessons. QuaverEd offers professional development, regular blog posts, and newsletters, and it uses social media actively to engage school-based partners. The lessons include physical activity and movement to connect with SEL.

SEL Journeys

The program SEL Journeys is provided by Coordinated Approach to Child Health (CATCH). SEL Journey aligns lessons for kindergarten through grade 12 with the CASEL competencies. The resources are grade-level banded in grades K through 5 and grades 6 through 12. Resources are provided in a digital platform to engage students in movement and cultural learning. SEL Journeys can be used as stand-alone lessons or integrated within other content areas to develop physical and mental health. CATCH aligns with the CDC's Whole Child, Whole School, Whole Community (WSCC) approach. The cornerstone of this SEL program is linked to authentic cultural connections aligned with CASEL's (2022a) equity and SEL framework through dance. SEL Journeys' content includes a variety of worldwide content with discussion, big ideas, application to life, traveling the world, engaging in physical activity, responding, and connecting.

SEL and Justice, Equity, Diversity, and Inclusion (JEDI)

There are different perspectives and characterizations for SEL linked to justice, equity, diversity, and inclusion (JEDI). SEL and equity are different bodies of work that can connect, but they must be elevated without losing one or the other. In review of the sample SEL curricula and resources, some explicitly focused on diversity, including appreciating and accepting differences. Keep in mind that providing *equality* for access to all SEL content assumes that all students need the same experiences and therefore should access the same SEL resources. The converse view is to develop an SEL approach that integrates *equity* as the cornerstone of development. An SEL equity approach includes working to overcome the institutional, systemic, and historical legacy of marginalization, discrimination, and lack of resources for disadvantaged groups as defined by race (Equity in Education, 2018; Minow, 2021). SEL work should expand on access to all marginalized groups, including gender, religion, socioeconomic status, sexual orientation, and others. SEL in **equity** is defined as providing what each individual student needs (as opposed to the one-size-fits-all phenomenon in equality). The topic of JEDI is further discussed in chapter 16.

In 2019, CASEL affirmed that a focus on JEDI is required. CASEL and presenters (2019) addressed the need of JEDI in the video presentation *SEL Learning Exchange: Building a Culture of Equity through SEL*. Within this presentation, various forms of social justice implications were identified, including personal responsible SEL—interpersonal justice; participatory SEL—procedural, restorative justice; and transformative SEL—distributive (equity) justice. Transformative SEL (tSEL) has a working definition as "a process whereby young people and adults build strong, respectful and lasting relationships that facilitate co-learning through critical examination of root cause of inequities, and the development of collaborative solutions to personal, community, and societal concerns" (CASEL, 2019, para. 6). The transformative SEL links intrapersonal, interpersonal, and institutional considerations for JEDI. Work on competencies is further aligned with JEDI as follows (CASEL, 2019):

1. *Self-awareness* includes issues of identity (e.g., racial, class, and gender identities).
2. *Self-management* includes issues of collective agency.
3. *Social awareness* includes issues of belonging and co-ownership.
4. *Relationship skills* includes collaboration and co-construction.
5. *Responsible decision making* includes distributive justice and collective well-being.

Some core features are power-sharing adults, youth, students, families, and other community stakeholders, but also rigor and relevance. Equity and excellence are directly connected through further research and work with the National Equity Project, a leadership and systems change organization whose mission is to transform the experiences and life options for children and families who have been historically underserved by institutions and systems.

TABLE 15.6 What SEL Can Look Like in Physical Education and Across the Content Areas for Students, Teachers, and Administrators: The What?

Self-Awareness	I affirm my intersectionality and recognize my cultural assets.
Self-Management	I can use positive skills to cope with acculturation stress, prejudice, and discrimination. *Acculturation stress*—Learning customs and traditions of a culture different than your own; the imposition or forced assimilation to a foreign culture (Hannigan, 2007).
Social Awareness	I recognize inequitable practices in school, community, and society.
Relationship Skills	I can relate and find commonality with those outside of my culture or in my group.
Responsible Decision Making	I pursue inclusive solutions for social conflicts.

From J. Greenberg and J. LoBianco, *Organization and Administration of Physical Education*, 2nd ed. (Human Kinetics, 2026). Developed by Cara D. Grant, Montgomery County Public Schools.

The goal of implementing and practicing SEL should occur in a manner that does not cause harm in the current structures of educational systems or erase bodies or groups of people's lived experiences and histories (Simmons, 2019).

Discussing and facilitating conversations about race, diversity, inclusion, sexual orientation, and the inequitable society people live in are difficult for many teachers; transformative SEL skill level of the teacher is key to balancing SEL and equity. Therefore, it is important for professionals to check their biases and beliefs at the schoolhouse door. This balance calls for the delivery of professional development opportunities for administrators on ways to teach teachers how to self-reflect and how to leverage the power of SEL to assist them in building relationships in the classroom.

Therefore, as a result, focusing on how to implement SEL through an equity lens is paramount. First, educators must develop a strong knowledge of SEL competencies with an equity lens. It begins with a reflection on self, getting to know one's own SEL strengths and weaknesses, including biases. A commitment to strong relationships and fostering classroom climates will extend the work of equity and SEL. In addition, educators can affirm all students' intersectional and cultural experiences. For example, a student who is Black, identifies as LGBTQ, and identifies as male will have a different cultural experience than a student who is Latino, identifies as female, and is middle class; and different from a White student, identifying as heterosexual, and lower class. Building relationships with students to learn the individual narrative will assist greatly with equity work and SEL implementation. A whole school approach to SEL will facilitate normalizing SEL competencies and equity conversations when practices are consistent from class to class across the content areas, as shown in table 15.6. Equity work has to be named alongside SEL to elevate and navigate difficult conversations about multicultural education, race, oppression, and bias. In short, achieving equity in SEL requires having courage and working through discomfort.

Srinivasan (2019) purports that transformative SEL is centered on justice and linked to interbeing; the idea of interbeing connects the collective of all people together. Relationships are key to equity and SEL, and they are key to developing an equitable and just society. Student voice and agency must be uplifted in a transformative SEL approach. Voices of all genders must be elevated regardless of their religion, native language, or ethnicity. Ishida (2019) shares that students must be co-creators with adults in SEL development and implementation within the classrooms and schools, and that this collaboration can be accomplished through a model of institutional work; this work is based on relationship-centered schools focused on investing in staff, valuing student voice, and creating spaces for relationship building. Safir (2016) further explains that there are six things that school staff can do to interrupt unconscious bias: (1) notice, (2) listen, (3) reflect,

TABLE 15.7 Equity Elaborations for Educators to Provide Instruction and Reflect on Practice

Self-Awareness	Examine the importance of various social identities. Derive constructive, positive meanings of social identities. Ground work and teaching within and affirming of cultural heritage.
Self-Management	Cope with acculturation stress. Cope with discrimination and prejudice.
Social Awareness	Discern the importance of diversity (situational). Understand the meaning of diversity in contexts (climate). Recognize cultural demands and opportunities. Cultivate collective efficacy.
Relationship Skills	Demonstrate cultural competence. Leverage cultural fluency.
Responsible Decision Making	Consider diversity salience and climate. Assess the impact of one's beliefs and biases. Pursue inclusive, mutually beneficial solutions. Reflect on the broader ethical consequences of one's decisions for intragroup, intergroup, and institutional relations.

From J. Greenberg and J. LoBianco, *Organization and Administration of Physical Education,* 2nd ed. (Human Kinetics, 2026). Developed by Cara D. Grant, Montgomery County Public Schools.

(4) connect, (5) affirm, and (6) act. Rivera (2019) states that creating and cultivating community is critical in transformative SEL. Listening to students is a foundational tool within implementing transformative SEL. Providing students with a platform to share what their narrative is will help drive the work forward.

SEL Equity Elaborations

To implement SEL and equity side by side, educators need to include the explicit naming of multiculturalism, marginalized groups, underserved groups, race, racism, oppression, and trauma—topics that are often left out due to discomfort. True SEL is about understanding your relationships with yourself and with others. SEL builds on knowing yourself as a holistic human being and being able to see the humanity in others to fight, together, for the world everyone deserves, which is rooted in justice, equity, diversity, and inclusion (Kaler-Jones, 2020). SEL cannot be carried out well without acknowledging equity as a stand-alone body of work that is integral to SEL. SEL and equity need to be part of every content area and every part of the student's day, as shown in table 15.7.

Connecting to Policies and Regulations

SEL implementation aligns with complementary well-being policies and procedures at the federal, state, and local levels. This alignment is evidenced through the connections found within the CDC's Whole School, Whole Community, Whole Child (WSCC) model, which aims to develop healthy and supportive school environments. Social and emotional climate is one of the 10 components found in the WSCC framework. The CDC names the psychosocial aspects as a key component in the development of student social and emotional development, further linking the school's climate to how students engage in the school setting and their academic identity. Additionally, the school's social and emotional climate is linked with relationship development across students, staff, family, and community. The aim is to foster SEL to develop a safe and supportive learning environment for students. The WSCC model also names physical education as a component to build connection with the students, school, family, and community.

The Healthy, Hunger-Free Kids Act of 2010 (updated February 26, 2014 and expired on September 30, 2015), which is still in effect, includes provisions under the final rule for local school wellness policy implementation under the U.S. Department of Agriculture (USDA). Local school wellness policies align with the WSCC model, and they include components that complement SEL instructional practices and procedures focusing on student health, well-being, and the ability to learn. The final rule requires schools to identify and promote school-based activities aligned with student wellness that are evidence based. As a result, schools are looking to CASEL as an opportunity to review the evidence-based programs identified in their database to serve student well-being. In a triennial assessment, schools report on how they are meeting or exceeding the final rule guidelines.

A local example of strategic planning for well-being and SEL is evidenced in a large Maryland school district through the development of the Be Well 365 program (Montgomery County Public Schools, n.d.). The program was developed as a local WSCC model implementation structure with the goal of enhancing student well-being, collecting student voice data, and elevating physical education, health education, psychological services, social workers, counselors, and community partners to foster connection for students and families. After implementation of Be Well 365, the Maryland district secured an anti-racist audit to align with the focus on equity. As the anti-racist audit was underway, the school system secured an SEL curriculum during the same time as traversing the COVID-19 pandemic. The strategic plan of the superintendent aligns with a focus on academic excellence; well-being and family engagement; and professional and operational excellence pillars resting on a foundation of respect, relationships, equity, excellence, and learning. These concepts and bodies of work come together to prepare and equip students in the district for college, career, and the community. This situation is an example of bringing together bodies of work to acknowledge equity, well-being, and the relationship with SEL to achieve academic gains for underserved students.

SEL Connections to Families and Community

Aligned with the CDC WSCC model, SEL can be used to foster connections with families and the community. Schools can extend and reinforce the SEL learning to build stronger connections, reinforcing student SEL development. Caregivers and families are the first educators of children; they bring with them culture, experiences, and developmental practices from the home. Schools can enlist families for input, voice, and feedback on SEL implementation in school as well as to carry out the continued lessons when students are at home. CASEL (2020) shares that when evidence-based programs are extended to home, students grasp SEL content more effectively. It can also help foster positive relationships with families and community members through enlisting various cultural backgrounds and practices within SEL work. Strategically partnering with historically marginalized groups and families through planning, implementing, and reflecting on SEL in the school will create a more inclusive SEL decision-making process. Various activities and partnerships can be formed with families leveraging SEL work. These activities include enhanced communication, child development professional learning opportunities, assisting the school in learning about different cultures and family backgrounds, offering volunteer opportunities in the school, and coordinating services for families aligned to the WSCC model.

Community partners are an integral component of developing SEL through connecting services, schools, and families. Community partners leverage different funding sources, and they have different structures and strengths to complement the SEL work in schools. Recreation programs, mentoring groups, and other clubs and activities within the community can provide students with opportunities to practice their social and emotional skills in authentic settings. Schools can partner with community groups to come into the school before or after the school day or at lunch to implement content for students as well. Partnering with community groups and enlisting them to extend SEL learning must be explicit through sharing the SEL efforts carried out in the schools with sharing common language and practices. Through connecting with families and community partners, SEL can be practiced in authentic settings and affirmed through various groups.

Barriers to Implementing SEL Programming

Success does not come without overcoming barriers. Challenges follow when change occurs in any organization. Challenges could include teacher professional development structures, educators' implementation fidelity, normalizing working SEL definitions, and understanding and implementing evidence-based SEL practices and curriculum in schools. Teachers struggle to effectively implement practices promoting SEL outcomes within their curricula (Gagnon, 2016). Competing demands, such as high-stakes testing and instructional minutes, affect the implementation structures of SEL programs and curriculum. The continued pressure of high-stakes testing and the demands of meeting curricular outcomes inhibit the extent to which teachers and instructors implement SEL (Gordon et al., 2016). Equity and cultural barriers exist within SEL as well (Blackshear & Culp, 2023). As with the implementation of any instructional program, there are numerous barriers within SEL program implementation to consider.

Successes in Implementing SEL Programming

There are numerous successes in implementation of SEL programming (CASEL, 2020). These successes are evidenced through different modalities and practices. With the goal of enhancing SEL competence for students, there are a variety of ways SEL can be explicitly taught or become a practice in the classroom. Explicit instruction of SEL skills and competencies can be taught and practiced in content-specific situations during physical education or in homeroom or advisory settings during the school day. To yield the greatest results, these skills should be taught and expressed in a developmentally and culturally responsive way (CASEL, 2020). Instructional practices within the content areas can successfully be integrated through cooperative learning structures and project-based learning. Integration of SEL across the content areas is evidenced through language arts, math, science, social studies, health education, and the performing arts. In physical education classes, this integration can look like an implementation of the SEM, TPSR, and TGfU practices where students engage in small teams and pairs.

CASEL (2020) shared a SAFE model that has demonstrated success in SEL implementation. This model has four elements: sequenced, active, focused, and explicit, which are represented by the acronym SAFE. SEL curricula and programs must follow a coordinated set of professional learning or training to develop the CASEL core competencies for staff and students. There is an active emphasis on the SEL competencies and learning structures to create opportunities to practice and gain confidence with the SEL skills. Educators must identify, name, and deliberately call out and focus on implementing CASEL core competencies. Students should know and be able to identify that they are directly working on these skills within the content areas or in isolation. Educators are explicitly defining and targeting the specific CASEL core competencies, skills, attitudes, and knowledge. Implementation of CASEL core competencies using the SAFE model is most effective within school and class climates that are nurturing, are positive, and include teachers who have developed routines and practices where students experience positive relationships. To do this work successfully and with culturally responsive practices, teachers must get to know each individual student. This process includes understanding the unique growth areas and strengths of all students as well as understanding their cultural backgrounds. Through developing a SAFE and warm learning environment with healthy relationships, teachers can create opportunities for greater inclusion and foster development of student agency in the SEL learning process.

A PEEK INSIDE IMPLEMENTATION OF SEL

Sample Case Studies in Physical Education Settings

Here are a few examples of SEL in physical education. These examples do not include all the ways to incorporate SEL, and they may not include every CASEL core competency.

Elementary School

It's Tuesday morning and time for physical education class. Students walk into the physical education classroom (gymnasium or multipurpose room) to begin class. As they are walking in, Ms. Hewitt is at the door welcoming students with a smile and giving them a high five. After the students give Ms. Hewitt a high five, they tap a poster of emojis on the wall, called the How Am I Feeling? board (see figure 15.4). This poster includes a check-in for students to identify how they are feeling (using a happy, silly, okay, sad, or worried emoji). Students start by walking or jogging around the physical education classroom. After all students are warmed up, Ms. Hewitt gives the signal, then students join her by the whiteboard. On the board, she has written the objective for the day and the agenda. Students repeat the objective out loud after Ms. Hewitt reads it, saying, "I can demonstrate meditation (mindful minute) for 20 seconds. I can identify when I want to use a mindful minute when I need it." The essential question is shared

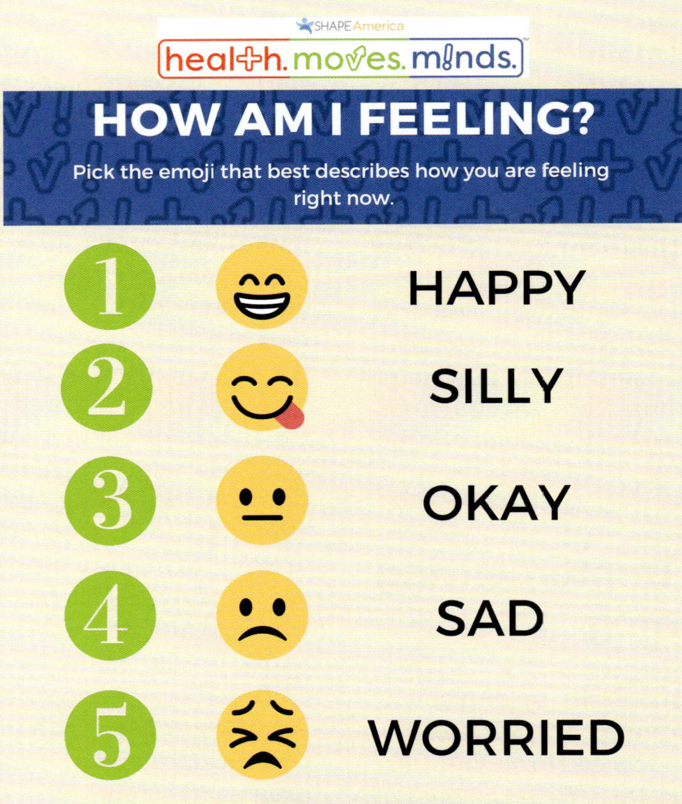

FIGURE 15.4 Students tap an emoji on the poster to indicate how they are feeling.

in call and response with the class: "What does it mean to be mindful?" Next, students are directed to find their personal space and are asked to put on their listening ears and bodies. Ms. Hewitt calls out different directions for students to move, and she reminds students to maintain personal space safely while moving.

Within the directions, the teacher asks students to stop, find a classmate, and say hello without using words; then, find another classmate to say hello nonverbally in a different way; and repeat this progression five times. Students then come back together, and Ms. Hewitt checks for student understanding by asking students to share examples of how they greeted and said hello to each other. She then asks how it made them feel. She shares that saying hello and greeting people—even if you do not know them—is a way to be kind and help people feel comfortable.

The next activity focuses on teaching the students a mindful minute. Students are asked to find a seat and sit cross-legged in personal space. Students are asked to think about what the word "mindful" is and what it means to them. Then, they are asked to share their answers with a person next to them. Ms. Hewitt then asks for students to share by pulling names randomly from a cup she has in the front of the class. Students share, and then Ms. Hewitt shares: "Being mindful is paying full attention to where you are and what you are doing. Being mindful helps us to be healthy, and we can think about what we are doing and how we feel in that moment. This mindfulness can help us when we feel unkind, sad, mad, or other feelings." She asks students to think about the feeling they touched on the way into class and lets them know that they will identify their feelings again. Now, she prompts them to close their eyes or look at a space in front of their seated position and soften their gaze, or focus, closing out distractions around them. She prompts them to notice what they hear around them (without saying it out loud) and how doing so can help them clear their mind and be mindful. She has students count to 10; each time they think of something, they restart counting from 1 to 10. She shares that this activity is a great way to relax and feel calm. After the minute has passed, she asks students to share how they feel. She asks them to turn to a partner and share how they may act when they feel stressed or anxious or overwhelmed. She asks whether this practice could help change that emotion or acknowledge the feeling.

The next activity brings students to a parachute. Students use the parachute to physically show breathing in mindful moments. Ms. Hewitt prompts the students to breathe in and breathe out with their hand on their chest while the parachute is on the ground. Next, she prompts them to hold the parachute and breathe in together while lifting the parachute; she explains, "Our belly pokes out when we breathe in, just as the parachute gets bigger." She then has them exhale and push down the parachute. Next, have students lift the parachute. While the parachute is still up she calls out a color; have all the students holding that color come to the center and greet each person however they wish. Next, students are prompted to lift the parachute and create a mushroom and move under it sitting down. During this time, Ms. Hewitt prompts them to practice mindful moments by sitting quietly and noting the environment around them (sounds and feelings). The next parachute activity includes having students come out of the mushroom and adding balls to the center. When the color ball bounces up that matches your color, students are prompted to share an emotion or feeling that is on their mind. Students are prompted to move the parachute quickly and think about how it feels when someone is mad, angry, or upset and how this can match the feeling of the balls. Then students are prompted to slow down the movement of the parachute. Ms. Hewitt asks what they notice and what emotion may match this movement. Students say they are sleepy, calm, and relaxed.

Ms. Hewitt transitions the group back to the board and asks students to close their eyes and think about their feelings now. She asks, "Why is it important to know your feelings?" and "How does a mindful minute help us when we know our feelings or do not know them?" As students leave the class, Ms. Hewitt prompts them to touch the "How am I feeling?" board sharing nonverbally how they feel as they exit the physical education class.

(continued)

A Peek Inside Implementation of SEL *(continued)*

Middle School

Physical education class is starting, and students are entering the teaching space; they are going to designated team areas and beginning dynamic stretches led by the student leader in athletic training. Student captains are prompted to come together with Mr. Khalifa to review the objective and agenda for the class. The student objective is "I can identify ways to be mindful and use positive self-talk to empower me." Mr. Khalifa has distributed kind message cards around the teaching space face down, and the coaches have shared the task with their teams. In their SEM teams, students designate one person to move around the space, pick up a card when the music stops, and bring the card back to their team. While the designated student is moving, the team has selected fitness component activities to work on. The next student goes and tries to find the matching card. The teams keep going until they find a match. At the end, the students are prompted to reflect on the messages they collected, and they are asked how the messages made them feel; all students on each team have an opportunity to share with one another how it made them feel.

The next activity brings the teams to sit cross-legged in a team circle. Mr. Khalifa prompts students to transition to a mindful minute. Some students have practiced the mindful minute before, and others have no idea what is going on. Team captains are encouraged to lead the mindful progression, sharing with their teams that it's time to sit and relax and asking team members to either close their eyes or focus on space in front of them. They are prompted to think about what they hear, notice what they smell, and focus on the breath going in and out of their body. The team captain models breathing in and out for 10 seconds. Then, Mr. Khalifa suggests that they will play relaxing music for one minute as students practice noticing things around them or practice breathing in and out for 10 seconds and repeating until the music stops. As the students are breathing, Mr. Khalifa then shares that being mindful is being aware of self. In a calm voice as students are practicing, he shares that they can think of their thoughts, emotions, body, and environment. The students can focus on the present, acknowledging that the past has already happened and that the future is not here yet. When the music stops, Mr. Khalifa prompts students to think about when the mindful minute would be useful and how it promotes overall health. He prompts teams to share with each other first, then have the team reporter stand when all teams have shared. The team reporter then summarizes what was shared to the class.

Team building is the next activity presented in class. Mr. Khalifa prompts students to get in their teams and line up behind the designated hula hoop. He prompts students that they will have to find the equipment list items one through six through exploring the space and items hidden under cones. Each team can send one person at a time to find the six items. Once the team has the equipment and cards for the activity, Mr. Khalifa shares that they will construct their task through cooperative learning and identifying what each team will build. Once the team has finished building, they can go to other teams and practice the kind messages from the first activity.

As students finish the task, Mr. Khalifa prompts them to go back to their teams for closure. He asks the team to practice a mindful minute again for 60 seconds. He reviews the effects of mindfulness on health. The team question for the day is "What are ways to be mindful and have positive self-talk?" Students begin with "All Hands In" where each team member puts a hand into the team circle. Once they have shared, they take their hand out until all team members have shared. Students are challenged by Mr. Khalifa to practice a mindful minute at home and share it with a friend.

This lesson sequence is adapted from Health.Moves.Minds. Empowered Mind & Body- Physical Education, SHAPE America 2019)

High School

Physical education class has started, and students have reported to their teaching location with Mrs. Garcia. Students have started doing different choice warm-up activities individually and in pairs. Students were prompted to go to the whiteboard, where the objective and agenda are up for the day. Mrs. Garcia shares, "Today we are focusing on personal and social relationships. By the end of the class, you will explore movement with others to learn about the impact of collective power in advocacy. Who has heard the word 'amplify?'" Some students raise their hands. "'Amplify' means to make something bigger and louder. By the end of class, we will see how we can amplify our task." Mrs. Garcia directs students to find two objects around the classroom and come back together. Next, she puts students in random equitable groups of four. She shares that the groups will need to build the tallest tower in groups of four with what they picked up around the classroom. She starts the music for students to build, then stops after a few minutes. She puts the countdown on the board. Mrs. Garcia provides a yardstick to each team to measure their building and sharing with the group, acknowledging the tallest structure. In the next progression, she combines the class for a total of three groups. She provides the same conditions for building a tall tower. She asks them if they can build a tower taller than before. This time, students get five minutes to build and then measure their tower. In the third progression, all students come together for one big team. They are given time to build the tallest tower with all equipment and measure it. They discuss and try to find a voice to lead, and they have some difficulty forming a consensus. Eventually, they agree on a plan and finish their building. They are unable to measure it with the yardsticks because it is so tall. The students are ecstatic. In closing out the task, Mrs. Garcia asks the class, "What were some of the positive things that came up as the groups increased in size?" Students share that they had more equipment to build with and more people to help. Next, she asks, "What were some challenges as groups got bigger?" Some students share that it was harder because everyone was talking at once and they did not know who was in charge. People were all yelling at each other. No one was listening. Some people sat out and did not participate. Mrs. Garcia shares that the task progression built from four people, to three groups, to the whole class; she asks, "How did this *amplify* our tasks?" Students share that they got more people and more equipment to build with. "How do the physical buildings you made link to amplifying? How would it work for advocacy?" says Mrs. Garcia. Students share that they can make more noise and create more change if they come together. They also share that this task is hard when the loudest single voice wins. She prompts them to think about how they played out in the whole-group team and how this task could work through cultural and equity framing. Students share that they need "to include all voices, cultures and perspectives before building." "Exactly!" says Mrs. Garcia. "It is more about the process and bringing together many voices than it is about the outcome sometimes. The more we come together as a community and elevate all voices, the more our work is amplified. Next class, we will practice building our own creative movement to music by combining sequences from different students. Have a great class! See you next time!"

This lesson is adapted from Health.Moves.Minds. Amplify Kindness-Building Together, SHAPE America 2022).

Conclusion

Social and emotional learning (SEL) is a long-standing structure and skill set that has historical foundations. Throughout the ages, educators have sought to foster the psychosocial development of students. This practice has occurred from ancient Greece through modern day. Character development, personal and social responsibility, teamwork development, communication, and other skills are part of the foundation of SEL that has evolved in balancing academic and psychosocial development. SEL skills and concepts were honed through the work of CASEL in the 1990s; since then, most evidence-based curricula and research align with their SEL competencies. These competencies aim to support the social and emotional development of students through practicing skills and concepts. The CASEL core competencies include self-awareness, self-management, social awareness, relationship skills, and responsible decision making. These skills can assist student learning and development as they navigate school, home, and the community. SEL integration must include a focus on adverse childhood experiences, trauma, and equity to be a culturally responsive practice over a color-blind approach to learning that perpetuates White cultural norms in education. Table 15.8 was developed to serve as a checklist for physical education teachers to ascertain if they are implementing SEL competencies. One way to conclude that the CASEL core competencies are included in physical education lessons is to use the sample implementation checklist in table 15.8.

TABLE 15.8 Sample CASEL Core Competencies Implementation

	CASEL Core Competencies				
Opportunities for SEL in Physical Education	**Self-Awareness**	**Self-Management**	**Social Awareness**	**Relationships**	**Responsible Decision Making**
Goal setting: Personal and collective					
Emotions, feelings, values					
Communication					
Cultural backgrounds					
Ability levels					
Recognizing personal strengths					
Mindset and reflection					
Personal, cultural, and linguistic assets					
Self-monitoring and feedback					
Peer monitoring and feedback					
Assumptions, biases					
Helping others					
Stress management					
Self-discipline					
Self-motivation, taking initiative					
Personal and collective agency					
Perspective taking					
Acknowledging diversity and ability differences					
Teamwork and collaboration					
Empathy and compassion					
Fostering a sense of belonging					
Celebrating personal and team successes					
Reviewing and reflecting on different conditions for learning					
Class environment structures					
Developing relationships (pairs, small groups, and teams)					
Respect					
Problem solving					
Conflict resolution skills					

Opportunities for SEL in Physical Education	CASEL Core Competencies				
	Self-Awareness	Self-Management	Social Awareness	Relationships	Responsible Decision Making
Leadership and followership					
Standing up for the rights of others					
Practicing open-mindedness in analyzing situations					
Identifying solutions linked to well-being					
Evaluating consequences					
Using data and feedback to inform decisions					

Review Questions

1. What SEL connections are already in place in your local physical education program?
2. What opportunities for enhancement and fostering explicit connections of SEL can you create for students?
3. How can you elevate student voices in development of SEL in linking equity and culturally responsive instruction in your program?
4. What are possible barriers and solutions for implementations of SEL and equity work?

» Visit HKPropel for reproducible forms.

CHAPTER 16

Diversity, Equity, and Inclusion: Underrepresented Teachers and Students in Physical Education

Wesley J. Wilson and Mara Simon

Photo courtesy of USA Field Hockey

LEARNING OBJECTIVES

After reading this chapter, you will be able to do the following:

- Describe the legal and historical backdrop that frames the experiences of underrepresented teachers and students in physical education.
- Describe the unique and often marginalizing experiences of teachers and students from various underrepresented populations in physical education.
- Describe administrator approaches that will elevate the participation of underrepresented teachers and students in physical education.
- Reflect on your own belief systems as they relate to teachers' and students' membership in underrepresented populations.

KEY CONCEPTS

Americans with Disabilities Act (ADA)
Brown v. Board of Education of Topeka
Defense of Marriage Act (DOMA)
Every Student Succeeds Act (ESSA)
inclusion
Individuals with Disabilities Education Act (IDEA)
No Child Left Behind Act
Obergefell v. Hodges
Plessy v. Ferguson
social groups
social justice
Title I
Title IX

Within the world of educational scholarship, a desire for equity, diversity, and inclusion (EDI) has proliferated (Perez et al., 2020). Notably, as part of this movement, there has been a call for teachers and administrators to embrace social justice as a pathway to create instructional spaces in which members of underrepresented—and often marginalized—**social groups** can be meaningfully included (Pugach et al., 2021). As coauthors of this chapter, we conceptualize **social justice** as "facilitating educational structures and experiences where students can embrace and name their ways of knowing in the world through critical understandings of themselves, their communities, and their place in wider society" (Lynch et al., 2020, p. 8). Inextricably linked to social justice is inclusion, which is often discussed in conversation with social justice and thus has numerous definitions (Wilson, Haegele, et al., 2020). However, our understanding of inclusion is that it only occurs when an individual (e.g., a student or a teacher) has subjective feelings of belonging, acceptance, and value in a particular space and context. We should note that this definition has been shaped and expanded from previous work in special education (Stainback & Stainback, 1996) and adapted physical education (Wilson et al., 2021).

For school administrators (including those who oversee health and physical education programs), creating inclusive, socially just spaces for learning requires being responsive to the lived experiences of not only the students receiving instruction but also to those of their teachers. Unfortunately, literature has highlighted threats to EDI in physical education contexts because of disability (Haegele, 2019), race and ethnicity (Douglas & Halas, 2013; Flintoff et al., 2015; Simon & Boyd, 2021), gender (Azzarito & Solomon, 2005; Dagkas et al., 2011; Oliver & Kirk, 2015), sexuality (Landi et al., 2020; Sykes, 2011), and socioeconomic status (Walker et al., 2020). Physical education has frequently been a space of hegemonic masculinity (Mooney & Hickey, 2012) and ableism (Alfrey & Jeanes, 2021) that dictates what types of bodies are valuable en route to bolstering exclusion.

This chapter aims to be a valuable resource for administrators of physical education programs as they consider the lived experiences of the physical educators they supervise and the students they teach. As the United States becomes more diverse, so too does the physical education classroom, which has tremendous implications for how programs are designed, organized, and implemented. The purpose of the chapter is to unpack the sociocultural and sociopolitical considerations of diversity in physical education, with reference to both the teacher and the students, and to provide recommendations for organizing and leading inclusive programming. Specifically, this chapter discusses five major social distinctions:

1. Disability
2. Race
3. Gender
4. Sexuality
5. Low socioeconomic status

Each section begins with a brief legal background (see chapter 11 for more on relevant laws) and a scenario from a physical educator's perspective. Then, it discusses that perspective before pivoting to a scenario from a student's viewpoint, along with further discussion. The end of each section provides recommendations for the empowerment of teachers and students belonging to the respective social grouping.

Finally, while it may seem that each group is presented monolithically, it is important to keep in mind that an individual can have membership in multiple social groups at once and that an individual's experiences in physical education could be viewed through multiple lenses (e.g., disabled *and* Black). The intersection of multiple marginalized identities can yield specific experiences that must be acknowledged in terms of oppression, privilege, access, and equity. However, because a discussion of such intersectionality is beyond the scope of this chapter, you are referred to the work by Simon, Lee, and colleagues (2021) for more information.

Disability in Physical Education

The most relevant federal laws regarding disability in physical education are the **Americans with Disabilities Act (ADA)** of 1990 and the **Individuals with Disabilities Education Act (IDEA)** of 2004. For physical educators who experience disability in the workplace, they are federally protected by the ADA (1990) from discrimination on the basis of disability from their employers and prospective employers. More specifically, Title I of the ADA prohibits public and private employers from discriminating against qualified applicants experiencing disability regarding hiring and firing procedures, career advancement, and compensation and that reasonable accommodations must be made should they allow the qualified individual to perform the essential functions of the job. The ADA (1990) does not provide a concrete definition of "reasonable accommodation" since it is open to interpretation, as many federal laws are, but some concrete examples include job restructuring and part-time or modified work schedules. For students in physical education, the IDEA (2004) federally mandates that all students who experience disability must receive special education services, including physical education. Further, these services must be free and appropriate education (FAPE) for the student; they may also include (if needed) related services such as speech and language therapy, physical therapy, and occupational therapy. IDEA (2004) does not define the specifics of what "appropriate" means, but it does stipulate that related services are designed to meet the child's unique needs and that prepares the child for further education, employment, and independent living.

Teacher Perspectives

» Cameron, five years removed from his teacher education program, identifies as a visually impaired adapted physical educator. In Cameron's own estimation, he is the only educator experiencing disability in his large public school district. While his impairment has prevented him from achieving many traditional milestones (e.g., driving), his love for movement and sports is what guides the physical education services he provides for his students who also experience disability. Of course, Cameron finds it amusing that he, a former student who absolutely hated physical education while growing up, is now responsible for teaching a caseload of over 100 students across eight different schools in the district. He remembers struggling to learn various sports skills, especially when no modifications were made by his physical education teachers. "So much for being included," he often reflects of his integrated physical education experience.

Now, even with five years of teaching within the district under his belt, he still feels as if he were a stranger—quite literally, as an itinerant adapted physical educator of multiple schools—and as an outsider, not only because of his visual impairment but also because of the subject he teaches. For example, more than once last week, Cameron found himself teaching his students in the hallway because the principal needed the gymnasium for an event. Even when Cameron has gymnasium space, he often does not have access to the physical educators' equipment closet, which forces him to rely only on what he can fit into his colleague's car, a midsized sedan. When he attempts to place one of his students into integrated physical education, more often than not, Cameron comes across resistance from the general physical educators. "Not my job," "I don't have the training," and "I am concerned that they will hurt themselves" are the common refrains. Even the well-meaning physical educators sometimes unwittingly marginalize his students by perpetuating able-bodied perspectives in their interactions with Cameron's students. Perhaps the last straw was when Cameron, a prolific track athlete in college, was denied the opportunity to coach high school track and field because the principal felt as if he would be better suited to coach the school's unified sports team. »

In this scenario, Cameron experiences much of the marginalization that has been perpetrated against adapted physical educators (those trained to work specifically with students experiencing disability). Being *itinerant*, as Cameron is, means that adapted physical educators may end up providing services in 10 or more schools, which has been shown to limit their ability to develop deep, supportive relationships with colleagues, administrators, and other school staff (Richards et al., 2021). Working across multiple schools may also leave adapted physical educators feeling as if they do not belong anywhere as well as lessen their ability to advocate for themselves and their students (Richards et al., 2020). Further, a growing body of evidence has indicted general physical educators, a marginalized group themselves (Laureano et al., 2014), as a primary perpetrator of marginalization against adapted physical educators and their students (Holland & Haegele, 2020; Wilson & Richards, 2019). For Cameron, one form of marginalization occurred through general physical educators who either did not believe it was their responsibility to teach students experiencing disability or did not feel as if they were prepared to work with the population, a regrettable lack of training that is well documented (Wilson, Kelly, et al., 2020). For some adapted physical educators, like Cameron, the beliefs, knowledge, and behaviors of general physical educators may force the former to keep students experiencing disability in self-contained (separate) settings rather than placing them in integrated physical education, even when the students would be successful (Wilson & Richards, 2019).

Another key feature from Cameron's scenario is his identity as a visually impaired educator. Beyond the challenges of being itinerant, he also felt as if he were an outsider because of disability, which presented itself as a barrier for his teaching career. Literature surrounding physical educators experiencing disability is virtually nonexistent to date, so the scenario presented is a composite of anecdotes. However, emerging research (e.g., Ware et al., 2022) among disabled educators more generally is troubling; it has highlighted significant discrimination and barriers to continued employment, including job retention and the capacity for career progression, which directly contradicts ADA (1990). For Cameron, his belief that he was overlooked for a coaching job because of his impairment, along with the marginalization he felt as an adapted physical educator, could prompt him to leave the field early (Mäkelä et al., 2014). Of further concern is the principal's suggestion that Cameron should instead consider coaching the school's unified sports team (a team that is composed of both students who do and students who do not experience disability), a perspective that may have dangerous ableist underpinnings in that his worth as a coach can be realized only if he leads a team that also has members of the disability community (Wilson et al., 2021). Such experiences may threaten a school administration's ability to create a work environment centered on inclusion—a culture where educators who identify as disabled or otherwise are able to provide physical education services to all students, particularly those experiencing disability themselves.

Student Perspectives

» Joao is a 14-year-old student who identifies as disabled; he has lived experience with Down syndrome. Joao has recently joined an integrated physical education class taught by a 20-year veteran physical educator, Coach, who also oversees the high school basketball team. Coach adopts a traditional sports-based curriculum, which centers on competition and team sports. Joao, who is overweight, routinely struggles to keep up with the pace of the drills during class. Lately, he has noticed that he is lower skilled than his classmates during the competitive play that dominates Coach's lessons. "This isn't fun," Joao says to his paraeducator as he begins to feel deficient; consequently, he pretends to feel sick to get out of participating in physical education. "I want to go back to

Ms. Debra's class and my friends," he says. Joao is referring to the self-contained physical education class (a placement in which only students experiencing disability participate) taught by Debra, the adapted physical education teacher. His friends, who also experience disability, enjoy Debra's class too.

Recently, however, the school administration adopted a full inclusion policy with the goal of placing all students who identify as disabled in integrated educational settings, regardless of available resources and individual student needs. Joao was among the first students to transition from the self-contained setting into integrated physical education. His paraeducator also joined him in support but did not know how to help Joao have a meaningful and inclusive experience. What has become abundantly clear is that Coach has no interest in changing his practices to create a more inclusive space for Joao, particularly because he spends class time going over his basketball practice notes. Accordingly, Joao does not feel as if he belongs, is accepted, or valued in integrated physical education. »

Joao's experience in integrated physical education is all too common (Haegele, 2019). For many students experiencing disability, physical education is a space for discrimination, bullying, and isolation (Haegele & Sutherland, 2015; Holland & Haegele, 2021). Exacerbating Joao's negative experiences in his class, Coach appears to have adopted a coaching orientation, like many other physical educators, rather than a student-focused approach (Curtner-Smith, 2017). The larger issue, however, is the school's decision to implement a "full inclusion" policy. While well-intentioned, the decision has resulted in worse educational outcomes for Joao; moreover, it is potentially noncompliant with federal special education law because it could eliminate more appropriate, alternative placements (Wilson, Haegele, et al., 2020). The IDEA (2004) guarantees that students experiencing disability will receive free appropriate public education (FAPE) in the least restrictive environment (LRE); that is, they will be educated alongside nondisabled students to the maximum extent appropriate. Importantly, the federal law goes on to state that if the student's education cannot be satisfactorily achieved in integrated settings due to the nature or severity of the impairment (even with supplementary aids), then the student may be removed and placed in a range of alternative placements (e.g., self-contained special classes, special schools, etc.).

In Joao's case, it is clear that he will not be able to satisfactorily achieve his educational goals in Coach's integrated physical education class; however, it may not be due to the nature or severity of his impairment but rather the inappropriate teaching practices of the physical educator. If Joao is removed from Coach's class and returns to Debra's, it will likely be the more appropriate placement for him to learn, but it also makes him a target of a so-called artificial LRE (Wilson, Kelly, et al., 2020), in that he was moved due not to his individual needs but rather as a function of an underqualified physical educator in Coach (after he was already arbitrarily moved once before because of the school's new full inclusion policy).

Recommendations for Physical Education Administrators

The two preceding scenarios presented several different challenges from the perspectives of educators who experience disability or provide physical education services to students experiencing disability as well as the perspectives of the students themselves. While it may seem like a daunting task to address these concerns, physical education administrators are uniquely positioned to support both the physical educators and the students who experience disability.

In districts that employ trained adapted physical educators, administrators are strongly encouraged to actively explore ways to increase their social capital. Since schools are socially constructed environments, social capital is required for adapted physical educators, who are often itinerant like Cameron, to advocate for themselves, their profession, and their students (Richards et al., 2023). One of the practical strategies to elevate their social status and prevent the potential for the teachers to feel like strangers across the schools they visit is to emphasize their integral role in the holistic education of students who experience disability. Inviting adapted physical educators to participate meaningfully in any decisions that affect their teaching or the students they serve is essential. Another useful practice is to attend physical education classes in which teachers are instructing students who experience disability, demonstrating a desire to build relationships with teachers who often work in areas of the school farthest away from the main centers. For itinerant teachers in particular, designating a home base—a school building in which they have an office with a space to make their own and to store their specialized equipment—may reduce feelings of isolation. For educators who identify as disabled, beyond adhering to the policies of ADA (1990), tremendous effort must be made to support their careers as they are forced to disrupt the status quo and the notion of able-bodiedness in education by their mere presence in schools (Ware et al., 2022). This includes creating a school culture that values their embodied knowledge—their lived experiences, values, and beliefs—rather than dismissing it (Goodwin & Rossow-Kimball, 2012). By acknowledging the discrimination and barriers that are embedded in society as well as more specifically within the school, those experiencing disability will be more likely to be empowered within their practice and workplace.

To improve the educational experiences of students who identify as disabled, all physical educators should be trained in how to work with them and be expected to work with them. Simply put, physical educators must first start with quality physical education in general so that they are not the disabling force in physical education spaces. Physical education administrators play an integral role in ensuring that training and professional development opportunities are made available to all physical education teachers and coaches. For teachers like Coach, providing roll-out-the-ball physical education does not work for students experiencing disability (or, in fact, for students in general). Research (e.g., Wilson & Richards, 2019) has shown that such physical educators can force students into less integrated settings even when the students could be successfully integrated, provided the presence of a student-centered approach. To that end, decisions about student placement should adhere to IDEA (2004), meaning that policies of full inclusion should be cautioned against, because they could render all alternative placements as reprehensible (Sherrill, 1994). Making placement decisions should be based on student need (the nature and severity of the disability) rather than on administrative convenience (e.g., high expense of hiring adapted physical educators, scheduling issues, not adequate support staff, etc.) (Wilson, Haegele, et al., 2020). For some students, a fully integrated setting will be appropriate; for others, alternative placements such as self-contained special classes will be required. Appropriate placement, along with student-centered instruction, will help foster physical educational spaces in which the students can feel that they belong, they are accepted, and they are valued, so that they may (re)take control of what types of bodies are valued in physical education (Petrie et al., 2018).

Race in Physical Education

Examining race dynamics in physical education requires an understanding of U.S. historical legal rulings, starting with ***Plessy v. Ferguson*** (1896), which upheld separate but equal educational facilities for students. For more than 50 years, school segregation was not only normalized but legal, yielding inequitable school experiences for students that directly correlated with their racial identities. However, the ***Brown v. Board of Education of Topeka*** rulings in 1954 and 1955 meant that schools were required to integrate, in spite of direct opposition from many communities. The *Brown* ruling is publicly revered as a highpoint of U.S. societal progress toward racial equality, is commonly discussed and analyzed in textbooks and history or law classes, and is frequently used as the basis of the argument for a color-blind educational perspective. However, the language of the *Brown* rulings was vague, was nondescript, and lacked a specific time frame, all of which provided numerous legal loopholes and allowed individual state and local districts autonomy in determining exactly how to interpret and implement the ruling (Ladson-Billings, 2004). Thus, in the decades that followed, schools did not become the imagined spaces of racial equality but rather demonstrated social backlash to integration; communities openly resisted the idea and funneled money and resources toward white schools while ignoring the schools that served Black, Latinx, Asian and Pacific Islander, and Native, among other racialized communities (Hughey, 2014). Today's public schools are more racially stratified than ever; both students and teachers of color (individuals who are constructed as racialized in comparison to whiteness) tend to be concentrated in schools serving low socioeconomic status households (National Center for Education Statistics [NCES], 2021), and the vision embedded within the *Brown* ruling of racially integrated schools is less of a reality than it was in the few decades immediately following the ruling. The passing of the **No Child Left Behind Act** of 2001 further exacerbated race-based school performance disparities, reinforcing a neoliberal discourse of individual achievement and positioning historically oppressed student populations as "underachieving" or "underperforming" (Leonardo, 2007, p.263). The fact that teaching about race and its history in the United States is currently perceived by many as controversial instead of essential indicates that there is still much work to be done to create equal school experiences for students of color.

Teacher Perspectives

» Dave, who is white, is a new teacher, having just graduated and received his teaching license. He was hired at a local school near his undergraduate college, a mid-sized, predominantly white private institution located at the outskirts of a former industrial city that now sees more than 90 percent of its public school students receiving free and reduced lunch. The school district's population has also more than 80 percent students of color who are predominantly Puerto Rican and Black. Dave's predominantly white physical education teacher education (PETE) program focused on models-based pedagogy, such as teaching games for understanding (TGfU) and the Sport Education Model (SEM). Models such as these have been embraced by PETE faculty and physical educators as developing inclusive learning environments for students of wide-ranging abilities and backgrounds. However, as Dave began his school year teaching and tried to implement a SEM approach to lacrosse, he was met with resistance. Half of the students refused to participate at all, opting to sit out or walk laps, while the other half goofed around, using the equipment improperly and not following directions. One time, the principal walked in unannounced for an informal observation and saw students disengaged and lacking a safe learning environment. At the end of that class, a student walked by Dave and asked, "Why we gotta learn these white people sports?" Dave could not understand what was going wrong. He was following the models he was taught to use in his PETE program, and he was presenting opportunities for students with a wide range of sport experience and ability to fully participate in the class. Nevertheless, the students remained disinterested and disengaged, often preferring to opt out of participation altogether. »

This scenario highlights cultural dissonance between Dave's teacher preparation experiences and the interests, desires, and cultures of the students he was teaching. Cultural dissonance, or disconnects between curricula and pedagogy that a teacher values in contrast with those that students value, can yield devastating results in physical education; it can lead to students who are disengaged at best, and disruptive, dismissive, or absent at worst. The need to address cultural dissonance through implementing culturally relevant pedagogy, similar in idea and intention to culturally responsive pedagogy (Gay, 2018) or cultural competency, is crucial for teaching contexts such as the one highlighted. Students of color deserve to be provided with a physical education experience that fosters student learning, reflects their cultural interests and values, and encourages the development of a critical consciousness (Ladson-Billings, 2004). Dave's approach to pedagogy meant that students' ways of being were not represented within the class; students did not see themselves, their cultures, their means of interacting and engaging, or their values and beliefs embedded within the physical education curricula and pedagogy. Given the racialized makeup of current school and teacher demographics in the

United States, a lack of cultural connections can have serious consequences for students; while over 50 percent of public school students are students of color, the teacher population is approximately 80 percent white and female, a number that has been consistent since before the 1990s (NCES, 2021).

Scholars have established the importance of physical education reflecting students' cultural knowledges; doing so can lead to enriching experiences that help students develop physical literacy in myriad culturally significant and fluent ways. This is not to say that students of color should not learn lacrosse; indeed, exposing students to new forms of physical activity, sport, and movement is a key component of physical education. However, the means of approach might need to be implemented differently from how Dave did so; new and novel topics in physical education should still be student centered and student led. For example, perhaps Dave might have begun a lacrosse unit by explaining the sport's historical connections to Native American peoples, a group who have been historically and catastrophically marginalized. Historical context might provide a jumping-off point for exploring Native American representation in lacrosse currently, which then could allow Dave's students to move toward exploring physical skills and tactical strategy. If Dave had addressed all three tenets of culturally relevant pedagogy—student learning, cultural competence, and sociopolitical consciousness (Ladson-Billings, 1995)—in his pedagogical approach to teaching, he might have seen greater success and higher student engagement.

Research on race, racism, and culturally relevant pedagogy reflects the vast experiences of both white physical educators and physical educators of color. White physical educators, both in-service and pre-service, often take up a racialized othering or deficit approach to teaching diverse student populations, relying on assumptions and stereotypes related to the intersection of race and low socioeconomic status (Flintoff et al., 2015; Shiver et al., 2020). For example, Flintoff and Dowling (2019) determined that the white physical educators in their study took up a so-called color-blind discourse when it came to teaching students of color, operationalizing whiteness as universal. Physical educators of color, particularly those located in predominantly white schools, often experience overt racism, marginalization, and othering, and they struggle to navigate educational contexts in which they feel they do not belong (Dagkas et al., 2011; Simon & Azzarito, 2018, 2019). Flory and McCaughtry (2011) mapped out a culturally relevant physical education framework that can be a useful approach for physical educators; the framework includes (1) knowing students, (2) identifying cultural distance, and (3) bridging the gap. While often cited in physical education literature, their framework is missing the sociopolitical consciousness piece, which Ladson-Billings (2014) admitted is often the most difficult for teachers to pursue. However, when teaching at schools with high percentages of racially minoritized students, helping students develop a critical understanding of dominant discourse on race in physical education can be a catalyst for a new level of engagement, interest, and action on the part of the students.

Student Perspectives

» Sahra headed slowly toward the locker room to change for her physical education class, wondering if she'd be singled out again in the class for her height. Despite the fact that she was planning to major in biochemistry in college, her physical education teacher kept insisting that, due to her height, she must love and want to play basketball. As a 5-foot, 10-inch tall Black female student, Sahra knew that basketball was important for many Black women; however, her family had left their homeland of Somalia under duress to move to the United States, and Sahra was far more concerned with academics than athletics. She grimaced as she entered the gymnasium to the thud of at least 10 basketballs bouncing on the floor; the physical education teacher had put the balls out for the students while he waited for the stragglers to arrive. Sahra chose to ignore the basketballs; instead, she started to walk a few laps around the gym to warm up. As she passed her teacher, he tossed her a basketball, which she fumbled, dropping it and catching it on the bounce. He smiled at her and said, "You sure you don't want to try out for the basketball team? We could really use someone with your height. I'm sure you'd make a great player." Sahra shook her

LEADERSHIP IN ACTION

Reflections on DEI in an Educational and Professional Journey

Lennie Parham, MS

New Jersey Department of Education

As a former K-12 athletic director and health and physical education supervisor for 10 years, I had the opportunity to collaborate with the building principals to implement state and national student learning standards as well as provide guidance for local curricula to include health and physical education (HPE) in the daily K-12 class schedules. In addition, I implemented specific professional development for all HPE educators in order to provide every classroom with high-quality instructional strategies; for teachers to meet the needs of every child; and for the whole child's social, emotional, and physical well-being. As an African American male, I encountered only one teacher of color throughout my K-12 and college educational journey, and through both my undergraduate and master's degrees. I know firsthand the impact of the lack of diversity in the teaching workforce across the country. The benefits of an inclusive, diverse instructional teacher population are imperative; each student must be seen, respected, valued, and supported to succeed academically, emotionally, and socially.

During my third year at the New Jersey Department of Education, I was invited by the organization Society of Health and Physical Educators (SHAPE America) to join their equity, diversity, and inclusion (EDI) advisory team. This opportunity to collaborate with other educators dedicated to EDI prompted me to contemplate my educational journey and confront the racial inequities I've encountered in various aspects of my life. The work around diversity, equity, and inclusion (DEI) at the New Jersey Department of Education continues, and it is an important goal of the commissioner. The department will provide the support and environment I need to continue this important work as the health and physical education coordinator in the Office of Standards. I continue to research and merge DEI resources for educators to our newly designed content-specific DEI Standards web page along with the department's annual state equity and diversity conference for educators and families. I will continue these important and challenging conversations along with my colleagues to collaborate with other state leaders, which will allow me to build my capacity and create solutions to inspire educators to think differently about teaching strategies, professional development, and opportunities for student voice and choice to be the bridge and the on-ramp to DEI for all teachers, students, and administrators.

---

head and reminded him that she preferred to focus on her schoolwork. Thinking to herself, "I don't even like basketball," she tossed the ball back to him. She wondered if that was how everyone at the school saw and valued her—as a potential basketball player, not a potential Rhodes scholar. »

Race is often conceptualized as biological in physical education, presuming that certain racialized groups, such as Black students, have superior athletic prowess in spite of the fact that the myth has been debunked over and over again in scholarly literature (McDonald, 2013). Athletic superiority as a racial stereotype can be particularly harmful because it can simultaneously foster negative beliefs about intelligence and potential for students of color to succeed academically (Hodge et al., 2008; Steele & Aronson, 1995). In Sahra's case, students and teachers made assumptions about her athletic capabilities and interests while disregarding her love for science and desire to learn and grow intellectually.

Traditional so-called raceless curricula, pedagogy, and policies taken up and enacted in physical education contexts ignore the disparities often forced on students of color in terms of participation and engagement. Physical education is not a space where teachers talk about race; however, race is a salient factor at play for students, particularly in light of how sport is often considered a gateway to financial success and how many professional athletes of color are championed in U.S. sport contexts. Thus, students experience a disconnect between their racialized selves engaging in physical education, physical activity, and sport, and how their teachers overlook or refuse to address racial disparities. Such a disconnect contrasts sharply with the few existing studies focusing on how critical curricula can engage students of color in physical education in meaningful and eye-opening ways, demonstrating culturally relevant pedagogy. Oliver and colleagues (2009) worked with elementary Latina girls to cocreate a curriculum that combined the duality of cultural femininity with the girls' desire to be physically active. Azzarito and colleagues (2016) developed and implemented the Body Curriculum to help high school students of color analyze body norms from a critical lens and reject media portrayals of the so-called ideal (white) body. Examples such as these ones present resounding evidence for the case for physical educators to address race and racism as interconnected with physical education, sport, fitness, and physical activity in an effort to help both white students and students of color to understand racialized power dynamics at play. Otherwise, students of color may experience physical education as a disconnected curriculum, a space where typically white teachers often focus on team sports and fitness without considering whether the content is applicable for students' daily lives outside of school.

Recommendations for Physical Education Administrators

If race is salient to the field of physical education, and both teachers and students of color recognize the need for reflection on and action toward this point, it becomes the responsibility of physical education administrators to encourage, support, and develop curricula, pedagogy, and policy to move the idea forward. First, administrators (who are assumed to be majority white much like the in-service and pre-service teachers) must engage in self-reflection related to their own belief systems. Interrogating whiteness is a formidable task, but utilizing resources provided by districts, professional organizations such as SHAPE America, and external sources (e.g., social media, organizations, foundations, books, etc.) can be an important first step for white administrators to engage in a racial reckoning with their own white privilege. From this reckoning emerges an awareness of systemic racialized inequity—an understanding that physical education students and teachers of color might be experiencing physical education in very different ways from their white counterparts.

Providing district physical education teachers with professional development opportunities related to culturally relevant pedagogy can demonstrate an administrator's support for engaging in talks about race in physical education, thus helping to facilitate teachers' comfort and ability with such pedagogical endeavors. Another important step for administrators is to make open and outright commitments to supporting students and teachers of color through culturally relevant pedagogy; such a stance sets the tone for the department and signals to all physical educators and students that, as a department and as a field, physical education is committed to furthering racial justice through a culturally competent sociopolitical lens. Finally, administrators can be conscious of and make changes to existing hiring practices that often perpetuate the predominantly white field by making an effort to recruit and retain teachers of color and then providing a supportive teaching environment in which they can thrive.

Gender in Physical Education

From its initial inception, physical education has relied on a gender binary (gender as two biological sexes versus a spectrum of identities), with differing activities, beliefs, expectations, and standards for boys and girls. Girls were often excluded from full (or even any) participation, or they were provided opportunities for modified, so-called gentle, physical activity. The reinforcement of sport and physical activity as a masculine domain has deep-seated, historical roots that are still present within the field. Increased gender inclusion in physical education can be traced directly to the passage of **Title IX** of the Education Amendments of 1972, which stated that no person shall be excluded from participation or discriminated against based on sex in any educational program that receives federal funding. (It has since been clarified that Title IX covers both sex *and* gender.) Prior to Title IX, physical education and sport participation for girls was often underfunded, overlooked, and deemed second class.

Title IX directly prohibits teachers from offering a lesser physical education experience for girls, although stereotypes and discrimination still show up in such contexts. While much progress has been made in terms of gender equity that directly correlates with the changes implemented on account of Title IX, research indicates that gender equity still has not yet been achieved (Cheypator-Thomson et al., 2000). Physical education teachers' and administrators' reliance on gender binary excludes students who identify on the gender spectrum outside the binary, such as those who are nonbinary and gender fluid. Furthermore, assumptions of gendered identity as biological often go hand-in-hand with transphobia (either outright or hidden), further marginalizing transgender students.

Teacher Perspectives

» As a relatively new physical educator and a woman in her late 20s, Zara was not a stranger to gender dynamics within her field. She recalled, rather grimly, as she set up equipment for her next class, the man at the national physical education conference who had asked to borrow a flash drive to store his presentation on, promising he'd remember to give it back to her since he "never forgot a pretty face." She squatted down to set up a row of cones, wondering if the yoga pants she'd chosen to wear today were too form fitting; perhaps she was better off wearing something baggier. She felt comfortable in yoga pants or leggings, but she sometimes worried about them being judged as too revealing. However, the khaki pants and polo shirt required at her undergraduate PETE program never had been what she wanted to wear while teaching or engaging in physical activity. Zara continued setting up as the high school students filed in for her first class of the day; she gave encouraging and friendly smiles as she directed students into their warm-up routine. Today's lesson was part of a touch football unit her male colleagues had pushed for, in spite of the fact that Zara did not know much or care about football. The male teachers she worked with, along with several others in the district, all participated in a fantasy football league, even getting together outside of school hours for the draft and to watch the games. Although she was invited, Zara had never joined them because of her parenting responsibilities. With two young children to manage, going out to watch a football game with colleagues was not something she chose to prioritize. She recalled the anxiety of telling her supervisor that she was pregnant, wondering if he'd secretly be upset or annoyed at the disruption and additional work to find a maternity leave replacement. Zara approached her students and began to explain the first task, involving some simple routes that students would practice: first without a ball, then with a ball hand-off, and finally while trying to catch a tossed ball. Throughout her explanation and demonstration, she noticed several of the boys smirking at one another; one finally raised his hand and contradicted one of the directions, based on what his football coach told him. Zara felt her cheeks flush at this student's direct confrontation of her content knowledge, wondering if he would have felt emboldened to do so if she had been a man. Zara knew better than to get upset, recognizing the harm that being labeled as emotional can cause women, and calmly told the student that for the purposes of class today, this was how the tasks would be performed. »

Given the intense gender segregation found within sport contexts and links between physical education and sport, it is evident that physical education is also a space in which gender issues are rooted, informed by traditional constructions of hegemonic masculinity that place highly skilled and competitive boys as most valuable. In Zara's narrative, she must negotiate multiple forms of sexism as a female physical educator, from the focus on her physical appearance, to navigating new motherhood, to feeling ostracized from her male physical education teacher counterparts, and being challenged on her subject matter content knowledge from male students.

While physical educators may intend to avoid gender bias in their classrooms, research on the topic suggests that inherent, implicit, and unconscious constructions of gender binaries can lead to very different experiences for students of all genders (Azzarito et al., 2006; Rich, 2004). Regardless of their own gender, physical educators tend to spend more time and attention on boys in their classes, including providing specific corrective and positive feedback, suggesting that the teachers believe boys are more invested in the class and therefore worth investing time and energy toward (Nicaise et al., 2007). Furthermore, particularly at the middle and high school levels, physical educators often emphasize competition, performance, and skill acquisition, which may leave girls feeling uncomfortable, unsafe, and unwilling to fully engage, even if they identify as athletic and wish to fully participate (Constantinou et al., 2009). Even female physical educators have been found to take up a neoliberal discourse of individualism toward disengaged girls in spite of often wanting to change gender norms and stereotypes within the field (Rich, 2004). Widespread ideologies on gender norms mean many teachers perceive certain physical education curriculum content as gendered, such as dance being for girls and weightlifting being for boys. Teachers often profess a commitment to gender equity within their classes by taking on a so-called gender-blind approach; in doing as much, teachers may inadvertently favor, allow, or expect certain behaviors from boys without reciprocating to girls, and also implement a sports-heavy, competition-focused curriculum (potentially ostracizing girls and low-skilled boys). However, they do so without recognizing and taking action toward inherent gender biases with a predisposition toward hegemonic masculinity, from a sports-heavy curriculum content to student behaviors and developing a rapport.

Student Perspectives

» Jess walked happily from the locker room to the baseball diamond on the school grounds, eager to be outside and ready to play. She loved physical activity; she was a three-sport varsity athlete, and she appreciated the entirely sport-focused nature of her physical education class. She only wished her teacher, Mr. Wilton, who had been teaching at the school for more than 30 years, recognized her love and engagement in class as well. Mr. Wilton gruffly surveyed the class, then barked out, "Two laps of the diamond," as he walked away to set up the playing equipment. Jess jogged the bases with her peers, who were students of all genders and abilities walking and running laps together. When they were finished, Mr. Wilton chose two of the most athletic boys in the class to be the team captains, who then were each instructed to choose teams, one student at a time. Jess was not picked first, but she was one of the first girls picked, once the captains had divided up the other highly-skilled boys in the group. She didn't care; she was happy to get to play because movement and sport were a welcome break from the high expectations of some of her other academic classes. Mr. Wilton served as the pitcher as the game began; the captain of Jess' team went up to bat first, making contact with the ball and sprinting to first base. After another two batters went, Jess walked up to the plate, confident and ready to hit. Mr. Wilton paused, then turned to the outfield and yelled "Move in, fielders!" insinuating that because Jess was a girl and would not hit the ball far, the outfielders did not need to be far in the outfield. After checking to make sure the catcher was ready (insinuating that Jess would strike out), Mr. Wilton pitched the ball in a long, slow underhand pitch—a noticeable difference from the overhand pitches he had sent the previous (male) batters. Jess' cheeks burned, and all she could think about was how she had better not strike out after her teacher's assumptions about her ability to bat. While she made contact with the ball on the pitch, she jogged slowly to first base, allowing herself to be tagged out, to avoid continuing to play under the assumption that she was not as good an athlete as her male counterparts. »

The idea of gender issues in physical education has historical precedent, back to physical education's initial roots. Classes were segregated by gender; the men did calisthenics and other strength and endurance exercises, while the women's classes focused on socializing amid so-called milder and gentler forms of exercise. With the space race competition of the 1950s against Russia (sometimes referred to as the Sputnik era), national attention turned toward physical education as a way to develop fit citizens, yielding curricula that emphasized form and function of the body. Gender inequity in physical education classes was firmly identified in the 1980s through the work of scholars such as Griffin (1984, 1985), who established patterns of discrimination and a lack of robust participation opportunities for girls. In the 1990s, Vertinksy (1992) theorized gender inequity in physical education as reflective of power differentials and dynamics, proposing to rethink the inherent patriarchal disposition of sport-based physical education curricula and pedagogy. Typical curricula prioritize a certain type of hegemonic masculinity by celebrating traits such as aggression, dominance, strength, fierce competition, and physical prowess (Azzarito & Solomon, 2006). As the example provided, Jess' physical education teacher focused on the highly-skilled boys by making them team captains and challenging them with faster, overhand pitches. Mr. Wilton's assumptions about Jess' physical capabilities (along with his complete ignoring of low-skilled students) implied that Jess was not as valued and not as skilled as the boys in the class. In doing so, girls and low-skilled boys are constructed as *the problem*—disengaged, unskilled, and unenthusiastic (Flintoff & Scraton, 2001; Oliver et al., 2009).

Recommendations for Physical Education Administrators

Given the propensity for gender issues in physical education, administrators have a responsibility to take specific steps in an effort to create a gender-equitable learning environment. Administrators should actively support physical educators in using best practices when it comes to recognizing gender as a spectrum rather than a binary. These practices might include using gender-neutral language (e.g., "folks" instead of "boys and girls"), ensuring gender-neutral spaces for students to change if needed, and avoiding dividing classes by gender (e.g., "girls line up, then boys line up"). It is also recommended that teachers try to offer students the choice of single-gender and mixed-gender opportunities to engage in physical education, based on students' input and preferences. For this suggestion, it is imperative that the impetus come from the students, not the teacher, in terms of which group students self-select into and how the classes are framed, created, and taught.

As ones who often play an active role in the hiring of new physical educators, administrators are reminded to be mindful of hiring practices that cultivate hegemonic masculinity within physical education spaces, such as hiring teachers solely for their coaching expertise instead of teaching, having unqualified coaches teach physical education, and focusing solely on sports and sports skills within curricula. Furthermore, administrators should encourage and support their teachers in developing curricula that go beyond traditional team sports; they can do so through professional development funding to increase subject matter knowledge and pedagogical content knowledge. Administrators should encourage their faculty to focus on a wider range of movement possibilities in an effort to engage low-skilled students in ways that do not facilitate humiliation and dominance or aggression. If physical educators identify times, places, and spaces where they are observing or experiencing gender issues, administrators should support the teachers in helping them to make changes toward gender equity. Supporting gender equity goes beyond student issues to issues of gender for physical educators; for example, administrators can encourage and support teachers to take parental leave without guilt or shame. Finally, administrators should make clear-cut, unequivocal, and overt statements along with department goals regarding gender equity.

Sexuality in Physical Education

Physical education contexts have historically been a space rooted in heteronormativity, maintaining an environment in which lesbian, gay, bisexual, transgender, queer, intersex, asexual or aromantic, and beyond (LGBTQIA+) members did not feel safe disclosing their sexuality (Morrow & Gill, 2003). On the other hand, physical education and sport have also long been a safe haven for women who identified outside the spectrum of heteronormativity, creating a clandestine culture of safety and support (Cahn, 2015). The widespread acceptance of a spectrum of sexualities can be linked to the upending of the **Defense of Marriage Act (DOMA)** of 1996, when the ***Obergefell v. Hodges*** ruling of 2015 declared that same-sex marriage was a fundamental and protected right. Similarly, the repealing of the U.S. military's "Don't ask, don't tell" (DADT) policy in 2011 signaled a national shift in perception to the legitimization and acceptance of LGBTQIA+ communities. However, significant homophobia and prejudice still abound within physical education contexts, highlighting the need to both support and protect LGBTQIA+ teachers and students.

Teacher Perspectives

» Jan winced as she heard her colleague greet their class at the door of the gymnasium: "Good morning, boys and girls!" While well-intentioned, it was like nails on a chalkboard for Jan because she recognized the problematic nature of reinforcing a gender binary, even though it was an innocent comment. Jan thought about how for most of her life, she had been placed into the category of *girl* even though she often did not feel entirely comfortable in that box. Even as an adult, her gender representation fell more toward the male side of things; she wore her hair short, could most commonly be found in a warm-up track suit, and carried herself in a way that belied an aura of masculinity. Jan was also a lesbian, in a long-term relationship with her partner, but that was something she did not share with her students or even most of her colleagues. In spite of the fact that she knew many female physical educators throughout her 40 years in the field who were out and proud, for her, physical education and sport had been an avenue to channel her energy and cultivate a sense of belonging, particularly when she had been younger and it had been far less socially acceptable to embody the intersection of gender and sexuality. Jan still could never fully shake off the worry about how students and colleagues would react if they learned of her female partner (which was probably the result of decades of internalized homophobia), wondering if there would be sideways glances, snide comments, hidden laughter, or even outright harassment. So, while she wanted to discuss the use of a gender-neutral way to address students with her colleague, she kept quiet for the sake of her own mental peace, safely protecting her private life with her female partner from potential scrutiny, criticism, and prejudice. »

Historical perspectives on LGBTQIA+ teachers' experiences in physical education provide insights into the experiences of a marginalized group. Jan's story embodies the tension of representing both a sporting body with an athletic build, where gender representation is not straightforward, and a lesbian identity. As a physical education teacher, Jan loved physical activity, sport, and movement for the space it provided her to be free and supported, but she also recognized the stereotypes and potential difficulties she might encounter if she were to be open with her sexuality to her students, colleagues, and administrators. Gender plays a role in understanding embodied subjectivity of LGBTQIA+ teachers; while sport and physical education were long considered a route for men to demonstrate and capitalize on their traditional modes of masculinity (e.g., strength, muscles, speed, power), women who actively engaged in such endeavors faced a direct questioning of their gender positioning that often went hand in hand with their sexuality (Cahn, 2015). For example, Woods and Harbeck (1992) explored the experiences of lesbian physical educators, all of whom feared employment termination if their sexuality was exposed while knowing that the stereotype of a female physical educator was to be a lesbian; subsequently, the teachers mostly aimed to conceal their lesbian identities and distanced themselves from their colleagues and students. Similarly, Griffin (1991, 1998) determined that lesbian physical educators engage in a range of management strategies to navigate an LGBTQIA+ identity in spaces of heteronormativity, such as trying to pass as straight, censoring their lesbian identities. They were also at times openly and proudly out, feeling that physical education and sport were spaces where they were valued and accepted. Clarke's (1996, 1998) findings highlighted the abuse, harassment, and vandalism that lesbian physical educators often encountered, forcing them to silence their queer selves to avoid connections to pedophilia. However, as Sykes (1996) pointed out, lesbian teachers were never truly silenced, instead finding means of resistance even in the face of marginalization and the oppression of queer rights in physical education spaces.

Notably absent, in both historic and current scholarship and discourse, is the experiences of gay male physical educators, highlighting the intersection of gender and sexuality discourse as one of intense heterosexism for men where a straight identity is the only acceptable way to be within sport and physical education. Sparkes (1997) and Landi (2018) are two of the very few published works exploring the danger of rejecting a heteronormative masculinity and existing as a gay male physical educator within a space that has traditionally been physically and emotionally dangerous for gay men.

Student Perspectives

» Xavier flinched as several boys in his class ran by him on their way to physical education class, slightly knocking him aside as if he were invisible; for his lack of athletic prowess, he might as well have been invisible in class. He had never been into sports, and he was not looking forward to another class of volleyball, full of potential embarrassment in a setting where his lack of interest and inability to bump, set, or spike the ball could be put on display. Between being overweight, uncoordinated, and gay (but not openly so), Xavier couldn't imagine being less suited for the physical education environment created by his teacher, an exorbitantly fit young man with a penchant for loud whistleblowing and referring to students by their last names while calling them out for not trying. Plus, there was the locker room torture; Xavier frequently heard the mildly homophobic and joking homoerotic slurs his classmates used while changing, and he knew that an openly gay man changing in the locker room would lead to serious social repercussions, possibly even harassment or physical danger. His sexuality was something he kept to himself; only a few close friends knew the truth, and physical education was certainly not the place he wanted it revealed. So, Xavier tried to make himself as invisible as possible at all points, from changing in the bathroom to standing on the periphery during class while making a few half-hearted attempts at participating. The fear of how his classmates would not only perceive him but also treat him if they knew he was gay, the potential for social ostracism, and even open antagonism made Xavier fearful of doing anything that would make him stand out. Physical education, with its culture of hegemonic masculinity and compulsive heterosexuality, where the most athletic and highly praised boys ruled the roost, was clearly not a space for Xavier. He wished he could skip or drop the class altogether. »

Physical education environments have been found to be overwhelmingly heteronormative and homophobic for students who represent queer-embodied identities (they see themselves as located within the LGBTQIA+ spectrum). *Heteronormativity* refers to the compulsory assumption of a heterosexual position and identity for students and teachers, while *homophobia* reflects the fear, revulsion, or uncomfortableness regarding the LGBTQIA+ community, complete with systemic oppression toward the group. Researchers have demonstrated that queer students often find physical education, sport, and physical activity settings to be exclusionary, such as in the scenario with Xavier, with both overt and covert forms of heteronormativity and homophobia positioning them as outsiders and unwanted (Gill et al., 2010; Sykes, 2011). For example, queer students experience homophobic name-calling, isolation, loneliness, and harassment; characterize physical education as distressing and problematic; and often look to avoid or disengage from physical education altogether (Berg & Kokkonen, 2022). Landi (2019) explored the tension LGBTQIA+ students experience in physical education as both a place of exclusion and a potential space for homoeroticism and desire, given the same-gender spaces for changing and even participation, curriculum, and class organization. It is evident that teachers cannot ignore the potential for harm that physical education spaces can cause LGBTQIA+ students but they can also understand that it has the potential to be a space of welcoming affirmation; it depends on the learning environment the teacher creates. Indeed, given the historical connections between lesbianism, sport, and physical education, there is no shortage of precedents for facilitating connections and encouragement for LGBTQIA+ students to fully engage in quality physical education experiences.

Recommendations for Physical Education Administrators

The culture of sport in physical education maintains a hierarchy of performance, strength, and skill, often excluding those who cannot perform at a predetermined satisfactory level. The registers of performance often align along gender and sexuality lines (e.g., hypermasculinity, including heterosexuality, is both dominant and prioritized). Physical education administrators can look to expand traditional curricula beyond the narrow view of physical education as sport, encouraging (or even requiring) curriculum content such as dance, outdoor education, martial arts, and leisure activities (e.g., biking or rollerblading). By redesigning curricula toward less competitive and more widely encompassing forms of physical activity, the potential exists for inclusion of students who do not fit traditional heteronormative forms of masculinity often prized in physical education and sport contexts. This focus may also better support the objective of teaching lifetime physical activity and wellness habits on their physical literacy journey.

A key aspect of physical education that has potential to cause harm for LGBTQIA+ students is the locker room (e.g., see Xavier's story). Typically separated by gender and often unsupervised, locker rooms are spaces where the intersection of sexuality and gender are often put publicly on display. Therefore, physical educators and administrators can offer safe, gender-neutral spaces for students to change as well as clarify and enforce rules for the locker room that maintain changing before and after class as an emotionally safe endeavor for LGBTQIA+ students. Administrators should also ensure that their teachers have a no tolerance policy for homophobic language and that their teachers are comfortable engaging in teachable moments when such instances occur. In addition, for LGBTQIA+ physical educators, supervisors should offer gender-neutral parental leave on the expansion of families. Moreover, they should provide professional development opportunities for teachers to recognize and critique how heteronormative and homophobic practices, however subtle they may be, can be disrupted and replaced with inclusive language and actions for both LGBTQIA+ students and teachers.

Low Socioeconomic Status in Physical Education

As an adopted provision of the **Every Student Succeeds Act (ESSA)** of 2015, schools with a high percentage of children from low-income families can receive additional federal assistance through **Title I**. Title I provides this supplemental funding to help students from low socioeconomic communities meet academic standards; however, it is unclear how much (if any) of this additional funding is channeled into physical education and other physical activity opportunities in Title I schools. Thus, issues of underfunded physical education programs (Aikens & Barbarin, 2008) may lead to the experiences described by physical educator Jacinta and student Laura in the following examples.

Teacher Perspectives

» Jacinta is a new physical educator at a Title I school in a low socioeconomic community. Growing up in a middle-class family in a different part of the country, she can admit to herself that she does not have shared experiences with the students that she teaches. She remembers how surprised she was when she learned that many of her students come from families experiencing food, clothing, and housing insecurity. Unsurprisingly, she also found the amount and status of her available physical education equipment to be below the standards she was accustomed to in her teacher education program. The challenge of insufficient equipment, which is further magnified by a high student-to-teacher ratio, often results in Jacinta's students waiting to participate. With no financial support for physical education feasible within the school's limited budget, Jacinta privately mutters choice words to equipment companies that charge "$70 for just six skin-coated foam balls?!" How is she supposed to be able to provide a meaningful physical education experience for her students, many of whom would not otherwise have access to physical activity opportunities? »

A lack of resources, including staffing, professional development, and equipment budgets, is

LEADERSHIP IN ACTION

The Importance of Equity, Diversity, and Inclusion in the School Setting

Jared A. Russell, PhD

Professor, School of Kinesiology, Auburn University

Diversity, equity, and inclusion (DEI) in physical education school settings are crucial for creating an educational environment where each student feels valued, supported, and empowered to participate fully in a curriculum that meets their respective academic needs. Educational settings that promote inclusivity support students' comprehensive and holistic development, foster educational equity, encourage participation and engagement with the curriculum, and reduce negative stereotypes and biases related to body image, gender roles, and physical ability. Moreover, the incorporation of DEI allows schools to address respective legal and ethical (as well as moral) standards associated with local, state, and federal antidiscrimination laws.

Administrators and teachers are critical in establishing a sustainable school culture that exemplifies DEI practices and principles. Collaboratively, school personnel must develop and communicate a clear vision of the implementation of DEI in their respective school settings. These efforts include creating and enforcing DEI policies and practices, allocating sufficient instructional resources, and providing professional development that promotes inclusive pedagogy, curriculum, and strategic initiatives. Finally, consistent monitoring, assessment, and evaluation of DEI efforts will allow school personnel to make data-informed strategic decisions focused on enhancing student participation, engagement, satisfaction, and additional student performance goals. By prioritizing DEI, teachers and administrators can create sustainable educational settings that not only promote well-being but also foster a sense of belonging that prepares students to thrive in an ever-increasingly diverse world.

---

a growing trend in physical education (Turner et al., 2017). More generally, schools in low socioeconomic communities are prone to be underresourced, which may negatively affect their students' academic progress and performance (Aikens & Barbarin, 2008). Since many public schools serving low-income families are facing financial crises, some scholars (e.g., Picus & Odden, 2011) have posited eliminating or greatly reducing the capacity of so-called electives, such as physical education. Such cost-saving measures may contribute to the estimated 30 percent of schools, many of which are likely in low socioeconomic communities, that report not having a physical education budget at all (Turner et al., 2017). For Jacinta, not having adequate equipment dictated how she taught her students, resulting in increased waiting time. Further, teachers like Jacinta, who face high student-to-teacher ratios, see decreased instruction time and lower physical activity among students during class (Bevans et al., 2010), which is contributed, in part, by understaffing a school's physical education department. While high student-to-teacher ratios, understaffing of full-time, well-trained physical educators, and low-to-nonexistent budgets are not unique to schools in low socioeconomic communities, it is reasonable to believe that physical education departments in such schools are disproportionately affected as school budgets are largely dictated by local tax revenue (NCES, 2022).

Student Perspectives

» Laura is a 12-year-old student in Mr. Jenkins' physical education class. While her family works hard, medical bills and other life circumstances have prevented their financial security. Thus, Laura feels different from her mostly middle-class fellow student classmates, particularly when it comes to family support, school lunch and breakfast, and clothing. She notices this difference particularly when it comes to the mostly hand-me-down clothing that she wears to school; Laura's peers giggle, and when teachers are not around, they tease her. However, in physical education, she feels as though she can excel; she is faster than any of her classmates, and they know it. For 30 minutes, Laura can outrun the teasing and staring.

This week, though, Laura has suddenly stopped wanting to participate. Mr. Jenkins, always enthusiastic about maximizing participation in his classes, walks over to her and gives his standard "You can do it!" speech, drawing the attention of Laura's fellow classmates. Laura further withdraws; she says, "I don't feel good, Mr. Jenkins." Eventually she relents and unconvincingly participates in the chasing and fleeing game. Several times over the course of the activity, Laura bends down and adjusts her shoes. Each time she has to adjust her shoes, she is slow to get back into the game, prompting additional encouragement from Mr. Jenkins. At her next physical education class, Laura strategically wears her old flip-flops. Surely Mr. Jenkins will not make her participate in flip-flops, right? She is relieved that Mr. Jenkins allows her to sit on the bleachers. Later at home, Laura retrieves her shoes from her book bag; they are coming apart at the seams. She wonders whether she will get a new pair for her birthday. »

Before commenting on Laura's scenario, it is essential to acknowledge the complex sociocultural and sociopolitical issues surrounding financial insecurity in the United States. According to the U.S. Department of Agriculture (USDA) (2022), 10.2 percent of households are food insecure[1], while approximately 25 percent of renting households are severely burdened[2] by housing instability (Joint Center for Housing Studies of Harvard University [JCHS], 2020). These statistics are illustrated through Laura's lived experiences; she comes to school each day carrying this weight. She feels the differences between herself and her classmates, particularly when it comes to the clothing that she wears at school and during physical education, contributing to her perception of family economic stress; this perception is known to affect emotional distress and academic performance in students (Mistry et al., 2009). Laura's social and emotional wellness is likely further affected by her teacher, Mr. Jenkins, who unwittingly cast light on aspects Laura was attempting to hide during physical education (her falling-apart shoes). Because her family could not readily afford another pair for physical education, Laura felt compelled to remove herself from class first by pretending that she did not feel well and then by bringing her flip-flops. She was ultimately successful in coping and avoiding (Åsebø & Løvoll, 2021). Despite Laura's initial enjoyment in physical education spaces, without intervention, she may lose out on physical activity opportunities not only during future classes but also during extracurricular activities. For example, students who grow up in financially insecure households are less likely to participate in organized sports (Katzmarzyk et al., 2018). For now, Laura would appear to be physically fit; after all, she is the fastest in her class. However, if she does lose out on those physical activity opportunities, she could be at risk of the troubling trends highlighted by a large-scale study (Walker et al., 2020), which found that economically disadvantaged students, particularly girls, had lower odds of meeting aerobic capacity fitness standards than students in schools within more affluent communities.

Recommendations for Physical Education Administrators

Financial insecurity among U.S. households is a significant, systemic problem that cannot reasonably be addressed within the confines of this chapter. However, some of the suggestions provided here may alleviate some symptoms of the root causes as they narrowly relate to physical education. First, note that research scholars have indicated that school and neighborhood conditions contribute more to socioeconomic differences in learning rates than characteristics of families (Aikens & Barbarin, 2008). This fact positions the school as a potentially powerful influence in addressing equity issues in the services provided to economically disadvantaged students.

Thus, as a physical education administrator, hiring and retaining quality physical educators is of paramount importance because students in schools within low socioeconomic communities are less likely to have highly trained teachers (Clotfelter et al., 2006) or simply physical educators at all (Carlson et al., 2014). Highly trained physical educators should, of course, have a mastery of content and pedagogical knowledge, and they should espouse student-centered

[1] Food insecurity is defined as at some point during the year, being uncertain of having or acquiring sufficient food to meet all family needs (USDA, 2022).

[2] Severely burdened is defined as spending more than 50 percent of household income on housing costs (JCHS, 2020).

practices. However, no amount of excellent teaching will replace or improve physical education equipment in schools with limited financial flexibility or spatial constraints. Accordingly, physical educators should also be trained to identify, write, and submit grants to local foundations and organizations. Funding can be requested not only for typical sports equipment but also for other supplies, such as spare shoes or physical education attire, which can be discreetly loaned to students in need to help them feel as if they belong, they are valued, and they are accepted in physical education. As discussed in chapter 14, while grant writing may not be within the standard skill set of many physical educators and may be perceived as additional burden, physical educators (like Jacinta) and administrators are encouraged to develop and leverage partnerships with PETE faculty at local universities and colleges, many of whom already actively seek and receive grants. Physical education administrators can also offer professional development opportunities to teachers in grant writing, enabling them to enhance their grant writing skills.

To further create an inclusive environment for economically disadvantaged students, physical educators should be trained to be responsive to such students' needs without being patronizing or highlighting the need. From the earlier scenario, Mr. Jenkins—although completely inadvertently—was pointing out that Laura did not have adequate shoes in a social environment in which she was already uncomfortable. Instead, Mr. Jenkins could have been more alert to Laura's atypical participation in his class and then could have spoken with her individually after class. Similarly, physical educators, particularly those working in low socioeconomic communities, should be alert to potential barriers that could diminish a student's participation during physical education. Then, it is important for physical educators to collaborate with one another, their administrators, and available PETE faculty to seek solutions.

Conclusion

This chapter aimed to inform, enrich, and challenge you to critically reflect on your own belief system as it relates to matters of equity, diversity, and inclusion (EDI). The conversations herein may be unfamiliar or even uncomfortable for some, and there are many systemic social issues to be addressed. Indeed, the relational space that physical education occupies has been historically (and contemporarily) marginalizing to the communities discussed in this chapter. As a collective *we*, teachers and administrators in physical education must continue to push for inclusive learning environments whereby *all* school staff, students, and their families, irrespective of embodied identity, feel belonging, acceptance, and value. Those in physical education administration—the leaders—are positioned to advocate for more socially just educational systems, where the ways of knowing and being are embraced and controlled by the individuals themselves, and they are elevated by the surrounding community.

Review Questions

1. How may you, as an administrator, influence the physical education participation of teachers and students who belong to underrepresented groups?
2. Reflect on a teacher in your school or district who identifies as a member of an underrepresented group on the basis of disability, race, gender, sexuality, or low socioeconomic status (or a combination). How may this individual perceive their experience teaching physical education in your school or district?
3. Reflect on a student in your school or district who identifies as a member of an underrepresented group on the basis of disability, race, gender, sexuality, or low socioeconomic status (or a combination). How may this individual perceive their experience learning physical education in your school or district?
4. What practical strategies may you employ to increase the inclusiveness of physical education toward teachers and students who belong to underrepresented groups?

References and Resources

Chapter 1

American Association of School Administrators (AASA). (2021). *The American Superintendent 2020 Decennial Study*. AASA.

Amanchukwu, R.N., Stanley, G.J., & Ololube, N.P. (2015). A review of leadership theories, principles and styles and their relevance to educational management. *Management, 5*(1), 6–14. https://doi.org/10.5923/j.mm.20150501.02

American Association of University Women (AAUW). (2016). *Barriers and bias: The status of women in leadership*. Retrieved May 5, 2018, from www.aauw.org/research/barriers-and-bias

Bass, B.M. (1985). *Leadership and performance beyond expectations*. The Free Press.

Bass, B.M., & Stogdill, R.M. (1990). *Bass and Stogdill's handbook of leadership: Theory, research, and managerial applications*. The Free Press.

Bell, E.L., & Nkomo, S.M. (2001). *Our separate ways: Black and white women and the struggle for professional identity*. Harvard Business School Press.

Bennis, W. (1990). Managing the dream: Leadership in the 21st century. *Training: The Magazine of Human Resource Development, 27*(5), 44–46.

Bennis, W.G. (2009). *On becoming a leader*. Perseus Books.

Bennis, W.G., Benne, K.D., & Chin, R. (1985). *The planning of change* (4th ed.). Holt, Rinehart & Winston.

Bennis, W.G., & Nanus, B. (2003). *Leaders: The strategies for taking charge* (2nd ed.). Harper Collins.

Bogardus, E.S. (1929). Leadership and attitudes. *Sociology and Social Research,* 13, 377–387.

Bryson, J.M., & Crosby, B.C. (1995). *Leadership roles in making strategic planning work*. Jossey-Bass.

Burns, J.M. (1978). *Leadership*. Harper & Row.

Center for American Women and Politics (CAWP). (2022). Women in the U.S. Congress 2022. Eagleton Institute of Politics, Rutgers.edu.

Charry, K. (2012). Leadership theories: 8 major leadership theories. Retrieved May 5, 2018, from http://psychology.about.com/od/leadership/p/leadtheories.htm

Conger, J.A. (2004). Developing leadership capability: What's inside the black box? *Academy of Management Executive, 18*(3), 136–139. https://doi.org/10.5465/ame.2004.14776188

Davis, K. (1963). The case for participative management. *Business Horizons*, 6, 55–60.

Davis, R.C. (1942). *The fundamentals of top management*, New York: Harper.

Educational Business Articles. (2015). The leadership versus management debate: What's the difference? *EBA*. www.educational-business-articles.com/leadership-versus-management

Evans, M.G. (1970). The effects of supervisory behavior on the path-goal relationship. *Organizational Behavior and Human Performance*, 5, 277–298.

Fiedler, F.E., & Chemers, M.M. (1974). *Leadership and effective management*. Scott Foresman.

Fisher, R., & Ury, W. (1981). *Getting to yes: Negotiating agreement without giving in*. Houghton Mifflin.

French, J. and Raven, B. (1959). The bases of social power. In *Studies in Social Power*, D. Cartwright, Ed., pp. 150–167. Institute for Social Research.

Gill, R. (2011). *Theory and practice of leadership*. Sage.

Greenleaf, R.K. (1991). *Servant leadership: A journey into the nature of legitimate power and greatness*. Paulist Press.

Groysberg, B., & Connolly, K. (2013, September). Great leaders who make the mix work. *Harvard Business Review, 91*(9): 68–76.

Harris, B.M., McIntyre, K.E., Littleton, V.C., Jr., & Long, D.F. (1985). *Personnel administration in education*. Allyn & Bacon.

Hersey, P., & Blanchard, K.H. (1988). *Management of organizational behaviour: Utilizing human resources* (5th ed.). Prentice Hall.

Herzberg, F. (1959). *The motivation to work*. John Wiley & Sons, New York.

Hinchliffe, E. (2023). Women CEO's run 10.4% of Fortune 500 companies. A quarter of the 52 leaders became CEO in the last year. *Fortune*, June 23 2023.

House, R.J. (1971). A path goal theory of leader effectiveness. *Administrative Science Quarterly,* 12, 556–571.

Jenson, C.R., & Overman, S.J. (2003). *Administration and management of physical education and athletic programs*. Waveland Press.

Kilmann, R.H. (2014). Celebrating the Thomas-Kilmann Instrument (TKI) and systemwide conflict management. Retrieved May 5, 2018, from www.kilmanndiagnostics.com/celebrating-thomas-kilmann-instrument-tki-and-systemwide-conflict-management

Koontz, H., & O'Donnell, C. (1955). *Principles of management: An analysis of managerial functions*. McGraw-Hill.

Kotter, J.P. (1990). *A force for change: How leadership differs from management*. The Free Press.

Kouzes, J., & Posner, B. (2007). *The leadership challenge* (4th ed.). Wiley.

Landsberger, H.A. (1958). *Management and the worker: It's critics, and developments in human relations in industry*. Cornell University.

Locke, E.A. (1991). *The essence of leadership: The four keys to leading successfully*. Lexington Books.

Marshall, C. (1985). Professional shock: The enculturation of the assistant principal. *Education and Urban Society, 18*, 28–58.

Maslow, A.H. (1943). A theory of human motivation. *Psychological Review, 50*, 370–396.

McGregor, D. (1960). Theory X and Y. *Organization Theory*, 358, 5.

Mechikoff, R.A., & Estes, S. (2006). *A history and philosophy of sport and physical education* (4th ed.). McGraw-Hill.

Moniz, R.J., Jr. (2010). *Practical and effective management of libraries: Integrating case studies, general management theory and self-understanding*. Chandos.

Nanus, B. (1992). *Visionary leadership: Creating a compelling sense of direction for your organization*. Jossey-Bass.

National Center for Education Statistics (NCES). (2023). Characteristics of Public School Teachers. U.S. Department of Education, Institute of Education Sciences. Retrieved September 22, 2024, from https://nces.ed.gov/programs/coe/indicator/clr

Nickles, W.G., McHugh, J.M., & McHugh, S.M. (2010). *Understanding business* (9th ed.). McGraw-Hill Irwin.

Northouse, P.G. (2013). *Leadership: Theory and practice* (6th ed.). Sage.

Parkinson, J.M. (1897). The natural road to learning. *American Journal of Education, 30*(1), 8.

Pew Research Center. (2015). Women and leadership. Retrieved May 5, 2018, from http://www.pewsocialtrends.org/2015/01/14/women-and-leadership

Pigors, M. (1935). *Leadership or domination*. Houghton Mifflin.

Rollinson, B.R. (n.d.). The basics of strategic planning, strategic management and strategy execution. Retrieved July 4, 2018, from https://balancedscorecard.org/Resources/Strategic-Planning-Basics

Scott, D. (2014). *Contemporary leadership in sport organizations*. Human Kinetics.

Spahr, P. (2014). *What is transactional leadership? How structure leads to results*. St. Thomas University Online. Retrieved from https://online.stu.edu/articles/education/what-is-transformational-leadership.aspx

Stogdill, R. (1974). *Handbook of leadership: A survey of theory and research*. The Free Press.

Thomas, K.W., & Kilmann, R.H. (1974). Thomas-Kilmann Conflict Mode Instrument. Retrieved September 22, 2024, from www.kilmanndiagnostics.com/brief-history-thomas-kilmann-conflict-mode-instrument

Thornton, L.F. (2013). *7 lenses: Learning* the principles *and practices of ethical* leadership. Leading in Context.

U.S. Department of Labor. (1995). The environmental scan: A fact-finding report of the Federal Glass Ceiling Commission. Retrieved September 22, 2024, from www.dol.gov/dol/aboutdol/history/reich/reports/ceiling.pdf

Urwick, L.F. (1953). *Leadership and morale*. Ohio State University, College of Commerce and Administration.

Warnick, G.M., & Schmidt, J. (2014). *An experiential learning approach to develop leadership competencies in engineering and technology students*. Paper presented at the 121st ASEE Annual Conference and Exposition, Indianapolis, IN.

Weber, M. (1968). *On charisma and institution building*. The University of Chicago Press.

Yukl. G., & Gardner, W.L. (2020). *Leadership in organizations* (9th ed.). Pearson Education.

Chapter 2

Atkinson, J.W. (1974). The mainstream of achievement-oriented activity. In J.W. Atkinson & J.O. Raynor (Eds.), *Motivation and achievement* (pp. 13–41). V.H. Winston.

Allport, G.W. (1937). *Personality: A psychological interpretation*. Henry Holt and Company

Beighle, A., Erwin, H., Castelli, D., & Ernst, M. (2009). Preparing physical educators for the role of physical activity director. *Journal of Physical Education, Recreation & Dance, 80*(4), 24–29.

Cantor, N., & Kihlstrom, J.F. (1987). *Personality and social intelligence*. Prentice Hall.

Carlyle, T. (1837). *The French Revolution: A history in three volumes*. James Fraser, England.

Carson, R. (2012). Certification and duties of a director of physical activity. *Journal of Physical Education, Recreation & Dance, 83*(6), 16–19.

Castelli, D.M., & Beighle, A. (2007). The physical education teacher as school activity director. *Journal of Physical Education,* Recreation & Dance, 78(5), 25–28.

Cattell, R.B. (1965). *The scientific analysis of personality*. Penguin Books.

Chelladurai, P. (2001). *Managing organizations for sport and physical activity: A systems perspective*. Holcomb Hathaway.

Chelladurai, P. (2005). *Managing organizations for sport and physical activity: A systems perspective.* Holcomb Hathaway; 2nd edition

Connor, D.R. (1995). *Managing at the speed of change: How resilient managers succeed and prosper where others fail.* Villard Books.

Cowley, W.H. (1931). Traits of face-to-face leaders. *Journal of Abnormal and Social Psychology,* 26, 304–313.

Drucker, P.F. (1954). *The practice of management.* Harper & Row.

Drucker, P.F. (1967). *The effective executive.* Harper & Row Publishers, New York.

Eysenck, H.J. (1967). *The biological basis of personality* (100–117). Springfield, IL: Thomas

Eysenck, H.J. (1970). *The structure of human personality.* Methuen.

Fayol, H. (1916). *General and industrial management.* Institute of Electrical and Electronics Engineering, Paris

Galton, F. (1869). *Heredity genius: An inquiry into its laws and consequences.* D. Appleton and Company.

Gardner, H. (1983). *Frames of mind: The theory of multiple intelligences.* Basic Books.

Goleman, D. (1995). *Emotional intelligence: Why it can matter more than IQ.* Bantam Books.

Goleman, D. (1998). *Working with emotional intelligence.* Bantam Books.

Goleman, D. (2006). *Social intelligence: The new science of human relationships.* Bantam Books.

Guilford, J.P. (1959). *Personality.* McGraw-Hill

Gulick, L. and Urwick, L. (1937). *Papers on the science of administration.* Institute of Public Administration, New York.

Hersey, P., & Blanchard, K.H. (1988). *Management of organizational behaviour: Utilizing human resources* (5th ed.). Prentice Hall.

Horn, T. (2008). *Advances in sport psychology* (3rd ed.). Human Kinetics.

Institute of Medicine. (2013). *Educating the* student *body: Taking physical activity and* physical education *to school.* National Academies Press.

Jensen, C.R., & Overman, S.J. (2003). *Administration and management of physical education and athletic programs* (4th ed.). Waveland Press.

Juneja, P. (n.d.). Emotional intelligence for leaders. Retrieved May 5, 2018, from www.managementstudyguide.com/emotional-intelligence-for-leaders.htm

Katz, R.L. (1974). Skills of an effective administrator. *Harvard Business Review, 52*(5), 90–101.

Kihlstrom, J.F., & Cantor, N. (2000). Social intelligence. In R.J. Sternberg (Ed.), *Handbook of intelligence* (pp. 564–581). Cambridge University Press. Retrieved September 22, 2024, from https://doi.org/10.1017/CBO9780511977244.029

Kim. M. (2021, December 2). *Transformational leadership in physical education.* PHE America. www.pheamerica.org/2021/transformational-leadership-in-physical-education/

Kohl, H.W., Craig, C.L., Lambert, E.V., Alkandaqri, J.R., Leetongin, G., & Kahlmeier, S. (2012). The pandemic of physical inactivity: Global action for public health. *Lancet, 380*(9838), 294–305.

Kotter, J.P. (1995, March-April). Leading change: Why transformation efforts fail. *Harvard Business Review,* 259–267.

Kotter, J.P. (2012, March-April). Leading change: Why transformation efforts fail. *Harvard Business Review,* 23; 44–58. (Original work published in 1995)

Kotter, J.P., & Schlesinger, L.A. (2008). Choosing strategies for change. *Harvard Business Review, 57*(2): 106–114.

Lewin, K. (1951). *Field theory in social science.* Harper & Row.

Masteralexis, L.P., Barr, C.A., & Hums, M.A. (2005). *Principles and practice of sport management* (3rd ed.). Jones and Bartlett.

McClelland, D.C. (1961). *The achieving society.* Van Nostrand.

Miner, J.B. (1965). *Studies in management education.* Organizational Measurement Systems Press.

Mintzberg, H. (1989). *Mintzberg on management. Inside our strange world of organizations.* The Free Press.

Mintzberg, H. (1990, March-April). The manager's job: Folklore and fact. *Harvard Business Review, 68*(2), 1–31.

Mumford, M.D., Zaccaro, S.J., Connelly, M.S., & Marks, M.A. (2000). Leadership skills: Conclusions and future directions. *Leadership Quarterly, 11*(1), 155–170.

Mumford, M.D., Zaccaro, S.J., Harding, F.D., Jacobs, T., & Fleishman, E.A. (2000). Leadership skills for a changing world: Solving complex problems. *Leadership Quarterly, 11*(1), 11–35.

Mumford, T.V., Campion, M.A., & Morgeson, F.P. (2007). The leadership skills strataplex: Leadership skill requirements across organizational levels. *Leadership Quarterly, 18,* 154–166.

Park, S., Hironaka, S., Carver, P., & Nordstrum, L. (2013). *Continuous improvement in education* [White paper]. Carnegie Foundation for the Advancement of Teaching.

Parks, J.B., & Quarterman, J. (2007). *Contemporary sport management* (3rd ed.). Human Kinetics.

Rink, J., Hall, T., & Williams, L. (2010). *Schoolwide physical activity.* Human Kinetics.

Salovey, P., & Mayer, J.D. (1990). Emotional intelligence. *Imagination, Cognition, and Personality, 9*(3), 185–211.

Spreitzer, G.M., McCall, W.W., Jr., & Mahoney, J.D. (1997). Early identification of executive potential. *Journal of Applied Psychology, 82*, 6–29.

Stogdill, R.M. (1974). *Handbook of leadership: A survey of the literature*. The Free Press.

Tannenbaum, R. and Schmidt, W.H. (1958) How to choose a leadership pattern. *Harvard Business Review*, 36, 95–101.

Tannenbaum, R., & Schmidt, W. (1973). How to choose a leadership pattern. *Harvard Business Review, 51*(3), 162–180.

Tate, W. (2009). *The search for leadership: An organizational perspective*. Trinity Press.

Thorndike, E.L. (1920). Intelligence and its use. *Harper's Magazine, 140*, 227–235.

Weinberg, R.S., & Gould, D. (2024). *Foundations of sport and exercise psychology* (8th ed.). Human Kinetics.

Yukl, G. & Gardner, W.L. (2020). *Leadership in organizations* (9th ed.). Pearson.

Chapter 3

Adapted Physical Education National Standards (APENS). (2018). Retrieved September 23, 2024, from www.ncpeid.org/apens-national-standards

American College of Sports Medicine (ACSM). (2011). Exercise is medicine [Global health initiative]. www.exerciseismedicine.org/

Active Schools (2022). *A guiding framework for active schools.* Action for Healthy Kids. Retrieved September 23, 2025, from www.ncpeid.org/apens-national-standards

Association for Supervision and Curriculum Development (ASCD), & Centers for Disease Control and Prevention (CDC). (2014). Whole School, Whole Child, Whole Community: A collaborative approach to learning and health. www.ascd.org/ASCD/pdf/siteASCD/publications/wholechild/wscc-a-collaborative-approach.pdf

Behringer, H.K., Saksvig, E.R., Boedeker, P.J., Elish, P.N., Kay, C.M., Calvert, A.M.M., & Gazmararian, J.A. (2022). Physical activity and academic achievement: An analysis of potential student- and school-level moderators. *International Journal of* Behavioral *Nutrition and Physical Activity, 19*, 110. https://doi.org/10.1186/s12966-022-01348-3

Beighle, A., Erwin, H., Castelli, D., & Ernst, M. (2009). Preparing physical educators for the role of physical activity director. *Journal of Physical Education, Recreation & Dance, 80*(4), 24–29.

Bezold, C.P., Konty, K.J., Day, S.E., Berger, M., Harr, L., Larkin, M., Napier, M.D., Nonas, C., Saha, S., Harris, T.J., and Stark, J.H.. (2014). The effects of changes in physical fitness on academic performance among New York City youth. *Journal of Adolescent Health, 55*(6), 774–781.

Burson, S.L., Mulhearn, S.C., Castelli, D.M., & van der Mars, H. (2021). Essential components of physical education: Policy and environment. *Research Quarterly for Exercise and Sport, 92*(2), 209–221, https://doi.org/10.1080/02701367.2021.1884178

Burton, L.J., & VanHeest, J.L. (2007). The importance of physical activity in closing the achievement gap. *Quest, 59*, 212–218.

Carson, R.L. (2010, July 19). *Reshaping physical activity and PE in schools via physical activity director (PAD) training* [Comment on the webpage Online PE 2020 forum]. American Alliance for Health, Physical Education, Recreation & Dance. Retrieved August 1, 2011, from www.aahperd.org/naspe/about/relatedLinks/pe2020/submission_details.cfm?customel_dataPageID_48369=7033

Carson, R.L. (2012). Certification and duties of a director of physical activity. *Journal of Physical Education, Recreation & Dance, 83*(6), 16–19, 29. https://doi.org/10.1080/07303084.2012.10598790

Carson, R.L. (2013). Calling all practitioners: Encourage and support the creation of active schools and school physical activity champions. *American Journal of Lifestyle Medicine, 7*(5), 343–345.

Carson, R.L. (2012). Certification and duties of a Director of Physical Activity. In J. Rink (Ed.), Implementing comprehensive school physical activity programs: The role of Directors of Physical Activity [Special issue]. *Journal of Physical Education, Recreation & Dance, 83*(6), 16–19, 29.

Carson, R.L., Beighle, A., & Castelli, D. (2010, December). *The needs and vision for a NASPE's physical activity director task force* [White paper]. American Alliance for Health, Physical Education, Recreation & Dance.

Carson, R.L., Castelli, D.M., Pulling Kuhn, A.C., Moore, J.B., Beets, M.W., Beighle, A., Aija, R., Calvert, H.G., and Glowacki, E.M. (2014). Impact of trained champions of comprehensive school physical activity programs on school physical activity offerings, youth physical activity and sedentary behaviors. *Preventive Medicine, 69*(Suppl.), S12-S19. https://doi.org/10.1016/j.ypmed.2014.08.025

Carson, R.L., Castelli, D.M., & Kulinna, P.H. (2017). CSPAP professional preparation: Takeaways from pioneering physical education teacher education programs. In P.H. Kulinna, R.L. Carson, & D.M. Castelli (Eds.), Integrating CSPAP in PETE programs: Sharing insight and identifying strategies

[Special issue]. *Journal of Physical Education, Recreation & Dance*, *88*(2), 43–51.

Carson, R.L., Abel-Berei, C.P., Russ, L., Shawley, J., Peal, T., Weinberger, C. (2020). Internal capacity building: The role of the CSPAP champion and other school professionals. In R.L. Carson & C.A. Webster, *Comprehensive School Physical Activity Programs: Putting research into evidence-based practice* (pp. 35–52). Human Kinetics.

Castelli, D.M., Barcelona, J.M., & Bryant, L. (2015). Contextualizing physical literacy in the school environment: The challenges. *Journal of Sport and Health Science*, *4*(2), 156–163.

Castelli, D.M., & Beighle, A. (2007). The physical education teacher as school physical activity director. *Journal of Physical Education, Recreation & Dance, 78*(5), 25–28.

Castelli, D.M., Hillman, C.H., Buck, S.M., & Erwin, H.E. (2007). Physical fitness and academic achievement in third- and fifth-grade students. *Journal of Sport and Exercise Psychology, 29*(2), 239–252.

Castelli, D.M., Carson, R.L., & Kulinna, P.H. (2017). PETE programs creating teacher leaders to integrate Comprehensive School Physical Activity Programs. In P.H. Kulinna, R.L. Carson, & D.M. Castelli (Eds.), Integrating CSPAP in PETE programs: Sharing insight and identifying strategies [Special issue]. *Journal of Physical Education, Recreation & Dance*, *88*(1), 8–10.

Centers for Disease Control and Prevention (CDC). (n.d.). *Developing program goals and measurable objectives*. U.S. Department of Health and Human Services. Retrieved May 14, 2018, from www.cdc.gov/healthyyouth/evaluation/pdf/brief3b.pdf

Centers for Disease Control and Prevention (CDC). (2010). *The association between school-based physical activity, including physical education, and academic performance*. U.S. Department of Health and Human Services.

Centers for Disease Control and Prevention (CDC). (2011). School health guidelines to promote healthy eating and physical activity. *Morbidity and Mortality Weekly Report, 60*(5), 2. Retrieved May 14, 2018, from www.cdc.gov/mmwr/pdf/rr/rr6005.pdf

Centers for Disease Control and Prevention (CDC). (2013a). *Comprehensive school physical activity programs: A guide for schools*. U.S. Department of Health and Human Services.

Centers for Disease Control and Prevention (CDC). (2013b). *A guide for developing comprehensive school physical activity programs*. U.S. Department of Health and Human Services.

Centers for Disease Control and Prevention (CDC). (2014a). *National framework for physical activity and physical education*. U.S. Department of Health and Human Services.

Centers for Disease Control and Prevention (CDC). (2014b). *School health policies and practices study*. U.S. Department of Health and Human Services.

Centers for Disease Control and Prevention (CDC). (2015a). Disability overview. Retrieved May 14, 2018, from www.cdc.gov/ncbddd/disabilityandhealth/disability.html

Centers for Disease Control and Prevention. (2015b). *Youth Risk Behavior Surveillance*. U.S. Department of Health and Human Services.

Centers for Disease Control and Prevention (CDC). (2016). *School health policies and practices study*. U.S. Department of Health and Human Services.

Centers for Disease Control and Prevention (CDC). (2017). *Increasing physical education and physical activity: A framework for schools*. U.S. Department of Health and Human Services.

Centers for Disease Control and Prevention (CDC). (2019). *Physical Education Curriculum Analysis Tool: PECAT 2019*. www.cdc.gov/healthyschools/physicalactivity/pdf/18_300595-A_PECAT_042619_508tagged.pdf

Centers for Disease Control and Prevention (CDC). (2021). High School Youth Risk Behavior Survey Data. www.cdc.gov/yrbs

Clements, R.L., & Rady, A.M. (2012). *Urban physical education: Instructional practices and cultural activities*. Human Kinetics.

Cooper, K.H., Greenberg, J.D., Castelli, D.M., Barton, M., Martin, S.B., & Morrow, J.R. (2016). Implementing policies to enhance physical education and physical activity in schools. *Research Quarterly for Exercise and Sport, 87*(2), 133–140. https://doi.org/10.1080/02701367.2016.1164009

Corbin, C. (2016). Implications of physical literacy for research and practice: A commentary. *Research Quarterly for Exercise and Sport, 87*(10), 14–27.

Corbin, C.B., & Le Masurier, G. (2021). *Fitness for life* (7th ed.). Human Kinetics.

Corbin, C.B., McConnell, K.E., Le Masurier, G.C., Corbin, D.E., & Farrar, T.D. (2014). *Health opportunities through physical education*. Human Kinetics.

Dai, Haizhi, & Xu, Shuisheng. (2022) The relationship between physical activity and academic performance of students. *International Journal of Physical Activity and Health, 1*(22), Article 4. https://doi.org/10.18122/ijpah.1.2.4.boisestate

Dauenhauer, B., Krause, J.M., Douglas, S., Smith, M., & Stellino, M.B. (2017). A newly revised master's degree in physical education and physical activity leadership at the University of Northern Colorado.

Journal of Physical Education, Recreation & Dance, 88(2), 14–19.

Davis, K.S., Burgeson, C.R., Brener, N.D., McManus, T., & Wechsler, H. (2005). The relationship between qualified personnel and self-reported implementation of recommended physical education practices and programs in U.S. schools. *Research Quarterly for Exercise and Sport, 76*, 202–211.

DeCorby, K., Halas, J., Dixon, S., Wintrup, L., & Janzen, H. (2005). Classroom teachers and the challenges of delivering quality physical education. *Journal of Educational Research, 98*, 208–220.

Donnelly, J.A. (2017). The relationship between physical fitness and school performance. *Journal of Social, Behavioral, & Health Sciences,* 11(1), 231–244. https://doi.org/10.5590/JSBHS.2017.11.1.16

Donnelly, J.E., Hillman, C.H., Castelli, D., Etnier, J.L., Tompowski, P., Lambourne, K., & Szabo-Reed, A.N. (2016). Physical activity, fitness, cognitive function, and academic achievement in children: A systematic review. *Medicine and Science in Sport and Exercise, 48*(6), 1197–1222.

Dwyer, T., Sallis, J.F., Blizzard, L., Lazarus, R., & Dean, K. (2001). Relation of academic performance to physical activity and fitness in children. *Pediatric Exercise Science, 13*(3), 225–237.

Dyson, B. (2014). Quality physical education: A commentary on effective physical education and teaching. *Research Quarterly for Exercise and Sport, 85*, 144–152.

Ennis, C.D. (2011). Physical education curriculum priorities: Evidence for education and skillfulness. *Quest, 63*, 5–18.

Faucette, N., McKenzie, T.L., & Patterson, P. (1990). Descriptive analysis of nonspecialist elementary physical education teachers' curricular choices and class organization. *Journal of Teaching in Physical Education, 9*, 284–293.

Faulkner, G.E.J., Dwyer, J.J.M., Irving, H., Allison, K.R., Adlaf, E.M., & Goodman, J.M. (2008). Specialist or nonspecialist physical education teachers in Ontario elementary schools: Examining differences in opportunities for physical activity. *Alberta Journal of Educational Research, 54*(4), 407–419.

Farrey, T., & Isard, R. (2015). *Physical literacy in the United States: A model, strategic plan, and call to action.* The Aspen Institute.

Gao, Z., & Kaplan, M. (2012). *Physical fitness, academic achievement and student behavior outcomes in Delaware Public Schools, SY 2010–11.* Delaware Department of Education.

Graham, G., Holt/Hale, S.A., & Parker, M. (2003). *Children moving: A reflective approach to teaching physical education* (6th ed.). McGraw-Hill.

Grissom, J.B. (2005). Physical fitness and academic achievement. *Journal of Exercise Physiology, 8*(1), 11–25. Retrieved September 23, 2024, from www.researchgate.net/publication/235914141_Physical_fitness_and_academic_achievement

Hillman, C.H., Castelli, D.M., & Buck, S.M. (2005). Aerobic fitness and neurocognitive function in healthy preadolescent children. *Medicine & Science in Sports & Exercise, 37*(11), 1967–1974.

Hillman, C.H., Erickson, K.I., & Kramer, A.F. (2008). Be smart, exercise your heart: Exercise effects on brain and cognition. *Nature Reviews Neuroscience, 9*(1), 58–65.

Holt/Hale, S., & Hall, T. (2016). *Lesson planning for elementary physical education*. Human Kinetics.

Institute of Medicine (IOM). (2013). *Educating the student body: Taking physical activity and* physical educa*tion to school*. National Academies Press.

Janak, J.C., Gabriel, K.P., Oluyomi, A.O., Perez, A., Kohl, H.W., & Kelder, S.H. (2014). The association between physical fitness and academic achievement in Texas State House legislative districts: An ecologic study. *Journal of School Health, 84*(8), 533–542.

Kasser, S.L., & Lytle, R.K. (2005). *Inclusive physical activity: A lifetime of opportunities.* Human Kinetics.

Kern, B.D., Graber, K.C., Shen, S., Hillman, C.H., & McLoughlin, G. (2018). Association of school-based physical activity opportunities, socioeconomic status, and third-grade reading. *Journal of School Health, 88*(1), 34–43. https://doi.org/10.1111/josh.12581

Lounsbery, M.A.F., Holt, K.A., Monnat, S.M., Funk, B., & McKenzie, T.L. (2014). JROTC as a substitute for PE. *Research Quarterly for Exercise and Sport, 85*(3), 414–419. https://doi.org/10.1080/02701367.2014.930408

Lewallen, T.C., Hunt, H., Potts-Datema, W., Zaza, S., & Giles, W. (2015). The Whole School, Whole Community, Whole Child model: A new approach for improving educational attainment and healthy development for students. *Journal of School Health, 85*(11), 729–739.

Lieberman, L.J., Houston-Wilson, C., & Grenier, M. (2025). (4th ed.). *Strategies for inclusion: Physical education for everyone.* Human Kinetics.

Lund, J., & Veal, M.L. (2013). *Assessment-driven instruction in physical education: A standards-based approach to promoting and documenting learning.* Human Kinetics.

Martin, L.T., & Chalmers, G.R. (2007). The relationship between academic achievement and physical fitness. *Physical Educator, 64*(4), 214–221.

McKenzie, T.L., Feldman, H., Woods, S.E., Romero, K.A., Dahlstrom, V., Stone, E.J., Strikmiller, P.K., Williston, J.M., & Harsha, D.W. (1995). Student activity levels and lesson context during third-grade physical education. *Research Quarterly for Exercise and Sport, 66*, 184–193. https://doi.org/10.1080/02701367.1995.10608832

McKenzie, T.L., & Lounsbery, M. (2013). Physical education teacher effectiveness in a public health context. *Research Quarterly for Exercise and Sport, 84*, 419–430.

McKenzie, T.L., Marshall, S.J., Sallis, J.F., & Conway, T.L. (2000). Student activity levels, lesson context, and teacher behavior during middle school physical education. *Research Quarterly for Exercise and Sport, 71*, 249–259.

Mears, D. (2010). Physical education waivers and young adult physical activity. *The Physical Educator, 67*(2), 90–101. https://js.sagamorepub.com/pe/article/view/2111

Metzler, M.W. (2017). *Instructional models in physical education* (3rd ed.). Routledge.

Michael, S.L., Merlo, C.L., Basch, C.E., Wentzel, K.R., & Weshler, H. (2015). Critical connections: Health and academics. Journal of School Health, 85(11), 740–758.

Michael, S. L., Brener, N., Lee, S., Clennin, M., & Pate, R. (2019). Physical education policies in US schools: Differences by school characteristics. *Journal of School Health, 89*(6), 494–502. https://doi.org/10.1111/josh.12762

Mitchell, S.A., & Walton-Fisette, J.L. (2016). *The essentials of teaching physical education: Curriculum, instruction, and assessment.* Human Kinetics.

National Consortium for Physical Education for Individuals with Disabilities (NCPEID), & Kelly, L.E. (2020). *Adapted physical education national standards* (3rd ed.). Human Kinetics.

Novelly, T. (2022). Even more young Americans are unfit to serve, a new study finds. Here's why. In *Military News, Military.com.* Retrieved September 23, 2024, from www.military.com/daily-news/2022/09/28/new-pentagon-study-shows-77-of-young-americans-are-ineligible-military-service.html

Physical Activity Alliance (2022a). *The 2022 United States Report Card on Physical Activity for Children and Youth.* https://paamovewithus.org/wp-content/uploads/2022/10/2022-US-Report-Card-on-Physical-Activity-for-Children-and-Youth.pdf

Physical Activity Alliance (2022b). *National Physical Activity Plan.* Retrieved September 23, 2023, from https://paamovewithus.org/national-physical-activity-plan/

Ratey, J.J. (2008). *SPARK: The evolutionary new science of exercise and the brain.* Little, Brown. https://pdfs.semanticscholar.org/54bf/23284d3772f476476efc045f6b2c94e83d03.pdf

Roetert, E.P., & MacDonald, L.C. (2015). Unpacking the physical literacy concept for K-12 physical education: What should we expect the learner to master? *Journal of Sport and Health Science, 4*, 108–112.

Rosenbaum, D.A., Carlson, R.A., & Gilmore, R.O. (2001). Acquisition of intellectual and perceptual-motor skills. *Annual Review of Psychology, 52*, 453–470.

Schempp, P.G., Manross, D., Dan, S.K., & Fincher, M.D. (1998). Subject expertise and teachers' knowledge. *Journal of Teaching in Physical Education, 17*, 342–356.

SHAPE America. (2009). *Appropriate instructional practice guidelines, K-12: A side-by-side comparison.* www.shapeamerica.org/Common/Uploaded%20files/uploads/pdfs/Appropriate-Instructional-Practices-Grid.pdf

SHAPE America. (2011). *PE Metrics: Assessing national standards 1-6 in secondary school.* NASPE.

SHAPE America. (2014). *National standards & grade-level outcomes for K-12 physical education.* Human Kinetics.

SHAPE America. (2015a). *The essential components of physical education.* www.shapeamerica.org/Common/Uploaded%20files/uploads/pdfs/TheEssentialComponentsOfPhysicalEducation.pdf

SHAPE America. (2015b). *Physical education is an academic subject* [Position statement]. www.shapeamerica.org/Common/Uploaded%20files/document_manager/advocacy/Physical-Education-Is-an-Academic-Subject-2.pdf.

SHAPE America. (2016). *Shape of the nation report.* SHAPE America, American Heart Association, and Voices for Healthy Kids. www.shapeamerica.org//Common/Uploaded%20files/uploads/pdfs/son/Shape-of-the-Nation-2016_web.pdf

SHAPE America. (2017). *National standards for initial physical education teacher education.* Reston, VA: Author.

SHAPE America. (2019). *PE Metrics: Assessing student performance using the national standards & grade-level outcomes for K-12 physical education* (3rd ed.). Human Kinetics.

SHAPE America (2023). *Comprehensive school physical activity programs: Opportunities and access for all.* [Position statement]. https://issuu.com/shapeamerica/docs/comprehensive_school_physical_activity_programs.fi?fr=sNmFlMzY0MDk5Mjc

SHAPE America. (2025). *National physical education standards* (4th ed.). Human Kinetics.

Stokes, R., & Schultz, S.L. (2007). *Personal fitness for you*. Hunter Textbooks.

Stoepker, P., Dauenhauer, B., Carson, R.L., McMullen, J., & Moore, J.B., (2021). Becoming a physical activity leader (PAL): Skills, responsibilities, and training. *Strategies, 34*(1), 23–28. https://doi.org/10.1080/08924562.2020.1841695

The Community Guide. (2018). *Physical activity: Enhanced school-based physical education*. Retrieved September 23, 2024, from www.thecommunityguide.org/findings/physical-activity-enhanced-school-based-physical-education.html.

Trost, S. (2007). *Active education: Physical education, physical activity and academic performance*. Active Living Research.

Trudeau, F., & Shephard, R.J. (2008). Physical education, school physical activity, school sports and academic performance. *International Journal of Behavioral Nutrition and Physical Activity, 5*(1), 10. https://doi.org/10.1186/1479-5868-5-10

United Nations Educational, Scientific and Cultural Organization (UNESCO). (2015a). *Quality physical education: Guidelines for policy-makers*.

United Nations Educational, Scientific and Cultural Organization (UNESCO). (2015b). *Revised International Charter of Physical Education, Physical Activity and Sport*. Retrieved May 14, 2018, from http://portal.unesco.org/en/ev.php-URL_ID=13150&URL_DO=DO_TOPIC&URL_SECTION=201.html

U.S. Department of Health and Human Services (HHS). (2008). *Physical activity guidelines for Americans*.

U.S. Department of Health and Human Services (HHS). (2012a). *Physical activity guidelines for Americans midcourse report: Strategies to increase physical activity among youth*.

U.S. Department of Health and Human Services (HHS). (2012b). *Healthy People 2020. Physical activity objectives*. www.healthypeople.gov/2020/topicsobjectives2020/objectiveslist.aspx?topicId=33

U.S. Department of Health and Human Services (HHS). (2018). *Physical activity guidelines for Americans*. (2nd ed.). https://health.gov/paguidelines/second-edition/pdf/Physical_Activity_Guidelines_2nd_edition.pdf

U.S. Department of Health and Human Services (HHS), Office of Disease Prevention and Health Promotion. (n.d.) Healthy People 2030. Retrieved September 23, 2024, from www.health.gov/healthypeople

Van Dusen, D.P., Kelder, S.H., Kohl, H.W., Ranjit, N., & Perry, C.L. (2011). Associations of physical fitness and academic performance among schoolchildren. *Journal of School Health, 81*(12), 733–740. https://doi.org/10.1111/j.1746-1561.2011.00652.x

Ward, D. (2011). *School policies on physical education and physical activity*. Active Living Research. www.activelivingresearch.org

Weaver, R.G., Webster, C.A., Beets, M.W., Brazendale, K., Chandler, J., Schisler, L., & Aziz, M. (2018). Initial outcomes of a participatory-based, competency-building approach to increasing physical education teachers' physical activity promotion and students' physical activity: A pilot study. *Health Education and Behavior, 45*(3), 359–370. https://doi.org/10.1177/1090198117731600

World Health Organization (WHO). (2017). *Global action plan on physical activity 2018–2030: More active people for a healthier world*. www.who.int/publications/i/item/9789241514187

Youth Sport Trust. (2022, March). Evidence paper – The link between physical activity and attainment in children and young people. www.youthsporttrust.org/media/zyyo133r/pe-and-attainment-evidence-paper-january-2022.pdf

Chapter 4

Ainsworth, L. (2003). *Power standards*. Lead Learn Press.

Ainsworth, L. (2013). *Prioritizing the common core: Identifying the standards to emphasize the most*. Houghton Mifflin Harcourt.

Ayers, S.F., & Sariscsany, M.J. (2011). *Physical education for lifelong fitness* (3rd ed.). Human Kinetics.

Bernstein, E., Phillips, S.R., & Silverman, S. (2011). Attitudes and perceptions of middle school students toward competitive activities in physical education. *Journal of Teaching in Physical Education, 30*(1); 69–83, Human Kinetics

Blackburn, B.R. (2017). *Rigor and assessment in the classroom*. Routledge.

Cairney, J., Kwan, M.Y., Velduizen, S. Hay, J., Bray. S.R., & Faught, B.E. (2012). Gender, perceived competence and the enjoyment of physical education in children: A longitudinal examination. *International Journal of Behavioral Nutrition and Physical Activity, 9*(26). https://doi.org/10.1186/1479-5868-9-26

Castillo, I., Molina-García, J., Estevan, I., Queralt, A., & Álvarez, O. (2020). Transformational teaching in physical education and students' leisure-time physical activity: The mediating role of learning climate, passion and self-determined motivation. *International Journal of Environmental Research and Public Health, 17*(13), 4844. https://doi.org/10.3390/ijerph17134844

Capel, S. & Blair, R. (2007). Making physical education relevant: Increasing the impact of initial teacher training. *London Review of Education*, 5(*1*), 15–34.

Carr, J.F. & Harris, D. (2009). *Improving standards-based learning.* Corwin.

Centers for Disease Control and Prevention (CDC). (2017a). Developing program goals and measurable objectives. Retrieved from www.cdc.gov/std/Program/pupestd/Developing%20Program%20Goals%20and%20Objectives.pdf

Centers for Disease Control and Prevention (CDC). (2017b). *Program performance and evaluation.* Retrieved from www.cdc.gov/eval/index.htm

Connecticut State Department of Education. (2006, November 3). *Guide to curriculum development: Purposes, practices, procedures.* www.sde.ct.gov/sde/cwp/view.asp?a=2618&q=321162

Chen, A. & Ennis, C.D. (2009). Motivation and achievement in physical education. In K.R. Wenzel & A. Wigfield (Eds.), *Handbook of motivation at school* (pp. 553–574). Routledge/Taylor & Francis Group.

Cothran, D.J. & Ennis, C.D. (1998). Curriculum of mutual worth: Comparison of students' and teachers' curricular goals. *Journal of Teaching in Physical Education, 14,* 467–477.

Ennis, C.D. (2014). What goes around comes around… Or does it? Disrupting the cycle of traditional sport-based physical education. *Kinesiology Review,* Feb; 3(1): 63–70, Human Kinetics.

Flory, S.B., & McCaughtry, N. (2011). Culturally relevant physical education in urban schools: Reflecting cultural knowledge. *Research Quarterly for Exercise and Sport, 82*(1), 49–60.

Glatthorn, A.A., Carr, J.F., & Harris, D.E. (2001). *Planning and organizing for curriculum renewal.* Association for Supervision and Curriculum Development (ASCD).

Graham, G., Holt/Hale, S., & Parker, M. (2013). *Children moving: A reflective approach to teaching physical education* (9th ed.). Mc-Graw Hill Companies.

Graham, D.J., Sirard, J.R., & Neumark-Sztainer, D. (2011). Adolescents' attitudes toward sports, exercise, and fitness predict physical activity 5 and 10 years later. *Preventive Medicine, 52*(2), 130–132. https://doi.org/10.1016/j.ypmed.2010.11.013

Great Schools Partnership. (2015a, August 12). *Curriculum.* http://edglossary.org/hidden-curriculum

Great Schools Partnership. (2015b, November, 10). *Assessment.* http://edglossary.org/assessment

Gurvitch, R., & Metzler, M. (2013). Aligning learning activities with instructional models. *Journal of Physical Education, Recreation & Dance, 84*(3), 30–37.

Hellison, D. (2011). *Teaching personal and social responsibility through physical activity* (3rd ed.). Human Kinetics.

Hill, G.M., & Cleven, B. (2006). A comparison of students' choices of 9th grade physical education activities by ethnicity. *The High School Journal, 89*(2), 16–23.

Houston, J., & Kulinna, P. (2014). Health-related fitness models in physical education. *Strategies: A Journal for Physical Education and Sport Education,* 27(2), 20–26. https://doi.org/10.1080/08924562.2014.879026

Kim., M. (2021). *Transformational leadership in physical education.* PHE America.

Ladwig, M.A., Ekkekakis, P., & Vazou, S. (2018). Childhood experiences in physical education may have long-term implications. *Medicine and Science in Sports and Exercise. 50*(5S): 319. https://doi.org/10.1249/01.mss.0000536130.78614.ad

Lambert, L.T. (1996). Standards-based program design: Creating a congruent guide for student learning. In S.J. Silverman & C.D. Ennis (Eds.), *Student learning in physical education* (2nd ed., pp. 129–146). Human Kinetics.

Leyton-Román, M., Núñez, J.L., & Jiménez-Castuera, R. (2020). The importance of supporting student autonomy in physical education classes to improve intention to be physically active. *Sustainability, 12*(10), 4251. www.mdpi.com/2071-1050/12/10/4251

Lund, J., & Tannehill, D. (2015). *Standards-based physical education curriculum development* (3rd ed.). Jones & Bartlett Learning.

Martin-Kniep, G.O. (2000). *Becoming a better teacher: Eight innovations that work.* Association for Supervision and Curriculum Development.

Manninen, M., & Yli-Piipari, S. (2021). Ten practical strategies to motivate students in physical education: Psychological need-support approach, *Strategies, 34*(2), 24–30. https://doi.org/10.1080/08924562.2020.1867270

Mitchell, S.A., Oslin, J.L., & Griffin, L.L. (2021). *Teaching sport concepts and skills: A tactical games approach for ages 7 to 18* (4th ed.). Human Kinetics.

Mitchell, S.A., & Walton-Fisette, J.F. (2016). *The essentials of teaching physical education: Curriculum, instruction, and assessment.* Human Kinetics.

Mitchell, S.A., & Walton-Fisette, J.F. (2022). *The essentials of teaching physical education* (2nd ed.). Human Kinetics.

Phillips, S.R., & Silverman, S. (2015). Upper elementary school student attitudes toward physical education. *Journal of Teaching in Physical Education, 34,* 461–473.

Quay, J., & Peters, J. (2008) Skills, strategies, sport, and social responsibility: Reconnecting physical education. *Journal of Curriculum Studies, 40*(5), 601–626. https://doi.org/10.1080/00220270801886071.

SHAPE America. (2014). *National Standards & Grade-Level Outcomes for K-12 Physical Education.* Human Kinetics.

SHAPE America. (2025). *National physical education standards.* (4th ed.). Human Kinetics.

Siedentop, D., Hastie, P.A., & van der Mars, H. (2020). *Complete guide to sport education* (3rd ed.). Human Kinetics.

Sierra-Díaz, M.J., González-Víllora, S., Pastor-Vicedo, J.C., & López-Sánchez, G.F. (2019) Can we motivate students to practice physical activities and sports through models-based practice? A systematic review and meta-analysis of psychosocial factors related to physical education. *Frontiers in Psychology, 10*(10), 2115. https://doi.org/10.3389/fpsyg.2019.02115 .PMID: 31649571; PMCID: PMC6795761.

Silverman, S. (2011). Teaching for student learning in physical education. *Journal of Physical Education, Recreation & Dance, 82*(6), 29–34.

Tannehill, D., van der Mars, H., & MacPhail, A. (2015). *Building effective physical education programs.* Jones & Bartlett Learning.

Trudeau, F., & Shephard R. (2008). Is there a long-term health legacy of required physical Houston

U.S. Department of Education. (n.d.) Individuals with Disabilities Act. Retrieved September 24, 2024, from https://sites.ed.gov/idea/

Wiggins, G., & McTighe, J. (2005). *Understanding by design* (2nd ed.). Association for Supervision and Curriculum Development.

Chapter 5

Ardoy, D.N., Fernandez, J.M., Jimenez-Pazon, D., Castillo, R., Ruiz, J.R., & Ortega, F.B. (2014). A physical education trial improves adolescents' cognitive and academic achievement: The EDUFIT study. *Scandinavian Journal of Medicine & Science in Sports, 24*, 52–61.

Aspen Institute (2015). *Physical literacy in the United States: A model, strategic plan, and call to action.*

Bernstein, E., Phillips, S.R., & Silverman, S. (2011). Attitudes and perceptions of middle school students toward competitive activities in physical education. *Journal of Teaching in Physical Education,* 30, 69–83.

Burgeson, C.R., Wechsler, H., Brener, N.D., Young, J.C., & Spain, C.G. (2001). Physical education and activity: Results from the School Health Policies and Programs Study 2000. *Journal of School Health, 71*(7), 279–293.

Burkhalter, T.M., & Hillman, C.H. (2011). A narrative review of physical activity, nutrition, and obesity to cognition and scholastic performance across the human lifespan. *Advances in Nutrition, 2*(2), 201S-206S.

Calkins, N.D. (2017). Self-regulation strategy development as an instructional approach to motor skill acquisition. *Strategies: A Journal for Physical Education and Sport Education, 30*(5), 41–44. https://doi.org/10.1080/08924562.2017.1345262

Canady, R., & Retting, M. (1995). *Block scheduling: A catalyst for change in high schools.* Taylor and Francis.

Centers for Disease Control and Prevention (CDC). (2010). *The association between school-based physical activity, including physical education, and academic performance.* U.S. Department of Health and Human Services.

Centers for Disease Control and Prevention (CDC). (2012). *Results from the School Health Policies and Practices study 2012.* www.cdc.gov/healthyyouth /data/shpps/pdf/shpps-results_2012.pdf

Centers for Disease Control and Prevention (CDC). (2014). Youth risk behavior surveillance—United States, 2013. *Morbidity and Mortality Weekly Report, 63*(4), 1–168.

Centers for Disease Control and Prevention (CDC). (2016). *Results from the School Health Policies and Practices Study 2016.* www.cdc.gov/healthyyouth /data/shpps/results.htm

Centers for Disease Control and Prevention (CDC). (2019). *Youth risk behavior survey data.* www.cdc .gov/yrbs

Centers for Disease Control and Prevention (CDC) (2019). *National Health Interview Survey.* National Center for Health Statistics. Retrieved September 24, 2024, from www.cdc .gov/nchs/nhis/physical_activity/pa_glossary .htm#:~:text=Physical%20activity%3A%20Any%20 bodily%20movement,that%20substantially%20 increases%20energy%20expenditure.

Centers for Disease Control and Prevention (CDC). (2021a). *Youth Risk Behavior Surveillance System (YRBSS).* www.cdc.gov/healthyyouth /data/yrbs/reports_factsheet_publications .htm#anchor_1596724918

Centers for Disease Control and Prevention (CDC). (2021b). *National Health and Nutrition Examination Survey (NHANES).* National Center for Health Statistics. Retrieved September 24, 2024, from www .cdc.gov/nchs/nhanes/index.htm

Child and Adolescent Health Measurement Initiative. (n.d.). *2021–2022 National Survey of Children's Health (NSCH).* Data Resource Center for Child and Adolescent Health supported by the U.S. Department of Health and Human Services (HHS) and Health Resources & Services Administration (HRSA), Maternal and Child Health Bureau (MCHB). Retrieved September 24, 2024, from www .childhealthdata.org

Daum, D.N., & Buschner, C. (2012). The status of high school online physical education in the United States. *Journal of Teaching in Physical Education, 31*, 86–100.

DeCorby, K., Halas, J., Dixon, S., Wintrup, L., & Janzen, H. (2005). Classroom teachers and the challenges of delivering quality physical education. *Journal of Educational Research, 98*(4), 208–220.

Donnelly, F.C., Mueller, S.S., & Gallahue, D. (2017). *Developmental physical education for all children: Theory into practice.* (5th ed.) Human Kinetics.

Ericsson, I. (2008). Motor skills, attention and academic achievements. An intervention study in school years 1–3. *British Educational Research Journal, 34*(3), 301–313.

Every Student Succeeds Act (ESSA). (2015). Pub L. No. 114–95. www.everystudentsucceedsact.org/

Fletcher, T. (2008). Grouping students by ability in physical education: The good, the bad and the options. *Physical & Health Education Journal, 74*(3), 6–10.

French, R., Henderson, H., Kinnison, L., & Sherrill, C. (1998). Revisiting Section 504, physical education and sport. *Journal of Physical Education, Recreation & Dance, 69*(7), 57–63.

Gabbei, R. (2004). Achieving balance: Secondary physical education gender-grouping options. *Journal of Physical Education, Recreation & Dance, 75*(3), 33–39.

Gagen, L., & Getchell, N. (2004). Combining theory and practice in the gymnasium. "Constraints" within an ecological perspective. *Journal of Physical Education, Recreation & Dance, 75*(5), 25–30.

Greenberg, J.D., Calkins, N.D, & Spinosa, L.S. (2022) *Designing and teaching fitness education courses.* Human Kinetics.

Grenier, M., Miller, N., & Black, K. (2017). Applying Universal Design for Learning and the inclusion spectrum for students with severe disabilities in general physical education. *Journal of Teaching in Physical Education, 88*(6), 51–56.

Gurvitch, R., & Metzler, M. (2013). Aligning learning activities with instructional models. *Journal of Teaching in Physical Education, 84*(3), 30–37.

Hardman, K. (2004). *An update on the status of physical education in schools worldwide: Technical report for the World Health Organization.* World Health Organization. Retrieved Retrieved September 24, 2024, from www. icsspe.org/portal/download/PEworldwide.pdf

Herman, J., Aschbacher, P., & Winters, L. (1992). A practic*al guide to alternative assessment.* ASCD.

Hillman, C.H., Pontifex, M.B., Raine, L.B., Casteli, D.M., Hall, E.E., & Kramer, A.F. (2009). The effect of acute treadmill walking on cognitive control and academic achievement in preadolescent children. *Neuroscience, 159*(3), 1044–1054.

Houston, J., & Kulinna, P. (2014). Health-related fitness models in physical education. *Strategies:* A Journal *for Physical Education and Sport* Education, *27*(2), 20–26. https://doi.org/10.1080/08924562.2014.879026

Institute of Medicine (IOM). (2013). *Educating the student body: Taking physical activity and physical education to school.* National Academy of Sciences.

Kirk, D. (2014). A defining time for physical education futures? Exploring the legacy of Fritz Duras. *Asia-Pacific Journal of Health, Sport and Physical Education, 5*(2), 103–116.

Lentillon-Kaestner, V., & Patelli, G. (2016). Effects of grouping forms, student gender and ability level on the pleasure experienced in physical education. *Journal of Teaching in Physical Education, 35*, 251–262.

Lieberman, L.J., Grenier, M., Brian, A., & Arndt, A., (2021). *Universal Design for Learning.* Human Kinetics.

Lieberman, L.J., Houston-Wilson, C., and Grenier, M. (2025). *Strategies for inclusion: A handbook for physical educators* (4th ed.). Human Kinetics.

McKenzie, T.L. (2007). The preparation of physical educators: A public health perspective. *Quest, 59*(4), 347–357.

McKenzie, T.L., Stone, E.J., Feldman, H.A., Epping, J.N., Yang, M., Strikmiller, P.K., Lytle, L.A., & Parcel, G.S. (2001). Effects of the CATCH physical education intervention: Teacher type and lesson location. *American Journal of Preventive Medicine, 21*(2), 101–109.

Metzler, M. (2011). *Instructional models for physical education* (3rd ed.). Holcomb Hathaway.

Metzler, M., & Colquitt, G.T. (2012) *Instructional models for physical education* (4th ed.). Routledge.

Mohnsen, B. (2012). Implementing online physical education. *Journal of Teaching in Physical Education, 83*(2), 42–47.

Morgan, P.J., & Hansen, V. (2008). Classroom teachers' perceptions of the impact of barriers to teaching physical education on the quality of physical education programs. *Research Quarterly for Exercise and Sport, 79*(4), 506–516.

Murphy, B., Dionigi, R.A., & Litchfield, C. (2014). Physical education and female participation: A case study of teachers' perspectives and strategies. *Issues in Educational Research, 24*(3), 241–259.

Murphy, K.L., & Beh, H.G. (2014). The standard of care and the assumption of risk defense in a negligent injury case in a physical education class. *Journal of Physical Education, Recreation & Dance, 85*(8), 41–43.

National Association for Sport and Physical Education (NASPE). (2006a). *Opposing substitution and waivers/exemptions for required physical education. Position Statement.* SHAPE America. Retrieved September 24, 2024, from www.shapeamerica.org/Common/Uploaded%20files/document_manager/advocacy/position-statements/Opposing-Substitution-and-Waiver-Exemptions.pdf

National Association for Sport and Physical Education (NASPE). (2006b). *Teaching large class sizes in physical education: Guidelines and strategies* [Guidance document].

National Association for Sport and Physical Education (NASPE). (2007). *Initial guidelines for online physical education* [Position paper].

National Center for Education Statistics. (2016). Digest of education statistics. Retrieved August 18, 2017, from https://nces.ed.gov/fastfacts/display.asp?id=64

National Center for Education Statistics. (2024). Students with disabilities. *Condition of Education.* U.S. Department of Education, Institute of Education Sciences. Retrieved September 24, 2024, from https://nces.ed.gov/programs/coe/indicator/cgg

National Center for Health Statistics. (2021). (U.S.) NHSR No. 158. National Health Statistics Reports. https://stacks.cdc.gov/view/cdc/106273

National Health and Nutrition Examination Survey 2017–March 2020. Prepandemic Data Files Development of Files and Prevalence Estimates for Selected Health Outcomes

National Institutes of Health (2021). *Classification of laws associated with school students (CLASS).* https://class.cancer.gov

Office of the Superintendent of Public Instruction. (2013). *Recommendations for waivers in high school physical education.* Olympia, WA Office of Superintendent of Public Instruction. www.k12.wa.us/HealthFitness/pubdocs/RecommendationsWaiversHighSchoolPhysicalEducation.pdf.

Perna, F.M., Oh, A., Chriqui, J.F., Mâsse, L.C., Atienza, A.A., Nebeling, L., Agurs-Collins, T., Moser, R., & Dodd, K.W. (2012). The association of state law to physical education time allocation in US public schools. *American Journal of Public Health, 102*(8), 1594–1599.

Piekarz-Porter, E., Lin, W., Leider, J., Perna, F., & Chriqui, J. (2021). State laws matter when it comes to school provisions for structured PE and daily PE participation. *Translational Behavioral Medicine,* Feb; *11*(2): 597–606. https://doi.org/10.1093/tbm/ibaa013.

Qi, J., & Ha, A.S. (2012). Inclusion in physical education: A review of literature. *International Journal of Disability, Development, and Education, 59*(3), 257–281.

Robinson, L.E., Webster, E.K., Logan, S.W., Lucas, W.A., & Barber, L.T. (2012). Teaching practices that promote motor skills in early childhood settings. *Early Childhood Education Journal, 40*(2), 79–86.

Sallis, J.F., McKenzie, T.L., Beets, M.W., Beighle, A., Erwin, H., & Lee, S. (2012). Physical education's role in public health: Steps forward and backward over 20 years and HOPE for the future. *Research Quarterly for Exercise and Sport, 83*(2), 125–135.

Sallis, J.F., McKenzie, T.L., Kolody, B., Lewis, M., Marshall, S., & Rosengard, P. (1999). Effects of health-related physical education on academic achievement: Project SPARK. *Research Quarterly for Exercise and Sport, 70*(2), 127–134.

SHAPE America. (2012). *Instructional framework for fitness education in physical education* [Guidance document].

SHAPE America. (2014). *National standards & grade-level outcomes for K-12 physical education.* Human Kinetics.

SHAPE America. (2015a). *The essential components of physical education* [Guidance document].

SHAPE America. (2015b). *The essential components of physical education* [Physical Education Program Checklist guidance document].

SHAPE America. (2016). *2016 Shape of the nation report: Status of physical education in the USA.*

SHAPE America. (2017). *What is CSPAP?* Retrieved August 23, 2017, from www.shapeamerica.org/cspap/what.cfm

SHAPE America (2018). *Guidelines for K-12 Online Physical Education.* (Guidance document).

SHAPE America. (2019). *PE Metrics* (3rd ed). Human Kinetics.

SHAPE America. (2025). *National physical education standards.* (4th ed.). Human Kinetics.

Trudeau, F., & Shepard, R.J. (2008). Physical education, school physical activity, school sports and academic performance. *International Journal of Behavioral Nutrition and Physical Activity, 5*, 10.

U.S. Congress. (1973). PL 93–112—Rehabilitation Act.

U.S. Department of Education. (2023). *Distance education.* Code of Federal Regulations. 34 CFR 600.2. Definitions. eCFR. Retrieved September 24, 2024, from www.ed.gov/sites/ed/files/policy/highered/reg/hearulemaking/2023/program-integrity

-and-institutional-quality-session-1-issue-paper-distance-education-final.pdf

U.S. Department of Education. (n.d.). Office of Special Education Programs, Individuals with Disabilities Education Act (IDEA) database. https://sites.ed.gov/idea/

U.S. Department of Education. (2023). Code of Federal Regulations. Distance Education, 34 CFR 600.2 – Definitions-eCFR Washington, DC. www.ecfr.gov/current/title-34/subtitle-B/chapter-VI/part-600/subpart-A/section-600.2

van der Fels, I.M., Te Wierike, S.C., Hartman, E., Elferink-Gemser, M.T., Smith, J., & Visscher, C. (2015). The relationship between motor skills and cognitive skills in 4–16 year old typically developing children: A systematic review. *Journal of Science and Medicine in Sport, 18*(6), 697–703.

Voss, T., Kunter, M., & Baumert, J. (2011). Assessing teacher candidates' general pedagogical/psychological knowledge: Test construction and validation. *Journal of Educational Psychology, 103*(4), 952–969. https://doi.org/10.1037/a0025125

Whitehead, M. (2019). *Physical literacy across the world*. Routledge.

Wilkins, J.L., Graham, G., Parker, S., Westfall, S., Fraser, R.G., & Tembo, M. (2003). Time in the arts and physical education and school achievement. *Journal of Curriculum Studies, 35*(6), 721–734.

Yelm, M.L. (1998). The legal basis of inclusion. Educational *Leadership, 56*(2), 70–73.

Zeng, H.Z., Hipscher, M., & Leung, R.W. (2011). Attitudes of high school students toward physical education and their sport activity preferences. *Journal of Social Sciences, 7*(4), 529–537.

Chapter 6

Agyapong, B., Obuobi-Donkor, G., Burback, L., & Wei, Yifeng. (2022). Stress burnout, anxiety and depression among teachers: A scoping review. *International Journal of Environmental Research and Public Health. 19*(17). https://doi.org/10.3390/jrerph191710706

Cardinal, B.J., Yan, Z., & Cardinal, M.K. (2013). Negative experiences in physical education and sport: How much do they affect physical activity participation later in life? *Journal of Physical Education, Recreation & Dance, 84*(3), 49–53. https://doi.org/10.1080/07303084.2013.767736

Centers for Disease Control and Prevention (CDC). (2019). *Physical Education Curriculum Analysis Tool*. Retrieved June 5, 2023, from www.cdc.gov/healthyschools/pecat/index.htm

Cervone, L., & Martinez-Miller, P. (2007). Classroom walkthroughs as a catalyst for school improvement. *Leadership Compass, 4*(4). www.naesp.org/resources/2/Leadership_Compass/2007/LC2007v4n4a2.pdf

Corbin, C.B. (2016). Implications of physical literacy for research and practice: A commentary. *Research Quarterly for Exercise and Sport, 87*(1), 14–27. http://doi.org/10.1080/02701367.2016.1124722

Danielson Group. (2022). *The Framework for Teaching*. Retrieved June 6, 2023, from https://danielsongroup.org/the-framework-for-teaching

Darling-Hammond, L. (2015). Can value added add value to teacher evaluation? *Educational Researcher, 44*(2), 132–137. Retrieved July 6, 2018, from https://doi.org/10.3102/0013189X15575346

Dweck, C.S. (2007). Mindset: The new psychology of success. Random House.

Ennis, C.D. (2014, March). The role of students and content in teacher effectiveness. *Research Quarterly for Exercise and Sport, 85*(1), 6–13.

Gabbei, R. (2004). Achieving balance: Secondary physical education gender-grouping options. *Journal of Physical Education, Recreation & Dance, 75*(3), 33–39.

Gerstein, J. (2014). *The educator with a growth mindset: A staff workshop*. August 28, 2014. Retrieved June 20, 2018, from https://usergeneratededucation.wordpress.com/2014/08/29/the-educator-with-a-growth-mindset-a-staff-workshop

Ginsberg, M.B., & Murphy, D. (2002). How walkthroughs open doors. *Beyond Instructional Leadership, 59*(8), 34–36.

Kane, T.J., & Staiger, D.O. (2012). *Gathering feedback for teaching: Combining high-quality observations with student surveys and achievement gains*. Met Project. Bill and Melinda Gates Foundation. https://files.eroc.ed.gov/fulltext/ED540960.pdf

Kane, T. J., McCaffrey, D.F., Miller, T., & Staiger, D.O. (2013). *Have We Identified Effective Teachers? Validating Measures of Effective Teaching Using Random Assignment*. Bill and Melinda Gates Foundation. Harvard Center for International Development. www.hks.harvard.edu/centers/cid/publications/have-we-identified-effective-teachers-validating-measures-effective

Lund, J., & Veal, M.L. (2013). *Assessment-driven instruction in physical education: A standards-based approach to promoting and documenting learning*. Human Kinetics.

Mandigo, J., Francis, N., Lodewyk, K., & Lopez, R. (2012). Physical literacy for educators. *Physical Education and Health Journal, 75*(3), 27–30.

Marzano, R.J. (2010). Using games to enhance student achievement. *Educational Leadership, 67*(5), 71–72.

Mazur, P.J., & Lynch, M.D. (1989). Differential impact of administrative, organizational, and personality factors on teacher burnout. *Teaching and Teacher Education*, *5*(4), 337–353. https://doi.org/10.1016/0742-051X(89)90031-0

McKenzie, T.L. (2015). SOFIT: *System for Observing Fitness Instruction Time*. Retrieved June 20, 2018, from http://activelivingresearch.org/sofit-system-observing-fitness-instruction-time

McKenzie, T.L., & Lounsbery, M.A. (2013). Physical education teacher effectiveness in a public health context. *Research Quarterly for Exercise and Sport*, *84*(4), 419–430.

McKenzie, T.L., Sallis, J.F., & Nader, P.R. (1991). SOFIT: System for Observing Fitness Instruction Time. *Journal of Teaching in Physical Education*, *11*, 195–205.

McKenzie, T.L., & van der Mars, H. (2015). Top 10 research questions related to assessing physical activity and its contexts using systematic observation. *Research Quarterly for Exercise and Sport*, *86*(1), 13–29. https://doi.org/10.1080/02701367.2015.991264

myTeachstone (2023). The Classroom Assessment Scoring System (CLASS). Retrieved June 6, 2023, from https://teachstone.com/class

National Education Association (NEA). (2010). *Teacher assessment and evaluation: The National Education Association's framework for transforming education systems to support effective teaching and improve student learning*. Retrieved June 20, 2018, from https://files.eric.ed.gov/fulltext/ED583104.pdf

Network for Public Education. (2016). *Educators on the impact of teacher evaluation*. https://networkforpubliceducation.org/wp-content/uploads/2016/04/NPETeacherEvalReportCompress.pdf

National Institutes of Health. (n.d.). Classification of Laws Associated with School Students (CLASS). National Cancer Institute, Division of Cancer Control & Population Sciences. https://class.cancer.gov/About

Rink, J. (2013). Measuring teacher effectiveness in physical education. *Research Quarterly for Exercise and Sport*, *84*(4), 407–418. https://doi.org/10.1080/02701367.2013.844018

Shakman, K., Breslow, N., Koechanek, J., Riordan, J., & Haferd, T. (2012). *Changing cultures and building capacity: An exploration of district strategies for implementation of teacher evaluation systems* [White paper]. Education Development Center, Inc. Learning and Teaching Division. Retrieved June 20, 2018, from https://eric.ed.gov/?id=ED566724

SHAPE America. (2014). *National standards & grade-level outcomes for K-12 physical education*. Human Kinetics.

SHAPE America (2015a). *Essential components of physical education*. Retrieved June 6, 2023, from www.shapeamerica.org//Common/Uploaded%20files/uploads/pdfs/TheEssentialComponentsOfPhysicalEducation.pdf

SHAPE America (2015b). *Physical education program checklist*. Retrieved June 6, 2023, from www.shapeamerica.org/MemberPortal/publications/products/pechecklist.aspx

SHAPE America. (2025). *National physical education standards* (4th ed.). Human Kinetics.

Skaalvik, E.M. & Skaalvik, S. (2020). Teacher burnout: relations between dimensions of burnout, perceived school context, job satisfaction and motivation for teaching. A longitudinal study. *Teachers and Teaching: Theory and Practice*. *26*(7) pp 602–616. https://doi.org/10.1080/13540602.2021.1913404

Chapter 7

Acrobranch. (2021). *7 major benefits of taking your students on a school trip*. Retrieved January 9, 2023, from acrobranch.co.za

After School Alliance. (2022). *America After* 3PM: Promot*ing Healthy Futures: Afterschool provides the supports parents want for children's well-being*. https://afterschoolalliance.org/documents/AA3PM/AA3PM-Healthy-Futures-Report-2022.pdf

Covell, D., Walker, S., Siciliano, J., & Hess, P.W. (2012). *Managing sports organizations: Responsibility for performance*. Routledge.

Greene, J., Kisida, B., & Bowen, D. (2013). The educational value of field trips. EducationNext, *The Journal*, *14*(1) www.educationnext.org/wp-content/uploads/2013/09/ednext_XIV_1_greene.pdf

Greenwell, T.C., Danzey-Bussell, L.A., & Shonk, D.J. (2014). *Managing sports events*. Human Kinetics.

Kelly, M. (2019, September 14). *Field trips: Pros and cons*. Thought Co. www.thoughtco.com/field-trips-pros-and-cons-8401

Lussier, R.N., & Kimball, D. (2024). *Applied sport management skills* (4th ed.). Human Kinetics.

Masteralexis, L.P., Barr, C.A., & Hums, M.A. (2005). *Principles and practice of sport management*. Jones and Bartlett.

Miami-Dade County Public Schools (2022). *Field trip guidelines*. Retrieved January 9, 2023, from ehandbooks.dadeschools.net/policies/131.pdf

National Education Association (n.d.). How field trips boost students' lifelong success. *Benefits*. Retrieved November 1, 2022, from www.neamb.com/work-life/how-field-trips-boost-students-lifelong-success

Parkhouse, B.L. (2005). *The management of sport: Its foundation and application*. McGraw-Hill.

Pedersen, P.M., & Thibault, L. (2022). *Contemporary sport management* (7th ed.). Human Kinetics.

U.S. Department of Health and Human Services (2024). *I Can Do It!* Administration for Community Living. Retrieved September 24, 2024, from https://acl.gov/programs/health-wellness/icdi.

Watt, D. (2004). *Sports management and administration* (2nd ed.). Routledge.

Chapter 8

American Society for Testing Materials. (n.d.). Retrieved September 24, 2024, from www.astm.org/about/overview.html

Brown, T., & Haines, D. (2009). *Space planning guidelines for campus recreation facilities*. Human Kinetics.

California Department of Education. (2017). Title 5, California Code of Regulations.

Center for Active Design. (2010). *Active design guidelines*. Retrieved May 31, 2018, from https://centerforactivedesign.org/guidelines

Centers for Disease Control and Prevention (CDC). (2016). *Playground safety*. Retrieved June 20, 2018, from www.cdc.gov/safechild/playground/index.html

Dougherty, N., & Seidler, T. (2007). Injuries in the buffer zone: A serious risk management problem. *Journal of Physical Education, Recreation & Dance, 78*(2), 4–7.

Florida Department of Education. (2014). *State requirements for educational facilities*. Office of Educational Facilities.

Greenberg, J., & Stokes, R. (2007). *Developing school site wellness centers*. National Association for Sport and Physical Education.

Hypes, M.G. (2006). Facility design and development: Planning and designing facilities. *Journal of Physical Education, Recreation & Dance, 77*(4), 18–22.

Illinois Department of Natural Resources. (2006). Outdoor recreation facilities guide. Retrieved June 20, 2018, from www.dnr.illinois.gov/AEG/Documents/IDNROutdoorRecreationFacilitiesGuide.pdf

Institute of Medicine. 2013. *Educating the student body: Taking physical activity and physical education to school*. The National Academies Press. https://doi.org/10.17226/18314

Lieberman, L.J., Grenier, M., Brian, A., & Arndt, A. (2021). *Universal design for learning in physical education*. Human Kinetics.

Maryland State Department of Education. (2011). *Physical education facilities guidelines for new construction and major renovations*.

National Federation of State High School Associations (NFHS). (2025). *Court and field diagram guide*.

National Strength and Conditioning Association (NSCA). (2017). *NSCA strength and conditioning professional standards and guidelines*.

National Women's Law Center. (2017). The battle for gender equity in athletics in elementary and secondary schools. Retrieved June 20, 2018, from https://nwlc.org/wp-content/uploads/2015/08/Battle-for-GE-in-Elementary-and-Secondary-Schools.pdf

National Intramural and Recreational Sports Association (NIRSA). (2009). *Campus recreational facilities: Planning, design, and construction guidelines*. Human Kinetics.

Partnership for a Healthier New York City. (2017). Active design toolkit for schools. Center for Active Design. Retrieved June 20, 2018, from https://centerforactivedesign.org/activedesigntoolkitforschools

Petersen, J.C., & Piletic, C.K. (2006). Facility design and development: Planning and designing safe facilities. *Journal of Physical Education, Recreation & Dance, 77*(5), 39–44.

Portland Public Schools. (2015). *Education specifications: Comprehensive high schools*.

Sanders, M. (Ed.). (2019). *American College of Sports Medicine health/fitness facility standards and guidelines* (5th ed). Human Kinetics.

Sawyer, T.H. (2013). *Facility planning and design for health, physical activity, recreation, and sport* (13th ed.). Sagamore.

Seidler, T.L. (2006). Facility accessibility: Opening the doors to all. *Journal of Physical Education, Recreation & Dance, 77*(5), 32–38.

SHAPE America. (2001). *The Council on Physical Education for Children (COPEC) of the National Association for Sport and Physical Education (NASPE), Position Statement, Guidelines for Facilities, Equip ment and Instructional Materials in Elementary School Physical Education*. NASPE.

SHAPE America. (2012). Instructional framework for fitness education in physical education [Guidance document]. www.shapeamerica.org/upload/Instructional-Framework-for-Fitness-Education-in-Physical-Education .pdf

SHAPE America (2022). Guidelines for facilities, equipment, instructional materials & technology in K-12 physical education. https://issuu.com/shapeamerica/docs/shape_america_guidelines_for_facilities_equipment_?fr=sNDE4ZTQ3NDU1MTM.

U.S. Access Board. (n.d.). ADA Accessibility Standards. Retrieved September 24, 2024, from www.access-board.gov/buildings.html

U.S. Consumer Product Safety Commission (CPSC). (2015). *Public playground safety handbook*.

U.S. Department of Education (1972). Title IX and sex discrimination. Office of Civil Rights.

www.ed.gov/laws-and-policy/civil-rights-laws/sex-discrimination/Title-IX-and-Sex-Discrimination.

U.S. Department of Education (2024). U.S. Department of Education releases final Title IX regulations, providing vital protections against sex discrimination. www.ed.gov/about/news/press-release/us-department-of-education-releases-final-title-ix-regulations-providing-vital-protections-against-sex-discrimination.

U.S. Department of Justice (1990). American with Disabilities Act. Civil Rights Division. Retrieved September 24, 2024, from www.ed.gov/about/news/press-release/us-department-of-education-releases-final-title-ix-regulations-providing-vital-protections-against-sex-discrimination

Virginia Department of Education. (2013). *Guidelines for school facilities in Virginia's public schools*. Commonwealth of Virginia Department of Education.

WELL Building Standard (n.d.). Well building standard. Retrieved September 24, 2024, from https://standard.wellcertified.com/well

Chapter 9

Becker, H.J. (2000). Findings from the teaching, learning, and computing survey. *Education Policy Analysis Archives, 8*, 51.

Center for Education Policy Research. (2024). *Proof Points: Some of the $190 billion in pandemic money for schools actually paid off.* Harvard University. Retrieved September 25, 2024, from https://cepr.harvard.edu/news/proof-points-some-190-billion-pandemic-money-schools-actually-paid.

Centers for Disease Control and Prevention (CDC). (n.d.). *HEADS UP: Rocket Blades*. Center for Injury and Violence Prevention. www.cdc.gov/heads-up/media/pdfs/resources/RocketBlades_HandoutforKids-a.pdf

Chaker, R. (2018). Animated micro-sequences and auto-observational learning: An experiment in physical education and sports classes. *International Journal of Educational Technology, 5*(2), 35–45.

Chen, L. (2016). Impacts of flipped classroom in high school health education. *Journal of Educational Technology Systems, 44*(4), 411–420. https://doi.org/10.1177/0047239515626371

Christakis, D.A. (2019). The challenges of defining and studying "digital addiction" in children. *Journal of the American Medical Association, 321*(23), 2277–2278. http://doi.org/10.1001/jama.2019.4690

Congress (2015). Every Student Succeeds Act, S.177-114th Congress (2015–2016). www.congress.gov/bill/114th-congress/senate-bill/1177

Davis, M.R. (2019). *K-12 districts wasting millions by not using purchased software, new analysis finds.* Edweek Market Brief. Accessed 6/30/2023, from https://marketbrief.edweek.org/marketplace-k-12/unused-educational-software-major-source-wasted-k-12-spending-new-analysis-finds

Daum, D.N., & Buschner, C. (2012). The status of high school online physical education in the United States. *Journal of Teaching in Physical Education, 31*, 86–100. https://doi.org/10.1123/jtpe.31.1.86

Duggan, M. (2017, July). *1 in 4 Black Americans have faced online harassment because of their race or ethnicity* [Report]. Pew Research Center. http://pewrsr.ch/2eLpMZN

Ertmer, P.A., & Glazewski, K.D. (2015). Essentials of PBL implementation: Fostering collaboration, transforming roles, and scaffolding learning. In A. Walker, H. Leary, C. Hmelo-Silver, & P.A. Ertmer (Eds.), *Essential readings in problem-based learning* (pp. 89–106). Purdue University Press.

Garcia, E., & Weiss, E. (2020). *COVID-19 and student performance, equity, and U.S. educational policy: Lessons from pre-pandemic research to inform relief, recovery, and rebuilding.* Economic Policy Institute. www.epi.org/publication/the-consequences-of-the-covid-19-pandemic-for-education-performance-and-equity-in-the-united-states-what-can-we-learn-from-pre-pandemic-research-to-inform-relief-recovery-and-rebuilding

Goad, T., Towner, B., Jones, E., & Bulger, S. (2019). Instructional tools in online PE: Using mobile technologies to enhance learner experiences. *Journal of Physical Education, Recreation & Dance, 90*(6), 40–47. https://doi.org/10.1080/07303084.2019.1614118

Gray, L., & Lewis, L. (2021). *Use of educational technology for instruction in public schools: 2019–20 (NCES 2021- 017).* U.S. Department of Education, National Center for Education Statistics. Retrieved September 25, 2024, from https://nces.ed.gov/pubsearch/pubsinfo.asp?pubid=2021017

Gray, S., Treacy, J., & Hall, E. (2019). Re-engaging disengaged pupils in physical education: An appreciative inquiry perspective. *Sport, Education and Society, 24*(3), 241–255.

Jones, S.D., & Workman, E. (2016). *ESSA's well-rounded education.* Education Commission of the States. www.ecs.org/wp-content/uploads/ESSAs-Well-Rounded-Education-1.pdf

Kesiraju, L., & Vogels, T. (2017, September 7). Health and fitness app users are going the distance with record-high engagement. *Flurry.* www.flurry.com/blog/health-fitness-app-users-are-going-the-distance/

Killian, C.M., & Woods, A.M. (2018). Expanding and extending MVPA using e-Learning: FLiP study pilot results. *Research Quarterly for Exercise and Sport*, *89*, A170-A171.

Koehler, M.J., & Mishra, P. (2009). What is technological pedagogical content knowledge? *Contemporary Issues in Technology and Teacher Education*, *9*(1). Retrieved June 20, 2018, from www.citejournal.org/volume-9/issue-1-09/general/what-is-technological-pedagogicalcontent-knowledge

Koehler, M.J. & Mishra P. (2009). What is technological pedagogical content knowledge (TPACK)?, *Contemporary Issues in Technology and Teacher Education,* 9(1), 60–70.

Krause, J.M., Franks, H., & Lynch, B. (2017). Current technology trends and issues among health and physical education professionals. *The Physical Educator*, *74*, 164–180.

Kretschmann, R. (2012). What do physical education teachers think about integrating technology in physical education? *European Journal of Social Sciences*, *27*, 444–448.

Kretschmann, R. (2015). Effect of physical education teachers' computer literacy on technology use in physical education. *The Physical Educator*, *72*, 261–277.

Liu, S.-H. (2012). A multivariate model of factors influencing technology use by pre-service teachers during practice teaching. *Educational Technology & Society*, *15*, 137–149.

Lortie, D. 1975. Schoolteacher: A Sociological Study. London: University of Chicago Press.

Lu, F., & Turner, K. (2013, September). *Improving adolescent fitness attitudes with a mobile fitness game to combat obesity in youth* [Conference presentation]. Games Innovation Conference (IGIC), 2013 IEEE International, Vancouver, Canada.

Mishra, P., & Koehler, M.J. (2006). Technological pedagogical content knowledge: A framework for teacher knowledge. *Teachers College Record*, *108*(6), 1017–1054.

National Education Association. (n.d.). *Preparing 21*st *century students for a global society: An educator's guide to the "Four Cs."* Retrieved June 20, 2018, from www.nea.org/assets/docs/A-Guide-to-Four-Cs.pdf

Osterlie, O., & Kjelaas, I. (2019). The perception of adolescents' encounter with a flipped learning intervention in Norwegian physical education. *Frontiers in Education*, *4*, 1–12. https://doi.org/10.3389/feduc.2019.00114

Purcell, K., Heaps, A., Buchanan, J., & Friedrich, L. (2013). *How teachers are using technology at home and in their classrooms.* Pew Research Center's Internet and American Life Project.

Russell, A. (1995). Stages in learning new technology: Naive adult email users. *Computers in Education*, *25*(4), 173–178.

Society of Health and Physical Educators (SHAPE America). (2016). *Shape of the nation: Status of physical education in the USA.*

Society of Health and Physical Educators (SHAPE America). (2020). *Guidelines for K-12 Online Physical Education.* [Guidance document]. www.shapeamerica.org/Common/Uploaded%20files/uploads/pdfs/2020/guidelines/Online-PE-Guidance-Document.pdf

SHAPE America. (2022). *Guidelines for facilities, equipment, instructional materials and technology in K-12 physical education.* [Guidance document]. https://issuu.com/shapeamerica/docs/shape_america_guidelines_for_facilities_equipment_?fr=sNDE4ZTQ3NDU1MTM

SHAPE America (2023). *Appropriate use of technology in physical education.* [Guidance document]. https://issuu.com/shapeamerica/docs/shape_america_appropriate_use_of_technology_in_phy?fr=xKAE9_4xWQg

Shulman, L.S. (1986). Those who understand: Knowledge growth in teaching. *Educational Researcher*, *15*(2), 4–14.

Stelitano, L., Doan, S., Woo, A., Diliberti, M., Kaufman, J.H., & Henry, D. (2020). *The digital divide and COVID-19: Teachers' perceptions of inequities in students' internet access and participation in remote learning.* Retrieved November 09, 2020, from www.rand.org/pubs/research_reports/RRA134-3.html

Tondeur, J., van Braak, J., Ertmer, P.A., & Ottenbreit-Leftwich, A. (2016). Understanding the relationship between teachers' pedagogical beliefs and technology use in education: A systematic review of qualitative evidence. *Educational Technology Research and Development*, *65*, 555–575, https://doi.org/10.1007/s11423-016-9481-2

U.S. Department of Education, Office of Educational Technology. (2017). *Reimagining the role of* technology *in education: 2017* National Education *Technology Plan update.* https://tech.ed.gov/files/2017/01/NETP17.pdf

Vogels, E.A., Gelles-Watnik, R., & Massarat, N. (2022, August). *Teens, social media and technology 2022.* [Report]. Pew Research Center. www.pewresearch.org/internet/2022/08/10/teens-social-media-and-technology-2022

Wang, Y.H. (2016). Could a mobile-assisted learning system support flipped classrooms for classical Chinese learning? *Journal of Computer Assisted Learning*, *32*(5), 391–415.

Williams, L. (2014). *A case study of virtual physical education teachers' experiences in and perspectives of online teaching* [Unpublished doctoral dissertation]. University of South Florida.

Wiggins, G., & McTighe, J. (2005). *Understanding by design*. Association for Supervision and Curriculum Development.

Yu, H., Kulinna, P.H., & Lorenz, K.A. (2018). An integration of mobile applications into physical education programs. *Strategies, 31*, 13–19.

Zielezinski, M.B., & Darling-Hammond, L. (2016). *Promising practices: A literature review of technology use by underserved students*. Stanford Center for Opportunity Policy in Education.

Chapter 10

Berlo, D.K. (1960). *The process of communication: An introductory to theory and practice*. Holt, Rinehart & Winston.

Cheney, G., & Ashcraft, K.L. (2007). Considering "the professional" in communication studies: Implications for theory and research within and beyond the boundaries of organizational communication. *Communication Theory, 17*, 146–175.

Cheney, G., Christensen, L.T., Zorn, T.E., Jr., & Ganesh, S. (2011). *Organizational communication in an age of globalization: Issues, reflections, practices*. Waveland Press.

Coursera (2023). What is active listening and how can you improve this key skill? Retrieved June 12. 2024, from www.coursera.org/articles/active-listening

Internal Revenue Service. (2016). "Direct" and "grass roots" lobbying defined. Retrieved June 20, 2018, from www.irs.gov/charities-non-profits/direct-and-grass-roots-lobbying-defined

James, G. (2010). How to write a press release, with examples. *CBS News, Moneywatch*. www.cbsnews.com/news/how-to-write-a-press-release-with-examples

Jensen, S.J., & Overman, C.R. (2003). *Administration and management of physical education and athletic programs* (4th ed.). Waveland Press.

Jones, S.D., & Workman, E. (2016*). ESSA's well-rounded education*. Education Commission of the States. www.ecs.org/wp-content/uploads/ESSAs-Well-Rounded-Education-1.pdf

Kneen, J. (2011). *Essential skills: Essential speaking and listening skills*. Oxford University Press.

Lehigh University, Library and Technology Services. (n.d.). *Telephone etiquette*. Retrieved June 20, 2018, from www.lehigh.edu/phones/phonevmetiquette.html

Lunenburg, F.C. (2010). Communication: The process, barriers, and improving effectiveness. *Schooling, 1*(1), 1–11.

Lunenburg, F.C., & Ornstein, A.C. (2011). *Educational administration: Concepts and practices* (6th ed., p. 166). Wadsworth Cengage Learning.

Lussier, R.N., & Kimball, D. (2024). *Applied sport management skills* (4th ed.). Human Kinetics.

Mortensen, C.D. (2007). *Communication theory*. Routledge.

National Association of County and City Health Officials. (2016). Building your advocacy toolbox: Advocacy vs. lobbying. Retrieved June 20, 2018, from www.naccho.org/uploads/downloadable-resources/flyer_advocacy-na16-002.pdf

National School Public Relations Association (NSPRA). (n.d.). *PR Resources: Starting a school public relations program*. Retrieved June 12, 2024, from www.nspra.org/PR-Resources/Starting-a-School-Public-Relations-Program

Pauley, J.A. (2010). *Communication: The key to effective leadership*. ASQ.

Rogers, C.R., & Farson, R.R. (1957). *Active listening*. The University of Chicago Press.

Romkema, J. (2023, December 11). 10 Tips for effective e-mail communication. *Global Learning Partners*. www.globallearningpartners.com/blog/10-tips-for-effective-e-mail-communication [originally published June 20, 2012]

Salisbury University, Office of Career Services. (n.d.). *Helpful phone etiquette tips*. Retrieved from www.salisbury.edu/careerservices/facstaff/officeetiquette/telephone.html

Schramm, W. (Ed.). (1969). *Mass communications*. University of Illinois Press.

Shannon, C.E., & Weaver, W. (1949). *The* mathematical *theory of communication*. University of Illinois Press.

Stoner, J.A.F., Freeman, R.E., & Gilbert, D.R. (2006). *Management*. (6th ed.). Pearson

Tardanico, S. (2012). 5 Habits of highly effective communicators. *Forbes*. www.forbes.com/sites/susantardanico/2012/11/29/5-habits-of-highly-effective-communicators/#548ccf9c19b6

Trust, T. (2013). *Using body language to your advantage during a job interview*. University of California, Santa Barbara, GradPost. Retrieved June 20, 2018, from http://archive.gradpost.ucsb.edu/career/2013/2/26/using-body-language-to-your-advantage-during-a-job-interview.html

University of Waterloo, Centre for Teaching Excellence. (n.d). *Effective communication: Barriers and strategies*. Retrieved September 25, 2024, from https://uwaterloo.ca/centre-for-teaching-excellence/teaching-resources/teaching-tips/communicating-students/telling/effective-communication-barriers-and-strategies; https://uwaterloo.ca/centre-for-teaching-excellence/catalogs/tip-sheets/effective-communication-barriers-and-strategies

Chapter 11

Alstot, A.E., & Alstot, C.D. (2015). Behavior management: Examining the functions of behavior. *Journal of Physical Education, Recreation & Dance, 86*(2), 22–28. https://doi.org/10.1080/07303084.2014.988373.

Anti-Bullying Alliance. (n.d.). Definition of Bullying. Retrieved September 27, 2024, from https://anti-bullyingalliance.org.uk/tools-information/all-about-bullying/understanding-bullying/definition.

A.S. v. State of Florida (1997). Retrieved September 27, 2024, from www.casemine.com/judgement/us/591481e6add7b0493448c516.

Barber, H., & Krane, V. (2007). Creating a positive climate for lesbian, gay, bisexual, and transgender youths. *Journal of Physical Education, Recreation & Dance, 78*(7), 6–7, 52. https://doi.org/10.1080/07303084.2007.10598047

Block, B.A. (2014). Supporting LGBTQ students in physical education: Changing the movement landscape. *Quest, 66*, 14–26. https://doi.org/10.1080/00336297.2013.824904

Borkowski, R.P. (n.d.). *Putting prevention into practice: A risk management primer for physical education teachers*. Educational Service District 112.

Bridgeman Bridgeman v. New Trier High school District NO 203. (1997). Retrieved September 27, 2024, from https://caselaw.findlaw.com/court/us-7th-circuit/1075334.html.

Burnham v. West (1987). Retrieved September 27, 2024, from https://law.justia.com/cases/federal/district-courts/FSupp/681/1160/1800267/

California Assembly Bill No. 1266. (2013). Retrieved June 20, 2018, from https://leginfo.legislature.ca.gov/faces/billNavClient.xhtml?bill_id=201320140AB1266

Carpenter, L.J. (2008). *Legal concepts in sport: A primer* (3rd ed.). Sagamore.

Commonwealth v. Carey (1990). Retrieved September 27, 2004, from https://law.justia.com/cases/massachusetts/supreme-court/1990/407-mass-528-3.html

DeMartini, A. (2016). Sexual hazing or harassment is a Title IX violation. *Journal of Physical Education, Recreation & Dance, 87*(4), 53–55. https://doi.org/10.1080/07303084.2016.1142204

DesROCHES BY DesROCHES v. Caprio (1997). Retrieved September 27, 2024, from https://law.justia.com/cases/federal/district-courts/FSupp/974/542/1450893/

Dougherty, N.J., Goldberger, A.S., & Carpenter, L.J. (2007). *Sport, physical activity, and the law* (3rd ed.). Sagamore.

Eisenberg M.E., Gower A.L., McMorris B.J., Rider N., Shea G., & Coleman E. (2017). Risk and protective factors in the lives of transgender/gender nonconforming adolescents. *Journal of Adolescent Health*. 61:521–526. https://doi.org/10.1016/j.jadohealth.2017.04.014.

Essex, N.L. (n.d.). Don't get sued: 5-step guide to teacher liability. Retrieved June 20, 2018, from www.teachhub.com/dont-get-sued-5-step-guide-teacher-liability

Findlaw. (2024). *Teachers' rights*. Retrieved June 13, 2024, from www.findlaw.com/education/teachers-rights.html#:~:text=The%20Equal%20Protection%20Clause%20of,academics%2C%20privacy%2C%20and%20religion.

Fitzgerald, A., & Deutsch, J. (2016). Limiting the risk of injury through safety guidelines in a physical education setting. *Journal of Human Science, 13*(2), 2856–2859. https://doi.org/10.14687/jhs.v13i2.3783

Florida State Statutes. (2024). Physical Education; assessment, 1003.455. Retrieved September 27, 2024, from www.leg.state.fl.us/statutes/index.cfm?App_mode=Display_Statute&URL=1000-1099/1003/Sections/1003.455.html

Foley, J.T., Pineiro, C., Miller, D., & Foley, M. (2016). Including transgender students in school physical education. *Journal of Physical Education, Recreation & Dance, 87*(3), 5–8. doi:10.1080/07303084.2016.1131544

Freeh Sporkin & Sullivan, LLP. (2012). *The Freeh Report: Report of the special investigative counsel regarding the actions of The Pennsylvania State* University *related to the child sexual abuse committed by Gerald A. Sandusky*. Retrieved from http://i2.cdn.turner.com/cnn/2017/images/08/03/freeh.report.pdf

Fuller, B., Gulbrandson, K., & Herman-Ukasick, B. (2013). Bully prevention in the physical education classroom, *Strategies, 26*(6), 3–8. https://doi.org/10.1080/08924562.2013.839425

Gibbone, A., & Manson, M. (2013). Bullying. *Journal of Physical Education, Recreation & Dance, 81*(7), 20–24. https://doi.org/10.1080/07303084.2010.10598504

Gladden, R.M., Vivolo-Kantor, A.M., Hamburger, M.E., & Lumpkin, C.D. (2014). *Bullying surveillance among youths: Uniform definitions for public health and recommended data elements, version 1.0.* National Center for Injury Prevention and Control, Centers for Disease Control and Prevention, and U.S. Department of Education.

Gray, G.R. (1995). Safety tips from the expert witness. *Journal of Physical Education, Recreation & Dance, 66*(1), 18–21. Taylor & Francis.

Graham v. Florida (2010). Retrieved September 27, 2024, from https://supreme.justia.com/cases/federal/us/560/48/

Hand, K.E. (2016). Creating a bully-free environment in physical education. *Journal of Physical Education, Recreation & Dance, 87*(7), 55–57. https://doi.org/10.1080/07303084.2016.1203685

Hoerr, T.R. (2013). Principal connection: Who's the bully on your staff? *ASCD, Educational Leadership, 70*(5), 82–83.

James v. Jackson (2005). Retrieved September 27, 2024, from https://caselaw.findlaw.com/court/la-court-of-appeal/1293395.html.

Juvonen, J., & Gross, E.F. (2008). Extending the school grounds: Bullying experiences in cyberspace. *Journal of School Health, 78*(90), 496–505.

Kelley, J., Sansfacon, A.P., Gelly, M.A., Chiniara, Lyne, & Chadi, N. (2022). School factors strongly impact transgender and non-binary youths well-being. *Children. 9*(10): 1520.

Mahoney, T.Q., Dodds, M.A., & Polasek, K.M. (2015). Progress for transgender athletes: Analysis of the School Success and Opportunity Act. *Journal of Physical Education, Recreation* & Dance, 86(6), 45–47. https://doi.org/10.1080/07303084.2015.1054202

Marsh, J.P. (2017). Harassment and the First Amendment. *Journal of Physical Education, Recreation & Dance, 88*(3), 51–52. https://doi.org/10.1080/07303084.2017.1271258

Miranda v. Arizona (1966). Retrieved September 27, 2024, from https://supreme.justia.com/cases/federal/us/384/436/

Moore v. Willis Independent School District (2000). Retrieved September 27, 2024, from https://caselaw.findlaw.com/court/us-5th-circuit/1287170.html.

National Center for Education Statistics. (2022). Bullying at school and electronic bullying. *Condition of Education*. U.S. Department of Education, Institute of Education Sciences. Retrieved September 27, 2024, from https://nces.ed.gov/programs/coe/indicator/a10.

Parsons, L. (2005). *Bullied teacher, bullied student: How to recognize the bullying culture in your school and what to do about it*. Pembroke.

Pittman, A.T. (2006a). Sexual harassment and due process. *Journal of Physical Education, Recreation & Dance, 77*(4), 10–11. https://doi.org/10.1080/07303084.2006.10597853

Pittman, A.T. (Ed.). (2006b). Negligence. *Journal of Physical Education, Recreation & Dance, 77*(9), 10–11. https://doi.org/10.1080/07303084.2006.10597933

Pittman, A.T. (2007). Pat-down inspections at sports events. *Journal of Physical Education, Recreation & Dance, 78*(8), 8–9. https://doi.org/10.1080/07303084.2007.10598067

Pittman, A.T., Sinelnikov, O.A., & Rawls, W.J. (2008). Strip searches in high school physical education. *Journal of Physical Education, Recreation & Dance, 79*(4), 10–11. https://doi.org/10.1080/07303084.2008.10598155

Prejean v. East Baton Rouge Parish School Board (1999). Retrieved September 27, 2024, from https://caselaw.findlaw.com/court/la-court-of-appeal/1154508.html.

Roper v. Simmons (2005). Retrieved September 27, 2024, from https://supreme.justia.com/cases/federal/us/543/551/

Rosenthal, M.B., Pagnano-Richardson, K., & Burak, L. (2010). Alternatives to using exercise as punishment. *Journal of Physical Education, Recreation & Dance, 81*(5), 44–48. https://doi.org/10.1080/07303084.2010.10598479

Sawyer, T.H., Carroll, M.S., & Connaughton, D.P. (2010). Bullying and legal liability. *Journal of Physical Education, Recreation & Dance, 81*(7), 51–53. https://doi.org/10.1080/07303084.2010.10598509

Sawyer, T.H., Miller, J., & Lanehart, B. (2013). Mismatching in youth sports. *Journal of Physical Education, Recreation & Dance, 75*(6), 14–15. https://doi.org/10.1080/07303084.2004.10607248

Sawyer, T.H. (Ed.), & Sawyer, T.H. (2010). Duty of care for informal recreational sports. *Journal of Physical Education, Recreation & Dance, 81*(5), 7–8. https://doi.org/10.1080/07303084.2010.10598471

Sawyer, T.H., Spengler, J.O., & Connaughton, D. (2003). School punishment and physical education. *Journal of Physical Education, Recreation & Dance, 74*(2), 12–13. https://doi.org./10.1080/07303084.2003.10608371

SHAPE America. (2025). *National physical education standards*. (4th ed.). Human Kinetics.

Snyder v. Morristown Central School District No. 1 (1990). Retrieved September 27, 2024, from https://casetext.com/case/snyder-v-morristown-central-sch-dist-no-1

Spengler, J.O., Anderson, P.M., Connaughton, D.P., & Baker, III, T.A. (2016). *Introduction to sport law* (2nd ed.). Human Kinetics.

State of New Hampshire V. Drake (1995). Retrieved September 27, 2024, from https://case-law.vlex.com/vid/state-v-drake-no-890429147

Stephens, T, & Hallas, J. (2006). *Bullying and sexual harassment*. Chandos.

StopBullying. (n.d.). Stop Bullying. Retrieved September 27, 2024, from www.stopbullying.gov/

Strauss, S.L. (2012). *Sexual harassment and bullying: A guide to keeping kids safe and holding schools accountable*. Rowman & Littlefield.

Tepper v. City of New Rochelle (1988). Retrieved September 27, 2024, from www.casemine.com/judgement/us/59148b72add7b04934522632

U.S. Const. amend. I. Retrieved September 27, 2024, from https://constitution.congress.gov/constitution/amendment-1/

U.S. Const. amend. V. Retrieved September 27, 2024, from https://constitution.congress.gov/constitution/amendment-5/

U.S. Const. amend. X. Retrieved September 27, 2024, from https://constitution.congress.gov/constitution/amendment-10/

U.S. Courts. (1969). Facts and Case Summary – Tinker v. Des Moines. Retrieved September 27, 2024, from www.uscourts.gov/educational-resources/educational-activities/facts-and-case-summary-tinker-v-des-moines

U.S. Courts. (1985). Facts and Case Summary – New Jersey v. T.L.O. Retrieved September 27, 2024, from http://"www.uscourts.gov/educational-resources/educational-activities/facts-and-case-summary-new-jersey-v-tlo

U.S. Courts. (2011). Facts and case Summary – J.D.B. v. North Carolina. Retrieved September 27, 2024, from www.uscourts.gov/educational-resources/educational-activities/facts-and-case-summary-jdb-v-north-carolina

U.S. Department of Education. (2010a). *Dear colleague letter, Office of the Assistant Secretary, bullying*. Office for Civil Rights. September 27, 2027, from www.ed.gov/laws-and-policy/education-policy/policy-guidance/dear-colleague-letter-from-assistant-secretary-for-civil-rights-russlynn-ali--pg-1

U.S. Department of Education. (2010b). *Title IX colleague letter (April 20, 2010) background, fast facts, and summary*. Office for Civil Rights. Retrieved June 20, 2018, from www2.ed.gov/about/offices/list/ocr/docs/title9-factsheet-20100420.pdf

U.S. Department of Education. (2012). *Dear Colleague Letter: Harassment and Bullying*. Retrieved September 27 2024, from: www2.ed.gov/about/offices/list/ocr/letters/colleague-201010.pdf

U.S. Department of Education. (2015). *Title IX and sex discrimination*. Office for Civil Rights. Retrieved September 27, 2024, from www.ed.gov/about/news/press-release/us-department-of-education-releases-final-title-ix-regulations-providing

U.S. Department of Justice. (2004). Americans With Disabilities Act. Retrieved September 27, 2024, from www.ada.gov/.

Westrick, R.L., & Lower, L.M. (2016). Transgender students: Are they a protected class? *Journal of Physical Education, Recreation & Dance, 87*(6), 44–46. https://doi.org/10.1080/07303084.2016.1192919

Chapter 12

Alliance for Excellent Education. (2007). *Tapping the potential: Retaining and developing high-quality new teachers*. Retrieved June 20, 2018, from http://all4ed.org/wp-content/uploads/2007/07/TappingThePotential.pdf

American Federation of Teachers. (2001, September). Beginning teacher induction: The essential bridge. *Policy Brief 13*.

American Federation of Teachers. (2017). *2017 Educator quality of work life study*. Retrieved June 20, 2018, from www.aft.org/sites/default/files/2017_eqwl_survey_web.pdf

Ballou, D., & Podgursky, M. (2000). Reforming teacher preparation and licensing: What is the evidence? *Teachers College Record, 102*(1): 2–7.

Barth, P., Dillon, N., Hull, J., & Holland Higgins, B. (2016). *Fixing the holes in the teacher pipeline: An overview of teacher shortages*. Center for Public Education (CPE). Retrieved October 22, 2024, from https://files.eric.ed.gov/fulltext/ED608871.pdf

Bowen, B. (2013). Measuring teacher effectiveness when comparing alternatively and traditionally licensed high school technology education teachers in North Carolina. *Journal of Technology Education, 25*(1), 82–100. https://eric.ed.gov/?id=EJ1020207

Boyd, D., Lankford, H., Loeb, S., & Wyckoff, J. (2004). The draw of home: How teachers' preferences for proximity disadvantage urban schools. *Journal* of Policy *Analysis and Management, 24*(1), 113–132.

Bureau of Labor Statistics. (2017). Number of jobs, labor market experience, and earning growth among Americans at 50: Results from a longitudinal study. Retrieved from www.bls.gov/news.release/archives/nlsoy_08242017.htm

Centers for Disease Control and Prevention (CDC). (2017). *Guide to promoting professional development*. U.S. Department of Health and Human Services (HHS).

Clement, M. (2008, January/February). Improving teacher selection with behavior-based interviewing. *Principal Magazine*, 44–47.

Cohen, D.K., & Hill, H.C. (2000). Instructional policy and classroom performance: The mathematics reform in California. *Teachers College Record, 102*(2), 294–343.

Curtis, R. (2010). Managing human capital to improve student achievement. In R.E. Curtis & J. Wurtzel (Eds.), *Teaching talent: A visionary framework for human capital in education* (pp. 17–37). Harvard Education Press.

Curtis, R., & Wurtzel, J. (2008). *Human capital framework for K-12 urban education:* Organizing *for success*. The Aspen Institute. Retrieved September 1, 2014, from www.aspeninstitute.org/sites/default/files/content/docs/pubs/FrameworkCombined_071708.pdf

Curtis, R., & Wurtzel, J. (Eds.). (2010). *Teaching talent: A visionary framework for human capital in education*. Harvard Education Press.

Darling-Hammond, L. (2000). Reforming teacher preparation and licensing: Debating the evidence. *Teachers College Record, 102*(1): 28–56.

Fink, S., & Markholt, A. (2011). *Leading for instructional improvement: How successful leaders develop teaching and learning expertise*. Jossey-Bass.

Fishman, B.J., Marx, R.W., Best, S., & Tal, R.T. (2003). Linking teacher and student learning to improve professional development in systemic reform. *Teaching and Teacher Education, 19*, 643–658.

Garet, M.S., Porter, A.C., Desimone, L.M., Birman, B.F., & Yoon, K.S. (2001). What makes professional development effective? Results from a national sample of teachers. *American Educational Research Journal, 38*(4), 915–945.

Gordon, R., Kane, T., & Staiger, D. (2006). *Identifying effective teachers using performance on the job*. The Brookings Institution.

Gray, L., & Taie, S. (2015). Public school teacher attrition and mobility in the first five years: Results from the first through fifth waves of the 2007–08 Beginning Teacher Longitudinal Study (NCES 2015–337). U.S. Department of Education. National Center for Education Statistics. http://nces.*ed*.gov/*pubsearch*

Guskey, T., & Sparks, D. (2004). Linking professional development to improvements in student learning. In E.M. Guyton & J.R. Dangel (Eds.), *Research linking teacher preparation and student performance: Teacher education yearbook XII* (pp. 233–247). Rowman & Littlefield Education.

Haj-Broussard, M., Hall, T., Allen, S., Stephens, C., Person, V., & Johnson, T. (2016). Alternative certification teacher and candidate retention: Measures of educator preparation, certification, and school staffing effectiveness. *Journal of the National Association for Alternative Certification, 11*(2), 4–13. https://eric.ed.gov/?id=EJ1122591

Ingersoll, R. (2003). *Is there really a teacher shortage?* Center for the Study of Teaching and Policy.

Ingersoll, R., & Smith, T. (2004). What are the effects of induction and mentoring on beginning teacher turnover? *American Educational Research Bulletin, 41*(3), 681–714.

Institute of Medicine (IOM). (2013). *Educating the student body: Taking physical activity and physical education to school*. The National Academies Press.

International Labour Organization. (2012). *Handbook of good human resource practices in the teaching profession*. Retrieved September 20, 2014, from www.ilo.org/wcmsp5/groups/public/---ed_dialogue/---sector/documents/publication/wcms_187793.pdf

Joiner, S., & Edwards, J. (2008). Novice teachers: Where are they going and why don't they stay? *Journal of Cross-Disciplinary Perspectives in Education, 1*(1), 36–43.

Jones, S.D., & Workman, E. (2016). *ESSA's well-rounded education*. Education Commission of the States. www.ecs.org/wp-content/uploads/ESSAs-Well-Rounded-Education-1.pdf

Karge, B.D., & McCabe, M. (2014). Quality alternative certification programs in special education ensure high retention. *Journal of the National Association for Alternative Certification, 9*(2), 24–43. https://eric.ed.gov/?id=EJ1019823

Kearns, P. (2005). *Human capital management*. Reed Business Information.

Kennedy, M. (1998). *Form and substance of inservice teacher education*. Research Monograph No. 13. University of Wisconsin–Madison, National Institute for Science Education.

Killion, J. (2007). *What works in the high school grades: Results-based staff development*. National Staff Development Council.

Konoske-Graf, A., Partelow, L., & Benner, M. (2016). *To attract great teachers, school districts must improve their human capital systems*. Center for American Progress. Retrieved September 27, 2024, from www.americanprogress.org/wp-content/uploads/sites/2/2016/12/HumanCapitalSurvey-report.pdf

Kraft, M.A., & Lyon, M.A. (2022). The rise and fall of the teaching profession: Prestige, interest, preparation, and satisfaction over the last half century (EdWorkingPaper: 22–679). Annenberg Institute at Brown University. https://doi.org/10.26300/7b1a-vk92

Liu, E., & Johnson, S.M. (2006). New teachers' experiences of hiring: Late, rushed, and information-poor. *Educational Administration Quarterly, 42*(3), 324–360.

Loucks-Horsley, S., & Matsumoto, C. (1999). Research on professional development for teachers of mathematics and science: The state of the scene. *School Science and Mathematics, 99*(5), 258–271.

Maciejewski, J. (2007). *Supporting new teachers*. District Administration. Retrieved September 9, 2014, from www.districtadministration.com/article/supporting-new-teachers

Milanowski, T., & Kimball, S. (2010). The principal as human capital manager. In R.E. Curtis & & J. Wurtzel (Eds.), *Teaching talent: A visionary framework for human capital in education* (pp. 69–90). Harvard Education Press.

National Center for Public Education. (2008, October 8). *Wanted: Good teachers*. Retrieved from www.centerforpubliceducation.org/Main-Menu/Staffingstudents/Wanted-Good-teachers

National Commission on Teaching and America's Future. (2003). *No dream denied: A pledge to* America's *children*. Retrieved September 9, 2014, from www.nctaf.org/documents/no-dream-denied_full-report .pdf

National Education Association. (n.d.). Collective bargaining: What it is and how it works. Retrieved October 25, 2014, from www.nea.org/assets/docs/120701-CBWhatisitandHow-itWorks-3page.pdf

National Labor Relations Act. 29 U.S.C. §§ 151–169. July 5, 1935. Retrieved October 25, 2014, from www.nlrb.gov/guidance/key-reference-materials/national-labor-relations-act#:~:text=In%201935%2C%20Congress%20passed%20the,FINDINGS%20AND%20POLICIES

New Teacher Project, The. (2012a, March). *Teacher talent toolbox*. Retrieved October 2, 2014, from http://tntp.org/assets/tools/RecruitmentandHiring_03.12_Final_3.pdf

New Teacher Project, The. (2012b). *The widget effect* (2nd ed.). Retrieved October 20, 2014, from http://tntp.org/assets/documents/TheWidgetEffect_2nd_ed.pdf

No Child Left Behind Act of 2001, P.L. 107–110, 20 U.S.C. § 6319 (2002).

Nyhus, J. (2024). *Why teacher recruitment needs to change*. Insight Educational Group. Retrieved September 27, 2024, from www.insighteducationgroup.com/blog/why-teacher-recruitment-needs-to-change#:~:text=In%20the%20end%2C%20every%20one,we%20can%20find%20and%20retain.&text=By%20retaining%20effective%20teachers%2C%20schools,and%20possibly%20increase%20student%20achievement.

OECD. (2019). *TALIS 2018 results (Volume I): Teachers and school leaders as lifelong learners*. OECD. https://doi.org/10.1787/1d0bc92a-en

Papay, J.P., & Qazilbash, E.K. (2021). *What do we know about teacher hiring? Using early, open, and intensive hiring processes to build the teacher workforce*. Annenberg Institute at Brown University. Retrieved September 27, 2024, from https://annenberg.brown.edu/sites/default/files/AIB%20-%20Teacher%20Hiring%20Brief%20-%20June%202021.pdf

Public Agenda. (2007). *Lessons learned: New teachers talk about their jobs, challenges and long-range plans*. National Comprehensive Center for Teacher Quality and Public Agenda. (Issue No. 2). Retrieved June 20, 2018, from https://files.eric.ed.gov/fulltext/ED499415.pdf

Public Agenda. (2008). *Lessons learned: New teachers talk about their jobs, challenges and long-range plans*. National Comprehensive Center for Teacher Quality and Public Agenda. (Issue No. 3). Retrieved June 20, 2018, from www.publicagenda.org/files/lessons_learned_3.pdf

Reaching Higher NH. (2024). *Teacher certification and student outcomes: What the research says*. Retrieved June 14, 2024, from https://reachinghighernh.org/2024/02/27/teacher-certification-and-student-outcomes-what-the-research-says

Rebore, R.W. (2001). *Human resources administration in education* (6th ed.). Allyn & Bacon.

Redding, C., & Smith, T.M. (2016). Easy in, easy out: Are alternatively certified teachers turning over at increased rates? *American Educational Research Journal*, *53*(4), 1086–1125. https://doi.org/10.3102/0002831216653206

Remer, C.W. (2017). *Educator policies and the Every Student Succeeds Act*. The Hunt Institute.

Schwartz, H.L., & Diliberti, M.K. (2022). *Flux in the educator labor market: Acute staff shortages and projected superintendent departures: Selected findings from the Fourth American School District Panel Survey*. RAND Corporation. www.rand.org/pubs/research_reports/RRA956-9.html

SHAPE America (2015). *Suggested job interview questions for prospective physical education teachers*. [Guidance document]. Retrieved June 14, 2024, from www.shapeamerica.org/Common/Uploaded%20files/document_manager/publications/resources/Job-Interview-Questions-for-Prospective-Physical-Education-Teachers.pdf

SHAPE America. (2025). *National physical education standards*. (4th ed.). Human Kinetics.

Stein, S., & Curtis, R. (2010). Principals as leaders of learning. In R.E. Curtis & J. Wurtzel (Eds.), *Teaching talent: A visionary framework for human capital in education* (pp. 91–109). Harvard Education Press.

Stovall, J.L., Smith Alvarez, K., Hinton, L., Pope, B., & Falol, A. (2024, May). *California policy opportunities to support teacher credentialing and diversity: Lessons from San Francisco* [Commentary]. Policy Analysis for California Education. https://edpolicyinca.org/newsroom/california-policy-opportunities-support-teacher-credentialing-and-diversity

Sutcher, L., Darling-Hammond, L., & Carver-Thomas, D. (2016). *A coming crisis in teaching? Teacher supply, demand, and shortages in the U.S.* Learning

Policy Institute. Retrieved June 20, 2018, from https://learningpolicyinstitute.org/product/coming-crisis-teaching-brief

Teachers of Tomorrow. (2023). *Every child deserves a great teacher.* Retrieved September 27, 2024, from www.teachersoftomorrow.org/

U.S. Department of Education. (2005, October 21). *Letter from Secretary of Education Margaret Spellings.* Retrieved October 2, 2014, from www2.ed.gov/policy/elsec/guid/secletter/051021.html

U.S. Equal Employment Opportunity Commission. (n.d.). *Prohibited employment policies/practices.* Retrieved September 12, 2014, from www.eeoc.gov/laws/practices/index.cfm

Wilson, S., Floden, R., & Ferrini-Mundy, J. (2001). *Teacher preparation research: Current knowledge, gaps, and recommendations.* Center for the Study of Teaching and Policy.

Woods, J.R. (2016). *Mitigating teacher shortages: Induction and mentoring.* Education Commission of the States. Retrieved June 20, 2018, from www.ecs.org/wp-content/uploads/Mitigating-Teacher-Shortages-Induction- Mentorship.pdf

Yoon, K.S., Duncan, T., Lee, S.W.-Y., Scarloss, B., & Shapley, K. (2007). *Reviewing the evidence on how teacher professional development affects student achievement (Issues & Answers Report, REL 2007–No. 033).* U.S. Department of Education, Institute of Education Sciences, National Center for Education Evaluation and Regional Assistance, Regional Educational Laboratory Southwest. Retrieved from http://ies.ed.gov/ncee/edlabs

Chapter 13

Buchmiller, A.A. (1979). *Planning-programming-budgeting-evaluating systems (revised).* Information Series 7(4). Division for Management, Planning, and Federal Services; Wisconsin Department of Public Instruction, p. 3. https://books.google.com/books?id=ex3cAAAAMAAJ&printsec=frontcover&source=gbs_ge_summary_r&cad=0#v=onepage&q&f=false

Center for Public Education. (2008). *Money matters: A primer on K-12 school funding.* National School Boards Association.

Department of Materials Management, Rockland, MD. (2016). *Montgomery County Public Schools procurement manual.* Waveland Press.

Ellerson, N. (2012). *School budgets 101.* American Association of School Administrators.

Florida Department of Education. (2023). *Funding for Florida school districts.* www.fldoe.org/core/fileparse.php/7507/urlt/Fefpdist.pdf

Florida Statutes. Section 112.313(2) (2024). Standards of conduct for public officers, employees of agencies, and local government attorneys. www.leg.state.fl.us/Statutes/index.cfm?App_mode=Display_Statute&Search_String=&URL=0100-0199/0112/Sections/0112.313.html

Florida Statutes. Section 112.313(3) (2024). Standards of conduct for public officers, employees of agencies, and local government attorneys. www.leg.state.fl.us/Statutes/index.cfm?App_mode=Display_Statute&Search_String=&URL=0100-0199/0112/Sections/0112.313.html

Florida Statutes. Section 112.313(7)a (2024). Standards of conduct for public officers, employees of agencies, and local government attorneys. www.leg.state.fl.us/Statutes/index.cfm?App_mode=Display_Statute&Search_String=&URL=0100-0199/0112/Sections/0112.313.html

Jensen, C.R., & Overman, S.J. (2003). *Administration and management of physical education and athletic programs.* Waveland Press.

Larkins, A. (2021, June 22). Everything you need to know about PPBS. *Decision Lens.* www.decisionlens.com/blog/everything-you-need-to-know-about-ppbs.

Miami-Dade County Public Schools. (2011). Code of Ethics for Conflict. Retrieved September 27, 2024, from https://districtartifacts.dadeschools.net/Standard%202/2.02/School%20Board%20Policy%20-%201210.01-Code%20of%20Ethics%20-%20Adminstrative.pdf

National Center for Educational Statistics. (2003). *Financial accounting for local and state school systems.* U.S. Department of Education.

Parkhouse, B.L. (2005). *The management of sport: Its foundation and application* (4th ed.). McGraw-Hill.

Pennsylvania Office of the Budget. (2017). *Chart of accounts for PA local educational agencies.* Retrieved June 20, 2018, from www.education.pa.gov/Documents/Teachers-Administrators/School%20Finances/Comptrollers%20Office/Chart%20of%20Accounts.pdf

Rennie Center for Educational Research and Policy. (2012). *Smart school budgeting: Resources for districts.*

Wisconsin Department of Public Instruction. (1979). *Planning programming budgeting evaluating systems* (Vol. 7, Number 4). Division for Management, Planning, and Federal Services.

Chapter 14

Brewer, E.W., Achilles, C.M., & Fuheiman, J.R. (1995). *Finding funding: Grantwriting and project management from start to finish* (2nd ed.). Corwin Press.

Browning, B.A. (2016). *Grant writing for dummies* (6th ed.). Wiley.

Florida Department of Education. (2023). Red Book: Chapter 8: School Internal Funds. Retrieved

September 27, 2024, from www.fldoe.org/core/fileparse.php/7507/urlt/REDBKCH8.pdf

Jones, S.D., & Workman, E. (2016). *ESSA's well-rounded education.* Education Commission of the States. www.ecs.org/wp-content/uploads/ESSAs-Well-Rounded-Education-1.pdf

Karsh, E., & Fox, A.S. (2014). *The only grant-writing book you'll ever need.* (4th ed.). Basic Books.

Moursand, D. (1996). Grantwriting for technology in education: Part 2 – The dollars and cents of grant writing. *Learning and Leading With Technology, 23*(5), 34–37.

National Institutes of Health. (n.d.). *Grants and funding.* Retrieved February 27, 2023, from https://grants.nih.gov/grants/how-to-apply-application-guide.html

Smith, N.B., & Works, E. (2006). *The complete book of grant writing.* Sourcebooks.

U.S. Department of Agriculture (USDA) (2024). *National School Lunch Program.* Food and Nutrition Services (FNS). Retrieved September 27, 2024, from www.fns.usda.gov/nslp

U.S. Department of Agriculture (USDA) (2024). *School Breakfast Program.* Food and Nutrition Services (FNS). Retrieved September 27, 2024, from www.fns.usda.gov/sbp/school-breakfast-program

Worth, M.J. (1993). *Educational fundraising: Principles and practices.* American Council on Education series. The Oryx Press.

Chapter 15

American Public Health Association (APHA). (2022a). *Healthy equity.* Retrieved October 10, 2024, from www.apha.org/Topics-and-Issues/Health-Equity

American Public Health Association (APHA). (2022b). *Racism and health.* Retrieved October 10, 2024, from www.apha.org/topics-and-issues/health-equity/racism-and-health

Bandura, A. (1997). *Self-Efficacy: The exercise of control.* W.H. Freeman.

Bessa, C., Hastie, P., Araújo, R., & Mesquita, I. (2019). What do we know about the development of personal and social skills within the sport education model: A systematic review. *Journal of Sports Science & Medicine, 18*(4), 812–829.

Blackshear, T., & Culp, B. (2023). *Critical race studies in physical education.* Human Kinetics.

CASEL (2019). Transformative SEL. Retrieved October 10, 2024, from https://casel.org/fundamentals-of-sel/how-does-sel-support-educational-equity-and-excellence/transformative-sel

CASEL. (2003). *Safe and sound: An educational leader's guide to evidence-based social and emotional learning (SEL) programs.*

CASEL. (2020). *CASEL SEL Framework.* Retrieved October 10, 2024, from https://casel.org/casel-sel-framework-11-2020.

CASEL. (2022a). *How does SEL support educational equity and excellence?* Brief. Retrieved October 10, 2024, from https://casel.org/fundamentals-of-sel/how-does-sel-support-educational-equity-and-excellence

CASEL. (2022b). *Program guide.* Retrieved October 10, 2024, from https://pg.casel.org/review-programs

CASEL. (2022c). *Mindful practices & class catalyst: An integrated SEL approach.* SEL Curriculum. Retrieved October 10, 2024, from https://pg.casel.org/mindful-practices-class-catalyst-an-integrated-sel-approach/

Casey, A. (2016). Models-based practice. In C.D. Ennis (Ed.), *Routledge handbook of physical education pedagogies* (pp. 54–67). Routledge.

Catalano, R., Berglund, M., Ryan, J., Lonczak, H., & Hawkins, J. (1998). Positive youth development in the United States: Research findings on evaluations of positive youth development programs. Retrieved October 10, 2024, from https://aspe.hhs.gov/reports/positive-youth-development-united-states-research-findings-evaluations-positive-youth-development-0

Centers for Disease Control and Prevention (CDC). (2018). *Physical activity guidelines for Americans* (2nd ed.). Retrieved October 10, 2024, from https://health.gov/our-work/nutrition-physical-activity/physical-activity-guidelines

Centers for Disease Control and Prevention (CDC). (2021a). *Components of the Whole School, Whole Community, Whole Child.* Retrieved October 10, 2024, from www.cdc.gov/healthyschools/wscc/components.htm

Centers for Disease Control and Prevention (CDC). (2021b). *Racism and health.* Retrieved October 10, 2024, from www.cdc.gov/minority-health/racism-health/index.html

Center for the Study and Prevention of Violence. (2019). *Blueprints for violence prevention.* University of Colorado Boulder, Institute of Behavioral Science, Center for the Study and Prevention of Violence. Retrieved October 10, 2024, from www.colorado.edu/cspv/blueprints

Character Strong. (2022). SEL and character education curriculum. Retrieved October 10, 2024, from https://characterstrong.com

Ciotto, C.M., & Gagnon, A.G. (2018). Promoting social and emotional learning in physical education. *Journal of Physical Education, Recreation & Dance, 89*(4), 27–33.

Committee for Children. (2011). *Second Step: Skills for social and academic success, Grade 2.*

Comer, J. (1988, November 1). Educating poor minority children. *Scientific American*. www.scientificamerican.com/article/educating-poor-minority-children.

Corcoran, R.P., Cheung, A.C.K., Kim, E., & Xie, C. (2018). Effective universal school-based social and emotional learning programs for improving academic achievement: A systematic review and meta-analysis of 50 years of research. *Educational Research Review, 25*(56–72). www.sciencedirect.com/science/article/abs/pii/S1747938X17300611.

Covey, F. (2022). *Leader in Me. The 7 habits of highly effective people. SEL Curriculum.* Retrieved October 10, 2024, from www.leaderinme.org/the-7-habits-of-highly-effective-people

Cross, T., Bazron, B., Dennis, K., & Isaacs, M. (1989). *Towards a culturally competent system of care* (Vol. I). Georgetown University Child Development Center, CASSP Technical Assistance Center. Retrieved October 10, 2024, from www.ojp.gov/ncjrs/virtual-library/abstracts/towards-culturally-competent-system-care-monograph-effective.

Durlak, J.A., Weissberg, R.P., Dymnicki, A.B., Taylor, R.D., & Schellinger, K.B. (2011). The impact of enhancing students' social and emotional learning: A meta-analysis of school-based universal interventions. *Child development, Society for Research in Child Development, 82*(1), 405–432. https://srcd.onlinelibrary.wiley.com/doi/10.1111/j.1467-8624.2010.01564.x

Dyson, B., & Casey, A. (2012). *Cooperative learning in physical education: A research-based approach.* Routledge.

Dyson, B., Howley, D., & Wright, P. (2020). *A scoping review critically examining research connecting social and emotional learning with three model-based practices in physical education: Have we been doing this all along?* https://doi.org/10.1177/1356336X20923710 https://journals.sagepub.com/eprint/HJBW2EKRQ5QBWTEC4AZQ/full

Ee, J., & Ong, C.W. (2014). Which social-emotional competencies are enhanced at a social emotional learning camp? *Journal of Adventure Education & Outdoor Learning, 14*(1), 24–41.

Edutopia. (2011). *Social and emotional learning: A short history.* Retrieved October 10, 2024, from www.edutopia.org/social-emotional-learning-history/

Equity in Education. (2018, June 13). Achievement Network. www.achievementnetwork.org/anetblog/eduspeak/equity-in-education

Evangelio, C., Sierra-Díaz, J., González-Víllora, S. & Fernandez-Rio, J. (2018). The Sport Education model in elementary and secondary education: A systematic review. *Movimento (ESEFID/UFRGS), 24*(3), 931.

Elias, M.J., Zins, J.E., Weissberg, R.P., Frey, K.S., Greenberg, M.T., Haynes, N.M., Kessler, R., Schwab-Stone, M.E. & Shriver, T.R. (1997). Promoting social and emotional learning: Guidelines for educators. *Association for Supervision and Curriculum Development*, VA. https://earlylearningfocus.org/wp-content/uploads/2019/12/promoting-social-and-emotional-learning-1.pdf

EVERFI. (2022). *Building healthy relationships and understanding compassion & empathy: Free digital character education lessons.* Retrieved October 10, 2024, from https://everfi.com/k-12/social-emotional-learning

Facing History and Ourselves. *SEL* curriculum. Retrieved October 10, 2024, from www.facinghistory.org

Federal Registrar. (2016). *Local school* wellness *policy implementation under the H*ealthy, Hunger-*Free Kids Act of 2010.* Retrieved October 10, 2024, from www.federalregister.gov/documents/2016/07/29/2016-17230/local-school-wellness-policy-implementation-under-the-healthy-hunger-free-kids-act-of-2010

Fernandez-Rio, J., & Iglesias, D. (2022) What do we know about pedagogical models in physical education so far? An umbrella review. *Physical Education and Sport Pedagogy, 29*(2), 190–205. https://doi.org/10.1080/17408989.2022.2039615

Ford, D. (2020). *Social-emotional learning for Black students is ineffective when it is culture-blind.* Diverse Issues in Higher Education. https://diverseeducation.com/article/166341

Gagnon, A.G. (2016). Creating a positive social-emotional climate in your elementary physical education program. *Strategies, 29*(3), 21–27.

Goleman, D. (1994). *Emotional Intelligence: Why it can matter more than IQ.* Bantam Books.

Gordon, B., Jacobs, J.M., & Wright, P.M. (2016). Social and emotional learning through a teaching personal and social responsibility based after-school program for disengaged middle-school boys. *Journal of Teaching in Physical Education, 35*(4), 358–369.

Haffar, S., Bazerbachi, F., & Murad, M. H. (2019). *Peer review bias: A critical review. Mayo Clinic Proceedings, 94*(4), 670–676. https://doi.org/10.1016/j.mayocp.2018.09.004

Hannigan, T.P. (2007). Homesickness and acculturation stress in the international student. In M. van Tilburg & A. Vingerhoets (Eds.), *Psychological aspects of geographical moves: Homesickness and acculturation stress* (2021, pp. 63–72). Amsterdam University Press. https://doi.org/10.1017/9789048504169

Hart, A. (2020). *The OPEN priority learning outcomes for trauma informed social and emotional learning.* OPEN. Retrieved October 10, 2024, from https://openphysed.org/best-practices/priority-outcomes.

Health.Moves.Minds. (2022). Amplify Kindness-Building Together. SHAPE America. Retrieved October 10, 2024, from www.shapeamerica.org/Document_manager/healthmovesminds/Grades 9-12/Mini%20Lessons_GR%209-12%20Amplify%20Kindness-Building%20Together_AUG22.pdf

Health.Moves.Minds. (2019). Being Mindful, Being Kind Lesson. SHAPE America. Retrieved October 10, 2024, from www.shapeamerica.org/uploads/pdfs/events/hmm/K-2Lessons_MAY19_Lesson1.pdf

Health.Moves.Minds. (2019). Empowered Mind & Body-Physical Education. SHAPE America. Retrieved October 10, 2024, from www.shapeamerica.org/uploads/healthmovesminds/resources/education-materials/6-8/lessons/6-8_PE-Lessons.pdf

Healthy, Hunger-Free Kids Act of 2010, Public Law 296, U.S. Statutes at Large 124 (2010): 3183-3266. www.govinfo.gov/app/details/STATUTE-124/STATUTE-124-Pg3183.

Hellison, D. (1995). *Teaching personal and social responsibility through physical activity.* Human Kinetics.

Jacobs, J., & Wright, P. (2014). Social and emotional learning policies and physical education. *Strategies 27*(6), 42–44.

Jones, S., Brush, K., Ramirez, T., Mao, Z. X., Marenus, M., Wettje, S., Finney, K., Raisch, N., Podoloff, N., Kahn, J., Barnes, S., Stickle, L., Brion-Meisels, G.. McIntyre, J., Cuartas, J., & Bailey, R. (2017). *Navigating SEL from the inside out: Looking inside & across 25 leading SEL programs: A practical resource for schools and OST providers (Elementary School Focus).* The Wallace Foundation.

Jones, S.M., & Doolittle, E.J. (2017). Social and emotional learning: Introducing the issue. *The Future of Children,* 27, 3–11. https://doi.org/10.1353/foc.2017.0000.

Kaler-Jones, C. (2020). *When SEL is used as another form of policing.* Communities for Just Schools Fund. https://medium.com/@justschools/when-sel-is-used-as-another-form-of-policing-fa53cf85dce4

Kendi, I. (2019). *How to be an anti-racist.* One World New York.

Korpershoek, H., Harms, T., de Boer, H., van Kuijk, M., & Doolaard, S. (2016). A meta-analysis of the effects of classroom management strategies and classroom management programs on students academic, behavioral, emotional, and motivational outcomes. *Review of Educational Research, 86*(3):643–680. https://doi.org/10.3102/0034654315626799

Love, B. (2016) Anti-Black state violence, classroom edition: The spirit murdering of Black children. *Journal of Curriculum and Pedagogy, 13*(1), 22–25. https://doi.org/10.1080/15505170.2016.1138258

Lubans, D., Plotnikoff, R., & Lubans, N. (2011). Review: A systematic review of the impact of physical activity programmes on social and emotional well-being in at-risk youth. *Child and Adolescent Mental Health, 17*(1), 2–13. https://doi.org/10.1111/j.1475-3588.2011.00623.x

Minow, M. (2021). EQUALITY VS. EQUITY. *American Journal of Law and Equality, 2021*(1), 167–193. https://doi.org/10.1162/ajle_a_00019

Mitchell, S., Oslin, J., Griffin, L. (2021). *Teaching sport concepts and skills* (4th Ed.). Human Kinetics.

Montgomery County Public Schools (n.d.). be Well 365. Retrieved October 10, 2024, from www.montgomeryschoolsmd.org/departments/studentservices/wellbeing/index-new/

National Association of School Psychologists (NASP). (2015). *Trauma: Brief facts and tips.* Retrieved October 10, 2024, from www.nasponline.org/resources-and-publications/resources/school-safety-and-crisis/trauma

NASPE (1995). *Moving into the future: National standards for physical education.* McGraw-Hill.

National Center for Injury Prevention and Control, Division of Violence Prevention. (2019). *Preventing adverse childhood experiences (ACEs): Leveraging the best available evidence.* Centers for Disease Control and Prevention (CDC).Retrieved October 10, 2024, from https://stacks.cdc.gov/view/cdc/82316

National Survey of Children's Health (NSCH). (2011). Data query from the Child and Adolescent Health Measurement Initiative, Data Resource Center for Child and Adolescent Health website. Retrieved October 10, 2024, from www.childhealthdata.org

National Child Traumatic Stress Network (NCTSN). (2019). *What is child trauma?* Retrieved October 10, 2024, from www.nctsn.org/what-is-child-trauma

Paluck, E., Porat, R., Clark, C., and Green, D. (2021). Prejudice reeducation: Progress and challenges. *Annual Review of Psychology 2021,* 72, 533–60. https://doi.org/10.1146/annurev-psych-071620-030619

PATHS (2022). SEL Curriculum. Retrieved October 10, 2024, from https://pathsprogram.com

Paluk, E., Porat, R., Clark, C., & Green, D. (2020). Replication Data for Prejudice reduction. Harvard Dataverse, V1, UNF:6:4Gp3QettX/qWjT-1fVDVOrQ== [fileUNF] Retrieved October 10, 2024, from https://dataverse.harvard.edu/dataset.xhtml?persistentId=doi%3A10.7910%2FDVN%2FODACR5

Playworks (2022). SEL Curriculum. Retrieved October 10, 2024, from www.playworks.org/services/playworks-pro/?utm_source=region_redirect&utm_content=greater-washington-dc®ion_redirect=greater-washington-dc

Price, A. (2019). Using outdoor learning to augment social and emotional learning (SEL) skills in young people with social, emotional and behavioural difficulties (SEBD). *Journal of Adventure Education and Outdoor Learning, 19*(4), 315–328.

QuaverEd. (2022). *SEL curriculum.* Retrieved October 10, 2024, from www.quavered.com/ready/

Retrieved October 10, 2024, from www.eduguide.org/content

Rivera, R.C., & Arauz, J.C. (2019). Understanding and practicing cultural competence in helping youth thrive. In D. Osher, M.J. Mayer, R.J. Jagers, K. Kendziora, & L. Wood. (Eds), *Keeping students safe and helping them thrive* (pp 142–158). Praeger.

Safir, S. (2016, March 14). *5 Keys to challenging implicit bias.* Retrieved October 10, 2024, from www.edutopia.org/blog/keys-to-challenging-implicit-bias-shane-safir

Second Step.(n.d.). *Early learning curriculum.* Retrieved October 10, 2024, from www.secondstep.org

Second Step. (n.d.). *Elementary curriculum.* Retrieved October 10, 2024, from www.secondstep.org

Second Step.(n.d.). *Middle school curriculum.* Retrieved October 10, 2024, from www.secondstep.org

SEL CATCH Journeys (2022). CATCH Coordinated Approach to Child Health. SEL Curriculum. Retrieved October 10, 2024, from https://catch.org/what-we-do/sel

SHAPE America. (2019), *Physical Education/SEL Crosswalk.* www.shapeamerica.org/standards/guidelines/sel-crosswalk.aspx

SHAPE America. (2022). *Health. moves. minds.* www.shapeamerica.org/MemberPortal/events/healthmovesminds/

Simmons, D. (2019, October). How to be an antiracist educator. *Education Update Newsletter, 61*(10). Association for Supervision and Curriculum Development. Retrieved October 10, 2024, from https://ascd.org/el/articles/how-to-be-an-antiracist-educator

Simmons, D. (2021, March). *Why SEL alone isn't enough, 78*(6). Association for Supervision and Curriculum Development. Retrieved October 10, 2024, from www.ascd.org/el/articles/why-sel-alone-isnt-enough

Srinivasan, M. (2019). Transformative social and emotional learning (SEL) as a catalyst for climate action. *Journal of Global Transformation. 21*(3). Retrieved October 10, 2024, from www.kosmosjournal.org/kj_article/sel-catalyst-climate-action/

Substance Abuse and Mental Health Services Administration (SAMHSA). *Trauma and violence.* Retrieved October 10, 2024, from www.samhsa.gov/trauma-violence#:~:text=SAMHSA%20addresses%20the%20impact%20of,the%20healing%20and%20recovery%20process

Sutherland, S., & Legge, M. (2016), The possibilities of "doing" outdoor and/or adventure education in physical education/teacher education. *Journal of Teaching in Physical Education, 35*(4), 299–312.

Taylor, R.D., Oberle, E., Durlak, J.A., & Weissberg, R.P. (2017). Promoting positive youth development through school-based sand emotional learning interventions: A Meta-Analysis of follow-up effects. *Child Development,* July:88(4):1156–1171. https://doi.org/10.1111/cdev.12864

Timken, G., & McNamee, J. (2012). New perspectives for teaching physical education: Preservice teachers' reflections on outdoor and adventure education. *Journal of Teaching in Physical Education, 31*(1), 21–38.

U.S. Department of Health and Human Services (HHS). (2018). *Physical activity guidelines for americans.* (2nd ed.). https://health.gov/our-work/nutrition-physical-activity/physical-activity-guidelines

Western States Center. (2003). Dismantling racism: A resource book for social change groups. *Global Library for Antiracism & Digital Citizenship.* Accessed October 10, 2024, from https://sacred.omeka.net/items/show/221

Will, M. & Najarro, I. (2022). Culturally Responsive Teaching. *Education Week.* October, 2024. Retrieved October 10, 2024, from www.edweek.org/teaching-learning/culturally-responsive-teaching-culturally-responsive-pedagogy/2022/04

Chapter 16

Aikens, N.L., & Barbarin, O. (2008). Socioeconomic differences in reading trajectories: The contribution of family, neighborhood, and school contexts. *Journal of Educational Psychology, 100*(2), 235–251.

Alfrey, L., & Jeanes, R. (2021). Challenging ableism and the 'disability as problem' discourse: How initial teacher education can support the inclusion of students with a disability in physical education. *Sport, Education and Society.* [Advance online publication]. https://doi.org/10.1080/13573322.2021.2019698

Americans with Disabilities Act of 1990, 42 U.S.C. § 12101 *et seq.* (1990). www.ada.gov/pubs/adastatute08.htm

Åsebø, S.E., & Løvoll, H.S. (2021). Exploring coping strategies in physical education. A qualitative case study. *Physical Education and Sport Pedagogy.* [Advance online publication]. https://doi.org/10.1080/17408989.2021.1976743

Azzarito, L., Simon, M., & Marttinen, R. (2016). "Stop photoshopping!": A visual participatory inquiry into students' responses to a body curriculum. *Journal of Teaching in Physical Education*, *35*(1), 54–69.

Azzarito, L., & Solomon, M.A. (2005). A reconceptualization of physical education: The intersection of gender/race/social class. *Sport, Education and Society*, *10*(1), 25–47.

Azzarito, L., Solomon, M.A., & Harrison Jr., L. (2006). ". . . If I had a choice, I would. . . ." A feminist poststructuralist perspective on girls in physical education. *Research Quarterly for Exercise and Sport*, *77*(2), 222–239.

Berg, P., & Kokkonen, M. (2022). Heteronormativity meets queering in physical education: The views of PE teachers and LGBTIQ+ students. *Physical Education and Sport Pedagogy*, *27*(4), 368–381.

Bevans, K. B., Fitzpatrick, L., Sanchez, B. M., Riley, A. W., & Forrest, C. (2010). Physical education resources, class management, and student physical activity levels: A structure-process-outcome approach to evaluating physical education effectiveness. *Journal of School Health*, *80*(12), 573–580.

Cahn, S.K. (2015). *Coming on strong: Gender and sexuality in women's sport*. University of Illinois Press.

Carlson, J.A., Mignano, A.M., Norman, G.J., McKenzie, T.L., Kerr, J., Arredondo, E.M., Madanat, H., Cain, K.L., Elder, J.P., Saelens, B.E., & Sallis, J.F. (2014). Socioeconomic disparities in elementary school practices and children's physical activity during school. *American Journal of Health Promotion*, *28*(Suppl 3), S47–S53.

Cheypator-Thomson, J.R., You, J., & Hardin, B. (2000). Issues and perspectives on gender in physical education. *Women in Sport and Physical Activity Journal*, *9*(2), 99–121.

Clarke, G. (1996). Conforming and contesting with (a) difference: How lesbian students and teachers manage their identities." *International Studies in Sociology of Education*, *6*(2), 191–209.

Clarke, G. (1998). Voices from the margins: Regulation and resistance in the lives of lesbian teachers. In M. Erben (Ed.), *Biography and education: A reader* (pp. 59–71). Falmer Press.

Clotfelter, C.T., Ladd, H.F., & Vigdor, J.L. (2006). Teacher-student matching and the assessment of teacher effectiveness. *Journal of Human Resources*, *41*(4), 778–820.

Constantinou, P., Manson, M., & Silverman, S. (2009). Female students' perceptions about gender-role stereotypes and their influence on attitude toward physical education. *Physical Educator*, *66*(2), 85.

Curtner-Smith, M. (2017). Acculturation, recruitment, and the development of orientations. In K.A.R. Richards & K.L. Gaudreault (Eds.), *Teacher socialization in physical education: New perspectives* (pp. 33–46). Routledge.

Dagkas, S., Benn, T., & Jawad, H. (2011). Multiple voices: Improving participation of Muslim girls in physical education and school sport. *Sport, Education and Society*, *16*(2), 223–239.

Douglas, D.D., & Halas, J.M. (2013). The wages of whiteness: Confronting the nature of ivory tower racism and the implications for physical education. *Sport, Education and Society*, *18*(4), 453–474.

Every Student Succeeds Act, 20 U.S.C. § 6301 (2015). www.congress.gov/bill/114th-congress/senate-bill/1177

Flintoff, A., & Dowling, F. (2019). 'I just treat them all the same, really': Teachers, whiteness and (anti) racism in physical education. *Sport, Education and Society*, *24*(2), 121–133.

Flintoff, A., Dowling, F., & Fitzgerald, H. (2015). Working through whiteness, race and (anti) racism in physical education teacher education. *Physical Education and Sport Pedagogy*, *20*(5), 559–570.

Flintoff, A., & Scraton, S. (2001). Stepping into active leisure? Young women's perceptions of active lifestyles and their experiences of school physical education. *Sport, Education and Society*, *6*(1), 5–21.

Flintoff, A., & Scraton, S. (2006). Girls and physical education. In D. Kirk, D. Macdonald, & M. O'Sullivan (Eds.), *The handbook of physical education* (pp. 767–783). Sage.

Flory, S.B., & McCaughtry, N. (2011). Culturally relevant physical education in urban schools: Reflecting cultural knowledge. *Research Quarterly for Exercise and Sport*, *82*(1), 49–60.

Gay, G. (2018). *Culturally responsive teaching: Theory, research, and practice*. Teachers College Press.

Gill, D.L., Morrow, R.G., Collins, K.E., Lucey, A.B, & Schultz, A.M. (2010). Perceived climate in physical activity settings. *Journal of Homosexuality*, *57*(7), 895–913.

Goodwin, D.L., & Rossow-Kimball, B. (2012). Thinking ethically about professional practice in adapted physical activity. *Adapted Physical Activity Quarterly*, *29*, 295–309.

Griffin, P.S. (1984). Girls' participation patterns in a middle school team sports unit. *Journal of Teaching in Physical Education*, *4*(1), 30–38.

Griffin, P.S. (1985). Boys' participation styles in a middle school physical education team sports unit. *Journal of Teaching in Physical Education*, *4*(2), 100–110.

Griffin, P.S. (1991). Identity management strategies among lesbian and gay educators. *International Journal of Qualitative Studies in Education*, *4*, 189–202.

Griffin, P.S. (1998). *Strong women, deep closets: Lesbians and homophobia in sport*. Human Kinetics.

Haegele, J.A. (2019). Inclusion illusion: Questioning the inclusiveness of integrated physical education. *Quest, 71*(4), 387–397.

Haegele, J.A., & Sutherland, S. (2015). Perspectives of students with disabilities toward physical education: A qualitative inquiry review. *Quest, 67*(3), 255–273.

Hodge, S.R., Kozub, F.M., Dixson, A.D., Moore III, J.L., & Kambon, K. (2008). A comparison of high school students' stereotypic beliefs about intelligence and athleticism. *Educational Foundations, 22*, 99–119.

Holland, K., & Haegele, J.A. (2021). Perspectives of students with disabilities toward physical education: A review update 2014–2019. *Kinesiology Review, 10*(1), 78–87.

Holland, S.K., & Haegele, J.A. (2020). Socialization experiences of first-year adapted physical education teachers with a master's degree. *Adapted Physical Activity Quarterly, 37*, 304–323.

Hughey, M. (2014). White backlash in the 'post-racial' United States. *Ethnic and Racial Studies, 37*(5), 721–730.

Individuals with Disabilities Education Act, 20 U.S.C. § 1400 (2004). https://sites.ed.gov/idea

Joint Center for Housing Studies of Harvard University (JCHS). (2020). America's rental housing 2020. www.jchs.harvard.edu/sites/default/files/reports/files/Harvard_JCHS_Americas_Rental_Housing_2020.pdf

Katzmarzyk, P.T., Denstel, K.D., Beals, K., Carlson, J., Crouter, S.E., McKenzie, T.L., Pate, R.R., Sisson, S.B., Staiano, A.E., Stanish, H., Ward, D.S., Whitt-Glover, M., & Wright, C. (2018). Results from the United States 2018 report card on physical activity for children and youth. *Journal of Physical Activity and Health, 15*(Suppl 2), S422-S424.

Ladson-Billings, G. (1995). But that's just good teaching! The case for culturally relevant pedagogy. *Theory into Practice, 34*(3), 159–165.

Ladson-Billings, G. (2004). *Crossing over to Canaan: The journey of new teachers in diverse classrooms.* John Wiley & Sons.

Ladson-Billings, G. (2004). Landing on the wrong note: The price we paid for *Brown. Educational Researcher, 33*(7), 3–13.

Ladson-Billings, G. (2014). Culturally relevant pedagogy 2.0: Aka the remix. *Harvard Educational Review, 84*(1), 74–84.

Landi, D. (2018). Toward a queer inclusive physical education. *Physical Education and Sport Pedagogy, 23*(1), 1–15.

Landi, D. (2019). Queer men, affect, and physical education. *Qualitative Research in Sport, Exercise and Health, 11*(2), 168–187.

Landi, D., Flory, S.B., Safron, C., & Marttinen, R. (2020). LGBTQ research in physical education: A rising tide? *Physical Education and Sport Pedagogy, 25*(3), 259–273.

Laureano, J., Konukman, F., Gümüşdăg, H., Erdŏgan, S., Yu, J., & Çekin, R. (2014). Effects of marginalization on school physical education programs: A literature review. *Physical Culture and Sport: Studies and Research, 64*, 29–40.

Leonardo, Z. (2007). The war on schools: NCLB, nation creation, and the educational construction of whiteness. *Race, Ethnicity and Education, 10*(3), 261–278.

Lynch, S., Sutherland, S., & Walton-Fisette, J. (2020). The A–Z of social justice physical education: Part 1. *Journal of Physical Education, Recreation & Dance, 91*(4), 8–13.

Mäkelä, K., Hirvensalo, M., & Whipp, P.R. (2014). Should I stay or should I go? Physical education teachers' career intentions. *Research Quarterly for Exercise & Sport, 85*, 234–244.

McDonald, B. (2013). The reproduction of biological 'race' through physical education textbooks and curriculum. *European Physical Education Review, 19*(2), 183–198.

Mistry, R.S., Benner, A.D., Tan, C.S., & Kim, S.Y. (2009). Family economic stress and academic well-being among Chinese-American youth: The influence of adolescents' perceptions of economic strain. *Journal of Family Psychology,* 23(3), 279–290.

Mooney, A., & Hickey, C. (2012). Negotiating masculine hegemony: Female physical educators in an all-boys' school. *Asia-Pacific Journal of Health, Sport and Physical Education, 3*(3), 199–212.

Morrow, R.G., & Gill, D.L. (2003). Perceptions of homophobia and heterosexism in physical education. *Research Quarterly for Exercise and Sport, 74*(2), 205–214.

National Center for Education Statistics (NCES). (2021). *Annual report: Condition of education.* Retrieved October 10, 2024, from https://nces.ed.gov/programs/coe/indicator/cge

National Center for Education Statistics (NCES). (2022). *Public school revenue sources.* https://nces.ed.gov/programs/coe/indicator/cma/public-school-revenue#fn3

Nicaise, V., Bois, J.E., Fairclough, S.J., Amorose, A.J., & Cogérino, G. (2007). Girls' and boys' perceptions of physical education teachers' feedback: Effects on performance and psychological responses. *Journal of Sports Sciences, 25*(8), 915–926.

Oliver, K.L., Hamzeh, M., & McCaughtry, N. (2009). Girly girls can play games/las niñas pueden jugar tambien: Co-creating a curriculum of possibilities with fifth-grade girls. *Journal of Teaching in Physical Education, 28*(1), 90–110.

Oliver, K.L., & Kirk, D. (2015). *Girls, gender and physical education: An activist approach*. Routledge.

Perez, R.J., Robbins, C.K., Harris, L.W., & Montgomery, C. (2020). Exploring graduate students' socialization to equity, diversity, and inclusion. *Journal of Diversity in Higher Education, 13*(2), 133–145.

Petrie, K., Devcich, J., & Fitzgerald, H. (2018). Working toward inclusive physical education in a primary school: 'Some days I just don't get it right'. *Physical Education & Sport Pedagogy, 22*(4), 345–357.

Picus, L.O., & Odden, A.R. (2011). Reinventing school finance: Falling forward. *Peabody Journal of Education, 86*, 291–303.

Pugach, M.C., Matewos, A.M., & Gomez-Najarro, J. (2021). Disability and the meaning of social justice in teacher education research: A precarious guest at the table? *Journal of Teacher Education, 72*(2), 237–250.

Rich, E. (2004). Exploring teachers' biographies and perceptions of girls' participation in physical education. *European Physical Education Review, 10*(2), 215–240.

Richards, K.A.R., Holland, S.K., Wilson, W.J., Trad, A., & Stearns, J. (2023). A qualitative inquiry into the workplace experiences of adapted physical education teachers. *Sport, Education and Society*. [Advance online publication]/www.tandfonline.com/doi/abs/10.1080/13573322.2021.2007874

Richards, K.A.R., Wilson, W.J., Holland, S.K., & Haegele, J.A. (2020). The relationship among perceived organizational support, resilience, perceived mattering, emotional exhaustion, and job satisfaction in adapted physical educators. *Adapted Physical Activity Quarterly, 37*, 90–111.

Sherrill, C. (1994). Least restrictive environments and total inclusion philosophies: Critical analysis. *Palaestra, 10*(3), 25–35.

Shiver, V.N., Richards, K.A.R., & Hemphill, M.A. (2020). Preservice teachers' learning to implement culturally relevant physical education with the teaching personal and social responsibility model. *Physical Education and Sport Pedagogy, 25*(3), 303–315.

Simon, M., & Azzarito, L. (2018). 'Singled out because of skin color . . .': Exploring ethnic minority female teachers' embodiment in physical education. *Sport, Education and Society, 24*(2), 105–120.

Simon, M., & Azzarito, L. (2019). "Putting blinders on": Ethnic minority female PE teachers' identity struggles negotiating racialized discourses. *Journal of Teaching in Physical Education, 38*(4), 367–376.

Simon, M., & Boyd, K. (2021). Cracks in the narrative: Black and Latinx pre-service PE teachers in predominantly white PETE programs. *Physical Education and Sport Pedagogy*, 1–17.

Simon, M., Lee, J., Evans, M., Sucre, S., & Azzarito, L. (2021). A call for social justice researchers: Intersectionality as a framework for the study of human movement and education. *Kinesiology Review, 11*(2), 1–9. https://doi.org/10.1123/kr.2021-0009

Sparkes, A.C. (1997). Ethnographic fiction and representing the absent other. *Sport, Education and Society, 2*(1), 25–40.

Stainback, W., & Stainback, S. (1996). Collaboration, support network and community construction. In S. Stainback & W. Stainback (Eds.), *Inclusion: A guide for educators* (pp. 223–232). Paul H. Brookes.

Steele, C.M., & Aronson, J. (1995). Stereotype threat and the intellectual test performance of African Americans. *Journal of Personality and Social Psychology, 69*, 797–811.

Sykes, H. (1996). Constr (i)(u)cting lesbian identities in physical education: Feminist and poststructural approaches to researching sexuality. *Quest, 48*(4), 459–469.

Sykes, H. (2011). *Queer bodies: Sexualities, genders, & fatness in physical education*. Peter Lang.

Turner, L., Johnson, T.G., Calvert, H.G., & Chaloupka, F.J. (2017). Stretched too thin? The relationship between insufficient resource allocation and physical education instructional time and assessment practices. *Teaching and Teacher Education, 68*, 210–219.

U.S. Department of Agriculture (USDA). (2022). Key statistics & graphics. www.ers.usda.gov/topics/food-nutrition-assistance/food-security-in-the-u-s/key-statistics-graphics/#children

Vertinsky, P.A. (1992). Reclaiming space, revisioning the body: The quest for gender-sensitive physical education. *Quest, 44*(3), 373–396.

Walker, T.J., Craig, D.W., Pavlovic, A., Thiele, S., & Kohl III, H.W. (2020). Associations between gender, school socioeconomic status, and cardiorespiratory fitness among elementary and middle school students. *BMC Public Health, 20*, 1–8.

Ware, H., Singal, N., & Groce, N. (2022). The work lives of disabled teachers: Revisiting inclusive education in English schools. *Disability & Society, 37*(9), 1417–1438. https://doi.org/10.1080/09687599.2020.1867074

Wilson, W.J., Haegele, J.A., & Kelly, L.E. (2020). Revisiting the narrative about least restrictive environment in physical education. *Quest, 72*(1), 19–32.

Wilson, W.J., Kelly, L.E., & Haegele, J.A. (2020). "We're asking teachers to do more with less": Perspectives on least restrictive environment implementation in physical education. *Sport Education and Society, 25*(9), 1058–1071.

Wilson, W.J., Theriot, E.A., Richards, K.A., Trad, A.M., & Shriner, L. (2021). Experiential learning and inclusion through service-learning: Recommendations for kinesiology to support students and people with impairments. *Quest, 73*(3), 245–263.

Wilson, W.J., & Richards, K.A.R. (2019). Socialization of preservice adapted physical educators: Influence of teacher education. *Adapted Physical Activity Quarterly, 36*(4), 472–491.

Woods, S.E., & Harbeck, K.M. (1992). Living in two worlds: The identity management strategies used by lesbian physical educators. *Journal of Homosexuality, 22*(3–4), 141–166.

Index

Note: The italicized *f* and *t* following page numbers refer to figures and tables, respectively.

D

F

G

H

I

Q

T

About the Authors

© Jayne Greenberg

Jayne Greenberg, EdD, is the North America chair for the International Sport and Culture Association, the educational advocate and policy specialist for the University of Miami Miller School of Medicine and Kidz Neuroscience center, and the youth movement ambassador for the Life Time Foundation. Previously, she served as the director of the I Can Do It! program for the U.S. Department of Health and Human Services and was the district director of physical education and health literacy for Miami-Dade County Public Schools for 22 years.

Throughout her professional educational career, she has served as special advisor on youth fitness to the President's Council on Physical Fitness and Sports, president of FAHPERD, and chair of the sport development committee for the United States Olympic Committee and USA Field Hockey. In addition, she coordinated the Olympic Torch Relay Miami Leg for the Olympic Winter Games in Salt Lake City.

Greenberg has received numerous awards and accolades throughout her career, including induction into the SHAPE America Hall of Fame in 2019, the 2016 North America Society of HPERD Professionals Award; and the Lifetime of Giving Award from Delta Psi Kappa in 2017. Other highlights include being named the 2005 National Physical Education Administrator of the Year by the National Association for Sport and Physical Education; being appointed by President Obama to serve on the President's Council on Sports, Fitness, and Nutrition in 2011; and being named education sector chair for the National Physical Activity Plan.

Greenberg has served as an international consultant in many capacities. She coordinated Olympic education programs in Canada; developed the sport science curriculum at the University of Malaya in Kuala Lumpar, Malaysia; and developed a math and science sailing curriculum for the National Maritime Museum and Royal Observatory in London, England, and Sydney, Australia. She also developed a conservation safari in South Africa and developed the drug education curriculum for Antigua. She has authored several books, published numerous articles, and been a speaker at numerous state, national, and international conventions and meetings, including presenting at an International Olympic Committee meeting in Singapore. In the past 12 years, she has secured over $35 million in federal and foundation grants for educational programs.

© Judy LoBianco

Judy LoBianco is the president and CEO of HPE Solutions LLC, a consulting firm that helps advance teacher practice. She was previously an adjunct professor at Monmouth University and a supervisor of health and physical education for Livingston Public Schools in New Jersey. With over 30 years of experience in health and physical education, she has taught all levels, from kindergarten through college.

Formerly of the South Orange–Maplewood School District, LoBianco won two federal grants from the U.S. Department of Education totaling $2.74 million to revolutionize the district's K-12 physical education program. She has dedicated her professional service to several organizations, serving as president of the New Jersey Association for Health, Physical Education, Recreation and Dance; president of the Eastern District of the American Alliance for Health, Physical Education, Recreation and Dance; and president of SHAPE America (Society of Health and Physical Educators). She was named the 2013 National PE Administrator of the Year.

About the Contributors

Nichole Barta, EdD, is the director for the Center of Teaching & Advising (CTA) at Gonzaga University in Spokane, Washington. She is an associate professor in the kinesiology and sport management department; she taught physical education pedagogy courses for seven years before transitioning to her current role in faculty development. Before joining Gonzaga, she was a district health and physical education instructional specialist for 2 years and a high school health and physical education teacher for 15 years. Dr. Barta has coauthored the book *Designing and Teaching Fitness Education Courses*, and she has written health and physical education curricula for several state organizations and school districts. Dr. Barta holds an MEd in curriculum and instruction with a concentration in teaching and learning, as well as an EdD in doctoral studies in education and a program administration certificate from Seattle Pacific University. She holds the National Strength & Conditioning Association (NSCA) Certified Strength and Conditioning Specialist (CSCS) and American College of Sports Medicine Certified Personal Trainer (ACSM-CPT) credentials.

Erin E. Centeio, PhD, is currently an associate professor in the College of Education, department of kinesiology and rehabilitation science at the University of Hawai'i at Mānoa. Dr. Centeio completed her undergraduate degree in kinesiology with an emphasis in physical education as well as her master's degree in kinesiology at the University of Illinois at Urbana-Champaign. She taught high school health and physical education for four years and elementary physical education for one year before pursuing her PhD in curriculum and instruction at the University of Texas at Austin.

Dr. Centeio currently serves as the program coordinator of the health and physical education program at the University of Hawai'i at Mānoa. Her research focuses on integrating physical activity before, during, and after school as well as understanding the implications of physical activity and fitness on children's health, including its cognitive and psychosocial benefits. Erin works with numerous community programmers, physical education teachers, and school districts in order to maximize potential for quality physical education and additional opportunities for physical activity before, during, and after school. She has been a principal investigator (PI) and co-PI on over $10 million in grant funding, authored or coauthored over 100 presentations at national and international conferences, and published 5 book chapters and over 56 peer-reviewed manuscripts that focus on integrating physical activity and healthy eating interventions into school and community settings.

David N. Daum, PhD, is an associate professor of kinesiology at San Jose State University. His areas of expertise include physical education teacher education, curriculum design, assessment, and technology. He provides service to the physical education community through active engagement with the California Association of Health, Physical Education, Recreation and Dance (CAHPERD) and the Society of Health and Physical Educators (SHAPE America). Additionally, he has a long history of presentations and publications that target both K-12 practitioners and researchers. His scholarship focuses on the preparation of future teachers, technology in physical education, and K-12 blended and online physical education. Dr. Daum is an advocate for quality physical education at all levels. He enjoys preparing and mentoring the next generation of educators.

Heather Erwin, PhD, earned her doctorate degree in pedagogical kinesiology from the University of Illinois at Urbana-Champaign and her master's degree in adapted physical education from the University of Arkansas. Her undergraduate degree is in K-12 physical education with teaching certification. She is currently a professor in the department of kinesiology and health promotion at the University of Kentucky, where she serves as department chair. She has taught public school physical education, and she has worked with teachers and administrators in school districts, recreation programs, and youth sport organizations across the country to promote youth to be physically active for a lifetime. She has authored over 100 articles, books, chapters, and position statements, both data-based and applied. She coauthored the 8th and 10th editions of the text *Dynamic Physical Education for Secondary School Children.*

Tyler Goad, PhD, is an assistant professor in the department of health, physical education, and recreation at Emporia State University, where he teaches undergraduate and graduate courses in health and physical education teacher education. He is an experienced educator and researcher who specializes in the integration of technology in physical education and the development of online physical education programs. With a strong academic background and a passion for innovation in teaching, Dr. Goad has made significant contributions to the field. Dr. Goad has instructed various courses at West Virginia University and Emporia State University covering topics such as mobile fitness, technology in physical education, methods of online instruction, and specialized physical activities. Additionally, he has designed and developed online courses, with a focus on leveraging technology to enhance teaching and learning experiences in physical education to create engaging and interactive learning environments. Dr. Goad has published research articles in reputable journals and has presented their findings at national and international conferences.

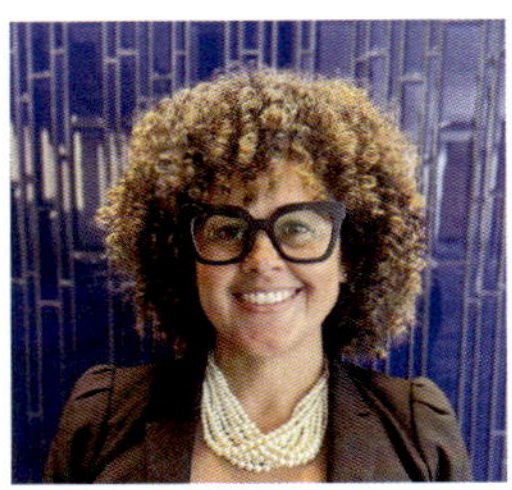

Cara D. Grant, EdD, has been working in the field of education for more than 20 years. She began in 2001 as an adapted physical education, health, and physical education teacher in Montgomery County (Maryland) Public Schools. She has had the opportunity to work in higher education as well as in PreK-12 education. In higher education, she developed the coursework for the physical education master's certification program at the University of Maryland at College Park. In PreK-12 education, she has worked to collaboratively supervise and coordinate teams of teachers to revise the PreK-12 framework in health and physical education. Dr. Grant has delivered professional development in her district, and she has been a keynote speaker for various conferences, including equity, diversity, and inclusion (EDI); wellness or well-being; educational leadership; adapted physical education; health education; and physical education. She has experience as a curriculum writer on the local county level, the state level, and the national level through developing content and curriculum for Discovery Education and the National Library of Medicine/National Institutes of Health (NIH). Grant is a published author on various topics. She has served SHAPE America in the past as a member of the board of directors, and she currently serves as president.

Lauren O'Mara, MS, is a talent strategy consultant who supports mission-driven K-12 organizations to build capacity and maximize their effectiveness. With deep experience in organizational change, systems thinking, and relationship management, Lauren's work focuses on helping clients refine human capital structures and processes; optimize recruitment, hiring, and selection; and enhance performance management systems. She has been employed by and consulted for a variety of public and nonprofit organizations, ranging from single-school charters to one of the largest school districts in the nation. An alumna of the Broad Residency, the Emerging Human Capital Leaders Initiative, and Teach For America, O'Mara holds master's degrees in educational leadership from The Broad Center for the Management of School Systems and a master's degree in education and social change from the University of Miami. She also earned dual undergraduate graduate degrees in broadcast news and French from the University of Georgia.

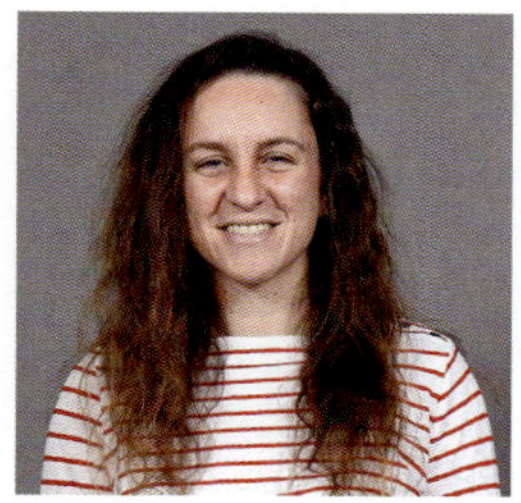

Mara Simon, EdD, is an associate professor in the department of physical education and health education at Springfield College. She received her doctor of education degree in teaching and curriculum in physical education from Teachers College, Columbia University in 2018, along with a master of education degree from Teachers College, Columbia University and a master of science degree in sport psychology from Ithaca College. She teaches elementary physical education methods as well as graduate-level courses on culturally relevant pedagogy and sport in society. Dr. Simon's research focuses on addressing racial disparities and working toward racial equity in physical education and sport, and her work has been recognized with multiple young scholar awards from various professional organizations.

John O. Spengler, JD, PhD, is a member of the sport management faculty at the University of Florida. He serves as a sport, recreation, and physical activity safety consultant nationwide. He is also a former professor and administrator at Texas A&M University. He was twice named University of Florida College of Health & Human Performance Teacher of the Year, a recognition for excellence in teaching. He is the author of four traditional classroom textbooks and several fiction novels. Dr. Spengler has published over 100 articles, and he has taught many thousands of students on topics relevant to sport, recreation, and physical activity. He is a former president of the Sport and Recreation Law Association, research partner for the Aspen Institute's Project Play, and he has served on the Science Board of the President's Council on Sport, Fitness & Nutrition (PCSFN). He has been recognized for his work through honors and awards presented by the Florida Sports Hall of Fame (Fame for Fitness award), Indiana University School of Public Health (Distinguished Alumnus), University of Florida Research Foundation (Distinguished Research award), and University of Florida College of Health & Human Performance (teaching excellence). He enjoys racket sports, outdoor recreation, reading, writing novels, and spending time with his family.

Wesley J. Wilson, PhD, is an assistant professor of adapted physical education and activity. He received his undergraduate degree in physical education and health education from Purdue University before continuing his studies in adapted physical activity at Oregon State University (master's) and adapted physical education at University of Virginia (PhD). Since graduation, Wilson has held faculty appointments at the University of Louisiana at Lafayette and the University of Utah. His scholarship focuses more broadly on adapted physical education and more specifically on the socialization of adapted physical educators. Wilson explores the lived experiences of adapted physical educators regarding their beliefs and behaviors related to inclusion, implementation of special education law, and experiences in teacher education and the workplace. He also examines the subjective experiences of people who experience disability within a variety of physical education and physical activity settings. More recently, Dr. Wilson's line of research has expanded to explore the influence of adapted physical activity service-learning programs on pre-service university students and the children they serve.

Carly Wright, Vice President for Advocacy and Equity, Diversity, and Inclusion (EDI) for the Society of Health and Physical Educators (SHAPE America), works on federal, state, and local initiatives related to improving, implementing, and assessing school health education and physical education programs and policies in schools. She also represents SHAPE America before the U.S. Congress and federal agencies, and she participates in national coalitions that work to elevate and promote health and physical education policies across the country.

Recently, Carly has taken on the responsibility of leading staff efforts related to equity, diversity, and inclusion (EDI) for SHAPE America. She is the staff liaison to the EDI task force, and works collaboratively with the board of directors, SHAPE America staff, and volunteers to advance EDI throughout the organization.

Carly has led numerous webinars, presentations, and trainings across the United States on advocating for health education, physical education, and the overall wellness of the nation's children. She has worked for SHAPE America for over 15 years. She loves working with passionate advocates from the health and physical education community.

About SHAPE America

SHAPE America – Society of Health and Physical Educators serves as the voice for more than 200,000 health and physical education professionals across the United States. The organization's extensive community includes a diverse membership of health and physical educators, as well as advocates, supporters, and over 50 state affiliate organizations.

Since its founding in 1885, the organization has defined excellence in physical education. For decades, SHAPE America's National Standards for K-12 Physical Education have served as the foundation for well-designed physical education programs across the country, just as SHAPE America's National Health Education Standards serve as the foundation for effective skills-based health education. Together, these national standards provide a comprehensive framework for educators to deliver high-quality instruction and make a positive difference in the health and well-being of every PreK-12 student.

SHAPE America provides programs, resources, and advocacy that support an inclusive, active, and healthier school culture, and the organization's newest program—health. moves. minds.©—helps teachers and schools incorporate social and emotional learning so students can thrive physically and emotionally.

Our Vision

A nation where all children are prepared to lead healthy, physically active lives.

Our Mission

To advance professional practice and promote research related to health and physical education, physical activity, dance, and sport.

To learn more, visit **www.shapeamerica.org**.

HUMAN KINETICS